TABLE A.3 Critical Values for the t Distribution

	One-tailed $\alpha = .10$	.05	.025	.01	.005
	Two-tailed $\alpha = .20$	.10	.05	.02	.01
df = 1	3.078	6.314	12.706	31.821	63.657
2	1.886	2.920	4.303	6.965	9.925
3	1.638	2.353	3.182	4.541	5.841
4	1.533	2.132	2.776	3.747	4.604
5	1.476	2.015	2.571	3.365	4.032
6	1.440	1.943	2.447	3.143	3.707
7	1.415	1.895	2.365	2.998	3.499
8	1.397	1.860	2.306	2.896	3.355
9	1.383	1.833	2.262	2.821	3.250
10	1.372	1.812	2.228	2.764	3.169
11	1.363	1.796	2.201	2.718	3.106
12	1.356	1.782	2.179	2.681	3.055
13	1.350	1.771	2.160	2.650	3.012
14	1.345	1.761	2.145	2.624	2.977
15	1.341	1.753	2.131	2.602	2.947
16	1.337	1.746	2.120	2.583	2.921
17	1.333	1.740	2.110	2.567	2.898
18	1.330	1.734	2.101	2.552	2.878
19	1.328	1.729	2.093	2.539	2.861
20	1.325	1.725	2.086	2.528	2.845
21	1.323	1.721	2.080	2.518	2.831
22	1.321	1.717	2.074	2.508	2.819
23	1.319	1.714	2.069	2.500	2.807
24	1.318	1.711	2.064	2.492	2.797
25	1.316	1.708	2.060	2.485	2.787
26	1.315	1.706	2.056	2.479	2.779
27	1.314	1.703	2.052	2.473	2.771
28	1.313	1.701	2.048	2.467	2.763
29	1.311	1.699	2.045	2.462	2.756
30	1.310	1.697	2.042	2.457	2.750
40	1.303	1.684	2.021	2.423	2.704
50	1.299	1.676	2.009	2.403	2.678
60	1.296	1.671	2.000	2.390	2.660
70	1.294	1.667	1.994	2.381	2.648
80	1.292	1.664	1.990	2.374	2.639
90	1.291	1.662	1.987	2.368	2.632
100	1.290	1.660	1.984	2.364	2.626
125	1.288	1.657	1.979	2.357	2.616
150	1.287	1.655	1.976	2.351	2.609
200	1.286	1.653	1.972	2.345	2.601
∞	1.282	1.645	1.960	2.326	2.576

Note: Table entry gives t^c corresponding to $\Pr(t \geq t^c) = \alpha$ for one-tailed tests and $\Pr(|t| \geq t^c) = \alpha$ for two-tailed tests.
Source: Computed using Fortran subroutines from the IMSL Library.

Economic Statistics
and Econometrics

Economic Statistics and Econometrics

THIRD EDITION

Thad W. Mirer
State University of New York at Albany

Prentice Hall, Upper Saddle River, NJ 07458

For Irene
and Paul
and Dan

Library of Congress Cataloging-in-Publication Data

Mirer, Thad W.
    Economic statistics and econometrics/Thad W. Mirer.--3rd ed.
        p. cm.
    Includes bibliographical references and index.
    ISBN 0-02-381831-X
    1. Economics—Statistical methods.   2. Econometrics.   I. Title.
HB137.M57   1995
330'.01'5195—dc20   94-8770
                                                CIP

Assistant Editor: Teresa Cohan
Production Editor: Katherine Evancie
Buyer: Paul Smolenski
Designer: Bob Freese
Cover Designer: Bob Freese
Illustrations by Carlisle Communications, Ltd.

© **1995 by Prentice-Hall, Inc.**
A Pearson Education Company
Upper Saddle River, NJ 07458

Earlier editions copyright © 1983 and 1988.

PRINTED IN THE UNITED STATES OF AMERICA
10 9 8 7 6 5 4 3

ISBN   0-02-381831-X

Prentice-Hall International (UK) Limited, London
Prentice-Hall of Australia Pty. Limited, Sydney
Prentice-Hall Canada Inc., Toronto
Prentice-Hall Hispanoamericana, S.A., Mexico
Prentice-Hall of India Private Limited, New Delhi
Prentice-Hall of Japan, Inc., Tokyo
Pearson Education Asia Pte. Ltd., Singapore
Editoria Prentice-Hall do Brasil, Ltda., Rio De Janeiro

Preface _____

Economic Statistics and Econometrics, third edition, is designed for courses in economic statistics and introductory econometrics that aim to mix the development of technique with its application to real economic analysis. No background in statistics is presumed. Calculus is not required, although it is used in some advanced sections and appendixes. Throughout, technical material is presented with careful explanation rather than oversimplification.

The core of the book (Chapters 1–13) is designed for courses in economic statistics or introductory econometrics that have no statistics prerequisite. Most texts that have a title such as *Statistics for Business and Economics* give detailed attention to topics in basic statistics, but they give short shrift to the use of regression in economics. This leaves students with very little to carry on to the rest of their studies. The core chapters in this text are designed for a course with the opposite priorities: Only those statistical topics that constitute a foundation for basic econometrics are covered, and regression models are treated in detail.

Chapters 14–19, which cover more advanced topics, are designed for more intensive courses or for courses in econometrics that have a statistics prerequisite.

In preparing the third edition, I have made the exposition clearer and simpler than in the previous editions, in order to make the book a more effective tool for learning and teaching. Hence, much of my work has involved editing and rewriting throughout the text. This has led to many small changes and quite a few large ones. In addition, a number of new topics have been added. The major features of the book and changes in the third edition are noted in the following summary outline. (A more complete description of the changes from the second edition is contained in the *Instructor's Manual.*)

Part I deals with data and descriptive statistics. A special chapter on the nature of economic data presents two data sets—cross-section and time-series—that provide the basis for most of the quantitative examples in the book. Chapter 2 includes a section on graphing time-series data that shows the logic underlying logarithmic time plots.

Part II deals with the specification, estimation, and interpretation of regression models. Questions of inference are treated in Part IV. Regression applications based on the text's data sets serve as mini case studies of the use of econometrics. A new section treats the case of regression through the origin, and applications appear in later chapters. Chapter 7 is devoted to the theory and application of multiple regression.

Part III is concerned with random variables and probability distributions. It begins with an optional chapter on basic probability theory and then presents the theory of random variables and probability distributions. The normal and t distributions are explained with an eye toward their use in Part IV, and an appendix on chi-square and F distributions provides background for topics appearing in Part V.

Part IV develops sampling theory and the methods of statistical inference wholly in the context of regression. This novel presentation focuses attention where it is most critical: on the regression coefficients. In Chapter 11 on sampling theory, the basic sections have been reorganized, and a section on interval estimation has been added. Hypothesis testing for single coefficients is developed in a series of special cases.

Part V covers a series of topics in econometrics that extend the methods presented earlier: F tests, dummy dependent variables, heteroscedasticity, autocorrelation, distributed lags, time-series use of regression, and simultaneous-equation models. The order of Chapters 14 and 15 has been reversed, allowing a smoother flow and more continuity for the time-series topics. There is new treatment of logit and probit models, expanded treatment of heteroscedasticity and autocorrelation, new treatment of Almon lags, and a new section on spurious regression.

Part VI covers standard topics in statistics: sampling and inference for the mean and variance of a random variable, chi-square tests, and a comparison of analysis of variance with regression. Parts of Chapters 18-19 can be studied in conjunction with earlier chapters.

The backmatter includes statistical tables, answers to selected problems, and a bibliography. The answers to all the problems in the book are in the *Instructor's Manual*, which is available from the publisher.

Special care has been taken in the production of the book to make it useful. Most drawings of important probability distributions were generated from the equations of their density functions; thus they are technically correct. The basic statistical reference tables were also computer generated. They are presented in a consistent format with accompanying directions for their use. The technical notation has been kept as simple and consistent as possible, and all equation displays are numbered for easy reference. The problems at the end of each chapter are separated by section, and a star marks those for which answers appear at the back of the book.

In teaching an economic statistics class based on the core chapters, I sometimes switch the order of treatment for Parts II and III. This yields the traditional separation between statistics and econometrics, while it maintains the separate exposition of modeling and inference in regression. Chapter appendixes that contain more difficult material can be skipped without loss of continuity. I skip Chapter 8 (basic probability) and usually do not cover Chapter 13.

I am grateful to many people for their help with the third edition. The following reviewers provided useful suggestions, and I hope that they will recognize the positive effects of their efforts: Phanidra Wunnava, Middlebury College; Kajal Lahiri, State University of New York at Albany; Burley Bechdolt, Northern Illinois University; and Gopa Chowdhury-Bose, Northeastern University.

My colleague Terrence Kinal provided helpful comments on a number of questions. Teresa Cohan, Jill Lectka, and Denise Abbott launched this project and kept it moving, and Margaret Comasky and Katherine Evancie guided it through production. My wife and children have been very patient with me, through three editions. I used to think it was merely tradition or writers' cant to thank one's family, but I have learned better.

T. W. M.

Contents

PART III
Probability Distributions   167

PART **VI**
Topics in Statistics

1

Introduction

When the Nobel Memorial Prize in Economic Science was first awarded, in 1969, it was given to Ragnar Frisch of Norway and Jan Tinbergen of The Netherlands for their pioneering work in econometrics. At the time, few people had heard of the subject and even fewer knew much about it. Today econometrics is widely recognized as the primary tool of empirical economic analysis.

Put simply, *econometrics* involves the development and use of special statistical methods within a framework that is consistent with the ways of economic inquiry. It is an extension of the field of *statistics,* which deals with techniques for collecting and analyzing data that arise in many different contexts. *Economic statistics* involves the application of these general techniques to economic questions.

1.1   The Nature of the Subjects

A time-honored example will illustrate the nature of the subjects and preview the topics covered in this book. In his *General Theory,* John Maynard Keynes developed the concept of an aggregate consumption function as a stable relation between consumer expenditures and aggregate income. Although the consumption function was only one part of his macroeconomic theory, its elaboration and testing were crucial in the validation and use of Keynes' other ideas. This was one of the first problems on which the then-young field of econometrics cut its teeth.

Econometric analysis starts from a statement about a behavioral relation. This statement, which may come from some sophisticated economic theory or from some plain reasoning, is then developed into an equation that specifies how the value of one variable is determined by the values of other variables. In the case of the Keynesian consumption function, the simplest specification is

$$C = \beta_0 + \beta_1 Y + u \tag{1.1}$$

In this equation, C stands for consumption and Y stands for income; these are the *variables* in the relation. The terms β_0 and β_1 are the *coefficients* in the equation (β is lowercase "beta," the Greek "b"); these coefficients are unknown constants, or parameters. The *disturbance* u is a random term that reflects all the factors in addition to income that help determine consumption. These factors may include variables that are individually unimportant, and therefore not explicitly mentioned as determinants of consumption, as well as pure chance and error in the measurement of C.

This behavioral, or structural, equation serves as a model of the economic process determining the level of consumption in the economy. As a model, it necessarily abstracts from reality by simplifying the complexity of the true economic process under consideration. It seeks to get down to the essentials. However, many of the techniques of statistics and econometrics are based on the premise that the specified model correctly describes the way the world works. If the model is wrong in its essentials, then all the quantitative and qualitative conclusions that are drawn from the analysis of data using these techniques may be far off the mark. The challenge of econometrics is to blend knowledge of economic behavior with knowledge of statistical techniques in order to produce well-specified models.

Not all equations in empirical economics are structural equations describing economic behavior. For example, the familiar GNP accounting identity

$$Y = C + I + G \tag{1.2}$$

has no unknown parameters and involves no disturbance term. The equation perfectly describes a relation among variables that holds true because of the way the variables are defined and measured. Here, there is no econometric problem.

Returning to the specification (1.1), the main task is to estimate the values of β_0 and β_1 using available data. Applying a technique known as *regression,* in Chapter 6 we estimate β_0 and β_1 to be 0.568 and 0.907, respectively, based on data presented in Chapter 2. We write the estimated model as

$$\hat{C} = 0.568 + 0.907Y \tag{1.3}$$

where $\hat{C}$ stands for the value of C that is predicted to occur in conjunction with any given value for Y. The result is illustrated schematically in Figure 1.1, where the estimated model is graphed through a scatterplot of data on C and Y. Since

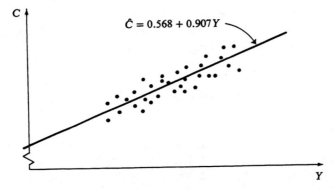

FIGURE 1.1 Each of the plotted points represents the paired values of consumption (C) and income (Y) in a particular year. The graphed line represents the estimated model of the aggregate consumption function, given as Equation (1.3). (The plotted points are merely illustrative; they are not the actual data points used in the estimation.)

the original specification includes a disturbance term, we recognize that the predictions made with this estimated model are always subject to some error. Also, since the numbers 0.568 and 0.907 are only estimates of the true β_0 and β_1, we recognize that there is a further source of error in our predictions.

In addition to, or instead of, making predictions we might have special interest in the values of the parameters themselves. For example, the essence of Keynes' consumption theory is that the marginal propensity to consume is less than 1; in terms of (1.1), this implies that $\beta_1 < 1$. Treating this as a hypothesis to be tested, we note that since our estimated value for β_1 is 0.907, it appears that the hypothesis is confirmed. However, remembering that 0.907 is only an estimate of β_1, and therefore subject to estimation error, should we really consider the hypothesis to be confirmed? To answer this question, which is related to questions regarding the errors associated with our estimates and predictions, we must gain a firm understanding of the statistical foundations on which econometrics is built.

The field of statistics is divided into two parts, descriptive statistics and statistical inference. *Descriptive statistics* is concerned with summarizing the information in data on one or more variables, and it provides the methods for estimating the values of various parameters, including the coefficients of an econometric model. *Statistical inference* is concerned with the relation between these estimates and the true values of the parameters, and it provides the basis for testing hypotheses and for assessing the errors that are always present in estimation.

As noted earlier, statistical analysis of economic questions need not be econometric in nature. For example, to estimate the extent of poverty in the United States, the U.S. Bureau of the Census takes an annual survey of more than 50,000 households, asking questions about income and related items.

Taking a representative survey involves sampling, and using the results to estimate the proportion of households that are poor involves inference. These techniques are statistical, but not econometric.

1.2 The Plan of This Book

This book is designed for students in courses in economic statistics or econometrics. These subjects get taught in a wide variety of ways at different levels, and the book aims to be as flexible as possible. A course in economic statistics might cover Parts I through IV, with the order of Parts II and III possibly being interchanged. An introductory course in econometrics might cover Parts II, IV, and V, plus whatever review of basic statistics is appropriate.

The field of statistics is quite broad and it has a wide variety of applications. This book covers only those fundamental statistical ideas that make up the foundations of econometrics. This coverage is satisfactory at the introductory level, but students planning advanced work in econometrics are well advised to learn statistics on its home ground (i.e., in departments of mathematics and statistics).

Econometrics is a broad field also. This book gives a thorough treatment of the fundamental principles of specification and estimation of single-equation regression models and of the corresponding procedures of statistical inference. The standard "advanced topics" in econometrics are treated in a straightforward way, aiming for appreciation and understanding rather than rigorous detail.

The subjects of statistics and econometrics are inherently technical, but this book is not for technicians. Instead, it aims to explain and apply the basic material in as careful a manner as possible. However, this does not make the book easy. It is necessary to have a certain level of technical appreciation and experience in order to apply the methods correctly. Most sophomores can easily learn to put numbers into a computer and get back statistical results. To do this wisely—to make the statistical analysis valid—requires a real understanding of the techniques involved.

The reader should bear in mind that each chapter is a self-contained unit, building on most of the previous chapters. Within each chapter, however, the importance and meaning of some material in early sections may not be clear until later sections are covered. Given the difficulty of some of the material, the chapters demand reading and then rereading, perhaps many times.

Each chapter has a set of problems at the end, separated according to the section on which they draw. The problems are meant to be learning aids, not simply chores to be done, and they can lead one through a review of the chapter after it has been read thoroughly. Those problems for which answers appear at the back of the book are marked by a star (*).

APPENDIX _____

Functions and Graphs

A function is a mathematical relation that associates a single value of the variable y with each value of the variable x. In very general form, we may write

$$y = f(x) \qquad (1.4)$$

In the graph of a function, the value of x is measured horizontally and the associated value of y is given by the height of the curve.

Figure 1.2 shows the graph of a straight line, which is associated with a function whose equation is

$$y = b_0 + b_1 x \qquad (1.5)$$

Such an equation is called a **linear equation.** If $x = 0$, then $y = b_0$, and therefore b_0 is the **intercept** of the line with the y axis drawn vertically through $x = 0$. The **slope** of a straight line is defined as the ratio of the change in y (i.e., Δy) to the change in x (i.e., Δx) resulting from moving from one point to another along the line. In other words,

$$\text{slope} = \frac{\Delta y}{\Delta x} \qquad (1.6)$$

(Δ is uppercase "delta," the Greek "D"). In (1.5) the slope is equal to b_1, the coefficient multiplying x. To see that this is true, let p' correspond to the y and x values y' and x', and let p'' correspond to y'' and x''. Since

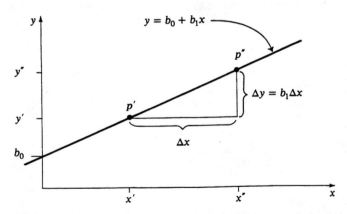

FIGURE 1.2 The graph of a linear equation is a straight line whose distinguishing features are its intercept and its slope. The intercept is the value of y corresponding to $x = 0$. The slope is given by the ratio $\Delta y/\Delta x$ associated with moving along the line from one point to another.

$$y'' = b_0 + b_1 x'' \quad \text{and} \quad y' = b_0 + b_1 x' \tag{1.7}$$

then

$$y'' - y' = (b_0 - b_0) + b_1(x'' - x') \quad \text{or} \quad \Delta y = b_1 \Delta x \tag{1.8}$$

Thus $b_1 = \Delta y/\Delta x$, the slope. If b_1 is positive, the line slopes upward from left to right; if b_1 is zero, it is horizontal; and if b_1 is negative, the line slopes downward from left to right. If the absolute value of the slope is large, the line is steep, and if the absolute value is small, the line is relatively flat.

In the special case where $\Delta x = 1$, we see that $b_1 = \Delta y$. Thus the coefficient b_1 gives the change in y that is associated with a unit change in x (i.e., $\Delta x = 1$). This interpretation is basic for understanding regression models, which are formulated as linear equations.

For example, if we start with the linear equation

$$y = f(x) = 2.5 + 0.9x \tag{1.9}$$

we see immediately that its slope is 0.9 and its intercept is 2.5. To graph the straight line corresponding to this equation, all we need to do is determine any two points on the line and then draw the line through them. In this example, we could use the intercept point ($x = 0$, $y = 2.5$) and the point corresponding to $x = 10$ and

$$y = 2.5 + (0.9)(10) = 2.5 + 9 = 11.5 \tag{1.10}$$

that is, the point ($x = 10$, $y = 11.5$).

Figure 1.3a shows the graph of a function that is not a straight line. The slope of this function is defined at each and every point on the curve as equal to the slope of the straight line that can be drawn tangent to the curve at that point. The

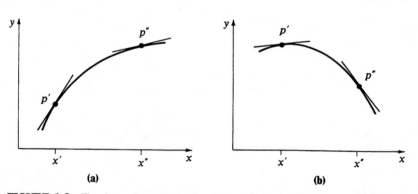

FIGURE 1.3 The slope of a nonlinear function usually varies from point to point along the curve. The slope at a particular point is defined as equal to the slope of the straight line that is tangent to the curve at that point. In (a), the slope is greater at p' than at p''. In (b), the slope at p' is algebraically greater than at p'', but the negative slope at p'' is greater in absolute value than that at p'.

slope of the function is greater at p' than at p''. In Figure 1.3b the slope at p' is positive, whereas that at p'' is negative but greater in absolute value.

Instead of thinking about the slope of a curve at a particular point as being the slope of the tangent line at that point, we can simply think of the slope as being the ratio of the change in y to the change in x that results from moving along the curve just a very small distance from the original point. To signify that the changes are very small we use dy instead of Δy and dx instead of Δx, so that

$$\text{slope} = \frac{dy}{dx} \tag{1.11}$$

which is calculus notation. Note that when the "curve" is a straight line, this definition is exactly the same as (1.6).

Elasticity

As just explained, the slope characterizes how the change in y is related to the change in x as we move along the graph of a function: the slope is the ratio of the two algebraic changes. Another way of characterizing how these changes are related is by the *elasticity*, which is a common term in economic discussion. For example, a demand curve expresses the quantity demanded (of some product) as being a function of price. The elasticity of demand with respect to price tells us something about how quantity changes are related to price changes.

The elasticity tells us how the proportional change in y is related to the proportional change in x as we move along the graph of the function. Note that a proportional change, such as $\Delta y/y$, equals the algebraic change (Δy) divided by the level or value of the variable (y). When the change in y is very small, the proportional change in y is given by dy/y.

The elasticity of a function at a particular point is defined as the ratio of the proportional changes:

$$\text{elasticity} = \frac{dy/y}{dx/x} \tag{1.12}$$

where the changes in y and x are very small. We say that this is "the elasticity of y with respect to x." Since this elasticity is defined at a particular point, it is called the *point elasticity*.

Simple algebra allows us to see that this elasticity definition can be reexpressed in various equivalent ways:

$$\text{elasticity} = \frac{dy/y}{dx/x} = \frac{dy/dx}{y/x} = \frac{\text{slope}}{y/x} = \text{slope} \cdot \frac{x}{y} \tag{1.13}$$

presuming that y is on the vertical axis and x is on the horizontal axis. Notice the close relation between elasticity and slope: in the next-to-last expression the elasticity is equal to the slope divided by the y/x ratio, and in the last expression it is equal to the slope multiplied by the x/y ratio. (The next-to-last expression may be the most useful in seeing how the elasticity is related to the slope in graphs of the function.)

For example, we determined earlier that the linear function in (1.9) has a slope equal to 0.9 and that one of the points on the line is ($x = 10$, $y = 11.5$). At this point the elasticity of y with respect to x is $(0.9)/(11.5/10) = 0.7826$. Another point on the line is ($x = 20$, $y = 20.5$), at which the elasticity is $(0.9)/(20.5/20) = 0.8780$.

Many people find the concept of elasticity difficult to understand, even though they find the concept of slope quite easy. To help develop an understanding, it is useful to realize that elasticity and slope both play the same role: they characterize how changes in y are related to changes in x as we move along the graph of the function $y = f(x)$. In some cases it is easier to talk about the slope, but in other cases it is easier to talk about the elasticity.

Two special cases provide an interesting comparison. In the case of a linear function, like (1.5), the slope takes on the same value (b_1) everywhere. However, unless $b_0 = 0$ the elasticity takes on a different value at each point. To see that this is true, we can draw a straight line from the origin to p' and another one from the origin to p'' in Figure 1.2. The slope of the first line is y'/x' and the slope of the second is y''/x''. From the figure it is clear that the first slope is greater than the second, so $y'/x' > y''/x''$. Hence, from the next-to-last expression in (1.13) we see that the elasticity at p' is smaller than the elasticity at p''.

The second special case is that of a function for which the value of the elasticity is constant, but the slope changes as we move along the relation. For such a nonlinear function, the elasticity provides a simple way to characterize how changes in y are related to changes in x, because one number holds at every point along the function. By contrast, the slope provides a complicated way to characterize this case, because it takes on a different value at every point along the function. This type of constant-elasticity function plays a useful role in applied econometrics, and it is explored in Chapter 6.

In general, as we move along the graph of a function, both the slope and the elasticity may change. For example, in Figure 1.3b we see that the slope is continuously decreasing in algebraic value, taking on a positive value at p' and a negative value at p''. In the range where the slope is negative, the elasticity is clearly changing: as x increases, the negative numerator in the next-to-last part of (1.13) increases in magnitude, while the positive denominator decreases. Thus as x increases the negative elasticity increases in magnitude. In Figure 1.3a, however, we cannot make such a sure determination by simple graphical analysis. At p'' the slope is smaller than at p', but the y/x ratio is also smaller. This is not enough information to determine how the elasticity at p'' compares with the elasticity at p'.

Both the slope and the elasticity are clearly defined at any single point along a function. However, these basic concepts need to be revised if they are to be applied to sizable movements from one point to another. For example, suppose that we are thinking of moving from p' to p'' along the function graphed in

Figure 1.3a. If we draw a straight line between p' and p'', its slope is the ratio between the Δy and the Δx in this case. Note, however, that this slope is smaller than the slope of the function at p' and greater than the slope at p''. Thus these two well-defined slopes do not correctly describe the ratio $\Delta y/\Delta x$ for the movement between the two points.

Similarly, if we compute the ratio of the proportional changes in y and x that occur in moving from one point (p') to another (p''), we obtain the **arc elasticity**:

$$\text{arc elasticity} = \frac{\Delta y/y}{\Delta x/x} \qquad (1.14)$$

A practical concern in computing the arc elasticity involves deciding what value of x (such as x', x'', or some other) and what value of y to use. The decision depends on the particular application involved. Usually the x value is taken to be the initial value x' or the average of x' and x'', and similarly for y. Because of these complications, we usually think of the point elasticity when using the elasticity concept in discussion.

When the proportional changes in x and y are relatively small, the arc elasticity is approximately equal to the point elasticity at the starting point. Hence, for a given proportional change in x, the proportional change in y can be approximated as

$$\frac{\Delta y}{y} \approx (\text{point elasticity}) \cdot \frac{\Delta x}{x} \qquad (1.15)$$

For example, if the elasticity of y with respect to x at a point is 1.5, a 2 percent change in x leads y to change by the proportion

$$\frac{\Delta y}{y} \approx (1.5)(0.02) = 0.03 \qquad (1.16)$$

or 3 percent. Computations like this are sometimes made in analyzing the implications of econometric models.

Problems _____

Section 1.1

    1.1   What specific economic factors other than income are likely to affect consumption? What noneconomic factors may affect consumption?

★ **1.2**   Based on the estimated model in Equation (1.3), determine the predicted value of consumption resulting from an income level of 1000 (the units have not been specified).

    ★ Answers for problems marked with a star are given at the end of the book.

1.3 Based on Equation (1.3), determine the impact on predicted consumption of an increase in income of 100.

1.4 Write down an equation that may serve as a simple model representing how the quantity demanded of a certain good depends on its price. What do you expect the signs of each of the coefficients to be? In your model is price the only factor that determines the quantity demanded?

★ **1.5** Write down an equation that may serve as a simple model representing how the quantity supplied of a certain good depends on its price. What differences are there between this and the demand model?

1.6 The equation $S = Y - C$ expresses the macroeconomic statement that saving equals income minus consumption. Is this a model that needs econometric analysis?

★ **1.7** It is important for the U.S. Department of Labor to obtain a fairly precise estimate of the nation's unemployment rate each month. Is this a task of econometrics?

1.8 It is important to know how the rate of inflation will be affected if the rate of growth of the money supply is increased. Is this a task of econometrics?

Appendix

For Problems 1.9–1.13, consider the linear equation $y = 1.0 + 0.5x$.

1.9 Determine the slope and the intercept, and graph this equation for the values of x from 0 to 10.

1.10 Let point A have $x = 3$ and point B have $x = 8$. Determine the y values of A and B algebraically and graphically.

★ **1.11** Using points A and B from Problem 1.10, determine the slope of the line.

★ **1.12** If x increases by 4, what is the associated change in y? If x decreases by 1, what is the associated change in y?

1.13 Determine the elasticity of this linear function when $x = 3$. Determine the elasticity when $x = 8$.

★ **1.14** The function $y = x^2$ has a slope equal to $2x$ at any point. Determine the slope and the elasticity when $x = 2$. Determine the slope and elasticity when $x = 4$.

1.15 For the function in Problem 1.14, determine the ratio $\Delta y/\Delta x$ for the movement between the point where $x = 2$ to the point where $x = 4$.

★ **1.16** For the function in Problem 1.14, determine the arc elasticity for the movement between the point where $x = 2$ to the point where $x = 4$.

1.17 Suppose that the elasticity of output with respect to labor input is 0.70. If labor input is increased by 3 percent, what effect does this have on output?

I

Data and Description

2

Economic Data

In this chapter we consider some general notions regarding data and present two sets of real economic data that serve as the bases for many of the examples presented later in the book. The appendix discusses the nature and use of natural logarithms, and in the last section of the chapter these are applied to a problem in graphing data.

2.1 General Considerations

Data (the plural of *datum*) are the quantitative facts or pieces of information that we deal with in any statistical analysis. In common parlance, data are usually referred to as "statistics," but we reserve that term for a very different technical meaning. Taken together, all the data we consider in any particular analysis constitute a *data set*.

In any economic process that we are studying empirically, the data present information about a set of cases or instances of the occurrence of that process. These cases or instances are called *observations*, and the nature of these cases or instances defines the *unit of observation*. For example, in macroeconomics the study of the consumption function focuses on an economy in aggregate as the unit of observation, and the observations may be different years' experiences of a single economy or they may be the experiences of different economies. At the microeconomic level, the study of consumption behavior usually focuses on the family as the unit of observation, because it is theorized that persons in a family make collective economic decisions. The observations may consist of data for the same family during different periods of time or for different families.

A *variable* is a measurable characteristic about which we collect data. For example, in a microeconomic study of consumption behavior the relevant variables might be consumption, income, family size, the number of children, and so on. Variables often are given symbolic names, such as X, Y, and Z. However, in reporting the results of data analysis it often makes sense to use variable names that are mnemonics for the corresponding characteristics (e.g., *CONSUM, INCOME, FAMSIZE*) or even to use plain words. We sometimes use the term "data variable" to distinguish what we are concerned with here from a "random variable," which is introduced in Chapter 9.

These basic concepts weave neatly together to make up the notion of a *rectangular data set.* Suppose that we have n observations on the variables Y, X, and Z. The data can be thought of as being in a rectangular array, with each row being an observation and each column containing the values of a variable, as in Table 2.1. Each element in the array is a value that is symbolized by the variable name with a subscript indicating the observation number. A typical observation, which we denote as the ith, consists of the values Y_i, X_i, and Z_i. An actual data set is a collection of numbers that can be thought of as being arranged in this format. Throughout this text, it is presumed that we have measurements on all the variables, for all the observations in the data set. In other words, there are no missing data.

Generally, variables are typed as being either discrete or continuous. The distinction between these types is precisely drawn in the probability theory dealing with random variables in Chapter 9, but in dealing with data the distinction is sometimes imprecise. A *discrete* data variable usually results from counting, and its values are usually integers. The number of distinct values taken

TABLE 2.1   Rectangular Data Set for Y, X, and Z

Observation Number	Y	X	Z
1	Y_1	X_1	Z_1
2	Y_2	X_2	Z_2
3	Y_3	X_3	Z_3
.			
.			
.			
i	Y_i	X_i	Z_i
.			
.			
.			
n	Y_n	X_n	Z_n

on by the variable is often rather limited, even when the number of observations in the data set is quite large. For example, the number of persons in a family is clearly a discrete variable; family size takes on only integer values, and even in a survey of many families its values may range only from 2 to 15 or so. By contrast, a *continuous* data variable usually results from measuring, possibly with great precision, and in principle its values can be any of the real numbers (perhaps within a specified interval). In practice, however, measurement problems often serve to impose some practical limit on the number of distinct values that the variable can take on. For example, the income of families might be measured very precisely (down to the penny, perhaps), and in a survey of 100 families there might well be 100 different values for the variable.

In some cases the type of a variable is unclear. For example, workers might report the exact number of days that they worked in the preceding five years. In such a case, where the number of different values occurring for a discrete variable is very large, the data tend to resemble those for a continuous variable. The number of days worked might be considered practically continuous, and it could be treated as such for some purposes. In Chapter 4 we explore methods of organizing and summarizing data that make use of the distinction between the two types of variables. Most of the other statistical techniques that we deal with treat discrete and continuous variables in exactly the same way.

A given set of observations is often thought of as being a *sample* drawn from some larger population. For example, the people interviewed in a survey might be chosen from among all the people in a certain geographic region or socioeconomic category. For some statistical purposes, such as estimating the nation's unemployment rate or describing the distribution of income, it is important that the sample be representative of the corresponding population. In these cases, sophisticated probability-based sampling techniques are used to select the people who are interviewed and who thereby become observations in a set of data.

By contrast, in econometric work much less attention is paid to selecting observations in such a way that they are representative of the corresponding population. For example, consider a microeconomic study of family consumption behavior in which consumption is theorized to depend on income, in a way that is similar to the Keynesian consumption function discussed in Chapter 1. Under certain commonly made assumptions, it is *not* of special concern that the percentages of families in the data set who have various levels of income correspond closely to the percentages in the entire population. That is, it is *not* important that the sample represent the population with regard to levels of income, or consumption. However, other considerations regarding the selection of data are important for econometric analysis, and some of these are examined in Part IV.

At this point we note a fundamental consideration that must be kept in mind when selecting data to be used in the econometric estimation of the parameters in a behavioral relation. Since the relation describes a particular economic process, all the observations should result from that process. That is, all the observations should follow the same behavioral pattern. For example, suppose that we have two groups of families and that the marginal propensity to consume is different in one group from what it is in the other. (Perhaps one group consists of young families with children and the other group consists of retired couples.) If one of the parameters in the behavioral relation is the marginal propensity to consume, it would not make sense to mix data from the two groups—because the model specifies that there is only one value for this parameter. In such cases, the data sets for the two groups might be used separately to estimate two different consumption functions. Sometimes it is possible to develop a more complex model that explicitly allows for a difference between the groups, and in such cases combining the data would be appropriate. What all this amounts to saying is that the data should correspond to the model being estimated, and vice versa.

In comparison with researchers in other disciplines, economists are not often involved in the collection of original data. In macroeconomics, most of the relevant data are prepared by government agencies. In microeconomics, governments are also a major source of data because of their administrative records and the information received through regulatory functions. In addition, governments carry out extensive surveys of economic behavior and conditions. Beyond government, there are business firms and research organizations that collect and disseminate data of various types. With this wealth of information on so many economic activities being easily available, it is rare to find economists or their students out in the field interviewing people or probing the records of economic units. Although this permits a greater share of research time and effort to be devoted to the analysis of data rather than its collection, it makes it more difficult for the researcher to judge the basic quality of the data that he or she is using. It should be noted, however, that economists are becoming more involved with survey techniques and the collection of data; the negative income tax experiments and similar projects are major examples of this activity.

2.2   Cross-Section Data

Cross-section data arise when the observations are data for different entities (such as persons, firms, or nations) for which a common set of variables is measured at about the same point in time. For example, the results of a survey in which various people are interviewed regarding their labor force activity and earnings constitute a cross-section data set, as do the revenue and expenditure figures for the 50 state governments in the United States in any particular year.

For use throughout this book, a small cross-section data set has been selected from the responses to the *Survey of Financial Characteristics of Consumers* and its sequel *Survey of Changes in Family Finances,* which were carried out for the Board of Governors of the Federal Reserve System in 1963 and 1964. In addition to being quite suitable for our purposes, these data are chosen because they were subjected to an especially interesting validation, which is discussed below.

The data set consists of 100 observations on 12 variables. These observations were selected from among those families headed by a male aged 25–54 who was not predominantly self-employed, in order to produce data relevant for estimating an earnings function. Also, in order to be able to examine normal behavior, families with wealth greater than $100,000 (in 1962 dollars) were not included. For convenience, the number of observations was reduced to 100 by a random selection. Normally, one would use as many observations as feasible, as long as they are appropriate for the estimation at hand.

The data are displayed in Table 2.2, arranged as a rectangular data set. The 12 variables refer to behavior or status during 1963, except as noted. Given mnemonic names, they are

1. *SIZE*   The number of persons in the family.
2. *ED*   The number of years of education received by the head.
3. *AGE*   The age of the head, in years.
4. *EXP*   The labor market experience of the head, in years, calculated as $EXP = AGE - ED - 5$.
5. *MONTHS*   The number of months during which the head worked.
6. *RACE*   The race of the head, coded 1 for whites and 2 for blacks.
7. *REG*   The region of residence, coded 1 for Northeast, 2 for North Central, 3 for South, and 4 for West.
8. *EARNS*   The wage and salary earnings of the head, expressed in thousands of dollars.
9. *INCOME*   The total income of the family members, expressed in thousands of dollars.
10. *WEALTH*   The wealth of the family on December 31, 1962, expressed in thousands of dollars.
11. *SAVING*   The saving (flow) of the family, expressed in thousands of dollars.
12. *ID*   The observation number, repeated as a variable for convenience.

The variable *EXP* is constructed from *AGE* and *ED,* and it is approximately equal to the number of years since a person left school. This is intended to serve as a proxy for true labor market experience. Since a proxy is not a true measure, the use of such a variable introduces potential for error and distortion. Variables *RACE* and *REG* contain coded information, which must be treated in special ways. The other variables are measured in natural units. Note that the financial variables are expressed in thousands of dollars, for convenience; as we shall see, this does not distort any of the statistical procedures. Each observation constitutes one row in the table, and the values of a single variable are contained in a single column. There are no missing values, because survey respondents who did not provide complete information were excluded from consideration.

Just looking at the data in the table conveys very little insight about how the economy works, although an experienced researcher can see things in the table

TABLE 2.2   Cross-Section Data Set

Obs.	(1) SIZE	(2) ED	(3) AGE	(4) EXP	(5) MONTHS	(6) RACE
1	4	2	40	33	12	2
2	4	9	33	19	12	1
3	2	17	31	9	12	1
4	3	9	50	36	12	1
5	4	12	28	11	12	1
6	4	13	33	15	12	1
7	5	17	36	14	12	1
8	5	16	44	23	12	1
9	5	9	48	34	12	2
10	5	16	31	10	12	1
11	10	9	41	27	12	1
12	4	10	41	26	12	1
13	7	11	36	20	12	1
14	5	14	31	12	12	1
15	5	7	27	15	12	1
16	5	8	42	29	12	1
17	4	12	28	11	11	1
18	2	6	46	35	12	2
19	3	12	47	30	12	1
20	7	8	35	22	12	1
21	3	9	41	27	9	1
22	4	17	30	8	12	1
23	6	12	38	21	12	1
24	3	11	48	32	12	1
25	3	10	36	21	12	1
26	3	12	45	28	12	1
27	6	8	44	31	6	1
28	4	10	44	29	12	1
29	3	3	46	38	12	1
30	4	12	26	9	12	1
31	5	12	50	33	12	1
32	4	8	46	33	11	1
33	5	8	33	20	12	1
34	4	12	41	24	12	1
35	5	17	33	11	12	1
36	4	12	41	24	12	1
37	3	12	29	12	11	2
38	9	11	27	11	12	1
39	5	12	42	25	12	1
40	5	16	39	18	12	1
41	6	12	36	19	12	1
42	4	8	34	21	12	1
43	4	12	40	23	12	1
44	4	12	37	20	12	1
45	5	17	44	22	12	1

(7) REG	(8) EARNS	(9) INCOME	(10) WEALTH	(11) SAVING	(12) ID
3	1.920	1.920	0.470	0.030	1
1	12.403	12.403	3.035	0.874	2
4	5.926	6.396	2.200	0.370	3
2	7.000	7.005	11.600	1.200	4
3	6.990	6.990	0.300	0.275	5
1	6.500	6.500	2.200	1.400	6
3	26.000	26.007	11.991	31.599	7
1	15.000	15.363	17.341	1.766	8
3	5.699	14.999	9.852	3.984	9
3	8.820	9.185	8.722	1.017	10
4	7.000	10.600	0.616	1.004	11
1	6.176	12.089	23.418	0.687	12
2	6.200	6.254	7.600	−0.034	13
3	5.800	9.010	0.358	−1.389	14
2	6.217	6.217	0.108	1.000	15
2	5.500	5.912	5.560	1.831	16
1	4.800	4.800	0.970	0.613	17
3	1.820	2.340	2.600	0.050	18
4	4.558	7.832	31.867	0.013	19
2	7.468	9.563	1.704	1.389	20
1	6.600	7.600	4.820	0.602	21
1	12.850	13.858	32.807	2.221	22
1	5.800	5.802	10.305	1.588	23
3	7.479	19.362	12.652	5.082	24
1	5.700	8.000	7.631	1.846	25
1	12.000	17.200	14.392	0.914	26
1	3.578	4.091	6.649	2.483	27
3	9.600	9.600	6.995	0.837	28
3	3.686	10.425	9.138	1.274	29
3	6.480	6.512	2.933	−0.275	30
4	6.383	7.675	38.260	1.092	31
1	5.610	12.418	12.661	1.157	32
1	6.000	6.079	0.820	0.340	33
2	6.300	6.979	21.286	0.373	34
1	10.513	10.517	9.723	3.307	35
2	30.000	30.996	95.187	10.668	36
1	3.427	5.283	0.171	1.105	37
2	8.500	8.511	3.105	3.500	38
1	11.300	12.700	7.385	0.541	39
3	16.960	16.770	16.049	3.020	40
1	8.300	8.300	0.050	0.650	41
2	5.375	5.375	4.464	0.989	42
4	4.770	6.265	7.203	2.532	43
2	4.320	8.520	9.145	6.120	44
4	10.720	24.226	54.524	−2.749	45

(*continued*)

TABLE 2.2   Cross-Section Data Set (*continued*)

Obs.	(1) SIZE	(2) ED	(3) AGE	(4) EXP	(5) MONTHS	(6) RACE
46	2	4	49	40	12	1
47	5	12	33	16	12	1
48	6	14	36	17	12	1
49	4	15	51	31	12	1
50	5	12	37	20	12	1
51	4	19	33	9	12	1
52	4	14	39	20	12	1
53	3	12	44	27	12	1
54	4	7	50	38	12	1
55	4	12	39	22	12	1
56	6	7	46	34	12	1
57	4	12	43	26	12	1
58	6	11	40	24	12	2
59	2	9	40	26	12	1
60	8	7	39	27	12	1
61	6	10	34	19	6	2
62	4	10	32	17	12	2
63	3	16	42	21	12	1
64	2	8	52	39	12	1
65	6	12	29	12	12	1
66	2	12	27	10	12	1
67	5	10	37	22	12	1
68	2	12	52	35	12	1
69	3	12	32	15	12	1
70	4	12	35	18	12	1
71	3	13	31	13	12	1
72	5	9	36	22	10	1
73	6	16	34	13	12	1
74	3	12	54	37	12	1
75	4	12	52	35	10	1
76	6	9	28	14	12	1
77	6	12	44	27	12	1
78	4	17	29	7	12	1
79	4	9	50	36	7	1
80	4	8	50	37	12	1
81	4	16	44	23	12	1
82	4	9	34	20	9	1
83	7	10	39	24	12	1
84	5	12	39	22	12	1
85	4	14	29	10	12	1
86	3	8	38	25	12	1
87	5	10	30	15	12	1
88	3	10	50	35	12	1
89	2	8	33	20	12	1
90	4	9	35	21	12	1

(7) REG	(8) EARNS	(9) INCOME	(10) WEALTH	(11) SAVING	(12) ID
3	0.750	0.750	4.000	0.000	46
4	7.310	7.356	6.800	−1.036	47
3	9.000	9.000	6.890	1.351	48
1	14.000	14.660	13.500	−1.150	49
2	3.900	5.593	9.837	−0.248	50
2	10.000	11.841	10.384	0.388	51
3	7.200	7.700	6.842	1.157	52
3	6.500	10.550	4.929	1.656	53
2	8.000	13.700	34.124	3.959	54
2	9.500	12.242	11.731	5.369	55
2	6.000	7.803	5.695	1.405	56
3	6.400	9.879	25.029	0.220	57
3	5.190	9.154	0.600	−0.298	58
3	4.548	7.067	45.105	−0.276	59
2	4.860	4.496	8.511	−0.578	60
4	2.736	4.636	20.205	−1.360	61
4	6.000	9.003	4.727	5.277	62
1	7.800	13.820	2.270	0.980	63
4	6.163	8.891	18.916	2.637	64
1	8.600	8.632	14.194	0.984	65
3	7.899	8.385	13.662	−0.076	66
4	5.048	5.403	0.159	0.902	67
2	4.133	8.573	21.700	10.733	68
3	6.500	6.516	1.180	0.716	69
2	6.000	6.000	5.900	0.200	70
4	10.116	16.778	2.531	0.006	71
1	6.000	9.504	44.461	1.464	72
4	8.950	8.953	4.863	0.948	73
4	4.952	8.703	8.534	0.835	74
1	8.681	12.667	26.085	−2.883	75
2	6.500	6.504	3.775	0.298	76
4	7.668	8.180	3.032	0.481	77
2	11.600	11.600	2.167	5.033	78
3	3.100	5.602	5.072	−0.111	79
3	4.586	10.390	4.100	0.000	80
2	27.000	30.610	51.892	4.115	81
1	1.500	3.941	1.260	2.575	82
3	1.789	2.936	17.128	−0.112	83
4	11.068	11.068	11.542	−5.577	84
4	8.338	8.338	2.272	2.750	85
3	2.943	6.683	6.100	0.095	86
1	7.212	7.212	0.857	1.348	87
1	7.500	10.411	3.678	0.178	88
3	5.250	8.850	1.650	−0.695	89
1	5.066	8.334	2.143	0.787	90

(continued)

TABLE 2.2   Cross-Section Data Set (*continued*)

Obs.	(1) SIZE	(2) ED	(3) AGE	(4) EXP	(5) MONTHS	(6) RACE
91	3	16	36	15	12	1
92	4	12	33	16	12	1
93	6	20	38	13	12	1
94	4	12	46	29	12	1
95	4	16	50	29	12	1
96	2	16	54	33	12	1
97	5	12	31	14	12	1
98	2	18	27	4	12	1
99	5	12	40	23	12	1
100	6	18	34	11	12	1

that another person might not. Statistical analysis, including econometrics, provides methods for learning about economic behavior from seemingly unfathomable masses of numbers such as this.

Errors in Data

Before any data are analyzed by statistical methods, the researcher should have a good understanding of exactly what characteristics the data variables purport to measure and of how good these measures are. In conjunction with the *Survey of Financial Characteristics of Consumers* (SFC) and with the cooperation of the Federal Reserve Board, a group of researchers undertook a validation study to assess the responses of interviewees to questions in the SFC regarding the ownership of savings accounts. The first step was to obtain bank records on savings accounts and their owners. Next, the owners were interviewed, following the same procedure that was used in the original SFC. Finally, the responses of the interviewees were matched with the corresponding bank records. The differences between the responses and the bank records are errors in the data, most of which are considered to be the fault of the respondents.

The findings of the study are quite interesting. The major source of error was the failure to report an existing savings account. Among the respondents to the validation survey, almost half failed to report an account that they owned, thus tending to underreport the amount of their wealth. (The amounts in savings accounts are a component of *WEALTH* and are very different from *SAVING*.) A second type of error was misreporting the size of an account. Among the accounts whose existence was reported, the size of small accounts was overreported and the size of large accounts was underreported. Among accounts that were actually smaller than $1000, the average reported value was $245 greater than the true value, and among the accounts larger than $10,000, the average reported value was $795 less than the true value.

(7) REG	(8) EARNS	(9) INCOME	(10) WEALTH	(11) SAVING	(12) ID
2	12.848	13.923	18.182	4.642	91
2	6.214	6.214	0.275	1.260	92
1	12.202	12.323	28.953	2.687	93
2	8.190	14.963	11.230	0.720	94
2	7.200	10.060	25.462	5.109	95
1	30.000	32.080	98.033	1.800	96
2	9.190	9.260	5.539	1.684	97
2	7.500	10.450	2.860	1.475	98
3	7.852	9.138	11.197	0.566	99
1	12.000	12.350	30.906	25.405	100

These types of errors in data should alert us to be careful in applying and interpreting statistical techniques. Unfortunately, there is not much that can be done to improve the quality of data once it is obtained. Some of the judgment involved in econometrics is deciding which variables in a given set of data are sufficiently good to work with. Also, it makes sense to examine each observation to see if there are any obvious errors, and then either correct them or delete the observation from further consideration. This is an inappropriate procedure, however, if there is any chance that the researcher would correct or delete observations that do not conform to established beliefs about the way the world works.

2.3   Time-Series Data

Time-series data arise when the observations are data for the same entity in different periods of time. For example, records of a person's employment and earnings in each year of his life constitute a time-series data set, as do the official National Income Accounts compiled by the Bureau of Economic Analysis in the U.S. Department of Commerce. The data are essentially historical, and the factor of time is usually very important.

One of the major uses of time-series econometric models is to make predictions about future events. In doing this, we assume that the economic process represented in data from the past will continue unchanged in the future. The observations in our data set, then, can be viewed as a sample from the results of a continuing economic process.

For use throughout this book, a small time-series data set has been selected from the series (variables) compiled by the U.S. President's Council of Economic Advisers and published in the *Economic Report of the President 1982*. The unit of observation is the aggregate American economy in a given year. The sample period spans the years 1956 through 1980, yielding a total of 25 observations. During this time period, which starts after the Korean War, the basic structure of the economy is presumed not to have changed. However, at least with regard to inflation and price determination, this assumption may be untenable for the last 5 or 10 years and deserves to be investigated further.

The data are displayed in Table 2.3, arranged as a rectangular data set. The 12 variables, given mnemonic names, are

1. **PGNP**   The implicit price deflator for gross national product, expressed as index numbers with $PGNP = 100.0$ for 1972.

2. **GNP**   (Real) gross national product (GNP), measured in billions of 1972 dollars.

3. **INV**   (Real) gross private domestic investment, measured in billions of 1972 dollars.

4. **CON**   (Real) personal consumption expenditures, measured in billions of 1972 dollars.

5. **DPI**   (Real) disposable personal income, measured in billions of 1972 dollars.

TABLE 2.3   Time-Series Data Set

Obs.	(Year)	(1) PGNP	(2) GNP	(3) INV	(4) CON	(5) DPI
1	(1956)	62.79	671.6	102.6	405.4	446.2
2	(1957)	64.93	683.8	97.0	413.8	455.5
3	(1958)	66.04	680.9	87.5	418.0	460.7
4	(1959)	67.60	721.7	108.0	440.4	479.7
5	(1960)	68.70	737.2	104.7	452.0	489.7
6	(1961)	69.33	756.6	103.9	461.4	503.8
7	(1962)	70.61	800.3	117.6	482.0	524.9
8	(1963)	71.67	832.5	125.1	500.5	542.3
9	(1964)	72.77	876.4	133.0	528.0	580.8
10	(1965)	74.36	929.3	151.9	557.5	616.3
11	(1966)	76.76	984.8	163.0	585.7	646.8
12	(1967)	79.06	1011.4	154.9	602.7	673.5
13	(1968)	82.54	1058.1	161.6	634.4	701.3
14	(1969)	86.79	1087.6	171.4	657.9	722.5
15	(1970)	91.45	1085.6	158.5	672.1	751.6
16	(1971)	96.01	1122.4	173.9	696.8	779.2
17	(1972)	100.00	1185.9	195.0	737.1	810.3
18	(1973)	105.69	1255.0	217.5	768.5	865.3
19	(1974)	114.92	1248.0	195.5	763.6	858.4
20	(1975)	125.56	1233.9	154.8	780.2	875.8
21	(1976)	132.11	1300.4	184.5	823.7	907.4
22	(1977)	139.83	1371.7	213.5	863.9	939.8
23	(1978)	150.05	1436.9	229.7	904.8	981.5
24	(1979)	162.77	1483.0	232.6	930.9	1011.5
25	(1980)	177.36	1480.7	203.6	935.1	1018.4

    6. *RINF1*   The annual rate of inflation in the GNP deflator, expressed as percent per annum.

    7. *RINF2*   The annual rate of inflation in the Consumer Price Index, expressed as percent per annum.

    8. *UPCT*   The unemployment rate, measured as a percent of the civilian labor force.

    9. *M1*   Money supply (M1), measured in billions of current dollars as the average of daily figures during December (the observations for 1956–1958 were obtained by splicing and adjusting comparable data from the 1980 *Report*).

    10. *RTB*   The interest rate on new issues of U.S. Treasury bills, expressed as percent per annum.

    11. *RAAA*   The interest yield of corporate bonds rated Aaa by Moody's Investors Service, expressed as percent per annum.

    12. *T*   Time, measured as the number of years since 1955 (i.e., 1 in 1956, 2 in 1957, etc.); this is the same as the observation number.

(6) *RINF1*	(7) *RINF2*	(8) *UPCT*	(9) *M1*	(10) *RTB*	(11) *RAAA*	(12) *T*
3.205	1.496	4.1	135.0	2.658	3.36	1
3.408	3.563	4.3	133.8	3.267	3.89	2
1.710	2.728	6.8	138.9	1.839	3.79	3
2.362	0.808	5.5	141.2	3.405	4.38	4
1.627	1.604	5.5	142.2	2.928	4.41	5
0.917	1.015	6.7	146.7	2.378	4.35	6
1.846	1.116	5.5	149.4	2.778	4.33	7
1.501	1.214	5.7	154.9	3.157	4.26	8
1.535	1.309	5.2	162.0	3.549	4.40	9
2.185	1.722	4.5	169.6	3.954	4.49	10
3.228	2.857	3.8	173.8	4.881	5.13	11
2.996	2.881	3.8	185.2	4.321	5.51	12
4.402	4.200	3.6	199.5	5.339	6.18	13
5.149	5.374	3.5	205.9	6.677	7.03	14
5.369	5.920	4.9	216.8	6.458	8.04	15
4.986	4.299	5.9	231.0	4.348	7.39	16
4.156	3.298	5.6	252.4	4.071	7.21	17
5.690	6.225	4.9	266.4	7.041	7.44	18
8.733	10.969	5.6	278.0	7.886	8.57	19
9.259	9.140	8.5	291.8	5.838	8.83	20
5.217	5.769	7.7	311.1	4.989	8.43	21
5.844	6.452	7.1	336.4	5.265	8.02	22
7.309	7.658	6.1	364.2	7.221	8.73	23
8.477	11.259	5.8	390.5	10.041	9.63	24
8.964	13.523	7.1	415.6	11.506	11.94	25

The meanings of most of these variables are discussed in books on macroeconomics. Variables 1–6 are based on the National Income Accounts, 7 and 8 on U.S. Department of Labor concepts, and 9–11 on Federal Reserve and private business reports.

Sometimes the definitions of variables and the measurement techniques used to collect data change over time. For example, in 1994 the U.S. Department of Labor changed the questions that are asked in the monthly survey that is used to determine the nation's unemployment rate. This means that older labor force data measure a slightly different concept than newer data, and some research shows that the newer concept results in slightly higher values for the unemployment rate. Similarly, in 1985 the Department of Commerce made extensive statistical and definitional changes in the National Income Accounts data, as it does from time to time. These revisions change our information about how the economy has functioned. For instance, real gross national product is now seen to have grown more slowly from 1972 to 1984 than was evident before the revisions. Clearly, economists working with time-series data must check to see whether the data being used are based on consistent definitions and measurement techniques over time. When the data are not consistent, it may be possible to develop models that take the changes into account.

Change and Growth

The observations in a time series have a natural order given by the historical sequence in which they occurred. Thus, differences in the value of the variable from one observation to another tell us something about the history of the variable: they tell us how it is changing or growing. (We use the words "change" and "growth" synonymously, so negative growth is possible.)

There are two concepts of change or growth in common use, and this sometimes leads to confusion. The simplest concept is that of *absolute change* or growth, which is simply the difference between one period's value and the previous one. For a time-series variable Y, the absolute growth in the ith period is given by the difference

$$\Delta Y_i = Y_i - Y_{i-1} \tag{2.1}$$

Note that ΔY_i may be negative; we are not dealing with the concept of "absolute value" here.

The concept of *relative change* relates the absolute change in a variable to its previous level: the relative growth of Y is defined as the proportionate change in Y. Relative change or growth in the ith period is measured by the *rate of change* or the *rate of growth:*

$$r_i = \frac{\Delta Y_i}{Y_{i-1}} = \frac{Y_i - Y_{i-1}}{Y_{i-1}} = \frac{Y_i}{Y_{i-1}} - 1 \tag{2.2}$$

Note that the word "rate" has different meanings in different contexts. When talking about change and growth, we reserve "rate" to mean the measure of relative change.

Both measures of growth deal with the same facts about how Y is changing. Although absolute growth is slightly simpler, relative growth is often more meaningful in economic analysis. The absolute change ΔY_i tells us how *much* Y is growing, and it is measured in the units of the variable (e.g., dollars). By contrast, the relative change r_i tells us how *fast* Y is growing, and it is measured as a pure number (a proportion, or a percentage).

For example, consider the data on *GNP* in Table 2.3. *GNP* was 800.3 billion dollars in 1962 and 832.5 billion in 1963. The absolute growth for 1963 was $\Delta GNP_8 = 32.2$ billion dollars. (Note that 1963 is the 8th observation.) For the same year the rate of growth was $32.2/800.3 = 0.0402$, or 4.02 percent; this is the measure of relative growth.

Similarly, *GNP* was 1436.9 billion dollars in 1978 and 1483.0 billion in 1979. The absolute growth for 1979 was 46.1 billion dollars, and the rate of growth was 3.21 percent. Comparing the 1979 changes with the 1963 changes, we see that the absolute growth was greater in 1979 than in 1963 but that the rate of growth was smaller.

Constructed Variables

Macroeconomic time-series variables are not always simple reports of observed magnitudes. Instead, some original data are adjusted to conform to certain statistical or economic concepts. Our time-series data set reflects four types of these adjustments.

First, some variables are presented as indexes. An *index* is constructed to measure the average of an underlying set of price or quantity variables in each year. The index itself is a series of numbers whose information is carried in the relative size of different years' values, not in their individual magnitudes. To give a base for comparing different values, a particular year is chosen as the benchmark and the index is set to an arbitrary value for that year. Some well-known indexes are the Dow Jones Index of Industrial Stock Prices, the Fed's Index of Industrial Output, and the Consumer Price Index.

In our data, *PGNP* is like an index of the prices of products and services in the economy. The benchmark is set as $PGNP = 100.0$ for 1972. The *PGNP* value for any other year reports the average level of prices in that year relative to the level in 1972. For example, in Table 2.3 we see that $PGNP = 62.79$ in 1956; this means that the average level of prices in 1956 was 62.79 percent as high as the average level of prices in 1972. Similarly, the value $PGNP = 177.36$ for 1980 means that prices in 1980 were 177.36 percent as high then as in 1972; in other words, the average level of prices in 1980 was 77.36 percent higher than the average level in 1972. Also, we may directly compare the prices in any two years: prices in 1980 were $177.36/62.79 = 2.82$ times as high as prices in

1956; in other words prices were 182 percent higher (but this expression is confusing).

Second, some variables are reported in *real* terms, after the corresponding *nominal* variable has been adjusted. For example, consider gross national product (GNP). When expressed in terms of the actual observable values based on prices and quantities in each particular year, the measure of GNP is known as the nominal GNP, which we denote by *NGNP*. Over time, *NGNP* has increased because prices have gone up and because the quantities of goods and services produced in the economy have gone up. In order to focus on the increase in quantities produced over time, which should be more closely related to employment and productivity changes, economists construct a measure known as real GNP, which we denote by *GNP*.

The adjustment of *NGNP* to get *GNP* aims to represent what the magnitude of GNP would have been in different years if the average level of prices had been constant at the level prevailing in the benchmark year 1972. The relation between real and nominal GNP is given by

$$GNP_i = \frac{NGNP_i}{PGNP_i/100} \tag{2.3}$$

That is, to get real GNP for the ith year, nominal GNP is deflated (i.e., divided) by the price index. In the denominator of (2.3), the price index *PGNP* is divided by 100 to offset its value in the benchmark year; as a result $GNP = NGNP$ in 1972, as it should. Reflecting what occurs in this defining formula, "real" magnitudes are sometimes described as "price-deflated." It should be clear that (2.3) can be rearranged to show that nominal GNP equals real GNP times the price index (divided by 100).

It is important to make a clear distinction between the units of measurement for nominal and real values. We say that *NGNP* is measured in "current dollars," and that *GNP* is measured in "constant dollars" or "1972 dollars." To say just "dollars" can be confusing. Note that when we say that *NGNP* in 1960 was $(737.2)(68.70/100) = 506.5$ billions of "current dollars" we mean that nominal GNP for that year is valued in 1960 prices, not today's prices.

The definition in (2.3) clearly generalizes, so that the real counterpart of any nominal time-series variable is obtained by dividing it by the appropriate price index. However, sometimes it is not clear what price index should be used. For example, the Federal Reserve releases data on the money supply in nominal terms (here, *M1*). It makes sense to deflate *M1* by *PGNP* to create real money supply data to reflect economy-wide behavior, but it also makes sense to deflate *M1* by the Consumer Price Index to reflect consumer behavior. The problem of deciding what price index to use is one of economics rather than statistics. Clearly, good economic judgment is needed in handling data even before statistical techniques are applied.

Third, some variables are expressed as the annual rate of change of some other variable. For example, in macroeconomics "inflation" means change in the level of prices. Usually this is understood to be the proportionate change from one period to another, computed as the rate of change. Hence, applying (2.2), inflation (as reflected in the growth of *PGNP*) is measured as

$$RINF1_i = \frac{PGNP_i - PGNP_{i-1}}{PGNP_{i-1}} \cdot 100 \qquad (2.4)$$

The multiplication by 100 here changes the result from a proportion to a percentage. In macroeconomics, more than one measure of inflation might be used. Table 2.3 also contains *RINF2*, which is the rate of change of the Consumer Price Index.

Fourth, some variables are constructed as ratios of two other variables. For example, the Bureau of Labor Statistics calculates the unemployment rate as the ratio of the number of unemployed persons to the number of persons in the labor force. The ratio is multiplied by 100 to express it in percentage points as the variable *UPCT* in our data set. Note that the unemployment "rate" is not a rate of change; it is simply a ratio.

2.4 Plotting a Time-Series Variable _____

A substantial amount of information about a time-series variable can be presented by constructing a graphical display of the data. In this section we look at two types of displays, and we see how they are related to the measures of growth defined in the previous section.

The simplest type of display is what we call a ***regular time plot***. Figure 2.1a presents such a plot for the data on the nominal money supply (*M1*) in Table 2.3. For each observation, the value of *M1* is plotted vertically above the corresponding value for the time variable *T*, which is defined as $T_i = i$ in Table 2.3. This figure is a natural way to display the data on *M1*; it clearly shows that *M1* has grown over time.

The second type of display is what we call a ***logarithmic time plot***, which differs from a regular time plot in that the logarithms of the values of the variable (rather than the regular values) are plotted vertically. In our work we use natural logarithms, which are discussed in the appendix to this chapter. Figure 2.1b displays the logarithmic time plot for *M1*. Overall the two time plots look fairly similar. As *M1* increases, ln(*M1*) increases also. However, each billion-dollar increase in *M1* leads to successively smaller increases in ln(*M1*). Hence, with these data on *M1* the logarithmic time plot in Figure 2.1b appears somewhat more linear than the regular time plot in Figure 2.1a.

The most important difference between these two graphs has to do with what they show about the growth of *M1*. To explain this difference we make reference to Figures 2.2b and d, which show the time plots for some variable *Y*.

In the regular time plot displayed as Figure 2.2b, the *i*th observation is the one associated with T_i, and it has a height of Y_i. The previous observation is plotted

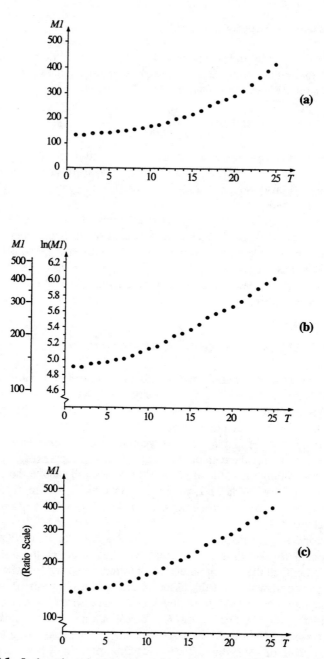

FIGURE 2.1 In these time plots, the slopes of imaginary lines connecting successive points give information about the growth of *M1*. Part (a) shows the regular time plot: where the slope is steeper, the absolute growth is greater. Parts (b) and (c) both show the logarithmic time plot: where the slope is steeper, the rate of growth is greater. The main vertical scale in (b) simply indicates various values for ln(*M1*), following normal graphing procedure. The vertical scale in (c) shows, instead, the antilogs of specially selected values for ln(*M1*), so the logarithmic nature of the plot is not explicit.

30

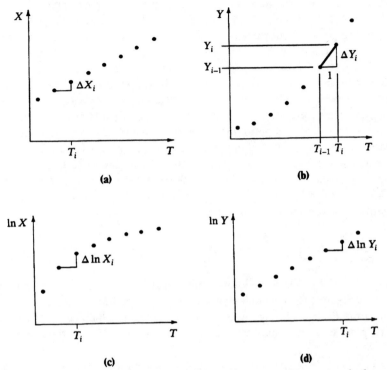

FIGURE 2.2 The constant slope in (a) shows that X increases with constant absolute growth. This implies that the rate of growth of X decreases over time, as evidenced by the decreasing slopes in the logarithmic time plot in (c). By contrast, the constant slope of the logarithmic time plot in (d) shows that Y increases at a constant rate of growth. This implies that the absolute growth of Y increases over time, as evidenced by the increasing slopes in the regular time plot in (b).

above T_{i-1}, and it has a height of Y_{i-1}. A straight line segment is drawn between the two plotted points. It is easy to prove that the slope of this line segment is equal to the absolute growth for Y in period i. Using the notation for graphs from the appendix to Chapter 1, the slope is given by $\Delta Y/\Delta T$. Now, mixing in notation for data concepts, the vertical distance ΔY between the two points is $Y_i - Y_{i-1}$, which equals ΔY_i from (2.1). The horizontal distance ΔT equals 1. Therefore,

$$\text{slope} = \frac{\Delta Y}{\Delta T} = \frac{\Delta Y_i}{1} = \Delta Y_i \tag{2.5}$$

That is, in a regular time plot the slope of the line segment leading up to the observation for period i is equal to ΔY_i, which is the absolute growth of Y in the ith period.

Looking at Figure 2.1a, it is easy to imagine line segments drawn between successive plotted points and to make comparisons among their slopes. Where the slope is steeper, the absolute growth is greater. For example, the figure clearly shows that the absolute growth for $M1$ in the 25th period is greater than that in the 3rd period. Unfortunately, it is not possible to compare rates of growth for these two periods in this plot. To do this we would need to compare the $\Delta M1_i/M1_{i-1}$ ratios for the two periods. For period 25, the figure shows that both the numerator and the denominator of this ratio are greater than the corresponding terms for period 3. Hence, we do not have enough information to determine whether the rate of growth r_i is greater in period 25 than in period 3, or less.

It turns out that a logarithmic time plot makes this possible: a visual comparison of slopes provides information about the rates of growth. In Figure 2.2d, where each height is ln Y (the natural logarithm of Y), our previous graphical logic leads us to realize that the slope of a line segment connecting the point for period $i - 1$ to that for period i is simply Δ ln Y_i. Using our knowledge of logarithms, we extend this to show that

$$\text{slope} = \frac{\Delta \ln Y}{\Delta T} = \frac{\Delta \ln Y_i}{1} = \Delta \ln Y_i = \ln Y_i - \ln Y_{i-1} = \ln \frac{Y_i}{Y_{i-1}} \qquad (2.6)$$

Reading from right to left, we know from (2.18) that the logarithm of a ratio is equal to the logarithm of the numerator minus the logarithm of the denominator.

Now, from (2.2) we know that $r_i = (Y_i/Y_{i-1}) - 1$, which can be rearranged as $Y_i/Y_{i-1} = 1 + r_i$. Thus, substituting $(1 + r_i)$ for Y_i/Y_{i-1} in the last term of (2.6),

$$\text{slope} = \ln(1 + r_i) \qquad (2.7)$$

That is, in a logarithmic time plot the slope of the line segment leading up to the observation for period i is equal to the logarithm of $1 + r_i$. Therefore, the slope increases with r_i. In other words, in a logarithmic time plot, the slope of the line segment drawn between two consecutive periods' observations is directly related to the rate of growth. For example, the slopes along the logarithmic time plot of $M1$ in Figure 2.1b provide information about the rates of growth of $M1$: where the slope is steeper, the rate of growth is greater.

The special cases in Figure 2.2 are interesting. In Figure 2.2a, the constant slope of the regular time plot for X tells us that X has constant absolute growth. In the corresponding logarithmic time plot, we see that the slope of ln X decreases as time passes; this tells us that the rate of growth of X decreases as time passes. That is, constant absolute growth for X implies that the rate of growth for X decreases over time. (This holds in all cases with positive growth for positive X.)

In Figure 2.2d, the constant slope of the logarithmic time plot for Y tells us that Y grows at a constant rate. This means that ΔY_i is increasing over time, as shown in Figure 2.2b. That is, constant relative growth for Y implies that the absolute growth for Y increases over time. (This holds in all cases with positive growth for positive Y.)

Logarithmic time plots are often more useful than regular time plots, because they permit a quick visual determination of what happens to the rate of growth of the variable as time passes. For this reason, logarithmic time plots are sometimes presented in nontechnical publications, even newspapers. To avoid mention of logarithms, the vertical scale is often relabeled with the antilogs of selected log values, as in Figure 2.1c. Often, a notation is made that the vertical axis has a "ratio scale." (Note that the only differences between Figures 2.1b and c are the marking and labeling on the vertical axis.)

Figure 2.1b shows how this relabeling is done for the case of the logarithmic time plot of *M1*. It would be possible simply to write the antilog values, instead of the ln(*M1*) values, next to the existing set of evenly spaced tick marks on the vertical axis (99.5 instead of 4.6, 121.5 instead of 4.8, 148.4 instead of 5.0, and so on), but this would be confusing. The standard approach is to choose a convenient set of evenly spaced label values (such as 100, 200, 300, and so on) and place the corresponding tick marks at the correct heights (4.605 = ln 100, 5.298 = ln 200, 5.704 = ln 300, and so on). Such a scale is shown offset to the left of the figure, with major tick marks corresponding to values of *M1* that are 100 billion dollars apart. The marking and labeling for this *M1* scale can be put directly on the main vertical axis, with no mention of logarithms, as in Figure 2.1c. The peculiar spacing of the tick marks signals the informed reader that this is a logarithmic time plot.

APPENDIX _____

Logarithms

Many people find logarithms to be mysterious and difficult to understand. This is unfortunate, because logarithms play a very useful role in econometric analysis: they simplify matters in certain cases.

To start with, we consider a relation between x and y of the form

$$x = b^y \tag{2.8}$$

In this relation, b is a **base** that is raised to a certain power, the **exponent** y. For example, for $b = 2$, the x values that correspond to the integer values for y from -3 to $+3$ are given in Table 2.4; these should be familiar computations. [Note that when an exponent is negative, the value of the expression is equal to the reciprocal of the base raised to the positive value of the exponent: $2^{-3} = 1/(2^3) = \frac{1}{8}$.] The information in this table is plotted as the points in Figure 2.3.

Applying a little mathematical finesse, we can view x as being a continuous function of y. This is suggested in Figure 2.3a by drawing a curve through the plotted points. For any possible value of y, the curve (function) determines a particular value of x. For example, if $y = 1.5$, $x = 2^{1.5} \approx 2.83$. Given that the base is positive, the x value of the function will always be positive. We will be

TABLE 2.4 Values of $x = 2^y$ and $y = \log_2 x$

y	x
-3	⅛ = 0.125
-2	¼ = 0.25
-1	½ = 0.5
0	1
1	2
2	4
3	8

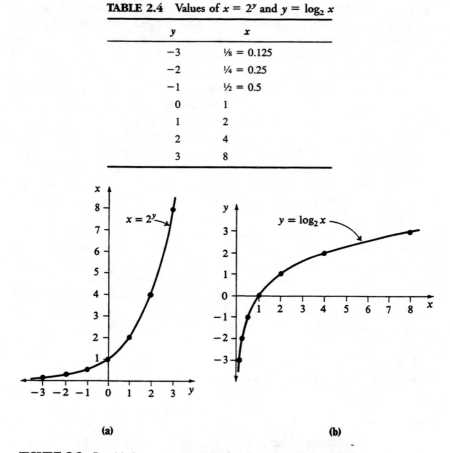

(a)   (b)

FIGURE 2.3 Part (a) shows an exponential function with base 2, and (b) shows its inverse—a logarithmic function. The plotted points are listed in Table 2.4.

interested in cases in which $b > 1$. In all these cases, the x value of the function will increase as y increases and the graph will be qualitatively similar to Figure 2.3a: $0 < x < 1$ for $y < 0$; $x = 1$ for $y = 0$; and $1 < x < \infty$ for $y > 0$.

This function, known as an *exponential function,* provides a unique one-to-one correspondence between x and y values. Hence it is possible to focus on the inverse relation: given a particular base, the exponent y is a function of x. This function is known as a *logarithmic function.* In other words, if x is the exponential of y, then y is the *logarithm* of x. Some simple notation to reexpress this is

$$\text{if} \quad x = b^y, \quad \text{then} \quad y = \log_b x \tag{2.9}$$

where $y = \log_b x$ is known as the logarithmic function.

Less formally, a logarithm is simply an exponent. The logarithm of x is the exponent to which a given base must be raised to yield the particular x value. The following tautology is useful to remember:

$$x = b^{\log_b x} \qquad (2.10)$$

For base 2, Table 2.4 shows the y values that correspond to certain x values; these y values are the logarithms (to the base 2) of the x values. Figure 2.3b, which shows the logarithmic function, is the same as Figure 2.3a but with the axes transposed.

Exponential and logarithmic functions may be set up for any positive base. In scientific and mathematical work it is convenient to use a number approximately equal to 2.718 as the base. This number is known as e, and logarithms using the base e are called *natural logarithms*. They may not seem very natural at first, but that is their proper name. The symbol "ln" is often used as a shorthand symbol instead of "$\log_e$," and we adopt this convention:

$$\text{if} \quad x = e^y, \quad \text{then} \quad y = \ln x \qquad (2.11)$$

where e is understood to be the base of natural logarithms.

Figure 2.4 shows the graph of the *natural logarithmic function* $y = \ln x$. Note that x is always positive but that y, the value of $\ln x$, may be negative or positive. Also, $\ln 1 = 0$ because $e^0 = 1$, as is true of any nonzero number raised to the zero power. The slope of $y = \ln x$ is always positive, but it decreases as x gets larger, meaning that as x increases $\ln x$ also increases but at a slower rate for larger values of x. Many electronic calculators can compute natural logarithms, and there also exist detailed tables to determine these values. Table

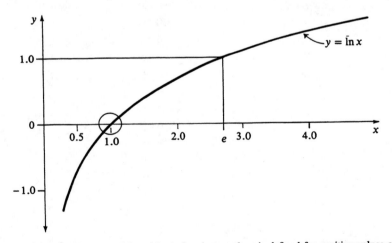

FIGURE 2.4 The natural logarithmic function $y = \ln x$ is defined for positive values of x, but y ranges from $-\infty$ to ∞. The slope of the function is always positive, but it decreases as x increases. The circled portion of the function is examined in Figure 2.5.

2.5 shows the natural logarithms of a few selected numbers. Note that the values of ln x do not get very large even when x does. Also, ln x gets very small (very negative) rapidly as x decreases below 1 toward zero.

The *antilog* of a number is the value of the exponential function using that number as the exponent. In the natural logarithmic system,

$$\text{``}x \text{ is the antilog of } y\text{''} \quad \text{means} \quad x = e^y \tag{2.12}$$

In other words, x is the antilog of y when y is the log of x. For example, from Table 2.5 we see that the antilog of 1.1 is 3.0, and the antilog of 9.21 is 10,000.

A useful approximation involving logarithms is illustrated in Figure 2.5. This figure enlarges the circled portion of Figure 2.4 and adds the line $y = x - 1$ for reference. This reference line is tangent to the curve $y = \ln x$ at the point $x = 1$, $y = 0$. For other values of x, the graph of $y = \ln x$ lies below the reference line. Thus, $\ln x \leq x - 1$. However, when x is close to 1 the difference is quite small, so

$$\ln x \approx x - 1 \quad \text{when} \quad x \text{ is close to 1} \tag{2.13}$$

TABLE 2.5 Selected Values of $y = \ln x$

x	$y = \ln x$
0.0	$-\infty$
0.0001	-9.21
0.001	-6.91
0.01	-4.61
0.1	-2.30
0.5	-0.69
0.90	-0.105
0.95	-0.051
1.00	0.000
1.05	0.049
1.10	0.095
1.5	0.41
2.0	0.69
2.5	0.92
(e) 2.718	1.00
3.0	1.10
5.0	1.61
10.0	2.30
50.0	3.91
100.0	4.61
1,000.0	6.91
10,000.0	9.21
1,000,000.0	13.82

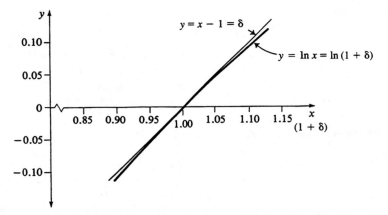

FIGURE 2.5 For values of x close to 1, $\ln x \approx x - 1$. Letting $\delta = x - 1$, this useful approximation can be restated as $\ln(1 + \delta) \approx \delta$ for δ close to 0. In this figure we see that the height of $y = \delta$ is only slightly greater than that of $y = \ln(1 + \delta)$ for a range of values where δ is close to zero (i.e., where x is close to 1).

This relation serves as a simple and useful method for determining the approximate value of $\ln x$, without the aid of a calculator or complicated formula. For example, a calculator gives $\ln(1.05) = 0.049$ to three decimal places, and using (2.13) the approximation $\ln(1.05) \approx 0.05$ is quite good. Similarly, a calculator gives $\ln(0.98) = -0.020$ to three decimal places, and the approximation $\ln(0.98) \approx -0.02$ is right on target for this degree of precision. Table 2.5 shows that the approximation is fairly good in the range of x values between 0.90 and 1.10, but that it is less accurate beyond there.

It is useful to recast this approximation in terms of differences. Let δ be the difference between x and 1, so that $\delta = x - 1$ and $x = 1 + \delta$. (Note that δ is lowercase "delta," the Greek "d.") In Figure 2.5, the graph of $y = \ln(1 + \delta)$ lies below that of the reference line $y = \delta$, except where they are tangent, and therefore $\ln(1 + \delta) \leq \delta$. The approximation (2.13) can be restated as

$$\ln(1 + \delta) \approx \delta \quad \text{for} \quad \delta \text{ close to zero} \tag{2.14}$$

Logarithmic Transformations

Our main use of logarithms will be to transform certain nonlinear equations into new equations that are linear. The *rules of logarithms,* which are used in these transformations, are based on the familiar rules of exponents in algebra. In what follows, the symbols y and x play different roles than in the earlier part of this appendix.

The most frequently used rule is

$$\text{if} \quad y = xz, \quad \text{then} \quad \ln y = \ln x + \ln z \tag{2.15}$$

Put differently,

$$\ln xz = \ln x + \ln z \tag{2.16}$$

meaning that the logarithm of a product of two terms is equal to the sum of the logarithms of those terms. To see that (2.15) is true, we note that $y = e^{\ln y}$, $x = e^{\ln x}$, and $z = e^{\ln z}$ by definition. Thus $y = xz$ can be rewritten as $e^{\ln y} = (e^{\ln x})(e^{\ln z})$. By the rules of exponents, $(e^{\ln x})(e^{\ln z}) = e^{(\ln x + \ln z)}$, so $e^{\ln y} = (e^{\ln x + \ln z})$. Thus $\ln y = \ln x + \ln z$.

A companion rule is based on division:

$$\text{if} \quad y = \frac{x}{z}, \quad \text{then} \quad \ln y = \ln x - \ln z \tag{2.17}$$

Put differently,

$$\ln \frac{x}{z} = \ln x - \ln z \tag{2.18}$$

meaning that the logarithm of a ratio of two terms is equal to the logarithm of the numerator minus the logarithm of the denominator.

Both (2.15) and (2.17) generalize to equations having more than two terms. Taking the logarithm of a complicated expression yields an expression involving the sums and differences of the logarithms of the terms. The logarithms of terms originally in the numerator are added together and the logarithms of terms originally in the denominator are subtracted. For example,

$$\text{if} \quad y = \frac{x}{wz} \cdot t, \quad \text{then} \quad \ln y = \ln x - \ln w - \ln z + \ln t \tag{2.19}$$

Often the basic multiplicative terms themselves involve exponentiation, and a final rule is helpful:

$$\text{if} \quad y = x^z, \quad \text{then} \quad \ln y = z \ln x \tag{2.20}$$

Put differently,

$$\ln x^z = z \ln x \tag{2.21}$$

To see that (2.20) is true, we note that $y = x^z$ can be rewritten as $e^{\ln y} = (e^{\ln x})^z$. By the rules of exponents $(e^{\ln x})^z = e^{z \ln x}$, so $e^{\ln y} = e^{z \ln x}$. Thus $\ln y = z \ln x$. Two special cases arise in econometric work. First, if z is a constant, we may replace it with c, so that

$$\ln x^c = c \ln x \tag{2.22}$$

Second, if x is a constant, we may replace it with c, so that

$$\ln c^z = z \ln c = zc' \tag{2.23}$$

where $c' = \ln c$.

Finally, we look at two examples. Consider first the specification of the Cobb–Douglas production function

$$Q = AK^aL^b \tag{2.24}$$

in which Q is output, K is capital services input, L is labor input, and A, a, and b are constants. Taking logarithms, we find that

$$\ln Q = \ln A + a \ln K + b \ln L \tag{2.25}$$

Thus we have transformed an equation that specifies Q as a nonlinear function of K and L into one that specifies $\ln Q$ as a linear function of $\ln K$ and $\ln L$. The importance of this will become apparent later.

The second example relates to modeling the growth of a time-series variable, such as population, that is assumed to grow at a steady rate. A constant-growth model in discrete terms is given in mathematical form by

$$P_i = P_0(1 + r)^i \tag{2.26}$$

where P_0 is an initial amount or level, r is the constant rate of growth, and P_i is the value of the variable i time periods later. In a discrete model, time is measured in whole periods, so that i takes on integer values only and P_i is the value of P at the end of period i. Taking logarithms of (2.26), we have

$$\ln P_i = \ln P_0 + i \ln(1 + r) \tag{2.27}$$

Since r is constant, $\ln P_i$ is a linear function of i.

In theoretical work, constant-growth models are often specified in continuous terms, such as

$$P_t = P_0 e^{gt} \tag{2.28}$$

where P_0 is the initial level, g is the constant rate of growth, t is a continuous measure of time, and P_t is the value of P at time t. In a continuous model every moment of time is numbered, so that t can take on fractional values (like 7.59) and P_t is the value of P at the exact time t. Taking logarithms, we have

$$\ln P_t = \ln P_0 + gt \tag{2.29}$$

Since g is constant, $\ln P_t$ is a linear function of t, just as $\ln P_i$ is a linear function of i in (2.27).

In practice, any constant-growth process can be described by either a discrete model or a continuous model. The models are equivalent, but the continuous-growth rate g will be smaller than the discrete-growth rate r. To see why, let our two measures of time be consistent, so that $t = i$ at the end of each period. After a certain number of periods, the value of the variable is denoted by P_t in the continuous model and P_i in the discrete model. Since these notations represent the same value, $P_t = P_i$. Inspection of (2.29) and (2.27) shows that $g = \ln(1 + r)$. Now, our earlier analysis of the natural logarithmic function revealed that $\ln(1 + r) < r$ unless $r = 0$. Putting these results together, we see that

$$g = \ln(1 + r) < r \quad \text{so} \quad g < r \tag{2.30}$$

[Recall from (2.14) that if r is small, $\ln(1 + r) \approx r$ and therefore $g \approx r$.] In other words, we see that in describing the same real growth process the continuous rate of growth (g) will be smaller than the discrete rate of growth (r), but these values will be close to each other when the rates are small.

In banking and finance, financial contracts are often described by more than one rate of return. For example, if a bank compounds interest frequently, the return on a savings account might be described as both a 5 percent interest rate and a 5.1 percent annual yield. The distinction between these two rate of return concepts is analogous to the distinction between continuous and discrete rates of growth. Let P be the value of the account, and let time be measured in years. If the bank compounds interest frequently, the concept of the interest rate corresponds to the rate of growth g in the continuous-growth model (although this is not obvious) and the concept of annual yield corresponds to the rate of growth r in the discrete-growth model. Since $g < r$, the interest rate is less than the annual yield.

Problems _____

Section 2.1

2.1 Consider a data set containing information relating to the number of employees, amount of output, number of plants, and number of different product lines for each of 200 firms in a given industry. Think of these data as being in a rectangular data set:
(a) How many rows and columns are there?
(b) How many numbers constitute one observation?
(c) How many observations are there?

★ **2.2** In the data set of Problem 2.1, which variables are discrete, and which are continuous?

★ **2.3** Why is it important that the sample used to estimate the nation's unemployment rate be representative?

2.4 Explain why combining time-series data from two decades governed by different marginal propensities to consume would be inappropriate for estimating a single aggregate consumption function. (A graph would help.)

Section 2.2

2.5 Look at the data on *ED* in Table 2.2:
(a) What are the minimum and maximum values of the variable?
(b) What value of the variable seems to be typical?
(c) If a person were chosen at random, what would be your guess of his *ED* value?

2.6 From among the variables in the cross-section data set, name one that is clearly discrete and one that is clearly continuous.

★ **2.7** Suppose it is true that the size of savings accounts held by individuals increases as a linear function of their total wealth: $S = \beta_0 + \beta_1 W$. Based on the discussion of errors in the SFC, what impact would these errors have on the apparent (i.e., estimated) value of β_1—assuming that W is measured without error? (A graph would help.)

2.8 Looking down Table 2.2, describe the relation between *INCOME* and *WEALTH* in the data. What are the economic links between the two variables?

2.9 Looking down Table 2.2, describe the relation between *SAVING* and *WEALTH* in the data. What are the economic links between the two variables?

Section 2.3

2.10 Look at the data on *GNP* in Table 2.3:
 (a) What are the minimum and maximum values of the variable?
 (b) What value of the variable seems to be "typical"?
 (c) What is your guess of the *GNP* value for 1981?

★ **2.11** Using the aggregate consumption function discussed in Section 1.1 as an example, explain why in making predictions about future consumption we must assume that the economic process represented in data from the past will continue unchanged. (A graph would help.)

2.12 Compute the amount of absolute growth and the rate of growth for real investment *INV* for each of the years 1976–1980.

2.13 Compute the real money supply for the years 1956–1958. For these years, is the real money supply greater or less than the nominal money supply? Why?

2.14 Compute the rate of inflation in *PGNP* for 1957 and for 1958. Compare your results with *RINF1*.

★ **2.15** Unlike the national accounts data, the Consumer Price Index is benchmarked in 1967 (i.e., *CPI* = 100 for 1967) in our data set. Using *RINF2*, determine the values of *CPI* for 1968 and 1969.

2.16 Based on the data for *PGNP*, how much higher were prices in 1980 than they were in 1970?

2.17 Determine the values of nominal GNP for the years 1971–1973.

Section 2.4

★ **2.18** For time periods 1 through 5, the five values for a time-series variable *X* are 10, 15, 22, 31, and 42. Graphically or algebraically determine what is happening to the absolute growth in *X* as time passes. Now determine the five values of ln X. What is happening to the rate of growth of X as time passes?

2.19 Let the value of X be 50 in time period 1. Determine the values of X in periods 2 through 5 if the absolute change in X is -20 each period. Now, determine the values of X in periods 2 through 5 if the rate of change is -20 percent per period.

★ **2.20** Extending Problem 2.19, sketch the graph of X and of ln X if the rate of change of X is -20 percent.

2.21 Suppose that five successive values for CON are 405, 461, 585, 697, and 824. Carefully construct both a regular time plot and a logarithmic time plot for CON.

Appendix

2.22 Using a calculator, prepare a two-column table showing the values of x and ln x for $x = 1.00$, 1.01, 1.02, $\ldots$, 1.20 (giving ln x to three decimals). Now add another column to the table, showing the approximate value of ln x computed according to Equation (2.13). For what values of x is the difference between the actual and approximate values of ln x less than 0.01?

★ **2.23** If a number is doubled, how is its logarithm affected?

★ **2.24** If $Q = AP^b$ is the equation of a demand curve, reexpress this relation in terms of how ln Q is related to ln P.

2.25 If $Y = Ab^x$, how is ln Y related to X?

2.26 If $Y = AX^b Z^{-c}$, reexpress this relation in terms of logarithms.

2.27 If ln $Y = a + b$ ln Z, reexpress this relation showing Y as a function of Z.

★ **2.28** If ln $Y = a + Z$ ln b, reexpress this relation showing Y as a function of Z.

★ **2.29** Suppose that $X = 10$ in an initial period, and that four periods later $X = 42$. Determine the rate of growth of X per period.

2.30 Suppose that $X = 10$ initially, and that four years later $X = 42$. Determine the continuous rate of growth of X.

2.31 If a bank offers a savings account with a 7 percent interest rate compounded continuously, what is the annual yield on this account?

3

Descriptive Statistics

In this chapter we examine basic concepts relating to variables on which we have a set of data. To summarize such data, we develop statistics that measure the typical value of a single variable and how much variation there is among the values of that variable. Also, we develop statistics that measure how much relation there is between any two variables. The appendix explains the use of the summation operator Σ.

In the sense used here, a *statistic* is a measure that is calculated from the values of variables in a given set of data. This technical definition constrasts with common usage, in which "statistics" is used to mean what we call data.

3.1 Univariate Statistics

Throughout this section we focus on a single variable for which we have n observations. Our examples use the variable measuring family income in the cross-section data set from Chapter 2; sometimes this variable is called X, and sometimes *INCOME*. Recall that in the full data set $n = 100$.

Measures of Central Tendency

A *measure of central tendency* is a statistic that measures the typical value that a variable takes on in data. Since "typical" is not a precise concept, it should not be surprising that a variety of measures have been developed.

The most common and useful measure is the **mean**. This is simply what most people call the "average," but that term is ambiguous to statisticians, who use it to refer to any measure of central tendency. The mean of a variable is conventionally symbolized by placing a bar over the variable name: the mean of X is $\overline{X}$, which is read as "X bar." Formally, the definition of the mean is

$$\overline{X} = \frac{1}{n} \sum_{i=1}^{n} X_i \tag{3.1}$$

which tells us that to calculate the mean of X we must add up all the values of X and multiply by $1/n$ (i.e., divide by n). It should be noted that the number produced by this calculation need not be a value that is actually taken on by any of the observations. In our data on family income, $\overline{X}^* = 9.941$, rounded to three decimals. (Throughout this book, when a symbol such as $\overline{X}$ defines a statistic, an asterisk is added to indicate its value in a specific set of data.)

Another useful measure of central tendency is the **median,** which can be denoted by X_{med}. The median value of X is the value of the middle observation on X, after the observations have been ordered from smallest to largest. If there are an odd number of observations, there is only one observation in the middle; X_{med} is the value of X for this observation. If there are an even number, there is no single middle observation. In this case, to determine X_{med} we take the two values of X that straddle the middle and average them. After ordering our data on *INCOME,* the "middle" is between the 50th and 51st observations. Hence, $X_{med} = (X_{50} + X_{51})/2 = (8.703 + 8.850)/2 = 8.777$ (rounded).

In econometric work, the mean plays an important role while the median is rather neglected. However, the median is often more useful for representing the typical value of a variable, and it is a useful tool in economic statistics. For example, consider a community in which different families have different incomes. Suppose that we desire that our measure of the typical family income should not be affected much by whatever happens to the richest family. If the richest family's income increases from one million to ten million dollars, while all other incomes remain constant, the mean would increase noticeably but the median would not change at all. Similarly, if the richest family moved away, the mean would decrease noticeably but the median would decrease only slightly. Hence, in this case the median would be preferred to the mean. In our data on *INCOME,* if we delete the five families with the greatest income, the mean drops markedly from 9.941 to 8.950, while the median drops only from 8.777 to 8.573 thousand dollars.

A third measure of central tendency is the **mode,** which is the most frequently occurring value. The mode is sometimes a useful statistic for identifying the typical value of a discrete variable, such as family size, but it is not too useful for continuous variables because every observation's value may be unique. (This is the case for *INCOME* in our data.)

Measures of Dispersion

After finding a measure of central tendency for the data on a variable, the next concern is to determine how spread out (or dispersed) the values are. A statistic that conveys this information is called a **measure of dispersion.**

One such measure is the **range,** which is simply the difference between the greatest (X_{max}) and the smallest (X_{min}) values of X among the n observations. In our *INCOME* data, X_{max} = 32.080 and X_{min} = 0.750, so the range is 31.330. The range is a simple concept that is often used, but it does not tell us anything about the distribution of the values of X—whether they are concentrated near the middle, spread out all over, or concentrated near the endpoints.

Several useful measures of dispersion are based on the deviations (differences) of the values of a variable from its mean. For the ith observation, the deviation of X from the mean is

$$d_i = X_i - \overline{X} \tag{3.2}$$

Since there are n observations, there are n deviations. Unless all the values of X are the same, some of the deviations are positive and some are negative. For *INCOME,* the deviations take on values between -9 and 20, roughly.

The most important measure that we develop is a statistic that represents the typical deviation of the values of X from its mean. An obvious candidate is the mean deviation ($\sum d_i/n$, because a mean is a typical value. However, the positive and negative values of d_i always cancel out in summation, so the mean deviation always equals zero. This makes it rather useless as a measure of dispersion. We can prove that the mean deviation equals zero by proving that the $\sum d_i$ always equals zero:

$$\sum d_i = \sum (X_i - \overline{X})$$
$$= \sum X_i - \sum \overline{X}$$
$$= n\overline{X} - n\overline{X} = 0 \tag{3.3}$$

In going from the second line to the third we make two simple substitutions: first, $\sum X_i = n\overline{X}$, as may be seen from (3.1), and second, $\sum \overline{X} = n\overline{X}$, since the constant $\overline{X}$ is being summed n times.

This problem of the positive and negative values canceling out suggests that we should seek a statistic that represents the "typical deviation, without regard to sign," and that is what we do. One possibility solves the problem by calculating the mean absolute deviation (*MAD*), which is ($\sum|d_i|)/n$. In our data on *INCOME* the *MAD* is about 3.771. This value seems reasonable as a measure of the typical deviation, since the $|d_i|$ for *INCOME* range from 0 to 20 roughly, with more small values than large values. Although the *MAD* appeals to our common sense, other statistics turn out to be more useful.

A second possibility solves the problem by squaring all the deviations and calculating their mean. This **mean squared deviation** of X is defined as

$$MSD_X = \frac{\sum\limits_{i=1}^{n} d_i^2}{n} = \frac{\sum\limits_{i=1}^{n} (X_i - \overline{X})^2}{n} \qquad (3.4)$$

For our data on *INCOME* the *MSD* is 30.869, which clearly is too large to be interpreted as the typical deviation; the difficulty, of course, is the squaring.

To fix this problem, we take the square root of the *MSD* to arrive at a useful way to measure the typical value of the deviation. This leads to the **root mean squared deviation** of X, which is denoted by $RMSD_X$:

$$RMSD_X = \sqrt{MSD_X} = \sqrt{\frac{\sum\limits_{i=1}^{n} d_i^2}{n}} = \sqrt{\frac{\sum\limits_{i=1}^{n} (X_i - \overline{X})^2}{n}} \qquad (3.5)$$

To understand this defining formula, one must be able to carry out the indicated operations. The name of the statistic, read backward, tells us exactly what to do. First, the deviation (from the mean) is computed for each observation separately. Second, each of these deviations is squared. Third, the n squared deviations are added up, and the sum is divided by n to yield the mean. Fourth, the square root is taken, and we end up with the root mean squared deviation. In our data on *INCOME* the *RMSD* is 5.556; from what we know about the data, this is a reasonable value for a statistic that claims to measure the typical deviation. The fact that the *RMSD* is larger than the *MAD* reflects the fact that the intermediate squaring gives extra weight to large deviations.

It turns out that a minor alteration of the *RMSD* yields a more useful statistic. Instead of dividing $\sum d_i^2$ by n, we divide by $n - 1$. This yields the **standard deviation** of X, for which the common symbol is S_X. The formal definition is

$$S_X = \sqrt{\frac{\sum\limits_{i=1}^{n} d_i^2}{n-1}} = \sqrt{\frac{\sum\limits_{i=1}^{n} (X_i - \overline{X})^2}{n-1}} \qquad (3.6)$$

It is easy to remember that the standard deviation is the same as the *RMSD* except that n is replaced by $n - 1$ in the denominator. This makes S_X larger than $RMSD_X$. To see how much larger, we note that S_X is simply $\sqrt{n/(n-1)}$ times $RMSD_X$. When $n = 20$ this term is 1.026, and when $n = 100$ it is 1.005. Thus S_X will be very close to $RMSD_X$, except when n is small. In our data on incomes $S_X^* = 5.584$, which is just slightly larger than $RMSD_X^* = 5.556$.

Sometimes, but not in this text, the root mean squared deviation is called the "standard deviation." One should be aware that calculators and computer programs may offer both options, and it is not always clear what definition of "standard deviation" is used. We adopt (3.6) in order to be consistent with procedures that are discussed later. The peculiar $n - 1$ term in this definition of the standard deviation is called the **number of degrees of freedom**. (Suppose that we know $n - 1$ values of the variable. The nth value can be determined if we know $\overline{X}$. In this sense, the nth observation is not "free.")

The name "standard deviation" proclaims the interpretation that we give to the statistic, since "standard" is a synonym for "typical." Given that S_X measures the typical deviation (without regard to sign), one might think that about half of the absolute deviations would be smaller than S_X and about half would be larger. This is not so. In practical data analysis, it often turns out that about two-thirds of the observations have absolute deviations $|d_i|$ that are smaller than S_X and about one-third have $|d_i|$ that are larger. In other words, the "standard" deviation is a relatively large standard. Nonetheless, it is a very useful statistic and it merits being interpreted as the typical deviation.

Another way of putting this yields an empirical approximation that is a useful rule of thumb: about 68 percent of the observations have values within one standard deviation of the mean—that is, in the interval $\overline{X} - S_X$ to $\overline{X} + S_X$. Similarly, about 95 percent of the observations have values within two standard deviations of the mean—that is, in the interval $\overline{X} - 2S_X$ to $\overline{X} + 2S_X$. These two rules add considerable interpretive power to the standard deviation as a measure of typical deviation. It happens that *INCOME* is not symmetrically distributed, as shown in Chapter 4, and the first rule does not work too well. The one-standard-deviation interval is 4.357 to 15.525 (i.e., 9.941 ± 5.584), and by actual count 85 percent of the observations lie in this interval. The two-standard-deviation interval is −1.227 to 21.109, and 95 percent of the observations lie therein.

If the mean of X equals zero, the standard deviation can be given a slightly different interpretation. Normally, we say that the typical value of X is measured by $\overline{X}$. However, a situation in which $\overline{X} = 0$ is often a special one, and in such a situation we probably are interested in knowing the typical value of X without regard to sign. Now, with $\overline{X} = 0$ we see that $d_i = X_i$. Hence, the typical (without regard to sign) X_i would be the same as the typical (without regard to sign) d_i. Thus, when $\overline{X} = 0$ the standard deviation S_X can be interpreted as the typical value of X (without regard to sign).

Finally, another measure of dispersion is the **variance**. This statistic is a minor alteration of the mean squared deviation (*MSD*) defined by (3.4), with $n - 1$ instead of n appearing in the denominator. Thus, the variance is equal to the square of the standard deviation S_X, and it is usually denoted by S_X^2. Formally,

$$S_X^2 = \frac{\sum\limits_{i=1}^{n} d_i^2}{n - 1} = \frac{\sum\limits_{i=1}^{n} (X_i - \overline{X})^2}{n - 1} \tag{3.7}$$

The variance and the standard deviation carry the same information about the variable they describe. Although the variance is often used as the main measure of dispersion in mathematical treatments of statistics, we focus on the standard deviation because of its meaningfulness as a measure of the typical deviation. For future reference we note that the numerator in the definition of the variance is called the **total variation** in X, and it serves as a measure of the overall variability among the values of X.

Computation

In practice, if the mean and standard deviation are to be calculated by hand, it makes sense to do it in a table format rather than by just substituting a long string of numbers into the appropriate formulas. For example, suppose that we wish to compute the mean and standard deviation for a sample consisting of the first 10 observations on *INCOME* in our data. Table 3.1 shows the X values listed in column (2). Summing these, we find that $\sum X = 106.768$, which yields a mean $\overline{X}^* = 10.6768$. For each observation, separately and one at a time, the deviation from the mean and its square are computed, as indicated in columns (3) and (4). The squared deviations are summed, $\sum d_i^2 = 420.388$, which then yields a variance of $S_X^{2*} = 46.710$ and a standard deviation of $S_X^* = 6.834$.

This procedure, which is based on the direct application of (3.1), (3.7), and (3.6), involves passing through the X values twice. On the first pass we accumulate $\sum X_i$ as we go through the data, and then $\overline{X}$ is determined at the end. On the second pass we go back to each observation to calculate d_i and d_i^2, and we accumulate $\sum d_i^2$ as we go through the data.

Is it possible to calculate all this in just one pass through the data? The answer is yes. To see how, we first show that

TABLE 3.1   First 10 Observations on Family Income and Computation of $\overline{X}$ and S_X

(1) i	(2) X_i	(3) $d_i = (X_i - \overline{X})$	(4) $d_i^2 = (X_i - \overline{X})^2$
1	1.920	−8.7568	76.682
2	12.403	1.7262	2.980
3	6.396	−4.2808	18.325
4	7.005	−3.6718	13.482
5	6.990	−3.6868	13.592
6	6.500	−4.1768	17.446
7	26.007	15.3302	235.015
8	15.363	4.6862	21.960
9	14.999	4.3222	18.681
10	9.185	−1.4918	2.225
	106.768	0.0	420.388

Mean: $\overline{X} = \sum X/n = 106.768/10 = 10.6768$

Variance: $S_X^2 = \sum d_i^2/(n-1) = 420.388/9 = 46.710$

Standard Deviation: $S_X = \sqrt{S_X^2} = 6.834$

Median = 8.095   Range = 24.087

Note: d_i is calculated to four decimals to illustrate that $\sum d_i = 0$; d_i^2 is rounded to three decimals for convenience.

$$\sum d_i^2 = \sum (X_i - \bar{X})^2$$
$$= \sum (X_i^2 - 2\bar{X}X_i + \bar{X}^2)$$
$$= \sum X_i^2 - 2\bar{X}\sum X_i + n\bar{X}^2$$
$$= \sum X_i^2 - 2\left(\frac{\sum X_i}{n}\right)\sum X_i + n\left(\frac{\sum X_i}{n}\right)^2$$
$$= \sum X_i^2 - 2\frac{(\sum X_i)^2}{n} + \frac{(\sum X_i)^2}{n}$$
$$= \sum X_i^2 - \frac{1}{n}(\sum X_i)^2 \qquad\qquad (3.8)$$

In this derivation, we move from line to line by applying the laws of algebra and summation, and substituting $\sum X_i/n$ for $\bar{X}$ in the fourth line. Focusing on

$$\sum d_i^2 = \sum X_i^2 - \frac{1}{n}(\sum X_i)^2 \qquad\qquad (3.9)$$

we note that $\sum X_i^2$ is a sum that can be accumulated in one pass through the X values: at each step we simply square the X value and accumulate it. Similarly, $\sum X_i$ can be accumulated in the same pass, simultaneously with the accumulation of $\sum X_i^2$ but independently of it. At the end of the pass we can calculate $\sum d_i^2$, using (3.9). Hence in one pass we can calculate the mean of X [from $\sum X_i$, using (3.1)] and the standard deviation [from $\sum d_i^2$, using (3.6)]. This computational procedure is useful for writing an efficient computer program, but it does not lead us through the basic concepts in the way that the table approach does. Hence, for our purposes, being able to work through the derivation (3.8) is more important than applying the result.

Finally, Figure 3.1a presents a graphical review of the basic descriptive statistics calculated in Table 3.1. The graph is one-dimensional, plotting values of X along the horizontal axis. (Note that four observations clump together near $X = 7$.) The range of 24.087 extends from $X_{min} = 1.920$ to $X_{max} = 26.007$. The median, $X_{med} = 8.095$, is halfway between the fifth and sixth ordered observations. The mean, $\bar{X} = 10.6768$, is larger. The span of the one-standard-deviation interval about the mean includes 8 of the 10 observations.

A good intuitive understanding of the mean and standard deviation allows one to guess their values simply by looking at a plot of data. For example, temporarily ignore the calculated statistics shown in Figure 3.1a, and look just at the plotted X values. It appears that the mean must be about 10—this is a middle-ish value, somewhat affected by one extremely high value of X. The standard deviation appears to be about 5, because the one-standard-deviation interval about the mean usually contains about two-thirds of the observations. As we know in fact, these guesses are quite good. We leave as a problem the task of guessing $\bar{Y}$ and S_Y in Figure 3.1b.

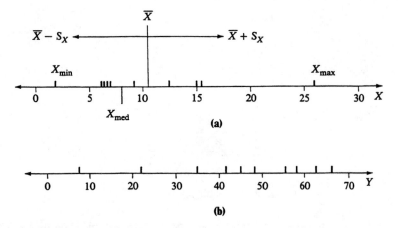

(a)

(b)

FIGURE 3.1   The one-dimensional graph in (a) plots the values of family income (X) from Table 3.1, and the values or positions of various statistics are indicated. The analysis of the data values plotted in (b) is left as a problem.

3.2   Linear Transformations

Sometimes a new variable (Y) is created as a transformation of an existing variable (X). Such a transformation is defined by a rule or equation, $Y_i = f(X_i)$, which may be simple or complex. For example, the U.S. personal income tax system defines tax liability to be a function of taxable income. If we start with data for n values of X, applying the transformation creates n values of Y.

Just as the data for X can be summarized by the descriptive statistics $\overline{X}$ and S_X, so too the n newly created values of Y can be summarized by computing $\overline{Y}$ and S_Y using the basic defining formulas (3.1) and (3.6). However, since each Y_i is related to the corresponding X_i in a known way, one might wonder whether there are simple ways to determine the values $\overline{Y}$ and S_Y directly from their counterparts $\overline{X}$ and S_X. The answer is generally "no," but for a certain class of transformations that are of considerable interest to us, the answer is "yes."

In econometric and statistical work, a common and useful type of transformation is the *linear transformation*. If Y is related to X according to

$$Y_i = a + bX_i \quad \text{for all } i \tag{3.10}$$

then Y is a linear transformation of X, and vice versa. In (3.10), a and b are constants, or parameters, while Y and X are variables. For each and every observation, the Y value is related to the X value in this way. For example, let X be family income measured in thousands of dollars. If b is the marginal tax rate and a is the (negative) tax credit in a simple linear tax system, then Y as defined by (3.10) is the net tax payment due.

As in the general case, the n values of Y can be summarized by $\overline{Y}$ and S_Y calculated according to basic procedures. However, in contrast to the general case, when Y is a linear transformation of X there are simple relations between their means, their variances, and their standard deviations. These are

$$\text{if} \quad Y_i = a + bX_i \quad \text{then} \quad \overline{Y} = a + b\overline{X} \tag{3.11}$$

$$S_Y^2 = b^2 S_X^2 \tag{3.12}$$

$$S_Y = |b| S_X \tag{3.13}$$

Thus in the income tax example with $a = -2$ and $b = 0.25$,

$$\overline{Y} = -2 + 0.25\overline{X} \quad \text{and} \quad S_Y = 0.25 S_X \tag{3.14}$$

In other applications, either a or b may take on the special values of zero or 1. For example, if every family is given 1.5 thousand dollars as a national dividend, the new income might be called Y, with $Y_i = 1.5 + X_i$. Implicitly, $b = 1$. The relations above enable us to see quickly that $\overline{X} = 1.5 + \overline{Y}$ and $S_Y = S_X$. Adding \$1500 increases every family's income by the same amount, so the dispersion among them remains the same. By contrast, suppose that every family's income is increased by 15 percent, leading to $Y_i = 1.15X_i$ (note that to increase by 15 percent is to multiply by 1.15). Here, $a = 0$. Then $\overline{Y} = 1.15\overline{X}$ and $S_Y = 1.15 S_X$. Increasing all incomes proportionately leads to an increase in dispersion (i.e., differences) in incomes as well as an increase in the mean.

As another example we might define Y as income expressed in dollars, while X is still income in thousands of dollars. Clearly, $Y_i = 1000X_i$. Thus, extending the results from earlier in the chapter, $\overline{Y}^* = 9941$ and $S_Y^* = 5584$, compared with $\overline{X}^* = 9.941$ and $S_X^* = 5.584$. Hence, as promised, measuring financial variables in thousands of dollars or other convenient units does not distort the statistical findings; it merely changes the units of measurement.

The nature of linear transformations is illustrated in Figure 3.2. In each case, the Y value corresponding to any X value is shown by the height up to the transformation line, and this value can be traced over to the Y axis. The four parts of the figure display the $X_{\min}$ and $X_{\max}$ values from the same set of n observations, and they also display the calculated $\overline{X}$ statistic. Equation (3.11) states that $\overline{Y}$ is the transformation of $\overline{X}$, and this is illustrated in all parts of the figure.

The various cases in Figure 3.2 provide some insight into (3.13), which gives the relation between the standard deviations S_Y and S_X. Although the standard deviations are not shown, we can compare the range of Y with the range of X in each case, and this indicates what the comparison of S_Y and S_X would be. Figure 3.2b shows that if a were to increase, the line of transformation would shift up in a parallel fashion. All the Y values would increase, but the range of Y would remain the same. That is, the range of Y is not affected by the value of a, and this holds true for the standard deviation also. This explains why the parameter a plays no role in (3.13).

Comparisons among the four parts of the figure illustrate the role of the parameter b. The slope b of the transformation in Figure 3.2a is greater than the

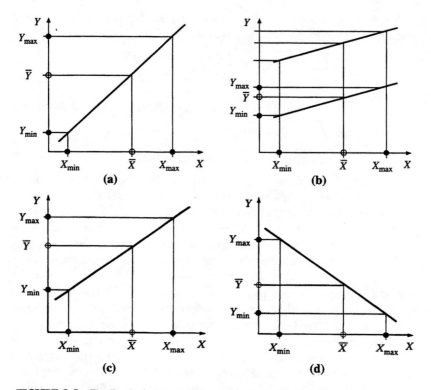

FIGURE 3.2 The line is the graph of the transformation $Y = a + bX$, with a and b taking on different values in each case. Part (b) shows that an increase in a does not affect the range of Y. Comparing the different cases, we see that the range of Y is greater when $|b|$ is greater. These findings regarding the range of Y also hold true for the standard deviation of Y, according to Equation (3.13).

slope b in Figure 3.2b, and we see that this causes the range of Y to be greater in the first case than in the second. This indicates that (for cases with $b > 0$) the greater is b, the greater is S_Y. The magnitudes of the slopes in Figures 3.2c and d are the same, but the signs are different. For the given set of X values we see that the range of Y is the same in both cases, and this indicates that S_Y would be the same in both cases also. That is, only $|b|$ matters in the comparison of S_Y with S_X.

The proofs of (3.11) and (3.12) are straightforward. For the mean,

$$\bar{Y} = \frac{1}{n} \sum Y_i = \frac{1}{n} \sum (a + bX_i) = \frac{1}{n} \sum a + \frac{1}{n} \sum bX_i$$

$$= \frac{1}{n} na + \frac{1}{n} b \sum X_i$$

$$= a + b\bar{X} \tag{3.15}$$

For the variance,

$$S_Y^2 = \frac{1}{n-1} \sum (Y_i - \bar{Y})^2$$

$$= \frac{1}{n-1} \sum (a + bX_i - a - b\bar{X})^2$$

$$= \frac{1}{n-1} \sum (bX_i - b\bar{X})^2$$

$$= \frac{1}{n-1} b^2 \sum (X_i - \bar{X})^2$$

$$= b^2 S_X^2 \tag{3.16}$$

The proof for the standard deviation follows from taking the square root of the variance.

It should be remembered that if $Y_i = f(X_i)$ is not a linear transformation, we cannot expect there to be simple relations between the corresponding statistics. For example if $Y_i = \ln X_i$, which is the logarithmic transformation, $\bar{Y} \neq \ln \bar{X}$.

3.3 Bivariate Statistics

Our ultimate objective in econometrics is to determine how some variables are related to others, and in this section we take a first step in that direction. We examine how much, or to what degree, two variables are related in a certain way.

We start with a data set that has n observations on two variables, X and Y. This means that there are n pairs of numbers, each of the form (X_i, Y_i). Each pair of numbers can be plotted, as in Figure 3.3, in a *scatter diagram* (or scatterplot) with X measured on the horizontal axis and Y on the vertical axis. In Figure 3.3a it looks as though X and Y are positively related: there is a tendency for high values of X to be associated with high values of Y. For a different set of data plotted in Figure 3.3b, it looks as though X and Y are negatively related.

One measure that quantifies how much the values of X and Y vary together is the *covariance*. The symbol used for the covariance of X and Y is S_{XY}, and its definition is

$$S_{XY} = \frac{1}{n-1} \sum_{i=1}^{n} (X_i - \bar{X})(Y_i - \bar{Y}) \tag{3.17}$$

Notice that X and Y enter this relation in basically the same way, so that there is no difference between the covariance of X and Y and that of Y and X. Neither variable is special in its relation to the other.

The values of X and Y enter the covariance formula as deviations from their means [i.e., as $(X_i - \bar{X})$ and $(Y_i - \bar{Y})$]. The impact of this may be seen by graphing a vertical line through $\bar{X}$ and a horizontal line through $\bar{Y}$, as in Figure

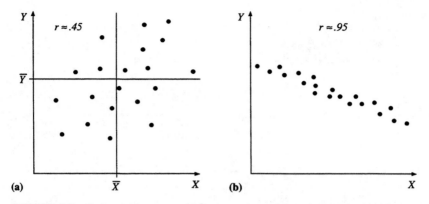

FIGURE 3.3 Each point in a scatter diagram represents a pair of numbers of the form X_i, Y_i. In (a), Y and X are positively but loosely correlated; the auxiliary axes show the positions of the data points relative to the means $\bar{X}$ and $\bar{Y}$. In (b), Y and X are negatively and strongly correlated.

3.3a. Each point, or observation, can be viewed in relation to these auxiliary axes. A point in the upper right quadrant has a positive X deviation $(X_i - \bar{X})$ and a positive Y deviation $(Y_i - \bar{Y})$. Thus the product $(X_i - \bar{X})(Y_i - \bar{Y})$ is positive, and it makes a positive contribution to the summation in (3.17). By contrast, a point in the upper left quadrant has a negative $(X_i - \bar{X})(Y_i - \bar{Y})$ product, because $(X_i - \bar{X})$ is negative and $(Y_i - \bar{Y})$ is positive, and it makes a negative contribution to the covariance. The signs for the products of points in the other quadrants are determined similarly. We come to the conclusion that if most of the points in the scatter diagram are in the upper right and lower left quadrants formed by the auxiliary axes through $\bar{X}$ and $\bar{Y}$, then the covariance probably will be positive; this is because most of the terms being summed will be positive, while a few will be negative. Similarly, if most of the points are concentrated in the upper left and lower right quadrants, the covariance probably will be negative. And if the points are scattered all over, it is hard to guess the sign of the covariance before it is actually calculated.

A difficulty with the covariance statistic is that the magnitude of the number is not easily interpreted. To remedy this, it is common to use an associated statistic, the *correlation coefficient,* which is defined as

$$r = \frac{S_{XY}}{(S_X)(S_Y)} \tag{3.18}$$

If we substitute the defining formulas for S_{XY}, S_X, and S_Y into this equation we end up with a formidable display of X's, Y's, Σ's, and $\sqrt{\ }$'s. We prove in the appendix to Chapter 5 that the effect of dividing the covariance of X and Y by the product of their standard deviations is to limit the possible values of r to be in the range from -1 to 1.

The interpretation of the correlation coefficient r relates to an imaginary line that can be fit through the data points. The correlation carries two pieces of information about the data and the line: the sign of r is the same as the sign of the slope of that line, and the magnitude (absolute value) of r measures the degree to which the points lie close to the line. The magnitude of r does *not* tell us the slope of the line.

If the points in the scatter diagram lie exactly along some straight line with a positive slope, then $r = 1$; if they lie exactly along a line with a negative slope, then $r = -1$. (If they lie along a vertical or horizontal line, then r will not be defined because S_X or S_Y is zero.) At the other extreme, if the points are scattered all over rather randomly, the correlation will be close to zero. In Figure 3.3a, $r \approx .45$ and we would say that Y and X are positively but loosely correlated: in Figure 3.3b, $r \approx -.95$ and we would say that Y and X are negatively and strongly correlated. It should be noted again that the correlation does not tell us whether a line drawn through the data would be steep or flat; it tells us only the sign of the slope.

Although the correlation coefficient is very useful, its weakness is that it measures only the degree of *linear* relation between the variables. Often this is interesting enough. However, if the data points in the diagram make a perfect $\vee$ shape, or $\cup$ shape, the correlation will be zero. If they lie neatly along an upward sloping snakelike shape, the correlation will be positive but not unity. Hence r is not a measure of general relation.

As an example of computation, consider the five observations on Y and X in Table 3.2, which are plotted in Figure 3.4. These are the first five observations on

TABLE 3.2 Descriptive Statistics for *SAVING* (Y) and *INCOME* (X)

(1) Y_i	(2) X_i	(3) $(X_i - \bar{X})$	(4) $(X_i - \bar{X})^2$	(5) $(Y_i - \bar{Y})$	(6) $(Y_i - \bar{Y})^2$	(7) $(X_i - \bar{X})(Y_i - \bar{Y})$
0.0	1.9	−5.04	25.4016	−0.56	0.3136	2.8224
0.9	12.4	5.46	29.8116	0.34	0.1156	1.8564
0.4	6.4	−0.54	0.2916	−0.16	0.0256	0.0864
1.2	7.0	0.06	0.0036	0.64	0.4096	0.0384
0.3	7.0	0.06	0.0036	−0.26	0.0676	−0.0156
2.8	34.7	0.0	55.5120	0.0	0.9320	4.7880

$$\bar{X} = \sum X_i/n = 34.7/5 = 6.94$$
$$\bar{Y} = \sum Y_i/n = 2.8/5 = 0.56$$
$$S_X = \sqrt{\sum (X_i - \bar{X})^2/(n - 1)} = \sqrt{55.512/4} = \sqrt{13.878} = 3.725$$
$$S_Y = \sqrt{\sum (Y_i - \bar{Y})^2/(n - 1)} = \sqrt{0.932/4} = \sqrt{0.233} = 0.483$$
$$S_{XY} = \sum (X_i - \bar{X})(Y_i - \bar{Y})/(n - 1) = 4.788/4 = 1.197$$
$$r = S_{XY}/(S_X S_Y) = 1.197/[(3.725)(0.483)] = .67$$

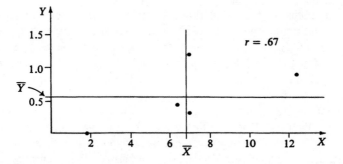

FIGURE 3.4 The scatter diagram displays the five observations on *SAVING* (*Y*) and *INCOME* (*X*) from Table 3.2, and the auxiliary axes showing the means $\overline{X}$ and $\overline{Y}$ are drawn in. There is a moderately strong, positive correlation between *Y* and *X* in these data.

SAVING (*Y*) and *INCOME* (*X*) from the cross-section data set, with the values rounded to one decimal position for simplicity. The correlation $r = .67$ indicates a moderately strong relation between *SAVING* and *INCOME,* which we investigate further in Chapter 5.

It is usually interesting, but never conclusive, to look at the correlations among possibly related variables in any data set. The correlation matrix for a selected set of the variables in the cross-section data set is shown in Table 3.3, in which each entry in the table gives the correlation between the variables indicated on the row and column headings. Only half the matrix is filled in, to avoid repetition. The correlation matrix for a selected set of our time-series variables is shown in Table 3.4.

It should be emphasized that finding a high correlation between two variables does not prove that there is a cause-and-effect relation between them. Why not? It could be the case that two variables are both strongly affected by a third variable. They may be different effects of the same cause and may have no direct link between them. In time-series data, especially, there often are high correlations between variables even when a true relation is lacking. This is because most variables tend to go steadily up, or steadily down, over time.

TABLE 3.3   Correlation Matrix from the Cross-Section Data Set ($n = 100$)

	EARNS	*ED*	*AGE*	*INCOME*	*SIZE*	*WEALTH*
EARNS	1.000					
ED	.534	1.000				
AGE	.057	−.214	1.000			
INCOME	.886	.457	.252	1.000		
SIZE	.002	.003	−.216	−.102	1.000	
WEALTH	.625	.251	.359	.673	−.132	1.000

TABLE 3.4   Correlation Matrix from the Time-Series Data Set ($n = 25$)

	GNP	CON	DPI	RAAA	M1	RINF1	UPCT
GNP	1.000						
CON	.998	1.000					
DPI	.998	.999	1.000				
RAAA	.945	.952	.954	1.000			
M1	.963	.974	.966	.948	1.000		
RINF1	.860	.866	.874	.915	.875	1.000	
UPCT	.351	.396	.390	.434	.488	.354	1.000

APPENDIX: Summation

Statistical calculations often involve adding together many numbers. When the addition is complicated by other algebraic operations, the use of a special summation notation simplifies matters considerably.

Suppose that we have data on the annual incomes, measured in thousands of dollars, of five families. We let the families be identified by a number from 1 to 5; this number is called the **index**, and its symbol for the typical case is i. We let X be the symbol denoting annual income, so X_i stands for the income of the ith family. The second column of Table 3.5 shows the hypothetical data: the income of the first family (X_1) is 21 thousand dollars, that of the second is 10, $X_3 = 32$, and so on.

The total income of this group of five families is 90 thousand dollars, this being the sum of the five X_i values. To symbolize this summation operation, we write

$$\sum_{i=1}^{5} X_i = X_1 + X_2 + X_3 + X_4 + X_5$$

$$= 21 + 10 + 32 + 12 + 15 = 90 \tag{3.19}$$

($\sum$ is uppercase "sigma," the Greek "S.") The left-hand side of (3.19) is read as "the sum of X_i, for i running from 1 to 5," and the first line of the right-hand side shows in simple algebraic terms what this operation means. The second line

TABLE 3.5   Hypothetical Income Data

(1) i	(2) X_i	(3) $0.25X_i$	(4) $-2 + 0.25X_i$
1	21	5.25	3.25
2	10	2.5	0.5
3	32	8.0	6.0
4	12	3.0	1.0
5	15	3.75	1.75

shows how the operation is performed. When no confusion is apt to occur, the indexing information below and above Σ may be partly or completely eliminated. For example, when it is clear that the operation involves all five families, the symbols

$$\sum_{i=1}^{5} X_i, \quad \sum_{i} X_i, \quad \sum X_i, \quad \text{and} \quad \sum X \tag{3.20}$$

are understood to be equivalent. The first form gives a complete statement of the summation, while the third strikes a nice balance between complexity of notation and possibility of confusion.

When the laws of algebra are brought into play in the summation of complicated expressions involving the X_i values, various properties of the summation operator become apparent and are worth remembering. To be general, let X be the name of a variable for which we have n different values, numbered 1 through n: $X_1, X_2, \ldots, X_n$. Let a and b be two constants—numbers that are the same for all i. Then, starting with an original X_i value we can think of a new value being defined as $a + bX_i$ and we can consider taking the sum of these n values: $\sum (a + bX_i)$. We can prove without much ado that

$$\sum_{i=1}^{n} (a + bX_i) = na + b \sum_{i=1}^{n} X_i \tag{3.21}$$

To do any simple proof, the basic method is to start with the expression on the lefthand side of the equation and use definitions and the laws of algebra to get to the righthand side. To wit:

$$
\begin{aligned}
\sum_{i=1}^{n} (a + bX_i) &= (a + bX_1) + (a + bX_2) + \cdots + (a + bX_n) \\
&= \underbrace{(a + a + \cdots + a)}_{n \text{ terms}} + (bX_1 + bX_2 + \cdots + bX_n) \\
&= na + b(X_1 + X_2 + \cdots + X_n) \\
&= na + b \sum_{i=1}^{n} X_i
\end{aligned}
\tag{3.22}
$$

Two important special cases arise. If $a = 0$, then $a + bX_i = bX_i$, and it should be clear from (3.21) that

$$\sum_{i=1}^{n} bX_i = b \sum_{i=1}^{n} X_i \tag{3.23}$$

If $b = 0$, then $a + bX_i = a$, and substituting in (3.21) we find that

$$\sum_{i=1}^{n} a = na \tag{3.24}$$

Although this is an odd-looking use of summation notation, it clearly states that the sum of a constant added up n times is simply equal to that constant multiplied by n.

To return to our hypothetical income data, suppose that the government imposes a 25 percent tax on all incomes and simultaneously declares a 2 thousand dollar tax credit (i.e., negative tax levy) for every family. The net tax due for a family with income X_i is $-2 + 0.25X_i$; note that this is of the form $a + bX_i$, with $a = -2$ and $b = 0.25$. The total net tax collection will be

$$\sum_{i=1}^{5}(-2 + 0.25X_i) = (5)(-2) + 0.25\sum_{i=1}^{5}X_i$$

$$= -10 + (0.25)(90) = 12.5 \qquad (3.25)$$

thousand dollars, by (3.21). The gross income tax collection is of the form $\sum bX_i = b\sum X_i$, which is 22.5 here, and the total negative tax levy is of the form $\sum a = na$, which is -10 here. Table 3.5 shows the gross and net tax payments for each family, in columns (3) and (4). The totals may be verified.

For a slight variation, let us reconsider (3.23). If b happens to be the inverse of another constant ($b = 1/c$), then the summation property still holds, so that

$$\sum_{i=1}^{n}\frac{X_i}{c} = \frac{\sum_{i=1}^{n}X_i}{c} \qquad (3.26)$$

Summations involving more complicated expressions than those considered here can be simplified or factored following the basic rules of algebra, along lines similar to those in (3.22).

Problems _____

Section 3.1

★ **3.1** Calculate the mean and median of *UPCT* for a sample consisting of the first 10 observations in the time-series data set.

3.2 Calculate the mean and median of *UPCT* for a sample consisting of the last 15 observations in the time-series data set.

3.3 Can the mean *UPCT* for all 25 observations be determined from your answers to Problems 3.1 and 3.2? If so, show how.

★ **3.4** Can the median *UPCT* for all 25 observations be determined from your answers to Problems 3.1 and 3.2? If so, show how.

3.5 Suppose that among a group of 10 families the mean number of persons in a family is 3.8. If all the families came together, how many people would be present?

3.6 Determine the mode of *SIZE* in the cross-section data set.

3.7 Using the tabular method presented in the text, calculate the mean, variance, and standard deviation of the first 10 observations on *UPCT*. Also calculate the range.

⋆ **3.8** Extending Problem 3.7, exactly what proportion of these 10 observations lie within one standard deviation of the mean? What proportion lie within two?

3.9 Suppose that data on a variable X consist of five observations for which $X = -1$ and five for which $X = 1$. For the whole data set of 10 observations, calculate the mean, root mean squared deviation, and standard deviation of X. In this case, is $RMSD_X$ or S_X a better measure of the typical deviation of X?

3.10 Prove that $S_X = \sqrt{n/(n-1)}\, RMSD_X$.

⋆ **3.11** Use the procedure associated with Equation (3.9) to help calculate the mean, variance, and standard deviation of the first 10 observations on *UPCT*. Compare the results with those from Problem 3.7.

⋆ **3.12** Guess the values of the mean and standard deviation of Y in Figure 3.1b.

3.13 Using the tabular method presented in the text, calculate the mean and standard deviation of the last 15 observations on *UPCT* in the time-series data set. What proportion of the observations lie within one standard deviation of the mean?

3.14 Using the data from Problem 3.13, plot the data on *UPCT* in a one-dimensional graph and indicate the values of the median, mean, and standard deviation.

Section 3.2

3.15 Suppose that X in Table 3.5 were survey data on the number of years of work experience of the head of each family and that each person had worked exactly X years (i.e., not X plus or minus a few months). Assume that $\overline{X}^* = 18$ and $S_X^* = 8.9$. Now, let Y_i stand for the number of months that the ith head of family has worked.
   (a) How is each Y_i related to the corresponding X_i?
   (b) Determine the mean and standard deviation of Y.

3.16 Let Z_i be the work experience, in years, of these same persons two years from the original survey.
   (a) How is each Z_i related to the corresponding X_i?
   (b) Determine the mean and standard deviation of Z.

⋆ **3.17** Let W_i be the work experience, in months, of these same persons two years from the original survey.
   (a) How is each W_i related to the corresponding X_i?
   (b) Determine the mean and standard deviation of W.

⋆ **3.18** Two common measures of cross-section income inequality are the standard deviation of income and the standard deviation of the logarithm of income. If all persons' incomes are increased by 20 percent, what happens to these measures of inequality?

3.19 Solve Equation (3.10) for X in terms of Y and write the equation in a form that makes it clear that X is a linear transformation of Y.

Section 3.3

3.20 Make a rectangular data set consisting of the first five observations on *UPCT* and *RINF1* from the time-series data set (for convenience, round *RINF1* to one decimal position). Make a scatterplot of *RINF1* against *UPCT* and guess the sign of the correlation coefficient.

★ **3.21** Calculate the covariance and the correlation between the data variables of Problem 3.20.

3.22 Suppose that the data on Y and X are identical (i.e., that $Y_i = X_i$ for all i). How does the covariance of Y and X compare with the variance of X?

★ **3.23** Suppose that we have data on Y and X, and then we create a new variable $Z = a + bX$ (with $b > 0$). How does the covariance of Y and Z compare with the covariance of Y and X?

3.24 In the context of Problem 3.23, prove that the correlation between Y and Z is equal to the correlation between Y and X.

3.25 Table 3.3 shows a negative correlation between *SIZE* and *INCOME*. What economic forces or patterns of behavior might lead to this? What might lead to a positive correlation?

4

Frequency Distributions

In this chapter we examine grouping and classification techniques for organizing and summarizing data on a single variable. The techniques are similar in the cases of discrete and continuous variables, but there are some important differences. Recall from Chapter 2 that a discrete variable usually results from counting and often it has relatively few distinct values actually occurring in the data. By contrast, a continuous variable usually results from measuring and it usually has many different values occurring in the data.

Most of the statistical methods of econometrics are based on calculations from raw data, as were those in Chapter 3. The techniques presented here are of interest to us because they are useful tools of economic statistics and because they provide a background for understanding the more abstract subject of probability theory that is presented in Chapter 9.

4.1 Discrete Data Variables

Suppose that we have data for n observations on a discrete variable X that takes on only m different values. In this case, it is possible to arrange the n observations into m different groups within which all the observations have exactly the same X value. The different groups ordered by their X values can be indexed by k with $k = 1, 2, \ldots, m$, so that the typical value can be denoted by X_k.

For example, we examine the 100 observations on *SIZE*, the size of families in our cross-section data set, and denote it by X. Inspection of the raw data reveals that X ranges from 2 to 10, so that $m = 9$. Table 4.1 displays the result of grouping. Each row corresponds to a different value of X, and the rows are ordered with $X_1 = 2$, $X_2 = 3, \ldots, X_9 = 10$. The first column shows the value of the group index k for each row and the second gives the value of X_k for that group. The third column gives the count of the number of observations among the original n that take on this value (here $n = 100$). This count is called the **absolute frequency,** and it is denoted by n_k. As a check on our counting we might add up the absolute frequencies, because in any frequency table

$$\sum_{k=1}^{m} n_k = n \tag{4.1}$$

That is, the sum of the number of observations having each particular value must equal the total number of observations.

The fourth column in the table contains the **relative frequency,** denoted by f_k, with which each X_k occurs. The relative frequency of X_k is the proportion of the n observations that have this value, and it is defined by

$$f_k = \frac{n_k}{n} \tag{4.2}$$

It is always true that the sum of the relative frequencies equals 1:

$$\sum_{k=1}^{m} f_k = 1 \tag{4.3}$$

TABLE 4.1   Frequency Table for *SIZE* ($n = 100$)

(1)	(2) Value of X	(3) Absolute Frequency	(4) Relative Frequency	(5)	(6)
k	X_k	n_k	f_k	$X_k n_k$	$(X_k - \overline{X})^2 n_k$
1	2	10	.10	20	55.2250
2	3	16	.16	48	29.1600
3	4	34	.34	136	4.1650
4	5	21	.21	105	8.8725
5	6	13	.13	78	35.3925
6	7	3	.03	21	21.0675
7	8	1	.01	8	13.3225
8	9	1	.01	9	21.6225
9	10	1	.01	10	31.9225
		100	1.00	435	220.7500

$$\overline{X} = \sum X_k n_k / n = 4.35$$

$$S_X = \sqrt{\sum (X_k - \overline{X})^2 n_k / (n-1)} = \sqrt{220.75/99} = 1.493$$

except that rounding error, if allowed, may cause a slight difference. Very simple algebra proves this:

$$\sum_{k=1}^{m} f_k = \sum_{k=1}^{m}\left(\frac{n_k}{n}\right) = \frac{1}{n}\sum_{k=1}^{m} n_k = \frac{1}{n}n = 1 \tag{4.4}$$

The values of X_k coupled with the corresponding f_k make up the *relative frequency distribution* of X, which is represented graphically in a line chart, as in Figure 4.1. The value of f_k for each class is measured vertically, and it is graphed as a vertical line rising from the horizontal X axis at the value X_k. This distribution is a concise restatement of the original data, and the only loss of information is the value of n.

Since the relative frequency distribution implicitly orders the X values, it is easy to find the median. We see that 26 percent of the observations are in groups 1 or 2, while another 34 percent are in group 3; hence the middle observations are in group 3, with $X_{\text{med}} = 4$ being the median value of X. Also, we see that 4 is the most frequently occurring value, making it the mode. Finally, we see that very few families have seven or more members—only 6 percent do.

The mean and standard deviation of X can be calculated from the frequency table, instead of the raw data, according to

$$\overline{X} = \frac{1}{n}\sum_{k=1}^{m} X_k n_k \tag{4.5}$$

$$S_X = \sqrt{\frac{\sum_{k=1}^{m}(X_k - \overline{X})^2 n_k}{n - 1}} \tag{4.6}$$

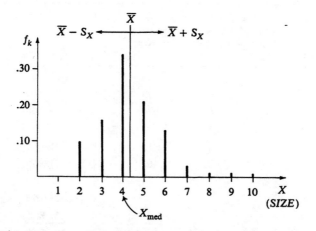

FIGURE 4.1 The relative frequency distribution of *SIZE*, a discrete variable, is graphed as a line chart. The height gives the relative frequency f_k corresponding to each group's X_k value. The mean and standard deviation calculated in Table 4.1 are displayed for reference.

Since grouping the data on a discrete variable involves no loss of information about the exact values of the variable, the statistics calculated from the frequency table are identical to those calculated from the underlying raw data.

To see that (4.5) is valid, first think of rearranging the n observations so that they are ordered by the value of X, with the smallest value being first and the largest being last. The mean defined in terms of the raw data as

$$\overline{X} = \frac{1}{n} \sum_{i=1}^{n} X_i = \frac{1}{n}(X_1 + X_2 + \ldots + X_n) \tag{4.7}$$

is $1/n$ times a summation of n terms, each of which is an observed X value. Now, the first n_1 of the ordered observations are equal to the same value (X_k with $k = 1$), the second n_2 are equal to another value (X_k with $k = 2$), and so on. Thus the summation is equal to $X_k n_k$ with $k = 1$, plus $X_k n_k$ with $k = 2$, and so on, and

$$\overline{X} = \frac{1}{n} \sum_{i=1}^{n} X_i = \frac{1}{n} \sum_{k=1}^{m} X_k n_k \tag{4.8}$$

The validity of (4.6) is similarly demonstrated.

The basic univariate descriptive statistics can also be stated in terms of relative frequencies. The mean and the root mean squared deviation of X are

$$\overline{X} = \sum_{k=1}^{m} X_k f_k \tag{4.9}$$

$$RMSD_X = \sqrt{\sum_{k=1}^{m} (X_k - \overline{X})^2 f_k} \tag{4.10}$$

and the standard deviation can be obtained from the $RMSD_X$:

$$S_X = \sqrt{n/(n-1)} \, RMSD_X \tag{4.11}$$

Although the definitions in terms of absolute frequencies provide a slightly easier method for computation, the definitions in terms of relative frequencies provide us with a better background for understanding probability distributions in Chapter 9.

In Table 4.1, columns (5) and (6) show the intermediate steps involved in calculating the mean and standard deviation for family size, according to (4.5) and (4.6). The calculated values are $\overline{X}^* = 4.35$ and $S_X^* = 1.49$, respectively. (Recall that an asterisk is used to denote the actual value of a statistic calculated in a data set.) The one-standard-deviation interval around the mean extends from $4.35 - 1.49$ to $4.35 + 1.49$; that is, it extends from 2.86 to 5.84. Since *SIZE* is discrete, only those observations with $X = 3$, 4, or 5 lie within this interval. By adding $f_2 + f_3 + f_4$ in Table 4.1 we see that 71 percent of the observations lie within one standard deviation of the mean. All the calculations in this paragraph yield exactly the same results as would be obtained by using the definitions in Chapter 3 with the raw data on *SIZE*. As noted above, grouping the data on a discrete variable involves no loss of information about the exact values of the variable; no approximations are introduced.

What is achieved by constructing the frequency table? First, we have transferred all the information in the original 100 observations into a nine-line table. If we had started with 25,000 observations, the economy resulting from this transfer would be even more striking. Second, the arrangement of the data in a frequency table displays the salient characteristics of the data on a single variable more readily than does presentation of the raw data: it is difficult to see any pattern in family size just by looking down the long column on *SIZE* in Table 2.2, but Table 4.1 and Figure 4.1 convey the pattern very clearly.

4.2 Continuous Data Variables _____

With a continuous variable (or with a discrete variable that is considered practically continuous), it would be impractical to set up groups within which all the observations have exactly the same value, because the number of groups would be very large. Instead, m classes are determined in such a way that every observation can be placed into one and only one class, which is defined to include an interval of values for the variable.

For our purposes, it is convenient to follow three principles in setting up the class intervals: (1) the number of classes should be between 5 and 15, (2) the width of each interval should be the same, and (3) the midpoint of each interval should be a convenient number.

For example, letting X now denote the income of families in our cross-section data set (*INCOME*), we recall that X ranges from 0.75 to 32.080 thousand dollars. One convenient classification is to set up nine intervals, each with a range of 4 thousand dollars: the first runs from 0 to 4, the second from 4 to 8, and so on. A difficulty with this scheme is that some observations may lie right on the boundary between two classes. Rather than adopt an arbitrary rule such as putting all such boundary cases into the lower class, it is better to randomize— such as by putting the first boundary case into the lower class, the second into the higher class, the third into the lower class, and so on. In many cases clever choice of the class intervals avoids the boundary problem. For example, if we were to treat *AGE* from Table 2.2 as practically continuous, then we might choose class boundaries such as 22.5 to 27.5, 27.5 to 32.5, and so on. The midpoints would be 25, 30, and so on, and no observations would lie on a boundary.

The *class mark* X_k is defined for each class as the midpoint of the class interval. The class marks here are $X_1 = 2$, $X_2 = 6$, and so on. The class mark is used to represent the value of each observation that is placed into a class, and as a result of this classification process the true value of each observation is lost. This loss of information contrasts sharply with the discrete case, in which there is no such loss.

The frequency table for family income (X) in our data is given in Table 4.2. The first column gives both the row index k and the boundary values for X that define the class. The second column gives the class mark, X_k. The third column gives the absolute frequency n_k, which is the number of observations in our data whose X value falls in each class. To construct a frequency table we must look at each of the observations, decide which class it corresponds to, and keep a running tally. After we have looked at all the observations, our tallies give us the absolute frequencies.

The relative frequency for a particular class, f_k, is the proportion of all the n observations that are in that class. The values of X_k coupled with the corresponding f_k make up the **relative frequency distribution** of X, which is represented graphically in a **histogram** as in Figure 4.2. The value of f_k for each class is measured vertically and is graphed as a horizontal line directly over the interval of X values that defines the class; then the area under each line is enclosed to make a bar.

Figure 4.3 shows some shapes that histograms commonly take on. When there is only one peak the resulting distribution is said to be **unimodal,** and when there are two it is **bimodal.** Among unimodal distributions, some are fairly symmetrical (Figure 4.3a) but others are not. The distribution in Figure 4.3c is said to be **skewed** to the right because it has a longer tail in that direction, and that in Figure 4.3d is skewed to the left.

The mean and standard deviation of a continuous variable whose data are classified in a frequency table are defined in exactly the same way as for a discrete variable, by (4.5) and (4.6). The calculations for family income are shown in Table 4.2, where we find that $\overline{X}^* = 10.120$ and $S_X^* = 5.755$. These

TABLE 4.2 Frequency Table for *INCOME* ($n = 100$)

(1)		(2) Class Mark X_k	(3) Absolute Frequency n_k	(4) Relative Frequency f_k	(5) $X_k n_k$	(6) $(X_k - \overline{X})^2 n_k$
k	Bounds					
1	(0– 4)	2	5	.05	10	329.672
2	(4– 8)	6	35	.35	210	594.104
3	(8–12)	10	35	.35	350	0.504
4	(12–16)	14	16	.16	224	240.8704
5	(16–20)	18	4	.04	72	248.3776
6	(20–24)	22	0	.00	0	0.0
7	(24–28)	26	2	.02	52	504.3488
8	(28–32)	30	2	.02	60	790.4288
9	(32–36)	34	1	.01	34	570.2544
			100	1.00	1012	3278.56

$$\overline{X} = \sum X_k n_k / n = 10.12$$

$$S_X = \sqrt{\sum (X_k - \overline{X})^2 n_k / (n - 1)} = \sqrt{3278.56/99} = 5.755$$

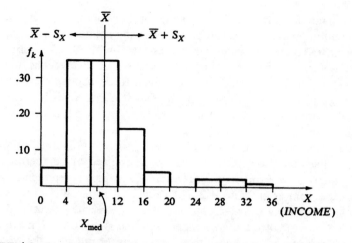

FIGURE 4.2 The relative frequency distribution of *INCOME*, a continuous variable, is graphed as a histogram. The height of each bar gives the relative frequency f_k for each class. The mean and standard deviation calculated in Table 4.2 are displayed for reference.

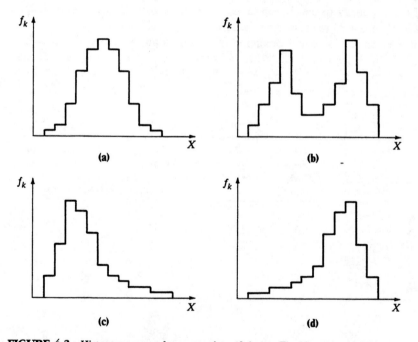

FIGURE 4.3 Histograms may take on a variety of shapes. The histogram in (b) is bimodal, whereas the others are unimodal. The histogram in (a) is symmetrical. The histogram in (c) is skewed to the right, and that in (d) is skewed to the left.

values are somewhat different from the statistics calculated in Chapter 3 from the raw data on *INCOME,* which were $\overline{X}^* = 9.941$ and $S_X^* = 5.584$. The differences are due to our now using the class marks to stand for the actual X values of the observations, and the error thereby introduced is part of the cost of achieving summarization through classification. The calculation of the median of a continuous variable from a frequency table is discussed below.

The calculations in Table 4.2 shed some light on a mystery from Chapter 3. There it was noted that the interval $\overline{X} - S_X$ to $\overline{X} + S_X$ contains 85 percent of the observations in the raw data for family income, and the discrepancy between this amount and the 68 percent rule of thumb was attributed to the lack of symmetry. We see in the table that the bulk of the observations lie in the first five classes, having *INCOME* less than 20 thousand dollars. However, in column (6) we see that more than half of the total variation in X is attributable to the five observations with the greatest amounts of income. These extreme observations boost up the standard deviation, and therefore they increase the range of the one-standard-deviation interval; this causes such a great proportion of the observations to lie therein.

To explore this further, we consider the frequency distribution for the sample with the five greatest X values deleted, leaving $n = 95$. The histogram for this reduced sample is the same as that for the whole sample, Figure 4.2, except that the three small bars lying at the right-hand side of the graph would not be present. The shape of the distribution for the reduced sample is clearly more symmetrical than that for the whole sample, although it is not perfectly so. Going back to the raw data ($n = 95$), we find $\overline{X}^* = 8.950$ and $S_X^* = 3.529$, and we find that 73 percent of the observations in the reduced sample lie within one S_X of $\overline{X}$. This makes the 68 percent rule look much better.

Finally, there is a special correspondence between relative frequencies and areas under a histogram, which arises from our method of construction. All the bars in the histogram have the same width, w, which is equal to the width used to define all the classes. The height of each bar is f_k, so the area of each is wf_k. The total area of the histogram is the total of all the bars' areas $\sum wf_k$. This is equal to w, because w is fixed and $\sum f_k = 1$. Thus the ratio of the area of the kth bar to the total area of the histogram is

$$\frac{wf_k}{\sum wf_k} = \frac{wf_k}{w \sum f_k} = \frac{wf_k}{w} = f_k \tag{4.12}$$

That is, the relative frequency f_k for any class can be determined graphically from the histogram as the area in the bar lying above the class interval, divided by the total area of the histogram. This link between relative frequencies and areas is an important feature of the classification technique.

Proportions

An interesting use of relative frequency distributions and histograms is making calculations that answer such questions as "What proportion of the observations have X values between X_a and X_b?" We may rephrase this question notationally as

$$\text{Prop}(X_a \le X \le X_b) = ? \tag{4.13}$$

where $X_a < X_b$. For example, from the classified data on *INCOME* we might want to determine the proportion of observations that lie in the one-standard-deviation interval 10.120 ± 5.755; that is, in (4.13), $X_a = 4.365$ and $X_b = 15.875$, with X being *INCOME*. Or, we might want to determine the proportion of observations having incomes less than or equal to 10 thousand dollars; in other words, $\text{Prop}(0 \le X \le 10)$.

If we were working with the raw data on X (or with the frequency distribution of a discrete variable), our method of answering this question would be to count up the number of observations that lie in the interval and reexpress this count as a proportion. The corresponding exact count generally cannot be made from the frequency distribution of a continuous variable, however, because we have thrown away information about the observations' exact X values and have let the class marks stand in their place. Thus whatever answer we come up with will be only an approximation to the answer obtained from the raw data.

The general approach to determining the proportion in question is to calculate the sum of the relative frequencies of the class intervals and parts of class intervals that make up the interval from X_a to X_b. The relative frequency of any whole class interval contained in the (X_a, X_b) interval is already known in the frequency table. If part of a class interval is involved, we must use some approximation technique to determine the relative frequency assignable to it.

For our purposes, we adopt the **uniform distribution assumption** that the X values of the observations in any class interval are spread smoothly, or uniformly, throughout it. (It helps to think that the number of observations is very large, so that there are no questions of spacing within the interval.) This assumption implies that the number of observations in any part interval is proportional to the range of that part interval. For example, if the range of a part interval constitutes one-third of the range (width) of the interval, we say that one-third of the observations in the interval lie in the part interval. Since the number of observations can be reexpressed as a proportion, the uniform distribution assumption implies that the relative frequency assigned to any part interval is proportional to the range of that part interval. For example, if the relative frequency for the whole interval is .30, a relative frequency value of .10 will be assigned to a part interval whose range constitutes one-third of the range of the whole interval.

As an example of applying this approach algebraically, we determine the proportion of observations lying in the one-standard-deviation interval for *INCOME*. Referring to Table 4.2, we see that the interval (4.365, 15.875) corresponds to part of the second class interval, all of the third, and part of the fourth class interval defined in the frequency table. First focusing on the second interval in the table, we see that the range for the whole interval is 4.0 (i.e., from

4 to 8) and the relative frequency of the interval is .35. The part interval from 4.365 to 8 has a range of 3.635; this range amounts to the fraction 3.635/4.0 of the range of the whole interval. By the uniform distribution assumption, we assign to the part interval a relative frequency equal to that fraction times the relative frequency of the whole interval. Since the relative frequency of the whole second interval is $f_2 = .35$, the part interval is assigned $(3.635/4.0)(.35) =$ .318 as its relative frequency. Now focusing on the whole third interval, we see in the table that its relative frequency is $f_3 = .35$. Finally focusing on the fourth interval, we see that we are interested only in the part interval from 12 to 15.875. This has a range of 3.875, and by our assumption we assign the relative frequency $(3.875/4.0)(.16) = .155$ to it. Adding the three relative frequencies together, we find that 82.3 percent of the observations on *INCOME* lie within one standard deviation of the mean in the frequency table.

These calculations can be summarized:

$$\text{Prop}(4.35 \le X \le 15.875) = \left(\frac{8 - 4.365}{4.0}\right) f_2 + f_3 + \left(\frac{15.875 - 12}{4.0}\right) f_4$$

$$= \left(\frac{3.635}{4.0}\right)(.35) + (.35) + \left(\frac{3.875}{4.0}\right)(.16)$$

$$= .318 + .35 + .155 = .823 \tag{4.14}$$

We recall from Chapter 3 that the interval $\overline{X} - S_X$ to $\overline{X} + S_X$ contained 85 percent of the observations in the raw data. The discrepancy between .823 and .85 is attributable to the loss of information that results from organizing the original raw data into classes.

An equivalent method for determining proportions based on the uniform distribution assumption involves comparing areas in the histogram. The key link between the assumption and this graphical method is our use of a horizontal line (as the top of a bar) to represent the relative frequency for each class in a histogram. We saw above, in (4.12), that the relative frequency for a whole class interval is equal to the area of the bar standing above that interval, divided by the total area of the histogram. Similarly, the relative frequency that we now assign to a part interval is equal to the area of the part bar standing above it, divided by the total area of the histogram. In the graphical approach, the proportion of observations in the (X_a, X_b) interval is taken to be equal to the sum of the areas lying above the class intervals and part intervals that make up the overall interval, divided by the total area of the histogram. This is illustrated in Figure 4.4a, in which $\text{Prop}(X_a \le X \le X_b)$ is given by the ratio of the shaded area to the total area in the histogram. The graphical approach can help us make some quick assessments of proportions, and it is helpful for understanding the probability theory in Chapter 9.

For example, consider again the problem of determining the proportion of observations lying in the one-standard-deviation interval for *INCOME*. Figure 4.5, which repeats the histogram from Figure 4.2, indicates the X_a and X_b values

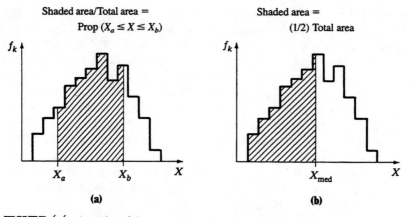

Shaded area/Total area =
Prop $(X_a \leq X \leq X_b)$

Shaded area =
(1/2) Total area

(a)

(b)

FIGURE 4.4 A portion of the area under a histogram, relative to the total area, gives the proportion of observations having values within the particular interval of X values. This idea is based on the uniform distribution assumption; a tally of the raw data would give a slightly different answer. Part (a) illustrates the general form of the proportion problem, given as Equation (4.13). Part (b) illustrates how this idea is used to determine the median, according to (4.17).

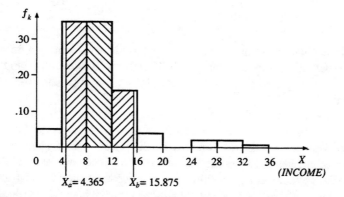

FIGURE 4.5 In accord with the uniform distribution assumption, Prop(4.365 $\leq X \leq$ 15.875) is calculated as the ratio of the shaded area to the total area in this figure. The shaded area is specified in Equation (4.15) as the sum of three component rectangular areas. The total area in this histogram is equal to 4.0; in general, the total area equals w, the width of each class interval.

for this problem and shows the three components of the shaded area lying above the (X_a, X_b) interval. Recalling that the width of each class interval in Table 4.2 is 4.0, we see that the shaded area is given by

$$\text{shaded area} = (8 - 4.365)f_2 + (4.0)f_3 + (15.875 - 12)f_4$$

$$= (4.0)\left[\left(\frac{8 - 4.365}{4.0}\right)f_2 + f_3 + \left(\frac{15.875 - 12}{4.0}\right)f_4\right] \quad (4.15)$$

In this calculation, the first line shows the three component bar and part bar areas, and the second line factors out the value 4.0.

Now, in (4.12) we found that the total area in the histogram equals w, which is equal to 4.0 in this example. Thus (4.15) can be rearranged as

$$\frac{\text{shaded area}}{\text{total area}} = \left(\frac{8 - 4.365}{4.0}\right)f_2 + f_3 + \left(\frac{15.875 - 12}{4.0}\right)f_4$$

$$= \text{Prop}(4.365 \le X \le 15.875) \quad \text{by u.d.a.} \quad (4.16)$$

The first line here is simply a restatement of our area computation. The expression on the right-hand side is identical to the right-hand side of the first line of (4.14). That is, the ratio of the shaded area to the total area is exactly equal to the algebraic calculation of $\text{Prop}(4.365 \le X \le 15.875)$ based on the uniform distribution assumption. This equivalence leads to the substitution in the second line of (4.16).

Another application of proportion calculations is determining the median. For a classified continuous variable, the median is defined as the value X_{med} such that

$$\text{Prop}(X \le X_{\text{med}}) = .5 \quad (4.17)$$

Figure 4.4b illustrates this definition for a general case. In our data for family income we see that the median is somewhere in the third class, since $\text{Prop}(X \le 8) = .40$ and $\text{Prop}(X \le 12) = .75$. The median value X_{med} can be visualized as lying at the end of a part interval that begins at the value $X = 8$ and stretches into the third interval in the frequency table. This part interval is of such a size that exactly .10 relative frequency is assigned to it, thus assuring that X_{med} satisfies (4.17). The median is calculated to be

$$X_{\text{med}} = 8 + \left(\frac{.10}{.35}\right)(4) = 9.14 \quad (4.18)$$

In this calculation, the fraction (.10/.35) is a ratio of relative frequencies. By the uniform distribution assumption, the ratio of the range of the part interval to the range of the class interval is equal to this ratio of relative frequencies. Hence, multiplying this fraction (.10/.35) by the range of the class interval ($w = 4$) gives us the range of the part interval (1.14). By construction the median lies at the end of this part interval, which begins at 8.

Similarly, these proportion calculations can be used to determine various *percentiles* of the variable X. In general, the pth percentile of X is the value X_p that satisfies

$$\text{Prop}(X \le X_p) = p \quad (4.19)$$

where $0 \le p \le 1$. For example, the 25th percentile ($p = .25$) for *INCOME* is that value of *INCOME* below which 25 percent of the observations lie. The method used for determining the median can be used to find any percentile. Indeed, comparing (4.19) with (4.17) we realize that the median X_{med} is simply the 50th percentile.

Problems _____

Section 4.1

4.1 Treating *REG* (from the cross-section data set, $n = 100$) as though it were a meaningful discrete variable, construct a frequency table and graph the relative frequency distribution.

4.2 Based on your answer to Problem 4.1, determine the mean, median, and standard deviation of *REG*.

★ **4.3** Based on your answers to Problems 4.1 and 4.2, what proportion of the observations have a value for *REG* that is within one standard deviation of the mean? What proportion are within two?

4.4 Starting from Equation (3.5) as the definition of *RMSD*, prove that Equation (4.10) is true for grouped discrete data.

4.5 Suppose that the frequency distribution of X is symmetric. Let $Y = 2X$. Explain why the distribution of Y is also symmetric.

★ **4.6** Suppose that the frequency distribution of X is symmetric. Let $Y_i = \ln X_i$, that is, let each Y_i be equal to the natural logarithm of X_i. Explain why the distribution of Y is skewed to the left.

4.7 Considering only those 60 families with *SIZE* 2, 3, or 4 in Table 4.1, construct a frequency table and graph the relative frequency distribution for *SIZE*. From this new table, determine the mean, median, mode, and standard deviation of *SIZE* for these observations.

4.8 Starting from Equation (4.5), show that Equation (4.9) is true.

Section 4.2

★ **4.9** Treating *ED* ($n = 100$) as a continuous variable, construct a frequency table and carefully graph the relative frequency histogram. Choose as class boundaries 1.5–4.5, 4.5–7.5, and so on. Why is this a good choice?

★ **4.10** Based on your answers to Problem 4.9, determine the mean and standard deviation of *ED*. Should we expect that these calculated values will be exactly equal to the statistics calculated from the raw data on *ED*? Why?

4.11 On the histogram from Problem 4.9, highlight the area under the histogram that is bounded by vertical lines drawn through the value for

ED equal to one standard deviation below the mean and the value for
ED equal to one standard deviation above the mean.

4.12 Based on your answers to Problems 4.9 and 4.10, what proportion of
the observations have a value for *ED* that is within one standard
deviation of the mean?

★ **4.13** Based on your answer to Problem 4.9, determine the median value of
ED.

4.14 Suppose that within each class interval the actual *X* values are
concentrated toward the left side. How would the mean calculated from
the frequency distribution compare with the mean calculated from the
raw data?

4.15 Treating the frequency distribution in Table 4.1 as though *SIZE* were a
continuous data variable, determine the proportion of observations that
could be considered to lie within one standard deviation of the mean.
Compare this with the proportion of actual observations that lie in this
range.

4.16 Treating the frequency distribution in Table 4.1 as though *SIZE* were a
continuous data variable, determine the median of size. Compare this
with the true median of *SIZE*.

4.17 The ninetieth percentile of any variable is that value of the variable
below which 90 percent of the observations lie. Based on Table 4.2,
determine the ninetieth percentile of *INCOME*.

II

Specification and Estimation of Regression Models

5

Simple Regression: Theory

As previewed in Chapter 1, regression analysis is a technique for estimating the values of the coefficients in a model of an economic process. In this chapter and the next we discuss simple regression, which applies to models involving just two variables. In Chapter 7 we discuss multiple regression, which applies to models that are more complex.

The discussion in this chapter deals with the theory and mechanics of estimating a simple regression model of regular form. In the next chapter we apply this theory in a variety of cases, and we see how the estimates and measures developed here are put into practice.

5.1 Specification of the Model

Simple regression is a statistical technique that is appropriate to use when it is believed that the values of one variable are systematically determined by the values of just one other variable. Attention is focused on learning about the systematic relation between the variables, rather than on describing the particular set of data on hand. In this section we look at how the relation is specified in equation form, and in the next section we see how data are used with this specification to arrive at an estimated model.

The kind of relation that we study in economics is usually based on behavior, as in the case of a consumption function. Sometimes, however, the relation is based on technology, as in the case of a production function. For simplicity we refer to either type as a behavioral relation. We can think of such a relation as being an *economic process.* The input and the output of the process are observable, but the actual operation of the process is not.

We theorize that the process produces a set of data in the following way. Suppose that we have n observations, each having a particular value for the variable X. A value for X is fed into the process as an input, and a value for Y is produced as an output. This is repeated for each of the n observations, and the matched pairs of X and Y values are collected as a data set of n observations on two variables. We envision there being some random factors at work as part of the process, but these are not observable.

Two aspects of this process should be noted. First, X is the only variable that affects Y; it is the only variable that feeds into the process. By explicit exclusion from the discussion, other variables that might be measured for each observation are understood to play no direct role in the determination of Y. Second, the values of X are taken as given. The economic process under consideration does not affect those values and it plays no role in their determination. In addition, we make no effort to understand why X takes on whatever values it does. Our interest is in how the value of Y is related to the value of X for any observation.

We move toward statistical analysis by making a more concrete specification of the process by which Y is determined; this specification is known as the *simple regression model.* We theorize that the value of variable Y for each observation is determined by the equation

$$Y_i = \beta_0 + \beta_1 X_i + u_i \qquad\qquad (5.1)$$

In this regression model, Y is called the *dependent variable,* and X is called the *explanatory variable* (sometimes X is called the *independent variable*). In the model, β_0 and β_1 are parameters that have fixed values throughout (β is lowercase "beta," the Greek "b"); they are called the *coefficients* of the regression model. The term u is called the *disturbance.*

The disturbance u is considered to be an unobservable random term that does not depend on the value of X. The disturbances are meant to represent pure chance factors in the determination of Y. Among these factors there may be one that is best described as luck. Also, we might believe that Y is affected by a host of minor factors that we cannot identify and whose combined impact is indistinguishable from pure chance. Finally, we recognize possible measurement error in Y (but we presume that there is no measurement error in X). For any particular observation, u can be positive or negative, small or large. Overall, the average disturbance is anticipated to be close to zero, but only by coincidence would it be exactly zero in any given set of data.

For example, consider the process by which families determine their annual saving. Economic theory suggests that saving depends mostly on income. Letting Y be family saving and X be family income, (5.1) is a simple model of family saving behavior in which different families are the observations. The model does not explain the level of income of each family; it takes this as given. The parameter β_0 is the saving (probably negative) of families with zero income, and β_1 is the increase in saving that would result from a unit increase in family income. In economic terms, β_1 is the marginal propensity to save.

Based on the simple regression specification (5.1), we can decompose each Y_i value into a systematic component $\beta_0 + \beta_1 X_i$ and a random component u_i. The value of the systematic component is called the ***expected value*** of Y for each observation:

$$E[Y_i] = \beta_0 + \beta_1 X_i \tag{5.2}$$

This concept will be given a precise statistical meaning in Chapter 11, but for now it seems fairly intuitive: given (5.1), it is the value that Y_i would take on if the disturbance were equal to zero. This decomposition of each Y_i value into its systematic and random components can be compactly rewritten as

$$Y_i = E[Y_i] + u_i \tag{5.3}$$

The model specified in (5.1) is represented graphically in Figure 5.1. The systematic part of the relation between Y and X is graphed as the line

$$E[Y] = \beta_0 + \beta_1 X \tag{5.4}$$

which is called the ***true regression line***. We consider only a specific set of n observations whose X values are somehow given and whose Y values are determined according to (5.1). The resulting data points are plotted.

Following (5.3), the value Y_i for a single observation can be decomposed vertically into the distance up to a point on the true regression line and the distance from that point to the observation. The decomposition is shown

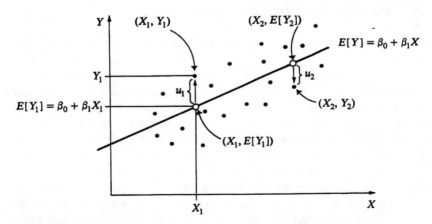

FIGURE 5.1 For each observation, the value Y_i can be decomposed into two parts: the systematic part $E[Y_i]$ (which equals $\beta_0 + \beta_1 X_i$) and the disturbance u_i. The systematic part is given by the height of the true regression line above the observation's X value, and the disturbance is given by the distance from the point on the regression line to the data point. The disturbance is positive for the first observation and negative for the second.

explicitly for two observations. For the first, which has the values X_1 and Y_1 for the two variables, the plotted point is shown and the X and Y values are traced to the axes. Directly above the value X_1 on the X axis we find a point on the true regression line; its vertical value is $E[Y_1]$, and this is traced over to the Y axis. The vertical distance from $E[Y_1]$ to Y_1 is u_i, which is shown also. The situation for the second observation (X_2, Y_2) is the same except that the data point lies below the true regression line, so the disturbance u_2 is negative.

In summary, the simple regression model illustrated in Figure 5.1 is a specification of the theoretical process that we use to describe the relation between two observable variables. For each observation the value X_i is determined outside the process. Given this X_i, the value Y_i is determined by (5.1). It will be convenient to say that the process generates the data on Y and X, even though the X values are determined outside.

Our theory is that the simple regression model actually reflects the way some economic behavior works. Surely this is a very simple model of how the values of a variable are determined: most economic variables systematically depend on more than one other variable, and that is why multiple regression is usually more appropriate. However, there are many instances in which simple regression is quite reasonable, and it is a useful tool of econometrics. Also, the presumption that the relation is strictly linear is not so constraining as it might seem. In some cases, we might well accept a linear model if we believe that the true relation is approximately linear. More important, we see in Chapter 6 that some truly nonlinear relations can be transformed into linear ones. In these cases we treat the transformed relation just as we treat the model specified in (5.1).

5.2   Estimation of the Model _____

When we believe that some economic behavior is correctly described by the simple regression model (5.1), the values of β_0 and β_1 are unknown. These values cannot be discovered: they are not written down anywhere, and there is no way that they can be directly measured. Instead, we seek to make estimates of these parameters. We do this by collecting a set of data, all of whose observations come from the economic process we are studying. These data provide the basis for making estimates of the unknown parameters.

Our job now is pictured in Figure 5.2. Temporarily ignore the line drawn there. The data we have are plotted, and these points represent all that we can observe. To say, as above, that we theorize that the data were generated by the process (5.1) means that we presume that there is some unobservable true regression line underlying the data. Figure 5.1, which illustrates the theory, explicitly shows a true regression line. Careful comparison of Figures 5.1 and 5.2 shows that the data points are exactly the same in both. In other words, Figure 5.1 presents our theory of how the data in Figure 5.2 were generated. Hence the true regression line in Figure 5.1 underlies the data in Figure 5.2. Of

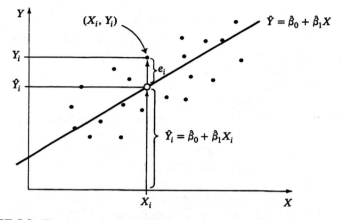

FIGURE 5.2 The estimated regression line is based on the data on Y and X, as plotted. It serves as an estimate of the true regression line in Figure 5.1, but it is generally different from it. For each observation, the value Y_i can be decomposed into two parts: the fitted value $\hat{Y}_i$ (which equals $\hat{\beta}_0 + \hat{\beta}_1 X_i$) and the residual e_i. The ordinary least squares criterion is to minimize the sum of the squares of these residuals.

course, we do not see it there, because it is not observable. But if we accept the theory that the true regression line underlies the data, we can use the data to estimate the parameters of the line.

The task of estimating the parameters β_0 and β_1 of the unobservable true regression line is carried out by drawing or fitting an actual line through the data. The intercept of this actual line is denoted by $\hat{\beta}_0$ and it serves as our estimate of β_0, the intercept of the true regression line. Similarly, the slope of the actual line is denoted by $\hat{\beta}_1$ and it serves as our estimate of β_1. (The circumflex looks like a hat, so $\hat{\beta}_1$ is conventionally read as "beta-one-hat.")

Suppose that the $\hat{\beta}_0$ and $\hat{\beta}_1$ we end up with correspond to the line

$$\hat{Y} = \hat{\beta}_0 + \hat{\beta}_1 X \tag{5.5}$$

drawn through the data in Figure 5.2. This is called the **estimated regression line** or the **fitted regression line.** For any data point such as (X_i, Y_i), this line decomposes the total value of Y_i into two parts. The first part, $\hat{Y}_i$, is the **fitted value** or **predicted value** for Y:

$$\hat{Y}_i = \hat{\beta}_0 + \hat{\beta}_1 X_i \tag{5.6}$$

which is the height up to a point on the estimated regression line, above X_i. The second part, e_i, is called the **residual,** or **error of fit:**

$$e_i = Y_i - \hat{Y}_i \tag{5.7}$$

which is the vertical distance from the line to the data point. Clearly,

$$Y_i = \hat{Y}_i + e_i \tag{5.8}$$

Note that if an observation lies below the estimated regression line, the actual value Y_i is less than the fitted value $\hat{Y}_i$. In this case, the residual e_i is negative.

How can we determine the parameters $\hat{\beta}_0$ and $\hat{\beta}_1$ of the estimated regression line? It seems reasonable to try to find the line that best fits the scatter of data. There are a variety of alternative techniques that might be used, and we consider several before focusing on the one we adopt.

One possibility is just to draw a line that seems to fit pretty well and accept that. In some cases this might be satisfactory, but it is not very precise. Two different persons analyzing the same data would undoubtedly come up with different estimates of the parameters, and we would have no basis for deciding which were better.

Another possibility is to measure the perpendicular distance from each point to the fitted line and then develop a method that calculates values for the parameters so as to minimize some overall measure of these distances. The results might be called "perpendicular estimators."

Instead of dealing with the perpendicular distances, what we actually do is based on another possibility: we measure the vertical distances from each point to the fitted line. These distances are the residuals, defined by (5.7).

Given this choice of what to measure, we next need to choose some overall function of the vertical distances so that a criterion can be specified to determine which line is the "best-fitting" one. We might try to find a line for which the sum of the residuals is zero. Unfortunately, it turns out that many lines satisfy this criterion, and some of them do not fit very well at all. Alternatively, we might try to minimize the sum of the absolute values of the residuals. This is reasonable, but somewhat awkward.

The standard approach in much practical work, which is the approach we adopt, is called the method of **ordinary least squares** (OLS). With this method, the criterion for being the best fit is that the line must make the **sum of the squared residuals** (SSR) as small as possible:

$$\text{OLS criterion:} \quad \text{minimize } SSR = \sum_{i=1}^{n} e_i^2 \tag{5.9}$$

Based on this criterion, we can develop mathematical rules or formulas for calculating $\hat{\beta}_0$ and $\hat{\beta}_1$.

Putting this more formally, suppose that we have n observations on Y and X, as illustrated in Figure 5.2. Any line drawn through the data will be of the form (5.5), and associated with particular $\hat{\beta}_0$ and $\hat{\beta}_1$ values are a set of residuals, e_i, that are determined by

$$e_i = Y_i - \hat{\beta}_0 - \hat{\beta}_1 X_i \tag{5.10}$$

Consider the sum of the squared residuals around a fitted line:

$$\sum_{i=1}^{n} e_i^2 = \sum_{i=1}^{n} (Y_i - \hat{\beta}_0 - \hat{\beta}_1 X_i)^2 \tag{5.11}$$

For a given set of data the X_i and Y_i are specific numbers, and our interest is in finding the $\hat{\beta}_0$ and $\hat{\beta}_1$ values that minimize this expression.

A calculus derivation, given in the appendix to this chapter, leads us to the following:

$$\hat{\beta}_1 = \frac{\sum\limits_{i=1}^{n} (X_i - \overline{X})Y_i}{\sum\limits_{i=1}^{n} (X_i - \overline{X})^2} \qquad (5.12)$$

and

$$\hat{\beta}_0 = \overline{Y} - \hat{\beta}_1 \overline{X} \qquad (5.13)$$

These are known as the OLS *estimators* of β_1 and β_0: they are the rules or formulas for calculating the $\hat{\beta}_1$ and $\hat{\beta}_0$ of the estimated regression line. In practice we calculate $\hat{\beta}_1$ first, and then use that value to calculate $\hat{\beta}_0$. Whenever we use these estimators we can be confident of getting the best-fitting line.

In the derivation of the OLS estimators, the only special assumption made is that the X values are not all identical. If this were the case, the denominator in (5.12) would be zero and $\hat{\beta}_1$ would be undefined. Graphically, this would be a case in which all the data points lie along a vertical line.

Three properties of the least squares fit always hold true. First, the sum of the residuals is exactly zero: $\sum e_i = 0$. Thus the average error of fit is also zero: $\overline{e} = 0$. This property holds true even though the sum of the squared residuals, which has been minimized, is some positive amount. Interestingly, the least squares line is not the only line for which the associated sum of residuals is zero; one could construct a very poor fitting line for which this also holds.

Second, the fitted regression line goes through the *point of means,* which is the point $(\overline{X}, \overline{Y})$. This property makes it easy to graph the line: one point on the estimated line is its intercept with the vertical axis $(0, \hat{\beta}_0)$, and a second point is $(\overline{X}, \overline{Y})$. We can graph the line through these two points. It should be noted that usually none of the observations in the data lie at the point of means, although this could happen by coincidence.

Third, there is zero correlation between the residuals and the explanatory variable. We already know that the average residual is zero. This third property assures us that for observations with X above $\overline{X}$, there is no tendency for the residuals to average differently from zero—and similarly for $X < \overline{X}$. To see what this means, think of all the data points as lying close to some straight line. The zero correlation between e and X assures us that the OLS fit cuts through the points rather than across them.

As an example of computation, consider the five observations on Y and X in Table 5.1. These are the first five observations on *SAVING* (Y) and *INCOME* (X) from our cross-section data set, with the values rounded to one decimal position for simplicity. As discussed above, the simple regression model (5.1) can be taken as a theoretical statement describing family saving behavior. The

TABLE 5.1   Calculation of Regression Estimates

(1) Y_i	(2) X_i	(3) $X_i - \overline{X}$	(4) $(X_i - \overline{X})^2$	(5) $(X_i - \overline{X})Y_i$
0.0	1.9	−5.04	25.4016	0.0
0.9	12.4	5.46	29.8116	4.914
0.4	6.4	−0.54	0.2916	−0.216
1.2	7.0	0.06	0.0036	0.072
0.3	7.0	0.06	0.0036	0.018
2.8	34.7	0.0	55.5120	4.788

$$\overline{X} = \sum X_i/n = 34.7/5 = 6.94$$

$$\overline{Y} = \sum Y_i/n = 2.8/5 = 0.56$$

$$\hat{\beta}_1 = [\sum (X_i - \overline{X})Y_i]/[\sum(X_i - \overline{X})^2] = 4.788/55.512 = 0.0863$$

$$\hat{\beta}_0 = \overline{Y} - \hat{\beta}_1\overline{X} = 0.56 - (0.0863)(6.94) = -0.0386$$

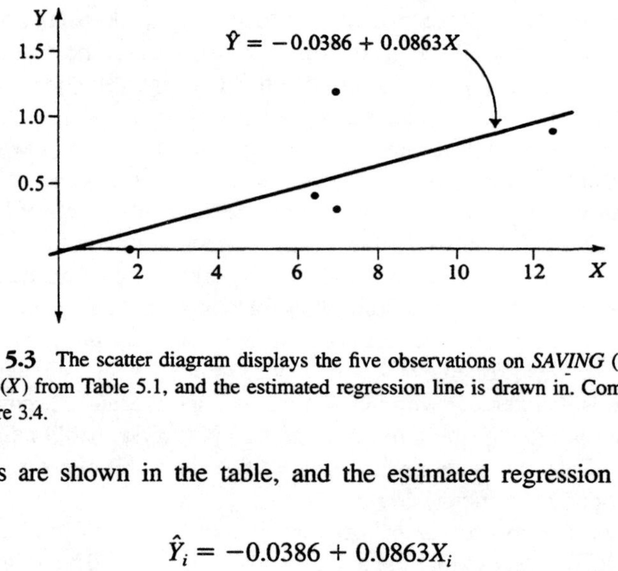

FIGURE 5.3   The scatter diagram displays the five observations on *SAVING* (*Y*) and *INCOME* (*X*) from Table 5.1, and the estimated regression line is drawn in. Compare this with Figure 3.4.

calculations are shown in the table, and the estimated regression is reported as

$$\hat{Y}_i = -0.0386 + 0.0863X_i \tag{5.14}$$

The data are plotted in a scatter diagram in Figure 5.3, and the fitted regression line is drawn in.

5.3   Interpretation of the Regression

As explained in the previous two sections, the econometric approach to analyzing data is based on the theory that some stable process of economic behavior underlies all the data we have. What we call the true regression is the equation that specifies the systematic part of the process, and what we call the estimated regression is the equation of the best-fitting line drawn through the data. The distinction between these two equations is of great importance.

To understand this distinction, suppose that we have a set of n observations on Y and X that were produced by an economic process correctly described by the simple regression model (5.1). The coefficients β_0 and β_1 in the true regression are unknown and unknowable, but the technique of ordinary least squares provides a method for making estimates. These estimates, which are coefficients in the estimated regression, are denoted by $\hat{\beta}_0^*$ and $\hat{\beta}_1^*$. (Asterisks are used to denote values that are actually computed from a set of data.)

Given this, how is $\hat{\beta}_0^*$ related to β_0 and how is $\hat{\beta}_1^*$ related to β_1? One might hope that the corresponding coefficients would be equal, so that $\hat{\beta}_0^* = \beta_0$ and $\hat{\beta}_1^* = \beta_1$. However, this would be tantamount to discovering the true values, and this is unlikely ever to occur. One could hardly expect to learn the precise values of the coefficients in the process (5.1) on the basis of a limited set of data generated by the process.

This thinking is reflected in Figure 5.4. Suppose that we are dealing with three observations, having actual X values X_1, X_2 and X_3. We do not explore why the observations take on these values; even in theory we accept them as given. We theorize that the actual Y values for the observations are produced by the process (5.1). Accordingly, in Figure 5.4 we graph the true regression line, which is the systematic part of the process, and we also plot the actual data points resulting from the process. Given these data, the estimated regression line is determined by the OLS estimators, and it is drawn in the figure also.

For the first observation, $E[Y_1]$ is the height of the point on the true regression line directly above the value X_1, and the disturbance u_1 is the vertical distance from there to the plotted data point. Similarly, the fitted value $\hat{Y}_1$ is the height of

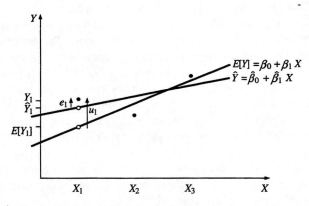

FIGURE 5.4 For the given set of X values, the Y values are determined around the true regression line as in Figure 5.1, with a large positive disturbance u_1 in this case. For these data on Y and X, the estimated regression line is also shown, as in Figure 5.2. The difference between the true regression and the estimated regression arises from the particular pattern of values taken on by the disturbances.

the point on the estimated regression line directly above the value X_1, and the residual e_1 is the vertical distance from there to the plotted point. The disturbances and residuals for the other two observations can be determined in the figure, but they are not explicitly identified.

For the data in Figure 5.4, the disturbance u_1 is large and positive, while u_2 and u_3 are relatively small. This causes the estimated regression line to have a flatter slope than the true regression line, in this case. It is usually true that the sum of the disturbances is not exactly equal to zero because they reflect uncontrolled random factors, and in this case it appears that $\sum u_i > 0$. However, it is always true that the sum of the residuals is exactly equal to zero, $\sum e_i = 0$, and that is illustrated here.

As in Figure 5.4, it is generally true that the difference between an estimated regression line and the underlying true regression line arises from the particular pattern of values that the disturbances happen to take on. If u_1 happened to be large and negative while u_2 and u_3 were the same as in Figure 5.4, the estimated regression would be steeper than the true regression. It is possible that the set of disturbances would be such that the estimated regression line would be the same as the true regression line, but we do not expect that this will occur in practice.

In general, then, $\hat{\beta}_0^* \neq \beta_0$ and $\hat{\beta}_1^* \neq \beta_1$. The difference between an estimated coefficient and its true value (e.g., $\hat{\beta}_1^* - \beta_1$) is said to be an estimation error. Since the true values β_0 and β_1 are unknown, we cannot determine the size of the estimation errors in any particular case. Although we hope that the errors are small, we can never be sure that they are. (Later, in Part IV, we develop methods of statistical inference that permit us to assess how large or small the estimation errors might be.)

In all the discussion above, we first considered some economic process and then presumed that we could gather data generated by the process to make estimates of the parameters. In practical work, the order is sometimes reversed: we might start with some data that is available and then specify a model of the process by which one of the variables is determined. This approach can be reasonable. However, in order to interpret regression results in the way we do, we must be willing to presume that all the data come from the economic process that we specify. Then, the regression fit to the data can be interpreted as an estimate of the true regression underlying the data. We note that it is possible to use OLS to fit a regression line through a scatter of data points without any thought of an underlying process, but this can result in misleading interpretations of the findings.

To foreshadow the analysis that we carry out in various applications in Chapter 6, consider again the estimated regression of family saving on family income that was calculated in Table 5.1:

$$\hat{Y}_i = -0.0386 + 0.0863X_i \qquad (5.15)$$

In what follows, remember that we used only five observations to calculate this example, so that these numerical results do not constitute a serious economic study.

The numerical coefficients in the estimated regression, $\hat{\beta}_0^* = -0.0386$ and $\hat{\beta}_1^* = 0.0863$, are the estimates of the corresponding parameters β_0 and β_1 in the behavioral relation.

Looking at the estimated slope, we see that if a family's income were to increase by 1 thousand dollars (i.e., $\Delta X = 1$) its predicted saving would increase by 0.0863 thousand dollars (i.e., \$86.30). This is a basic interpretation that we can make without any computation. If a family's income were to increase by \$2500 (i.e., $\Delta X = 2.5$), we use our knowledge of slopes (see the appendix to Chapter 1) to compute

$$\Delta \hat{Y} = 0.0863 \, \Delta X = (0.0863)(2.5) = 0.21575 \qquad (5.16)$$

thousand dollars. That is, predicted saving increases by about \$216. Notice that the intercept plays no role in a computation like this.

Looking at the estimated intercept, we see that if a family's income were zero, its predicted saving would be -0.0386 thousand dollars (i.e., minus \$38.60). Although this may seem odd at first, it does make economic sense: many families with temporarily low incomes do have some accumulated wealth that they would spend if their income were zero, and decreases in wealth are measured as negative saving.

Finally, just as the theoretical true regression line underlying the data determines the systematic part of saving for a family with a given income, so too the estimated regression line can be used to make predictions of saving for a family with some specified income. A family whose income is 8 thousand dollars has a predicted saving of

$$\hat{Y}_i = -0.0386 + (0.0863)(8.0) = 0.6518 \qquad (5.17)$$

thousand dollars (i.e., about \$652). Notice that in predicting a level for the dependent variable we are finding the height of the estimated regression line corresponding to a specific level of X.

5.4   Measures of Fit

The technique of ordinary least squares guarantees that the estimated regression line is the best-fitting line that can be drawn through the data, in the sense that it has the smallest possible sum of squared residuals. Although it is the best-fitting line, whether it fits well or not so well depends on the data. If the data points in the scatterplot seem to lie close to some line, the best-fitting line will fit very well; but, if the points are widely dispersed, the best-fitting line will not fit very well. In this section we develop two statistics that allow us to quantify how well the regression fits the data.

Starting from a set of data on Y and X, the estimated regression line yields a set of fitted values, or predictions, for the actual Y_i values. These are given by

$$\hat{Y}_i = \hat{\beta}_0 + \hat{\beta}_1 X_i \qquad (5.18)$$

The associated errors of fit are given by the residuals

$$e_i = Y_i - \hat{Y}_i \tag{5.19}$$

These residuals serve as the basis for our two measures of fit.

The Standard Error of the Regression, *SER*

The n residuals constitute a data variable e that can be described by the methods of Chapter 3. As noted above, it is a property of OLS estimation that the mean residual is always zero: $\bar{e} = 0$. The standard deviation of the residuals (S_e) will be some positive number, and its usual interpretation will still be valid: S_e measures the typical deviation of e from its mean, without regard to sign.

Since $\bar{e} = 0$, each deviation $(e_i - \bar{e})$ is the same as the value of the variable (e_i) itself. Hence the standard deviation can be interpreted here as the typical value of the variable, without regard to sign. Thus S_e could serve as a measure of how well the regression fits the data: it answers the question, "What is the typical error of fit?" To satisfy some purposes discussed in Chapter 11, the actual measure we adopt is a slight modification of S_e.

The *standard error of regression* (*SER*), which is sometimes called the "standard error of estimate," is defined by

$$SER = \sqrt{\frac{\sum_{i=1}^{n} e_i^2}{n - 2}} \tag{5.20}$$

and its value is interpreted as a measure of the typical error of fit. (Notice that if $n - 2$ were replaced by $n - 1$, the expression on the right-hand side would equal S_e.) The denominator in this expression is referred to as the number of degrees of freedom.

To illustrate how the *SER* is computed, we continue with the previous example dealing with family saving behavior. Table 5.2 starts with the same data on Y and X as Table 5.1. For each observation, separately, the fitted or predicted value $\hat{Y}_i$ is determined from the estimated regression (5.14) by substituting in the X_i value, and the results are shown in column (3). Then, again for each observation separately, the residual (5.19) is calculated and squared, with results shown in columns (4) and (5). The sum of the items in column (5) is shown at the bottom of the column; this is $\sum e_i^2$. Finally, the *SER* is then calculated directly according to (5.20).

The units of measurement of the *SER* are always the same as those of the dependent variable Y, because each residual is equal to the actual value Y_i minus the fitted value $\hat{Y}_i$. In this case, since family saving is measured in thousands of dollars, we would report that the typical error of fit (*SER*) for the regression of family saving on family income is 0.416 thousand dollars.

In general, the smaller is the *SER* the better is the fit of the estimated regression to the scatter of data. In any particular case, however, whether the

TABLE 5.2 Calculation of R^2 and SER

(1) Y_i	(2) X_i	(3) $\hat{Y}_i$	(4) e_i	(5) e_i^2	(6) $Y_i - \overline{Y}$	(7) $(Y_i - \overline{Y})^2$
0.0	1.9	0.125	−0.125	0.0157	−0.56	0.3136
0.9	12.4	1.031	−0.131	0.0171	0.34	0.1156
0.4	6.4	0.513	−0.113	0.0129	−0.16	0.0256
1.2	7.0	0.565	0.635	0.4030	0.64	0.4096
0.3	7.0	0.565	−0.265	0.0703	−0.26	0.0676
			0.0	0.5190	0.0	0.9320

$$R^2 = 1 - \sum e_i^2 / [\sum(Y_i - \overline{Y})^2] = 1 - 0.5190/0.9320 = .443$$

$$SER = \sqrt{\sum e_i^2/(n-2)} = \sqrt{0.5190/3} = 0.416$$

SER should be considered small or large depends on a comparison with some other value. What comparison should be made depends on the context. For example, if we are using the estimated model to make a prediction, a comparison of the SER with the $\hat{Y}_i$ value suggests how much in error the prediction might be. (A probabilistic analysis of prediction errors is given in Chapter 13.) Similarly, if we are considering the overall goodness of fit of the regression, a comparison of the SER with the mean of Y is useful. For example, in the saving regression, the SER is \$416 and $\overline{Y}$ is \$560; the typical error of fit is relatively large, indicating a fairly poor fit. However, simple comparisons with the mean are sometimes misleading; if the same residuals had been obtained with families having greater income and saving levels (and thus greater $\overline{Y}$), the SER would not seem so large.

As evident in Table 5.2 and Figure 5.3, one of the residuals is much larger than the others in absolute value. This, combined with the small size of the sample, leads the SER to be larger than four of the five residuals. (The mean absolute residual is 0.254 here, which is substantially smaller than the SER.) Because of this, we might hesitate before accepting the conclusion that the fit is "fairly poor."

The Coefficient of Determination, R^2

The second measure we develop to quantify how well the estimated regression line fits the data yields a pure, dimensionless number. Like the magnitude of the correlation, this measure varies between zero and 1, with a higher value indicating a better fit. We go through several steps of a formal development because these are useful for understanding the interpretation we make.

Looking at Figure 5.5, it should be clear that for any observation i,

$$(Y_i - \overline{Y}) = (\hat{Y}_i - \overline{Y}) + (Y_i - \hat{Y}_i) = (\hat{Y}_i - \overline{Y}) + e_i \tag{5.21}$$

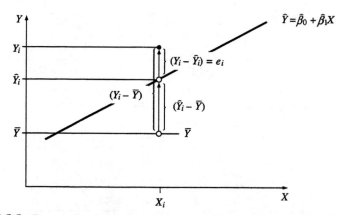

FIGURE 5.5 For any observation, the total deviation of Y_i from the mean $(Y_i - \bar{Y})$ can be decomposed into two parts: the unexplained deviation $(Y_i - \hat{Y}_i)$, which is just the residual e_i, and the explained deviation $(\hat{Y}_i - \bar{Y})$. The coefficient of determination R^2 is defined as the ratio of an overall measure of the explained deviations to an overall measure of the total deviations. The standard error of the regression *SER* is a measure of the typical unexplained deviation—that is, it is a measure of the typical error of fit e_i.

This is a decomposition, which means simply that the quantity $Y_i - \bar{Y}$ is viewed as being equal to the sum of two component parts. As shown, for any observation the total deviation of the observed Y_i from the mean is equal to the deviation of the fitted value from the mean plus the error of fit. Given the data, it is the regression that determines or "explains" the fitted value, while the error of fit is left "unexplained." Hence, giving new names to the items in the decomposition, we can say that the *total deviation* of Y_i from $\bar{Y}$ is equal to the *explained deviation* plus the *unexplained deviation.*

If we square the leftmost and rightmost portions of (5.21), we get

$$(Y_i - \bar{Y})^2 = (\hat{Y}_i - \bar{Y})^2 + e_i^2 + 2e_i(\hat{Y}_i - \bar{Y}) \tag{5.22}$$

and if we add up the n equations like (5.22) that hold for each i, we get

$$\sum(Y_i - \bar{Y})^2 = \sum(\hat{Y}_i - \bar{Y})^2 + \sum e_i^2 + 2\sum e_i(\hat{Y}_i - \bar{Y}) \tag{5.23}$$

It can be shown that the last term on the right-hand side of (5.23) is equal to zero, so that what remains is

$$\sum(Y_i - \bar{Y})^2 = \sum(\hat{Y}_i - \bar{Y})^2 + \sum e_i^2 \tag{5.24}$$

All the terms in this equation are positive or zero because they are sums of squares. The expression on the left-hand side is called the *total variation* in Y, because it is the sum of squares of the total deviations identified above. Similarly, the first expression on the right-hand side is called the *explained variation* and the second is called the *unexplained variation.* Thus, as a consequence of the original decomposition illustrated in Figure 5.5, we can say that the total variation in Y is equal to the variation that is explained by the regression plus the unexplained variation.

Rearranging (5.24) and dividing by the total variation, we get

$$1 - \frac{\Sigma\, e_i^2}{\Sigma(Y_i - \overline{Y})^2} = \frac{\Sigma(\hat{Y}_i - \overline{Y})^2}{\Sigma(Y_i - \overline{Y})^2}$$

(5.25)

$$1 - \frac{\text{unexplained variation}}{\text{total variation in } Y} = \frac{\text{explained variation}}{\text{total variation in } Y}$$

The right-hand side of this equation is the ratio of the explained variation to the total variation. The numerator and the denominator are positive, and since the numerator is a component of the denominator the ratio can take on values only between zero and 1. This ratio could serve as a measure of goodness of fit, and we adopt it for that purpose. The left-hand side of (5.25) is often easier to compute. In part for that reason, we use the left-hand side in the definition but give it the interpretation that applies directly to the right-hand side.

The *coefficient of determination,* which is usually denoted by R^2 and read as "R-squared," is defined by

$$R^2 = 1 - \frac{\sum\limits_{i=1}^{n} e_i^2}{\sum\limits_{i=1}^{n} (Y_i - \overline{Y})^2} = \frac{\text{explained variation}}{\text{total variation in } Y}$$

(5.26)

The general form of our interpretation of R^2 is that it measures "the proportion of the total variation in Y that is explained by the regression." Since the regression model explains the values of Y on the basis of the given values of X, we might say instead that R^2 measures "the proportion of the total variation in Y that is explained by X."

The computation of R^2 is illustrated in Table 5.2. In addition to calculating $\Sigma\, e_i^2$, which was done already for the *SER*, we need to calculate the total variation in Y. This is given by the sum of the items in column (7). Finding $R^2 = .443$, we say that "the regression explains about 44 percent of the variation in family saving" or that "in the regression, family income explains about 44 percent of the variation in family saving."

In the appendix to this chapter it is proved that R^2 is equal to the square of r, the correlation between X and Y. Thus these two measures serve in the same way to quantify how well the estimated regression line fits the data. In econometric analysis we usually talk in terms of R^2 rather than r, partly because of its useful interpretation in terms of explaining the total variation in Y.

The R^2 is a zero-to-1 dimensionless measure of fit, and knowing the numerical value in any case helps us form an image of the scatterplot in our minds. An R^2 of .443 is usually associated with a scatterplot in which the data are fairly dispersed around the estimated regression. In our example, we might qualify this description by noting that one residual is much larger than the others.

Our assessment of the magnitude of R^2 depends on the nature of the economic process being analyzed. The R^2 is often high in time-series work because Y and X often have a common trend. By contrast, the R^2 tends to be lower in cross-section work because there is no trend and because of the substantial natural variation in individual behavior. If $R^2 = .443$ were reported for a macroeconomic time-series saving function, it would be judged quite low; experienced researchers expect a regression of aggregate saving on income to have an R^2 of .95 or higher. However, an R^2 of .443 for a large-sample, cross-section saving function would be quite high compared with those for similar studies, and the regression would be judged to have a relatively good fit.

We note here that various writers and computer programs use different terminologies and notations to describe the decomposition in (5.24). The total variation in Y is often called the total sum of squares (TSS), which is clear. In some places, the explained variation is called the explained sum of squares and is denoted by ESS, while the unexplained variation is called the residual sum of squares and is denoted by RSS. In other places, the explained variation is called the regression sum of squares and is denoted by RSS, while the unexplained variation is called the error sum of squares and is denoted by ESS. Clearly, there is room for confusion!

Finally, both R^2 and SER are useful measures of how well an estimated regression fits the data. Computer programs for regression analysis routinely compute these statistics along with the estimated coefficients. It is common to report the results in a display such as

$$\hat{Y}_i = -0.0386 + 0.0863X_i$$
$$R^2 = .443 \quad SER = 0.416$$

(5.27)

The R^2 tells us that about 44 percent of the variation in family saving is explained by the regression. The SER tells us that the typical error of fit for saving is 0.416 thousand dollars (i.e., \$416). In Chapter 11 we develop additional calculations in regression estimation that will be added to this reporting style.

5.5   The Effects of Linear Transformation _____

The units in which we measure variables are arbitrarily chosen. For example, GNP for 1980 might be measured as 1,480,700,000,000 dollars, 1480.7 billion dollars, or 1.4807 trillion dollars. In this section we see what impact this choice has on our regression results. It turns out that even though the estimated coefficients do depend on the units of measurement, the economic meaning of the estimated regression does not.

Suppose that we start with data on Y and X. The most common form of units adjustment involves multiplying a variable by a constant. We view this as transforming the original variables Y and X into new variables y and x according to

$$y_i = b_y Y_i \quad \text{and} \quad x_i = b_x X_i \tag{5.28}$$

where lowercase notation for the names of variables is introduced here to distinguish a new form from an original one. For example, if Y is the unemployment rate expressed as a proportion of the labor force (like .062) and if $b_y = 100$, then y is the unemployment rate expressed in percentage points (like 6.2). Similarly, if X is GNP in billions of dollars (like 1480.7) and if $b_x = 1/1000$, then x is GNP in trillions of dollars (like 1.4807).

Using the original data, let the estimated regression of Y on X be denoted as usual by

$$\hat{Y}_i = \hat{\beta}_0 + \hat{\beta}_1 X_i \tag{5.29}$$

Now using the transformed data, let the estimated regression of y on x be denoted by

$$\hat{y}_i = \hat{\gamma}_0 + \hat{\gamma}_1 x_i \tag{5.30}$$

The choice of notation here makes it clear that the estimated intercepts may be different in the two regressions and that the estimated slopes may be different also. (Note that γ is lowercase "gamma," the Greek "g.")

The question is this: how are $\hat{\gamma}_0$ and $\hat{\gamma}_1$ related to $\hat{\beta}_0$ and $\hat{\beta}_1$? In other words, how do the new coefficients compare with the old ones? It can be shown that

$$\hat{\gamma}_0 = b_y \hat{\beta}_0 \quad \text{and} \quad \hat{\gamma}_1 = \frac{b_y}{b_x} \hat{\beta}_1 \tag{5.31}$$

That is, when Y and X are transformed by multiplicative constants as specified in (5.28) and then the OLS estimators are used to determine the intercept and slope from the new data, the new coefficient estimates are related to the original ones by (5.31). Knowing this allows us to apply these rules to determine the new coefficients from the old coefficients without actually carrying out new OLS calculations.

For example, the data on saving (Y) and income (X) that led to the regression

$$\hat{Y}_i = -0.0386 + 0.0863 X_i \tag{5.32}$$

in earlier examples are measured in thousands of dollars. If both variables were transformed to express the amounts in dollars, the new variables would be generated by

$$y_i = 1000 Y_i \quad \text{and} \quad x_i = 1000 X_i \tag{5.33}$$

That is, in the notation of (5.28), $b_y = 1000$ and $b_x = 1000$. For example, $Y_i = 15$ thousand dollars is transformed into $y_i = 15,000$ dollars. Hence, from (5.31) we see quickly that the new regression of saving on income would be

$$\hat{y}_i = -38.6 + 0.0863x_i \qquad (5.34)$$

That is, the slope is unchanged but the new intercept is 1000 times greater than the old one. The intercept in (5.32) tells us that if income is zero, saving will be negative 0.0386 thousand dollars; in (5.34), if income is zero saving will be negative 38.6 dollars, which has the same economic meaning.

Starting from the original data leading to (5.32) again, if saving were transformed to dollars while income remained in its original form ($b_y = 1000$ and $b_x = 1$), the regression of saving on income would be

$$\hat{y}_i = -38.6 + 86.3x_i \qquad (5.35)$$

If income increases by 1 thousand dollars, saving increases by 86.3 dollars—which has the same economic meaning as the slope in (5.32).

Which of the alternative regressions is the best to report? The choice is a matter of judgment. It usually does not make sense to report a regression with financial variables measured in different units, because this leads to confusing interpretations; this argues against (5.35). In choosing between (5.32) and (5.34), the latter appears somewhat better. In (5.32), the leading zeros in the intercept lend themselves to mistakes in reading and transcription, and the value of the intercept leads to the awkward phrase "-0.0386 thousand dollars"; these problems with the intercept are avoided in (5.34).

We note that the R^2 in both of these new regressions is the same as that in the original regression; it is always true that R^2 is unaffected by linear transformations of variables. By contrast, the SER in a transformed regression is b_y times the SER in the original regression. In both of the cases leading to (5.34) and (5.35), $b_y = 1000$. In both of these equations, y is measured in dollars and the new SER $= (1000)(0.416) = 416.0$ dollars.

The question of units choice can be generalized somewhat to the following problem. Suppose that we have data on Y and X and have estimated the regression

$$\hat{Y}_i = \hat{\beta}_0 + \hat{\beta}_1 X_i \qquad (5.36)$$

Suppose now that we create a new variable, y, from Y according to the linear transformation

$$y_i = a_y + b_y Y_i \qquad (5.37)$$

and a new variable, x, according to

$$x_i = a_x + b_x X_i \qquad (5.38)$$

(Note that a_y and b_y need not be related to a_x and b_x at all; the notation is used just to economize on symbols.) If we estimate an OLS regression of y on x, we get

$$\hat{y}_i = \hat{\gamma}_0 + \hat{\gamma}_1 x_i \tag{5.39}$$

and we ask: how are $\hat{\gamma}_0$ and $\hat{\gamma}_1$ related to $\hat{\beta}_0$ and $\hat{\beta}_1$? It can be shown that

$$\hat{\gamma}_0 = a_y + b_y \hat{\beta}_0 - \frac{a_x b_y}{b_x} \hat{\beta}_1 \tag{5.40}$$

and

$$\hat{\gamma}_1 = \frac{b_y}{b_x} \hat{\beta}_1 \tag{5.41}$$

For example, suppose that after-tax income (x) is related to before-tax income (X), both expressed in thousands of dollars, by

$$x_i = 2 + 0.75 X_i \tag{5.42}$$

Comparing this to (5.38), we have $a_x = 2$ and $b_x = 0.75$. Suppose now that we are interested in the relation between saving and after-tax income. The saving concept is unchanged: $y_i = Y_i$, so $a_y = 0$ and $b_y = 1$. Without estimating another regression, we can determine from (5.32) that the regression of saving on after-tax income is

$$\hat{y}_i = \left[0 + (1)(-0.0386) - \frac{(2)(1)}{0.75}(0.0863) \right] + \left[\frac{1}{0.75}(0.0863) \right] x_i$$
$$= -0.269 + 0.115 x_i \tag{5.43}$$

The R^2 of the original and new regressions would be the same; in this case the SER is also unchanged because the units of measurement for saving, the dependent variable, are unchanged.

Understanding the effects of units adjustment and linear transformation is useful to us in two ways. First, given an estimated regression, we are able to restate it to make more sensible reports without actually computing new estimates from transformed data. For example, if a co-worker brought us an estimated saving regression like (5.35), with saving measured in dollars and income measured in thousands of dollars, we could determine and report a new regression (in which both variables are measured in the same units) by simply applying our rules.

Second, and more important, this analysis makes us aware that the magnitude of an estimated regression coefficient depends in part on the units of measurement that happen to have been used in the data. Without knowing what the units are in any particular regression, finding a coefficient equal to 3400.0 is no more interesting or important than finding 0.00034 as the estimated value.

5.6   Regression Through the Origin _____

Consider again the simple regression model (5.1), which states that the value of variable Y for each observation is determined by the equation

$$Y_i = \beta_0 + \beta_1 X_i + u_i \tag{5.44}$$

Sometimes economic theory leads to a firm belief that the intercept β_0 is zero. In this special case, the model can be rewritten as

$$Y_i = \beta X_i + u_i \tag{5.45}$$

so as to incorporate the idea that $\beta_0 = 0$ as part of the specification. (We use β, without a subscript, to denote the slope in this case.)

This model is represented graphically in Figure 5.6a. The true regression line is

$$E[Y] = \beta X \tag{5.46}$$

and data points are produced as vertical deviations (of size u_i) around this line. To make an estimate of β we could proceed by determining the slope of the best-fitting line through the data points in exactly the same way as in Section 5.2. However, this would ignore the theoretical specification that the intercept is zero.

When the process underlying the data is (5.45), a better approach is to determine an estimated regression line of the form

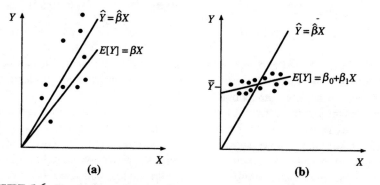

(a)   (b)

FIGURE 5.6   Part (a) shows the case of regression through the origin. The data are generated around a true regression that has a zero intercept, and the estimated regression is restricted to have a zero intercept also. In (b) the data are generated around a true regression that has a positive intercept, but an estimated regression through the origin is fit to the data. In such a situation, the estimated slope $\hat{\beta}$ tends to be larger than the true slope β_1.

$$\hat{Y} = \hat{\beta}X \qquad (5.47)$$

which is graphed in Figure 5.6a for the hypothetical data shown there. Since both the true regression and the estimated regression have zero intercepts, their graphs go through the origin. This gives rise to the name we attach to this special case of simple regression.

To estimate β, we apply the principle of least squares again. In order to minimize the sum of squared residuals in this case, it turns out that the OLS estimator for the slope is given by

$$\hat{\beta} = \frac{\sum X_i Y_i}{\sum X_i^2} \qquad (5.48)$$

which is different from the OLS estimator (5.12) for the slope in the regular case.

The case of regression through the origin differs from the regular case in other ways also. In this case, the OLS estimation no longer has the property that $\sum e_i = 0$. In addition, it turns out that the R^2 measure of fit as defined by (5.26) can be negative.

Comparing this special case with the regular model illustrates some interesting features of regression. Suppose that the true process is given by (5.45), but that we apply the regular method of simple regression and obtain a line whose equation is

$$\hat{Y} = \hat{\beta}_0 + \hat{\beta}_1 X \qquad (5.49)$$

Although one might think that $\hat{\beta}_0$ would be equal to zero, this is not usually true. Effectively, there is a true β_0 that is equal to zero, but $\hat{\beta}_0$ will not equal this because of the occurrence of estimation error (as discussed in Section 5.3). Similarly, for a given set of data one might think that $\hat{\beta}_1$ from (5.49) would be identical to $\hat{\beta}$ from (5.47), but this is not true either. Hence, the two different methods of estimating the best-fitting line through the data will give us different results.

Now, changing the situation, we consider an economic process that is correctly specified by the regular simple regression model (5.44). As an example, suppose that the true regression line and a set of data produced by this process are as shown in Figure 5.6b. Now suppose that, for some reason, we estimate a regression through the origin, with the result shown in the figure. For these data, the $\hat{\beta}$ is clearly greater than the true slope β_1. Similarly, for almost any data set generated by the process in this example, the $\hat{\beta}$ will be larger than the true slope β_1. That is, in this situation the estimation error tends to be positive and large.

To avoid such systematic and large estimation errors, standard practice is to use the special model of regression through the origin only when there are strong reasons for doing so. In Chapter 12 we discuss how to test a hypothesis about a coefficient. With this procedure, we can estimate a simple regression of regular form and then test the hypothesis that $\beta_0 = 0$. In effect, this allows us to test whether regression through the origin is appropriate.

Finally, it is possible to see in Figure 5.6b how the regular R^2 could be negative. Imagine a horizontal line drawn through the mean, $\bar{Y}$, indicated on the vertical axis. The vertical distances from this line to the plotted points are the total deviations, as defined in Section 5.4. Now look at the vertical distances from the estimated regression line to the plotted points; these are the unexplained deviations. In the figure, we can see that some of the total deviations are small and that some of the unexplained deviations are small also. However, it appears that there are many more large unexplained deviations than there are large total deviations. Hence it appears that the sum of squared unexplained deviations will be larger than the sum of squared total deviations. Looking at the definition of R^2 in (5.26), one sees that this would lead it to be negative.

APPENDIX _____

Derivation of the OLS Estimators

The derivation of the OLS estimators is a standard calculus minimization problem in which the objective function to be minimized is the sum of squared residuals [see (5.9)]. Given a set of data, all the values like Y_i and X_i are fixed numbers. Our task is to find the values of $\hat{\beta}_0$ and $\hat{\beta}_1$ that make SSR as small as possible. In this context, $\hat{\beta}_0$ and $\hat{\beta}_1$ are variables (arguments of the function) while the Ys and Xs are constants.

The sum of squared residuals is given by

$$\sum_{i=1}^{n} e_i^2 = \sum_{i=1}^{n}(Y_i - \hat{\beta}_0 - \hat{\beta}_1 X_i)^2 \tag{5.50}$$

To find the values of $\hat{\beta}_0$ and $\hat{\beta}_1$ that minimize this expression, we take the partial derivatives of (5.50) with respect to $\hat{\beta}_0$ and $\hat{\beta}_1$ and set them equal to zero:

$$\frac{\partial}{\partial \hat{\beta}_0}\left[\sum\left(Y_i - \hat{\beta}_0 - \hat{\beta}_1 X_i\right)^2\right] = 0 \tag{5.51}$$

$$\frac{\partial}{\partial \hat{\beta}_1}\left[\sum\left(Y_i - \hat{\beta}_0 - \hat{\beta}_1 X_i\right)^2\right] = 0 \tag{5.52}$$

Evaluating these partial derivatives gives us

$$-2\sum(Y_i - \hat{\beta}_0 - \hat{\beta}_1 X_i) = 0 \tag{5.53}$$

$$-2\sum(Y_i - \hat{\beta}_0 - \hat{\beta}_1 X_i)X_i = 0 \tag{5.54}$$

Next, we divide each equation by -2, leaving each side equal to zero, and then rearrange terms to get

$$\sum Y_i = n\hat{\beta}_0 + \hat{\beta}_1 \sum X_i \tag{5.55}$$

$$\sum Y_i X_i = \hat{\beta}_0 \sum X_i + \hat{\beta}_1 \sum X_i^2 \tag{5.56}$$

This pair of equations is a set of two simultaneous equations in which $\hat{\beta}_0$ and $\hat{\beta}_1$ are unknown and all the X_i and Y_i values are known.

A convenient way to solve these equations is to solve (5.55) for

$$\hat{\beta}_0 = \{\sum Y_i - \hat{\beta}_1 \sum X_i\}/n \tag{5.57}$$

and substitute this for $\hat{\beta}_0$ in (5.56). That equation then can be solved to yield

$$\hat{\beta}_1 = \frac{n \sum X_i Y_i - \sum X_i \sum Y_i}{n \sum X_i^2 - (\sum X_i)^2} \tag{5.58}$$

For theoretical and computational convenience, we note that this expression can be arranged in various ways, including

$$\hat{\beta}_1 = \frac{\sum(X_i - \bar{X})(Y_i - \bar{Y})}{\sum(X_i - \bar{X})^2} \tag{5.59}$$

and

$$\hat{\beta}_1 = \frac{\sum(X_i - \bar{X})Y_i}{\sum(X_i - \bar{X})^2} \tag{5.60}$$

which is the same as (5.12). Now (5.57) can be manipulated to yield

$$\hat{\beta}_0 = \bar{Y} - \hat{\beta}_1 \bar{X} \tag{5.61}$$

which is the same as (5.13). We could find instead an expression that gives $\hat{\beta}_0$ solely in terms of X and Y values, but this is not useful.

The property that $\sum e_i = 0$ follows from (5.53) and that e and X are uncorrelated follows from (5.54).

Equivalence of R^2 and $(r)^2$

The value of R^2 is exactly equal to the square of r, the correlation between X and Y. To see this, first note that

$$\sum_{i=1}^{n}(\hat{Y}_i - \bar{Y})^2 = \sum_{i=1}^{n}(\hat{\beta}_0 + \hat{\beta}_1 X_i - \hat{\beta}_0 - \hat{\beta}_1 \bar{X})^2$$

$$= \sum_{i=1}^{n}[\hat{\beta}_1(X_i - \bar{X})]^2$$

$$= (\hat{\beta}_1)^2 \sum_{i=1}^{n}(X_i - \bar{X})^2 \tag{5.62}$$

Now,

$$R^2 = \frac{\sum_{i=1}^{n}(\hat{Y}_i - \bar{Y})^2}{\sum_{i=1}^{n}(Y_i - \bar{Y})^2}$$

$$= \frac{(\hat{\beta}_1)^2 \sum (X_i - \bar{X})^2}{\sum(Y_i - \bar{Y})^2} = (\hat{\beta}_1)^2 \frac{\sum(X_i - \bar{X})^2}{\sum(Y_i - \bar{Y})^2}$$

$$= \left[\frac{\sum (X_i - \bar{X})(Y_i - \bar{Y})}{\sum (X_i - \bar{X})^2}\right]^2 \frac{\sum (X_i - \bar{X})^2}{\sum (Y_i - \bar{Y})^2}$$

$$= \frac{[\sum(X_i - \bar{X})(Y_i - \bar{Y})]^2}{\sum(X_i - \bar{X})^2 \sum(Y_i - \bar{Y})^2}$$

$$= \left[\frac{\sum(X_i - \bar{X})(Y_i - \bar{Y})}{\sqrt{\sum(X_i - \bar{X})^2}\sqrt{\sum(Y_i - \bar{Y})^2}}\right]^2$$

$$= (r)^2 \tag{5.63}$$

Since we showed earlier that the maximum value of R^2 is 1 and the minimum is 0, the equivalence of R^2 and $(r)^2$ proves that the maximum value of r is 1 and the minimum is -1.

Problems _____

Section 5.1

5.1 In a simple linear regression model of market demand involving the quantity demanded and the price of a product, which variable is the dependent one and which is the explanatory one? Draw a figure showing the true regression line and plot some of the observations that might be observed.

★ **5.2** In the simple regression model illustrated in Figure 5.1, is it possible that all the actual Y_i values would lie above the true regression line? Explain.

5.3 Suppose that the quantity demanded in a market depends on the price of the product and the income of consumers. Would a simple regression model explaining the quantity demanded be appropriate? Could income be considered part of the disturbance?

5.4 Suppose that the true regression line is $E[Y] = 2 + 3X$. Determine the value of the disturbance for an observation having (X_i, Y_i) values (3, 8). Determine the disturbance for an observation (6, 21).

Section 5.2

5.5 In an OLS regression estimation, is it possible that all the actual Y_i values would lie above the estimated regression line? Explain.

★ **5.6** Construct a diagram to show a case for which $\sum e_i = 0$ around a line that is clearly not the best-fitting line.

5.7 In the following table Y stands for *EARNS* and X stands for *ED* from the cross-section data set, and the data are for observations 26 through 30 (with *EARNS* rounded). Plot Y and X in a scatter diagram, with Y on the vertical axis.

Y	X
12.0	12
3.6	8
9.6	10
3.7	3
6.5	12

5.8 Based on the data of Problem 5.7, estimate the coefficients of the OLS regression of Y on X and graph the estimated regression line through the scatter diagram of Problem 5.7. (Use a table format to organize your calculations.)

5.9 For a data set of three observations whose (X_i, Y_i) values are (10, 5), (8, 7), and (12, 9), estimate the regression of Y on X. Calculate the sum of the residuals and the covariance between e and X. Verify that the regression goes through the point of means.

5.10 Calculate the sum of squared residuals for the estimated regression in Problem 5.9. Now, add 0.5 to the intercept to get another line through the data, and calculate the sum of squared residuals for this line. Which of the two calculated *SSR*s is smaller? Why?

Section 5.3

★ **5.11** Draw a scatter diagram of the first five observations on *EARNS* and *ED* from the cross-section data set, and roughly draw in the best-fitting line. How does comparing this to the graph from Problem 5.8 illustrate the existence of estimation errors?

5.12 Based on the estimated regression (5.15), determine the predicted saving of a family whose income is 25 thousand dollars. For what level of income would predicted saving be zero?

Section 5.4

★ **5.13** Based on Problem 5.8, compute the values of R^2 and *SER*.

5.14 OLS finds the best-fitting line, while R^2 measures the goodness of fit. Does this mean that R^2 will always be high if the OLS technique is used?

5.15 Prove that the last term in Equation (5.23) is equal to zero. [*Hint:* At one stage use the fact that $\sum e_i X_i = 0$, which stems from Equation (5.54).]

5.16 Compute the values of R^2 and *SER* for the regression estimated in Problem 5.9.

5.17 In Figure 5.3 and Table 5.2, the observation with the large residual could be called an "outlier." Recompute the estimated regression, the R^2, and the *SER* after deleting this outlier (i.e., using only four observations) and compare the results to those gathered in Equation (5.27).

Section 5.5

★ **5.18** Based on Problems 5.7 and 5.8, suppose that *EARNS* is transformed into dollars (from thousands of dollars). What would be the new estimated regression of earnings on *ED*?

5.19 Based on the saving function presented in Equation (5.27), what would be the estimated regression of saving on income if income were transformed to dollars but saving remained in the original form?

5.20 Derive the relations presented as Equations (5.40) and (5.41).

Section 5.6

5.21 Using the data of Problem 5.7, estimate the regression of Y on X based on the model of regression through the origin. Compare this estimated regression with that from Problem 5.8.

★ **5.22** For a data set of three observations whose (X_i, Y_i) values are (1, 4), (3, 6), and (5, 5), estimate two separate regression models of Y on X: the first based on the assumption that the intercept is not zero, and the second based on the assumption that the intercept is zero. Compute the R^2 statistic for the second regression.

Appendix

5.23 Prove that Equations (5.60) and (5.59) are equivalent. [*Hint:* Start from the numerator in (5.59).]

5.24 Show why Equation (5.54) is equivalent to stating that e and X are uncorrelated.

★ **5.25** Derive the OLS estimator for the regression through the origin model, as displayed in Equation (5.48).

6

Simple Regression: Application

The simple regression model developed in Chapter 5 can be used to estimate the behavioral relation between two variables whenever we believe that the model accurately describes the process by which Y is determined. Although this model is too simple to describe most economic relations, it has many useful applications. In all these, the task of estimating the unknown coefficients is the same as in the general case, and the technique needs no further elaboration. What remains is to interpret the estimated model, and the first two sections of this chapter focus on that problem.

When we believe that the true process is more complex than the basic model, there are several paths open to us. If the true relation involves two variables in a nonlinear fashion, it is sometimes possible to transform the relation into a linear one and then apply the basic techniques already developed. Much of this chapter is devoted to exploring these possibilities. If more than one variable plays a systematic role in the determination of Y, we are led to multiple regression (Chapter 7).

6.1   Interpretation of the Coefficients

As presented in Chapter 5, the simple regression model

$$Y_i = \beta_0 + \beta_1 X_i + u_i \tag{6.1}$$

105

is a theoretical statement of the process by which the value of Y for each observation is determined on the basis of the given value of X for that observation. The systematic part of the relation is specified by the true regression line

$$E[Y] = \beta_0 + \beta_1 X \qquad (6.2)$$

where $E[Y]$ denotes the expected value of Y associated with any particular value of X. This is graphed in Figure 6.1, which illustrates that $E[Y]$ is a linear function of X.

When we have data on Y and X, an estimated regression line

$$\hat{Y} = \hat{\beta}_0 + \hat{\beta}_1 X \qquad (6.3)$$

can be determined by the method of ordinary least squares. This line is the empirical counterpart of the true regression line, and it serves as an estimated model of the systematic relation between Y and X. We should keep in mind, however, that this model is only an estimate of the true relation—in the sense that $\hat{\beta}_0$ and $\hat{\beta}_1$ are only estimates of β_0 and β_1. Figure 6.1 illustrates an estimated regression line that (hypothetically) is based on data produced by the process described by the true regression line in the same figure. As explained in Section 5.3, the differences between the estimated and true regressions arise from the particular pattern of disturbances in the data set.

After estimation, our interest moves on to interpreting and using the estimated model. For this we blend together economic reasoning and some mathematical analysis. Since (6.3) is the equation of a straight line, the mathematics is easy.

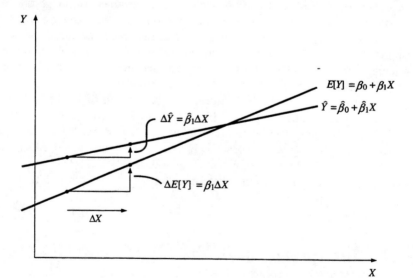

FIGURE 6.1   The systematic part of the simple regression model is specified by the true regression line, whose intercept is β_0 and whose slope is β_1. The estimated regression line fit to a particular set of data produced by this process has an intercept of $\hat{\beta}_0$ and a slope of $\hat{\beta}_1$. In each case, the slope coefficient is the basis for assessing how changes in X affect Y.

The parameter $\hat{\beta}_0$ in the estimated regression is called the **intercept** because it is the intercept of the estimated regression line with the vertical axis drawn through $X = 0$. In mathematical terms, the intercept gives the predicted value of Y for an observation with $X = 0$. In some cases this interpretation is of special interest. However, in many cases such an interpretation does not make economic sense. For example, with an aggregate consumption function it would be absurd to use a real-world model to predict what consumption would be if income were equal to zero: in all probability, either everyone would starve or chaos would reign as inventories of food and products were consumed.

The parameter $\hat{\beta}_1$ is called the **slope coefficient.** Based on the simple analytics of a straight line (see the appendix to Chapter 1), we know that the change in predicted Y that would be associated with any particular change in X is given by

$$\Delta \hat{Y} = \hat{\beta}_1 \Delta X \qquad (6.4)$$

In this context, a "change in X" that is economically interesting might be the difference between the values of X for two observations or it might be a hypothetical change in the value of X for a particular observation. In either case, we are considering moving from one point to another along the estimated regression line.

Based on (6.4), we can see that if X changes by 1, $\hat{Y}$ will change by $\hat{\beta}_1$. That is,

$$\text{if} \quad \Delta X = 1, \quad \text{then} \quad \Delta \hat{Y} = \hat{\beta}_1 \qquad (6.5)$$

This simple relation is the basis of the general form of our usual interpretation of a slope coefficient: we say that $\hat{\beta}_1$ is the change in $\hat{Y}$ that results from a unit change in X. (Note that a "unit change in X" means $\Delta X = 1$; this is different from a change in the units of measurement for X.)

In analyzing and discussing an estimated regression, it is natural to consider the question, "What is the effect of X on Y?" In many cases, as we will see in various examples, a satisfactory answer is given simply by reporting the slope coefficient and giving its usual interpretation. Sometimes we say that this gives the **impact** of X on $\hat{Y}$. Indeed, one of the reasons why regression is so useful is that the estimated parameters lend themselves to economically meaningful interpretations in such a simple way. However, we are not limited to the simplest interpretations. For example, in some cases analysts prefer to discuss the effect of X on Y in terms of the elasticity rather than the simple impact. The point elasticity can be computed from the slope $\hat{\beta}_1$ and a particular (X, Y) combination on the estimated regression line, using the definition given in the appendix to Chapter 1.

The same form of interpretation can be applied to the coefficients of the true regression (6.2) of course. Thus, we say that β_1 is the change in $E[Y]$ that results from a unit change in X, and that β_0 is the value of $E[Y]$ for an observation having $X = 0$. Also, since $\hat{\beta}_1$ is an estimate of β_1, we might say that $\hat{\beta}_1$ is an estimate of the impact of X on $E[Y]$.

A semantic problem arises in discussing the effect of the explanatory variable in a regression. Everyday use of the English language makes it natural to use the word "significant" when the effect is big or noteworthy in an economic sense. Unfortunately, the use of "significant" in statistical discussion has been pre-empted by a technical meaning that is different from ordinary usage. As explained in Chapter 12, the meaning of "significant" in a basic hypothesis test is simply "not zero." Some writers make a distinction between "economic significance" and "statistical significance," but this is not universal. A simple way to avoid confusion is to use the word "significant" only in its technical meaning and to use the word "important" in connection with an assessment of the magnitude of a coefficient. We follow this usage.

Finally, since $\hat{\beta}_1$ estimates the effect of X on Y, it is tempting to jump to the conclusion that the larger is the $\hat{\beta}_1$ value in a regression the more important is X in explaining Y. This conclusion is valid when thinking about different possible values for the coefficient in a particular regression. However, the conclusion is invalid when thinking about the importance of a single coefficient, or when thinking about a comparison of coefficients in different regressions. As shown in Section 5.5, the magnitude of a coefficient is affected by the units of measurement of the variables in the data. Therefore, the magnitude by itself does not indicate the importance of the coefficient. For example, if all we know about an estimated slope coefficient is that $\hat{\beta}_1^* = 0.0000014$, we do not know whether this indicates an important effect or an unimportant effect.

6.2   The Earnings Function and the Consumption Function _____

In this section we present two examples of regular simple regression that serve as small case studies of econometric research. In both cases we start with a theory or belief about the form of the relation. The actual calculations are not shown, because they are standard applications of the methods of Chapter 5 and because we nearly always rely on a computer to carry them out anyway. The emphasis is on interpreting and using the estimated model.

The Earnings Function

We start with a simple theory that labor markets serve to determine persons' earnings according to their educational attainment as specified in

$$EARNS_i = \beta_0 + \beta_1 ED_i + u_i \tag{6.6}$$

using mnemonic variable names instead of Y and X. The theory might be based on the idea that education enhances productivity, which is rewarded in labor markets with greater earnings. Alternatively, it might be based on the ideas that educational attainment mainly certifies the existence of potential abilities, and that earnings are based on this certification. In either case, (6.6) is an appropriate model.

Using the 100 observations in our cross-section data set, in which $EARNS$ measures earnings in thousands of dollars and ED measures years of schooling, and applying (5.12) and (5.13) to calculate the OLS coefficients, we find that

$$\widehat{EARNS}_i = -1.315 + 0.797ED_i$$

$$R^2 = .285 \quad SER = 4.361$$

(6.7)

In this estimated regression, the finding that $\hat{\beta}_1^* = 0.797$ is interpreted to mean that an extra year of education leads to 0.797 thousand dollars greater annual earnings. In other words, in this labor market the effect of education is to increase annual earnings by $797 for each additional year of schooling. Is this an important effect? In considering this question of economics, remember that the data refer to labor market conditions in 1963. Given the relative ease of acquiring another year of education and taking into account the magnitude of this impact in comparison with the variation in earnings that exists among the observations, most economists (and educators) would say that education has a fairly important effect on earnings in this model.

The intercept $\hat{\beta}_0^* = -1.315$ tells us that the predicted earnings of a person with no education is -1.315 thousand dollars (or $-$1315$). Since labor markets do not offer negative earnings, this unrealistic finding needs careful attention. We briefly consider some alternatives. One possibility is that the model (6.6) is fully correct, with a positive β_0 that gives the expected earnings of a worker with no schooling. In this case, the negative $\hat{\beta}_0^*$ in (6.7) would be associated with a large estimation error resulting from the particular outcomes for the disturbances in our data. A second possibility is that the model (6.6) is fully correct, but with $\beta_0 < 0$. In economic terms, this might mean that a worker with no schooling would have negative productivity in a job, and therefore such a worker would not be hired. In this case the estimated model (6.7) would be in accord with the true behavior of the labor market, but our simple interpretation of the intercept would be misleading because it attempts to apply the model to a value of ED that is not economically appropriate. A third possibility is that the model (6.6) is incorrect: perhaps the true form of the relation between $EARNS$ and ED is nonlinear, with positive earnings for workers with no education. In this case, the attempt to fit a straight line to the data would lead to an incorrect analysis of the determination of earnings for workers with no education. We leave this issue unresolved, but note that the minimum value for ED in our data is 2 years and that the model (6.7) predicts positive earnings in this case.

The R^2 indicates that about 29 percent of the variation in earnings in our data is explained by the level of educational attainment. This may seem low, but it is similar to the R^2 values found in other cross-section studies of earnings.

Another assessment of how well the regression fits the data is provided by the SER, which indicates that the typical error of fit is 4.361 thousand dollars. To make this meaningful, the magnitude can be compared with values of *EARNS*, which is the dependent variable. In the data, *EARNS* ranges from 0.750 to 30.000 and has a mean of 7.911 thousand dollars. Taking the mean as a standard for comparison, the *SER* seems quite large; this indicates that the fit is not especially good.

Using (6.7) we can predict the earnings of a college graduate (*ED* = 16) to be

$$\widehat{EARNS} = -1.315 + (0.797)(16) = 11.437 \qquad (6.8)$$

thousand dollars. It should be remembered that our data pertain only to male heads of families in the 25–54 age range, in 1963. Making predictions or assessing the effect of education on the basis of this estimated earnings function is appropriate only with reference to this particular group. We do not expect that it would adequately predict women's earnings, for example, nor earnings in 1995.

Although the *SER* gives the typical error of fit for the estimated regression, when we use the regression to make a prediction for an observation that is not in the original data (sample) we have a new situation. In Chapter 13 we see that the typical error of prediction for an out-of-sample observation is greater than the *SER* of the estimated regression.

The Consumption Function

As discussed in Chapter 1, an aggregate consumption function based on simplified Keynesian ideas can be specified as

$$CON_i = \beta_0 + \beta_1 DPI_i + u_i \qquad (6.9)$$

where CON_i is aggregate personal consumption expenditure in year i, and DPI_i is aggregate disposable personal income in the same year. β_1 can be interpreted as the marginal propensity to consume, because (6.9) implies that if *DPI* increases by 1 dollar, then $E[CON]$ will increase by β_1 dollars (assuming that both variables are measured in the same units).

Using the 25 observations for the years 1956–1980 in our time-series data set, in which *CON* and *DPI* are both measured in billions of 1972 dollars, and calculating the ordinary least squares estimates, we find that

$$\widehat{CON}_i = 0.568 + 0.907DPI_i$$
$$R^2 = .997 \quad SER = 8.935 \qquad (6.10)$$

The estimated marginal propensity to consume ($\hat{\beta}_1^*$) is 0.907, which is consistent with Keynes' conjecture. The fit is extraordinarily good: the R^2 of .997 means that nearly 100 percent of the variation in *CON* over this period is explained by the regression (i.e., is explained by variation in *DPI*). Although it seems that we might have discovered some fundamental economic law, judgment must be reserved on this question. Very high R^2 values are common in time-series studies because most variables tend to increase over time, and therefore high correlations will exist among them even if cause-and-effect relations are absent or weak. Also, other specifications of the process determining consumption behavior may be preferred in economic research.

We can use (6.10) to predict how high *CON* will be when *DPI* is 1.2 trillion dollars:

$$\widehat{CON} = 0.568 + (0.907)(1200) = 1088.97 \tag{6.11}$$

billion dollars. Also, if *DPI* were to decrease by 20 billion dollars (from whatever level it might be at), the estimated model predicts a change in consumption of

$$\Delta\widehat{CON} = (0.907)(-20) = -18.14 \tag{6.12}$$

billion dollars. Note that the estimated intercept plays no role in a calculation like this.

6.3 Alternative Model Specifications _____

As already noted, the appropriateness of using the regular simple regression model is contingent on its being an accurate description of the particular process being studied. Most important, the model requires that for each observation the expected value of *Y* be a linear function of the value of *X* and that no other variable be systematically involved in the determination of *Y*. In the cases of the earnings function and consumption function, this was taken to be an appropriate specification of the relations. The general technique can be applied to many other economic relations in the same straightforward way.

In other cases, however, simple regression can be applied even when the theory that describes the determination of a particular variable is more complex than the model seems to allow. The key to doing this is realizing that the *Y* and *X* in the regular model (6.1) need not be the original variables involved in the process. Instead, *Y* and *X* in the regression model can be variables that are constructed from the original variables. To keep this clear, it is common to refer to *Y* as the **regressand** rather than the dependent variable and to *X* as the **regressor** rather than the explanatory variable.

In this section we look at some examples in which a relation involving more than two variables is respecified in such a way that simple regression can be applied. Also, we look at cases in which the relation involves variables that are measured in different time periods. In succeeding sections we look at special cases in which inherently nonlinear relations between two variables can be respecified in linear form.

Ratios of Variables

Part of the controversy surrounding the Keynesian consumption theory focused on the average propensity to consume (*APC*), which is defined as

$$APC_i = \frac{CON_i}{DPI_i} \tag{6.13}$$

One tradition and body of evidence viewed the consumption–income ratio as an economic constant that did not change over time. By contrast, Keynes conjectured that the APC would decline as income rose over time.

One way to look at the data and provide evidence on this question begins by assuming that the average propensity to consume is a simple linear function of time. The variables CON and DPI from the time-series data set are used to construct a new variable APC defined by (6.13). A regression model is specified and then estimated, using APC as the regressand and the time trend T as the regressor. With $n = 25$, the results are

$$\widehat{APC_i} = 0.911 - 0.000213T_i$$
$$R^2 = .020 \quad SER = 0.011$$

(6.14)

Sometimes regressions like this one are reported as

$$\left(\widehat{\frac{CON_i}{DPI_i}}\right) = 0.911 - 0.000213T_i$$

(6.15)

to make it clear that the regressand is constructed as the ratio of two variables.

These results show that the average propensity to consume decreases over time, seemingly in conformity with the Keynesian view. Each year, the APC is estimated to decrease by about 0.000213. Is this a lot or a little? In the middle year of the sample (1968, with $T = 13$) the predicted APC is $0.911 - (0.000213)(13) = 0.908$, and the annual decrease (0.000213) is very small compared with this. The annual decrease seems quite unimportant. Hence some persons might be inclined to say that for all practical purposes the average propensity to consume is constant.

Differences of Variables

In financial economics, it is theorized that the return to the stock of a particular company (RS) depends on the return to all stocks in the market (RM) and the return to a riskfree asset (RF) such as a government bond. That is, RS depends on two variables, and the situation seems to call for a multiple regression. However, in the standard formulation, the relation is simplified by defining two new variables:

$$Y = RS - RF \quad \text{and} \quad X = RM - RF$$

(6.16)

With these definitions, Y is the risk premium for the particular stock being studied and X is the market risk premium. Then, a simple regression model involving the regressand Y and the regressor X is specified.

According to some financial theory, the appropriate model is

$$Y_i = \beta_0 + \beta_1 X_i + u_i$$

(6.17)

which is the same as the regular simple regression model (6.1). In the language of finance, the slope coefficient β_1 is known as the stock's "beta." This coefficient is theorized to depend on the particular risk characteristics of the company, which are presumed to remain constant over time. Different companies have different risk characteristics, and therefore each has its own separate beta.

Starting from time-series data on the three underlying variables (all measured in percentage points), we can construct time series for Y and X and estimate the regression for a particular company. For example, the results in a particular case are

$$\hat{Y}_i = 0.792 + 0.920X_i \qquad (6.18)$$

Instead of trying to apply our usual method of interpreting the coefficients ("a one-point increase in the market risk premium leads to ..."), we might simply state that we have estimated the stock's beta to be 0.920. In the theory of finance, this means that the company's stock is somewhat less risky than the market as a whole.

An important theory in finance, the Capital Asset Pricing Model, states that β_0 in (6.17) should be exactly zero. This leads to a model of regression through the origin,

$$Y_i = \beta X_i + u_i \qquad (6.19)$$

which was discussed in Section 5.6. In this formulation, the coefficient β is also known as the stock's beta. Using the same data as before, the results are

$$\hat{Y}_i = 0.958X_i \qquad (6.20)$$

which gives us a slightly different estimate for the same company's beta.

Lagged Variables and First Differences

The regular simple regression model is specified so that Y_i is related to X_i. In a time-series context, this means that the values of Y and X are to be measured in the same time period. However, economic behavior is dynamic, and an effect may occur substantially later than its cause. For example, a firm's investment decision may be made at one point in time but the machines might not be produced and delivered until a year or more later. Similarly, people may budget their consumption expenditures on the basis of last year's income rather than its current level. In these cases the explanatory variable is said to determine the dependent variable with a *lag*.

If there is a one-period lag between cause and effect, it is natural to formulate a simple regression model as

$$Y_i = \beta_0 + \beta_1 X_{i-1} + u_i \qquad (6.21)$$

where X_{i-1} is the value of X one period before i. In other words, the current (ith period) value of Y depends on the one-period lagged value of X and the current disturbance. This formulation appears to complicate the estimation of the coefficients, because the paired Y_i, X_{i-1} values are no longer a row in a rectangular data matrix and the OLS estimators are no longer appropriately defined.

However, the creation of a new regressor straightens out these difficulties. Table 6.1 illustrates the procedure. The table shows some data on two variables Y and X. A new regressor is created in such a way that each of its values is equal to the previous period's value of X. Appropriately, this new regressor is called *XLAG*. In period i, the value $XLAG_i$ is equal to X_{i-1}, and

$$Y_i = \beta_0 + \beta_1 XLAG_i + u_i \tag{6.22}$$

has the same meaning as (6.21). In this specification the earlier difficulties disappear, and the coefficients can be estimated in the ordinary way. It should be noted that in the construction of *XLAG*, no value could be assigned to $XLAG_1$ because X_0 is not in the data set. Hence in estimating (6.22) we must ignore the first observation in the data, and use only 2 through n.

For example, using observations 2 through 25 of the time-series data set, an aggregate consumption function embodying the theory that *DPI* affects *CON* with a one-period lag is estimated as

$$\widehat{CON}_i = 10.913 + 0.923 DPILAG_i$$
$$R^2 = .993 \quad SER = 14.953 \tag{6.23}$$

The results differ slightly from the contemporaneous model (6.10). The standard error of regression, which measures the typical error of fit, is about 50 percent greater here, but the R^2 is only slightly lower. Although the original specification provides a better fit, we do not have a statistical basis yet for choosing between the two. This lag specification is so common and easy to understand that reports

TABLE 6.1 Construction of the Transformed Variables

i	Y	X	$XLAG$	$FDIFFX$
1	405.4	446.2	—	—
2	413.8	455.5	446.2	9.3
3	418.0	460.7	455.5	5.2
.				
.				
.				
$i-1$	Y_{i-1}	X_{i-1}	$XLAG_{i-1}$	$FDIFFX_{i-1}$
i	Y_i	X_i	$XLAG_i$	$FDIFFX_i$
.				
.				
.				
n				

of equations like (6.23) often are written with DPI_{i-1} rather than $DPILAG_i$ on the right-hand side, because no confusion is likely to occur.

Another common specification in time-series modeling involves letting the regressand or regressor, or both, be the *first difference* of a variable. The first difference is a constructed variable whose value in any period is equal to the value of the original variable in that period minus its lagged value. For example, starting with data on X, the new variable $FDIFFX$ is defined by

$$FDIFFX_i = X_i - X_{i-1} \qquad (6.24)$$

The first difference $FDIFFX_i$ is the same as the absolute change ΔX_i defined in Chapter 2.

The construction of the first difference is illustrated in Table 6.1. Notice, for example, that $FDIFFX_2 = 455.5 - 446.2 = 9.3$. Starting with n observations on X, the values of $FDIFFX$ are defined only for observations 2 through n.

One model formulation involving a first difference is

$$Y_i = \beta_0 + \beta_1 FDIFFX_i + u_i \qquad (6.25)$$

The estimation of the coefficients this regression is equivalent to finding the best fitting line drawn through the scatterplot of data points on Y and $FDIFFX$ from Table 6.1, for observations 2 through n.

For example, the accelerator theory of aggregate investment behavior is based on the idea that changes in the level of GNP are the main determinant of the level of investment spending by business. This leads to a model like (6.25) in which the regessand is INV and the regressor is the first difference of GNP. It is common to denote the regressor simply by ΔGNP.

Using observations 2 through 25 from the time-series data set in Chapter 2, where INV is real gross private domestic investment, the estimated model is

$$\widehat{INV}_i = 136.6 + 0.691\ \Delta GNP_i$$
$$R^2 = .175 \quad SER = 40.4 \qquad (6.26)$$

The positive intercept gives the estimated amount of investment (136.6 billion dollars) that would occur if GNP were not growing (i.e., if $\Delta GNP = 0$); this might reflect investment to replace depreciated assets. The estimated slope is substantially smaller than predicted by simple accelerator theory, which suggests that (6.26) might not be an appropriate model of investment behavior.

6.4   The Reciprocal Specification

Sometimes economic theory predicts that the systematic relation between two variables is nonlinear. If the nonlinearity is not too severe, it might be reasonable to use the regular simple regression model as an approximation. However, this is not usually advisable because it prevents us from investigating the nonlinear features. An alternative approach involves finding a nonlinear mathematical form to specify a relation that is appropriate for the economic process and that is transformable into a linear relation.

One such mathematical form is the **reciprocal** relation

$$Y = \beta_0 + \frac{\beta_1}{X} \quad \text{or} \quad Y = \beta_0 + \beta_1 \left(\frac{1}{X}\right) \tag{6.27}$$

The geometry of the reciprocal relation is illustrated in the left side of Figure 6.2. Y may be positive or negative. We focus only on cases in which all the X values are positive; although the reciprocal relation is defined for negative X values, it is rarely used in these cases. In part (a) we see that if β_1 is negative, the slope of the relation between Y and X is positive and it becomes flatter as X increases. Y never rises above the value $Y = \beta_0$, and in fact it never quite reaches it. In part (b) we see that if β_1 is zero, Y is constant. In part (c) we see that if β_1 is positive, the slope of the relation between Y and X is negative and becomes flatter as X increases. Y never reaches or falls below the value $Y = \beta_0$.

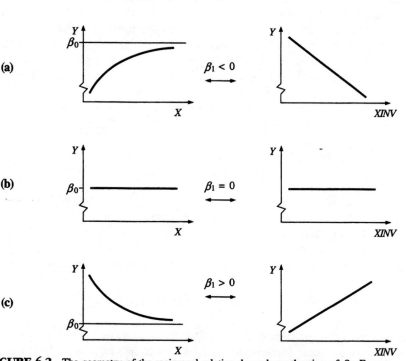

FIGURE 6.2 The geometry of the reciprocal relation depends on the sign of β_1. Except when $\beta_1 = 0$, Y is a nonlinear function of X; as X increases, Y increases ($\beta_1 < 0$) or decreases ($\beta_1 > 0$) and approaches the asymptotic limit β_0. Although Y is a nonlinear function of X, it is a linear function of the inverse of X—which is denoted by $XINV$.

Now consider a new variable, *XINV*, that is equal to the reciprocal (i.e., inverse) of *X*. In other words, let $XINV = 1/X$. It follows from (6.27) that *Y* is a linear function of *XINV*:

$$Y = \beta_0 + \beta_1 XINV \tag{6.28}$$

The relation between *Y* and *XINV* is illustrated on the right side of Figure 6.2, with three cases depending on the value of β_1. We see that the specific form of the nonlinear relation (6.27) implies a linear relation between *Y* and *XINV*.

Using the word "inverse" in describing relations requires special care. If *Y* decreases as *X* increases, it is commonly said that *Y* is inversely related to *X*. This usage is quite separate from what we are dealing with here, and it can lead to confusion. For example, the previous paragraphs explain that the relation between *Y* and *X* in the left side of Figure 6.2a can be described by saying that *Y* is linearly related to the inverse of *X*. It could never be said of this figure that *Y* is inversely related to *X*.

The potential for applying this bit of mathematical analysis to econometric regression modeling should be clear. If we have a theory or belief that the systematic part of the relation between *Y* and *X* is reciprocal, like (6.27), this theory can be reexpressed to state that *Y* is linearly related to *XINV*. Further, the parameters β_0 and β_1 of the linear relation (between *Y* and *XINV*) are the same as the parameters of the reciprocal relation (between *Y* and *X*). If we add a disturbance term to (6.28), we have the specification of a regression model.

For example, before the combined high inflation and unemployment of the 1970s, the systematic part of the Phillips curve relation between the rate of inflation and the unemployment rate was considered to be nonlinear and to resemble the left side of Figure 6.2c. Hence a reciprocal relation between inflation and unemployment was considered to be an appropriate form, and we use 15 annual observations (1956–1970) to estimate the model.

The regressand is simply *RINF1*. The regressor is a new variable, equal to the inverse of *UPCT*:

$$UINV_i = \frac{1}{UPCT_i} \tag{6.29}$$

The estimated regression is

$$\widehat{RINF1}_i = -1.984 + 22.234 UINV_i \tag{6.30}$$
$$R^2 = .549 \quad SER = 0.956$$

Results such as these are commonly reported with $1/UPCT$ written in place of *UINV*, but we wish to stress here that the actual regressor is a transformed variable.

The results of regressions involving transformed variables require care in interpretation. Since $\hat{\beta}_1^*$ is positive, the actual estimated regression resembles the right side of Figure 6.2c. However, the economic interpretation is best carried out in terms of the implied relation between predicted *RINF1* and *UPCT*, which resembles the left side of Figure 6.2c. Looking first at the estimated intercept, we see that as *UPCT* increases, *RINF1* decreases and approaches a lower limit of −1.984 percent. The sign of the estimated slope tells us the general shape (here, like the left side of Figure 6.2c), but interpreting the magnitude requires some extra effort.

The quantitative implications of the estimated slope are best understood by comparing the predicted values for the rate of inflation at various levels of the unemployment rate. For example, if *UPCT* = 3 percent, the predicted value of *RINF1* is −1.984 + (22.234)(1/3) = 5.43 percent. Similarly, the predicted values of *RINF1* when *UPCT* = 4, 5, and 6 percent are *RINF1* = 3.57, 2.46, and 1.72 percent, respectively. Thinking of movements along the relation between *RINF1* and *UPCT*, the values of $\Delta RINF1$ when $\Delta UPCT = 1$ at *UPCT* = 4, 5, and 6 percent are −1.86, −1.11, and −0.74 percent, respectively. These successive differences give us a quantitative assessment of the diminishing effect that increasing unemployment has on reductions in inflation.

The restriction of the data to observations from the period 1956–1970 reflects the fundamental requirement that all the data used to estimate a model must have been generated by the same economic process. We believe that after 1970 expectations of continuing inflation began to get built into the behavior of the economy in a way that they had not been in the earlier period. In other words, the behavioral pattern changed. This means that although the model (6.30) may be quite appropriate for the earlier period, it cannot be used to make predictions after 1970. For this later period, a more complicated model is required.

6.5   Logarithmic Functional Forms _____

As seen in Section 6.4, in some cases a transformation of a nonlinear relation leads to an equivalent linear relation involving newly created variables. The benefit of this is that a linear regression model can be used to estimate the parameters. The focus of our interest and interpretation, however, remains with the original nonlinear relation.

Certain nonlinear relations become linear when they are transformed with logarithms. The wide range of nonlinearities that can be captured and the associated ease of interpretation make these specifications very popular with applied econometricians. These relations and their transformations are explored in this section, and the appendix to this chapter contains the derivations of some of the interpretations given here.

The Log-Linear Specification

As in the previous section, we begin with some mathematical analysis. Consider an exact relation between *Y* and *X* given by

$$Y = (e^{\beta_0})(X^{\beta_1}) \tag{6.31}$$

where e is the base of natural logarithms and e^{β_0} is some positive constant. Taking natural logarithms of both sides of the equation, we obtain

$$\ln Y = \beta_0 + \beta_1 \ln X \qquad (6.32)$$

which is a linear relation between $\ln Y$ and $\ln X$. Since (6.32) involves the logarithms of Y and X, the relation is defined only if all the values of Y and X are positive. Equations (6.31) and (6.32) describe a *log-linear* relation between Y and X.

An important feature of the log-linear relation is that the graph of the original relation between Y and X can take on a wide variety of shapes, even though the relation between $\ln Y$ and $\ln X$ is always linear. Figure 6.3 shows the geometry of (6.31) and its logarithmic transformation (6.32) when β_1 takes on different values. In part (a) we see that if β_1 is negative, the relation between Y and X is downward sloping and its slope becomes flatter as X increases. In part (b) we see that if β_1 is zero, Y is constant. In part (c) we see that if β_1 is between 0 and 1, the relation between Y and X extends out from the origin and slopes upward, with the slope becoming flatter as X increases. In part (d) we see that if β_1 is equal to 1, the relation between Y and X extends out from the origin and is linear; in this case, Y is proportional to X. In part (e) we see that if β_1 is greater than 1, the relation between Y and X extends out from the origin and slopes upward, with the slope becoming steeper as X increases.

A second important feature of the log-linear relation is that β_1 is equal to the elasticity of Y with respect to X. More precisely, β_1 is equal to the point elasticity, which is constant over the whole range of the relation. That is,

$$\beta_1 = \frac{dY/Y}{dX/X} \qquad (6.33)$$

where dY and dX can be thought of as very small changes (Δ's) in Y and X. For this reason, the log-linear relation is sometimes called the *constant-elasticity* relation. (The concept of elasticity is discussed in the appendix to Chapter 1.)

Since the coefficient β_1 is an elasticity, it has a straightforward interpretation and it can be applied to make useful calculations. Consider a movement from one point to another along a relation like (6.31). Let "pc of X" denote the proportionate change in X, and let "pc of Y" denote the resulting proportionate change in Y. (Note that "pc of X" is an alternate notation for $\Delta X/X$.) As shown in the appendix to this chapter,

$$\text{pc of } Y \approx (\beta_1)(\text{pc of } X) \qquad (6.34)$$

This approximation is quite good when the proportionate changes are small, and in such a situation we apply (6.34) as though it were an equality. For example, if the elasticity β_1 equals 1.2, a 5 percent change in X (i.e., pc of $X = 0.05$) will cause Y to change by the proportion $(1.2)(0.05) = 0.06$, or 6 percent. In applying (6.34), the "pc" can be replaced by the percentage-point change (e.g., 0.05 can be replaced by 5.0). This leads to no problem so long as the usage is consistent for Y and X. In the previous example, a 5 percent change in X will lead to a $(1.2)(5) = 6.0$ percent change in Y.

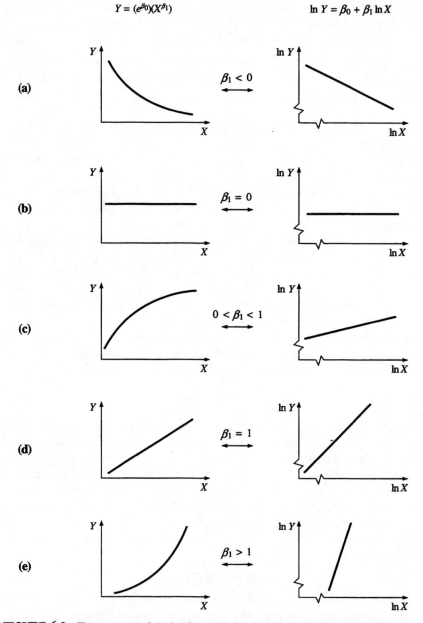

$$Y = (e^{\beta_0})(X^{\beta_1}) \qquad\qquad \ln Y = \beta_0 + \beta_1 \ln X$$

FIGURE 6.3 The geometry of the log-linear relation depends on the sign of β_1. When Y decreases as X increases [case (a), with $\beta_1 < 0$], it is concave upward. When Y increases with X (with $\beta_1 > 0$), the concavity may be upward or downward, depending on the magnitude of β_1. Although Y is a nonlinear function of X, $\ln Y$ is a linear function of $\ln X$; the slope of that line is the same β_1 as in the original formulation. The parameter β_1 is the elasticity of Y with respect to X.

So far we have focused on an exact relation between variables Y and X. Moving toward econometrics, (6.32) can be taken as a statement of the systematic relation between Y and X for the ith observation. Adding a disturbance term to recognize the role of random factors in the determination of Y, we have a simple regression model

$$\ln Y_i = \beta_0 + \beta_1 \ln X_i + u_i \tag{6.35}$$

where the regressand is $\ln Y$ and the regressor is $\ln X$.

For example, consider the aggregate demand for money in the United States. Monetary theory leads us to specify the model in real terms, so we must first construct a new variable that gives the real quantity of money (see Section 2.3), based on variables in our data set:

$$M_i = \frac{M1_i}{PGNP_i/100} \tag{6.36}$$

Note that $M1$ is identified in Chapter 2 as the nominal supply of money. Since financial markets adjust rapidly to changing conditions, the quantity demanded will be equal to the quantity supplied under prevailing conditions. Hence, the data on $M1$ also serve as data on the nominal demand for money.

Monetary theory suggests that the demand for money depends on national income (GNP) and also that it is reasonable to specify the relation in constant-elasticity form:

$$\ln M_i = \beta_0 + \beta_1 \ln GNP_i + u_i \tag{6.37}$$

Comparing this with the general specification of the regular simple regression model (6.1), it should be clear that the regressand $\ln M$ plays the role of Y and that the regressor $\ln GNP$ plays the role of X. That is, the regressand and regressor of this model are transformed variables: they are the logarithms of M and GNP, respectively. For notational convenience we let the names of the new variables be LNM and $LNGNP$.

The necessary construction of data for this estimation is illustrated in Table 6.2, which presents data for the first three observations in the time-series data set from Chapter 2. Variables $M1$, $PGNP$, and GNP are taken directly from Table 2.3, and the construction of M was just discussed. Variables LNM and $LNGNP$ are determined simply as the natural logarithms of the values of M and GNP. All this work can be done easily with a computer, or not so easily with a calculator.

TABLE 6.2 Construction of the Transformed Variables

i	$M1$	$PGNP$	M	GNP	LNM	$LNGNP$
1	135.0	62.79	215.00	671.6	5.3706	6.5097
2	133.8	64.93	206.07	683.8	5.3282	6.5277
3	138.9	66.04	210.33	680.9	5.3487	6.5234

The actual regression model is specified like (6.37), with LNM_i replacing ln M_i, and $LNGNP_i$ replacing ln GNP_i. Only the variables in the last two columns of Table 6.2 are used in the actual regression. Thus, estimating the regression is the same as finding the best-fitting line drawn through the scatterplot of data points on LNM and $LNGNP$.

Using the 25 observations in the time-series data set, the estimated regression is

$$\widehat{LNM_i} = 3.948 + 0.215LNGNP_i$$

$$R^2 = .780 \quad SER = 0.0305$$

(6.38)

Since $0 < \hat{\beta}_1^* < 1$, we see that the estimated regression is like the right side of Figure 6.3c and the implied relation between M and GNP is like the left side.

We interpret the estimated slope $\hat{\beta}_1^* = 0.215$ by saying "the elasticity of M with respect to GNP is 0.215," with the understanding that this means that if GNP increases by 1 percent, predicted M will increase by 0.215 percent. (No one wants to hear or read about how changes in $LNGNP$ will affect LNM.) To determine the effect of other-sized changes in GNP, we usually work through (6.34) rather than the estimated regression itself. For example, a 5 percent increase in GNP leads to a $(0.215)(5) = 1.075$ percent increase in predicted M. However, when the changes in GNP or M are large, the approximation based on the point elasticity is not too precise. A method for making exact calculations in this situation is shown in the appendix to this chapter.

Now, suppose that we wish to predict the demand for money when $GNP = 1000$. We must work through the estimated regression for this problem. First, we determine $\ln(1000) = 6.908$. Next, we calculate the predicted value of ln M to be $3.948 + (0.215)(6.908) = 5.433$. Finally, we take the antilog of this number, yielding a predicted demand for money of 222.8 billion dollars. (A refinement of this procedure is presented in Section 16.2.)

The constant elasticity model is probably the second most useful specification for a simple regression, after the regular linear form. This is because economic theory often characterizes relations in elasticity terms, and the model provides a simple method for estimating an elasticity. It should be noted that the presumption that the elasticity is constant throughout the relation is a strong one—but so is the corresponding assumption that the slope is constant in a regular linear model.

The Semilog Specification

Returning to mathematical analysis again, suppose that the exact relation between Y and X is

$$Y = (e^{\beta_0})(e^{\beta_1 X})$$

(6.39)

Taking natural logarithms of both sides of the equation, we obtain

$$\ln Y = \beta_0 + \beta_1 X \tag{6.40}$$

which is a linear relation between $\ln Y$ and X. Equations (6.39) and (6.40) describe a *semilog* relation between Y and X. (Another variant, which we do not consider, specifies Y as a function of $\ln X$.)

The geometry of (6.39) and (6.40) is illustrated in Figure 6.4. For the semilog relation, X may take on positive or negative values, but Y must be positive if $\ln Y$ is to be defined. In part (a) we see that if β_1 is negative, Y decreases as X increases and the slope of the relation becomes flatter. In part (b) we see that if β_1 is zero, Y is constant. In part (c) we see that if β_1 is positive, Y increases as X increases and the slope of the relation becomes steeper.

Part of the usefulness of the semilog relation arises from the ease of interpreting β_1. Thinking of dY and dX as very small changes resulting from

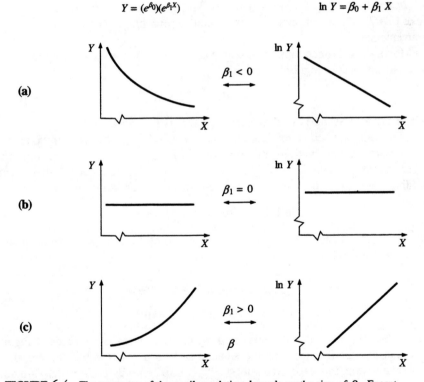

FIGURE 6.4 The geometry of the semilog relation depends on the sign of β_1. Except when $\beta_1 = 0$, Y is a nonlinear function of X. As X increases, Y decreases ($\beta_1 < 0$) or increases ($\beta_1 > 0$), and the relation is concave upward in both cases. Although Y is a nonlinear function of X, $\ln Y$ is a linear function of X; the slope of that line is the same β_1 as in the original formulation. The parameter β_1 can be interpreted as the proportional change in Y that results from a unit change in X.

movement along the relation between Y and X, it is shown in the appendix to this chapter that

$$\beta_1 = \frac{dY/Y}{dX} \tag{6.41}$$

That is, β_1 is the ratio of the proportionate change in Y to the absolute change in X.

When the change in X is not very small, it is denoted by ΔX. The corresponding proportionate change in Y that results from moving from one point to another along the relation is denoted by "pc of Y," as before. As shown in the appendix, (6.41) implies that

$$\text{pc of } Y \approx \beta_1 \, \Delta X \tag{6.42}$$

If $\Delta X = 1$, we see that $\beta_1 \approx$ pc of Y. Hence, the coefficient β_1 can be interpreted as the proportionate change in Y that results from a unit change in X. The "pc of Y" determined in calculations with this approximation is always a proportion (like 0.107). The result can be reexpressed in percentage points (like 10.7), for convenience.

Moving toward econometrics, it is easy to see that the exact relation (6.40) leads to the simple regression model

$$\ln Y_i = \beta_0 + \beta_1 X_i + u_i \tag{6.43}$$

where the regressand is $\ln Y$ and the regressor is simply X.

The semilog specification has often been applied to the human capital theory of earnings determination. In one formulation, the theory states that the logarithm of earnings is linearly related to the level of educational attainment. Adding a disturbance term, this yields the semilog regression model

$$\ln EARNS_i = \beta_0 + \beta_1 ED_i + u_i \tag{6.44}$$

Based on the 100 observations in our cross-section data set, the estimated earnings function is

$$\widehat{LNEARNS}_i = 0.673 + 0.107 ED_i$$

$$R^2 = .405 \quad SER = 0.446 \tag{6.45}$$

Since $\hat{\beta}_1^* > 0$, we see that the estimated regression is like the right side of Figure 6.4c and that the implied relation between $EARNS$ and ED is like the left side.

We interpret the estimated slope $\hat{\beta}_1^* = 0.107$ through the approximation (6.42). In this case, we say that "the estimated slope coefficient means that an additional year of schooling increases earnings by the proportion 0.107, or 10.7 percent." (No one wants to hear or read about $LNEARNS$.) Using (6.42) again, we can calculate that a three-year increase in schooling will increase earnings by the proportion $(0.107)(3) = 0.321$, or 32.1 percent, approximately. (The method for making exact calculations is shown in the appendix to this chapter.)

It is interesting to compare these findings with those from (6.7), in which the effect of each additional year of schooling is to increase annual earnings by $797. Which model is more appropriate for the earnings function? In principle, we look to economic theory for guidance in specifying the model. When this is not sufficient, we may try alternative forms and compare the results. One way to compare (6.7) with (6.45) is to graph the residuals against the explanatory variable, ED. If the residuals appear to be unrelated to ED in one case, but related to ED in a $\cap$ or $\cup$ shape in the other, then the case with the unrelated residuals may be judged better because it is in greater conformity with regression theory.

We note that $R^2 = .405$ in the semilog model is substantially larger than $R^2 = .285$ in the linear model. However, this does not mean that the semilog model is better. When the regressands of two models are different transformations of the same economic variable, the R^2 values in the two models are not comparable.

Another common application of the semilog specification is to estimating the trend rate of growth in a time-series variable. For this type of analysis, it is assumed that the rate of growth underlying the time series is constant.

Consider a simple model of growth

$$Y_i = Y_0(1 + r)^i \tag{6.46}$$

where r is the rate of growth of Y, and i indicates the number of years since period 0. Since the value of time trend T introduced in Chapter 2 is equal to the observation number i, we can write

$$Y_i = Y_0(1 + r)^{T_i} \tag{6.47}$$

Taking logarithms yields

$$\ln Y_i = \ln Y_0 + T_i \ln(1 + r) \tag{6.48}$$

Now, $\ln Y_0$ and $\ln(1 + r)$ are both constants, which we can rename β_0 and β_1, respectively. Adding a disturbance term for econometric reality, (6.48) becomes

$$\ln Y_i = \beta_0 + \beta_1 T_i + u_i \tag{6.49}$$

which is suitable for OLS estimation using the transformed variable $\ln Y$ as the regressand. Following (6.42), we see that β_1 is the proportionate change in Y that results from a unit increase in T. Since T counts years, this means that β_1 is the rate of growth of Y, expressed as a proportion. [Note that since $\beta_1 = \ln(1 + r)$, we know from Chapter 2 that $\beta_1 \approx r$.] The disturbance u_i allows for random fluctuation of Y from its trend each year, so the data would not actually display a constant rate of growth each year.

For example, an estimated model of the growth of real GNP is given by

$$\widehat{LNGNP}_i = 6.456 + 0.0354 T_i$$

$$R^2 = .988 \quad SER = 0.0297$$

(6.50)

using the 25 observations for 1956–1980 in the time-series data set. The annual rate of growth of GNP is estimated to be 3.54 percent.

APPENDIX: The Coefficients in Logarithmic Models _____

In this appendix we derive several results relating to the slope coefficients in log-linear and semilog models: (1) we derive the exact meanings of the coefficients, (2) we derive the approximations (6.34) and (6.42), which are useful for applying the estimated coefficients to practical questions, and (3) we derive formulas for making exact calculations to answer the same questions.

For the log-linear functional form, we use calculus to show that β_1 is equal to the point elasticity of Y with respect to X:

$$\ln Y = \beta_0 + \beta_1 \ln X$$

$$d(\ln Y) = d\beta_0 + d(\beta_1 \ln X)$$

$$dY/Y = 0 + \beta_1(dX/X)$$

(6.51)

$$\beta_1 = \frac{dY/Y}{dX/X}$$

The ratio in the last line of (6.51) is the elasticity, and the derivation shows that this is equal to β_1, which is a constant.

For discrete changes in X and Y we consider moving from p' to p'' along the relation between Y and X illustrated in Figure 6.5. Letting X_1 and Y_1 correspond to p', and X_2 and Y_2 correspond to p'', we find that

$$\ln Y_2 = \beta_0 + \beta_1 \ln X_2$$

$$\ln Y_1 = \beta_0 + \beta_1 \ln X_1$$

$$\ln Y_2 - \ln Y_1 = \beta_0 - \beta_0 + \beta_1 \ln X_2 - \beta_1 \ln X_1$$

$$\ln(Y_2/Y_1) = \beta_1 \ln(X_2/X_1)$$

(6.52)

$$\beta_1 = \frac{\ln(Y_2/Y_1)}{\ln(X_2/X_1)} = \frac{\ln(1 + pc \text{ of } Y)}{\ln(1 + pc \text{ of } X)} \approx \frac{pc \text{ of } Y}{pc \text{ of } X}$$

where "pc of Y" denotes the proportionate change in Y, which might also be denoted by $\Delta Y/Y$, and similarly for X. The first two lines in the derivation are statements of the relation holding at p'' and p', and the third line results from subtracting the second line from the first. The fourth and fifth lines solve for

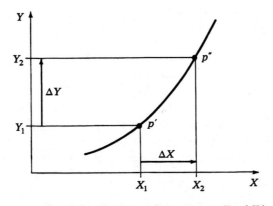

FIGURE 6.5 Moving from p' to p'' along a relation between Y and X is viewed as a change in Y (i.e., ΔY) resulting from a given change in X (i.e., ΔX). In the linear form (not illustrated here), Y and X are related in such a way that ΔY is a constant multiple of ΔX. In the log-linear form, Y and X are related in such a way that $\Delta Y/Y$ is a constant multiple of $\Delta X/X$, approximately; that is, the elasticity is constant, and therefore it does not vary with the level of X. In the semilog form, Y and X are related in such a way that $\Delta Y/Y$ is a constant multiple of ΔX, approximately; that is, the proportionate change in Y resulting from a given ΔX does not depend on the level of X.

β_1 in terms of the proportionate changes of Y and X; the manipulations draw on the discussion of logarithms in Chapter 2.

Parts of the last line of (6.52) can be rearranged to yield

$$\text{pc of } Y \approx (\beta_1)(\text{pc of } X) \qquad (6.53)$$

which is the same as (6.34). The approximation is quite good when the proportionate changes in X and Y are small. This is the basis for our usual interpretation of the slope coefficient in a log-linear model: we say that β_1 is the percentage change in Y that results from a 1 percent increase in X. [Note that multiplying both sides of (6.53) by 100 allows us to describe the changes in percentage-point terms.]

The exact effect on Y that results from any given change in X, small or large, is more difficult to calculate. Restating parts of the last line of (6.52) leads to

$$\ln(1 + \text{pc of } Y) = \beta_1 \ln(1 + \text{pc of } X)$$
$$1 + \text{pc of } Y = \exp[\beta_1 \ln(1 + \text{pc of } X)] \qquad (6.54)$$
$$\text{pc of } Y = \exp[\beta_1 \ln(1 + \text{pc of } X)] - 1$$

where $\exp[\cdot]$ is the antilog of the expression in brackets (i.e., $\exp[\cdot] = e^{[\cdot]}$).

For example, in the demand for money equation (6.38) the estimated slope is $\hat{\beta}_1^* = 0.215$. If GNP were to increase by 100 percent (pc $= 1.00$), as it does over the 1956–1980 sample period, the approximation (6.53) indicates that M would increase by 21.5 percent. However, the exact proportionate effect on M is determined from (6.54) to be

$$\text{pc of } Y = \exp[(0.215) \ln(1 + 1.00)] - 1$$
$$= \exp[(0.215)(0.693)] - 1 \quad (6.55)$$
$$= 0.161$$

or 16.1 percent. In this case, with such large changes in X and Y, the approximation (6.53) is not very accurate.

For the semilog form, the precise meaning of β_1 is derived using calculus:

$$\ln Y = \beta_0 + \beta_1 X$$
$$d(\ln Y) = d\beta_0 + d\beta_1 X = \beta_1 dX \quad (6.56)$$
$$\beta_1 = \frac{d(\ln Y)}{dX} = \frac{dY/Y}{dX}$$

For discrete changes in X and Y we consider moving from p' to p'' in Figure 6.5 again:

$$\ln Y_2 = \beta_0 + \beta_1 X_2$$
$$\ln Y_1 = \beta_0 + \beta_1 X_1$$
$$\ln Y_2 - \ln Y_1 = \beta_0 - \beta_0 + \beta_1 X_2 - \beta_1 X_1 \quad (6.57)$$
$$\ln(Y_2/Y_1) = \beta_1 \Delta X$$
$$\beta_1 = \frac{\ln(1 + \text{pc of } Y)}{\Delta X} \approx \frac{\text{pc of } Y}{\Delta X}$$

Parts of the last line of (6.57) can be rearranged to yield

$$\text{pc of } Y \approx \beta_1 \Delta X \quad (6.58)$$

which is the same as (6.42). The approximation is quite good when the proportionate changes in X and Y are small. This is the basis for our usual interpretation of the slope coefficient in a semilog model: letting $\Delta X = 1$, we say that β_1 is the proportionate change in Y that results from a unit change in X.

The exact effect on Y that results from any given change in X is derived as follows. Restating parts of the last line of (6.57) leads to

$$\ln(1 + \text{pc of } Y) = \beta_1 \Delta X$$
$$1 + \text{pc of } Y = \exp[\beta_1 \Delta X] \quad (6.59)$$
$$\text{pc of } Y = \exp[\beta_1 \Delta X] - 1$$

For example, in the earnings function (6.45) the estimated slope coefficient, 0.107, was interpreted as meaning that each additional year of schooling increases earnings by the proportion 0.107, or 10.7 percent. The actual computed increase is $e^{0.107} - 1 = 0.113$, or 11.3 percent. A three-year increase in schooling increases earnings by the proportion $e^{0.321} - 1 = 0.379$, or 37.9 percent. This is substantially larger than the 32.1 percent computed by the approximation (6.58).

Problems

Section 6.1

★ **6.1** If the expected value of Y for the ith observation is 35, how could it be that the actual value is 33?

6.2 Suppose that an appropriately estimated regression is $\hat{Y}_i = 3 + 4X_i$.
(a) Determine the change in $\hat{Y}$ associated with $\Delta X = 2$.
(b) Comparing two particular observations in the data, it turns out that $\Delta Y = 9$ while $\Delta X = 2$. What accounts for the difference between this ΔY and your answer to part (a)?

6.3 In regressions of saving on income reported in Section 5.5, the slope coefficient was 86.3 in one case and 0.0863 in another. In which case is income more important in explaining saving? Why?

Section 6.2

6.4 Based on the regression reported as Equation (6.7),
(a) Determine the predicted value of *EARNS* corresponding to *ED* = 12.
(b) Determine the change in predicted *EARNS* associated with a change from *ED* = 12 to *ED* = 16.
(c) Thinking of $\Delta ED = 1$, is the effect on earnings of the senior year in college the same as for the sophomore year?

★ **6.5** Suppose that Equation (6.6) is the correct specification of the relation between *EARNS* and *ED*. If the regression (6.7) explains 28.5 percent of the variation in earnings in the sample, what accounts for the rest of the variation?

★ **6.6** Suppose that in 1980 all earnings levels had been inflated by a factor of 100 percent compared with the levels of 1963. If the relation between *EARNS* and *ED* otherwise remained unchanged, what would be the impact of an additional year of schooling on predicted earnings in 1980?

6.7 Based on Equation (6.10), how much of an increase in *DPI* is required to increase predicted *CON* by 1 billion dollars?

6.8 Interpret the estimated intercept in Equation (6.10).

Section 6.3

6.9 Suppose that instead of T in Equation (6.14) we had used the actual year number t as the regressor (i.e., $t_1 = 1956$, $t_2 = 1957$, etc.). What would be the estimated regression of APC on t?

★ **6.10** From Table 2.3, find the actual values of CON and DPI for 1974. What is the actual value for the APC? What is the predicted value of the APC based on Equation (6.14)?

6.11 Assuming that DPI increases steadily over time, what does Equation (6.10) imply about what happens to the average propensity to consume over time?

★ **6.12** Based on Equations (6.16) and (6.18), suppose that RM and RF both increase by one percentage point. What effect would this have on RS?

6.13 Based on Equations (6.16) and (6.20), what is the effect on RS of a one-percentage-point increase in RM (assuming that RF is constant)?

★ **6.14** Based on Equation (6.23), what is the predicted value of consumption for 1974? What is the predicted value based on Equation (6.10)?

6.15 Based on Equation (6.26), determine the predicted level of investment for 1976.

Section 6.4

6.16 Suppose that in normal times the yield on bonds increases with the time to maturity, but that it increases at a decreasing rate and that it never goes above some natural level. Explain how a regression model can best be used to estimate the relation between yield and time to maturity.

6.17 Based on the estimated Phillips curve (6.30), what level of unemployment would have been required to bring the predicted rate of inflation down to zero?

Section 6.5

6.18 With reference to Equation (6.31), what happens to the value of all possible observations on Y if β_0 is increased by a constant amount?

6.19 Based on the slope coefficient in Equation (6.38), what would be the proportional impact on predicted M of the actual increase in GNP that occurred between 1967 and 1968? What was the actual proportional change in M? (See Table 2.3.)

★ **6.20** Suppose that $\ln Y = 1.0 + 0.25 \ln X$. Compute the values of Y for these four values of X: 100, 500, 1000, 1500.

6.21 Plot the four Y, X points determined in Problem 6.20. How does the shape of this graph compare with Figure 6.3?

★ **6.22** Suppose that X increases from 500 to 1000. Based on your calculations for Problem 6.20, what is the percentage increase in predicted Y? How does this compare with the estimated elasticity?

  6.23 Based on Equation (6.45), what is the proportional change in predicted earnings that would result from gaining a college education rather than stopping after completing high school?

★ **6.24** Consider the specification of a demand curve $Q = AP^b$. Interpret the meaning of b. Based on examination of Figure 6.3 and knowledge of economics, is b likely to be positive or negative? How could you use simple regression to estimate the value of b?

  6.25 Suppose that the labor force has been growing at a steady rate over time. Explain how a regression model can be used to estimate the rate of growth.

Appendix

★ **6.26** Based on the relation in Problem 6.20, follow the procedure in Equation (6.54) to determine the exact predicted percentage increase in Y associated with a 100 percent increase in X. Compare this result with that in Problem 6.22.

  6.27 Based on Equation (6.59), what is the exact proportionate change for Problem 6.23? Compare this with the simpler calculation.

7

Multiple Regression:
Theory and Application

Most economic relations, and the processes they describe, involve more than one determinant of some particular dependent variable. For example, the earnings function examined in Chapter 6 presumes that education is the only variable that affects a person's earnings. Surely many more variables are directly relevant, and in this chapter we go on to examine the roles of experience, demographic characteristics, and other variables.

This chapter covers both the theory and application of multiple regression, which involves more than one explanatory variable in a single regression equation. Most of the ideas regarding simple regression carry over, so there are relatively few new concepts to learn.

7.1 Two Explanatory Variables

As a first step in learning about multiple regression, we consider an economic process in which the variable Y is determined by two explanatory variables, X_1 and X_2. For example, a worker's earnings might depend on both education and experience.

Our thinking is that n observations are subjected to this process, one at a time. For each observation separately, the values of X_1 and X_2 are fed in, and the value of Y is determined. The n values of X_1, X_2, and Y are all observable, and they can be collected as a set of data. We envision there being some random factors at work as part of the process, but these are not observable.

Two aspects of this process should be noted. First, X_1 and X_2 are the only variables that directly affect Y. Other variables that might be measured for each observation are understood to play no direct role in the determination of Y. Second, the values of X_1 and X_2 are taken as given. These are determined outside the process under consideration, and we make no effort here to understand why they take on whatever values they do. (In Section 7.6 we look more deeply into the causal nexus surrounding the determination of Y. The variables that help determine X_1, for example, may be said to have an indirect effect on Y, but these are excluded from our conceptualization of the process determining Y. Only variables that have a direct effect on Y are treated as inputs of the process.)

The observations in a data set generated by this process can be plotted in a three-dimensional scatter diagram. We rely on our visual imagination to see this. The explanatory variables X_1 and X_2 are measured along the two axes defining the base, and the dependent variable Y is measured vertically. Each observation is graphed as a single point in this three-dimensional space, and together the plotted points resemble a cloud.

We move toward statistical analysis by making a more concrete specification of the process by which Y is determined. We theorize that for each observation the value of variable Y is determined by the *linear multiple regression model*

$$Y_i = \beta_0 + \beta_1 X_{1i} + \beta_2 X_{2i} + u_i \qquad (7.1)$$

Variable Y is the dependent variable (or regressand), and X_1 and X_2 are the explanatory variables (or regressors). A double-subscript notation is used to refer to particular observations for the explanatory variables, so that X_{1i} denotes the ith observation on X_1, and X_{2i} denotes the ith observation on X_2. The disturbance u is considered to be a random term that represents pure chance factors in the determination of Y.

Based on (7.1), we can decompose each observed Y_i value into a systematic component and a random component:

$$Y_i = E[Y_i] + u_i \qquad (7.2)$$

In this decomposition, the systematic component $E[Y_i]$ is the expected value of Y for the ith observation. As with simple regression, $E[Y_i]$ is the value that Y_i would be, according to (7.1), if the disturbance u_i were equal to zero.

The systematic part of the relation between Y, X_1, and X_2 is specified by

$$E[Y] = \beta_0 + \beta_1 X_1 + \beta_2 X_2 \qquad (7.3)$$

which we call the true regression. This is the equation of a plane graphed in three dimensions, but it is also known as a linear equation. For each observation, the height up to the plane is the value $E[Y_i]$, and the vertical distance from the plane to the observed value Y_i is the disturbance u_i. Thus the whole data set consists of a cloud of points that are generated as points above or below the true regression.

Given this theoretical statement of how observable data are generated, our econometric task is to estimate the coefficients β_0, β_1, and β_2. When we fit a plane to the three-dimensional scatter of data points, it has an equation of the form

$$\hat{Y} = \hat{\beta}_0 + \hat{\beta}_1 X_1 + \hat{\beta}_2 X_2 \tag{7.4}$$

This plane is called the estimated regression. It decomposes each actual Y_i value into its fitted (or predicted) value

$$\hat{Y}_i = \hat{\beta}_0 + \hat{\beta}_1 X_{1i} + \hat{\beta}_2 X_{2i} \tag{7.5}$$

and its residual

$$e_i = Y_i - \hat{Y}_i = Y_i - \hat{\beta}_0 - \hat{\beta}_1 X_{1i} - \hat{\beta}_2 X_{2i} \tag{7.6}$$

The OLS technique calculates $\hat{\beta}_0$, $\hat{\beta}_1$, and $\hat{\beta}_2$ so as to make the sum of squared residuals as small as possible, and a derivation similar to that given in the appendix to Chapter 5 leads to estimators for the coefficients (i.e., rules or formulas for calculating them). To simplify the presentation, we temporarily adopt the notation that a lowercase letter stands for the deviation of a variable from its mean. Thus

$$y = Y - \overline{Y}, \quad x_1 = X_1 - \overline{X}_1, \quad \text{and} \quad x_2 = X_2 - \overline{X}_2 \tag{7.7}$$

The estimators are

$$\hat{\beta}_2 = \frac{(\sum x_2 y)(\sum x_1^2) - (\sum x_1 y)(\sum x_1 x_2)}{(\sum x_1^2)(\sum x_2^2) - (\sum x_1 x_2)^2} \tag{7.8}$$

$$\hat{\beta}_1 = \frac{(\sum x_1 y)(\sum x_2^2) - (\sum x_2 y)(\sum x_1 x_2)}{(\sum x_1^2)(\sum x_2^2) - (\sum x_1 x_2)^2} \tag{7.9}$$

$$\hat{\beta}_0 = \overline{Y} - \hat{\beta}_1 \overline{X}_1 - \hat{\beta}_2 \overline{X}_2 \tag{7.10}$$

Since most regression calculations are carried out by computer programs, one may never have to apply these formulas in practice. They are presented here for several insights that they offer into how multiple regression works. First, notice that the estimators for all three coefficients involve all the values for all the variables. For example, $\hat{\beta}_2$ depends not only on Y and X_2, but on X_1 as well. This means that $\hat{\beta}_2$ is different from the slope coefficient of a simple regression of Y on X_2. Further, the multiple regression coefficients cannot be obtained by estimating two simple regressions, one of Y on X_1 and the other of Y on X_2.

There is an exception to this. If the correlation between X_1 and X_2 is zero, then $\sum x_1 x_2 = 0$ by definition. Looking at (7.8), the right-hand terms in both the numerator and denominator would be equal to zero. In the remaining ratio, identical terms in the numerator and denominator would cancel out, leaving $\hat{\beta}_2$ equal to the estimated slope in a simple regression of Y on X_2. The corresponding result holds for $\hat{\beta}_1$ as determined by (7.9). This special case, in which the correlation between X_1 and X_2 is equal to zero, is known as *orthogonal regression.* This situation rarely occurs in practical econometrics.

The normal situation, then, is one in which the correlation between the explanatory variables is not zero; it might be positive or negative. Multiple regression allows for a determination of the separate effects of two explanatory variables even when they are correlated. The meaning of this will be explained shortly, when we consider how the coefficients are interpreted.

The final insight that arises from looking at the estimators is seeing the possibility of a case of *perfect multicollinearity*. If X_1 and X_2 are perfectly correlated, so that $r = +1$ or $r = -1$, it can be shown that the denominator in (7.8) and (7.9) is equal to zero. Hence, the OLS estimators are not defined in this case, and the regression coefficients cannot be computed. (One might say that both coefficients are equal to infinity, but this does not help much.) It might seem that perfect multicollinearity is a terrible problem, but this is not so. When two explanatory variables are perfectly correlated, it would be logically impossible to disentangle their separate effects and one could not expect a statistical technique to do so. For example, if we try to estimate a regression of family saving (Y) on family income measured in dollars (X_1) and also family income measured in thousands of dollars (X_2), the two explanatory variables would be perfectly correlated and perfect multicollinearity would be present. However, the model is illogical, and our inability to estimate its coefficients is therefore of no consequence.

After the estimated regression is calculated, our attention turns to interpreting the estimated coefficients. The interpretation differs somewhat from the case of simple regression, but is consistent with it. To begin, we note that if two observations (either actual or hypothetical ones) are compared, they may differ with regard to the values of X_1, X_2, and $\hat{Y}$. These differences are linked by

$$\Delta\hat{Y} = \hat{\beta}_1 \Delta X_1 + \hat{\beta}_2 \Delta X_2 \qquad (7.11)$$

This is derived by subtracting an equation like (7.5) specified for one point from the corresponding equation specified for another. This equation determines how changes in the values of the explanatory variables affect the predicted value of the dependent variable. Graphically, this equation compares two points on the estimated regression plane and shows how differences in the three dimensions are related.

Now, if only one explanatory variable changes in value while the other remains the same, then

$$\Delta\hat{Y} = \hat{\beta}_1 \Delta X_1 \quad \text{when} \quad \Delta X_2 = 0 \qquad (7.12)$$

and

$$\Delta\hat{Y} = \hat{\beta}_2 \Delta X_2 \quad \text{when} \quad \Delta X_1 = 0 \qquad (7.13)$$

These equations allow us to calculate the effect on Y of a change in just one of the explanatory variables.

When we let $\Delta X_1 = 1$ in (7.12), this equation provides the basis for interpreting the slope coefficient $\hat{\beta}_1$ as the effect of X_1 on $\hat{Y}$. Looking at (7.12), we say that $\hat{\beta}_1$ is the change in $\hat{Y}$ that results from a unit change in X_1, holding constant the value of X_2. This phrasing corresponds closely to the concept *ceteris paribus* ("other things being equal"), which is commonly used in economic analysis. The interpretation does not suggest that X_2 is held constant in normal economic activity when X_1 increases. Rather, the interpretation is based on a sensible mathematical interpretation of the equation that we use to represent behavior. What we are saying is that if X_2 were somehow held constant, $\hat{\beta}_1$ would give the change in $\hat{Y}$ that would result from a unit change in X_1.

The same logic holds when we let $\Delta X_2 = 1$ in (7.13). We say that $\hat{\beta}_2$ is the change in $\hat{Y}$ that results from a unit change in X_2, holding X_1 constant. These general-form interpretations of the estimated regression coefficients will be illustrated and enhanced in later examples and discussion.

The same measures of fit that are used for simple regression are used for multiple regression also, and they carry the same interpretation. The *SER* measures the typical error of fit, and R^2 gives the proportion of the variation in Y that is explained by the regression. The defining formula for the *SER* is modified from its specification for simple regression, and it is presented in the next section. The defining formula for R^2 is unchanged.

The technique of multiple regression with two explanatory variables can be applied to a variety of economic behaviors, whenever we believe that one variable is systematically determined by just two other variables in a direct way.

The Earnings Function

As an example, we extend our analysis of the earnings function explored in Chapter 6. Suppose that labor market theory suggests that in addition to formal education, experience working in the labor force has a direct effect on workers' earnings. This may be because experience represents on-the-job training and thereby increases a person's productivity and wage, or it may be because of some other considerations. If this theory is correct and if the relation is linear, it is appropriate to formulate the multiple regression model

$$EARNS_i = \beta_0 + \beta_1 ED_i + \beta_2 EXP_i + u_i \tag{7.14}$$

Turning to estimation, the 100 observations in the cross-section data set in Chapter 2 are used to obtain the estimated regression

$$\widehat{EARNS}_i = -6.179 + 0.978 ED_i + 0.124 EXP_i$$

$$R^2 = .315 \quad SER = 4.288 \tag{7.15}$$

It should be clear that these results come from applying the OLS estimators (7.8)–(7.10) to the data with *EARNS* being thought of as *Y*, *ED* being thought of as X_1, and *EXP* being thought of as X_2. A computer program for regression is normally used to carry out the calculations.

We interpret the estimated coefficient $\hat{\beta}_2^* = 0.124$ by saying "holding constant the level of education, an additional year of experience increases earnings by 0.124 thousand dollars ($124)." As noted above, the *ceteris paribus* qualification "holding constant the level of education" is an interpretation based on (7.13); it does not mean that we or the computer hold some values fixed during the estimation. To help assess the importance of this estimated effect of *EXP*, we use (7.13) directly to calculate the effect on earnings of the difference in years of experience between the youngest and oldest men in the sample. This $\Delta X_2 = 30$ leads to a $(0.124)(30) = 3.720$ thousand dollar difference in annual earnings. On this basis, one might make an economic judgment that experience is a moderately important factor in the determination of earnings.

Similarly, the estimated coefficient $\hat{\beta}_1^* = 0.978$ means that an additional year of schooling increases earnings by 0.978 thousand dollars ($978), holding constant the level of experience. We note that this estimate of the effect of education on earnings is substantially greater than the estimate in the simple regression in Chapter 6, which was $\hat{\beta}_1^* = 0.797$. The data did not change, so the difference in the estimates must arise from the change in the specification of the regression, from simple to multiple. We return to this later.

In this particular case, the method of constructing *EXP* provides auxiliary information that leads us to ask this question: Taking into account that for a specific individual an increase in *ED* means an equal decrease in *EXP*, what is the total economic effect on earnings of going to school for two more years? In this question we want to determine the joint effect of $\Delta ED = 2$ and $\Delta EXP = -2$. Applying (7.11), we find that the change in earnings is

$$\widehat{\Delta EARNS} = (0.978)(2) + (0.124)(-2) = 1.708 \qquad (7.16)$$

thousand dollars per year. Note that this is somewhat smaller than the *ceteris paribus* effect of gaining two more years of education.

The estimated model (7.15) can be used to predict earnings for given values of *ED* and *EXP* in the usual way. For example, the predicted earnings (in 1963) for a college graduate with five years of experience is

$$\widehat{EARNS_i} = -6.179 + (0.978)(16) + (0.124)(5) = 10.089 \qquad (7.17)$$

thousand dollars.

The R^2 in the multiple regression is .315, which is somewhat higher than the .285 in the simple regression. Does the fact that R^2 increases by only .030 mean that the impact of experience is marginal, compared with that of education? No, not necessarily. *ED* could seem to get most of the credit simply because we considered it first. The R^2 of a simple regression of *EARNS* on *EXP* in these data could be fairly high, although in fact it is not in this case.

7.2   The General Case

The **general linear multiple regression model** is a particular specification of some economic process in which the values of a dependent variable (or regressand) are determined by several explanatory variables (or regressors). In general we may say that Y depends on k explanatory variables:

$$Y_i = \beta_0 + \beta_1 X_{1i} + \beta_2 X_{2i} + \cdots + \beta_k X_{ki} + u_i \qquad (7.18)$$

where the names of the variables are $X_1, X_2, \ldots, X_k$. A typical variable is denoted by X_j, and a typical coefficient by β_j. When a particular observation is referred to, a second subscript is used, so the ith observation on the jth variable is X_{ji}.

As with simple regression, our notion is that this model accurately reflects the way some process works. Indeed, this notion is more acceptable with multiple regression because this technique allows us to take into account all the relevant variables that help determine the value of the dependent variable. Since most economic processes involve multiple causes of a single effect, this feature is especially important.

When $k = 1$, this model reduces to that of simple regression

$$Y_i = \beta_0 + \beta_1 X_{1i} + u_i \qquad (7.19)$$

in which X_1 is the same as X in (5.1). With simple regression, the observations can be plotted in a two-dimensional graph, and the estimated regression is the line that provides the best possible fit to the scattered points. When $k = 2$, the general model reduces to the case with two explanatory variables, as specified by (7.1). In this case, the observations can be plotted in a three-dimensional graph, and the estimated regression is the plane that provides the best possible fit to the scattered points.

By extension from these simpler cases, the observations in the general case can be thought of as plotted in a $(k + 1)$-dimensional graph, and the estimated regression can be thought of as the best-fitting hyperplane going through the scattered points. Of course, it is easier to say this than to visualize it. The mathematics becomes easier than the graphics.

As in the simpler cases, an estimated regression fit to the data allows us to decompose Y_i into the fitted value and the residual:

$$Y_i = \hat{Y}_i + e_i, \quad \text{where} \quad \hat{Y}_i = \hat{\beta}_0 + \hat{\beta}_1 X_{1i} + \cdots + \hat{\beta}_k X_{ki} \qquad (7.20)$$

for the ith observation. The OLS technique calculates the estimated coefficients so as to make the sum of squared residuals as small as possible:

$$\text{OLS criterion:} \quad \text{minimize} \quad SSR = \sum_i e_i^2 \tag{7.21}$$

Suffice it to say that we end up with a set of estimators analogous to those for the simpler cases. All the data are used together to solve simultaneously for the $k + 1$ coefficients; it is not the case that we just estimate k simple regressions. A computer can carry out the necessary calculations, and we rely on this facility.

The discussion in Section 5.3 regarding the comparison of the estimated regression coefficients with the corresponding true regression coefficients applies fully to multiple regression. Although one might wish that each estimated coefficient were equal to the corresponding true coefficient, so that $\hat{\beta}_j^* = \beta_j$, this is unlikely ever to occur. (As before, the asterisk indicates the computed values in a set of data.) The difference between $\hat{\beta}_j^*$ and β_j arises from the particular pattern of values taken on by the disturbances. (Just how the value of $\hat{\beta}_j$ might be related to β_j is the subject of sampling theory, which is discussed in Chapter 11.) Overall, we recognize that the estimated regression will be different from the true regression, but we hope that the differences are not too great.

To interpret and apply the estimated regression model, we need to see how changes in the regressors affect the predicted value of the regressand. The estimated regression is given by

$$\hat{Y} = \hat{\beta}_0 + \hat{\beta}_1 X_1 + \hat{\beta}_2 X_2 + \cdots + \hat{\beta}_k X_k \tag{7.22}$$

For any given set of changes in the explanatory variables,

$$\Delta\hat{Y} = \hat{\beta}_1 \, \Delta X_1 + \hat{\beta}_2 \, \Delta X_2 + \cdots + \hat{\beta}_k \, \Delta X_k \tag{7.23}$$

provides the method for calculating the effect on the predicted value of Y of specified changes in the X_j's. Graphically, this equation compares two points on the estimated regression hyperplane and shows how differences in the $k + 1$ dimensions are related.

If only one explanatory variable changes in value while all the others remain the same, then

$$\Delta\hat{Y} = \hat{\beta}_j \, \Delta X_j \quad \text{holding all other regressors constant} \tag{7.24}$$

Under these conditions, we see that $\Delta\hat{Y} = \hat{\beta}_j$ when we let $\Delta X_j = 1$. This provides the basis for the general form of the interpretation of any single coefficient: we say that $\hat{\beta}_j$ is the change in $\hat{Y}$ that results from a unit change in X_j, holding constant the values of all the other variables. The latter qualification closely corresponds to the economic concept of *ceteris paribus,* and it is an important part of our interpretation. This does not require or imply that there are no relations among the explanatory variables, but it leaves these relations unaccounted for in assessing the effect of each variable. (Note that a "unit change in X_j" means that $\Delta X_j = 1$.)

In working with multiple regression models, the only effects revealed are the *ceteris paribus* effects given by the individual regression coefficients, and these are usually what we are interested in. However, we recognize that in reality a change in X_j may cause changes in other explanatory variables, and we recognize that the total economic effect on $\hat{Y}$ includes the *ceteris paribus* effect plus the effects of the consequent changes in the other variables, through (7.23). Additional information about how the explanatory variables affect each other would be needed to make this calculation, but usually it is not available. Sometimes such information arises from hypothetical considerations or from other economic knowledge.

Some of the properties of the estimated regression, which is often called a line even though it is not one, are the same as for simple regression. First, it turns out that $\Sigma\, e_i = 0$; that is, the positive and negative residuals cancel out in summation, so the average error is zero. Second, the point $\overline{Y}, \overline{X}_1, \overline{X}_2, \ldots, \overline{X}_k$ lies on the fitted line; that is, the regression goes through the point of means. Third, the correlation between the residuals and any explanatory variable is zero.

The standard error of regression is given by

$$SER = \sqrt{\frac{\sum\limits_{i=1}^{n} e_i^2}{n - k - 1}} \tag{7.25}$$

and it measures the typical error of fit. Notice that the denominator is equal to n minus the number of coefficients (including $\hat{\beta}_0$) that are estimated; this count is the number of degrees of freedom for the estimation.

How well the estimated regression fits the data is also measured by the coefficient of determination R^2, which is calculated as in the case of simple regression

$$R^2 = 1 - \frac{\sum\limits_{i=1}^{n} e_i^2}{\sum\limits_{i=1}^{n} (Y_i - \overline{Y})^2} \tag{7.26}$$

Since each residual e_i is the part of Y_i that *is not* explained by the regression, R^2 is again interpreted as the proportion of the variation in Y that *is* explained by the regression. In other words, R^2 is the proportion of the variation in Y that is explained by the variation in the X_j's.

Comparing Regressions

In practical econometrics we often estimate more than one regression involving the same dependent variable. For example, so far we have estimated two earnings functions: one involving *ED* as the only explanatory variable, and a second involving both *ED* and *EXP* as explanatory variables. In comparing regressions like these it is useful to have a statistic or an indicator that tells us which regression fits better. Our natural candidates are the *SER* and R^2.

The R^2 is the more popular measure of fit for any single regression. However, for comparing regressions like our earnings functions, it always gives the same answer: the regression with additional variables included fits better. This is because the addition of an explanatory variable to an original regression model cannot raise the sum of squared residuals *SSR*. (Since OLS is acting to minimize this sum, it need not allow an additional specified variable to increase the *SSR;* it could effectively ignore the new variable rather than let it increase the *SSR*.) This sum, which is $\sum e_i^2$, appears in the numerator of the ratio in (7.26). Thus for a given set of data on a dependent variable Y, the addition of an explanatory variable to a regression model cannot decrease R^2, and in practice it always increases it at least a bit.

However, the increase in R^2 is obtained at a statistical cost: the inclusion of another variable. An indicator of whether the new equation "really" fits better should assess whether the decrease in *SSR* achieved by including a new regressor is substantial enough to outweigh the cost of doing so.

A statistic that does this is known as the **adjusted** or **corrected** R^2, which is denoted by $\overline{R}^2$ and defined as

$$\overline{R}^2 = 1 - \frac{\sum_{i=1}^{n} e_i^2/(n - k - 1)}{\sum_{i=1}^{n} (Y_i - \overline{Y})^2/(n - 1)} \tag{7.27}$$

The symbol $\overline{R}^2$ is conventionally read as "R bar squared." A comparison of (7.27) with (7.26) shows that $\overline{R}^2$ is less than R^2, except if $R^2 = 1$. A direct method for calculating $\overline{R}^2$ from R^2 is shown in Problem 7.10.

To examine what happens to $\overline{R}^2$ when another variable is added to a regression, we need look only at the numerator of the ratio in (7.27) because the denominator stays fixed. The numerator itself is a ratio. Adding a variable to a regression causes both $\sum e_i^2$ and $n - k - 1$ to decrease. The crucial point depends on which term decreases faster. If adding a variable causes $\sum e_i^2$ to decrease proportionately more than $n - k - 1$ decreases, the ratio in the numerator will decrease and therefore $\overline{R}^2$ will increase. By contrast, if adding a variable causes $\sum e_i^2$ to decrease proportionately less than $n - k - 1$ decreases, $\overline{R}^2$ will decrease. Note that the decrease in the number of degrees of freedom, $n - k - 1$, is the link to the "statistical cost" of adding another variable.

The $\overline{R}^2$ measure of fit is commonly calculated by regression programs, and it is often reported along with the basic regression results. It can be used for comparing the fit of different regressions, as just discussed. However, $\overline{R}^2$ does not have as straightforward an interpretation as R^2 does, and it can even be negative.

We make little use of $\overline{R}^2$ here because it is redundant: the $\overline{R}^2$ functions in exactly the same way as *SER* as an indicator of whether the addition of an explanatory variable "really" improves the fit. To see that this is true, one can easily show from (7.27) that

$$\overline{R}^2 = 1 - \frac{(SER)^2}{S_Y^2} \tag{7.28}$$

where S_Y^2 is the variance of Y. Now, S_Y^2 is the same in the different regressions that we are comparing. Thus, whether $\overline{R}^2$ would be higher or lower in comparable regressions can be determined by examining the SERs. A decrease in the SER always accompanies an increase in $\overline{R}^2$, and an increase in the SER always accompanies a decrease in $\overline{R}^2$.

An implication of all this is that our two basic measures of fit, SER and R^2, can sometimes give conflicting signals. Whenever a variable is added to the specification of a regression, R^2 will increase and we say that the overall fit is improved. However, when the increase in R^2 is relatively small, SER may increase and in this case we would say that the typical error of fit got worse.

In other situations we may want to compare regressions that cannot be viewed as differing by the inclusion of some additional explanatory variable(s). For example, we might compare two simple earnings functions—one in which $EARNS$ depends on ED, and the other in which $EARNS$ depends on EXP. When the regressions are based on the same set of observations, R^2 and the SER can be used to compare the fits. These measures give consistent comparisons when the regressions have the same number of regressors, but they may give conflicting signals when the regressions have different numbers of regressors.

Sometimes we may estimate the same regression model with two sets of data. For example, consider a study of family consumption behavior in which a simple regression model relating consumption to income correctly describes the behavioral process. Suppose that we have a set of data consisting of observations from the process. Now suppose that two regressions are estimated—one with all the data, and the other only with families in the middle range of incomes. Since the variation in consumption will be much greater in the whole sample than in the more homogeneous sample, the R^2 will tend to be greater in the whole sample. In terms of overall fit, the regression with the whole sample will be better, but this does not mean that this model is more correct: in both cases, the true regression model correctly describes the process generating the data.

Finally, it generally is not very meaningful to compare the measures of fit for regressions having different dependent variables, even when the regressions are based on the same set of observations. For example, as noted in Chapter 6, if one earnings function is estimated with $EARNS$ as the regressand and another is estimated using $LNEARNS$, we cannot judge which equation is better on the basis of a simple comparison of the R^2 or SER. The situation is like one of comparing apples with oranges.

The Consumption Function

The original Keynesian idea that aggregate consumption is determined primarily by income can be expanded to include other potentially relevant explanatory variables. We might think that the rate of interest available on savings and the rate of inflation in consumer prices are relevant. Economic theory does not specify strictly whether these effects would be positive or negative, so we approach the data with an exploratory frame of mind.

Using the 25 annual observations from our time-series data set, we estimate

$$\widehat{CON}_i = -2.370 + 0.910DPI_i + 0.500RAAA_i$$
$$- 0.562RINF2_i \tag{7.29}$$
$$R^2 = .997 \quad SER = 9.309$$

In this regression, the coefficient on *DPI* gives the estimated marginal propensity to consume: a one-billion-dollar increase in *DPI* leads to a 0.910 billion-dollar increase in predicted *CON*, holding *RAAA* and *RINF2* constant. The coefficient on *RAAA* means that a one-percentage-point increase in the long-term interest rate is estimated to increase consumption by 0.500 billion dollars, holding other variables constant. Similarly, holding other variables constant, a one-point increase in the rate of inflation decreases consumption by 0.562 billion dollars. (Reports of econometric research often leave out the phrase "holding other variables constant." The reader is expected to understand that a regression coefficient gives the *ceteris paribus* effect of a change in an explanatory variable.)

In comparison with the simple regression of *CON* on *DPI* reported in (6.10), we see that the estimated marginal propensity to consume is changed only slightly—from 0.907 there to 0.910 here. The overall fit is somewhat better here because R^2 is slightly higher (in the fifth decimal position, not shown), but the typical error of fit is bigger here (suggesting a worse fit) because the *SER* increases from 8.935 to 9.309 billion dollars. As noted above, in this situation the $\bar{R}^2$ must be lower in the present model (indeed, it falls slightly from .9969 to .9966).

We see that the addition of *RAAA* and *RINF2* to the simple form has not led to a model with appreciably more explanatory power. This, in itself, does not mean that the new variables do not belong in the model. If *DPI* were treated as a "new" variable and compared with a simple regression of *CON* on *RAAA* or *RINF2*, then it might appear to have little additional explanatory power. Indeed, we see from Table 3.4 that the correlation between *CON* and *RAAA* is .952, so we know that a simple regression of *CON* on *RAAA* would have an R^2 of .906. In Chapter 12 we present formal hypothesis tests that also bear on this question.

7.3 Dummy Variables _____

In all the regression models considered so far, every variable has been a cardinal measure of some economic characteristic. For example, *CON* measures aggregate consumption in billions of constant dollars and *ED* measures the years of schooling completed by individual persons. These variables are included in a regression model in a natural way, so that changes in the numerical value of an explanatory variable have consistent numerical effects on the dependent variable.

Another type of data variable introduced in Chapter 2 carries information that is essentially categorical, such as a person's race, gender, or region of residence. This information can be used to classify or categorize observations or to separate them in some way, but the characteristic cannot be measured in any meaningful way. For example, the variable *REG* in the cross-section data set is equal to 1 if the worker lives in the Northeast, 2 if he lives in the North Central region, and so on. The variable *REG* indicates where the worker lives, but the values 1, 2, 3, and 4 do not result from measuring or counting anything. Hence the information contained in *REG* cannot be included directly into a regression model.

However, when the numerical outcome of an economic process depends in part on some categorical characteristic of the observation, this information must be brought into the regression specification somehow. This is necessary in order for the model to correctly describe the process. The technique for doing this involves constructing new regressors known as **dummy variables** and treating them exactly like other regressors in the multiple regression framework. (The meaning of "dummy" here is that these variables "represent" categorical information.)

To start with the simplest case, suppose that some characteristic of the observations allows them to be identified or categorized as being in one of two groups. For example, persons might be identified as men or women, and firms might be categorized as unionized or not unionized; in time-series data, years might be categorized as being either before 1981 or after 1980, or they might be categorized as being in wartime or peacetime. For reasons that will make sense later, one group is called the **excluded group** and the other is called the **included group.** These names do not imply that one group is in any way better off than the other, and switching the names attached to the two groups does not change the results of our analysis.

Suppose now that there is some economic behavior that could appropriately be described by a simple regression model in which Y depends on X. There are several ways in which this relation could interact with the categorizing information in the data. One possibility is that Y is determined quite differently for observations in one group than it is for observations in the other. In this case, there are essentially two separate processes occurring, and we would split the observations into two separate data sets and carry out separate regression analyses.

Another possibility is that the effect on Y of a change in X is the same for both groups, but that there is a systematic difference with regard to the levels of Y associated with each particular value of X. This idea is further refined and represented in Figure 7.1, which shows that $E[Y]$ is a separate linear function of X for each group, with the same slope for both groups but different intercepts for each. The common slope is denoted by β_1, and the intercept for the excluded

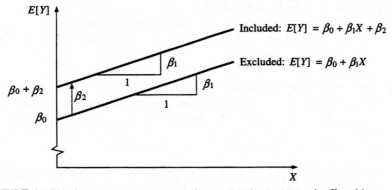

FIGURE 7.1 This figure represents an economic process whose outcome is affected by categorical information about the observations. Among observations having the same value of X, the expected value of Y for those in the included group is different from the expected value of Y for those in the excluded group. Despite this, the process is such that the impact on Y of a change in X is the same for all observations. Assuming linearity, the parameterization in the diagram leads naturally to a regression model with a dummy variable.

group is denoted by β_0. We let the intercept for the included group be denoted by $\beta_0 + \beta_2$, so that β_2 is the difference between the intercepts. Since the two lines are parallel, β_2 also is the difference in $E[Y]$ between observations in the included group and the excluded group that have the same value of X. As drawn in the figure, β_2 is positive, so that the relation for the included group lies above that for the excluded group. In some other case, β_2 might be negative.

In order to represent this specification in equation form, we create a dummy variable. This new variable, D, is set equal to 1 for every observation that is in the included group, and it is set equal to 0 otherwise (i.e., for every observation that is in the excluded group). Now, consider the equation

$$E[Y] = \beta_0 + \beta_1 X + \beta_2 D \qquad (7.30)$$

For observations that are in the excluded group (with $D = 0$), the right-hand side of (7.30) equals $\beta_0 + \beta_1 X$, so that the relation between $E[Y]$ and X is a line whose intercept is β_0 and whose slope is β_1. For observations that are in the included group (with $D = 1$), the right-hand side of (7.30) can be rearranged as $(\beta_0 + \beta_2) + \beta_1 X$, which is a line whose intercept is $\beta_0 + \beta_2$ and whose slope is β_1. Hence (7.30) is an equation that fully describes the relations in Figure 7.1.

The coefficient β_2 on the dummy variable in (7.30) has two related meanings. The simple graphical interpretation is that this coefficient represents the difference between the intercepts for the included and excluded groups. However, the economic interpretation of intercepts is often not meaningful, and our attention turns to the vertical difference in $E[Y]$ between observations in the two groups. That is, in terms of economic interpretation, the coefficient on the dummy variable represents the impact on the expected value of Y of an observation's being in the included group rather than the excluded group, holding all the other regressors constant. Sometimes a dummy variable is called a shift variable, because it simply causes a shift in the relation between $E[Y]$ and the other variables in the equation; it does not otherwise alter that relation.

Equation (7.30) specifies the systematic relation between Y and X, taking into account the differences between two groups of observations. Hence, it specifies the relation for both groups together. Adding a disturbance term for econometric reality, this leads naturally to the specification of a multiple regression model

$$Y_i = \beta_0 + \beta_1 X_i + \beta_2 D_i + u_i \qquad (7.31)$$

This model can be estimated by OLS by use of a data set that combines both groups of observations together.

For example, suppose theory suggests that earnings depends linearly on educational attainment but that there is a shiftlike difference between races. Data from Chapter 2 are available for *EARNS* and *ED,* and the values for the first 10 observations are shown in Table 7.1. The cross-section data set also includes the variable *RACE,* which was coded in the interview as 1 for whites and 2 for blacks; no persons of other races are present in the data. We use this variable to construct a new regressor, *DRACE,* which is a dummy variable taking the value 0 for whites and 1 for blacks. Thus, white workers are the excluded group and black workers are the included group. Algebraically,

$$DRACE_i = RACE_i - 1 \qquad (7.32)$$

and the values of *DRACE* for the first 10 observations are shown in Table 7.1. Although we know that *DRACE* is like a code, in the data set it appears to be just another discrete variable. Nothing in the theory of regression prevents us from using it as a regressor.

TABLE 7.1 First 10 Observations for
Estimating Equation (7.33)

Obs.	EARNS	ED	DRACE
1	1.920	2	1
2	12.403	9	0
3	5.926	17	0
4	7.000	9	0
5	6.990	12	0
6	6.500	13	0
7	26.000	17	0
8	15.000	16	0
9	5.699	9	1
10	8.820	16	0

These ideas about how earnings are determined lead to a multiple regression with a dummy variable. Using all 100 observations based on the cross-section data set in Chapter 2, the estimated regression is

$$\widehat{EARNS}_i = -0.778 + 0.762ED_i - 1.926DRACE_i \tag{7.33}$$

$$R^2 = .293 \quad SER = 4.356$$

In general, the graph of an estimated multiple regression with two regressors is a plane in three dimensions. However, with this special dummy variable specification, the regression can be analyzed in a two-dimensional graph like Figure 7.1, with *EARNS* on the vertical axis and *ED* on the horizontal axis. The equation describes two parallel lines, each with a slope of 0.762. The intercept for whites ($DRACE = 0$) is simply the estimated intercept of the equation: $\hat{\beta}_0^* = -0.778$. The graphical intercept of the line corresponding to the relation for blacks is $\hat{\beta}_0^* + \hat{\beta}_2^* = -0.778 + (-1.926) = -2.704$.

In this multiple regression, the coefficient $\hat{\beta}_1^* = 0.762$ can be given an interpretation of the usual form: the impact on earnings of an additional year of schooling is 0.762 thousand dollars, holding *DRACE* constant. As a result of the special features of a dummy variable regression specification, a better way of saying this is that "an additional year of schooling increases earnings by $762, for both blacks and whites." The specification of the regression model necessarily leads to the finding that the impact is the same for both groups, but the data determine the estimate of this impact.

A good economic interpretation of the estimated coefficient on the dummy variable, $\hat{\beta}_2^* = -1.926$, is "holding constant the level of education, the earnings of blacks are $1926 less than those of whites." Note that the *ceteris paribus* qualification is particularly useful here: our finding is very different from saying that the mean level of earnings for blacks is $1926 less than the mean level of earnings for whites. Also, recall that our usual interpretation of a regression coefficient is based on the effect of a unit change in the regressor. In the present case, however, it would not make sense to talk about a worker having an additional amount of *DRACE*. Instead, the most meaningful phrasing that we can attach to $\Delta DRACE = 1$ is based on a change from $DRACE = 0$ to $DRACE = 1$. For this change, $\Delta DRACE = 1$ means "being black rather than white." Hence, one might say that the regression shows that "holding constant the level of education, being black rather than white leads to a decrease in earnings of $1926."

Finally, if *DRACE* had been created to have the value 1 for whites and 0 for blacks, the substance of our findings would not have changed. That is, the two-dimensional graph implied by the estimated regression would be exactly the same as that implied by (7.33). The coefficient on *ED* would be exactly the same. The coefficient on the new *DRACE* would have the opposite sign of the corresponding coefficient in (7.33) but the same magnitude: the new $\hat{\beta}_2^* = 1.926$. We would say that holding constant the level of education, the earnings of whites are $1926 greater than those of blacks. The new $\hat{\beta}_0^*$ would give the graphical intercept for black workers (the new excluded group, with new $DRACE = 0$); this would be $\hat{\beta}_0^* = -2.704$. The graphical intercept for white workers (new $DRACE = 1$) would be $\hat{\beta}_0^* + \hat{\beta}_2^* = -2.704 + 1.926 = -0.778$.

In time-series regressions it may be that for some periods the relation between a dependent variable and a set of explanatory variables is shifted by a constant amount. For example, during war years the consumption function might shift down at all levels of income, because of the decrease in production of consumer goods and the special incentives given to saving. In this case, a model of the form

$$CON_i = \beta_0 + \beta_1 DPI_i + \beta_2 WAR_i + u_i \qquad (7.34)$$

would be appropriate. The dummy variable WAR takes on the value 1 for war-time observations and zero for others; the coefficient β_2 is the shift in the consumption function, and we expect that $\hat{\beta}_2$ will be negative.

Another example is provided by the Phillips curve, which represents the trade-off between inflation and unemployment. It is conjectured that the relation shifted up in the middle of the 1960s because of the Viet Nam War and structural changes in the economy. To examine this conjecture, we add a dummy variable to the model earlier specified (6.30):

$$RINF1_i = \beta_0 + \beta_1 \left(\frac{1}{UPCT_i} \right) + \beta_2 D_i + u_i \qquad (7.35)$$

where $D_i = 0$ for the observations 1956–1964 and $D_i = 1$ for 1965–1970. With 15 observations in total, we find that

$$\widehat{RINF1_i} = -0.803 + 15.030 \left(\frac{1}{UPCT_i} \right) + 0.894 D_i$$

$$R^2 = .600 \quad SER = 0.936 \qquad (7.36)$$

(Note that the first regressor is actually $UINV$ as defined previously.) The coefficient on the dummy variable indicates that the Phillips curve shifted up by 0.894 percentage point in the latter part of the sample period as compared with where it was earlier. The two estimated Phillips curves are shown in Figure 7.2.

More Than Two Categories

Using categorical information with the dummy variable technique is more complicated when there are more than two categories associated with a particular characteristic. For example, the variable REG in our cross-section data set carries information about the region of the country in which the person lives. The information is coded 1 for Northeast, 2 for North Central, 3 for South, and 4 for West.

Suppose that we are focusing on a linear relation between Y and X, and that we want to take region into account. Would the specification

$$E[Y] = \beta_0 + \beta_1 X + \beta_2 REG \qquad (7.37)$$

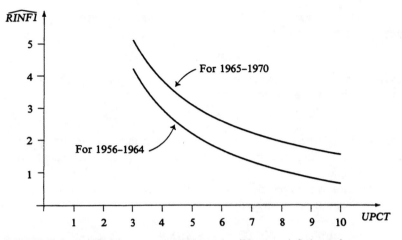

FIGURE 7.2 The Phillips curve shows the trade-off between inflation and unemployment. Using a dummy variable specification, Equation (7.36) finds evidence that is consistent with the conjecture that the curve shifted upward in the middle of the 1960s, as compared with its position earlier. The reciprocal specification of the effect of unemployment on inflation leads to the nonlinear relation shown here.

make sense? No. This specification does show a common impact of X on $E[Y]$ among the regions, but holding X constant it specifies that $E[Y]$ is β_2 greater in the North Central region than in the Northeast, $2\beta_2$ greater in the South, and $3\beta_2$ greater in the West. There is no reason why the actual differences should be so ordered or why they should be multiples of one another.

To bring in multiple-category information like region, we must construct a set of dummy variables. One way to think about doing this is to create a separate dummy variable for each category (region), taking on the value 1 if the observation belongs to that category and 0 if it does not. From *REG*, we can create four dummy variables: *DNEAST, DNCENT, DSOUTH,* and *DWEST,* to use mnemonic names. As before, each dummy variable serves to identify each observation as being in one of two groups (i.e., in the specified region or not). In formulating the regression model, one of the dummy variables must be excluded. Then, the coefficient on each of the included dummy variables represents the difference between the intercepts of that category and the excluded category. The intercept for the excluded category is simply β_0. If all four dummy variables were included, there would be one more coefficient than we could interpret logically. This would be a situation of perfect multicollinearity, so that the OLS estimators would not be defined and could not be estimated. (Perfect multicollinearity is discussed in Sections 7.1 and 7.6.)

Revising (7.37), we have

$$E[Y] = \beta_0 + \beta_1 X + \beta_2 DNCENT + \beta_3 DSOUTH$$
$$+ \beta_4 DWEST \qquad (7.38)$$

If a person lives in the excluded Northeast, the value of each of the included dummy variables is zero and

$$E[Y] = \beta_0 + \beta_1 X \qquad (7.39)$$

If a person lives in one of the other regions, the corresponding dummy variable is 1 but the other two are 0; thus

$$E[Y] = \beta_0 + \beta_1 X + \beta_j \quad (j = 2, 3, \text{ or } 4) \qquad (7.40)$$

The economic interpretation of each dummy variable coefficient (β_j) is the difference in $E[Y]$ of living in that region rather than the excluded Northeast region, holding X constant.

For example, we reconsider the simplest earnings function. Now taking region into account, the estimated regression is

$$\widehat{EARNS_i} = -0.803 + 0.794ED_i + 0.288DNCENT_i$$
$$-0.828DSOUTH_i - 1.992DWEST_i \qquad (7.41)$$
$$R^2 = .310 \quad SER = 4.351$$

which is graphed in Figure 7.3. The coefficients on the dummy variables estimate shiftlike differences among the predicted earnings for persons living in different regions. It does not matter for the ultimate interpretation which of the region dummies is excluded, but it does affect the constant and dummy coefficients that are actually found.

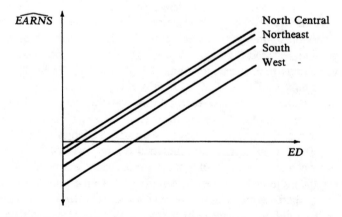

FIGURE 7.3   The simplest earnings function taking region into account uses three dummy variables to estimate the shiftlike differences among the regions. In Equation (7.41), the dummy for the Northeast region is excluded, and the other dummy-variable coefficients give the shift between each of the other regions and the Northeast. If a different region were excluded, the resulting graphical representation would be exactly the same as shown here, but the dummy variable coefficients and the regression intercept would be different because of the change of reference.

The dummy variable technique can be extended to cases with more than one categorizing variable. For example, if theory specifies that earnings is a function of education, race, and region, then the regression model would include *DRACE* and the three dummy variables for region. For men in the sample who are white and live in the Northeast, the values of all the dummy variables are zero; this is the reference group to which other observations are compared.

7.4 Polynomial Specifications

In Chapter 6 a variety of functional forms were introduced that allow the linear regression model to be used even when the basic behavioral relation is essentially nonlinear. The idea is that transformations of variables create new variables that can be examined in a regression framework. In the multiple regression extension of this idea, the same transformation can be applied to all the original variables, or different transformations can be applied to different variables. The important requirement is that a linear relation be specified between the regressand and the regressors.

In this section we look at another functional form that enhances the flexibility of the regression model. In the example provided, one of the original explanatory variables is left unchanged while the other is treated in the new way.

We begin with some mathematical analysis before we come to a regression specification. Suppose that the exact relation between Y and X is given by the quadratic function

$$Y = \beta_0 + \beta_1 X + \beta_2 X^2 \qquad (7.42)$$

The graph of this relation is a parabola, which can take on the forms illustrated in Figure 7.4. If $\beta_2 > 0$, the parabola is concave upward, and if $\beta_2 < 0$, the parabola is concave downward. Note that the point at which the parabola reaches its minimum or maximum value for Y can have either a positive or negative value for X and a positive or negative value for Y. When Y and X are economic variables, it may be that only a portion of this relation is relevant. For example, the left-hand portion of Figure 7.4b looks like a production function with diminishing returns.

The slope of the relation is given by

$$\text{slope of parabola} = \beta_1 + 2\beta_2 X \qquad (7.43)$$

Corresponding to the shapes shown in Figure 7.4, the slope increases as X increases if $\beta_2 > 0$, and the slope decreases as X increases if $\beta_2 < 0$. As usual, we know that when $\Delta X = 1$, the corresponding ΔY is approximately equal to the slope.

$$Y = \beta_0 + \beta_1 X + \beta_2 X^2$$

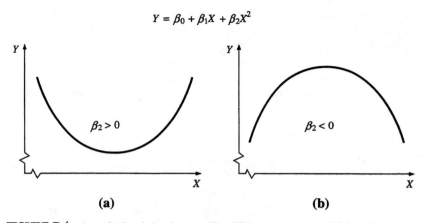

(a)   **(b)**

FIGURE 7.4   A quadratic relation between Y and X is concave upward if $\beta_2 > 0$ and concave downward if $\beta_2 < 0$. Although Y is a nonlinear function of X, Y also can be viewed as a linear function of X and X^2 together. This allows a multiple regression model to specify a quadratic function for the systematic relation between Y and X.

Returning to econometrics, think of creating two regressors. Let X_1 be equal to the original variable X, and let X_2 be equal to its square, X^2. It should be clear that the systematic part of the linear multiple regression model

$$Y_i = \beta_0 + \beta_1 X_{1i} + \beta_2 X_{2i} + u_i \tag{7.44}$$

mimics the quadratic function (7.42). This is even clearer when we rewrite (7.44) as

$$Y_i = \beta_0 + \beta_1 X_i + \beta_2 X_i^2 + u_i \tag{7.45}$$

which is a common form of presentation.

Although the regression model specifies that Y is a linear function of two regressors, we have relatively little interest in the usual *ceteris paribus* interpretation of the coefficients. This is because we know that X^2 must change if X does, so that the usual interpretation makes no sense. Our interest lies in the nonlinear relation between Y and X that is evident in Figure 7.4, and our approach to interpreting the regression coefficients will be based on the slope of this relation. Looking at (7.45), we would say that the impact on $E[Y]$ of a unit change in X is given approximately by the slope of the quadratic relation as determined from (7.43).

For example, in studies of earnings functions it sometimes is suggested that the impact of experience diminishes and perhaps even becomes negative as the amount of experience increases. This is based on notions of physical and mental aging, diminishing returns, and optimal investment in human capital. Holding constant the level of education, the relation between earnings and experience is theorized to look like a hill-shaped parabola as in Figure 7.4b.

These ideas lead us to specify a multiple regression that includes *ED* in the usual way, but includes *EXP* as a quadratic function. Letting *EXPSQ* be the name of the regressor that is equal to the square of *EXP*, the 100 observations in our cross-section data lead to the estimated earnings function

$$\widehat{EARNS_i} = -9.791 + 0.995ED_i + 0.471EXP_i$$
$$- 0.00751EXPSQ_i \tag{7.46}$$
$$R^2 = .329 \quad SER = 4.267$$

In reporting regressions like this, the last regressor might be denoted by EXP^2.

In interpreting what this regression says about the effect of education on earnings, we can use our knowledge that the last two regressors in the equation are both based on experience. Thus we say that holding experience constant, an additional year of education increases earnings by $995.

In assessing the relation between earnings and experience, we can think of *ED* being fixed at some particular level. This allows us to rewrite (7.46) temporarily as

$$\widehat{EARNS_i} = \text{constant} + 0.471EXP_i - 0.00751EXPSQ_i \tag{7.47}$$

where the "constant" depends on the particular value chosen for *ED*. It should be clear that the relation between *EARNS* and experience (*EXP*) is a hill-shaped parabola, as in Figure 7.5. If the fixed value for *ED* were higher, the relation graphed in the figure would shift upward by a constant amount (0.995 ΔED).

From (7.43) we know that the slope of this relation is

$$\text{slope} = 0.471 + (2)(-0.00751)EXP \tag{7.48}$$

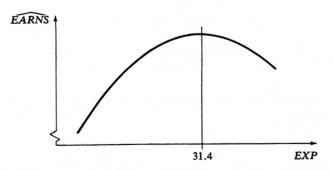

FIGURE 7.5 The earnings function (7.46) includes a quadratic specification for the partial relation between earnings and experience. Holding education constant at any level, the relation between predicted earnings and the level of experience is illustrated here. The slope, which is given by Equation (7.48), gives the impact on predicted earnings of a one-year increase in experience. For any given level of education, predicted earnings reach a peak at 31.4 years of experience.

Using this, we find that a man with five years of experience will have his earnings increased by about \$396 after gaining another year, but a man with 20 years of experience will have his earnings increased by about only \$171 after gaining another year. To find the level of experience that corresponds to the peak of earnings, we solve (7.48) for the *EXP* value associated with a zero slope. Here, peak earnings occurs after about 31 years of experience, and beyond that negative returns to experience set in. All this holds true regardless of what the level of education is.

To assess the effect on predicted earnings of any particular change in experience two approaches are reasonable. The first, which makes sense for small changes in experience, makes use of the slope at the original point to make an approximation:

$$\Delta EARNS \approx [0.471 + (2)(-0.00751)EXP_i]\Delta EXP \qquad (7.49)$$

The second approach makes use of (7.23) to find the exact change along the estimated regression:

$$\Delta EARNS = 0.471 \, \Delta EXP - 0.00751 \, \Delta EXPSQ \qquad (7.50)$$

In this computation, note that $\Delta EXPSQ$ is not equal to the square of ΔEXP.

For example, consider a worker with 10 years of experience. The effect on *EARNS* of gaining another two years can be approximated using (7.49) as

$$\Delta EARNS \approx [0.471 + (2)(-0.00751)(10)](2) \qquad (7.51)$$

$$\approx [0.3208](2) = 0.6416$$

thousand dollars greater annual earnings. Alternatively, an exact computation using (7.50) determines the effect to be

$$\Delta EARNS = (0.471)(2) - (0.00751)(44) = 0.61156 \qquad (7.52)$$

thousand dollars greater annual earnings. Note that for a worker with $EXP = 10$, increasing experience by 2 years means that *EXPSQ* increases from 100 to 144, so $\Delta EXPSQ = 44$.

It sometimes is theorized that the relation between Y and X is specified by a higher-order polynomial, such as

$$Y = \beta_0 + \beta_1 X + \beta_2 X^2 + \beta_3 X^3 \qquad (7.53)$$

Clearly, our technique can be extended to bring in the values of X, X^2, and X^3 as three separate regressors in order to make estimates of the unknown parameters. These applications are rare, however, in contrast to the more common quadratic specification.

7.5   Logarithmic Specifications _____

If the regressand in a multiple regression is the logarithm of a regular variable, then the regressors might be any combination of logarithmic, regular, and dummy variable forms. The model might be pure log-linear, pure semilog, or a hybrid of types.

The Demand for Money

Although the demand for money depends importantly on the level of income because money holdings are used to finance the transactions that generate income, it probably also depends on the rate of interest because money is held as an asset, as part of wealth. In addition, even the money balances held for transactions purposes may be interest sensitive. For both reasons, the interest impact is theorized to be negative. Thus a multiple regression in which the amount of money demanded is related to both the level of income and the rate of interest seems more appropriate than the simple model proposed in Chapter 6.

The most common specification in money demand regressions is the pure log-linear form, because it yields constant elasticity estimates. Using the 25 annual observations from 1956 through 1980, we find

$$\widehat{LNM}_i = 3.759 + 0.246 LNGNP_i - 0.0205 LNRTB_i \tag{7.54}$$

$$R^2 = .785 \quad SER = 0.0309$$

where M is the real quantity of money [see(6.36)], GNP is real national income, and RTB is the rate of interest on Treasury bills. As theory predicts, the income elasticity (0.246) is positive and the interest elasticity (-0.0205) is negative.

How important is the interest rate relative to the level of income? We may directly compare the regression coefficients, because they are elasticities: a 1 percent increase in income leads to a 0.246 percent increase in the predicted demand for money, while a 1 percent increase in the interest rate leads to a 0.0205 percent decrease. Thus the interest rate appears to be much less important than income, but this comparison is misleading. In the short run the interest rate is proportionately much more variable than income: year-to-year changes of 25 percent (not percentage points!) or more often occur in the interest rate, while changes of only 5 percent or more in income occur with roughly the same frequency. Comparing these two hypothetical changes in RTB and GNP, we find the resulting impact of the interest rate to be about half as much as that of the level of income. Thus the rate of interest should be viewed as having a moderately important impact on the demand for money.

Comparing this regression with the simple regression reported earlier (6.38), we see that the estimated income elasticity is somewhat greater (0.246 versus 0.215). Although the R^2 is somewhat larger here (.785 versus .780), so is the SER (0.0309 versus 0.0305). Thus whether the new equation fits better is debatable.

The Earnings Function

In applied labor market research, the preferred form for earnings functions specifies the regressand to be the logarithm of earnings. When education is the only explanatory variable, we have a pure semilog form as in (6.44). As more variables are taken into account, the form of the function may become mixed.

For example, we consider a model in which the logarithm of earnings depends on the level of education, the amount of experience (entered quadratically), the logarithm of the number of months worked (to yield an elasticity), and the person's race and region of residence. Based on our cross-section data set, the estimated regression is

$$\widehat{LNEARNS_i} = -2.031 + 0.106ED_i + 0.0501EXP_i$$
$$- 0.000930EXPSQ_i + 0.908LNMONTHS_i$$
$$- 0.239DRACE_i - 0.00468DNCENT_i \qquad (7.55)$$
$$- 0.193DSOUTH_i - 0.162DWEST_i$$

$$R^2 = .511 \quad SER = 0.420$$

Each coefficient is interpreted in the same way as in simpler formulations.

The coefficient on ED is interpreted as in a semilog model: an additional year of schooling increases the level of earnings by approximately 10.6 percent, which is quite close to the finding in the simple semilog model (6.45). Experience enters quadratically, through two regressors. After a simple calculation, we see that the level of earnings increases with the amount of experience up to a peak at about 27 years of experience, and that it decreases thereafter. The number of months worked enters in log-linear form, so we say that the elasticity of $EARNS$ with respect to $MONTHS$ is 0.908. (All these are understood to be *ceteris paribus* effects.)

With the regressand being a logarithm, each of the coefficients on dummy variables can be interpreted in the same way as the coefficient on a regular variable in a semilog model. For each dummy variable, the coefficient gives the proportional change in $EARNS$ that results from an observation being in the included group rather than in the excluded group, because this corresponds to $\Delta D = 1$. Thus, the coefficient on $DRACE$ means that earnings for blacks are approximately 23.9 percent lower than for whites, holding other variables constant. (Recall that the approximation is not very precise when the percentage is this large.) Similarly, the coefficients on the regional dummies show that earnings are lower in all these regions than in the Northeast, which is the excluded category. Holding other variables constant, earnings are approximately 1/2 of 1 percent lower in the North Central region, 19 percent lower in the South, and 16 percent lower in the West.

The R^2 value indicates that more than half of the variation in observed $LNEARNS$ has been explained by the regression, which is fairly good for this type of regression.

7.6   Specification Questions _____

In our development and use of multiple regression, we have followed a consistent approach in all cases. We start from the presumption that there is some stable process determining the values of some variable. Next we set up a multiple regression model that correctly describes the process in mathematical terms. Finally, we use data to estimate the unknown parameters and interpret or apply the estimated model according to our needs.

One of the difficulties with this approach is that we must correctly describe the process in terms of a regression model. This is a very demanding requirement. To meet it, or at least to come close to meeting it, we need to know more about how to specify regression models. In this section we limit ourselves to questions relating to the selection of variables for a linear model.

The Causal Nexus

In thinking about how several variables together affect or determine another one, it is natural to make a distinction between direct and indirect effects. Figure 7.6 sketches the causal linkages in a hypothetical case, with arrows indicating the paths and directions of causation. Variable X_1 is directly affected by X_3 and unlabeled variables. Variable X_2 is directly affected by X_1 and an unlabeled variable, and it is indirectly affected by X_3 and the other unlabeled variables. Variable Y is directly affected by X_1 and X_2, and it is indirectly affected by X_1, X_3, and the unlabeled variables. Note that X_1 has both direct and indirect effects

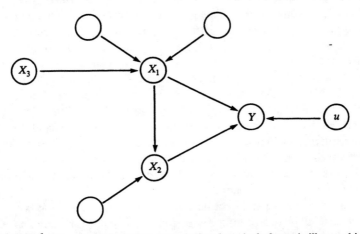

FIGURE 7.6   The causal nexus determining Y in a hypothetical case is illustrated in this schematic diagram. Arrows indicate the paths and directions of causation, and unlabeled circles contain other variables. This behavioral process is properly specified by Equation (7.56), assuming linearity. A regression model that mistakenly excludes X_2 or one that mistakenly includes X_3 misspecifies this process, but these two types of misspecification have very different consequences.

on Y. Also, note that the disturbance u has a direct effect on Y and no linkage at all to any of the other variables.

For example, in thinking about the aggregate demand for money in macro-economics, theory suggests that it depends directly on the level of GNP and on some interest rate and indirectly on the Federal Reserve discount rate. Through bank behavior and the action of financial markets, the discount rate affects the general level of the interest rate. Through expenditure decisions, the level of the interest rate affects GNP; and through the behavior of firms and individuals, the interest rate and the level of GNP affect the demand for money. In a commonsense way, this logic is represented in Figure 7.6, with Y being the demand for money, X_1 being the interest rate, X_2 being the level of GNP, and X_3 being the Federal Reserve discount rate.

Suppose that the correct form of the model determining Y is linear. Which variables should be included? The answer here is that only X_1 and X_2 should be included as explanatory variables, so that the proper model is

$$Y_i = \beta_0 + \beta_1 X_{1i} + \beta_2 X_{2i} + u_i \tag{7.56}$$

That is, in the specification of a multiple regression model, all the variables that have direct effects should be included, and variables that have only indirect effects (or no effects at all) should not be included.

The validity of this general rule depends on specific notions of what "direct" and "indirect" mean. For our purposes, a variable has a direct effect on Y only if in our general thinking about the process determining Y it is true that a change in the variable would lead to a change in Y while all other variables affecting Y are held constant. In other words, if a variable truly has a *ceteris paribus* effect on Y, then it has a direct effect. This leads to the general rule for specifying the regression model, because each coefficient is only a *ceteris paribus* effect.

In the causal nexus illustrated in Figure 7.6, variable X_3 has only an indirect effect. We recognize its effect as working this way: a change in the value of X_3 affects X_1, and any change in X_1 affects Y. There is no other path along which X_3 affects Y. Thus if X_1 somehow remains constant, there is no way for X_3 to affect Y. Since X_3 has no *ceteris paribus* effect, it does not have a direct effect and it should not be included in the regression model. In the demand for money example, neither firms nor individuals care about the Federal Reserve discount rate. It affects the demand for money only through the general interest rate. If the general interest rate somehow remains constant, changes in the discount rate will not affect the demand for money.

The distinction between direct and indirect effects means that we must be especially careful in interpreting regression coefficients for variables like X_1, which has both kinds. The proper interpretation of β_1 is that it gives the change in Y that results from a unit change in X_1, holding constant the value of X_2. This is the direct effect. The indirect effect of X_1 works through consequent changes in X_2. If we knew the amount of change in X_2 that would be associated with the initial change in X_1, we would have a basis for calculating the magnitude of the indirect effect. However, a regression model does not provide any information about the linkages between or among its explanatory variables, so generally it does not provide enough information to determine the magnitude of an indirect effect like that of X_1. Thus a regression model always tells us about the partial effects of the explanatory variables, but it is silent on the question of total effects. In applied research it is often true that there are some linkages between or among explanatory variables, and therefore careful interpretation is usually needed.

In thinking about what determines some economic outcome, sometimes it is natural to consider a variable that has only an indirect effect, and sometimes this indirect effect may be of special interest to us. For example, we may want to know what effect the Federal Reserve discount rate has on the demand for money. If the variable, like X_3, is not included in the model, how can we learn about its effect? What is needed is a second regression model that describes how X_1 is determined by X_3 and other variables. This model and (7.56) taken together form a recursive system of equations that can be used to analyze the effect X_3 has on Y. Such a system is a special case of *simultaneous-equation models,* which are discussed in Chapter 17. Until then our attention will be focused on single-equation models, which we realize are necessarily limited in scope.

Consequences of Misspecification

Sometimes it is difficult to know whether a variable under consideration for inclusion in a regression model has a direct effect, only an indirect effect, or no effect at all. Hence it is difficult to decide which variables should be included in the model, and it is likely that some models we see or create will be misspecified.

Let us return to the causal nexus illustrated in Figure 7.6. The process is correctly described by (7.56), as explained above. Variables X_1 and X_2 are known as *relevant variables* because they should be included in the regression, and all other variables (such as X_3) are known as *irrelevant variables* because they should be excluded. Suppose that we have data on all the necessary variables. The estimated form of the correct model is

$$\hat{Y}_i = \hat{\beta}_0 + \hat{\beta}_1 X_{1i} + \hat{\beta}_2 X_{2i} \qquad (7.57)$$

In carrying out our research we might make either of two mistakes, unfortunately: we might exclude a relevant variable from the regression, or we might include an irrelevant one. What are the consequences of these mistakes?

Suppose first that we leave out a relevant variable, say X_2, from the equation and estimate just the simple regression

$$\hat{Y}_i = \hat{\gamma}_0 + \hat{\gamma}_1 X_{1i} \qquad (7.58)$$

(γ is lowercase gamma, the Greek "g"). Here $\hat{\gamma}_1$ denotes the estimated coefficient on X_1. In general, the value of $\hat{\gamma}_1$ in (7.58) will be different from the value of $\hat{\beta}_1$ in (7.57) when the regressions are estimated from the same set of data. This is because the formulas used are different: the simple regression slope coefficient is calculated by (5.12), and it depends only on the values of Y and X_1; the multiple regression slope coefficient on X_1 is calculated by (7.9), and it depends on the values of X_2 as well as on the values of Y and X_1.

In general we believe that the $\hat{\beta}_1$ in the estimated multiple regression provides the best estimate of the true *ceteris paribus* effect of X_1 on Y, which is denoted by β_1 in the true regression model (7.56). This idea is explored further in Chapter 13. Since $\hat{\gamma}_1$ is different from $\hat{\beta}_1$, it makes sense to say that it should be considered a not-so-good estimate of the true effect. Mathematical analysis of the estimating formulas shows that $\hat{\gamma}_1$ differs from $\hat{\beta}_1$ by factors that represent the relation between X_1 and X_2 and the relation between Y and X_2. Loosely speaking, the calculation of $\hat{\gamma}_1$ captures both the direct effect of X_1 on Y and some part of the direct effect of X_2 on Y. The latter effect is captured because of the correlation between X_2 and X_1 in the data. Hence $\hat{\gamma}_1$ is systematically distorted from the true value β_1, which is only the direct effect of X_1 on Y.

For example, consider the earnings functions (7.15) and (6.7). In the estimated multiple regression the coefficient on *ED* is 0.978. In the estimated simple regression the coefficient on *ED* is 0.797, which is substantially smaller. This difference is consistent with what would be expected if the multiple regression were the true model. To see this we note that *ED* and *EXP* are negatively correlated ($r = -.57$) in the data. This means that higher-than-average *ED* values tend to be accompanied by lower-than-average *EXP* values among the observations. Since experience is estimated to have a positive direct effect [$\hat{\beta}_2 = 0.124$ in (7.15)], observations with higher-than-average values of *ED* tend to have their earnings diminished by their lower-than-average values of *EXP*. Thus it would be expected that $\hat{\gamma}_1$ would be smaller than $\hat{\beta}_1$.

Suppose now that we make the mistake of including an irrelevant variable, say X_3, in the regression specification and that we end up with

$$\hat{Y}_i = \hat{\delta}_0 + \hat{\delta}_1 X_{1i} + \hat{\delta}_2 X_{2i} + \hat{\delta}_3 X_{3i} \tag{7.59}$$

(δ is lowercase delta, the greek "d"). In comparison with (7.57), the inclusion of the irrelevant variable affects the estimates of the other coefficients in the sense that $\hat{\delta}_2 \neq \hat{\beta}_2$, $\hat{\delta}_1 \neq \hat{\beta}_1$, and $\hat{\delta}_0 \neq \hat{\beta}_0$. However, the effects on these estimates are rather random and usually mild. The coefficient $\hat{\delta}_3$ serves to estimate the true impact of X_3 on Y, which is zero (because X_3 is irrelevant). However, because of the randomness introduced into the data by the disturbances, the actual estimated value is not likely to be zero. Hence inclusion of the irrelevant variable can lead to misinterpretation of the true economic process.

In deciding whether or not to include a variable in a regression specification, the consequences of these two types of mistake must be compared. In most cases the introduction of additional randomness into the estimation process is less serious than the introduction of systematic distortion. Hence, including an irrelevant variable is usually considered to be less of a problem than excluding a relevant one. If one has good theoretical reasons for including a variable, it is best to do so. However, this should not be taken as a suggestion to hunt for variables with the hope that some might turn out to look good. In practice, most researchers estimate more than one specification of the process they are studying and then try to determine which of them is best. This judgment must be based on a blending of economic and econometric analysis, including considerations covered in Chapters 11 through 13.

Finally, it is often the case that our interest is in determining just the effect of one variable on another. For example, we might want to estimate the effect of education on earnings but we might be unconcerned with the role of experience. It is tempting to estimate just a simple regression of earnings on education and look at the slope coefficient. However, this is not what we are interested in. The analysis above shows that the estimate of the slope in the simple regression is not a good estimate of the *ceteris paribus* effect of education on earnings. Also, it is not a good estimate of what was identified in the preceding section as the total effect of education on earnings, because to calculate that we would need a simultaneous-equation model.

To generalize this, even when we are interested in the effect of a particular variable, it is necessary to specify and estimate a regression model that fully reflects the behavior of the economic process at work. Sometimes the variables that we are not interested in are called **statistical controls**. For example, we might say that the multiple regression (7.15) estimates the effect of education on earnings, controlling for experience. Similarly, the coefficient on *DRACE* in (7.33) estimates the effect of race (i.e., the effect of being black rather than white) on earnings, controlling for education. What all this amounts to saying is that the only effects that can be estimated in a single-equation, multiple regression model are the *ceteris paribus* (direct) effects and that the proper way to estimate these effects is with a correctly specified model.

Multicollinearity

In the data used to estimate a multiple regression model, it is usually the case that there is some correlation or (more technically) some degree of linear dependence among the explanatory variables. For example, in Figure 7.6 a case is illustrated in which there is a direct relation between X_1 and X_2. In other cases there may be a correlation between explanatory variables even when they are not connected by a behavioral relation. The general model and our method of estimation accept this situation as valid; indeed, the absence of any relations among the explanatory variables is a very special case that we rarely encounter in econometrics. The main consequence of this situation, so far, has been that we must be careful to interpret regression coefficients as direct effects and to recognize that there may be indirect effects as well.

In addition, when two explanatory variables have a very high correlation or when there are some other special relations among the explanatory variables, the situation has some unfortunate consequences for statistical inference. We will examine these in Chapter 13. Loosely speaking, it becomes very difficult to disentangle the separate effects of the explanatory variables on the dependent variable. For example, suppose that aggregate consumption depends on aggregate income, the Treasury bill rate, and the interest rate on consumer debt. Because of the behavior of financial markets, there is likely to be a high correlation between the two interest rates over time. One might guess that it would be difficult to determine the effects of each interest rate separately with any great precision, because the two variables might be nearly linear transformations of each other. A common consequence of this is that if we happen to add a few new observations to the data set, or drop a few from it, the new regression coefficients may be very different from the original ones.

This situation is known as *multicollinearity.* From the point of view of specifying the model, it does not indicate any mistake. Rather, multicollinearity arises from the nature of the data, and usually we have to accept it as part of reality. Multicollinearity is common in time-series regressions, because several of the explanatory variables may increase over time and therefore be highly correlated.

However, consider the possibility that there is a perfect correlation ($r = 1$) between a pair of explanatory variables, or (more generally) that there is a perfect linear dependence among the explanatory variables. Technically, this is a limiting case of multicollinearity, and indeed it is called *perfect multicollinearity.* As discussed in the case with two explanatory variables, in Section 7.1, the OLS method cannot produce estimates in this situation.

Although this would seem to complicate matters for us immensely, it turns out not to be much of a problem. In contrast to regular multicollinearity, which is a situation that occurs naturally in data, perfect multicollinearity nearly always is the result of making a mistake in the specification of the model. The remedy is simple: respecify the model appropriately. To understand this, we consider several cases in which perfect linear dependence can arise in a regression model. These mistakes share the characteristic that they include in the specification some variable that is not really needed or that does not bring new information to the model; in this sense, the mistaken specification is redundant.

A very special case of perfect linear dependence occurs if an explanatory variable X_j is a constant. In this case, the coefficient β_j plays the same role as the intercept β_0 in the regression specification: β_0 and the term $\beta_j X_j$ are constants that are just added in during the determination of Y. There is no unique way for any statistical technique to assign some of the constancy to β_0 and the rest to $\beta_j X_j$.

Perfect linear dependence also occurs if one variable is simply a multiple of another. For example, suppose that we are trying to explain the exports of cars from Japan to the United States and that we include both the price of these cars in Japan (measured in yen) and the price in the United States (measured in dollars) among the explanatory variables. If all our observations are from a period of fixed exchange rates during which all the dollar prices were the same multiple of the yen prices, then the two price variables measure exactly the same set of economic facts. It does not make sense to include them both, and because of the linear dependence we could not.

Perfect linear dependence also occurs if some set of the explanatory variables satisfy an additive identity. For example, suppose that we are interested in estimating the marginal propensities to consume (mpc's) out of labor income, property income, and total income. We might think of regressing consumption on these three income variables in one equation. However, since total income equals labor income plus property income, it must be that the mpc out of total income equals the sum of the two type-specific mpc's. Trying to estimate three mpc's is redundant and therefore not necessary; since it involves a linear dependence among the explanatory variables, it is also impossible.

A final case of perfect linear dependence occurs if dummy variables for all the groups of a categorical variable are included in the regression. For example, in our treatment of region in Section 7.3 we distinguished four groups but included only three in the specified earnings function. This was adequate to specify the theory behind the model, because each dummy variable coefficient specified the difference between the estimated intercept for that group and the intercept (β_0) for the excluded group. Including the fourth dummy variable would be redundant and would introduce a linear dependence.

As might be realized from these cases, it is quite possible to specify a model with perfect multicollinearity if the work is done with insufficient thought. Usually, a computer program will detect the situation and give some kind of error message. However, because of either imprecision in the data or design of the computational algorithm, it is possible that a computer program might not detect the situation and it would produce some calculations. In this case, the user might think that the computer produced an estimated regression when in fact it produced nonsense.

Problems _____

Section 7.1

7.1 Formulate a multiple regression model showing how the quantity demanded of a certain product depends on both the price of the product and the income of consumers. What are the anticipated signs of the coefficients?

7.2 What is the graphical interpretation of the demand model estimated from the specification in Problem 7.1?

★ **7.3** Continuing Problem 7.2, if income is fixed at a certain amount, what is the graphical interpretation of the relation between predicted demand and price? How does this graph illustrate the *ceteris paribus* concept?

7.4 Based on Equation (7.15), what is the impact on predicted earnings of gaining a college education ($ED = 16$) rather than stopping after completing high school ($ED = 12$)? Assume that EXP is held constant.

★ **7.5** Consider two men of age 35. Suppose that the first has four more years of schooling than the second and therefore has four fewer years of working experience. Based on Equation (7.15), who has greater predicted earnings? By how much?

7.6 Show that the denominator in Equation (7.8) equals zero if X_1 and X_2 are perfectly correlated.

Section 7.2

7.7 Based on Equation (7.29), what is the impact on predicted consumption of an increase in the interest rate from 5 percent to 7 percent?

7.8 Suppose that inflationary forces increase both the interest rate and the rate of inflation by three percentage points. Based on Equation (7.29), determine the effect of these changes on predicted consumption.

7.9 Suppose that a one-percentage-point increase in the rate of interest causes DPI to decrease by 200 million dollars. Based on Equation (7.29), determine the total effect of this change in the rate of interest.

7.10 Prove that $\overline{R}^2 = R^2 - [k/(n - k - 1)](1 - R^2)$.

7.11 Using the relation in Problem 7.10, determine the values of $\overline{R}^2$ for Equations (7.29) and (6.10).

Section 7.3

★ **7.12** Based on Equation (7.33), what is the predicted level of earnings for a black man with 16 years of schooling? For a white man with 12 years of schooling?

7.13 Graph the estimated regression (7.33), clearly labeling all its features.

7.14 Based on Equation (7.41), determine the predicted levels of earnings for high school graduates ($ED = 12$) in each of the four regions of the country.

★ **7.15** Suppose that you want to estimate the impact of education and marital status on the earnings of women. If the data show three marital status categories (single, married, and divorced), how would you set up a regression model?

7.16   Based on Equation (7.41) and Figure 7.3, determine the coefficients of the estimated regression of *EARNS* on *ED* and the regional dummies if the West is the excluded region.

7.17   Does the estimated coefficient on *DRACE* in Equation (7.33) give the total effect of race on earnings? Explain.

7.18   Based on Equation (7.36), determine the predicted rate of inflation in 1960 and compare this with the actual rate. Now, try to predict the rate of inflation for 1980, and compare whatever prediction you make with the actual rate. Explain.

Section 7.4

7.19   Based on Equation (7.46), what is the effect on the predicted earnings of a person with 25 years of experience gaining one more year? What about a person with 35 years of experience?

7.20   Based on Equation (7.46), determine the effect on predicted earnings of a five-year increase in experience for a worker already having 20 years of experience. Do this first using an approximation based on the slope of the implied relation and then using an exact calculation in the estimated regression.

7.21   Verify that the peak in earnings in Figure 7.5 occurs at about 31.4 years of experience.

7.22   Suppose that we have data on a factory's average cost of production and the amount of output in different periods. Specify a regression model that could estimate a U-shaped average cost curve.

Section 7.5

7.23   Suppose that the quantity demanded of a certain product depends on its price and consumers' income. Formulate a constant-elasticity regression model for estimating this demand relation. What are the anticipated signs of the estimated elasticities?

★ **7.24**   In a cross-section context, suppose that output depends on labor and capital inputs. Formulate a regression model for estimating the output elasticities of labor and capital.

★ **7.25**   In a time-series context, suppose that "disembodied technical progress" leads the output yielded by all combinations of capital and labor inputs to grow at a fixed rate per year. Assuming constant output elasticities for labor and capital, formulate a regression model for estimating the rate of disembodied technical progress.

7.26   Modify the model formulated in Problem 7.25 to take account of the effect of "energy restrictions" that prevailed during three years. Explain clearly the econometric assumption underlying this modification.

7.27 In the earnings function estimated as Equation (7.55), would it make sense to have all the regressors in logarithmic form? Explain.

Section 7.6

7.28 Supposing that the rate of inflation affects the interest rate, and making any other economic assumptions that seem appropriate, illustrate the causal nexus determining aggregate consumption as estimated in Equation (7.29). Where could the Federal Reserve discount rate enter?

7.29 Suppose that a properly specified earnings function includes *ED*, *EXP*, and *DRACE* as explanatory variables. Illustrate the causal nexus determining earnings and explain the linkages.

7.30 Compare the estimated effect of education in Equations (7.33) and (6.7) from the point of view of possible misspecification.

7.31 Suppose that we wish to estimate the effect of being a union member on workers' earnings, using cross-section data. Specify a regression model that would be appropriate for estimating this effect. What theory or assumptions are required to make it appropriate?

7.32 Consider the Phillips curve model in Equation (7.36). Could this be estimated using data just for 1965 through 1970? Explain.

7.33 Suppose that the fourth dummy variable *DNEAST* were added to the regression specification in Equation (7.41) and that a computer provided "estimates." Try to interpret all the coefficients.

III

Probability Distributions

8

Probability Theory

The theory of statistical inference, which allows us to assess the relations between the estimated coefficients in a regression model and the true values of these parameters, is based on the discussion of random variables and probability distributions in Chapters 9 and 10. As helpful background for understanding that material, this chapter discusses some elementary probability theory. However, later chapters are written so that this one can be skipped without any loss of continuity.

8.1 Outcomes and Probabilities

Notions of probability arise in situations of uncertainty, where several possible outcomes are candidates to be the one actual outcome of an *activity.* (In more formal presentations, these basic activities are called "experiments.") Some of the best examples are gambling games, and it was in their study that the subject of probability was developed.

To provide a context for introducing some basic probability concepts, consider flipping a coin. We assume that a coin never lands on its edge, and so we identify only two possible *outcomes:* the coin lands on its head side (H) or it lands on its tail side (T). In general, each possible outcome is denoted by e_i. In coin flipping the two outcomes are denoted by e_1 and e_2, and they are identified as $e_1 = H$, $e_2 = T$. In general, all the possible outcomes of an activity are collectively known as the *sample space,* which is denoted by S. For coin flipping, $S = \{e_1, e_2\}$.

We consider two ways of arriving at the concept of probability. First, we could take a given coin and (hypothetically) flip it a great many times, recording the actual outcomes. At any stage, we could calculate the proportion of flips that resulted in heads and the proportion that resulted in tails. These two proportions are relative frequencies and they sum to 1. Now, if we think of the number of flips as approaching infinity, we could define the *probability* of H occurring as the proportion of flips that result in H. This probability is denoted by $\Pr(H)$ or $\Pr(e_1)$. Although this is not a practical approach to determining probabilities, it is a useful conceptual approach. Second, we could analyze the coin physically in order to determine the symmetry of its design and weight distribution. If our understanding of the natural laws of physics is correct, this analysis could lead us to proclaim knowledge of $\Pr(e_1)$ and $\Pr(e_2)$ without any experimenting. This approach focuses on characterizing the uncertainty regarding the single result of an activity that will occur, and the practicality of repeating the activity is not an issue. We rely on both approaches for interpretation.

Based on these concepts, two properties of probabilities emerge. Thinking of probabilities as relative frequencies, we realize that none can be negative and that none can be greater than 1. For convenience in describing some sample spaces, we allow a probability to be zero. Hence for any outcome

$$0 \leq \Pr(e_i) \leq 1 \tag{8.1}$$

And again thinking of probabilities as relative frequencies, we realize that they must sum to 1:

$$\sum \Pr(e_i) = 1 \tag{8.2}$$

where the summation is understood to include all the outcomes in the sample space.

As an example, we consider a *fair* coin. By this we mean that if the coin were flipped a great many times, then in the limit half the actual outcomes would be H and half would be T. Hence $\Pr(H) = \frac{1}{2}$ and $\Pr(T) = \frac{1}{2}$. Alternatively viewed, we mean that the physics of the coin is such that each possible outcome is judged equally likely. Since there are two outcomes, $\Pr(H) = \frac{1}{2}$ and $\Pr(T) = \frac{1}{2}$.

It is possible to use the game of flipping a fair coin to define a variety of different activities. The first activity we consider is just the flip of one coin. As we have seen, there are two outcomes, and $\Pr(e_1) = \frac{1}{2}$ and $\Pr(e_2) = \frac{1}{2}$. The second activity is flipping a coin twice in a row; here it is important to identify the sequence as well as the result of each flip in distinguishing the outcome. There are four outcomes: $e_1 = HH$, $e_2 = HT$, $e_3 = TH$, and $e_4 = TT$. A little physics and logic lead to the conclusion that these outcomes are equally likely, so $\Pr(e_i) = \frac{1}{4}$ for each. The third activity is flipping a coin three times in a row. There are eight outcomes, identified in Table 8.1, and $\Pr(e_i) = \frac{1}{8}$ for each of

TABLE 8.1 Outcomes for Three Flips of a Coin

Outcome		Pr (e_i)	A	B	C	D
HHH	e_1	⅛			✔	
HHT	e_2	⅛	✔			
HTH	e_3	⅛	✔			✔
THH	e_4	⅛	✔	✔		
HTT	e_5	⅛				✔
THT	e_6	⅛		✔		
TTH	e_7	⅛		✔		✔
TTT	e_8	⅛		✔		✔

them. It should be noted that these outcomes can be identified and labeled in any order; none has any special claim to being e_1.

8.2 Events

Often we have special interest in groups, or sets, of outcomes. For example, we might be concerned with getting exactly two heads in the activity of flipping a coin three times. Referring to Table 8.1, we see that e_2, e_3, and e_4 are all the outcomes meeting this description. It is convenient to define an *event* as a set of outcomes. Letting A be the event of getting exactly two heads, then

$$A = \{e_2, e_3, e_4\} \tag{8.3}$$

Our basic concepts lead us to define the probability of an event as being equal to the sum of the probabilities of the constituent outcomes. In this case,

$$\Pr(A) = \Pr(e_2) + \Pr(e_3) + \Pr(e_4) \tag{8.4}$$

The logic of this is best seen in terms of the proper treatment of relative frequencies. By $\Pr(A)$ we mean what would be the number of actual outcomes with two heads as a proportion of the number of repetitions of the three-flip activity, in the limit. A little algebra justifies (8.4) and the general definition.

Similarly, we might be concerned with getting a tail on the first flip. This event B is defined as

$$B = \{e_4, e_6, e_7, e_8\} \tag{8.5}$$

and $\Pr(B) = \frac{1}{2}$. A third event C is getting no tails at all. This leads to

$$C = \{e_1\} \tag{8.6}$$

with $\Pr(C) = \frac{1}{8}$.

Two events are said to be ***mutually exclusive*** if they have no outcomes in common. In our three-flip activity, A and C are mutually exclusive; also, B

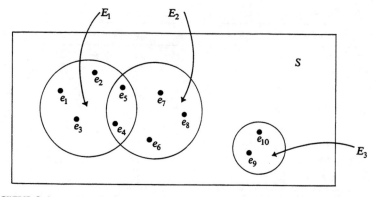

FIGURE 8.1 A Venn diagram illustrates all the outcomes of an activity and some events defined as sets of the outcomes. In this case, we see that events E_1 and E_2 are not mutually exclusive, because they have outcomes e_4 and e_5 in common. The outcomes e_4 and e_5 constitute the intersection $E_1 \cap E_2$.

and C are mutually exclusive. A and B are not mutually exclusive because they have e_4 in common.

The basic notions used in defining events are sometimes illustrated in **Venn diagrams.** In this type of diagram a point is used to represent an outcome, and groups of points make up events. A Venn diagram for an undescribed activity is given in Figure 8.1. The points represent all the outcomes (i.e., the sample space) of the activity, and this set of points is enclosed in a boundary to indicate this. Three events are defined as

$$E_1 = \{e_1, e_2, e_3, e_4, e_5\} \tag{8.7}$$

$$E_2 = \{e_4, e_5, e_6, e_7, e_8\} \tag{8.8}$$

$$E_3 = \{e_9, e_{10}\} \tag{8.9}$$

Events E_3 and E_1 are mutually exclusive, as are E_3 and E_2. Graphically, we see that E_3 has no points in common with either E_1 or E_2. By contrast, E_1 and E_2 have e_4 and e_5 in common, so they are not mutually exclusive.

A Venn diagram can be drawn to reflect the design of the activity. For example, in the two-flip activity the outcomes can be arranged in a matrix like that in Figure 8.2. In more complicated cases such a diagram can help simplify the identification of the outcomes that constitute an event defined in terms of the procedure of the activity.

8.3   Unions and Intersections _____

Sometimes events are defined as special combinations of other events. One type of combination is the union of events, and another is their intersection.

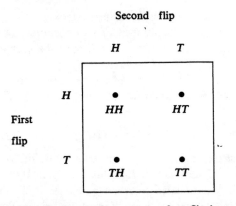

FIGURE 8.2   In this Venn diagram the four outcomes from flipping a coin twice are arranged in a matrix. The first row contains all the outcomes having a head on the first flip, and the second row contains all those having a tail on the first flip. Similarly, the first column contains all the outcomes having a head on the second flip, and the second column contains all those having a tail on the second flip.

The **union** of two events is a new event whose constituent outcomes are all those in either or both of the two events. Notationally, the union of E_1 and E_2 is $E_1 \cup E_2$, which is read as "E_1 union E_2." A specific outcome is in $E_1 \cup E_2$ if it is in E_1 only, or if it is in E_2 only, or if it is in both. Although we could assign a new name to this event, such as E_3 (defined as $E_3 = E_1 \cup E_2$), we usually refer to it simply as $E_1 \cup E_2$. In our three-flip example

$$A \cup B = \{e_2, e_3, e_4, e_6, e_7, e_8\} \qquad (8.10)$$

$$A \cup C = \{e_1, e_2, e_3, e_4\} \qquad (8.11)$$

$$B \cup C = \{e_1, e_4, e_6, e_7, e_8\} \qquad (8.12)$$

Notice that since (8.10) just identifies the constituent outcomes of $A \cup B$, there is no double listing for e_4, which is in both A and B.

The **intersection** of two events is a new event whose constituent outcomes are only those in both of the two events. Notationally, the intersection of E_1 and E_2 is $E_1 \cap E_2$, which is read as "E_1 intersect E_2." A specific outcome is in $E_1 \cap E_2$ if it is in E_1 and if it is also in E_2. This "and" combination contrasts with the "either-or-both" combination of a union. In our three-toss example

$$A \cap B = \{e_4\} \qquad (8.13)$$

$$A \cap C = \phi \qquad (8.14)$$

$$B \cap C = \phi \qquad (8.15)$$

where ϕ indicates an empty set, in which there are no outcomes. There are no outcomes in $A \cap C$ and no outcomes in $B \cap C$. This occurs because A and C are mutually exclusive, as are B and C.

The probability of an event that is defined either as a union or an intersection is equal to the sum of the probabilities of its constituent outcomes. This basic definition is the same as our previous definition of the probability of any event. For example, $\Pr(A \cup B) = \frac{6}{8}$ while $\Pr(A \cap B) = \frac{1}{8}$.

Moving up from the basic definition, the probability of a union also can be determined from the probabilities of the combining events according to an *addition rule:*

$$\Pr(E_1 \cup E_2) = \Pr(E_1) + \Pr(E_2) - \Pr(E_1 \cap E_2) \qquad (8.16)$$

The logic of this stems from the basic probability definition. The outcomes in $E_1 \cap E_2$ are in E_1 and they are in E_2. Thus, the sum $\Pr(E_1) + \Pr(E_2)$ double counts the probability associated with the outcomes in $E_1 \cap E_2$, and therefore $\Pr(E_1 \cap E_2)$ is subtracted once to keep the counting right. Note that if E_1 and E_2 are mutually exclusive, $\Pr(E_1 \cap E_2)$ is zero and no double counting exists. In our three-flip activity,

$$\Pr(A \cup B) = \Pr(A) + \Pr(B) - \Pr(A \cap B)$$

$$= \frac{3}{8} + \frac{4}{8} - \frac{1}{8} = \frac{6}{8} \qquad (8.17)$$

$$\Pr(A \cup C) = \Pr(A) + \Pr(C) - \Pr(A \cap C)$$

$$= \frac{3}{8} + \frac{1}{8} - 0 = \frac{4}{8} \qquad (8.18)$$

$$\Pr(B \cup C) = \Pr(B) + \Pr(C) - \Pr(B \cap C)$$

$$= \frac{4}{8} + \frac{1}{8} - 0 = \frac{5}{8} \qquad (8.19)$$

In the Venn diagram of an undescribed activity shown in Figure 8.1, the union of E_1 and E_2 (i.e., $E_1 \cup E_2$) consists of the outcomes e_1 through e_8. The intersection of E_1 and E_2 (i.e., $E_1 \cap E_2$) consists of e_4 and e_5 only. With regard to the probability of a union such as $\Pr(E_1 \cup E_2)$, it is clear that $\Pr(e_4)$ and $\Pr(e_5)$ are double counted in the sum $\Pr(E_1) + \Pr(E_2)$. Since the outcomes e_4 and e_5 constitute $E_1 \cap E_2$, $\Pr(E_1 \cap E_2)$ is subtracted away in the addition rule.

These concepts extend easily to more than two events entering into a combination. A union of events consists of the outcomes in any or all of the combining events, whereas an intersection of events consists only of the outcomes in all the combining events.

8.4   Conditional Probability and Independence _

Our basic idea of probability is that any of the possible outcomes in the sample space might occur as the actual outcome of the activity, and concern often focuses on the occurrence of some subset of the possible outcomes. For example, in the activity of flipping a coin three times, $\Pr(A)$ is "the probability of two heads occurring, given that the set of outcomes that might possibly occur is the sample space S." The condition that any of the outcomes in S may occur helps determine the calculation of the probability that two heads will occur. To highlight this, we may denote $Pr(A)$ by the fuller statement $Pr(A|S)$. This is read as "the probability of A, given S," which concisely conveys our basic idea.

Now, it might be that we already know that the first flip resulted in a tail, or it might be that we are considering the hypothetical situation that the first flip results in a tail. In either context, suppose that we are still concerned with the occurrence of two heads, and we wish to determine "the probability of two heads occurring, given that the set of outcomes that might possibly occur is B," where B is the event of getting a tail on the first flip. This probability, which we denote by $Pr(A|B)$, is known as a **conditional probability,** and it might be equal to or different from the unconditional probability amount $Pr(A)$.

Returning to Table 8.1, we see that if B occurs (tail on first), then the final result must be e_4, e_6, e_7, or e_8. Among these outcomes, only e_4 also corresponds to A (two heads). Hence our concern now is focused on the occurrence of e_4, given that e_4, e_6, e_7, or e_8 is the set of now-possible outcomes of the activity. Since each of these four outcomes is equally likely, the probability of e_4 occurring is $\frac{1}{4}$ now. Thus we may state that $Pr(A|B) = \frac{1}{4}$. This conditional probability is different from the unconditional $Pr(A)$, which is $\frac{3}{8}$. Notice that to determine $Pr(A|B)$ we calculate a ratio in which the numerator is based on the set of outcomes that corresponds both to A (two heads) and B (tail on first); this is the set $A \cap B$. The denominator of the ratio is based on the set of outcomes that corresponds to B; this is simply the set B.

The probability calculation in this example generalizes quite readily. For any two events E_1 and E_2,

$$Pr(E_1|E_2) = \frac{Pr(E_1 \cap E_2)}{Pr(E_2)} \tag{8.20}$$

This expression determines the conditional probability of E_1 given E_2. In essence, (8.20) uses the conditioning information (i.e., the occurrence of E_2) to restrict our concern for the occurrence of E_1 to just those outcomes that occur in conjunction with E_2 (i.e., to just $E_1 \cap E_2$). In the previous example, where we followed more basic principles, we formed the ratio of the numbers of equally likely outcomes. Following (8.20) instead, we calculate the ratio of probabilities, yielding

$$Pr(A|B) = \frac{Pr(A \cap B)}{Pr(B)} = \frac{\frac{1}{8}}{\frac{4}{8}} = \frac{1}{4} \tag{8.21}$$

as before.

In some probability applications it is easy to determine probability amounts like $Pr(E_1|E_2)$ and $Pr(E_2)$ but difficult to get down to the basic level to determine $Pr(E_1 \cap E_2)$. In such a case, (8.20) can be reexpressed as

$$Pr(E_1 \cap E_2) = Pr(E_1|E_2) \cdot Pr(E_2) \tag{8.22}$$

This is especially helpful in the case of independence.

Among the events of an activity, two events E_1 and E_2 are said to be statistically *independent* if and only if

$$\Pr(E_1|E_2) = \Pr(E_1) \quad \text{for } E_1, E_2 \text{ independent} \tag{8.23}$$

That is, when we say that E_1 and E_2 are independent (of each other), this means that the conditional probability of E_1 occurring is equal to the unconditional probability of its occurring. Independence is symmetric, so that $\Pr(E_2|E_1) = \Pr(E_2)$ holds along with (8.23) when E_1 and E_2 are independent. [It should be noted that $\Pr(E_1|E_2) \neq \Pr(E_1)$ corresponds to E_1 and E_2 being not independent.]

For example, returning again to the activity of flipping a coin three times, let D be the event of getting a tail on the second flip and recall that B is the event of getting a tail on the first flip. Are D and B independent? From Table 8.1 we see that

$$D = \{e_3, e_5, e_7, e_8\}$$
$$B = \{e_4, e_6, e_7, e_8\} \tag{8.24}$$
$$D \cap B = \{e_7, e_8\}$$

For this activity with eight equally likely outcomes, we know from basic principles that $\Pr(D) = \frac{4}{8}$, $\Pr(B) = \frac{4}{8}$, and $\Pr(D \cap B) = \frac{2}{8}$. Thus, applying (8.20) we see that

$$\Pr(D|B) = \frac{\Pr(D \cap B)}{\Pr(B)} = \frac{\frac{2}{8}}{\frac{4}{8}} = \frac{1}{2} \tag{8.25}$$

Since $\Pr(D|B) = \Pr(D)$, events D and B meet the definitional requirement (8.23) for being independent.

When two events are independent, the conditioning information that one of them did or must occur does not alter the chance that the other event might occur. In coin flipping, the independence of D and B means that the occurrence of a tail on the first flip in no way affects the chance of a tail occurring on the second flip. This independence arises because of the physical laws that govern the activity of flipping a coin.

For events that are independent, we may substitute $\Pr(E_1)$ for $\Pr(E_1|E_2)$ in (8.22), yielding the *multiplication rule*

$$\Pr(E_1 \cap E_2) = \Pr(E_1) \cdot \Pr(E_2) \quad \text{for } E_1, E_2 \text{ independent} \tag{8.26}$$

This rule holds true if and only if E_1 and E_2 are independent, and it may be taken as an alternative form of the definition (8.23).

The multiplication rule for independent events is helpful in determining the probabilities of outcomes in activities that are designed as sequences of repetitions of simpler activities. For example, suppose that we have an unfair coin for which $\Pr(H) = \frac{2}{3}$ and $\Pr(T) = \frac{1}{3}$. Consider the activity of flipping a coin two times, for which the Venn diagram is given in Figure 8.2. Let H_1 be the event of getting a head on the first toss and H_2 be the event of getting a head on the second toss. A physical analysis of the activity leads one to realize that H_1 and H_2 are independent. Thus we realize that $\Pr(H_1) = \Pr(H_2) = \Pr(H)$. A similar analysis holds for T_1 and T_2. Therefore, the multiplication rule can be used to determine the probabilities of the four outcomes:

$$\Pr(HH) = \Pr(H_1) \cdot \Pr(H_2) = (\tfrac{2}{3})(\tfrac{2}{3}) = \tfrac{4}{9} \qquad (8.27)$$

$$\Pr(TH) = \Pr(T_1) \cdot \Pr(H_2) = (\tfrac{1}{3})(\tfrac{2}{3}) = \tfrac{2}{9} \qquad (8.28)$$

$$\Pr(HT) = \Pr(H_1) \cdot \Pr(T_2) = (\tfrac{2}{3})(\tfrac{1}{3}) = \tfrac{2}{9} \qquad (8.29)$$

$$\Pr(TT) = \Pr(T_1) \cdot \Pr(T_2) = (\tfrac{1}{3})(\tfrac{1}{3}) = \tfrac{1}{9} \qquad (8.30)$$

8.5 A Pair of Dice

Rolling a pair of dice is an activity that nicely illustrates the probability concepts developed in this chapter. In this example we view the dice as distinguishable: one is red and the other is green.

Since any of the outcomes on the red die can occur in conjunction with any on the green die, there are 36 possible outcomes for the activity. These are enumerated in Figure 8.3, which arranges the outcomes of the activity in matrix form according to the outcome on each die. Since the laws of physics show that each of the outcomes of the activity is equally likely, the probability of each is 1/36. Alternatively, we might start by recognizing that the six outcomes for one die are equally likely events, so that the probability of each is $\tfrac{1}{6}$. Then,

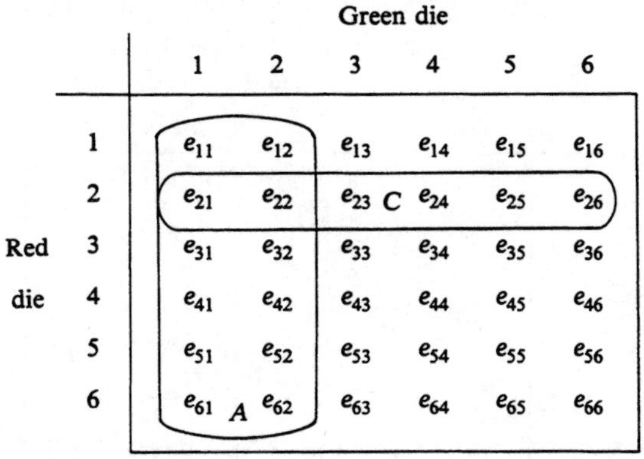

FIGURE 8.3 The 36 outcomes from rolling a pair of dice are illustrated in a Venn-like diagram that arranges the outcomes in a matrix. Each row contains all the outcomes having a particular value occurring on the red die, and each column contains all those having a particular value on the green die. This arrangement facilitates the identification of some events. For example, event A is "getting a 2 or less on the green die," and C is "getting a 2 on the red die."

recognizing that the outcomes on the two dice are independent, we obtain the probability of each of the 36 outcomes of the activity by using the multiplication rule—each $\Pr(e_i) = 1/36$.

Determination of the probabilities associated with events is straightforward, but needs some care. For example, let event A be defined as "getting a 2 or less on the green die." Since this definition places no restriction on the red die, the outcomes making up A are given in the first two columns of the matrix in Figure 8.3. Hence $\Pr(A) = 12/36$.

In dice throwing, the outcomes often are characterized by the sum of the two numbers occurring. Figure 8.4 shows the matrix of Figure 8.3 rewritten with sums replacing the outcome identifiers. The event B, defined as "getting a sum of 5," is shown to correspond to four outcomes. Hence $\Pr(B) = 4/36$.

The event $A \cap B$, "getting a 2 or less on the green die and a sum of 5," corresponds to $\{e_{41}, e_{32}\}$ only, and $\Pr(A \cap B) = 2/36$. This event $A \cup B$ corresponds to all the outcomes in the first two columns, plus e_{23} and e_{14}. Thus, from the basic principles, $\Pr(A \cup B) = 14/36$. Alternatively, from the addition rule,

$$\Pr(A \cup B) = \Pr(A) + \Pr(B) - \Pr(A \cap B) \tag{8.31}$$
$$= 12/36 + 4/36 - 2/36 = 14/36$$

As noted, $\Pr(B) = 4/36$. However, if we wish to determine the probability of "getting a sum of 5, given that the green die is 2 or less," then we formulate and calculate

$$\Pr(B|A) = \frac{\Pr(B \cap A)}{\Pr(A)} = \frac{2/36}{12/36} = \frac{6}{36} \tag{8.32}$$

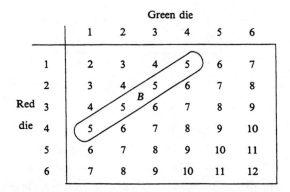

FIGURE 8.4   In this diagram the outcome identifiers are replaced with the sum of the values occurring on the dice for that outcome. This facilitates the identification of events defined in terms of the sum of the dice values. Event B is "getting a sum of 5." "Getting a 2 or less on the green die" (event A in Figure 8.3) corresponds to all the outcomes in the first two columns.

In this case $\Pr(B|A) > \Pr(B)$, and we realize that A and B are not independent.

Since the outcome on the green die cannot affect the outcome on the red die, events defined solely in terms of one die are independent of events defined solely in terms of the other. Let C be "getting a 2 on the red die," for which $\Pr(C) = 6/36$. Then the probability of "getting a 2 or less on the green die and a 2 on the red die" is given by

$$\Pr(A \cap C) = \Pr(A)\cdot\Pr(C) = (12/36)(6/36) = 2/36 \qquad (8.33)$$

using knowledge of independence. Alternatively, basic principles identify $A \cap C$ as $\{e_{21}, e_{22}\}$, and yield the same probability of course.

It should be noted that the activity of rolling a single die two times in succession is basically the same as rolling a pair of dice once. Unless the die has a memory, the outcomes on successive rolls will be independent. Hence, the probability analysis of events defined in terms of two successive rolls of a single die is exactly the same as that for a single roll of a pair of dice.

Problems

Section 8.1

8.1 Take a fair coin and flip it 20 times. After each flip, calculate the proportion of flips up to that point that have resulted in H and record the results in a table or graph. As the number of flips increase, does the proportion that are heads tend toward .5?

★ **8.2** Suppose that the four sides of a tetrahedron are labeled 1, 2, 3, and 4, and that the result of any flip is the number that is face down.
 (a) List all the outcomes for the activity of flipping a tetrahedron twice.
 (b) What is the probability of each of these outcomes?
 (c) How many outcomes are there in a three-flip activity with a tetrahedron?

Section 8.2

8.3 For the three-flip coin activity, define (in terms of their constituent outcomes) the following events and determine their probabilities:
 (a) Three tails.
 (b) No heads.
 (c) Head on first flip with tail on second.
 (d) Two tails.

8.4 Draw a Venn diagram similar to Figure 8.1 to represent the outcomes of the three-flip coin activity, and identify on it the events A, B, and C defined in Table 8.1.

8.5 Devise a simple three-dimensional diagram to represent the outcomes of the three-flip coin activity, and identify on it the four events defined in Table 8.1.

★ **8.6** Suppose that there are 10 balls in a hat: one labeled 5, two 6, three 7, and four 8.
  (a) What is the probability of drawing a particular ball?
  (b) What is the probability of drawing a ball labeled 5? a 6? a 7? an 8?
  (c) In a draw from the hat, what is the probability that the number on the ball will be less than or equal to 7?

★ **8.7** For the three-flip activity, are the two events in each of the following pairs mutually exclusive?
  (a) Two tails, two heads.
  (b) Head on first flip, two tails.
  (c) Tail on first flip, tail on third flip.

Section 8.3

★ **8.8** For the unions of the pairs of events in Problem 8.7, write out the set listings of the outcomes in each combination, and apply basic probability concepts to determine the probabilities of each union.

8.9 For the intersections of the pairs of events in Problem 8.7, do the same analysis as in Problem 8.8.

★ **8.10** Use the addition rule to determine the probability of the union of each of the pairs of events in Problem 8.7.

8.11 Draw a Venn diagram illustrating a case in which the intersection of three events has one outcome. Label all the two-event intersections in the diagram.

Section 8.4

8.12 For the three-flip coin activity, what is the probability of getting a tail on the third flip given that
  (a) There is a tail on the first flip?
  (b) There is a tail on the first two flips?
  (c) There is a total of one tail?
  (d) There is a total of two tails?

★ **8.13** Suppose that a worker is twice considered for a bonus, that each time the chance of getting it is 20 percent, and that getting it once does not affect the chance of getting it again. Determine the probability of the worker's
  (a) Never getting a bonus.
  (b) Getting it once.
  (c) Getting it twice.

Section 8.5

8.14 The game of craps is played by rolling a pair of dice. If a player rolls a sum of 7 or 11 on the first roll, he wins; if he rolls a sum of 2, 3, or 12 (craps), he loses.

    (a) What is the probability of winning on the first roll?

    (b) What is the probability of losing on the first roll?

    (c) What is the probability of neither winning nor losing on the first roll?

★ **8.15** In the game of craps, if a player neither wins nor loses on the first roll, whatever sum appeared is called the "point." After a point is established, the player keeps on rolling the dice until his point appears (an ultimate win) or a 7 appears (an ultimate loss).

    (a) What is the probability of winning given that the point is 8?

    (b) What is the probability that a player just approaching the table will ultimately win with a point of 8 in his first game?

9

Random Variables and Probability Distributions

In this chapter and the next we develop the theory of random variables and probability distributions, which is part of the general study of mathematical statistics. The topics are rather abstract, and we rely on intuition rather than formal derivation as much as possible.

In Chapters 2 through 4 we used the term data variable to mean a measurable characteristic for which we might have some data. Now we are interested in developing a theoretical framework for thinking about processes that can generate such data, and these processes are called random variables. Our treatment of random variables and probability distributions emphasizes their similarity to data variables and frequency distributions, so it would be helpful to review Chapter 4 at this time.

9.1   Discrete Random Variables

Consider a process that produces numbers. It may be helpful to imagine that some activity is going on inside a box: there might be a woman throwing dice, a man picking numbers out of a hat, or a computer churning away. As part of the process, a number is associated with each outcome of the activity. From where we stand, all that we see is that some number appears each time the activity is repeated.

For example, suppose that there are 10 numbered balls in a hat. The hat is shaken well, a single ball is drawn out, its number is read aloud, and the ball is replaced. This activity can be repeated over and over, thereby producing a series of numbers.

In this setting, the process is called a *random variable,* and the numbers that get produced are called the *values* of the random variable. The process can continue forever, thereby producing an unlimited number of values. However, the number of different values that can possibly occur for a particular random variable may be quite limited.

Among random variables, a distinction is made between discrete and continuous types. A *discrete* random variable is one for which a countable number of possible values can occur, as in the balls-in-hat example. A *continuous* random variable is one for which the set of possible values is some range or interval of real numbers; this type is discussed in Section 9.4.

When we observe a set of numbers that were produced by a random variable, this series of values is a *sample* from the random variable. The sample is a set of data, and the methods of descriptive statistics presented in Chapters 3 and 4 to summarize data can be used to analyze it. The distinction between a random variable and a sample is important: a random variable is a process that produces numbers, and a sample is a set of these numbers.

Suppose that among the 10 balls in the hat one is labeled 5, two are labeled 6, three 7, and four 8. Presuming that the balls are physically identical except for their labels, it is equally likely that any one of the ten balls will be picked in a particular draw. Simple logic leads us to say that the probability of getting a 5 is 1/10, of getting a 6 is 2/10, of getting a 7 is 3/10, and of getting an 8 is 4/10. For now we can proceed with a commonsense notion of what "probability" means, and we will use the term interchangeably with "chance."

This information about the process is arranged in Table 9.1. Four possible values can occur for this random variable, which is named X. Each row in the table refers to one of the possible values, and the first column simply indexes the rows. The column headed X_k shows a list of all the possible values, and the column headed $p(X_k)$ shows the probability of each of these values occurring in any particular draw. This information can be graphed in a simple way, as in

TABLE 9.1   Probability Distribution of X

k	X_k	$p(X_k)$
1	5	.1
2	6	.2
3	7	.3
4	8	.4

Figure 9.1. Also, this information about values and probabilities can be presented in an equation format:

$$p(X_k) = \frac{X_k - 4}{10} \quad \text{for } X = 5, 6, 7, 8 \tag{9.1}$$

An equation format may not seem to be a useful way of writing down information in this example, but in other cases it will be.

This balls-in-hat example illustrates the general features of a discrete random variable. To describe or characterize the random variable, we focus our attention on a particular occurrence—for instance, the next value to be produced. Letting X denote the name of the random variable, our knowledge about the value of X on this future occurrence has two components, which together are called the **probability distribution** of X. The first component is a list of the possible values that X might take on, and we denote this generally by $\{X\}$. The second component is a function $p(X)$ that gives information about the probability that the number produced by X will be equal to each of the possibly occurring values. The probability distribution for the balls-in-hat example is displayed three different ways: in Table 9.1, in Figure 9.1, and in Equation (9.1).

Letting X_k denote a particular value, we let "$\Pr(X = X_k)$" be a shorthand way of writing "the probability that the random variable X will be equal to X_k." In saying this we are focusing on a particular occurrence—perhaps the next value to be produced. For a discrete random variable, the component $p(X)$ of its probability distribution gives the probability values corresponding to each possible value of X. Hence

$$p(X_k) = \Pr(X = X_k) \tag{9.2}$$

[This meaning for $p(X)$ does not hold for continuous random variables.]

An important idea about random variables is that the values produced are **independent** of each other. This means that the value produced on one

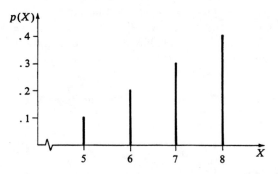

FIGURE 9.1   This graph represents the probability distribution of X, a discrete random variable that is also represented by Equation (9.1) and Table 9.1. For each specific value X_k, the value $p(X_k)$ is the probability that X will be equal to X_k; that is, $p(X_k)$ is $\Pr(X = X_k)$.

occurrence is not affected by whatever values occurred previously. This idea may lead to surprises for people who are not accustomed to games of chance. For example, in the balls-in-hat game, suppose that a 7 has just occurred twice in a row. One might think that the chance of a 7 occurring as the next value would be diminished by the fact that two 7s just occurred, but this is not so: since the balls have no memory and since they are shaken up after the previous draw is returned to the hat, the previous history cannot affect the probabilities of the different values in $\{X\}$ occurring this time. The implication of independence is that $\Pr(X = 7)$ is still 3/10.

Two simple aspects of discrete probabilities should be noted. First, if X_k is a possibly occurring value for X, we must mean that its probability is positive. That is,

$$p(X_k) > 0 \quad \text{for } X_k \text{ in } \{X\} \tag{9.3}$$

Second, the sum of the probabilities associated with all the possible values of X is exactly equal to 1:

$$\sum p(X_k) = 1 \quad \text{including all } X_k \text{ in } \{X\} \tag{9.4}$$

These two aspects are in accord with our commonsense understanding of what "probability" means.

As another example, consider a random variable Y that has the probability distribution given by Table 9.2 and by Figure 9.2. One can verify that $\sum p(Y_k) = 1$. Without thinking about any underlying activity, it should be understandable that Y is some chance process such that the probability that the value will be zero is 1/64, that the value will be 1 is 6/64, and so on.

It is straightforward to use a probability distribution to determine the probability or chance that the value of the random variable will be in some range or interval of numbers. In general, an *event* is a set of possible values of a

TABLE 9.2 Probability Distribution of Y and Computation of μ_Y and σ_Y

(1) k	(2) Y_k	(3) $p(Y_k)$	(4) $Y_k p(Y_k)$	(5) $(Y_k - \mu_Y)^2 p(Y_k)$
1	0	1/64	0	9/64
2	1	6/64	6/64	24/64
3	2	15/64	30/64	15/64
4	3	20/64	60/64	0
5	4	15/64	60/64	15/64
6	5	6/64	30/64	24/64
7	6	1/64	6/64	9/64
			192/64	96/64
			$\mu_Y = 3$	$\sigma_Y^2 = 1.5$
				$\sigma_Y = 1.22$

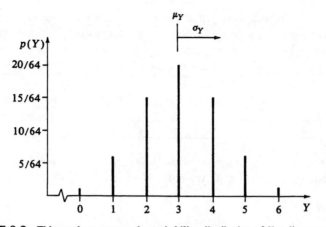

FIGURE 9.2 This graph represents the probability distribution of Y, a discrete random variable that is also represented by Table 9.2. The values of the mean and standard deviation of Y, which are calculated in Table 9.2, are also indicated here ($\mu_Y = 3$, $\sigma_Y = 1.22$). One possible description of Y is that it is the number of heads that might result from tossing a fair coin six times. In Section 9.3 we see that Y has a binomial distribution with $n = 6$ and $P = 1/2$.

random variable, and for a discrete random variable the probability of an event is the sum of the probabilities associated with each of the values that make up the event. For example, in the balls-in-hat game

$$\Pr(X \leq 7) = p(5) + p(6) + p(7)$$
$$= 1/10 + 2/10 + 3/10 = 6/10 = .6 \qquad (9.5)$$

and in the second example above it is easy to see that

$$\Pr(Y \leq 3) = 42/64 \qquad (9.6)$$

Similarly, it is possible to consider evaluating probabilities such as $\Pr(X_1 \leq X \leq X_2)$—the probability that X takes on a value between two specified values X_1 and X_2, including these endpoint values. It should be clear that

$$\Pr(6 \leq X \leq 8) = .9 \qquad (9.7)$$

and

$$\Pr(2 \leq Y \leq 4) = 50/64 \qquad (9.8)$$

Often we work with "greater than" inequalities such as

$$\Pr(X \geq 7) = p(7) + p(8) = .7 \qquad (9.9)$$

Mean and Standard Deviation

The final concepts we need to develop for our treatment of discrete random variables are the summary features of their probability distributions. Recall that in working with data variables, we found that the mean and standard deviation could summarize a relative frequency distribution. The same ideas apply here.

The **mean** of a random variable X is denoted by μ_X or by $E[X]$, and its definition is

$$\mu_X = E[X] = \sum X_k p(X_k) \tag{9.10}$$

(μ is lowercase "mu," the Greek "m"). As with data variables, the mean is a typical value, but because of the probabilistic nature of random variables the mean is referred to as the **expected value**. Most often, we use the notation μ_X when we want to say "mean" and the notation $E[X]$ when we want to say "expected value." Comparing (9.10) with (4.9), we note how similar the definition of μ_X is to that of $\overline{X}$: the difference is that a probability now appears, in place of a relative frequency.

The **variance** of X is denoted by σ_X^2 or $\sigma^2(X)$, and its definition is

$$\sigma_X^2 = \sigma^2(X) = \sum (X_k - \mu_X)^2 p(X_k) \tag{9.11}$$

(σ is lowercase "sigma," the Greek "s"). We use two alternative notations for the variance because sometimes the symbolic name of the random variable is too large to write as a subscript.

The **standard deviation,** denoted by σ_X or $\sigma(X)$, is simply the square root of the variance

$$\sigma_X = \sigma(X) = \sqrt{\sigma_X^2} = \sqrt{\sum (X_k - \mu_X)^2 p(X_k)} \tag{9.12}$$

and it is a measure of the typical (in the sense of "expected") deviation of X from its mean. The definition of σ_X is similar to that of the root mean squared deviation (*RMSD*) of a data variable [see (4.10)], except that a probability now appears instead of a relative frequency.

A worked-through set of calculations for the mean, variance, and standard deviation of the random variable Y is given in Table 9.2. It is helpful to do the calculations in a neat table like this rather than to try to plug numbers into formulas. The values of μ_Y and σ_Y are graphed in Figure 9.2, which shows the probability distribution of Y.

9.2   Random Variables and Samples of Data ____

As explained in the previous section, a random variable can be thought of as a process that produces numbers. Its uncertain nature is completely characterized by a probability distribution, which consists of $\{X\}$ and $p(X)$. For a discrete random variable, $p(X_k)$ is the probability that the random variable takes on the specific value X_k, as stated in (9.2). In this section we examine the relation between a random variable and the data it generates, and we consider what is meant by "probability."

If we collect a series of values of a random variable, we have a sample. This sample is a set of data: each value is an observation. The data can be summarized by a relative frequency distribution and analyzed with the methods of descriptive statistics. In a sample from a discrete random variable, each relative frequency value f_k gives the proportion of the observations that take on the specific value X_k.

Consider again the balls-in-hat game and its description as a discrete random variable X. Its probability distribution is given in Table 9.1 and Figure 9.1. Suppose that we take a sample of just three observations ($n = 3$) and get two 8s and a 6. The complete relative frequency distribution for this sample is given in Table 9.3. Although the relative frequencies in this table differ greatly in magnitude from the probabilities in Table 9.1, we are not greatly surprised that this is the situation in such a small sample. (Note that with $n = 3$, at least one of the four f_k values must be zero. This sample could not possibly be summarized by the frequency distribution in Table 9.4, in which no f_k is zero.)

Now suppose that we take a sample of 100 observations from the same random variable X and that the relative frequency distribution for this sample is given in Table 9.4. Although the f_k values are not equal to the corresponding $p(X_k)$ values of the probability distribution, they are quite similar. This is in accord with commonsense expectations. By contrast, we would be greatly surprised if the frequency distribution turned out to be the one in Table 9.3: this would mean that we got thirty-three 6s and sixty-seven 8s. This would surely be an unlikely result, but we should realize that our understanding of the balls-in-hat game does not preclude it from occurring.

Three general ideas emerge from this thinking. First, we realize that the relative frequency values f_k, which describe a sample of data taken from a random variable, cannot be expected to be identical to the corresponding probability values $p(X_k)$.

TABLE 9.3 First Relative Frequency Distribution

k	X_k	f_k
1	5	.00
2	6	.33
3	7	.00
4	8	.67

TABLE 9.4 Second Relative Frequency Distribution

k	X_k	f_k
1	5	.11
2	6	.18
3	7	.33
4	8	.38

Second, we expect that the similarity between the relative frequency values and the corresponding probability values will tend to be greater in large samples than in small samples.

Third, we expect that the frequency distributions for two samples of the same size, taken from the same random variable, will be similar to each other but probably somewhat different. This difference illustrates the phenomenon of *sampling variability*, which is very important.

Now, consider taking a sample from some random variable X. It can be shown that as the size of the sample approaches infinity, the relative frequency f_k associated with each possible value X_k approaches some limiting amount. In the limit, each f_k is equal to the corresponding $p(X_k)$. That is, the relative frequencies for an infinite sample will be equal to the corresponding probabilities of the random variable. (Also, in the limit, $\overline{X}$ in the sample equals μ_X, and S_X in the sample equals σ_X.)

Turning this idea around, we now have a way of defining what we mean by "probability": the probability of X_k occurring as the value of X is given by the proportion of observations that would take on the value X_k in an infinite sample. In other words, an infinite historical record of the various numbers produced by X informs us about what to expect regarding the value produced on any single occurrence. Although this is not a practical way to determine the probabilities characterizing a process, it helps us understand what "probability" means. Also, we might be willing to accept the relative frequencies calculated in a large sample as estimates of the underlying probabilities.

An alternative approach to conceptualizing how we determine probabilities is based on making an a priori analysis of the process. For the balls-in-hat game, a thorough understanding of the laws of physics, coupled with a careful examination of the materials and the procedure, would allow us to determine the probability values. In the preceding section we used logic and common sense in lieu of this scientific approach.

In this chapter and the next, our attention is focused on learning about the nature of random variables and their probability distributions. Later in the book we again will be concerned with the relation between random variables and samples of data.

9.3 The Binomial Distribution _____

It is possible for a group of different random variables to be related to each other in such a way that their probability distributions share a common mathematical form. Under certain circumstances their distributions might be recognized as being members of a particular *family.*

One of the most important families of discrete distributions is that of the *binomial distribution.* This family is built up from combinations of a basic chance process known as a *Bernoulli trial* (named after the mathematician James Bernoulli). Each Bernoulli trial is a process that has only two possible outcomes: either a "success" or a "failure." In any trial the probability of a success occurring is denoted by P, and therefore the probability of a failure is $1 - P$. In a series of trials the probability of a success remains fixed at P, so the outcomes of the trials are independent: the previous history of successes or failures does not affect the probability of success in any given trial. For example, flipping a coin can be described as a Bernoulli trial, with the probability of getting "heads" (a success, say) being P. If the coin is physically symmetrical, the laws of physics tell us that $P = .5$; if the coin is specially weighted, it might be that $P = .6$.

Now suppose that we are going to examine the results of a series of n Bernoulli trials. Let X be the number of successes that occur over this whole series. Clearly, the minimum number of successes is 0 and the maximum is n. Also, X can take on any integer value between 0 and n, so X is discrete. A statement of the probability distribution of X consists of a list of the possibly occurring values of X and the probabilities that X will take on each of these values. It can be shown mathematically that this probability distribution is given by

$$p(X) = \frac{n!}{X! \, (n - X)!} \, (P)^X (1 - P)^{n-X}, \quad X = 0, 1, 2, \ldots, n \qquad (9.13)$$

In this notation, the exclamation mark stands for the factorial operation, which specifies that the given integer is to be multiplied by all the lower positive integers. Thus, $5! = (5)(4)(3)(2)(1)$, for example. By special definition, $0! = 1$. [In (9.13), the ratio of factorials gives the number of ways of getting exactly X successes in n independent trials, and the other terms give the probability of one of those ways occurring.]

For example, suppose that we think of tossing a fair coin six times and that we are interested in the number of heads that might occur. Each toss is a Bernoulli trial with $P = 1/2$. Let Y denote the number of heads. Clearly, Y is a random variable having a binomial distribution with $n = 6$ and $P = 1/2$. Using (9.13), we can compute the probability of each specific number of heads occurring; for example, the probability of getting exactly 2 heads in the 6 tosses is

$$p(2) = \frac{6!}{2! \, 4!} \left(\frac{1}{2}\right)^2 \left(\frac{1}{2}\right)^4 = \frac{(6)(5)(4)(3)(2)(1)}{(2)(1)(4)(3)(2)(1)} \left(\frac{1}{2}\right)^2 \left(\frac{1}{2}\right)^4 = \frac{15}{64} \qquad (9.14)$$

The complete probability distribution of Y is given in Table 9.2 and Figure 9.2, which we considered earlier without knowing its origin.

In general, it can be shown that if $P = .5$, the graphed probability distribution is symmetrical around the midpoint of the range of X values. If $P < .5$, there is a tendency for relatively low values of X to occur more frequently, so that the distribution is skewed with a tail to the right. If $P > .5$, the distribution is skewed to the left. When n is large, the distribution appears to be fairly symmetrical even if $P \neq .5$, as long as P is not extremely small or large; however, if $P \neq .5$, this fairly symmetrical distribution is not centered at the middle of the range of X.

A particular binomial distribution can be summarized by its mean and standard deviation. These can be calculated according to (9.10) and (9.12), as in Table 9.2. However, for a binomially distributed random variable, it turns out that the exact mean and standard deviation also are given by

$$\mu_X = nP \tag{9.15}$$

and

$$\sigma_X = \sqrt{nP(1 - P)} \tag{9.16}$$

For example, in the series of 6 tosses of a fair coin, the mean of Y (i.e., the expected number of heads) is $(6)(1/2) = 3$, and the standard deviation is $\sqrt{(6)(1/2)(1/2)} = 1.22$. It should be noted that these values are the same as those calculated in Table 9.2.

The binomial distribution is not frequently used in econometrics, although it is quite important in other applications of statistics. Nonetheless, this and similar distributions do play an important role in some types of economic analysis, such as search theory. For example, consider the situation of an unemployed worker who plans to look for a job for 5 weeks. Suppose that the probability of getting a job offer in any week is .3, that this probability is not affected by the results in previous weeks, and that not more than one offer is received in any week. Given all this, a week's search is a Bernoulli trial. Let X be the number of offers that the searcher gets in the five-week period. Clearly, X is a random variable having a binomial distribution with $n = 5$ and $P = .3$. For the worker, the expected number of job offers is 1.5. However, it is possible that no offers will be received, and the probability of this occurring is computed from (9.13) as

$$p(0) = \frac{5!}{0!5!}(.3)^0(.7)^5 = .1681 \tag{9.17}$$

The complete probability distribution, with each value similarly computed from (9.13), is given in Table 9.5 and Figure 9.3.

TABLE 9.5　Distribution of the Number of Job Offers

k	X_k	$p(X_k)$
1	0	.1681
2	1	.3602
3	2	.3087
4	3	.1323
5	4	.0284
6	5	.0024

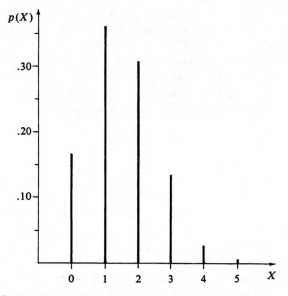

FIGURE 9.3 The discrete random variable X is the number of job offers received by a searcher in a five-week period. As discussed, X has a binomial distribution with $n = 5$ and $P = .3$; in this distribution, $\mu_X = 1.5$ and $\sigma_X = 1.02$. Since $P < .5$, the distribution is skewed with a tail to the right.

Suppose now that a large group of unemployed workers all face the same situation as the worker just discussed, so that the random variable X applies to each of them. In this case, the experience of the group constitutes a sample from the random variable. Based on our previous results, we predict that about 17 percent of workers searching for a job for five weeks would not get even one job offer.

9.4 Continuous Random Variables _____

A *continuous random variable* is one for which the possible values that might occur are all the real numbers in some interval. This interval might be of fixed length, or it might extend to infinity. In either case, an uncountably infinite number of possible values can occur. We maintain the idea that a random variable represents a chance process that can generate an unlimited number of independent values, one after another.

As in the case of a discrete random variable, all the probability information about a continuous random variable X is given by its probability distribution, which has two important components. The first is a statement $\{X\}$ of the possibly occurring values, and the second is a function $p(X)$ that gives information about probabilities. Both of these components differ from those for discrete random variables.

For example, consider the activity of shooting arrows for distance, in the sport of archery. Let X be the distance that an arrow travels in an open field. For a particular archer, suppose that the arrow never travels less than X_{min} nor more than X_{max}. In this case, the range of possibly occurring values $\{X\}$ can be stated as $X_{min} \leq X \leq X_{max}$. Notice that the possible values of X are specified as an interval of numbers, rather than as a list.

Providing information about probabilities is more difficult here than for discrete random variables. To appreciate the difficulty, consider how we might determine the probability that X will take on the particular value X_k. In the case in which each of the infinite number of possible values for X has an equally likely chance of occurring, we would think that the probability of X_k occurring is $1/\infty$, which is zero. Although this seems odd, it makes sense: with an infinite number of possible values for X, there is essentially no chance that any one of them will be the exact value that occurs. Similar logic extends to cases in which the possible values are not equally likely, and so we accept the notion that for a continuous random variable the probability of any particular value occurring is zero: $Pr(X = X_k) = 0$. Since this statement does not provide useful or interesting information, we no longer focus on this type of probability.

Instead, the basic probability concept for continuous random variables relates to the occurrence of an event defined as the value of X being in some specific interval. For example, we might be concerned with $Pr(X \geq 50)$. Since $Pr(X = 50) = 0$, it follows that $Pr(X \geq 50) = Pr(X > 50)$, so either inequality notation can be used. This generalizes to all probability statements for continuous random variables. [Note that for discrete random variables $Pr(X \geq 50) \neq Pr(X > 50)$ if $p(50) > 0$.]

Our task now is to understand how information about probabilities for a random variable can be provided by a function $p(X)$. To help with this, first think of taking a large sample from the random variable. If we watch an archer shoot all day and record the distances, we have such a sample. These data can be presented in a relative frequency histogram, as in Figure 9.4a. If our attention were focused on the occurrence of values between X_3 and X_4, we could compute $Prop(X_3 \leq X \leq X_4)$, using a method presented in Chapter 4. As discussed there, this proportion is given by the ratio of the shaded area to the total area under the histogram.

Now, if the sample were very large, we could categorize the data into many narrow intervals. With an extremely large number of intervals, the outline of the resulting histogram would suggest a fairly smooth relation between f_k and X, as in Figure 9.4b, rather than a jagged sequence of steps. As before, the proportion of values that occurred in any interval of X would be given by the corresponding shaded area divided by the total area in the histogram.

We can extend this thinking to the theoretical case of an infinite sample. As discussed in Section 9.2 for discrete random variables, an infinite historical record of the values generated by X informs us about what to expect on any future occurrence. For the continuous case, this suggests that the probability of X occurring in some specific interval is equal to the proportion of observations in

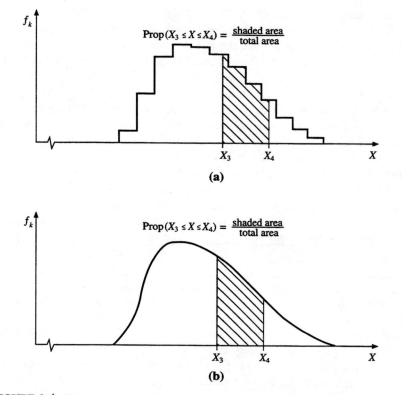

FIGURE 9.4 For samples of data from a continuous random variable, the height f_k in the histogram shows the proportion of values occurring in each class interval. Part (a) shows the histogram for a large sample whose values are categorized into twelve classes. Part (b) shows the histogram for a sample that is so large that the width of each interval can be made very narrow, resulting in an apparently smooth top to the histogram. As explained in Chapter 4, Prop($X_3 \leq X \leq X_4$) is given by the ratio of the shaded area to the total area in each case.

an infinite sample that would occur in this interval. Although we do not actually collect information in this way, we can still use these ideas as the basis for thinking about what a probability distribution is.

The method for organizing information about probabilities for a continuous random variable is analogous to the method for categorizing data into a histogram. Information about probabilities is given by a ***probability density function*** $p(X)$. This function can be thought of as being defined from the smooth relation between f_k and X that would be shown by the histogram for an infinite sample from the random variable. The heights $p(X)$ are proportional to the corresponding f_k, and they are scaled so that the area under $p(X)$ equals 1.

When information about probabilities is presented as the graph of a probability density function, probabilities correspond to areas—just as proportions correspond to areas in a histogram. For example, suppose that Figure 9.5a gives

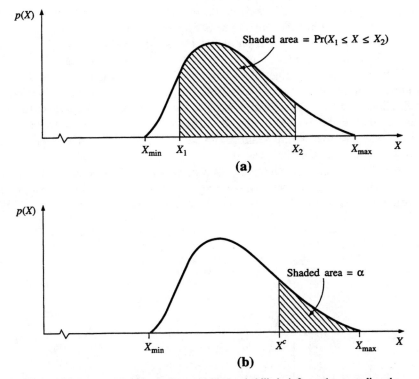

FIGURE 9.5 For a continuous random variable, probabilistic information regarding the random variable is contained in a probability density function (or probability distribution). The same distribution is graphed in (a) and (b). In both, the total area under $p(X)$, from X_{min} to X_{max}, is equal to 1, as must be true for any density function. In (a), the shaded area gives $\Pr(X_1 \leq X \leq X_2)$. In (b), the shaded area is specified to be an amount α, and this determines the value X^c such that $\Pr(X \geq X^c) = \alpha$.

$p(X)$ for a particular archer. Then, the probability that the value of X will occur between X_1 and X_2 is given by the shaded area under $p(X)$ lying above the interval. That is,

$$\Pr(X_1 \leq X \leq X_2) = \text{shaded area} \tag{9.18}$$

There is no need to relate the shaded area to the total area, because the total area equals 1. Calculation of this probability is not usually an easy task: calculus is needed to find areas, except in some cases where simple geometry is sufficient.

Similarly, suppose that we want to determine the value X^c such that

$$\Pr(X \geq X^c) = \alpha \tag{9.19}$$

where α is a given probability amount, $0 \leq \alpha \leq 1$ (α is lowercase "alpha," the Greek "a"). That is, suppose that we want to find the specific value X^c such that the probability that the value of the random variable X will be greater than or equal to X^c is α. The X^c value is determined from the probability density function $p(X)$, as illustrated in Figure 9.5b: the X^c we seek is the value that bounds exactly α area to the right of itself under the curve.

In order to provide an example that permits computation, consider the activity of shooting arrows at a target placed on a wall. Let X be the horizontal distance from the center of the target to where the arrow hits, with positive values indicating distance to the right and negative values indicating distance to the left. Suppose that no hit is ever farther from the center than 1 meter (left or right). Further, suppose that we are dealing with a good archer who is more likely to hit close to the center than far away.

We can formalize this description in a particular case by considering X to be a continuous random variable whose probability density function is graphed in Figure 9.6a. As described, the range of possible values is $-1 \leq X \leq 1$. We

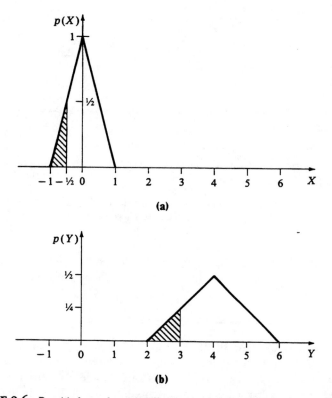

(a)

(b)

FIGURE 9.6   Part (a) shows the probability density function of a continuous random variable X that measures the distance from the center for outcomes of a specific target-shooting activity. In this distribution, $\mu_X = 0$ and $\sigma_X = 0.4$, roughly. The shaded area gives $\Pr(X \leq -1/2)$. Part (b) shows the probability distribution (i.e., density function) of Y, which is defined as a linear transformation of X: $Y = 4 + 2X$. The graph of $p(Y)$ is obtained from $p(X)$ by expanding $p(X)$ by a factor of 2 and then moving the result four units to the right. The shaded area gives $\Pr(Y \leq 3)$, which is equal to $\Pr(X \leq -1/2)$.

suppose that the inverted-V shape of $p(X)$ is the appropriate specification for this particular archer. Since the total area under $p(X)$ must be equal to 1, simple geometry implies that the peak height $p(0)$ is also equal to 1 in this case. Although the various heights of $p(X)$ can be determined geometrically, we can represent $p(X)$ in equation form:

$$p(X) = 1 - |X| \quad \text{for } -1 \leq X \leq 1 \tag{9.20}$$

Thus, for example, $p(.35) = .65$ and $p(-.75) = .25$.

Determining probabilities for this random variable demands only that we know that the area of a triangle is equal to one-half its base times its height. For example, general principles tell us that the probability that the arrow will land farther than 1/2 meter to the left of the target's center, $\Pr(-1 \leq X \leq -1/2)$, is given by the shaded triangular area in Figure 9.6a. A simple geometric calculation leads us to see that this area equals 1/8. More complex problems can be broken down into problems based on triangles, or other geometric calculations can be made. For example, with a little manipulation we can find that $\Pr(-1/2 \leq X \leq 1/2) = 3/4$, so there is a 75 percent chance that the arrow will land within 1/2 meter of the center. Somewhat more manipulation allows us to work with a problem like (9.19): the X^c value such that $\Pr(X \geq X^c) = .18$ is found to be $X^c = .4$ (in this case X^c is found after we realize that the triangle to the right of X^c must have a base and height of .6).

Now we turn to some general considerations regarding continuous random variables. First, two important aspects of the probability density function for any continuous random variable should be noted: (1) $p(X) > 0$ for any value in $\{X\}$, and (2) the area under the graph of $p(X)$ lying above the whole range $\{X\}$ is exactly equal to 1. These two aspects of $p(X)$ are analogous to $p(X_k) > 0$ and $\sum p(X_k) = 1$ for discrete random variables.

Second, it is important to contrast the information given by the function $p(X)$ for a continuous random variable with that given by $p(X)$ for a discrete one. Whereas for a discrete random variable $p(X_k)$ is the probability associated with the value X_k, this is not so in the present case: for a continuous random variable, $p(X_k)$ does *not* give $\Pr(X = X_k)$, because that probability is equal to zero. Note also that whereas $p(X_k) \leq 1$ for a discrete random variable, $p(X_k)$ may be greater than 1 for a continuous random variable. For example, if an inverted-V density function similar to that in Figure 9.6a covered only the interval $-1/2 \leq X \leq 1/2$, the height at the center would have to be $p(0) = 2$ for the total area to be 1.

What can be said about $p(X)$ here? For a continuous random variable X, we say that $p(X_k)$ gives the **likelihood** of X_k occurring. The numerical value of this likelihood makes sense only when it is compared with the likelihood for another value of X, because this allows us to make a statement about probabilities. For example, in Figure 9.5a it appears that $p(X_1)$ is twice as high as $p(X_2)$. The information in $p(X)$ allows us to say that it is twice as likely that the value of X will be near X_1 as it is that the value will be near X_2. To see why this is so and to understand what this means, think of constructing two small intervals of the same width around X_1 and X_2. The areas of the thin bars above these intervals give the probabilities of X being in the intervals. Since the two bars have equal widths, a ratio comparison of their areas is the same as a ratio comparison of their heights, $p(X_1)$ and $p(X_2)$. Putting this in reverse, the ratio of one height to another is equal to the ratio of the probability of being near one value of X to the probability of being near the other.

This concept of likelihood allows us to talk about $p(X)$ in a simple yet meaningful way. For example, we can describe Figure 9.6a by saying that the most likely value for X is zero and that the likelihood of different values occurring for X decreases linearly with the distance of X from zero.

Third, just as the histogram of sample values can be summarized by the mean $\overline{X}$ and standard deviation S_X, so too the density function $p(X)$ can be summarized by a mean μ_X and standard deviation σ_X. For continuous random variables, the definitions of μ and σ are given by calculus expressions (integrals) that are analogous to (9.10) and (9.12). As stated in Section 9.2, it can be shown that the mean μ_X of a random variable is equal to the mean $\overline{X}$ of the values in an infinite sample drawn from the random variable. Similarly, the standard deviation σ_X of a random variable is equal to the standard deviation S_X of the values in an infinite sample. For the case of the inverted-V distribution in Figure 9.6a, the mean of X is obviously 0, and the standard deviation looks as though it might be between 1/3 and 1/2. (Calculus is required for the exact determination; it turns out that $\sigma_X = \sqrt{1/6} \approx 0.4$.)

Fourth, recall that every probability distribution has two components: a statement $\{X\}$ of the values that X might ever take on and a function $p(X)$ giving probability information. To economize on terminology and notation, we sometimes refer to the function $p(X)$ simply as "the probability distribution," both in the discrete and continuous cases. So long as $\{X\}$ is specified explicitly or implicitly, this should cause no confusion. Also, in the continuous case this allows us to refer to $p(X)$ as either the "probability distribution" or the "density function."

Finally, the concept of a *family* of probability distributions, which was introduced in Section 9.3, also applies in the continuous case. For example, different archers have different styles and abilities, but it could be that a group of archers have a common mathematical form for the probability distributions that characterize their activity. For instance, it might be that a group of archers are known as "inverted-V" archers, because the probability distribution of X for any one of them is given by

$$p(X) = \frac{1}{h} - \frac{1}{h^2}|X - c| \quad \text{for } c - h \leq X \leq c + h \tag{9.21}$$

where X is the distance from the center of the target, $h > 0$, and c can be any value. The graph of this equation is an inverted V with a center at c and a base of $2h$ (so that h is half the base). Each archer in the group is characterized by a particular combination of values for the c and h parameters. The archer of Figure 9.6a has $c = 0$ and $h = 1$, and the archer of Figure 9.6b has $c = 4$ and $h = 2$.

9.5 Transformations

Suppose that we have a random variable X and know its probability distribution $p(X)$. Given this, we can create a new random variable Y by transforming X according to some fixed rule, as we did with data variables, and we can determine the new probability distribution $p(Y)$.

A useful class of transformations is that of linear transformations, whose general form is

$$Y_k = a + bX_k \qquad (9.22)$$

This transformation establishes a one-to-one correspondence between Y_k and X_k values, unless $b = 0$, and it leads to an important equivalence between probabilities defined for the original and transformed random variables. This equivalence applies somewhat differently in discrete and continuous cases.

For discrete random variables related by (9.22), the transformation relabels the possible values of X, but it does not affect the probabilities of their occurring. In other words, the probability equivalence is that $\Pr(Y = Y_k) = \Pr(X = X_k)$ for Y_k and X_k related through (9.22). In graphical terms, $p(Y)$ is obtained from $p(X)$ by horizontally compressing (for $|b| < 1$) or expanding (for $|b| > 1$) the distribution and then shifting it to the left or right; the heights of all the vertical lines remain the same. (If $b < 0$, there is also a change of order.) For example, starting with the random variable X described by Figure 9.7a and Table 9.1, the transformation $Y = -1 + (1/2)X$ yields a new random variable whose probability distribution $p(Y)$ is given in Figure 9.7b and Table 9.6.

For continuous random variables related by the linear transformation (9.22), the situation is similar: $p(Y)$ is obtained from $p(X)$ by horizontally compressing (for $|b| < 1$) or expanding (for $|b| > 1$) the distribution and then shifting it to the left or right. (If $b < 0$, there is also a change of order.) However, since the area under all density functions must equal unity, compression will cause all the $p(Y)$ values to be proportionately greater than the corresponding $p(X)$ values, and

TABLE 9.6 Probability Distribution of Y [$Y = -1 + (1/2)X$]

k	Y_k	$p(Y_k)$
1	1.5	.1
2	2.0	.2
3	2.5	.3
4	3.0	.4

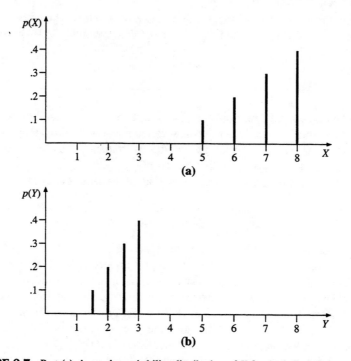

FIGURE 9.7   Part (a) shows the probability distribution of X for the balls-in-hat example of Section 9.1. Part (b) shows $p(Y)$, where Y is defined by the linear transformation $Y = -1 + (1/2)X$. To obtain $p(Y)$ graphically, $p(X)$ is compressed and then shifted to the left. With discrete random variables related through a linear transformation, the probability associated with a particular X_k is also associated with the corresponding Y_{k-}. Thus the heights $p(\cdot)$ are preserved.

expansion will cause all of them to be proportionately smaller. For example, starting with the random variable X whose probability distribution is given in Figure 9.6a, the transformation $Y = 4 + 2X$ yields a new random variable whose probability distribution is given in Figure 9.6b. Notice that in going from X to Y, the width of the probability distribution has been expanded by a factor of 2 and all the corresponding heights have been cut in half.

For continuous random variables, the probability equivalence is that the probability associated with Y being in a certain interval of Y values is equal to the probability of X being in the corresponding interval of X values. In other words, if Y_k corresponds to X_k through (9.22), then $\Pr(Y \le Y_k) = \Pr(X \le X_k)$. Applying this to the distributions in Figure 9.6, suppose that we are interested in determining $\Pr(Y \le 3)$. (Although we could determine this directly by computing the triangular shaded area, we shall determine it indirectly by probability equivalence.) We see that the X_k value that corresponds to any Y_k is found by solving (9.22) for X_k:

$$X_k = \frac{Y_k - a}{b} \qquad (9.23)$$

In this case, starting with $Y_k = 3$ we find the corresponding $X_k = (3 - 4)/2 = -1/2$. Now, in Section 9.4 we determined that $\Pr(X \le -1/2) = 1/8$; since $\Pr(Y \le 3)$ is equivalent to $\Pr(X \le -1/2)$, this 1/8 is the answer we seek.

For both discrete and continuous random variables, the discussion above explains how the complete probability distribution $p(Y)$ can be determined from the original probability distribution of X and the parameters a and b in (9.22). Once $p(Y)$ is determined, we could use basic definitions to determine its mean, variance, and standard deviation. However, these summary characteristics of Y can be determined from the corresponding characteristics of X, without even determining the complete $p(Y)$, by knowing that

$$\mu_Y = a + b\mu_X \qquad (9.24)$$

$$\sigma_Y^2 = b^2 \sigma_X^2 \qquad (9.25)$$

$$\sigma_Y = |b|\sigma_X \qquad (9.26)$$

These relations, whose proofs follow along lines similar to the corresponding results for data variables in Section 3.2, are often useful to us. For example, the mean and standard deviation of the discrete random variable Y described in Table 9.6 can be determined directly from that probability distribution. However, once μ_X and σ_X are determined (a task that has been left as a problem), it would be easier to determine μ_Y and σ_Y from the relations $\mu_Y = -1 + (1/2)\mu_X$ and $\sigma_Y = (1/2)\sigma_X$ than from applying basic definitions to Table 9.6.

APPENDIX

This appendix extends the discussion of random variables and probability distributions to cases involving two or more random variables.

Joint Probability Distributions

Our concept of a single random variable likens it to a number-generating process whose values are governed by the probability distribution of the random variable. Now we can think of a more complex process that produces two numbers simultaneously. A gambling activity that serves as an example is throwing a pair of dice, one red and the other green. A second example is the economic process that determines a person's earnings (labor income) and wealth at a particular time. The key idea in both cases is that two numbers are produced, but that they are separately identifiable. In the first example, one number is red and the other green; in the second, one is earnings and the other wealth. Although in each example the two numbers are separately identifiable, they are jointly determined: the number-generating process produces the two numbers simultaneously. Were we to draw a sample from this process, each pair of simultaneously produced numbers would constitute an observation.

To generalize, we can think of a number-generating process that determines jointly two separately identifiable numbers, which are values of the random variables Y and X. The overall statement that describes the likelihood that different combinations of Y and X values will be produced is called the *joint probability distribution* of Y and X. This joint distribution can be presented as a mathematical equation, a three-dimensional figure, or (in the case of discrete Y and X) a table. The actual representation is not important to us, but we can denote it by $p(Y, X)$. For discrete Y and X, the joint distribution $p(Y, X)$ gives the probability of occurrence for each possible combination of Y and X values.

Although Y and X are jointly determined, it is possible to focus on one of the variables, such as Y. Since Y is a random variable, it has a regular (univariate) probability distribution $p(Y)$ that describes the probability or likelihood that Y will take on different values. This distribution has a mean μ_Y and variance σ_Y^2. It turns out that the exact specification of $p(Y)$ can be determined from the joint distribution $p(Y, X)$ if that is given. Similarly, from the joint distribution $p(Y, X)$ it is possible to determine the probability distribution of X alone, $p(X)$, along with its mean μ_X and variance σ_X^2. In the context of thinking that Y and X are jointly determined in a process described by $p(Y, X)$, the regular (univariate) distributions $p(Y)$ and $p(X)$ are known as *marginal probability distributions* because they can be displayed easily in the margins of a table that gives the joint distribution (for a discrete random variable).

A numerical example will help make these fundamental ideas clearer. Let Y and X be two jointly determined discrete random variables; we will not consider what physical or economic process they represent. The possible values $\{X\}$ are 5 and 10, and the possible values $\{Y\}$ are 4, 5, and 6. The joint distribution $p(Y, X)$ is shown in Figure 9.8, along with the marginal distributions. Each entry in the joint distribution is the probability that a specific pair of Y and X values will

$p(Y, X)$

Y \ X	5	10	
4	.15	.05	.20
5	.10	.30	.40
6	.05	.35	.40
	.30	.70	

X	$p(X)$
5	.30
10	.70

Y	$p(Y)$
4	.20
5	.40
6	.40

FIGURE 9.8 The left side of this figure displays the joint probability distribution $p(Y, X)$ for two discrete random variables. On the right side are the marginal probability distributions for X and for Y, which are shown also as the column and row sums, respectively, in the joint distribution.

occur. For example, the probability that the pair $(Y = 5, X = 10)$ occurs is 30 percent. Notice that the marginal probabilities for Y are simply the row sums in the joint distribution. For example, the event that Y equals 5 corresponds both to the pair $(Y = 5, X = 5)$ and the pair $(Y = 5, X = 10)$; hence $p(Y)$ for $Y = 5$ is the sum of the two probabilities in the joint distribution. Similarly, the marginal probabilities for X are simply the column sums in the joint distribution.

Now, it is also possible to focus on what would be the probability distribution of Y if X takes on a specific value X_k. This distribution, which is denoted by $p(Y|X_k)$, is known as the **conditional probability distribution** of Y (i.e., the probability distribution of Y conditional on a specific value for X). In the case of dice tossing, the conditional distributions of Y (the red value) for the different possible values of X (the green value) are all exactly the same as the unconditional (marginal) probability distribution $p(Y)$. This is because the physics of tossing fair dice tells us that whatever happens to the green die has no effect on what happens to the red die. Hence, the likelihood of different values occurring on the red die is not affected by the actual value on the green die. In our new terminology, this means that the conditional probability distributions for Y, $p(Y|X_k)$, are all identical to the unconditional (marginal) probability distribution for Y, $p(Y)$. By contrast, the likelihood of a person's receiving various possible levels of earnings (Y) is probably related to how much wealth (X) the person has; the economic process is probably such that persons with considerable amounts of wealth have a greater chance also to have high levels of earnings. Hence, at least some of the conditional probability distributions of earnings, $p(Y|X_k)$, for different levels of wealth (X_k) are different from each other and different from $p(Y)$, the unconditional probability distribution of earnings.

Suppose that Y and X are two random variables having a joint probability distribution $p(Y, X)$. If all the conditional distributions $p(Y|X_k)$ are identical to each other, so that the likelihood of different values occurring for Y is not at all affected by the X value that is simultaneously determined, then Y and X are **independent.** In the case of tossing a pair of dice, Y (the red value) and X (the green value) are independent. On the other hand, if not all the conditional distributions $p(Y|X_k)$ are identical to each other, so that the likelihood of different values occurring for Y may be affected by the X value that is simultaneously determined, then Y and X are not independent. In the joint determination of earnings and wealth, Y (earnings) and X (wealth) are not independent.

In the example of Figure 9.8, the conditional probability distributions for Y are denoted by $p(Y|X = 5)$ and $p(Y|X = 10)$. When $X = 5$ the most likely value for Y is 4; when $X = 10$ the most likely value for Y is 6. Since the value that would occur for Y is affected by the value of X with which it is jointly determined, Y and X are not independent. [The conditional distribution $p(Y|X = 5)$ is obtained from the first column of the joint distribution by dividing each of the three entries by $p(X)$ for $X = 5$. Since that $p(X)$ value is obtained marginally by adding up the probabilities in the first column, the effect of dividing each of the entries in the first column by the $p(X)$ value for that column is to make the sum of the "new entries" equal to 1.]

A measure of the relation, or dependence, between two random variables having the joint distribution $p(Y, X)$ is given by the **covariance** between them. For the discrete case,

$$\sigma_{YX} = \sigma(Y, X) = \Sigma(Y - \mu_Y)(X - \mu_X)p(Y, X) \qquad (9.27)$$

This is a somewhat cumbersome calculation and we do not dwell on it. Suffice it to say that the covariance σ_{YX} between two random variables is the theoretical analog of the covariance S_{YX} between two data variables. As might be expected, one can define the **correlation** between two random variables:

$$\rho_{YX} = \frac{\sigma_{YX}}{\sigma_Y \sigma_X} \qquad (9.28)$$

where ρ is the theoretical analog of the correlation coefficient r between two data variables (ρ is lowercase "rho," the Greek "r"). If two random variables are independent, the covariance between them is zero and therefore so is the correlation. However, the converse of this statement is not always true: if the covariance and correlation between two jointly determined random variables is zero, it is not necessarily true that they are independent.

All the basic ideas presented here are symmetrical. There are conditional distributions $p(X|Y_k)$ of the same nature as the $p(Y|X_k)$ discussed above, $\sigma_{XY} = \sigma_{YX}$, and independence is a mutual relation—Y cannot be independent of X without X being independent of Y.

These concepts regarding jointly determined random variables can be extended to any number of separately identifiable numbers occurring simultaneously. We can denote the different random variables as $X_1, X_2, \ldots, X_n$ and consider that their values are governed by a joint probability distribution $p(X_1, X_2, \ldots, X_n)$. This distribution is characterized in part by n means, n variances, and $(n^2 - n)/2$ different covariances. All covariances are pairwise relations, and there is no similar concept that encompasses more than two variables together. If all the n variables are pairwise independent, the value occurring for any one has no effect on the likelihood of different values occurring for any of the others and all the covariances are zero.

Linear Combinations

Sometimes we might want to define a new random variable, say W, in terms of two random variables Y and X that have a joint distribution $p(Y, X)$. One of the possible ways in which W might be defined in terms of X and Y is as a linear combination of the general form

$$W = a_1 Y + a_2 X \qquad (9.29)$$

For example, if Y and X are the numbers on the red and green dice, $W = Y + X$ (i.e., $a_1 = 1$, $a_2 = 1$) is a variable that gives the sum of the values. If Y and X are earnings and wealth, and if 0.07 is the annual rate of return to wealth, then $W = Y + 0.07X$ (i.e., $a_1 = 1$, $a_2 = 0.07$) is a variable giving total annual income.

Since W is a random variable, it has a (univariate) probability distribution $p(W)$ that describes the probability or likelihood of its taking on various values. The exact form of $p(W)$ depends on the joint distribution $p(Y, X)$ and the linear combination defining W. Determining $p(W)$ can be very complex. However, $p(W)$ is a genuine distribution with mean μ_W and variance σ_W^2, and these two summary characteristics are nicely related to the characteristics of $p(Y, X)$. It turns out that

$$\mu_W = a_1\mu_Y + a_2\mu_X \tag{9.30}$$

$$\sigma_W^2 = (a_1)^2\sigma_Y^2 + (a_2)^2\sigma_X^2 + 2(a_1)(a_2)\sigma_{YX} \tag{9.31}$$

If Y and X are independent, the covariance between Y and X is zero, and therefore the last term in (9.31) is equal to zero. In the example of the dice, $\mu_W = \mu_Y + \mu_X$ and $\sigma_W^2 = \sigma_Y^2 + \sigma_X^2$ because Y and X are independent. In the earnings and wealth example, $\mu_W = \mu_Y + 0.07\mu_X$ and $\sigma_W^2 > \sigma_Y^2 + 0.0049\sigma_X^2$, assuming it is true that labor income and wealth are positively related (i.e., $\sigma_{YX} > 0$).

Extending these ideas to the special case of n independent random variables having a joint distribution $p(X_1, X_2, \ldots, X_n)$ with all covariances equal to zero, we can consider a linear combination

$$W = a_1X_1 + a_2X_2 + \cdots + a_nX_n = \sum_{j=1}^{n} a_jX_j \tag{9.32}$$

It turns out that the means are related as

$$\mu_W = a_1\mu_1 + a_2\mu_2 + \cdots + a_n\mu_n = \sum_{j=1}^{n} a_j\mu_j \tag{9.33}$$

and (in the case of independence) the variances as

$$\sigma_W^2 = (a_1)^2\sigma_1^2 + (a_2)^2\sigma_2^2 + \cdots + (a_n)^2\sigma_n^2 = \sum_{j=1}^{n}(a_j)^2\sigma_j^2 \tag{9.34}$$

where μ_j is the mean of X_j and σ_j^2 is the variance of X_j.

This analysis of linear combinations will be an important element in the derivation of certain results later in the book. Outside the field of statistics, it is also used in economics and finance to determine features of the probability distribution of the return to a mutual fund when the fund is made up of stocks whose return is uncertain.

Problems

Section 9.1

9.1 For the random variable X described in Table 9.1, determine
(a) $\Pr(X = 6)$.
(b) $\Pr(X \leq 6)$.
(c) $\Pr(X \geq 7)$.
(d) $\Pr(6 \leq X \leq 8)$.

9.2 For the random variable Y described in Table 9.2, determine
(a) $\Pr(Y = 2)$.
(b) $\Pr(Y \leq 2)$.
(c) $\Pr(Y \geq 3)$.
(d) $\Pr(2 \leq Y \leq 4)$.

★ **9.3** Consider "$p(Y_k) = Y_k/20$ for $Y = 1, 2, 3, 4, 5, 6$." Could this be the probability distribution of a random variable? If so, graph the distribution.

9.4 Consider "$p(X_k) = (X_k)^2/10$ for $X = -2, -1, 0, 1, 2$." Could this be the probability distribution of a random variable? If so, graph the distribution.

★ **9.5** Calculate the mean and standard deviation of X, the random variable defined in Table 9.1.

★ **9.6** Let X be the outcome on the toss of a fair die. Construct the probability distribution of X and determine its mean and standard deviation.

9.7 In the balls-in-hat game, if the first two balls drawn are 7s and if they are not replaced after being drawn, what is the probability of getting a 7 on the third draw?

9.8 Suppose that X takes on the value 1 with probability P and the value 0 with probability $(1 - P)$. Determine the mean and variance of X.

Section 9.2

9.9 Consider the process of flipping a single coin. Let $X = 1$ if a head occurs, and let $X = 0$ if a tail occurs. For a fair coin, $\Pr(X = 0) = 1/2$ and $\Pr(X = 1) = 1/2$. Based on this information, construct a table that gives the probability distribution of X. Now, flip a real coin 10 times, thereby taking a sample from X. Construct a relative frequency distribution table for this sample and compare it with the probability distribution of X.

9.10 Extending Problem 9.9, flip a fair coin 10 more times and construct a relative frequency table for this sample. Compare it with the relative frequency distribution from Problem 9.9.

* **9.11** Continuing with coin flipping from Problem 9.9, let $X = 2$ if the coin lands on its edge. Suppose that $\Pr(X = 2) = 1/1000$. Is the frequency distribution determined for a particular sample likely to be identical to the probability distribution of X?

9.12 Construct the relative frequency distributions that might reasonably describe two different samples of size 5 taken from the random variable X defined in Table 9.1.

9.13 Determine the means of X for the samples in Tables 9.3 and 9.4. What would be the mean of X in an infinite sample drawn from the random variable described in Table 9.1?

Section 9.3

9.14 Suppose that X has a binomial distribution with $n = 3$ and $P = 1/3$. Construct the complete probability distribution of X and graph it. Determine the mean and standard deviation.

* **9.15** Suppose that a worker plans to look for work for five weeks and that the probability of getting an offer in any week is 1/5. What is his expected number of job offers? What is the probability that he will get fewer than the expected number?

9.16 Among members of the binomial family all having the same value of n, which has the largest variance? (Try the set of values $P = .1, .3, .5, .7, .9$, or use calculus.)

Section 9.4

9.17 Based on Figure 9.5a, which is greater: $\Pr(X \leq X_2)$ or $\Pr(X \geq X_2)$?

9.18 Based on $p(X)$ shown in Figure 9.6a, determine
   (a) $\Pr(X \geq 0)$.
   (b) $\Pr(X \geq 1/2)$.
   (c) $\Pr(0.2 \leq X \leq 0.8)$.
   (d) X^c such that $\Pr(X \geq X^c) = .32$.

* **9.19** Based on $p(X)$ shown in Figure 9.6a, explain why the chance that X will be about 0.2 is greater than the chance that X will be about 0.8.

9.20 Let X be a continuous random variable that takes on values only between 0 and 1 and for which $p(X) = 2X$ over this interval.
   (a) Graph the density function and verify that the area under $p(X)$ equals 1.
   (b) Determine $\Pr(X \geq 0.5)$.
   (c) Determine X^c such that $\Pr(X \geq X^c) = .5$.

9.21 Suppose that a sample of size 10 is taken from the random variable described by Figure 9.6a. Using four class intervals (-1 to -0.5, -0.5 to 0, etc.), construct a frequency table and relative frequency histogram that might reasonably describe the sample.

Section 9.5

9.22 Comparing Y and X in Figure 9.6,

    (a) What Y values correspond to the following X values: 0, 1/4, 1/2, 1?

    (b) What X values correspond to the following Y values: 2, 3, 4, 5, 6?

9.23 For Y given in Figure 9.6b,

    (a) Determine $\Pr(Y \geq 4.5)$.

    (b) Given that $\mu_X = 0$ and $\sigma_X \approx 0.4$, determine the mean and standard deviation of Y.

★ 9.24 From its probability distribution, calculate the mean and standard deviation of Y, the random variable defined in Table 9.6. Compare the results with those from Problem 9.5.

Appendix

9.25 Based on the discussion in the text, draw (on the same set of axes) the probability distribution of earnings for a person with a small amount of wealth and the probability distribution of earnings for a person with a large amount of wealth.

★ 9.26 Let W be the sum of the outcomes of a pair of dice. Determine the mean and standard deviation of W.

9.27 Based on Figure 9.8, construct a small table showing

    (a) $p(Y|X = 5)$.

    (b) $p(X|Y = 4)$.

10

The Normal
and t Distributions

In this chapter we examine several families of continuous probability distributions that are of importance in statistics and econometrics. The two main sections of the chapter discuss the normal and t distributions, which provide the foundation for the next three chapters and beyond. The appendix discusses the chi-square and F distributions, which are somewhat more advanced.

10.1 The Normal Distribution

In this section we consider a family of continuous probability distributions that is of fundamental importance in the field of statistics. Many magnitudes that occur in nature or that result from measurement error seem to be samples drawn from random variables that have normal probability distributions. We first consider the basic member of the family, and then we go on to consider other family members.

The Standard Normal

A random variable Z whose possibly occurring values run all the way from $-\infty$ to ∞ is said to have a *standard normal distribution* if its probability distribution (i.e., density function) is of the form

$$p(Z) = \frac{1}{\sqrt{2\pi}} \exp\left[-\frac{1}{2}Z^2\right], \quad -\infty < Z < \infty \tag{10.1}$$

where π is the number 3.14 . . . , and the notation exp[·] indicates that the term in brackets is an exponent to which e, the base of natural logarithms, is to be raised. It is common to use Z, rather than X or Y, as the name for a standard normal random variable in order to give it instant recognition.

This probability distribution is defined so that $p(Z) > 0$ for all values of Z. The area under $p(Z)$ over the range $-\infty < Z < \infty$ is equal to 1, as is required for $p(Z)$ to be a genuine density function. It turns out that Z has a zero mean ($\mu_Z = 0$) and unit standard deviation ($\sigma_Z = 1$), and thus $p(Z)$ is sometimes called the *unit normal distribution*. The distribution has a bell-shaped curve, as shown in Figure 10.1.

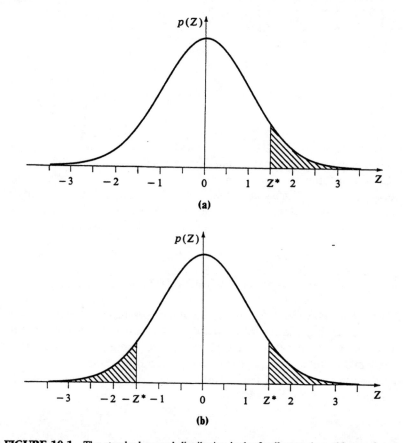

(a)

(b)

FIGURE 10.1   The standard normal distribution is the family member with $\mu = 0$ and $\sigma = 1$. A random variable having a standard normal distribution is usually denoted by Z. In (a), the shaded area represents $\Pr(Z \geq Z^*)$. In (b), the shaded area represents $\Pr(|Z| \geq Z^*)$, and half the probability is located in each tail. In practice, probability calculations such as these are made using Table A.1.

Suppose that we wish to determine $\Pr(Z \geq 1.5)$. Applying basic principles, we know that this probability is given by the area under $p(Z)$ to the right of the value $Z = 1.5$, which is shown in Figure 10.1a as the shaded area to the right of Z^*. Because of the complex form of $p(Z)$, area calculations like this are extremely difficult and are best left to computers. We can proceed, however, by making use of a table that gives us a record of many computer calculations. In an appendix at the end of the book, the entries in Table A.1 give $\Pr(Z \geq Z^*)$ for various positive values of Z^*. In Figure 10.1a, the shaded area represents this probability for the Z^* indicated. By taking advantage of the symmetry of the distribution, it is possible to use this information to solve a wide variety of probability problems involving the standard normal distribution.

The first class of probability problems that we commonly confront are of the form

$$\text{Find } \alpha \text{ such that} \quad \Pr(Z \geq Z^*) = \alpha \tag{10.2}$$

where Z^* is a specified value of Z and α is a probability amount. For example, if $Z^* = 1.5$, then α is equal to the area in the tail of the distribution to the right of $Z = 1.5$. A quick glance at Table A.1 gives the answer: $\alpha = .067$. In other words, the probability that a random variable with a standard normal distribution will take on a value greater than 1.5 is 6.7 percent. Because of the symmetry of the standard normal distribution around its zero mean, if Z^* is a particular positive value, then

$$\Pr(Z \leq -Z^*) = \Pr(Z \geq Z^*) \tag{10.3}$$

Hence, $\Pr(Z \leq -1.5) = .067$, for example. In this way, Table A.1 can be used for negative values of Z as well as positive values.

We often are interested in determining the probability amounts in two symmetrical tails of the distribution. It is helpful in this connection to use absolute value notation:

$$|Z| \geq Z^* \quad \text{means} \quad Z \leq -Z^* \quad \text{and} \quad Z \geq Z^* \quad \text{together} \tag{10.4}$$

That is, the range of Z values for which the absolute value of Z is greater than or equal to Z^* consists of the Z values less than or equal to $-Z^*$ and the Z values greater than or equal to Z^*. Thus it should be clear that the probability of being in one tail or the other is

$$\Pr(|Z| \geq Z^*) = \Pr(Z \leq -Z^*) + \Pr(Z \geq Z^*)$$
$$= 2 \Pr(Z \geq Z^*) \tag{10.5}$$

In Figure 10.1b the shaded areas together represent this probability. The probability of not being in either tail, $\Pr(|Z| \leq Z^*)$, is represented by the unshaded area. Since a value of Z is either in the tails or not,

$$\Pr(|Z| \leq Z^*) = 1 - \Pr(|Z| \geq Z^*) \tag{10.6}$$

For example, since $Pr(Z \geq 1.5) = .067$, then $Pr(|Z| \geq 1.5) = .134$ and $Pr(|Z| \leq 1.5) = .866$.

More complex probability calculations can be carried out using simple tail areas and basic knowledge of probabilities. In complex problems, as well as simple ones, it is always useful to draw a diagram to represent the probabilities as areas. For example, if we wish to determine $Pr(-0.31 \leq Z \leq 1.5)$, we realize that we need to determine the shaded area in Figure 10.2. The shaded area equals the total area minus the unshaded areas; these unshaded areas represent simple tail probabilities, whose amounts are given in Table A.1. Mathematically, the desired probability equals $1 - Pr(Z \leq -0.31) - Pr(Z \geq 1.50)$, which equals $1 - .378 - .067 = .555$.

The second class of probability problems that are important for us are of the form

$$\text{Find } Z^c \text{ such that } \quad Pr(Z \geq Z^c) = \alpha \tag{10.7}$$

where α is a specified amount of probability and Z^c is the **critical value** of Z that bounds exactly α probability in the right-hand tail. To solve these problems we use Table A.1 in the opposite way: for the given probability, we search for the corresponding Z value. For example, to find Z^c such that $Pr(Z \geq Z^c) = .25$, we use the table to see that Z^c is between 0.67 and 0.68. Taking the closer value, we say that Z^c is about 0.67; if more precision is needed, interpolation can be used. Because of the symmetry of the standard normal distribution, we see that the critical value $-Z^c$ such that $Pr(Z \leq -Z^c) = .25$ is about -0.67. (For consistency throughout this book, critical value notation like "Z^c" always refers to a positive value. A negative critical value is clearly signed: here, $-Z^c \approx -0.67$.)

We often deal with a two-tailed probability of the general form

$$\text{Find } Z^c \text{ such that } \quad Pr(|Z| \geq Z^c) = \alpha \tag{10.8}$$

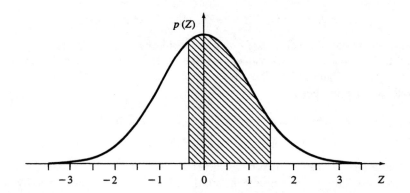

FIGURE 10.2 In this graph of the standard normal distribution, the shaded area gives $Pr(-0.31 \leq Z \leq 1.5)$. This may be determined by first using Table A.1 to find the probabilities in the unshaded tail areas.

Referring to Figure 10.1b, if we let α be the probability measure of all the shaded area, then the area in each tail is $\alpha/2$. Thus we solve (10.8) by determining Z^c such that

$$\Pr(Z \geq Z^c) = \frac{\alpha}{2} \tag{10.9}$$

For example, a common problem is to determine the symmetrical values of Z that bound a total of 5 percent of the probability in both tails. We solve this by finding Z^c such that $\Pr(Z \geq Z^c) = .025$. In the body of Table A.1 we find that $Z^c = 1.96$; the foot of the table shows that $Z^c = 1.960$ precisely to three decimals because this is such an important reference value.

As before, we may be interested in the probability of not being in the tails. For example, an interesting question is: what symmetrical values of Z contain between them 50 percent of the total probability? This can be rephrased as: find Z^c and $-Z^c$ such that $\Pr(|Z| \leq Z^c) = .5$. These are found by determining Z^c such that $\Pr(Z \geq Z^c) = .25$. As before, we choose the closest Z value in Table A.1 and say that Z^c is about 0.67. Thus, the answer to our question is that the Z values -0.67 and 0.67 contain between them (about) 50 percent of the probability. (A more precise determination shows that Z^c is about 0.6745.)

Other Normal Distributions

A random variable X whose possibly occurring values run all the way from $-\infty$ to ∞ is said to have a **normal distribution** if its probability distribution (i.e., density function) is of the form

$$p(X) = \frac{1}{b\sqrt{2\pi}} \exp\left[-\frac{1}{2}\left(\frac{X-a}{b}\right)^2\right], \quad -\infty < X < \infty \tag{10.10}$$

where $b > 0$ and a can be any value. It can be shown that $\mu_X = a$ and $\sigma_X = b$, so it is common to think of (10.10) as

$$p(X) = \frac{1}{\sigma_X\sqrt{2\pi}} \exp\left[-\frac{1}{2}\left(\frac{X-\mu_X}{\sigma_X}\right)^2\right], \quad -\infty < X < \infty \tag{10.11}$$

Since a and b can take on many different values, we recognize that there is a whole family of normal probability distributions, all of which have density functions of the form (10.10). Each member of the family is characterized by a pair of a and b values, which is to say that each is characterized by its mean and standard deviation. Since there are an unlimited number of combinations of these two parameter values, there are an unlimited number of members of the family. One member of the family is the standard normal, for which $\mu = 0$ and $\sigma = 1$. To see that this is true, note that if $a = 0$ and $b = 1$, the form of (10.10) reduces to that of (10.1).

The general shape of $p(X)$ for all normal distributions is the same: it is the bell-shaped curve illustrated in Figure 10.3. We cannot tell which member of the family this is, because there is no numerical scale on the horizontal axis.

Figure 10.4 shows three normal distributions on the same set of axes. We temporarily adopt a new form of notation, letting X_1, X_2, and X_3 be the names of the three random variables. The probability distributions of X_1 and X_2 have the same standard deviation but different means, and the density functions look alike

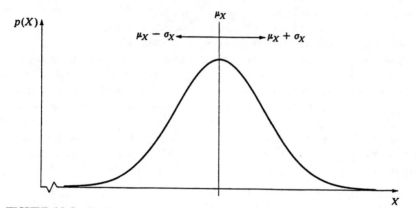

FIGURE 10.3 The density function for a continuous random variable having a normal distribution is given by Equation (10.11). Members of the family of normal distributions differ only with regard to two parameters: the mean μ_X and the standard deviation σ_X. For any member of the family, 68.2 percent of the probability is concentrated within one standard deviation of the mean. That is, the probability that the random variable will take on a value between $\mu_X - \sigma_X$ and $\mu_X + \sigma_X$ is .682.

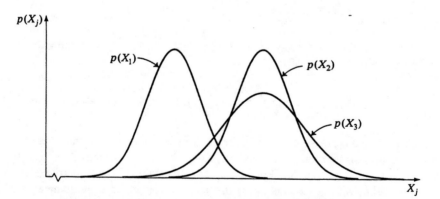

FIGURE 10.4 In this graph, three members of the normal distribution family are plotted together. The probability distributions of X_1 and X_2 have different means but the same standard deviation. The probability distributions of X_2 and X_3 have the same mean, but $\sigma(X_3) > \sigma(X_2)$. Any member of the normal family can be obtained as a linear transformation of some other member. Thus, the graph of one distribution can be obtained from that of another by compressing or expanding it and then shifting it to the left or right.

except that $p(X_2)$ is shifted over to the right relative to $p(X_1)$. The probability distributions of X_2 and X_3 have the same mean but different standard deviations; they are centered at the same value, but $p(X_3)$ has a greater standard deviation and is shorter at the mean value. When drawn on the same axes, all normal distributions have the same amount of graphical area under them: the area equals 1.

Any probability question posed for a member of the normal family can be solved, in principle, by applying the basic ideas governing all continuous random variables. For example, in Figure 10.5a we know that $\Pr(X > 6)$ is given by the shaded area under $p(X)$ to the right of $X = 6$. Instead of actually carrying out the calculation of this area, we might hope to have a table similar to Table A.1 for this specific distribution. Unfortunately, we do not have one. Therefore, in order to solve this problem we follow an indirect approach that takes advantage of the fact that all members of the normal distribution family can be viewed as being linear transformations of each other. Loosely speaking, one distribution can be obtained from any other by compressing or expanding it and then shifting it to the left or right.

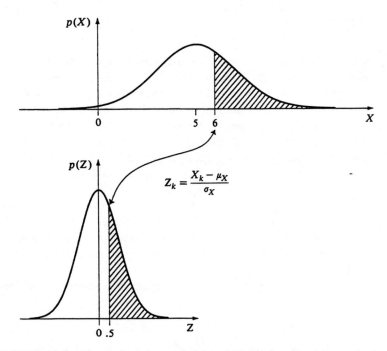

FIGURE 10.5 When two continuous random variables such as X and Z are related through a linear transformation, the probability associated with X being in a certain interval of X values is the same as that of Z being in the corresponding interval of Z values. Hence, a probability problem involving any member of the normal family can be solved by seeing it as equivalent to a problem involving the standard normal distribution. In turn, this problem is solved using Table A.1. In the case illustrated here $\mu_X = 5$ and $\sigma_X = 2$, so the Z value corresponding to $X_k = 6$ is $Z_k = 0.5$. The shaded area in both distributions is the same probability amount, $\alpha = .309$.

In particular, any member can be thought of as a transformation of the standard normal distribution. Starting with a standard normal random variable Z and two parameters a and b, we can create a new random variable X by letting each possible value Z_k be transformed into a value X_k according to

$$X_k = a + bZ_k \tag{10.12}$$

Given that the probability distribution of Z is as stated in (10.1), it can be shown that the probability distribution of X is given by (10.10). That is, X is normally distributed with $\mu_X = a$ and $\sigma_X = b$. Hence it is common to think of the correspondence as

$$X_k = \mu_X + \sigma_X Z_k \tag{10.13}$$

Putting all this in reverse, if we start with a normal random variable X having mean μ_X and standard deviation σ_X, it is possible to think of each value X_k as corresponding to the Z_k value found by

$$Z_k = \frac{X_k - \mu_X}{\sigma_X} \tag{10.14}$$

which is just (10.13) solved for Z_k.

Now, recall the fundamental probability equivalence between two continuous random variables, such as X and Z, that are related by a linear transformation: the probability associated with X being in a certain interval of X values is the same as that of Z being in the corresponding interval of Z values. Thus $\Pr(X \geq X_k)$ is exactly the same as $\Pr(Z \geq Z_k)$ when Z_k and X_k correspond to each other through (10.13) or (10.14). Hence, any probability problem involving a normal variable X can be solved by seeing it as equivalent to a probability problem involving Z, a standard normal variable. For example, suppose that X-has a normal probability distribution with $\mu_X = 5$ and $\sigma_X = 2$, and that we want to determine $\Pr(X \geq 6)$. The value $X_k = 6$ corresponds to a particular Z value, determined by $Z_k = (X_k - \mu_X)/\sigma_X = (6 - 5)/2 = 0.5$. We know from Table A.1 that $\Pr(Z \geq 0.5) = .309$; because of the probability equivalence between X and Z, this probability amount is the same as $\Pr(X \geq 6)$ and it is the answer to our problem. This is illustrated in Figure 10.5.

For future reference we may rework and generalize this example more formally:

$$\alpha = \Pr(X \geq X_k)$$

$$= \Pr(Z \geq Z_k), \quad \text{where} \quad Z_k = \frac{X_k - \mu_X}{\sigma_X}$$

$$= \Pr(Z \geq 0.5) = .309 \tag{10.15}$$

The first line restates the problem in a general form. The second line formulates the equivalent problem in terms of Z, which is a linear transformation of X, preserving the probability amount α. Finally, the third line computes Z_k for this example and shows the probability value determined from Table A.1.

More complex probability calculations for normally distributed random variables can be carried out by transforming them into equivalent problems stated in terms of the standard normal. For example, continuing with the random variable X having a normal distribution with $\mu_X = 5$ and $\sigma_X = 2$, we might seek to determine $\Pr(4.38 \leq X \leq 8.00)$. Using (10.14) and the fundamental fact of probability equivalences, this probability is equal to $\Pr(-0.31 \leq Z \leq 1.5)$; this was calculated earlier to be .555 and that is the answer to the current problem also.

We can now entertain two familiar problems. First, what is the probability that a normal random variable X will take on a value within one standard deviation of its mean? This question is formally posed and solved as

$$\alpha = \Pr(\mu_X - \sigma_X \leq X \leq \mu_X + \sigma_X)$$

$$= \Pr(Z_1 \leq Z \leq Z_2), \quad \text{where} \quad Z_1 = \frac{(\mu_X - \sigma_X) - \mu_X}{\sigma_X} = -1$$

$$Z_2 = \frac{(\mu_X + \sigma_X) - \mu_X}{\sigma_X} = +1$$

$$= \Pr(-1 \leq Z \leq 1) = .682 \tag{10.16}$$

Second, we can show that the probability that any normal random variable X will take on a value within two standard deviations of its mean is .954 [i.e., $\Pr(\mu_X - 2\sigma_X \leq X \leq \mu_X + 2\sigma_X) = .954$]. These two findings, combined with the fact that in many cases observed relative frequency distributions are similar to those taken from normal random variables, are the source of the empirical approximation that about 68 percent of the observations on a data-variable lie within one standard deviation of the mean and about 95 percent lie within two.

The previous calculations illustrate a useful interpretation of the Z value that corresponds to any particular value of X. In (10.14), which defines the correspondence, the numerator $(X_k - \mu_X)$ measures how far X_k is from the mean of X. Dividing the numerator by σ_X expresses this distance in terms of how many standard deviations (of X) it constitutes. For example, for the normal random variable X in earlier examples ($\mu_X = 5$, $\sigma_X = 2$), we saw that the value $X_k = 6$ corresponds to $Z_k = 0.5$. We see now that this means the X_k value is one half of a standard deviation (of X) above the mean (of X).

Similarly, for example, suppose that X is a normal random variable and that X_k is known to be one and a half standard deviations above the mean. Then without further steps we can determine from Table A.1 that $\Pr(X \geq X_k) = 6.7$ percent, because $Z_k = 1.5$ here.

This understanding allows us to see that the generic normal distribution in Figure 10.3 truly represents every single member of the family. In the figure, the values of μ_X and σ_X are specified graphically. Although there is no numerical scale on the X axis, each value of X can be identified graphically in terms of how many standard deviations away from the mean it is. This is sufficient to determine the answer to any probability problem regarding X, using Table A.1.

10.2   The *t* Distribution _____

Another important family of continuous probability distributions is that of the *t distribution,* which is sometimes referred to as "Student's *t* distribution" after the pseudonym of its originator, W. S. Gossett. (It is said that Gossett did not want his work known to his employer, Guiness Brewery.)

The members of this family have probability distributions that have the same general equation form but differ with regard to the value of one parameter. That parameter, which is known as the *number of degrees of freedom* and is denoted here by "df," takes on only positive integer values 1, 2, 3, . . . , ∞. To distinguish a random variable having a *t* distribution from others, it is common to use *t*, rather than X or Y, as the name of the variable.

The equation of the probability density function $p(t)$ is quite complex, so we indicate it here simply by

$$p(t) = f(t; \text{df}), \quad -\infty < t < \infty \tag{10.17}$$

The general shape of $p(t)$ for all t distributions is similar to that of the standard normal distribution, except that it is a bit fatter. The distribution $p(t)$ is symmetrical and bell-shaped; the mean equals zero, and the standard deviation equals $\sqrt{(\text{df})/(\text{df}-2)}$ when df > 2.

When we compare different members of the *t* family, as the number of degrees of freedom increases, the distribution $p(t)$ becomes more compressed and the standard deviation decreases toward a lower limit of one. Figure 10.6a compares the *t* distributions with 5 and 50 degrees of freedom. The overall difference between the two distributions appears to be small, but their standard deviations are 1.29 and 1.02, respectively. Also, the differences in tail areas [e.g., Pr($t \geq 2$)] are substantial, and these are of special importance.

In the limit, as the number of degrees of freedom approaches infinity, the *t* distribution becomes identical with the standard normal distribution. Figure 10.6b shows a *t* distribution with 5 degrees of freedom and also a standard normal distribution. The overall difference between these two distributions is barely greater than the difference between those in Figure 10.6a, and we realize that a *t* distribution having 50 or more degrees of freedom is nearly indistinguishable from a standard normal distribution.

In contrast to the normal family, the different *t* distributions are not linear transformations of each other. Thus, it is necessary to carry out separate mathematical computations to determine probabilities for each distribution. Some of this work is already done, and the results are given in Tables A.2 and A.3. Since each distribution is different, these tables can display only a limited

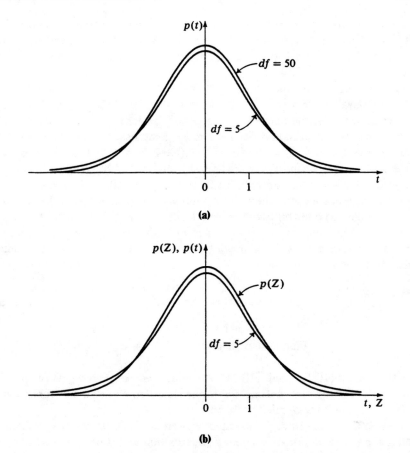

FIGURE 10.6   Part (a) compares two *t* distributions, those with 5 and 50 degrees of freedom. The overall difference between them is small, but the differences in the tails are more substantial. Part (b) compares the *t* distribution with 5 degrees of freedom with the standard normal. As the number of degrees of freedom approaches infinity, the limiting form of the *t* distribution is the standard normal. Comparing the two parts of this figure, we realize that when df = 50, the *t* distribution is already quite close to its limiting form.

amount of probability information for each of a limited number of members of the *t* distribution family. This turns out to be satisfactory in practice, and computers can be used to determine specific probability amounts that are not given in the tables.

One type of probability problem that we sometimes encounter is of the form

$$\text{Find } \alpha \text{ such that} \quad \Pr(t \geq t^*) = \alpha \tag{10.18}$$

where *t* is a random variable having a *t* distribution with some particular number of degrees of freedom and t^* is a specified value of *t*. Table A.2 is arranged to provide the answer to a problem of this form. In the table, each row provides probability information about a *t* distribution with a particular df. The table entries in the row give the probabilities that a random variable having this particular distribution will exceed the corresponding $t*$ values specified in the column headings. In other words, each entry gives the probability α that we are seeking in (10.18).

For example, we see that for df = 5, $\Pr(t \geq 1.5) = 0.97$ and $\Pr(t \geq 2.5) = .027$. Looking down any column, we see that the probability of exceeding the value $t*$ decreases as the number of degrees of freedom increases. This reflects the fact that the t distribution becomes more compressed as df increases. For example, $\Pr(t \geq 2.0) = .051$ when df = 5, $\Pr(t \geq 2.0) = .025$ when df = 50, and $\Pr(t \geq 2.0) = .023$ when df = ∞. [The last result should be compared with the finding that for a standard normal distribution $\Pr(Z \geq 2.0) = .023$ also.]

Our most frequent use of the t distribution is to determine what value t^c leads to a certain desired probability (α) being bounded in one or both tails. In the case of two tails, half the probabililty ($\alpha/2$) is to be in each tail. For the random variable t having a t distribution with df degrees of freedom, we encounter problems of the forms

$$\text{Find } t^c \text{ such that } \quad \Pr(t \geq t^c) = \alpha \qquad (10.19)$$

$$\text{Find } t^c \text{ such that } \quad \Pr(t \leq -t^c) = \alpha \qquad (10.20)$$

$$\text{Find } t^c \text{ such that } \quad \Pr(|t| \geq t^c) = \alpha \qquad (10.21)$$

Problem forms (10.19) and (10.21) are illustrated in Figure 10.7a and b, respectively. For obvious reasons, the former is called a one-tailed problem and the latter is called a two-tailed problem.

Table A.3 is arranged to provide the answers to these probability problems. Each row provides information about a t distribution with a particular number of degrees of freedom. The double row of column headings provides a selection of five different probability amounts (α) separately for one- and two-tailed problems. The table entries are the t^c values that satisfy (10.19) or (10.21). For example, if df = 20 and α = .05, the t^c is found to be 1.725 in the one-tailed problem and 2.086 in the two-tailed problem. Notice that a one-tailed problem like (10.20) is solved by symmetry, because $\Pr(t \leq -t^c) = \Pr(t \geq t^c)$ for any given t^c.

Notice that the one-tailed α is exactly half as large as the two-tailed α in the heading for each column of Table A.3. For example, a one-tailed α = .05 and a two-tailed α = .10 both lead to the same t^c = 1.725 when df = 20. Looking at this another way, it can be seen in Figure 10.7b that the same t^c that bounds a total of α in two tails also bounds $\alpha/2$ in one tail. Notice also that (for any given α) the two-tailed t^c is larger than the one-tailed t^c, but it is *not* twice as large. This can be seen by comparing the two parts of Figure 10.7.

More complex probability problems can be handled using these basic elements. To avoid errors, it is always a good idea to draw a diagram to represent the probabilities as areas.

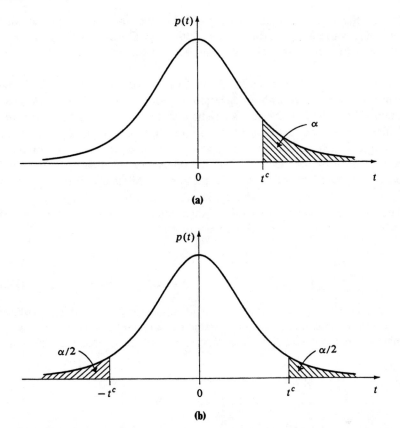

FIGURE 10.7 Suppose that a certain random variable is known to have a t distribution. We often need to determine what value (t^c) leads to a certain probability amount (α) being bounded in one or both tails. In (a), the shaded area represents $\Pr(t \geq t^c) = \alpha$; in (b), the shaded area represents $\Pr(|t| \geq t^c) = \alpha$, with $\alpha/2$ probability being bounded in each tail. In both cases, when α is specified, t^c can be determined from Table A.3.

APPENDIX

In this appendix we discuss two families of probability distributions that are related to the normal distribution.

The Chi-Square Distribution

Suppose that we have d independent random variables $Z_1, Z_2, \ldots, Z_d$, each having a standard normal distribution. We can define a new random variable χ^2 as

$$\chi^2 = \sum_{j=1}^{d} (Z_j)^2 \tag{10.22}$$

where χ^2 should be thought of as the name of the variable, rather than as the square of a variable (χ is lowercase "chi," the Greek "ch"). The possibly occurring values of χ^2 are all nonnegative, because χ^2 is defined as a sum of squares.

A random variable that can be thought of as arising through (10.22) has a *chi-square distribution* with *d* degrees of freedom. The number of degrees of freedom, df $= d$ here, is the characteristic that makes one member of the family different from another. As illustrated in Figure 10.8, the graph of the probability distribution is skewed to the right with a tail that extends out to infinity. However, the shape of the distribution becomes more symmetric as the number of degrees of freedom increases. The mean of a chi-square distribution with *d* degrees of freedom equals *d*, and the standard deviation equals $\sqrt{2d}$.

The chi-square distribution is of practical importance to us in Chapters 18 and 19, where we encounter problems of the forms

$$\text{Find } (\chi^2)^c \text{ such that } \Pr(\chi^2 \geq (\chi^2)^c) = \alpha \tag{10.23}$$

$$\text{Find } (\chi^2)^c \text{ such that } \Pr(\chi^2 \leq (\chi^2)^c) = \alpha \tag{10.24}$$

Table A.4 is arranged to provide directly the answer to a problem posed like (10.23). For example, if a random variable has a chi-square distribution with 10 degrees of freedom and if we are concerned with $\alpha = .10$, then the random

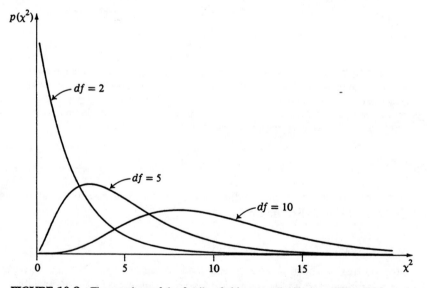

FIGURE 10.8   The members of the family of chi-square distributions differ with regard to only one parameter, the number of degrees of freedom (df). The distributions are skewed to the right, but they become more symmetric as df increases. Table A.4 is used to find the critical values of χ^2 that bound specified probability amounts in the right-hand tail.

variable will take on a value greater than or equal to $(\chi^2)^c) = 15.99$ with the stated probability. A problem like (10.24) seeks the critical value that bounds α probability in the left-hand side. If $\alpha = .05$, for example, then this problem is equivalent to one posed like (10.23) with $\alpha = 1 - .05 = .950$. For df $= 10$, the critical value is $(\chi^2)^c = 3.94$.

The chi-square distribution is a bridge between the standard normal distribution and two other families that are of interest to us. Mathematically, a t distribution arises in the following way. Suppose that Z has a standard normal distribution and χ_d^2 has a chi-square distribution with d degrees of freedom. If Z and χ_d^2 are independent,

$$t = \frac{Z}{\sqrt{(\chi_d^2)/d}} \tag{10.25}$$

defines a new random variable t that has a t distribution with d degrees of freedom.

The F Distribution

Suppose that we have two independent random variables χ_n^2 and χ_d^2 having chi-square distributions with n and d degrees of freedom, respectively. We can define a new random variable F as the ratio of these independent chi-squares:

$$F = \frac{(\chi_n^2)/n}{(\chi_d^2)/d} \tag{10.26}$$

A random variable that can be thought of as arising this way is said to have an **F distribution** with n and d degrees of freedom, and we use the notation $F_{n,d}$ to indicate this. Note that n and d are so named because they are the parameters in the numerator and denominator, respectively, of (10.26). In econometric applications n is often relatively small, but d may be small or large because it is closely related to the number of observations.

The F distribution is defined for the range $0 \leq F < \infty$. The members of the family differ from each other with regard to the values of the parameters n and d. As illustrated in Figure 10.9, the shape of the distribution is skewed to the right (i.e., there is a long tail coming out to the right). However, as n and d become large the F distribution becomes more symmetric. When $d > 2$, the mean of F equals $d/(d - 2)$.

In Chapters 14 and 19 we encounter problems of the form

$$\text{Find } F^c \text{ such that } \quad \Pr(F_{n,d} \geq F^c) = \alpha \tag{10.27}$$

Table A.5 gives the F^c values for various combinations of n and d when $\alpha = .05$, and Table A.6 gives F^c when $\alpha = .01$. For example, for an F distribution with 5 and 10 degrees of freedom, the critical value that bounds 5 percent probability in the right-hand tail is 3.33. For an F distribution with 10 and 1500 degrees of

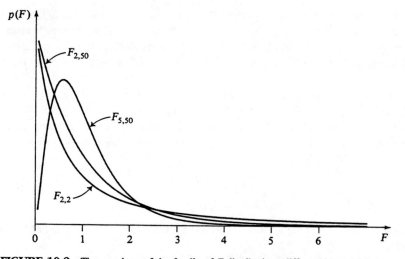

FIGURE 10.9 The members of the family of F distributions differ with regard to two parameters, which are known as the numbers of degrees of freedom in the numerator (n) and denominator (d), respectively. Table A.5 is used to find the critical value of F that bounds 5 percent probability in the right-hand tail, and Table A.6 is used for 1 percent.

freedom, the critical 5 percent probability value is $F^c = 1.83$, using ∞ to approximate the high number of degrees of freedom in the denominator.

Finally, consider a random variable t^2 that is defined as the square of a random variable having a t distribution with d degrees of freedom. From (10.25) we see that t^2 can arise from

$$t^2 = \frac{Z^2}{(\chi_d^2)/d} = \frac{(\chi_1^2)/1}{(\chi_d^2)/d} \tag{10.28}$$

Comparing the rightmost expression with (10.26), we see that $p(t^2)$ is the same as an F distribution with 1 and d degrees of freedom. In Chapter 14 we see that this equivalence has an interesting application to testing a hypothesis about a regression coefficient.

Problems

Section 10.1

10.1 For the random variable Z having a standard normal distribution, determine the following probabilities and draw figures showing the areas representing these probabilities:

(a) $\Pr(Z \geq 1.1)$.
(b) $\Pr(Z \leq -0.5)$.
(c) $\Pr(0.5 \leq Z \leq 1.5)$.
(d) $\Pr(-0.5 \leq Z \leq 1.5)$.

(e) $\Pr(|Z| \geq 0.5)$.

(f) $\Pr(|Z| \leq 1.5)$.

★ **10.2** For the random variable Z having a standard normal distribution, determine the value of Z^c such that

(a) $\Pr(Z \geq Z^c) = .02$.

(b) $\Pr(Z \leq -Z^c) = .10$.

(c) $\Pr(Z \leq Z^c) = .85$.

(d) $\Pr(|Z| \geq Z^c) = .02$.

(e) $\Pr(|Z| \geq Z^c) = .10$.

(f) $\Pr(|Z| \leq Z^c) = .85$.

10.3 What symmetrical values of Z contain between them 20 percent of the total probability?

10.4 Consider a variable X having a normal distribution with mean 100 and standard deviation 15. Determine

(a) $\Pr(X \geq 100)$.

(b) $\Pr(X \geq 110)$.

(c) $\Pr(X \leq 90)$.

(d) $\Pr(90 \leq X \leq 110)$.

(e) $\Pr(-10 \leq X - \mu_X \leq 10)$.

★ **10.5** For X defined in Problem 10.4

(a) What symmetrical values of X contain between them 60 percent of the total probability?

(b) What is the probability of X occurring within one-half standard deviation of its mean?

10.6 For the standard normal distribution, compute the value of $p(Z)$ for $Z = 0, 1, 2$, and 3.

10.7 For normal distributions, compute the value of $p(X)$ at the mean (i.e., $X = \mu_X$) in the following cases: $\sigma_X = 0.2, 0.5, 1.0, 2.0$, and 10.0.

10.8 For a normally distributed random variable u having a mean of zero, determine

(a) $\Pr(u \geq 7)$ if $\sigma_u = 3$.

(b) $\Pr(u \geq 7)$ if $\sigma_u = 13$.

(c) $\Pr(|u| \leq 5)$ if $\sigma_u = 4$.

(d) u^c if $\Pr(u \geq u^c) = .05$ with $\sigma_u = 5$.

(e) u^c if $\Pr(|u| \leq u^c) = .25$ with $\sigma_u = 5$.

Section 10.2

10.9 For a variable t having a t distribution with 21 degrees of freedom, determine

(a) $\Pr(t \geq 1.00)$.

(b) $\Pr(|t| \geq 1.50)$.

(c) $\Pr(t \leq -2.00)$.

(d) $\Pr(t \leq 2.00)$.

★ **10.10** Compare $Pr(Z \geq 1.00)$ with $Pr(t \geq 1.00)$ for t distributions with various degrees of freedom. What does this show about the shape of the probability distribution of t?

★ **10.11** For a variable t having a t distribution with 21 degrees of freedom, determine t^c such that
(a) $Pr(t \geq t^c) = .01$.
(b) $Pr(t \leq -t^c) = .05$.
(c) $Pr(t \leq t^c) = .90$.
(d) $Pr(|t| \geq t^c) = .01$.
(e) $Pr(|t| \geq t^c) = .05$.
(f) $Pr(|t| \leq t^c) = .90$.

10.12 Use a diagram to compare the results of Problem 10.11 parts (b) and (e).

10.13 For a random variable t having a t distribution, under what conditions is
(a) $Pr(|t| \geq 2) \approx .05$?
(b) $Pr(|t| \geq 2) \leq .05$?
(c) $Pr(|t| \geq 1.7) \leq .10$?
(d) $Pr(|t| \geq 1.25) \leq .30$?

10.14 For a random variable t having a t distribution with 1000 degrees of freedom, determine t^c such that
(a) $Pr(t \geq t^c) = .05$.
(b) $Pr(|t| \geq t^c) = .05$.
(c) $Pr(t \geq t^c) = .15$.
(d) $Pr(|t| \geq t^c) = .25$.

Appendix

10.15 For a random variable χ^2 having a chi-square distribution with 20 degrees of freedom, determine $(\chi^2)^c$ such that
(a) $Pr(\chi^2 \geq (\chi^2)^c) = .025$.
(b) $Pr(\chi^2 \geq (\chi^2)^c) = .100$.
(c) $Pr(\chi^2 \geq (\chi^2)^c) = .900$.
(d) $Pr(\chi^2 \leq (\chi^2)^c) = .025$.
(e) $Pr(\chi^2 \leq (\chi^2)^c) = .010$.

★ **10.16** In each column of Table A.4, the values of $(\chi^2)^c$ increase with the number of degrees of freedom. What does this illustrate about the probability distributions in the chi-square family?

★ **10.17** For a random variable $F_{5,20}$, find F^c such that $Pr(F_{5,20} \geq F^c) = .05$.

10.18 Except for cases in which the number of degrees of freedom in the denominator is very small, use the F^c values in Table A.5 to describe the differences among the probability distributions in the F family.

IV

Inference
in Regression

11

Sampling Theory
in Regression

While discussing the estimation of regression coefficients in Chapter 5, we noted that the calculated $\hat{\beta}_0^*$ and $\hat{\beta}_1^*$ values will not be equal to the true β_0 and β_1 values of the economic process that generated the data, except by coincidence. Our interest now is in going beyond the estimates themselves and making some probabilistic statements about the true values of the parameters. The key to doing this is based on the theories of *sampling* and *statistical inference,* which we develop and apply to regression in this and the next two chapters.

Some of the material in these chapters is fairly difficult and contains some subtle reasoning. These difficult topics are worth mastering, because only then can the results be applied properly and with understanding.

11.1   The Normal Regression Model

In this section we develop a theoretical framework that enlarges our discussion of the simple regression model presented in Section 5.1. Our attention is focused on the probabilistic nature of the process that generates the data for Y, the dependent variable.

The basic model of simple regression states that for a given set of values for the variable X, the corresponding values of Y are determined by

$$Y_i = \beta_0 + \beta_1 X_i + u_i \tag{11.1}$$

229

for $i = 1, 2, 3, \ldots, n$. As previously explained, the expression $\beta_0 + \beta_1 X_i$ is the systematic portion of the determination of Y_i, and the disturbance u_i is the random portion.

The disturbance is meant to represent a host of factors that help determine Y, including the effects of unconsidered explanatory variables and possible error in the measurement of Y. These determinants are considered to be secondary in importance to the explanatory variable X, and their effects on Y are not analyzed directly. Instead, these factors collectively are considered equivalent to pure chance, and the disturbance is treated as a random variable. The random nature of the disturbance is extremely important in the development of sampling theory.

To begin, we focus on the determination of Y for a typical observation, the ith. The value of the explanatory variable X_i is fixed by some other economic process, and the value of the systematic portion $\beta_0 + \beta_1 X_i$ is thereby determined. With regard to the disturbance, we assume that u_i is a random variable having a probability distribution that is normal (in the sense of Chapter 10) with

$$E[u_i] = 0 \qquad \qquad (11.2)$$

$$\sigma(u_i) = \sigma_u \qquad \qquad (11.3)$$

That is, u_i is assumed to be a normal random variable with a mean of 0 and a standard deviation of σ_u. By (11.1), the value of Y_i depends on the value of this random variable u_i, and therefore Y_i itself is a random variable. Indeed, Equation (11.1) can be read as stating that the random variable Y_i is determined as a linear transformation of the random variable u_i:

$$Y_i = a + bu_i, \quad \text{where} \quad a = \beta_0 + \beta_1 X_i \quad \text{and} \quad b = 1 \qquad (11.4)$$

(Note that a is a parameter for each observation because X_i is fixed, but a takes on different values for different observations.)

It is essential to understand that the result of assuming the disturbance to be a random variable is that the value of Y_i we observe in a set of data is simply one possible value that might have occurred for the dependent variable for the ith observation. Pure chance might have led to a different value, even though X_i is fixed. For example, suppose that we observe the value of a person's earnings in the labor market. Our understanding is that the same labor market process that produced this observed value might have produced a different value of earnings for the same person. Had this person applied for work at the same company on a different day, or at a different company on the same day, the observed level of earnings would have turned out to be a different value. For economy of notation we do not distinguish between Y_i used as the name of the random variable (e.g., the level of earnings that the ith person might receive) and as its value (e.g., the level of earnings that the ith person actually receives in our data). This use of the notation Y_i requires us to ascertain its meaning from the context.

In this view of things, the determination of Y_i is illustrated in Figure 11.1, which shows $p(Y_i)$, the probability distribution of Y_i. The asterisk (*) indicates the particular value that we observe and that we denote by Y_i in our data. Since the random variable Y_i is a linear transformation of u_i, as shown in (11.4), $p(Y_i)$ can be obtained by moving the probability distribution of u_i (normal, $\mu = 0$, $\sigma = \sigma_u$) over to the right or left by the amount $\beta_0 + \beta_1 X_i$. Thus Y_i has a probability distribution that is normal. Its mean is

$$E[Y_i] = \beta_0 + \beta_1 X_i \tag{11.5}$$

and its standard deviation is

$$\sigma(Y_i) = \sigma_u \tag{11.6}$$

Equation (11.5) provides the technically correct basis for the nontechnical use of this notation in Chapter 5.

With Y_i being viewed as a random variable, we are in a position to make probabilistic statements about the value that we might observe in data. For example, suppose we know that the true regression specification is

$$Y_i = 7 + 12X_i + u_i \tag{11.7}$$

and that the disturbance has a normal distribution with $E[u_i] = 0$ and $\sigma(u_i) = 5$. Note that the numbers in this equation are the true regression coefficients β_0 and β_1, not estimates. For an observation having $X_i = 5$, we calculate that $E[Y_i] = 67$. Hence, our new view of Y_i leads us to see that Y_i is normally distributed with $\mu = 67$ and $\sigma = 5$. Hence any probability question regarding Y_i can be answered using the methods developed for the normal family in Section 10.1. For

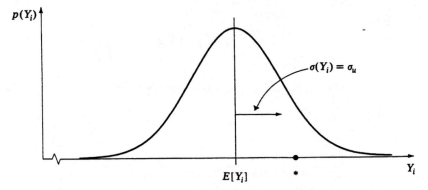

FIGURE 11.1 In the normal regression model, X_i is fixed and Y_i is thought of as a random variable because it is determined, in part, by a random disturbance. The probability distribution of Y_i is normal, with a mean equal to $\beta_0 + \beta_1 X_i$ and a standard deviation equal to σ_u. The value we denote by Y_i in a data set now is thought of as one outcome from this probability distribution, and such a value is indicated by the asterisk in this figure.

example, we can calculate that the probability that Y_i would be greater than 70 is 27.4 percent.

Now we consider the situation for all the observations looked at together. Each observation is characterized by its own value for X, although more than one observation can have the same value. For each observation, separately, the value of Y is determined according to the process just discussed.

We make two explicit assumptions about the relations among the disturbances for the different observations. First, we assume that all the u_i are independent: the value of the disturbance for one observation in no way affects the value that occurs for another. Second, as already embodied in (11.3), we assume that $\sigma(u_i)$ = σ_u, the same for all observations. These two assumptions imply that the disturbance values for the different observations can be thought of as different values drawn from the same random variable u, which has a normal probability distribution with a mean equal to 0 and standard deviation equal to σ_u.

Figure 11.2 illustrates the theory for a set of three observations in which the X values are given as X_1, X_2, and X_3. This figure represents a three-dimensional diagram in which the familiar X and Y axes are drawn on a horizontal base. The line graphed there is the true regression line. For each observation the probability distribution of Y_i is shown, as though it were taken from Figure 11.1 and placed upright on the X, Y plane. Thus the vertical axis measures probability density values. A set of values of the Y_i are shown; these are traced over to the

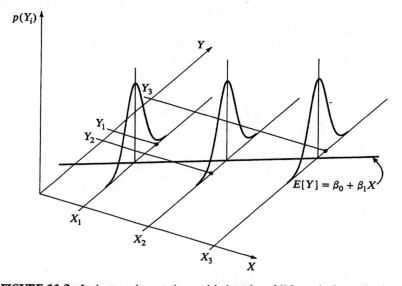

FIGURE 11.2 In the normal regression model, the value of Y for each observation is considered to be an outcome of a separate normal probability distribution. Each distribution has a mean of $\beta_0 + \beta_1 X_i$ and a standard deviation of σ_u as in Figure 11.1. In this three-dimensional diagram, probability density values are drawn vertically. The set of values labeled here as Y_1, Y_2, and Y_3 are thought of as just one possible set of values for Y corresponding to the three given values of X.

Y axis and labeled as Y_1, Y_2, and Y_3. The information on the horizontal base—the three plotted observations together with the true regression line—is similar to that in Figure 5.1. In this figure we see more about the probabilistic nature of the process by which the Y_i values are determined. Since each Y_i is a random variable, we realize that some other set of Y_i values might have occurred instead of this one. That other set would be an equally valid outcome for this situation.

Note that the assumptions we have made about the disturbances, together with the basic tenet that the X values are determined outside the process described by the regression model, imply that the disturbance values are not related to the X values. Thus, for instance, the disturbance is no more likely to be positive when X_i is large than when it is small.

The determination of Y values as discussed in this section is known as the *normal regression model.* The ideas extend to multiple regression without substantial change, except that a three-dimensional diagram no longer suffices. That is, for a given set of values for k explanatory variables, the corresponding values of Y are determined by (7.18). We assume that the disturbance u_i has a probability distribution that is normal, with mean and standard deviation specified by (11.2) and (11.3).

11.2   An Experiment in Sampling _____

In basic econometrics, we assume that the actual data on Y and X that we are working with were generated by a process described by the normal regression model, which includes (11.1) and assumptions about the disturbances. Our main statistical task is to make estimates of the unknown parameters β_0 and β_1 of the model.

We recognize that the coefficients we actually calculate, $\hat{\beta}_0^*$ and $\hat{\beta}_1^*$, are simply estimates of the unknown true parameters and that these estimates will not be equal to the true values, except by coincidence. The explanation of how and why this occurs is called *sampling theory.* This theory provides the basis for making judgments about the true values β_0 and β_1 based on calculations that we make from our data.

Sampling theory involves several layers of reasoning, and it is quite complicated. In order to gain some insight into the theory, we first discuss a thought experiment: we think about making calculations without actually making them. The various steps that we go through do not reflect the actual steps of applied statistical analysis. Rather, they are aimed at illustrating some occurrences that we will later look at in a more theoretical way. Econometricians sometimes carry out numerical experiments that are similar to what we think through here. These are known as *Monte Carlo experiments,* after the town best known for its casino.

The experiment involves applying the ordinary least squares estimators for simple regression, from Chapter 5, to sets of data that are generated by the same normal regression model. These different sets of data are *samples* from the process. An important aspect of this experiment is that the same X values are used in each sample. As we will see, what differ from sample to sample are the values of Y.

For the first step of the experiment, we take a sample of size $n = 3$ for which the X values are given as X_1, X_2, and X_3. Following the discussion in the previous section, the Y values are determined in part by the values for the disturbance terms. We now have a set of data with three observations: (X_1, Y_1), (X_2, Y_2), and (X_3, Y_3). These are plotted in the top panel of Figure 11.3, where the true regression line with height $\beta_0 + \beta_1 X_i$ is also shown. This true regression line is the systematic part of the process described by (11.1). For each observation, whether the actual Y_i value is greater or less than $\beta_0 + \beta_1 X_i$ depends on pure chance; that is, it depends on the value of the disturbance u_i. The OLS estimated regression line, which is based on the three plotted observations, is also drawn in.

In the next step of the experiment we keep the same three X_i values and generate three new values for the disturbances, yielding a new set of Y_i values. This new set is plotted in the second panel of Figure 11.3, where the true regression line is repeated and the new sample's estimated regression line is also drawn. Except by coincidence, the Y_i values in this second sample will be different from the corresponding Y_i values in the first sample because of the random nature of the disturbances. Hence, the estimated values $\hat{\beta}_0^*$ and $\hat{\beta}_1^*$ will also be different from those in the first sample. In the cases illustrated, $\hat{\beta}_1^* < \beta_1$ in the first sample but $\hat{\beta}_1^* > \beta_1$ in the second sample. The value of β_1 is the same in both cases, of course.

In the same fashion we can draw a total of N samples, all having the same three X values. The Y values differ from sample to sample, but they are all based on the same true regression. In each sample we calculate the values $\hat{\beta}_0^*$ and $\hat{\beta}_1^*$, and we collect these values for future use. Our experimental finding that different values for $\hat{\beta}_0^*$ and $\hat{\beta}_1^*$ occur in different samples drawn from the same economic process illustrates the phenomenon of *sampling variability*.

Now, the N different values calculated for $\hat{\beta}_0^*$ are numbers that can be thought of as N different values of a data variable named $\hat{\beta}_0^*$. Thus these N values can be summarized and described by the methods of descriptive statistics presented in Chapters 3 and 4. Similarly, the N different values for $\hat{\beta}_1^*$ can be thought of as N different values of a data variable named $\hat{\beta}_1^*$.

Accordingly, we take the N different $\hat{\beta}_0^*$ values and display them in a relative frequency histogram, and we take the N different $\hat{\beta}_1^*$ values and display them similarly. This is done near the bottom of Figure 11.3, in the figures showing $f(\hat{\beta}_0^*)$ and $f(\hat{\beta}_1^*)$ on the vertical axes. Without introducing notation here, we realize that each of these frequency distributions can be summarized by its mean and its standard deviation—just as the frequency distribution for a data variable X can be summarized by its mean $\overline{X}$ and its standard deviation S_X. That is, thinking of the N different $\hat{\beta}_0^*$ values as a data variable, we understand that there

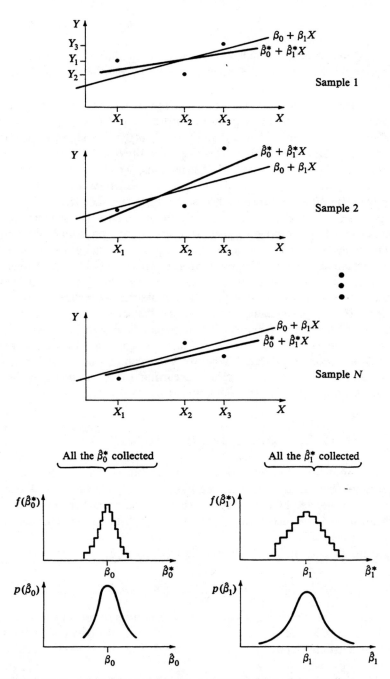

FIGURE 11.3 A thought experiment helps explain the nature of the sampling distributions of the OLS estimators of β_0 and β_1. The same three X values are used in each sample, but different sets of Y values are produced because different values for the disturbances occur in each sample. The $\hat{\beta}_0^*$ and $\hat{\beta}_1^*$ values computed in each sample are collected, and their frequency distributions are constructed. The sampling distribution of an estimator is the limiting form of the frequency distribution as N approaches infinity. The actual $\hat{\beta}_0^*$ and $\hat{\beta}_1^*$ that we calculate from a set of data are thought of as just one pair of outcomes from these sampling distributions.

is a mean of $\hat{\beta}_0^*$ and a standard deviation of $\hat{\beta}_0^*$. Similarly, the frequency distribution $f(\hat{\beta}_1^*)$ is summarized by the mean of $\hat{\beta}_1^*$ and the standard deviation of $\hat{\beta}_1^*$.

Mathematical analysis shows that if N is increased toward infinity in an experiment like this, the relative frequency distributions $f(\hat{\beta}_0^*)$ and $f(\hat{\beta}_1^*)$ becomes smoother and each approaches a limiting form: $p(\hat{\beta}_0^*)$ and $p(\hat{\beta}_1^*)$, respectively. These limiting forms can be interpreted as probability distributions, as discussed in Chapter 9. These two probability distributions, which are illustrated at the bottom of Figure 11.3, are called the *sampling distributions* of $\hat{\beta}_0$ and $\hat{\beta}_1$, respectively, because they arise in the context of taking samples.

In practice, of course, we work with only one set of data. The sampling theory that is illustrated by our thought experiment leads us to view a set of real data as though it is just one sample from an underlying process that produces data. We realize that another sample drawn from this process would have different Y values associated with the same X values, and thus this other sample would produce different values for $\hat{\beta}_0^*$ and $\hat{\beta}_1^*$. In other words, we realize that when we have a set of data our situation might be like that of any one of the samples illustrated or hinted at in Figure 11.3, but we cannot know which one.

Before we actually look at our set of data, we might think about the values of $\hat{\beta}_0$ and $\hat{\beta}_1$ that will be calculated. What we know can be summarized by saying that the likelihood of different values occurring for $\hat{\beta}_0$ is governed by the sampling distribution $p(\hat{\beta}_0)$, and similarly for $\hat{\beta}_1$.

11.3   The Sampling Distributions: Theory _____

The sampling distributions discussed in the previous section can be developed theoretically. We start by supposing we have a set of data on Y and X that we believe was generated by a process described by the normal regression model, which includes (11.1) and assumptions about the disturbances. Our task is to make estimates of β_0 and β_1.

Focusing first on β_1, we would use the OLS estimator

$$\hat{\beta}_1 = \frac{\sum (X_i - \overline{X})Y_i}{\sum (X_i - \overline{X})^2} \tag{11.8}$$

developed in Chapter 5. For a given set of X values, we see from this equation that the value of $\hat{\beta}_1$ depends on the Y values in the data. In the previous sections we came to understand that these Y values can be viewed as one set of values of the Y_i random variables.

In this view, $\hat{\beta}_1$ itself is a random variable because it depends on random variables. The likelihood of different values occurring for $\hat{\beta}_1$ is described by a probability distribution $p(\hat{\beta}_1)$, which is called the sampling distribution of $\hat{\beta}_1$. The estimate that we actually calculate from our data, $\hat{\beta}_1^*$, is viewed as being just one outcome from this distribution.

Based on the assumptions of the normal regression model, it is shown in the appendix to this chapter that $p(\hat{\beta}_1)$ is normal with mean and standard deviation given by

$$E[\hat{\beta}_1] = \beta_1 \tag{11.9}$$

$$\sigma(\hat{\beta}_1) = \sigma_u \sqrt{\frac{1}{\Sigma(X_i - \overline{X})^2}} \tag{11.10}$$

For reasons discussed below, the standard deviation in a sampling distribution is called the **standard error** of the estimator. Thus, we say that $\sigma(\hat{\beta}_1)$ is the standard error of $\hat{\beta}_1$. Recall that the expression $\Sigma(X_i - \overline{X})^2$, which appears in (11.10), is known as the total variation in X.

All these ideas carry over to estimation of the intercept, β_0. For the given set of data on X, the value of the OLS estimator $\hat{\beta}_0$ also depends on the Y_i values. Hence, $\hat{\beta}_0$ is a random variable having some probability distribution that is called the sampling distribution for $\hat{\beta}_0$. It can be shown that this distribution, $p(\hat{\beta}_0)$, is normal with

$$E[\hat{\beta}_0] = \beta_0 \tag{11.11}$$

$$\sigma(\hat{\beta}_0) = \sigma_u \sqrt{\frac{\Sigma X_i^2}{n \Sigma(X_i - \overline{X})^2}} \tag{11.12}$$

These sampling distributions, $p(\hat{\beta}_1)$ and $p(\hat{\beta}_0)$, are illustrated at the bottom of Figure 11.3. Each of these distributions gives a description of the likelihood of various possible values occurring as the estimate of the corresponding coefficient. When we work with a set of actual data, the $\hat{\beta}_0^*$ and $\hat{\beta}_1^*$ that we calculate are thought of as just one pair of outcomes from their respective sampling distributions. Thus we realize that chance might have led to other values.

In multiple regression also, each of the estimated coefficients is thought of as being the outcome of the sampling distribution for the estimator of that coefficient. It can be shown that for the jth coefficient, the sampling distribution $p(\hat{\beta}_j)$ is normal, with

$$E[\hat{\beta}_j] = \beta_j \tag{11.13}$$

and a standard deviation that depends on σ_u and the values of all the regressors.

Since $E[\hat{\beta}_j] = \beta_j$ for any regression coefficient, the OLS estimator $\hat{\beta}_j$ is said to be **unbiased.** This means that on average (i.e., in expectation) the estimate is right on target. However, we realize that in any particular case the actual estimated coefficient $\hat{\beta}_j^*$ will be different from β_j, except by coincidence.

The difference $\hat{\beta}_j - \beta_j$ is the **estimation error** that arises in using $\hat{\beta}_j$ to estimate β_j:

$$\text{estimation error for } \hat{\beta}_j = \hat{\beta}_j - \beta_j \tag{11.14}$$

Since this error is equal to the random variable $\hat{\beta}_j$ minus the constant β_j, the estimation error is a random variable having a normal distribution with a mean of zero and a standard deviation equal to $\sigma(\hat{\beta}_j)$. Now, since the expected estimation error equals zero, we may say that the size of the typical estimation error (without regard to sign) is given by its standard deviation $\sigma(\hat{\beta}_j)$. Using "standard" as a synonym for "typical," we may rephrase this as saying that $\sigma(\hat{\beta}_j)$ measures the standard estimation error—or, simply, the standard error. This is the basis for using the term "standard error" to refer to the standard deviation in a sampling distribution.

Probability Calculations

This sampling theory permits us to pose and answer questions about our estimates. For example, suppose we know that the specification of the true regression process is

$$Y_i = 7 + 12X_i + u_i \tag{11.15}$$

and that the u_i satisfy all the assumptions of the normal regression model with $\sigma_u = 5$. We do not face an estimation problem at all, because we know that $\beta_0 = 7$ and $\beta_1 = 12$. For the fun of it, however, we can do some experiments with data.

Suppose first that from this process we select a set of data for which the total variation in X is equal to 9. Given this set of X values, the corresponding Y values that we find are thought of as having been produced by the normal regression model (11.15). Hence, focusing on $\hat{\beta}_1$, we realize that the $\hat{\beta}_1$ we calculate by applying (11.8) is not likely to be equal to 12, the true value. Rather, we realize that the $\hat{\beta}_1$ we calculate is one outcome from a sampling distribution that is normal with a mean of 12 and a standard deviation calculated from (11.10) to be

$$\sigma(\hat{\beta}_1) = \sigma_u \sqrt{\frac{1}{\Sigma(X_i - \overline{X})^2}} = 5\sqrt{\frac{1}{9}} \approx 1.67 \tag{11.16}$$

With this knowledge of the sampling distribution, we can answer any probability question regarding $\hat{\beta}_1$. For example, we might ask ourselves what the chance is that $\hat{\beta}_1$ in this sample would turn out to be between 11 and 13. Applying the method of determining probabilities in a normal distribution, the probability amount α is about 45 percent:

$$\alpha = \Pr(11 \le \hat{\beta}_1 \le 13)$$

$$= 1 - 2\Pr(\hat{\beta}_1 \ge 13)$$

$$= 1 - 2\Pr(Z \geq Z_k), \quad \text{where} \quad Z_k = \frac{(\hat{\beta}_1)_k - E[\hat{\beta}_1]}{\sigma(\hat{\beta}_1)} = \frac{13 - 12}{1.67} = 0.6$$

$$= 1 - 2\Pr(Z \geq 0.6) = 1 - (2)(.274)$$

$$= .452 \tag{11.17}$$

As a second experiment, suppose that we now select a set of data for which the total variation in X is equal to 25. In this case the standard error computed from (11.10) is $\sigma(\hat{\beta}_1) = 1.0$, rather than 1.67 as before. The probability that $\hat{\beta}_1$ in this sample would turn out to be between 11 and 13 is about 68 percent, rather than about 45 percent as before.

Comparing these two experiments, we see that when the standard error is smaller there is a greater probability that $\hat{\beta}_1$ will take on a value in some interval centered on the true β_1 value (e.g., in the interval 12.0 ± 1.0). If we think of some interval around β_1 that we would want to call "close" to β_1, we see that the smaller is the standard error of $\hat{\beta}_1$ the greater will be the probability that the value of $\hat{\beta}_1$ will be "close" to the true β_1 value. Because of this, we say that the smaller is the standard error, the more **precise** is $\hat{\beta}_1$ as an estimator of β_1. Generally speaking, we would prefer to have the standard errors of our estimated coefficients be small rather than large, because this makes the estimators more precise.

Also, the key difference between these two experiments is the value of the total variation in X. As can be seen in (11.10), the greater is the total variation in X, the smaller will be the standard error. Thus, if there is any choice regarding the selection of data, it is generally better to make the total variation in X as large as possible. Based on definitions in Chapter 3, the total variation in X equals $(n - 1)S_X^2$. Thus, it is generally better to have a large sample size (n) than a small one, and a lot of dispersion among the values of X (as measured by S_X or S_X^2) rather than a little.

We can also use our knowledge of sampling distributions to make statements that hold in general across all applications. For example, we earlier defined the estimation error for $\hat{\beta}_j$ to be the difference $\hat{\beta}_j - \beta_j$. We might think of comparing this with the standard error, which gives the typical estimation error that might occur. To do this, we define a new statistic Z as the ratio

$$Z = \frac{\text{estimation error for } \hat{\beta}_j}{\text{standard error of } \hat{\beta}_j} = \frac{\hat{\beta}_j - \beta_j}{\sigma(\hat{\beta}_j)} \tag{11.18}$$

Because of the context in which it arises, Z is called a **sampling statistic**. This Z measures the size of the estimation error for any outcome relative to the standard error. For example, $Z = -1.4$ indicates a negative estimation error that is 1.4 times as large as the standard error. As explained in Chapter 10, since $\hat{\beta}_j$ is a random variable having a probability distribution that is normal with mean β_j

and standard deviation $\sigma(\hat{\beta}_j)$, the Z defined by (11.18) is a random variable having a standard normal distribution ($\mu = 0$, $\sigma = 1$). Hence probability calculations regarding the sampling statistic Z can easily be made.

For example, we might ask what the chance is that the estimation error for a regression coefficient will be more than one and a half times as large as its standard error. Allowing for both positive and negative errors, this translates into asking what the chance is that $|Z|$ is larger than 1.5. From Table A.1 we see that $\Pr(|Z| \geq 1.5) = (2)(.067) = .134$, or 13.4 percent.

Similarly, suppose that a statistical experiment produces an estimation error that is three times as large as the standard error. In this case, $Z = 3$. In assessing this result, we might note that $\Pr(|Z| \geq 3) \approx .002$, so that it would be quite unusual to see such a large Z value. That is, we would be quite surprised to find a situation in which the estimation error is more than three times as large as the standard error.

Finally, we note that the probability problem solved in (11.17) can be solved in two stages, making use of the Z statistic defined in (11.18). First, knowing that $\beta_1 = 12$, we translate the question regarding $\hat{\beta}_1$ being between 11 and 13 into a question regarding the estimation error for $\hat{\beta}_1$ being less than 1 (in absolute value). After determining that the standard error of $\hat{\beta}_1$ is 1.67, the question translates into one regarding the Z statistic being less than 0.6 (in absolute value). The second stage is based on the realization that the Z statistic defined in (11.18) has a standard normal distribution. Therefore determining $\Pr(|Z| \leq 0.6)$ is a simple problem solved by using Table A.1.

11.4   The Sampling Distributions: Application ___

In practical applications, we apply sampling theory to help analyze the $\hat{\beta}_0^*$ and $\hat{\beta}_1^*$ that we calculate from the data we have. We view these values as outcomes from the sampling distributions $p(\hat{\beta}_0)$ and $p(\hat{\beta}_1)$, which are normal.

According to sampling theory, the means of these sampling distributions are β_0 and β_1. These values are unknown, of course.

The standard errors $\sigma(\hat{\beta}_0)$ and $\sigma(\hat{\beta}_1)$ are also unknown, because they depend on the unknown value σ_u in addition to the known X values [see (11.12) and (11.10)]. To make progress in practical applications, the standard errors must be estimated. To do this, we let the standard error of the regression, SER, serve as an estimate of σ_u. [Recall that the SER is approximately equal to the standard deviation of the residuals (S_e), so that it should serve reasonably well as an estimate of the standard deviation of the disturbances (σ_u).] When SER replaces σ_u in (11.12) and (11.10), the resulting estimators of the standard errors $\sigma(\hat{\beta}_0)$ and $\sigma(\hat{\beta}_1)$ are denoted by $s(\hat{\beta}_0)$ and $s(\hat{\beta}_1)$:

$$s(\hat{\beta}_0) = SER \sqrt{\frac{\sum X_i^2}{n \sum(X_i - \overline{X})^2}} \qquad (11.19)$$

$$s(\hat{\beta}_1) = SER\sqrt{\frac{1}{\Sigma(X_i - \overline{X})^2}} \qquad (11.20)$$

Computer programs used for regression analysis routinely report the estimated standard errors along with the estimated regression coefficients.

(Without dwelling on extra complexity, we note that these estimators are random variables and have sampling distributions that describe the relative likelihood of different values occurring. To understand this, consider again the thought experiment from Section 11.2. The residuals are different in each sample, so the SERs also will differ from sample to sample. Hence, the estimated standard errors will differ from sample to sample.)

For example, the simplest earnings function reported in Chapter 6 is based on the presumption that the true process determining earnings is

$$EARNS_i = \beta_0 + \beta_1 ED_i + u_i \qquad (11.21)$$

The estimated form of the model is

$$\widehat{EARNS}_i = -1.315 + 0.797 ED_i$$
$$(1.540) \quad (0.128) \qquad (11.22)$$
$$R^2 = .285 \quad SER = 4.361$$

In this style of reporting, which is fairly common, the estimated standard errors of the coefficient estimators are shown in parentheses below the corresponding coefficients. In this case, the report tells us that $\hat{\beta}_1^* = 0.797$ and $s^*(\hat{\beta}_1) = 0.128$. Similarly, $\hat{\beta}_0^* = -1.315$ and $s^*(\hat{\beta}_0) = 1.540$.

The information we have about β_1 is illustrated in Figure 11.4: the sampling distribution of $\hat{\beta}_1$ is normal, with a mean equal to the unknown β_1 and a standard

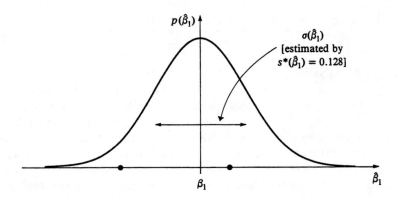

FIGURE 11.4 The sampling distribution of $\hat{\beta}_1$ in the earnings function is normal, with a mean equal to β_1 (unknown) and a standard deviation (i.e., standard error) estimated to be 0.128. The estimate of β_1 is $\hat{\beta}_1^* = 0.797$; this might correspond to either of the unlabeled points on the horizontal axis.

deviation estimated to be 0.128. It might be that the calculated $\hat{\beta}_1^*$ lies at the unlabeled point to the right, in which case the true β_1 would be less than 0.797. Or, it might be that $\hat{\beta}_1^*$ lies at the unlabeled point to the left, in which case the true β_1 would be greater than 0.797. It is of fundamental importance to realize that in any practical situation we never know where the calculated $\hat{\beta}_1^*$ lies relative to the true β_1.

Probability Calculations

Suppose someone makes a conjecture that $\beta_1 = 1.0$ in (11.21). Our estimate of β_1 is $\hat{\beta}_1^* = 0.797$, so we might start to say that the conjecture is wrong. However, sampling theory makes us realize that if $\beta_1 = 1.0$, the value of $\hat{\beta}_1$ could be 0.797 or even less.

If the conjecture that $\beta_1 = 1.0$ were true, the estimation error in our reported regression would be equal to $0.797 - 1.0 = -0.203$. This is about 1.586 times as large as the standard error $s^*(\hat{\beta}_1) = 0.128$. The situation would correspond roughly to our estimate being the unlabeled point to the left in Figure 11.4. What does this suggest about the validity of the conjecture?

To provide the basis for some numerical analysis of this question, we need to assert a new result from probability theory. As a starting point, consider the sampling statistic Z defined in the previous section as

$$Z = \frac{\hat{\beta}_j - \beta_j}{\sigma(\hat{\beta}_j)} = \frac{\text{estimation error for } \hat{\beta}_j}{\text{standard error of } \hat{\beta}_j} \tag{11.23}$$

As noted previously, this Z is a random variable that has a standard normal distribution ($\mu = 0$, $\sigma = 1$). Now consider the sampling statistic t defined as

$$t = \frac{\hat{\beta}_j - \beta_j}{s(\hat{\beta}_j)} = \frac{\text{estimation error for } \hat{\beta}_j}{\text{(estimated) standard error of } \hat{\beta}_j} \tag{11.24}$$

Since the random variable t defined this way is similar to Z defined in (11.23), differing only by a replacement in the denominator, we might anticipate that their probability distributions would also be similar. Indeed this is so: it can be shown that this t has a t distribution with $n - k - 1$ degrees of freedom (n is the number of observations, k is the number of regressors). As we know from Chapter 10, a t distribution is quite similar to the standard normal, except when the number of degrees of freedom is small.

Therefore, if the conjecture that $\beta_1 = 1$ in the earnings function is true, then

$$t = \frac{\hat{\beta}_1 - 1}{s(\hat{\beta}_1)} \tag{11.25}$$

has a t distribution with df $= 100 - 1 - 1 = 98$. From our regression report we have values for the two random variables in the ratio, so we calculate

$$t^* = \frac{\hat{\beta}_1^* - 1}{s^*(\hat{\beta}_1)} = \frac{0.797 - 1}{0.128} = -1.586 \qquad (11.26)$$

Since t has a t distribution, we can try to use Table A.2 to determine $\Pr(t \leq -1.586)$. Using df $= 100$ as the closest value to df $= 98$, and interpolating between columns, we determine that the probability is about 6 percent. (A computer calculation yields 5.80 percent.) That is, if $\beta_1 = 1.0$, the chance that data would yield a $\hat{\beta}_1$ with a negative estimation error that is more than 1.586 times as large as the estimated standard error is about 6 percent.

Comparing this probabilistic analysis of the estimated regression with the conjecture, we might find ourselves a bit surprised. Although the results could have arisen with data from an earnings determination process in which $\beta_1 = 1$, it seems rather unlikely that this would have occurred. Hence we conclude by saying that the evidence casts some doubt on the conjecture. In Chapter 12 we extend this thinking to a formal treatment of hypothesis testing.

11.5 Interval Estimation

Until now, our notion of the "estimation" of an unknown regression coefficient has been the calculation of a single value that serves as our best guess of the coefficient's true value. In statistical terms, this value is a *point estimate.* Since sampling theory makes it clear that every estimate is accompanied by some estimation error, it is useful to provide information regarding this error when reporting the value of the point estimate. This is accomplished to some extent by the common practice of reporting the standard error along with each estimated coefficient as in (11.22).

A more structured approach is to specify a range of values that is likely to include the true value of the unknown coefficient. This range of values is called an *interval estimate,* and it is constructed in the general form

$$\hat{\beta}_j^* \pm h \quad \text{or} \quad (\hat{\beta}_j^* - h) \text{ to } (\hat{\beta}_j^* + h) \qquad (11.27)$$

where $\hat{\beta}_j^*$ is the point estimate and h is the half-width of the interval. Sampling theory allows us to determine the size of h in association with a probability amount so that we can make statements like "I am 95 percent confident that the true β_1 is in the interval $\hat{\beta}_1^* \pm h$." Usually we decide in advance what probability amount is to be used, so the problem is to determine the appropriate size for h.

To see how this is done, we start with the unrealistic situation in which the true standard deviation of the disturbance, σ_u, is known. For the given values of the explanatory variables in our data, this allows us to determine the standard error $\sigma(\hat{\beta}_j)$. In this situation, then, sampling theory tells us that the sampling distribution of the estimator $\hat{\beta}_j$ is normal with an unknown mean β_j and a known standard deviation $\sigma(\hat{\beta}_j)$.

Figure 11.5 illustrates this distribution. The figure is set up like one for a two-tailed probability problem, with $\alpha/2$ probability in each tail. Since the two bounding points must be symmetrically located on either side of the mean, they can be denoted by $\beta_j - h$ and $\beta_j + h$, where h is simply the distance from the mean to either bounding point. Given the construction in this figure, it is clear that the greater α is, the smaller h will be.

Focusing on the right-hand tail in the figure, we see that

$$\frac{\alpha}{2} = \Pr(\hat{\beta}_j \geq \beta_j + h)$$

$$= \Pr(Z \geq Z_k), \quad \text{where} \quad Z_k = \frac{(\beta_j + h) - \beta_j}{\sigma(\hat{\beta}_j)} = \frac{h}{\sigma(\hat{\beta}_j)}$$

$$= \Pr\left(Z \geq \frac{h}{\sigma(\hat{\beta}_j)}\right) \tag{11.28}$$

In the first line we start with a probability statement involving the normal random variable $\hat{\beta}_j$, and in the next two lines we set up the equivalent statement involving the standard normal variable Z. Now, using general notation that conforms with our reference tables, the statement

$$\Pr(Z \geq Z^c) = \frac{\alpha}{2} \tag{11.29}$$

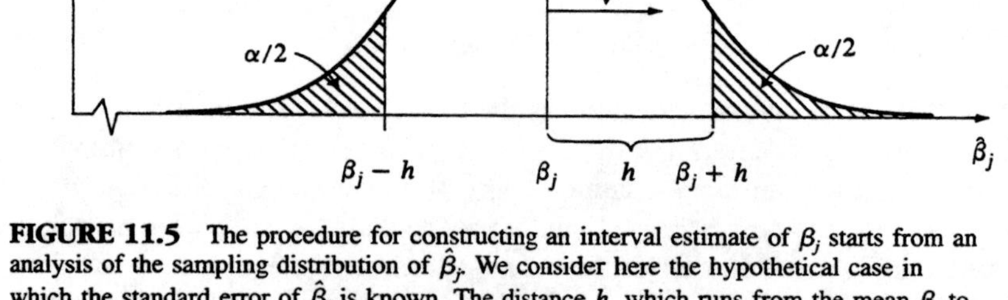

FIGURE 11.5 The procedure for constructing an interval estimate of β_j starts from an analysis of the sampling distribution of $\hat{\beta}_j$. We consider here the hypothetical case in which the standard error of $\hat{\beta}_j$ is known. The distance h, which runs from the mean β_j to the bounding point $\beta_j + h$, is associated with the probability amount $(\alpha/2)$ that it bounds in the tail. By construction, the probability that $\hat{\beta}_j$ will fall within h of the true β_j is $1 - \alpha$. Hence, the probability that the interval $\hat{\beta}_j \pm h$ contains the true β_j is $1 - \alpha$.

identifies the critical value Z^c that bounds $\alpha/2$ in the right-hand tail. In (11.28), $h/\sigma(\hat{\beta}_j)$ also plays this role. Hence, $Z^c = h/\sigma(\hat{\beta}_j)$. Thus we can say that

$$h = Z^c \sigma(\hat{\beta}_j) \tag{11.30}$$

where Z^c depends on the given value of α, through (11.29). That is, based on the construction of Figure 11.5, we have developed a two-step method for determining the h associated with any given α.

Now focusing on the unshaded area in the figure, we see that

$$\Pr(\beta_j - h \le \hat{\beta}_j \le \beta_j + h) = 1 - \alpha \tag{11.31}$$

That is, the probability that the estimate $\hat{\beta}_j$ will fall within h of the true β_j is $1 - \alpha$.

To put this in action, suppose that we adopt the procedure of using the interval

$$\hat{\beta}_j^* \pm h, \quad \text{where} \quad h = Z^c \sigma(\hat{\beta}_j) \tag{11.32}$$

to serve as an *interval estimate* of β_j, with the understanding that Z^c depends on the chosen α, through (11.29). Referring to Figure 11.5, if the $\hat{\beta}_j^*$ value happens to fall in the range $\beta_j - h$ to $\beta_j + h$, then $\hat{\beta}_j^*$ is clearly within h of the true β_j. That is, under this condition, β_j is in the interval $\hat{\beta}_j^* \pm h$. Continuing this reasoning, if $\hat{\beta}_j^*$ happens to fall outside the range $\beta_j - h$ to $\beta_j + h$ (either to the left of $\beta_j - h$ or to the right of $\beta_j + h$), it is clear that $\hat{\beta}_j^*$ and β_j are farther than h away from each other. That is, β_j is not in the interval. Thus, the interval $\hat{\beta}_j^* \pm h$ will contain β_j if and only if $\hat{\beta}_j^*$ happens to fall in the range $\beta_j - h$ to $\beta_j + h$. By (11.31), the probability of this occurring is $1 - \alpha$.

Based on this reasoning, we can be confident that an interval constructed according to this method will contain the true β_j about $(1 - \alpha) \cdot 100$ percent of the times we make such an estimate. Because of this interpretation, the interval is known as a *confidence interval*, and the probability amount $1 - \alpha$ is known as the *level of confidence*. Note, for example, that $\alpha = .05$ leads to the 95 percent level of confidence.

In practical applications, the standard deviation of the disturbance is unknown. In this situation we proceed along similar lines but use $s(\hat{\beta}_j)$ instead of $\sigma(\hat{\beta}_j)$. As in Section 11.4, the substitution of $s(\hat{\beta}_j)$ for $\sigma(\hat{\beta}_j)$ leads us to find that a certain sampling statistic has a t distribution instead of a standard normal distribution.

We show in the appendix that the interval

$$\hat{\beta}_j^* \pm h, \quad \text{where} \quad h = t^c s^*(\hat{\beta}_j) \tag{11.33}$$

and where t^c is determined from

$$\Pr(t \geq t^c) = \frac{\alpha}{2} \qquad (11.34)$$

can be used to construct an interval estimate of an unknown β_j at the $1 - \alpha$ level of confidence. In (11.34), the sampling statistic t has a t distribution with $n - k - 1$ degrees of freedom (n is the number of observations, k is the number of regressors).

This procedure is easy to apply. For example, consider again the aggregate consumption function

$$\widehat{CON_i} = 0.568 + 0.907DPI_i$$
$$(6.973) \quad (0.010)$$
$$R^2 = .997 \quad SER = 8.935 \qquad (11.35)$$

where parentheses contain standard errors. Suppose that we wish to construct a 95 percent confidence interval for estimating the marginal propensity to consume, β_1. In terms of our general notation, we see that $\alpha = .05$. Thus t^c must be such that

$$\Pr(t \geq t^c) = \frac{\alpha}{2} = .025 \qquad (11.35)$$

for a t distribution with 23 degrees of freedom. Table A.3 gives the value $t^c = 2.069$. Hence

$$h = t^c s^*(\hat{\beta}_1) = (2.069)(0.010) = 0.021 \qquad (11.36)$$

and the interval is

$$\hat{\beta}_1^* \pm h = 0.907 \pm 0.021 \quad \text{or} \quad 0.886 \text{ to } 0.928 \qquad (11.37)$$

That is, our best estimate is that β_1 is 0.907, and we are 95 percent confident that β_1 is between 0.886 and 0.928.

Suppose, instead, that we wish to construct a 99 percent confidence interval for estimating β_1 in the consumption function. All the steps of the procedure are the same, except that $t^c = 2.807$ instead of 2.069. Thus, h will be greater and so will the whole width of the confidence interval. It should be clear, generally, that the greater the level of confidence desired, the wider the confidence interval must be. Putting this in reverse and in other words, the less precise our interval estimate is, the greater confidence we can have that it contains the true value of the coefficient.

What level of confidence should be used? In principle, the answer involves a conscious choice involving the precision/confidence tradeoff just discussed. In practice, the level of confidence is chosen by convention. The most common choice is 95 percent, but 90 percent and 99 percent are also used.

Sometimes confidence intervals are reported less formally, using a rule of thumb that sets $t^* = 2$. This produces a "two-standard-error confidence interval" of the form $\hat{\beta}_j^* \pm 2s^*(\hat{\beta}_j)$. In effect, this rule chooses h and lets the level of confidence $1 - \alpha$ be whatever probability is associated with that. It turns out that a two-standard-error confidence interval is approximately the same as a 95 percent confidence interval. To see why, we note that the exact level of confidence is given by

$$1 - \alpha = 1 - \Pr(|t| \geq 2) \tag{11.39}$$

From Table A.2, when there are 10 degrees of freedom we see that the exact level of confidence for a two-standard-error confidence interval is .926; when df = 25 we see that $1 - \alpha = .944$; and when df = 100 we see that $1 - \alpha = .952$. Thus the approximation is quite good, except when the number of observations is small.

11.6   A Compendium of Reported Regressions _____

Tables 11.1 through 11.6 bring together nearly all the regressions reported in Chapters 6 and 7. This style is a common way of reporting alternative

TABLE 11.1   Earnings Functions (Dependent Variable: *EARNS*, *n* = 100)

	(6.7)	(7.15)	(7.46)	(7.33)	(7.41)
Constant	−1.315	−6.179	−9.791	−0.778	−0.803
	(1.540)	(2.780)	(3.780)	(1.615)	(1.778)
ED	0.797	0.978	0.995	0.762	0.794
	(0.128)	(0.153)	(0.152)	(0.131)	(0.130)
EXP		0.124	0.471		
		(0.060)	(0.254)		
EXPSQ			−0.00751		
			(0.00536)		
DRACE				−1.926	
				(1.759)	
DNCENT					0.288
					(1.166)
DSOUTH					−0.828
					(1.184)
DWEST					−1.992
					(1.329)
R^2	.285	.315	.329	.293	.310
SER	4.361	4.288	4.267	4.356	4.351

TABLE 11.2 Semilog Earnings Functions
(Dependent Variable: *LNEARNS*, $n = 100$)

	(6.45)	(7.55)
Constant	0.673	−2.031
	(0.158)	(0.974)
ED	0.107	0.106
	(0.013)	(0.016)
EXP		0.0501
		(0.0253)
EXPSQ		−0.000930
		(0.000533)
LNMONTHS		0.908
		(0.375)
DRACE		−0.239
		(0.177)
DNCENT		−0.00469
		(0.116)
DSOUTH		−0.193
		(0.119)
DWEST		−0.162
		(0.130)
R^2	.405	.511
SER	0.446	0.420

TABLE 11.3 Consumption Functions (Dependent Variable: *CON*)

	(6.10)	(6.23)	(7.29)
Constant	0.568	10.913	−2.370
	(6.973)	(12.167)	(10.024)
DPI	0.907		0.910
	(0.010)		(0.034)
DPILAG		0.923	
		(0.017)	
RAAA			0.500
			(3.902)
RINF2			−0.562
			(1.444)
R^2	.997	.993	.997
SER	8.935	14.953	9.309
n	25	24	25

TABLE 11.4 Trend Analyses (Dependent Variable: As Indicated)

	(6.14) *APC*	(6.50) *LNGNP*
Constant	0.911	6.456
	(0.0046)	(0.012)
T	−0.000213	0.0354
	(0.000309)	(0.00082)
R^2	.020	.988
SER	0.011	0.0297
n	25	25

TABLE 11.5 Phillips Curves (Dependent Variable: *RINF1*, $n = 15$)

	(6.30)	(7.36)
Constant	−1.984	−0.803
	(1.219)	(1.524)
UINV	22.234	15.030
	(5.594)	(7.965)
D (1965–70)		0.894
		(0.717)
R^2	.549	.600
SER	0.956	0.936

TABLE 11.6 Money Demand Functions (Dependent Variable: *LNM*, $n = 25$)

	(6.38)	(7.54)
Constant	3.948	3.759
	(0.165)	(0.325)
LNGNP	0.215	0.246
	(0.024)	(0.053)
LNRTB		−0.0205
		(0.0304)
R^2	.780	.785
SER	0.0305	0.0309

specifications of regressions having the same dependent variable. Each column displays a separate estimated regression, and a blank entry indicates that the variable listed in the left-hand stub is not included in the specification. When only one or two regressions are reported, the style of (11.22) is satisfactory.

The number in parentheses below each estimated coefficient is the corresponding standard error. Often researchers report results following another convention:

instead of giving the standard error, the number that appears in parentheses is the ratio of the estimated coefficient to its standard error: $\hat{\beta}_j^*/s^*(\hat{\beta}_j)$. This ratio is the same as the outcome of the sampling statistic t defined in (11.24) *if and only if* $\beta_j = 0$. (In the next chapter we see why this is interesting to consider.) Both styles of reporting give essentially the same information: given the estimated coefficient, the t ratio can be determined from the standard error, and vice versa.

APPENDIX

Derivation of a Sampling Distribution

In this appendix we derive the sampling distribution of $\hat{\beta}_1$ in the simple regression model and show some related results.

We start by accepting the specification of the simple regression model, including all the assumptions about the disturbances, as presented in Section 11.1. Based on (5.12), the ordinary least squares estimator of β_1 is given by

$$\hat{\beta}_1 = \frac{\Sigma(X_i - \overline{X})Y_i}{\Sigma(X_i - \overline{X})^2} = \Sigma\left[\frac{(X_i - \overline{X})}{\Sigma(X_i - \overline{X})^2}\right]Y_i$$

$$= \Sigma\, w_i Y_i, \quad \text{where} \quad w_i = \frac{(X_i - \overline{X})}{\Sigma(X_i - \overline{X})^2} \qquad (11.40)$$

Since the X values are taken as fixed rather than as random variables, the w_i values are constants. Substituting for Y_i yields

$$\hat{\beta}_1 = \Sigma\, w_i(\beta_0 + \beta_1 X_i + u_i)$$
$$= \beta_0 \Sigma\, w_i + \beta_1 \Sigma\, w_i X_i + \Sigma\, w_i u_i \qquad (11.41)$$

From the definition of w_i, it can be shown that $\Sigma\, w_i = 0$ and $\Sigma\, w_i X_i = 1$. Hence

$$\hat{\beta}_1 = (\beta_0)(0) + (\beta_1)(1) + \Sigma\, w_i u_i = \beta_1 + \Sigma\, w_i u_i \qquad (11.42)$$

Let us define

$$V = \Sigma\, w_i u_i \qquad (11.43)$$

Recall that the u_i are independent identical random variables each having a normal distribution with mean 0 and variance σ_u^2 and that each w_i is a constant. Since V is a linear combination of normally distributed random variables, it can be shown that V itself is normally distributed. Based on (9.33) and (9.34), the mean and variance of V are

$$E[V] = \Sigma\, w_i \mu_u = \Sigma\, w_i 0 = 0 \qquad (11.44)$$

$$\sigma^2(V) = \Sigma(w_i)^2 \sigma_u^2 = \sigma_u^2 \Sigma(w_i)^2 \qquad (11.45)$$

Noting that the denominator in the ratio called w_i is the same for all i, we have

$$\Sigma(w_i)^2 = \Sigma\left[\frac{(X_1 - \overline{X})}{\Sigma(X_i - \overline{X})^2}\right]^2 = \frac{\Sigma(X_i - \overline{X})^2}{[\Sigma(X_i - \overline{X})^2]^2}$$

$$= \frac{1}{\Sigma(X_i - \overline{X})^2} \tag{11.46}$$

so that

$$\sigma^2(V) = \sigma_u^2 \frac{1}{\Sigma(X_i - \overline{X})^2} \tag{11.47}$$

Now, since $\hat{\beta}_1 = \beta_1 + V$, $\hat{\beta}_1$ is a random variable equal to the random variable V plus a constant. Thus

$$E[\hat{\beta}_1] = \beta_1 + E[V] = \beta_1 + 0 = \beta_1 \tag{11.48}$$

$$\sigma^2(\hat{\beta}_1) = \sigma^2(V) = \sigma_u^2 \frac{1}{\Sigma(X_i - \overline{X})^2} \tag{11.49}$$

Since V has a normal distribution, so does $\hat{\beta}_1$. Equation (11.48) underlies (11.9), and taking the square root of (11.49) gives (11.10).

A similar derivation shows that the sampling distribution of $\hat{\beta}_0$ in a simple regression is normal with mean and variance given by

$$E[\hat{\beta}_0] = \beta_0 \tag{11.50}$$

$$\sigma^2(\hat{\beta}_0) = \sigma_u^2 \frac{\Sigma X_i^2}{n \, \Sigma(X_i - \overline{X})^2} \tag{11.51}$$

Finally, we note that $\hat{\beta}_0$ and $\hat{\beta}_1$ depend on the same X values and the same disturbance terms. Their individual sampling distributions can be thought of as being derived from a joint sampling distribution $p(\hat{\beta}_0, \hat{\beta}_1)$, and it should not be surprising to find a nonzero covariance between $\hat{\beta}_0$ and $\hat{\beta}_1$. The form of this joint distribution turns out to be "bivariate normal," and the covariance between $\hat{\beta}_0$ and $\hat{\beta}_1$ is

$$\sigma(\hat{\beta}_0, \hat{\beta}_1) = \frac{-\overline{X}\sigma_u^2}{\Sigma(X_i - \overline{X})^2} \tag{11.52}$$

Since σ_u^2 and $\Sigma(X_i - \overline{X})^2$ are always positive, the sign of the covariance is opposite to that of $\overline{X}$. Suppose that $\overline{X}$ is positive. If $\hat{\beta}_1^*$ turns out to be greater than β_1 in a particular sample, we would expect that $\hat{\beta}_0^*$ in that sample would be less than β_0. In other words, too high an estimate of β_1 tends to be compensated for by too low an estimate of β_0.

Derivation of the Confidence Interval

In practical applications, when σ_u is unknown, a confidence interval is determined by (11.33) and (11.34). A demonstration of the validity of this procedure must take into account that both $\hat{\beta}_j$ and $s(\hat{\beta}_j)$ depend on the values of the disturbances. That is, two random variables are involved.

We start with a probability statement that defines the critical t values, t^c and $-t^c$, such that

$$\Pr(-t^c \le t \le t^c) = 1 - \alpha \qquad (11.53)$$

As explained in Section 11.4, the sampling statistic

$$t = \frac{\hat{\beta}_j - \beta_j}{s(\hat{\beta}_j)} \qquad (11.54)$$

has a t distribution with $n - k - 1$ degrees of freedom.

By substituting (11.54) into (11.53), we have a probability statement involving the random variables $\hat{\beta}_j$ and $s(\hat{\beta}_j)$:

$$\Pr\left(-t^c \le \frac{\hat{\beta}_j - \beta_j}{s(\hat{\beta}_j)} \le t^c\right) = 1 - \alpha \qquad (11.55)$$

This can be arranged to yield

$$\begin{aligned}
1 - \alpha &= \Pr\left(-t^c \le \frac{\hat{\beta}_j - \beta_j}{s(\hat{\beta}_j)} \le t^c\right) \\
&= \Pr(-t^c s(\hat{\beta}_j) \le \hat{\beta}_j - \beta_j \le t^c s(\hat{\beta}_j)) \\
&= \Pr(\hat{\beta}_j - t^c s(\hat{\beta}_j) \le \beta_j \le \hat{\beta}_j + t^c s(\hat{\beta}_j)) \qquad (11.56)
\end{aligned}$$

In going from the second line to the third, we first subtract $\hat{\beta}_j$ from each of the three terms, then multiply through by -1 (which switches the direction of the inequalities), and then do a left-right swap to reswitch the direction of the inequalities.

Now we focus on the end and beginning of (11.56):

$$\Pr(\hat{\beta}_j - t^c s(\hat{\beta}_j) \le \beta_j \le \hat{\beta}_j + t^c s(\hat{\beta}_j)) = 1 - \alpha \qquad (11.57)$$

This is a probability statement about the ***random interval*** $\hat{\beta}_j \pm t^c s(\hat{\beta}_j)$, not about the parameter β_j. The interpretation of (11.57) is that the probability that an interval of the form $\hat{\beta}_j \pm t^c s(\hat{\beta}_j)$ will include the value β_j within it is $1 - \alpha$. In other words, we can be $(1 - \alpha) \cdot 100$ percent confident that an interval of the form (11.33) contains the true value β_j.

Problems _____

Section 11.1

11.1 Consider a regression model in which $\sigma_u = 2.5$. If the expected value of Y is 10 for a given observation, what is the probability that its actual value will be between 9 and 11?

★ **11.2** Suppose that three observations are observed sequentially. If the disturbance is positive for the first two, what is the probability that the disturbance will be positive for the third observation?

★ **11.3** Suppose that the mean of the disturbance is not zero, but a constant for all observations. How could the regression model (11.1) be rewritten to conform to the assumption in Equation (11.2)?

11.4 Show graphically what the generated data might look like if the disturbance is negative for low values of X and positive for high values of X.

11.5 Suppose that the true regression model is $Y_i = 18 - 2X_i + u_i$, with $\sigma_u = 3$. If $X_i = 7$, determine the probability that Y_i will be negative.

Section 11.2

★ **11.6** Suppose that a Monte Carlo experiment produced 10 estimates of the slope: 1.3, 1.6, 1.7, 1.9, 2.1, 2.2, 2.3, 2.4, 2.6, and 2.9. Determine the mean and standard deviation of these estimates.

11.7 Using the situation of Problem 11.6, make a frequency table classifying the data into four groups: 1.0 to 1.5, 1.5 to 2.0, and so on. Sketch the relative frequency histogram, and describe its relationship to Figure 11.3.

Section 11.3

11.8 Consider the relative frequency histograms in Figure 11.3.
(a) How are they affected by increases in N?
(b) How are they affected by increases in n?

11.9 Suppose we know that $\beta_1 = 10$ and that the standard deviation of the sampling distribution of its estimator is 1.2. What is the probability that the actual estimate of β_1 will be between 8.5 and 11.5?

★ **11.10** Suppose we know that $\beta_1 = 10$ and $\sigma(\hat{\beta}_1) = 8$. What is the probability that the actual estimate of β_1 will be negative?

11.11 In a statistical experiment, suppose that the true regression line is $E[Y] = 19 - 2X$. If the standard error for $\hat{\beta}_0$ equals 2, what is the probability that $\hat{\beta}_0$ will be greater than 20?

★ **11.12** Suppose that we are doing a statistical experiment in which we know that $E[Y] = 5 + 3X$, $\sigma_u = 2$, and the total variation of X is 1.

Determine the probability that an estimate of β_1 will be less than 2. If the total variation of X were 9, what would this probability be?

⋆ **11.13** In simple regression, if the total variation of X is quadrupled, what happens to the standard error of $\hat{\beta}_1$?

11.14 Suppose that the exact standard errors for coefficient estimators are known in a statistical experiment. What is the chance that the absolute value of an estimation error will be more than twice as large as the standard error?

Section 11.4

11.15 Suppose that a simple regression is estimated with 22 observations. What is the chance that the absolute value of an estimation error will be more than twice as large as the calculated standard error?

⋆ **11.16** In the consumption function reported as Equation (6.10), the estimated intercept is 0.568 and the calculated standard error for $\hat{\beta}_0$ is 6.973. Would these results be surprising if we knew that the true β_0 were equal to zero?

11.17 Suppose it is somehow known that the true value of the impact of *ED* on *EARNS* is 0.73.
   (a) Determine the value of the t statistic for the regression reported in Equation (11.22).
   (b) Use Table A.2 to determine, approximately, the probability that a t statistic would turn out to be this large or larger in absolute value.

⋆ **11.18** Suppose it is conjectured that the true value of the impact of *ED* on *EARNS* is zero. What is the value of the t statistic for the regression reported in Equation (11.22)? Is it likely that such an outcome would often occur?

Section 11.5

⋆ **11.19** Construct a 95 percent confidence interval for estimating the impact of education on earnings, based on the regression (11.22).

11.20 Construct a 90 percent confidence interval for estimating the marginal propensity to consume, based on the regression (11.35). Now construct a 99 percent confidence interval for the same parameter, and compare the two interval estimates.

⋆ **11.21** It is important for the U.S. Treasury to have a good estimate of the marginal propensity to consume in order to recommend tax changes. Would a 100 percent confidence interval be ideal?

⋆ **11.22** Suppose that we perform a statistical experiment, taking many samples of the same size from a given economic process. In each sample we construct a 95 percent confidence interval for estimating the coefficient β_j.

(a) In roughly what proportion of the samples does the confidence interval contain the value β_j?

(b) Assume that β_j is unknown. If we look at just one sample, can we tell from the confidence interval whether in fact it contains the value β_j?

11.23 In a simple regression, what happens to the interval estimate for the slope if the data are selected with a lot of variation in the X values rather than with a smaller amount?

Appendix

11.24 Show that $\sum w_i = 0$.

11.25 Show that $\sum w_i X_i = 1$.

12

Hypothesis Testing

In this chapter we develop methods for testing hypotheses about individual coefficients in simple and multiple regression models. Our attention is limited to a procedure known as a *significance test.* Tests of hypotheses involving more than one coefficient are discussed in Chapter 14.

12.1 Specification of Hypotheses

In regression analysis, a hypothesis is a statement or conjecture about the value of a particular coefficient β_j that is made before the empirical analysis is undertaken. (In simple regression j is either 0 or 1, representing the intercept or the slope; in multiple regression β_j represents any of the coefficients.) The statement may be deduced from theoretical principles or induced from previous empirical findings.

Formal hypothesis testing involves a choice between two contradictory hypotheses. One is called the *null hypothesis* and is denoted by H_0, and the other is called the *alternative hypothesis* and is denoted by H_1. For the procedures that we develop here, the null hypothesis must state that the true value of the regression coefficient β_j is equal to a specific value, which is sometimes denoted by β_j^0. The alternative hypothesis must be one of three vague (or "composite") forms, as shown in the following three sets of hypotheses:

$$H_0: \beta_j = \beta_j^0 \qquad H_0: \beta_j = \beta_j^0 \qquad H_0: \beta_j = \beta_j^0$$
$$\text{or} \qquad \text{or}$$
$$H_1: \beta_j \neq \beta_j^0 \qquad H_1: \beta_j > \beta_j^0 \qquad H_1: \beta_j < \beta_j^0 \qquad (12.1)$$

Note that hypotheses are statements about the true regression coefficient β_j. They are not about the estimated coefficient $\hat{\beta}_j^*$ nor are they phrased in terms of the explanatory variable X_j.

For example, a researcher might be concerned with whether or not the true slope coefficient in a simple regression is equal to 25. A test between the hypotheses $\beta_1 = 25$ and $\beta_1 \neq 25$ is clearly relevant, and the hypotheses would be presented formally as

$$H_0: \beta_1 = 25$$
$$H_1: \beta_1 \neq 25 \qquad (12.2)$$

Note that the null hypothesis is specific and the alternative is vague in an appropriate way.

Whether it is the null hypothesis or the alternative that the researcher thinks is more interesting or believable is not a factor that is built into the testing procedure. For example, the hypotheses in (12.2) would be used to test a theory that predicts $\beta_1 = 25$, and they also would be used to test a theory that predicts $\beta_1 \neq 25$. In the first case the interesting proposition is formulated as the null hypothesis, whereas in the second case the interesting proposition is formulated as the alternative.

In the procedures of hypothesis testing that we develop, the null and the alternative hypotheses play very different roles. Attention is focused on the null hypothesis, which is a specific statement about the true value of a coefficient. The role of the alternative hypothesis is to help shape a decision rule that leads us either to reject the null hypothesis in favor of the alternative or to not reject it.

In most situations the ideas of a researcher regarding a coefficient's true value are not so precise as suggested by the example above. How are the hypotheses chosen? As we shall see, the most common choice for the value of β_j^0 is zero, and in many others the choice for β_j^0 is 1. Choosing the proper form for the alternative, from among the three possibilities in (12.1), calls for careful thought about economics and also about the testing procedure.

12.2   The Basic Significance Test _____

The most common test in regression analysis, which we call the *basic significance test*, involves the following hypotheses:

$$H_0: \beta_j = 0$$
$$H_1: \beta_j \neq 0 \qquad (12.3)$$

where β_j is one of the coefficients in a regression model. In terms of our general notation, $\beta_j^0 = 0$ in these hypotheses.

The basic significance test serves to answer the question "Does X_j affect Y?" If the null hypothesis H_0 is true, the term $\beta_j X_j$ in the true regression is equal to zero no matter what the value of X_j is, and therefore the explanatory variable X_j has no effect on the dependent variable Y. Alternatively, if H_1 is true, the term $\beta_j X_j$ does depend on the value of X_j and therefore X_j affects Y. (If β_j is the intercept, the hypotheses simply state that β_0 is or is not equal to zero.)

It may seem odd to raise the question of whether an explanatory variable affects the dependent variable, because in the specification of regression models we have always presumed that it does. However, the validity of our presumption is always open to question, and this hypothesis test can provide support for the specification of the model. Also, a conclusion that a particular variable has no effect on the dependent variable can be very interesting.

We proceed slowly by explaining some of the basic logic underlying the test, and then we reformulate the mechanics in a way that makes the procedure simple to apply in practice.

The Underlying Logic

All the tests we work with are based on the sampling theory developed in the previous chapter. Recall that the estimator $\hat{\beta}_j$ has a normal distribution with a mean equal to β_j and a standard deviation $\sigma(\hat{\beta}_j)$ that depends on the variability of the random disturbance and on the values of the explanatory variables. We view the estimated coefficient $\hat{\beta}_j^*$ as being an outcome from this distribution.

If the null hypothesis is true, so that $\beta_j = 0$, sampling theory implies that $\hat{\beta}_j$ can take on any value from $-\infty$ to ∞ because the value of a normal random variable can occur anywhere in this range. Hence, no value $\hat{\beta}_j^*$ that we ever find in an estimated regression is totally inconsistent with the null hypothesis. Therefore, no value $\hat{\beta}_j^*$ can stand as evidence that the null hypothesis is definitely false. Similarly, if the alternative hypothesis is true, so that $\beta_j \neq 0$, the estimated coefficient $\hat{\beta}_j$ can also take on any value from $-\infty$ to ∞.

These implications of sampling theory make us realize that hypothesis testing can be very tricky. It will never be possible to conclude that one hypothesis is right and the other is wrong, because every possible value $\hat{\beta}_j^*$ is theoretically consistent with both hypotheses. For this reason, procedures have been developed that lead us to make conclusions based on probabilistic reasoning. Although the procedures may seem a bit awkward, they are easy to apply and they prevent us from making unreasonable judgments. Even our reasonable judgments, however, may sometimes be in error.

The testing procedure treats the null and the alternative hypotheses very differently. Attention focuses on the null hypothesis H_0. Instead of trying to decide whether H_0 or H_1 is the better hypothesis, our goal is to choose between two conclusions: "Reject H_0" or "Do not reject H_0."

The essence of the test involves a comparison of the estimated coefficient $\hat{\beta}_j^*$ with the value β_j^0 stated in H_0, which is zero for the basic significance test. Simple logic leads us to say that if $\hat{\beta}_j^*$ is very different from zero, then the evidence could be judged sufficiently inconsistent with the null hypothesis to allow us to reject it.

In view of what sampling theory says can occur, a *decision rule* of the form

$$\text{Reject } H_0 \text{ if } |\hat{\beta}_j^*| \geq \hat{\beta}_j^c \qquad (12.4)$$

would make sense, presuming that $\hat{\beta}_j^c$ is positive. This rule is illustrated in Figure 12.1. In the rule, $\hat{\beta}_j^c$ is the *critical value* for $\hat{\beta}_j$, and the two-part range of values $\hat{\beta}_j \geq \hat{\beta}_j^c$ and $\hat{\beta}_j \leq -\hat{\beta}_j^c$ is known as the *critical region*. Thus the decision rule says, in effect, "Reject H_0 if $\hat{\beta}_j^*$ is in the critical region."

With this decision rule, a value $\hat{\beta}_j^*$ that is much larger than 0 on the positive side or much smaller than 0 on the negative side leads to the rejection of H_0. Although such an outcome could occur if H_0 were true, it seems more in line with H_1. By contrast, a $\hat{\beta}_j^*$ that is close to 0, either on the positive or negative side, would lead to not rejecting H_0. Of course, such an outcome could occur if H_0 were not true. For instance, if β_j were a small positive number, it would be fairly likely that $\hat{\beta}_j^*$ would be close to zero.

We see that applying a decision rule like (12.4) can lead to two types of mistakes: (1) we may decide to reject the null hypothesis when in fact it is true, or (2) we may decide to not reject the null hypothesis when in fact it is false. These mistakes are known formally as *Type I* and *Type II error*, respectively. A classification of the possible errors and correct decisions that can be made in hypothesis testing is shown in Figure 12.2.

In principle, the critical value in the decision rule is chosen after careful consideration of the relative undesirability of making Type I and Type II errors in a particular empirical setting. The probabilities of making these errors depend on the exact value of β_j and on the $\hat{\beta}_j^c$ used in the decision rule. Since β_j is only vaguely specified in the alternative hypothesis, the chance of making a Type II error cannot be determined. Our concern for Type II error is therefore kept in the

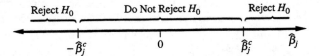

FIGURE 12.1 The logic underlying the basic significance test recognizes that no value for the estimated coefficient is totally inconsistent with the null hypothesis "H_0: $\beta_j = 0$." We plan to use a decision rule like "Reject H_0 if $|\hat{\beta}_j^*| \geq \hat{\beta}_j^c$." The extreme values for $\hat{\beta}_j$ that lead us to reject H_0 (namely, $\hat{\beta}_j \geq \hat{\beta}_j^c$ and $\hat{\beta}_j \leq -\hat{\beta}_j^c$) are collectively known as the critical region. The idea is that values of $\hat{\beta}_j$ in the critical region are quite inconsistent with H_0 because they are quite far away from $\beta_j = 0$.

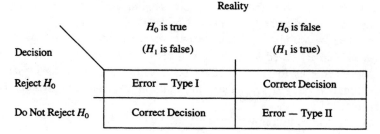

Reality

	H_0 is true (H_1 is false)	H_0 is false (H_1 is true)
Reject H_0	Error — Type I	Correct Decision
Do Not Reject H_0	Correct Decision	Error — Type II

FIGURE 12.2 The possible errors and correct decisions that can be made in hypothesis testing are classified in this array. The probability of making a Type I error is determined by the choice of the level of significance. This choice affects the probability of making a Type II error, but does not alone determine it.

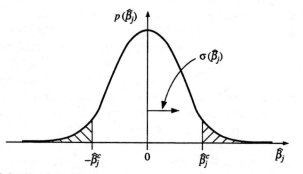

FIGURE 12.3 If the null hypothesis that $\beta_j = 0$ is true, sampling theory tells us that the OLS estimator $\hat\beta_j$ has a normal distribution with a mean of zero and a standard deviation of $\sigma(\hat\beta_j)$, as illustrated here. If we apply the decision rule (12.4), which is illustrated in Figure 12.1, there is some probability that $\hat\beta_j$ will occur in the critical region. That is, we may decide to reject H_0 even though it is true. The shaded area illustrates this probability amount, which is the probability of making a Type I error. This probability amount is also known as the "level of significance" of the test.

background. By contrast, since β_j is uniquely specified in the null hypothesis, the chance of making a Type I error can be determined exactly. This allows us to choose the critical value with knowledge of the associated probability of making a Type I error.

If the null hypothesis is true, so that $\beta_j = 0$, the sampling distribution for $\hat\beta_j$ is normal with a mean of zero and standard deviation $\sigma(\hat\beta_j)$. This distribution is illustrated in Figure 12.3, and a critical value $\hat\beta_j^c$ and its negative $-\hat\beta_j^c$ are shown. If it happens that $\hat\beta_j^* \geq \hat\beta_j^c$ or that $\hat\beta_j^* \leq -\hat\beta_j^c$, the decision rule (12.4) will lead us to reject H_0. However, this decision is incorrect if the null hypothesis is true, and so a Type I error would occur. The probability of making this Type I error is given by the shaded area in tails of Figure 12.3. Clearly, the greater is $\hat\beta_j^c$ the smaller will be the associated probability. Hence, the critical value is uniquely related to the probability of making a Type I error.

The probability of making a Type I error is also known as the *level of significance* of a test. Thus, as just explained, the critical value in the decision rule is uniquely related to the level of significance. The standard procedure is to choose the level of significance that we wish our test to have and allow this to determine what the critical value is. In practice, researchers "choose" a conventional level rather than try to make an independent assessment of the appropriate level: 5 percent is the most common value, but 1 percent and 10 percent are also used frequently. The consequences of this choice can be quite important, as we see in Section 12.3. We let α denote the level of significance, so $\alpha = .05$ will be the most common level for our tests.

Choosing a small level of significance makes the test conservative, which is usually appropriate. When the null hypothesis is rejected, we interpret this as evidence that X_j affects Y. In most cases this is what the researcher is really hoping to show. Therefore, making the test conservative means that there will be only a small chance that this conclusion is in error.

When the level of significance is small, the possible values for $\hat{\beta}_j$ that constitute the critical region for the decision rule have only a small chance of occurring if H_0 is true—the chance is simply α. Thus when we use a decision rule like (12.4), the empirical findings that lead us to reject a null hypothesis are those findings that (1) are more in line with H_1 than other possible findings and (2) are unlikely to occur if the null hypothesis is true.

Reformulation

The appropriate procedure is simpler to carry out if we reformulate the decision rule for the test. We do this first for the hypothetical situation in which $\sigma(\hat{\beta}_j)$ is known, and then we modify the procedure for the realistic situation in which we use the estimated standard error $s(\hat{\beta}_j)$ instead.

Consider a test statistic defined as

$$Z = \frac{\hat{\beta}_j}{\sigma(\hat{\beta}_j)} \qquad (12.5)$$

which is simply the estimate of a coefficient divided by its (true) standard error. (A *test statistic* is simply a statistic that is used in the decision rule of a hypothesis test.) Although sampling theory leads us to view $\hat{\beta}_j$ as a random variable, $\sigma(\hat{\beta}_j)$ is a constant. Thus Z is a simple linear transformation of $\hat{\beta}_j$, and (as for any linear transformation) there is a point-to-point correspondence between values of $\hat{\beta}_j$ and values of Z.

Since the test statistic Z is a linear transformation of $\hat{\beta}_j$, the decision rule (12.4) can be reformulated as

$$\text{Reject } H_0 \text{ if } |Z^*| \geq Z^c \qquad (12.6)$$

In effect, each possible value for $\hat{\beta}_j$ on the scale in Figure 12.1 can be relabeled with its equivalent Z value; the critical region consists of the same set of outcomes.

Now, recall again that sampling theory tells us that $\hat{\beta}_j$ has a normal distribution with an unknown mean of β_j and a standard deviation of $\sigma(\hat{\beta}_j)$. For a short time, we will make the notation Z do double duty. As explained in Chapter 10, the linear transformation

$$Z = \frac{\hat{\beta}_j - \beta_j}{\sigma(\hat{\beta}_j)} \tag{12.7}$$

yields a random variable Z that has a standard normal distribution ($\mu = 0$, $\sigma = 1$).

If the null hypothesis is true, so that $\beta_j = 0$, the test statistic Z in (12.5) is the same as the Z in (12.7), so it too has a standard normal distribution. If the null hypothesis is not true, the test statistic Z has some other probability distribution.

In order to apply the decision rule (12.6), we need to determine the critical value Z^c for the test statistic in such a way that the probability of making a Type I error is equal to the chosen level of significance α. To do this, the critical value Z^c is determined from

$$\Pr(|Z| \geq Z^c) = \alpha \tag{12.8}$$

on the condition that H_0 is true (which is the condition under which the test statistic Z has a standard normal distribution). For example, if $\alpha = .05$ the critical value is determined from Table A.1 to be $Z^c = 1.96$; note that the area in the right hand tail of $p(Z)$ is $\alpha/2 = .025$ for this example. Similarly, if $\alpha = .10$ the critical value is $Z^c = 1.645$.

The value for the test statistic is determined from the estimated coefficient $\hat{\beta}_j^*$ by

$$Z^* = \frac{\hat{\beta}_j^*}{\sigma(\hat{\beta}_j)} \tag{12.9}$$

To reach the conclusion of the test we simply compare the value of this ratio to the critical value, according to the decision rule (12.6).

Practical Application

In practical work $\sigma(\hat{\beta}_j)$ is never known, but it can be estimated by $s(\hat{\beta}_j)$, the estimated standard error. Parallel to the creation of the test statistic Z in the previous case, we consider a new test statistic t defined as

$$t = \frac{\hat{\beta}_j}{s(\hat{\beta}_j)} \qquad (12.10)$$

In contrast to the previous situation, this t is not a simple point-to-point transformation of $\hat{\beta}_j$ because sampling theory implies that $s(\hat{\beta}_j)$ would take on different values in different samples. That is, $s(\hat{\beta}_j)$ is a random variable, not a constant.

We can see, however, that values of $\hat{\beta}_j$ that are much larger than the hypothesized value $\beta_j = 0$ will tend to correspond to large values of t, and similarly on the negative side. Hence the logic underlying the decision rule (12.4) suggests that large values of t, positive or negative, are the outcomes that should lead us to reject the null hypothesis. Looked at another way, if H_0 is true then the estimation error is $\hat{\beta}_j - 0$, or simply $\hat{\beta}_j$ itself. Hence, t measures the size of the estimation error implied by H_0 in comparison with the standard error. For example, $t = 2.5$ means that the estimation error implied by H_0 is 2.5 times as large as the standard error. Large values of t are relatively unlikely to occur if the null hypothesis is true, and they seem more in line with H_1 than with H_0. Hence they are the possible outcomes that are used as evidence against H_0.

Thus, we can reformulate the decision rule (12.4) in terms of this test statistic as

$$\text{Reject } H_0 \text{ if } |t^*| \geq t^c \qquad (12.11)$$

As before, the values of t such that $|t| \geq t^c$ are known as the critical region. Thus the decision rule says, in effect, to reject H_0 if t^* is in the critical region.

To determine the critical value t^c, we need to recall a result introduced in Chapter 11. Here, we make the notation t do double duty. Consider a new random variable t defined as

$$t = \frac{\hat{\beta}_j - \beta_j}{s(\hat{\beta}_j)} \qquad (12.12)$$

Since t defined this way is similar to Z defined in (12.7), differing only by a substitution in the denominator, we might anticipate that $p(t)$ would be similar to $p(Z)$. Indeed this is so: it can be shown that this random variable has a t distribution with $n - k - 1$ degrees of freedom (n is the number of observations, k is the number of regressors).

If the null hypothesis is true, so that $\beta_j = 0$, the test statistic t in (12.10) is the same as the t in (12.12), so it too has a t distribution with df $= n - k - 1$. If the null hypothesis is not true, the test statistic t has some other probability distribution.

As usual, the critical value t^c is determined under the condition that the null hypothesis is true. This allows us to determine t^c so that the probability of making a Type I error is equal to the chosen level of significance α. Thus, the critical value t^c is determined from

$$\Pr(|t| \geq t^c) = \alpha \tag{12.13}$$

in which the test statistic t has a t distribution with $n - k - 1$ degrees of freedom. This is illustrated in Figure 12.4. Since the critical region $|t| \geq t^c$ underlies the two shaded areas in the figures, the basic significance test is called a **two-tailed test**. For example, if we have a regression model with 3 regressors that is estimated with data having 25 observations (so that df $= 25 - 3 - 1 = 21$), we see from Table A.3 that $t^c = 2.080$ for a test at the 5 percent level of significance and that $t^c = 1.721$ for a 10 percent test.

The value of the test statistic is calculated as

$$t^* = \frac{\hat{\beta}_j^*}{s^*(\hat{\beta}_j)} \tag{12.14}$$

Because the basic significance test is so commonly used, most computer programs for regression analysis compute this t^* automatically. It is usually labeled "t ratio" or "t statistic."

To reach the conclusion of the test, we follow the mandate of the decision rule (12.11): if the value of the t statistic (t^*) is in the critical region, the null hypothesis is rejected; if t^* is not in the critical region, H_0 is not rejected. If the null hypothesis is rejected, it is common to say that "the estimated coefficient is **significant**" or "... significantly different from zero," or even that "the

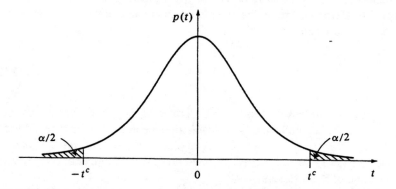

FIGURE 12.4 If the null hypothesis that $\beta_j = 0$ is true, the test statistic $t = \hat{\beta}_j / s(\hat{\beta}_j)$ has a t distribution with $n - k - 1$ degrees of freedom. The possible values of t range from $-\infty$ to ∞, so no value t^* is totally inconsistent with the null hypothesis. In the basic significance test the decision rule is: Reject H_0 if $|t^*| \geq t^c$. This specifies a two-tailed critical region, which bounds $\alpha/2$ probability in each tail. Therefore, if the null hypothesis is true, the probability of deciding to reject it (i.e., of making a Type I error), is α. In this figure, $\alpha = .05$.

explanatory variable X_j is significant" or "... has a significant effect on Y." If the null hypothesis is not rejected, we use the terms "insignificant(ly)" or "not significant(ly)" in each of these expressions.

In these interpretations that are attached to the conclusion of the test, the word "significant" can be thought of as a translation of "Reject H_0." Thus, whether or not an explanatory variable is "significant" is different from whether or not it is "important." Often the two findings go hand in hand, but they need not do so. The question of significance has to do with whether or not a hypothesis test indicates that an explanatory variable has *some* effect on the dependent variable. By contrast, the question of importance has to do with whether or not an economic assessment of the estimated coefficient indicates that the explanatory variable has a *big* effect on the dependent variable. To emphasize the distinction, sometimes the term "statistically significant" is used instead of just "significant" when reporting the results of a hypothesis test.

For completeness, it is a good idea to carry out the following five steps in conducting the test:

1. State the hypotheses clearly.
2. Choose the level of significance α.
3. Construct the decision rule.
4. Determine the value of the test statistic t^*.
5. State and interpret the conclusion of the test.

Most of the work comes in the third step. Notice that the first three steps should not depend on the actual findings in the data (except that the values of n and k are needed in the third step). In other words, the test should be set up without regard to any hint of what the data show.

For example, the simplest earnings function reported in Chapter 6 is

$$\widehat{EARNS}_i = -1.315 + 0.797ED_i$$
$$(1.540) \quad (0.128) \tag{12.15}$$
$$R^2 = .285 \quad SER = 4.361$$

with standard errors reported in parentheses beneath the corresponding coefficients. If we are interested in the question "Does education affect earnings?" then we carry out the basic significance test:

1. We clearly state the hypotheses, as in (12.3).
2. We choose $\alpha = .05$, by convention.
3. The decision rule is of the form (12.11). Given that $\alpha = .05$ and noting that the number of degrees of freedom (df) is 98, we see from Table A.3 that $t^c = 1.984$ approximately. Thus our decision rule is "Reject H_0 if $|t^*| \geq 1.984$."

4. We compute the value $t^* = \hat{\beta}_1^*/s^*(\hat{\beta}_1) = 0.797/0.128 = 6.23$.

5. Seeing that t^* is in the critical region, we decide to reject the null hypothesis and we conclude that education has a significant effect on earnings.

Note that it is not possible to look only at the magnitude of the estimated coefficient and judge immediately whether it is significant. In one situation a $\hat{\beta}_j^* = 0.0032$ might be significant, and in another situation $\hat{\beta}_j^* = 4372.35$ might be insignificant. The t statistic compares the estimated coefficient with the standard error. Only when this ratio is large (i.e., when $|t^*| \geq t^c$) do we judge the coefficient to be significantly different from zero.

This implies that the conclusion of a hypothesis test is not affected by the units of measurement for the data. For example, if the units of measurement for earnings in the data underlying (12.15) were changed to dollars (from thousands of dollars), the estimated coefficient on *ED* would be 797.0, which is a much larger magnitude. However, the standard error would also increase by a factor of 1000, so t^* would be 6.23 as before.

Experienced researchers know that it is possible to reach the conclusion of the test very quickly in many cases, without actually going through the complete procedure. Looking at Table A.3 we see that the critical value t^c is never less than 1.0 at conventional levels of significance, and t^c is not more than 5.0 except when the number of degrees of freedom is less than four. Hence, if $|t^*|$ is less than 1.0, it is clear that the coefficient is not significant by conventional standards. Similarly, if $|t^*|$ is greater than 5.0, it is clear that the coefficient is significant (unless one is working with an uncommonly low number of degrees of freedom). For example, looking quickly at the earnings function reported in (12.15), one can determine without a calculator that the intercept is not significant (because $|t^*| < 1$) but that the slope is significant (because $|t^*| > 5$). However, there is plenty of room for ambiguity and error, and carrying out a complete test is advisable.

In a similar spirit, practical researchers sometimes use a rule-of-thumb procedure in which an estimated coefficient is judged to be significant if $|t^*| \geq 2$. In formal terms, this amounts to setting the critical value $t^c = 2$ and letting the probability of making a Type I error be whatever results from this. Looking at Table A.2, we see that this probability will be about 5 percent so long as df is not small: in Table A.2, we double the values under the heading "$t^* = 2.00$." Closely related to this rule-of-thumb is the realization that for a basic significance test carried out at the 5 percent level of significance, the critical value t^c is roughly 2, except when the df is quite small (see Table A.3).

The testing procedure in multiple regression is the same as in simple regression. For example, consider the consumption function (7.29), which is reported fully in Table 11.3. In this multiple regression model, consumption is theorized to depend on income (*DPI*), the interest rate (*RAAA*), and the rate of inflation (*RINF2*). In Section 7.2 we noted that economic theory does not clearly specify whether the effects of *RAAA* and *RINF2*, individually, would be positive, negative, or zero. Thus the basic significance test is quite appropriate for these two variables separately:

1. For each of these tests, the hypotheses are given in (12.3).
2. We choose a 5 percent level of significance, by convention.
3. In each test, the critical value is $t^c = 2.080$ because there are 21 degrees of freedom. The decision rule is "Reject H_0 if $|t^*| \geq 2.080$."
4. Looking at Table 11.3, we see quickly that $|t^*| < 1$ in both cases, because the estimated coefficients are smaller in absolute value than their standard errors. It is hardly necessary to calculate the $|t^*|$ values with any greater precision.
5. Since the $|t^*|$ values are not in the critical region, we do not reject the null hypothesis in either case. The conclusions of the two separate tests are that both the interest rate and the rate of inflation are insignificant.

When we conclude that a variable is *insignificant,* we mean that we cannot reject the null hypothesis that it has no effect on the dependent variable. The test does not prove that the variable has no effect. Although it is possible that the variable has no effect ($\beta_j = 0$) it is also possible that the variable does have some effect ($\beta_j \neq 0$) and that we have made a Type II error. In any case, our best guess of the effect of a variable is given by the point estimate of its coefficient, $\hat{\beta}_j^*$. For example, in the consumption function just examined our best estimate is that a one percentage point increase in the rate of inflation decreases aggregate consumption by 0.562 billion dollars; however, according to standard statistical procedures we say that our result is insignificant. Although this sounds like doublespeak, it is really just a compact way of conveying information about what can be learned from the data.

12.3   The Test for Sign

Sometimes economic theory leads us to hypothesize that β_j is positive. For example, we would expect that the marginal propensity to consume in a simple aggregate consumption function would be positive. Although the complete logical opposite to this is that β_j is negative or zero, the formal procedure of hypothesis testing leads us to set up the following:

$$H_0: \beta_j = 0$$
$$H_1: \beta_j > 0$$
(12.16)

It is important to understand that $\beta_j > 0$ cannot be used as the null hypothesis: the null hypothesis must be specific so that we can determine the critical value for the test statistic that is associated with the level of significance that we choose.

The appropriate test for these hypotheses, which we call the **test for positive sign,** serves to answer the question "Does X_j have a positive effect on Y?" Clearly, the alternative hypothesis corresponds to the answer "yes," and the null is consistent with "no." The logic of the testing procedure is very similar to that of the basic significance test.

The alternative hypothesis here plays an important role in the design of the decision rule, a role that was somewhat hidden in our discussion of the basic significance test. The test statistic is the same as before:

$$t = \frac{\hat{\beta}_j}{s(\hat{\beta}_j)} \tag{12.17}$$

and any value from $-\infty$ to ∞ is possible under either hypothesis. However, since large positive values for $\hat{\beta}_j^*$ are more in line with H_1 than with H_0, we use occurrences of t^* being positive and large as evidence against the null hypothesis and in favor of the alternative. Note that t^* being positive and large reflects a situation in which $\hat{\beta}_j^*$ is positive and large relative to its standard error. Although large negative values for $\hat{\beta}_j^*$ or t^* cast doubt on the null hypothesis as stated, they are not consistent with the alternative. Hence, these values are not taken to be evidence against the null hypothesis in this case.

The decision rule is of the form

$$\text{Reject } H_0 \text{ if } t^* \geq t^c \tag{12.18}$$

If the null hypothesis is true, so that $\beta_j = 0$, then the test statistic t in (12.17) has a t distribution with $n - k - 1$ degrees of freedom, as shown in Figure 12.5. Under this condition, the value of t^c is determined from

$$\Pr(t \geq t^c) = \alpha \tag{12.19}$$

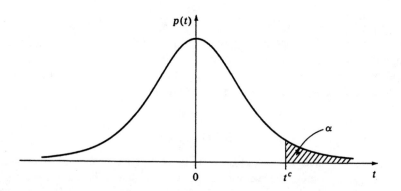

FIGURE 12.5 In the test for positive sign, the decision rule is to reject the null hypothesis if $t^* \geq t^c$. This specifies a one-tailed critical region, which bounds α probability in the right-hand tail. In this figure, $\alpha = .05$.

where α is the chosen level of significance. As illustrated in Figure 12.5, the critical region consists only of the values $t \geq t^c$, which underlie the right-hand tail of the distribution. For this reason, the test for sign is a *one-tailed test*. The critical value t^c is found in Table A.3. For example, at the 5 percent level of significance, $t^c = 1.708$ when df = 25. Note that for a given α, the critical value t^c is smaller in a one-tailed test than in a two-tailed test because in a two-tailed test t^c is chosen to bound just $\alpha/2$ probability in each tail.

When the null hypothesis is rejected in a test for positive sign, we conclude that "the estimated coefficient is significantly positive," or that "X_j has a significantly positive effect on Y." Again, one should bear in mind that significance is different from importance: a statement that X_j has a significantly positive effect on Y does not indicate that it has a *big* positive effect, but just that it has *some* positive effect. When the null hypothesis is not rejected, we conclude that "the estimated coefficient is not significantly positive," or that "X_j does not have a significantly positive effect on Y."

As is true of any significance test, a test for sign is going to lead us to make mistakes sometimes. Of course, we never know whether or not we have made a mistake: no flag is waved. However, we do know that the probability of incorrectly rejecting the null hypothesis (i.e., of making a Type I error) is exactly α, the chosen level of significance. This is because a mistake of this type occurs if the outcome of the test statistic t falls in the critical region when H_0 is in fact true. By (12.19) the probability of this occurring is α.

For example, we return to the estimated earnings function (12.15). Suppose economic theory predicts that the impact of education on earnings is positive. A test of this theory can be made by testing the hypothesis that $\beta_1 > 0$ in the underlying true regression model. We are clearly interested in the test for positive sign. Our procedure leads us to set up the null hypothesis "H_0: $\beta_1 = 0$" and to use the theoretical prediction as the alternative. The complete test is based on five steps:

1. We state the hypotheses, as in (12.16).
2. We choose $\alpha = .05$, by convention.
3. The decision rule is of the form (12.18). Given that $\alpha = .05$ and noting that df = 98, we see from Table A.3 that $t^c = 1.660$ approximately for this one-tailed test. Thus the decision rule is "Reject H_0 if $t^* \geq 1.660$."
4. We compute the value $t^* = \hat{\beta}_1^*/s^*(\hat{\beta}_1) = 0.797/0.128 = 6.23$.
5. Seeing that t^* is in the critical region, we decide to reject the null hypothesis and we conclude that education has a significantly positive effect on earnings.

The two earnings function tests that we have used as examples (here and in the previous section) provide a comparison of one- and two-tailed tests, and this raises the question of what hypotheses should be tested. A useful comparison can be made by choosing the same level of significance ($\alpha = .05$) in the two tests, for which the appropriate critical regions are shown in Figure 12.6. Adding some

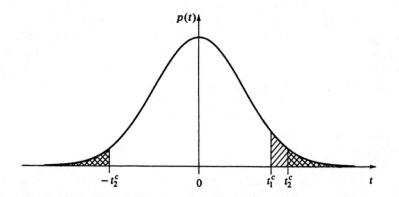

FIGURE 12.6 To compare the possible results of using a test for positive sign rather than the basic significance test, we use the same level of significance in both cases. The most important point of comparison to note is that if t^* happens to fall in the range between t_1^c and t_2^c, the tests give seemingly contradictory results. In the basic significance test we would conclude that the coefficient is not significant, whereas in the test for positive sign we would conclude that the coefficient is significantly positive. Since the conclusion of a test can be very sensitive to its technical specification, proper procedure calls for the hypotheses to be clearly stated before any results of the estimation are seen.

notation, we found that $t_2^c = 1.984$ in the two-tailed basic significance test and that $t_1^c = 1.660$ in the one-tailed test for positive sign. It turned out that $t^* = 6.23$, so the outcome is in the critical region for both tests. Other situations are possible, of course. If t^* occurs in the unshaded region between $-t_2^c$ and t_1^c, we would not reject H_0 in either test.

However, the conclusions from the two tests can seem to be contradictory in some cases. Suppose that $t^* = 1.8$, so that the outcome occurs in the range between t_1^c and t_2^c in Figure 12.6. In the basic significance test we would conclude that $\hat{\beta}_1^*$ is not significant, but in the test for positive sign we would conclude that the same $\hat{\beta}_1^*$ is significantly positive. Similarly, if t^* occurs in the range to the left of $-t_2^c$, the basic significance test would conclude that $\hat{\beta}_1^*$ is significant, but the test for sign would conclude that $\hat{\beta}_1^*$ is not significantly positive. It is clear that the qualitative conclusion can be very sensitive to the initial specification of hypotheses.

For example, in Section 7.3 we looked at a Phillips curve with a dummy variable allowing for a shift during the 1965–1970 period. The complete estimated regression ($n = 15$), also reported fully in Table 11.5, is

$$\widehat{RINF1}_i = -0.803 + 15.030 UINV_i + 0.894D_i$$
$$\qquad\quad (1.524) \quad (7.965) \qquad\quad (0.717) \tag{12.20}$$

$$R^2 = .600 \quad SER = 0.936$$

The t^* for the coefficient on *UINV*, the inverse of the unemployment rate, is $t^* = 1.886$. With df $= 12$, we see from Table A.3 that $t_1^c = 1.782$ and $t_2^c = 2.179$

at the 5 percent level of significance. The conclusion of the basic significance test is that the unemployment regressor *is not* significant, whereas the conclusion of the test for positive sign is that the regressor *is* significantly positive. In this case, economic theory and an understanding of the reciprocal specification naturally lead to the proposition that $\beta_1 > 0$, so the test for positive sign is appropriate.

Such a case, in which t^* falls between t_1^c and t_2^c, can lead to an awkward situation. If our initial economic theory is that $\beta_1 > 0$, the test for positive sign would be appropriate and we would be satisfied with the conclusion that $\hat{\beta}_1^*$ is significantly positive. On the other hand, if we begin with no particular theory and carry out a basic significance test, we would find that $\hat{\beta}_1^*$ is not significant. If this finding disappoints us, we would notice that a switch to a one-tailed test for positive sign would lead to "significance." On formal grounds, however, this is wrong because it invalidates the meaning of the level of significance. But, in our disappointment, we might realize that if we doubled the level of significance, the new t_2^c would equal the old t_1^c—so that the regression result would be significant in the two-tailed test. By extending this strategy, almost any finding can be made to look significant; this does not seem wise.

The proper choice of hypotheses and levels of significance requires good judgment, both of economic and statistical matters. Although there are no hard and fast rules, prudence calls for (1) determining the hypotheses to be tested before seeing any results, (2) choosing a 5 percent level of significance, and (3) reporting additionally, as appropriate, how changes in the hypotheses or the level of significance would alter the qualitative conclusion.

To specify the hypotheses after looking at the results of estimation, or to plan a sequence of tests that depends on the observed results, invalidates the formal validity of the hypothesis testing procedure. We have presented two different tests regarding the effect of education on earnings for the sake of providing examples and to introduce the question of the choice of test. In practice, only one test should be applied to any coefficient.

Almost as an afterword, we consider the situation in which the hypothesis of interest is that $\beta_j < 0$. This leads us to the **test for negative sign** in which the hypotheses are

$$H_0: \beta_j = 0$$
$$H_1: \beta_j < 0$$

(12.21)

and the decision rule is

$$\text{Reject } H_0 \text{ if } t^* \leq -t^c$$

(12.22)

where t^c is determined as in (12.19). All that was said about the test for positive sign holds for this test also.

Finally, we return to a consideration of why the hypotheses in the test for positive sign were not specified to be

$$H_0: \beta_j \leq 0$$
$$H_1: \beta_j > 0$$

$$(12.23)$$

In fact, sometimes they are written this way. The test procedure that is used in conjunction with this specification is exactly the same as that used here, so there is no real difference between the two approaches. We write the null hypothesis in specific form in order to be fully consistent with the procedure for determining the critical value t^c, which presumes that $\beta_j = 0$ if the null hypothesis is true.

12.4   Tests for Specific Coefficient Values _____

Sometimes the interesting proposition that we wish to test involves a specific value, β_j^0, that is not zero. For example, if theory suggests that β_1 equals 1, we would test

$$H_0: \beta_1 = 1$$
$$H_1: \beta_1 \neq 1$$

$$(12.24)$$

Similarly, if theory implies that β_1 is less than 1, we would test

$$H_0: \beta_1 = 1$$
$$H_1: \beta_1 < 1$$

$$(12.25)$$

In both cases the null hypothesis is of the form "$H_0: \beta_j = \beta_j^0$."

As with the other tests we have developed, the procedure involves constructing a decision rule that leads to rejecting the null hypothesis under clearly stated conditions. In every case, the test statistic is given by the ratio

$$t = \frac{\hat{\beta}_j - \beta_j^0}{s(\hat{\beta}_j)}$$

$$(12.26)$$

Given the results from an estimated regression, the value of t is

$$t^* = \frac{\hat{\beta}_j^* - \beta_j^0}{s^*(\hat{\beta}_j)}$$

$$(12.27)$$

In every case, sampling theory tells us that the test statistic t has a t distribution with $n - k - 1$ degrees of freedom if the null hypothesis is true.

When the alternative hypothesis is that $\beta_j \neq \beta_j^0$, as in (12.24), the decision rule is the same as that for the basic significance test:

$$\text{Reject } H_0 \text{ if } |t^*| \geq t^c$$

$$(12.28)$$

where t^c is determined from

$$\Pr(|t| \geq t^c) = \alpha \tag{12.29}$$

That is, we set up a two-tailed test in which finding t^* to be very large or very small (negatively) leads us to reject the null hypothesis. These values for t^* correspond to estimated coefficients $\hat{\beta}_j^*$ that are very different from β_j^0, and which therefore are taken as evidence against H_0. In other words, the values of t^* that lead to rejecting H_0 correspond to coefficients that would imply estimation errors that are much larger (in absolute value) than the standard error if H_0 were true. If the null hypothesis is rejected, we say that "$\hat{\beta}_j^*$ is significantly different from β_j^0."

Similarly, when the alternative hypothesis is that $\beta_j < \beta_j^0$, as in (12.25), the decision rule is the same as that for the test of negative sign:

$$\text{Reject } H_0 \text{ if } t^* \leq -t^c \tag{12.30}$$

where t^c is determined from

$$\Pr(t \geq t^c) = \alpha \tag{12.31}$$

That is, we set up a one-tailed test in which finding very small (negative) values of t^* leads us to reject the null hypothesis. In this case, these values of t^* correspond to estimated coefficients that are much less than β_j^0. If the null hypothesis is rejected, we say that "$\hat{\beta}_j^*$ is significantly less than β_j^0."

To complete the set of possibilities, we note that if the alternative hypothesis states that $\beta_j > \beta_j^0$, the decision rule is the same as that for the test of positive sign:

$$\text{Reject } H_0 \text{ if } t^* \geq t^c \tag{12.32}$$

where t^c is determined from

$$\Pr(t \geq t^c) = \alpha \tag{12.33}$$

For example, consider the aggregate consumption function reported in Chapter 6:

$$\widehat{CON}_i = 0.568 + 0.907DPI_i$$
$$(6.973) \quad (0.010) \tag{12.34}$$
$$R^2 = .997 \quad SER = 8.935$$

where the numbers in parentheses are the standard errors for the corresponding coefficients. As noted in Chapter 1, Keynes theorized that the marginal propensity to consume would be less than 1, which is a testable proposition about β_1.

1. The proper hypotheses are given by (12.25), which calls for a one-tailed test.
2. We choose the conventional 5 percent level of significance.

3. The decision rule is of the form (12.30). Noting that $\alpha = .05$ and df $= n - 2 = 23$, we see from Table A.3 that $t^c = 1.714$. Thus, our decision rule is "Reject H_0 if $t^* \leq -1.714$."

4. We compute the value

$$t^* = \frac{\hat{\beta}_1^* - \beta_1^0}{s^*(\hat{\beta}_1)} = \frac{0.907 - 1.0}{0.010} = -9.3 \qquad (12.35)$$

5. Seeing that t^* is in the critical region, we decide to reject the null hypothesis. We conclude that the marginal propensity to consume is significantly less than 1, supporting Keynes' theory.

Finally, if $\beta_j^0 = 0$ in the test for a specific value, we are back to the basic significance test or the test for sign. Thus all the tests presented in this chapter can be considered special cases of a general procedure. The most important distinction among the cases is not the value of β_j^0, but the specification of the alternative hypothesis. This distinction is made in Table 12.1, which summarizes the procedure for testing individual coefficients in regression models.

Hypothesis Testing and Confidence Intervals

There is an important equivalence between creating a confidence interval and carrying out a two-tailed test of the hypotheses

$$H_0: \beta_j = \beta_j^0$$
$$H_1: \beta_j \neq \beta_j^0 \qquad (12.36)$$

Suppose that the confidence interval and the significance test are based on the same value for α. For example, suppose that a 95 percent confidence interval is compared with a hypothesis test at the 5 percent level of significance. Whenever the confidence interval contains the value β_j^0, the null hypothesis is not rejected. And, whenever the confidence interval does not contain β_j^0, the null hypothesis is rejected.

TABLE 12.1 Summary of Regression t Tests

If the Alternative Hypothesis Is of the Form	Then the Decision Rule Is of the Form	Where t^c Is Determined by
$H_1: \beta_j \neq \beta_j^0$	Reject H_0 if $|t^*| \geq t^c$	$\Pr(|t| \geq t^c) = \alpha$
$H_1: \beta_j > \beta_j^0$	Reject H_0 if $t^* \geq t^c$	$\Pr(t \geq t^c) = \alpha$
$H_1: \beta_j < \beta_j^0$	Reject H_0 if $t^* \leq -t^c$	$\Pr(t \geq t^c) = \alpha$

Notes:
1. In all cases, $H_0: \beta_j = \beta_j^0$.
2. The level of significance is α.
3. The degrees of freedom is df $= n - k - 1$, where k is the number of regressors.
4. In all cases, $t^* = (\hat{\beta}_j^* - \beta_j^0)/s^*(\hat{\beta}_j)$.

This equivalence can be understood informally along the following lines. As explained in Chapter 11, the confidence interval for estimating β_j is the range

$$\hat{\beta}_j^* - t^c s^*(\hat{\beta}_j) \quad \text{to} \quad \hat{\beta}_j^* + t^c s^*(\hat{\beta}_j) \tag{12.37}$$

where t^c is determined from

$$\Pr(t \geq t^c) = \frac{\alpha}{2} \tag{12.38}$$

The decision rule for a two-tailed hypothesis test is

$$\text{Reject } H_0 \text{ if } |t^*| \geq t^c \tag{12.39}$$

where t^c is determined from

$$\Pr(|t| \geq t^c) = \alpha \tag{12.40}$$

Comparing (12.38) and (12.40), we see that t^c is the same in both procedures, so long as α is the same.

Now, if the null hypothesis is rejected with a positive t^*, it must be that $t^* \geq t^c$. In other words,

$$\frac{\hat{\beta}_j^* - \beta_j^0}{s^*(\hat{\beta}_j)} \geq t^c \tag{12.41}$$

Rearranging, we see that this implies that

$$\beta_j^0 \leq \hat{\beta}_j^* - t^c s^*(\hat{\beta}_j) \tag{12.42}$$

That is, β_j^0 lies to the left of (or on) the lower boundary of the confidence interval. Similarly, the conditions under which the null hypothesis is rejected with a negative t^* correspond to β_j^0 lying to the right of (or on) the upper boundary of the confidence interval. Further analysis along the same lines shows that the conditions under which the null hypothesis is not rejected, $|t^*| < t^c$, correspond to β_j^0 lying within the confidence interval.

For example, consider the question of whether or not the intercept in a simple consumption function is equal to zero. Based on (12.34), our best estimate is that the intercept is 0.568 billion dollars, which is not zero. However, the 95 percent confidence interval for estimating the underlying β_0 is

$$\hat{\beta}_0^* \pm h = 0.568 \pm (2.069)(6.973) \quad \text{or} \quad (-13.859) \text{ to } (14.995) \tag{12.43}$$

Since the confidence interval contains zero, we realize that a basic significance test with $\alpha = .05$ would lead to the conclusion that the intercept is not significantly different from zero. To verify this, we see quickly that $|t^*| < 1$ and therefore that the conclusion is correct. (Note that in a complete 5-step test, $t^c = 2.069$ in this case.)

Because the two methods overlap, a "test" of the hypotheses in (12.36) can be carried out by constructing a confidence interval and then checking to see if β_j^0 is included or not. Although this procedure is correct, it is not recommended. Standard practice calls for carrying out a hypothesis test when we want to talk about hypotheses or about the significance of a coefficient and for making a confidence interval when we want to provide an interval estimate of the coefficient.

12.5   *P*-Values

The essence of a significance test is a comparison of a test statistic calculated from a set of data with the probability distribution that would prevail for that statistic if the null hypothesis were true. In the formal test procedure described above, a level of significance is chosen and a clear decision rule for rejecting the null hypothesis is formulated. This decision rule can be reformulated in terms of a new concept, the *P*-value.

Also, we saw in Section 12.3 that the conclusion of a hypothesis test can be very sensitive to its technical specification—that is, to the choice of α and the alternative hypothesis. In a sense, the formality of the procedure can interfere with our learning from the data. The *P*-value can be used in a less formal way to interpret the findings in a reasonable probabilistic framework.

Consider, for example, the test for positive sign, in which the hypotheses are

$$H_0: \beta_j = 0$$
$$H_1: \beta_j > 0 \tag{12.44}$$

The decision rule is

$$\text{Reject } H_0 \text{ if } t^* \geq t^c \tag{12.45}$$

where t^c is determined from

$$\Pr(t \geq t^c) = \alpha \tag{12.46}$$

for a chosen level of α. If the null hypothesis is true, the probability distribution of the test statistic

$$t = \frac{\hat{\beta}_j}{s(\hat{\beta}_j)} \tag{12.47}$$

is as illustrated in Figure 12.7a. In this figure, the critical regions for two levels of significance, .05 and .10, are shown by the values of t underlying the shaded areas.

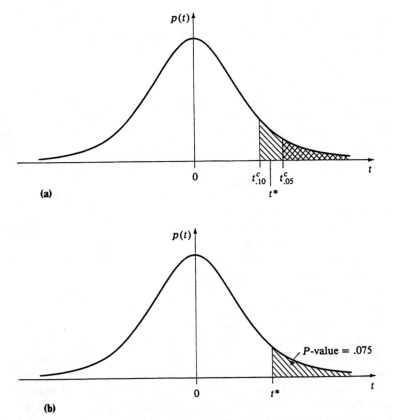

FIGURE 12.7 Part (a) shows the critical regions for the test of positive sign when $\alpha = .05$ and $\alpha = .10$. For the t^* indicated, the tests show significance at the 10 percent level but not at the 5 percent level. In (b), $\Pr(t \geq t^*)$ is shown by the shaded area. This probability is known as the P-value of the test, and it embodies all the information needed for statistical inference without setting up the formal decision rule and choosing the level of significance. When the P-value equals .075, we realize that a one-tailed test would show significance at 10 percent, but not at the 5 percent level.

Now, focusing on the t^* obtained in the data, we can compute a probability amount known as the **P-value** under the condition that the null hypothesis is true:

$$P\text{-value} = \Pr(t \geq t^*) \quad \text{(one-tailed)} \qquad (12.48)$$

Such a probability is given by the area under the distribution to the right of t^*, as shown in Figure 12.7b. Comparing (12.46) with (12.48), we see that whenever t^* is greater than t^c in a test for positive sign, the P-value will be less than α. Similarly, whenever t^* is less than t^c, the P-value will be greater than α. Thus, the standard decision rule (12.45) can be reformulated as

$$\text{Reject } H_0 \text{ if } P\text{-value} \leq \alpha \qquad (12.49)$$

The standard decision rule and its P-value reformulation are fully equivalent.

The P-value, by itself, is the probability that the t statistic would be as large as or larger than it actually is if the null hypothesis were true. A low P-value casts doubt on the null hypothesis, because it indicates that it is unlikely that a t statistic as large as or larger than t^* would occur if H_0 were true.

This interpretation of P-values is consistent with the standard formulation of hypothesis tests. If the P-value is small, say $P = .035$, then the result is quite unlikely and leads to formally rejecting the null hypothesis at $\alpha = .05$. If the P-value is a bit larger, say $P = .075$, then the result is still fairly unlikely. It would not lead to formal rejection at $\alpha = .05$ but it would at $\alpha = .10$; this case is illustrated in Figure 12.7a. Finally, if $P = .125$, the result is moderately unlikely—there is only a 12.5 percent chance that t^* would be as large as or larger than it actually is if H_0 were true—but it would not lead to significance at the conventional levels of significance.

Although rephrasing the test in terms of P-values permits us to carry out the formal procedure in just a slightly different language, it also permits us to proceed less formally and thereby to avoid the strictness involved with choosing the level of significance in the formal procedure. The difficulty with that strictness is that it invites inappropriate posturing: we have seen that a result can be made "significant" merely by changing the α, which serves as the formal criterion for significance. Also, if one has blind allegiance to the 5 percent level, a result for which $P = .06$ would be declared to be insignificant with no further analysis. Reporting the P-value of a test in addition to, or instead of, the formal decision is a way of concisely conveying some information about what is going on in the data.

For a two-tailed test, a two-tailed P-value can be calculated as

$$P\text{-value} = \Pr(|t| \geq t^*) \quad \text{(two-tailed)} \qquad (12.50)$$

and compared with the formal level of significance or interpreted directly.

Although practice varies, some statisticians suggest that calculation and reporting of the P-value ought to be done without any reference to the alternative hypothesis—that is, that the P-value ought to be computed only for the single tail of the sampling distribution in which the t^* happens to fall. This practice breaks away from the formal procedure, but for a very practical reason: often the appropriate null hypothesis to consider is objectively clear to the researcher, but whether the alternative hypothesis should be one-tailed or two-tailed is unclear. Since it invalidates the formal procedure to choose H_1 on the basis of sample evidence for t^*, the researcher may be left in a quandary. The suggested *P*-value procedure is simply a probabilistic calculation involving the null hypothesis and the sample results. It is up to the researcher or the reader to provide the substantive interpretation, rather than to rely on the formal decision rule.

For example, in the Phillips curve reported in Section 12.3, the t statistic for the unemployment variable is $t^* = 1.886$, having the anticipated sign. Interpolating in Table A.2, with df $= 12$, we find that the one-tailed *P*-value is

$$P\text{-value} = \Pr(t \geq 1.886) \approx .04 \tag{12.51}$$

(A computer calculation yields 4.19 percent.) Thus, if the null hypothesis were true ($\beta_1 = 0$), there would be only a 4 percent chance of getting a t^* of 1.886 or larger. This casts doubt on the null hypothesis, and the coefficient might be judged fairly significant. We see immediately that on a formal one-tailed test it would be significant at $\alpha = .10$ or $\alpha = .05$, but not significant at $\alpha = .01$.

P-values are not commonly reported in econometric studies, partly because standard t tables do not contain sufficient detail to allow them to be determined from t^* values. However, some computer programs for regression routinely print out the two-tailed *P*-value that is appropriate for the basic significance test. Even when the *P*-value is not calculated by a program, it can often be approximated by using Table A.1, because the t distribution is practically the same as the standard normal for large samples.

A common practice in reporting regression results is to indicate whether each of the coefficients is significant at any of the conventional levels of significance (e.g., 1, 5, and 10 percent). This conveys information similar to that of the *P*-value, but with less succinctness and less precision.

Finally, thinking in terms of *P*-values helps clarify the relation between the size of the t^* value in a formal hypothesis test and its meaning for the decision to reject or not reject the null hypothesis. Consider, for example, a one-tailed test with 30 degrees of freedom, for which Table A.2 can be used to determine selected *P*-values. If $t^* = 1.0$, so that $P = .163$, the null hypothesis would not be rejected at any of the commonly reported levels of significance (.10, .05, and .01). If t^* moved up to 1.5 with $P = .072$, the result would be significant (i.e., H_0 would be rejected) at the .10 level but not the others. If t^* moved up to 2.0 with $P = .027$, the result would be significant at the .10 and .05 levels, but not at the .01 level. If t^* moved up to 2.5 with $P = .009$, the result would be significant at all these levels. Thus, relatively modest differences in t^* when it is near 2.0 in value can have important implications for the conclusions of our tests. By contrast, we see that there is no difference of practical consequence between getting a t^* value of 5 or a t^* of 50: in both cases it is nearly impossible that the sample value would have occurred if the null hypothesis were true, and therefore the coefficient is judged significant.

Problems

Section 12.1

★ **12.1** For each of the following, could it be the statement of a null hypothesis? Could it be an alternative hypothesis?
(a) $\beta_1 < 60$.
(b) $\beta_1 \neq 60$.
(c) $\beta_1 = 60$.
(d) $\beta_1 > 60$.

12.2 Set up the appropriate null and alternative hypotheses for testing the proposition that
(a) $\beta_1 = 0$.
(b) $\beta_1 < 0$.
(c) $\beta_1 \neq 100$.
(d) $\beta_1 > 100$.

Section 12.2

12.3 Carry out a complete basic significance test for the effect of *DPI* on *CON* in Equation (12.34).

★ **12.4** In the earnings function (7.33), reported fully in Table 11.1, does a person's race affect his earnings?

★ **12.5** In the earnings function (7.15), reported fully in Table 11.1, does experience affect earnings? Carry out the basic significance test at the 10 percent level and then do it again at the 5 percent level.

12.6 In the demand for money regression (7.54), reported fully in Table 11.6, does income have a significant effect?

12.7 Among the five earnings functions reported in Table 11.1, in which equations is the intercept significantly different from zero?

12.8 In the earnings function (7.41), reported fully in Table 11.1, assess the significance of each of the coefficients on the regional dummy variables. Discuss the implications of these three tests taken together.

12.9 Under what condition would the rule-of-thumb procedure using $|t| > 2$ as the critical region be precisely the same as a regular 5 percent significance test?

Section 12.3

12.10 In the consumption function (12.34), determine quickly if the intercept is significantly positive.

12.11 Is the rate of growth of *GNP* estimated in regression (6.50), and reported fully in Table 11.4, significantly positive?

★ **12.12** In the demand for money regression (7.54), reported fully in Table 11.6, is the interest elasticity significantly negative?

* **12.13** For a 5 percent significance test with df $= 100$, determine the values that correspond to t_1^c and t_2^c in Figure 12.6.

  12.14 In the earnings function (7.46), reported fully in Table 11.1, is the coefficient of *EXPSQ* significant at the 10 percent level? Based on general economic knowledge, what would be the appropriate test for sign in this case? Carry out this test at the 10 percent level and compare its conclusion with that of the basic significance test.

  12.15 Suppose that $H_0: \beta_j = 0$ is true, and consider the following procedure. If the estimated coefficient $\hat{\beta}_j^*$ is positive, set up a 5 percent significance test for positive sign; if $\hat{\beta}_j^*$ is negative, set up a 5 percent significance test for negative sign. Now, viewing the situation before the estimate is calculated, what is the probability that this procedure will lead to a Type I error?

Section 12.4

  12.16 In a study with a very large number of observations, the price elasticity of demand for gasoline was estimated to be -0.90 with a standard error of 0.06; is the estimated elasticity significantly different from -1.0?

  12.17 In a study with a very large number of observations, the income elasticity of demand was estimated to be 0.70 with a standard error of 0.12. Is the elasticity significantly less than 1.0?

* **12.18** In the semilog earnings function (7.55), reported fully in Table 11.2, is the elasticity of *EARNS* with respect to *MONTHS* worked significantly different from 1?

  12.19 Use a confidence interval to test the hypothesis that the income elasticity of the demand for money, estimated in regression (7.54) and reported in Table 11.6, is equal to 1.0.

  12.20 Use a confidence interval to assess whether experience affects earnings, based on regression (7.15) as reported in Table 11.1.

Section 12.5

  12.21 Using Table A.2, determine (approximately) and interpret the one-tailed *P*-values for the tests in
  (a) Problem 12.4.
  (b) Problem 12.5.
  (c) Problem 12.10.
  (d) Problem 12.11.
  (e) Problem 12.12.

13

Estimation and Regression Problems

This chapter covers a variety of topics relating to the estimation of regression models. The first section applies the procedure of making a confidence interval to the task of making a prediction. The second section presents a general consideration of the properties of estimators. The succeeding sections use these concepts in reconsiderations of the topics of multicollinearity, misspecification, and sample selection.

The appendix generalizes the concept of expected values, which is used throughout this chapter.

13.1   Confidence Intervals for Prediction _____

One use of regression models is to make predictions of the dependent variable for observations that are not included in the data used for estimation. In time-series work this usually means considering an observation that occurs after the time period covered by the data, and such a prediction is called a *forecast*. In cross-section work, this usually means considering an observation that is in the same population as the data but that was not selected in the data collection. In either case, we call it an out-of-sample observation.

We consider the case of simple regression and focus on an out-of-sample observation whose value for the explanatory variable is X_p. Presuming that the economic process that determines Y_p is the same as that which produced the data used for estimation (which is an assumption that we must make if we are to use the estimated regression), the actual value of Y_p will be

$$Y_p = \beta_0 + \beta_1 X_p + u_p \tag{13.1}$$

In the prediction context, this Y_p is unknown. Given the value X_p, we predict Y_p to be

$$\hat{Y}_p = \hat{\beta}_0 + \hat{\beta}_1 X_p \tag{13.2}$$

using the coefficients from the estimated regression.

Associated with such a prediction is a **prediction error**

$$e_p = \hat{Y}_p - Y_p = (\hat{\beta}_0 - \beta_0) + (\hat{\beta}_1 - \beta_1)X_p - u_p \tag{13.3}$$

We see that there are two sources of error in the prediction. First, there are estimation errors $\hat{\beta}_0 - \beta_0$ and $\hat{\beta}_1 - \beta_1$ involved with the coefficients. Second, the prediction ignores the disturbance u_p, which will be a component of the actual Y_p.

The expected prediction error is equal to zero:

$$E[e_p] = 0 \tag{13.4}$$

(see the appendix to this chapter). Therefore, we can say that the predictions from (13.2) are unbiased.

In any particular situation the prediction error will not be zero (except by coincidence), and an estimate of the typical error is given by

$$s_p = SER \sqrt{1 + \frac{1}{n} + \frac{(X_p - \overline{X})^2}{\Sigma(X_i - \overline{X})^2}} \tag{13.5}$$

which is the **standard error of prediction**. Regarding (13.5), we see that the sum of the terms under the square-root sign is greater than 1, so the typical error of an out-of-sample prediction (s_p) is always greater than the typical error of fit within the sample (*SER*).

Also, the typical error of prediction depends on $X_p - \overline{X}$, which is the difference between the value of X for the observation being predicted and the mean of X for the observations in the data set. If the new observation is like the typical observation in the data (i.e., if X_p is close to $\overline{X}$), the typical prediction error is relatively small. However, if $|X_p - \overline{X}|$ is large, the typical prediction error is relatively large. This is unfortunate for time-series applications, because $X_p - \overline{X}$ is likely to be relatively large for the observation being predicted.

Confidence intervals for the prediction are of the form

$$\hat{Y}_p \pm h, \quad \text{where} \quad h = t^c s_p \tag{13.6}$$

where t^c is determined from

$$Pr(t \geq t^c) = \frac{\alpha}{2} \tag{13.7}$$

Note that both the construction and the interpretation of this confidence interval are basically the same as for the confidence intervals developed in Chapter 11.

For example, *DPI* in 1981 was 1040.2 billion dollars. Based on the consumption function (6.10) estimated for 1956–1980,

$$\hat{Y}_p = 0.568 + (0.907)(1040.2) = 944.03 \tag{13.8}$$

and

$$s_p = 8.935 \sqrt{1 + \frac{1}{25} + \frac{(1040.2 - 705.7)^2}{875,270}} = 9.656 \tag{13.9}$$

We predict with 95 percent confidence that Y_p is in the interval 944.03 ± (2.069)(9.656) = 944.03 ± 19.98, or between 924.05 and 964.01. (The actual value was Y_p = 959.1, which lies within the interval.)

Since the width of the confidence interval depends on s_p, then for any given level of confidence the confidence interval is wider the greater is the difference $|X_p - \overline{X}|$. This is illustrated in Figure 13.1, which shows schematically the 95 percent confidence bands for making predictions in a simple regression model. For an observation with X_p, the prediction of $\hat{Y}_p$ is read off the fitted regression line. The confidence interval for predicting Y_p extends vertically from the lower confidence band to the upper one.

The prediction methods discussed here take the X_p value as given, or known with certainty. This may be appropriate in cross-section applications, but for

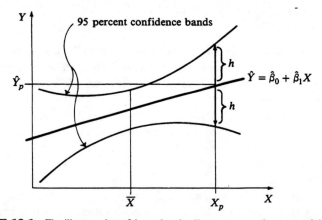

FIGURE 13.1 The illustrated confidence bands allow us to see the range of the 95 percent confidence interval for predictions made with the estimated regression model. For example, when $X = X_p$ the prediction interval runs from $\hat{Y}_p - h$ to $\hat{Y}_p + h$. As illustrated, the width of the confidence interval increases with the distance of X_p from $\overline{X}$.

time-series forecasting it often is not. When X_p also must be predicted, the actual errors involved in predicting Y_p are more complex. However, if the regressor in a time-series model is lagged variable, X_p may already be observed and we are in a position to make predictions of Y_p with (13.2).

13.2   Comparing Alternative Estimators _____

In all our work with regression so far, the method used to estimate the coefficients has been ordinary least squares (OLS) and our sampling theory has presumed that the estimators are applied to a correctly specified model. We should realize, however, that there can be alternative estimators for the coefficients and thus that the same data can yield more than one estimated value for a given parameter.

Alternative estimators arise from two sources. First and foremost, a method other than ordinary least squares may be adopted as the criterion for deriving the estimator of a coefficient. The method will lead to a rule or formula for determining an estimate of the coefficient from observed data; this rule or formula is the estimator. For example, in Chapter 5 we noted that one approach to determining the best-fitting line is to measure the error of fit from a plotted point to the fitted line by determining the perpendicular distance. (By contrast, in OLS we determine the vertical distance, $Y_i - \hat{Y}_i$.) For any given set of data, the "perpendicular estimates" of the coefficients will be different from the OLS estimates, and the corresponding sampling distributions of the estimators will be different also.

A second source of alternative estimators is the use of some estimator in a model specified differently from the one for which it was derived. For example, if we were to use the regular simple regression OLS estimator for β_1 to estimate the coefficient of the first explanatory variable in a multiple regression, we would obtain an estimate for the impact of that variable. Whether this should be considered to be a misapplication of OLS or the application of an "alternative estimator" is perhaps semantic, and we will return to this in Section 13.4.

For the purpose of discussion here, suppose that we are interested in estimating a particular coefficient, β_j, in a properly specified normal regression model. One way to make the estimate is to apply the appropriate OLS estimator, which we denote as usual by $\hat{\beta}_j$. A second way is to apply an alternative estimator, which we denote by $\tilde{\beta}_j$. What difference might it make whether we use $\hat{\beta}_j$ or $\tilde{\beta}_j$ to estimate β_j? To answer this question, we need to compare the sampling distributions of the estimators.

In Chapter 11 we noted the features of $p(\hat{\beta}_j)$, the sampling distribution of $\hat{\beta}_j$: it is normal, its expected value is equal to β_j, and its standard deviation is a known function of σ_u and the values of the explanatory variable(s). The sampling distribution $p(\tilde{\beta}_j)$ of the alternative estimator $\tilde{\beta}_j$ may be quite different:

its form may be not-normal, its mean may be greater or less that β_j, and its standard deviation may be greater or less than $\sigma(\hat{\beta}_j)$. Figure 13.2 illustrates one possible situation. As compared with $p(\hat{\beta}_j)$, the sampling distribution $p(\tilde{\beta}_j)$ of the alternative estimator has a smaller mean and a larger standard deviation.

In the general analysis of an estimator, statistical theory usually focuses on certain characteristics of the sampling distribution in relation to β_j. These are known as **properties** of the estimator. The statistical properties of estimators fall into two classes: those that hold true regardless of the sample size, and those that hold true only as the sample size approaches infinity. The latter are called *large-sample* properties, and by contrast the former are called *small-sample* properties even though they hold true in large samples also. We are concerned with small-sample properties relating to the mean and to the variance of the sampling distribution and with one large-sample property that combines the two.

The **bias** of an estimator is defined as the expected estimation error. For some estimator $\tilde{\beta}_j$ of β_j

$$\text{bias of } \tilde{\beta}_j = E[\tilde{\beta}_j - \beta_j] = E[\tilde{\beta}_j] - \beta_j \qquad (13.10)$$

If the bias equals zero, the estimator is said to be **unbiased;** otherwise it is said to be **biased.** In Figure 13.2 the estimator $\tilde{\beta}_j$ has a negative bias, because $E[\tilde{\beta}_j] - \beta_j < 0$. By contrast, for the OLS estimator,

$$\text{bias of } \hat{\beta}_j = E[\hat{\beta}_j - \beta_j] = E[\hat{\beta}_j] - \beta_j = 0 \qquad (13.11)$$

and we see that it is unbiased. The essence of unbiasedness is that on average (i.e., in expectation) the point estimate is right on target; a biased estimator yields point estimates that tend to be too large or too small. Unbiasedness is a desirable property for an estimator to have, but it is not essential.

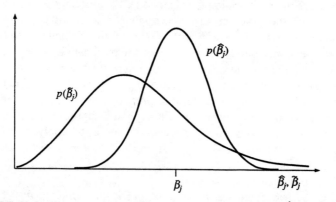

FIGURE 13.2 Two alternative estimators of β_j are denoted here by $\hat{\beta}_j$ and $\tilde{\beta}_j$. The OLS estimator $\hat{\beta}_j$ has a normal distribution and is unbiased. The alternative estimator $\tilde{\beta}_j$ illustrated here does not have a normal distribution, and it is negatively biased because $E[\tilde{\beta}_j] < \beta_j$.

It is desirable also that the sampling distribution of an estimator have a small standard deviation or variance, so that large estimation errors are not likely to occur. Comparing all possible estimators of β_j, the one with the smallest variance is called the ***minimum variance*** estimator. When we compare all unbiased estimators, the one with the smallest variance is said to be ***efficient***.

Suppose that one estimator ($\tilde{\beta}_j$) has a smaller variance than another estimator ($\hat{\beta}_j$), but that the bias of $\tilde{\beta}_j$ is larger than the bias of $\hat{\beta}_j$. In this situation, if we had to choose between using $\tilde{\beta}_j$ or $\hat{\beta}_j$, we would have to balance off our desire for minimum variance against our desire for least bias. One criterion for doing this is to choose the estimator with the smaller ***mean squared error*** (*MSE*). The mean squared error is defined as the expected value of the square of the estimation error. For an estimator $\tilde{\beta}_j$ used to estimate β_j, it is shown in the appendix that

$$MSE = E[(\tilde{\beta}_j - \beta_j)^2] = \sigma^2(\tilde{\beta}_j) + (E[\tilde{\beta}_j - \beta_j])^2 \qquad (13.12)$$

That is, the *MSE* equals the sampling variance of the estimator plus the square of its bias. The square root of the *MSE* is a measure of the typical estimation error that would result from using $\tilde{\beta}_j$ as an estimator of β_j. Thus the *MSE* criterion amounts to saying that the better estimator is the one that yields the smaller typical error.

In statistical theory, as the sample size increases toward infinity an estimator is said to be ***consistent*** if its sampling distribution becomes totally concentrated at the value of the unknown parameter it seeks to estimate. In other words, if $\tilde{\beta}_j$ is a consistent estimator of β_j, both $E[\tilde{\beta}_j - \beta_j]$ and $\sigma^2(\tilde{\beta}_j)$ head toward zero as the sample size increases. Consistency is a desirable property for an estimator to have. However, in small or finite-size samples, a consistent estimator may be biased or it may be inefficient. Conceivably, in small samples a consistent estimator may be less preferred than one that is inconsistent. A reason for being interested in large-sample properties is that for some techniques it is difficult to determine the small-sample properties. In these cases, the large-sample properties provide some basis for choosing among alternative estimators.

Although it is desirable for an estimator to have good properties, they need not be ideal in order for the estimator to be useful. For example, the standard error of regression (*SER*) can be used to estimate the standard deviation of the disturbances (σ_u), but it is a biased estimator.

Under the assumptions of the normal regression model, the ordinary least squares coefficient estimators are unbiased and consistent. Also, among possible estimators that are unbiased and that are defined as linear combinations of the observed Y values, the OLS estimators have the smallest variance. Technically, the OLS estimators are the "best linear unbiased estimators" for the regression coefficients. This result is known as the ***Gauss–Markov Theorem***, and it contributes to the high regard in which OLS is held.

13.3   Multicollinearity _____

As discussed in Chapter 7, the term *multicollinearity* names the situation that arises when there is a substantial degree of linear dependence among the regressors in the data we are using. This may result from there being high correlations among some of the regressors. Such a situation frequently occurs in macroeconomic time-series models, in which many of the variables tend to rise together over time. It also may occur in cross-section models—either naturally or as a result of specification, such as when we include a variable and its square as regressors.

The consequence of multicollinearity, especially when it is severe, is that the sampling distributions of the coefficient estimators have relatively large standard errors. As we know, the larger is the standard error, the greater is the probability that the estimated coefficient will be "far" from its expected value. In other words, multicollinearity makes the estimates imprecise.

To gain some insight into this problem, we consider an exploratory situation in which we can take more than one sample (set of data) from the same economic process. For example, suppose that among some population of workers the true process determining earnings is given by

$$EARNS_i = \beta_0 + \beta_1 ED_i + \beta_2 EXP_i + u_i \tag{13.13}$$

We choose two samples so that they are characterized by different degrees of multicollinearity and then compare the properties of the estimators in the samples. We focus on a cross-section model in this exploration, because planned sample selection is more practical with it than with a time-series model.

The first sample is a selection among workers who are about 30 years old. In this sample there will be a strong negative correlation between *ED* and *EXP*, because experience is measured approximately by the number of years since leaving school. Those workers with more-than-average years of education will tend to have fewer-than-average years of experience. The second sample is one in which a wide variety of ages are represented. This will result in a smaller correlation between *ED* and *EXP*. (For this exploration, the two sets of data should be selected so that the total variation in *ED* is the same in both samples, and similarly for the total variation in *EXP*. This will make the intersample differences in the sampling distributions be due to the intersample difference in the correlation between *ED* and *EXP*.)

It should be clear that both sets of data are appropriate for estimating the coefficients of the true process (13.13). The same OLS estimators are used in both cases, but the corresponding sampling distributions will differ because their standard errors depend on the values of the regressors in the different data sets.

Since the estimators in the two sets of data are appropriate OLS estimators, we know that each one is unbiased and has a normal sampling distribution. It turns out, however, that the standard errors of the sampling distributions are larger in the first sample—the one with a high correlation between the explanatory variables. Figure 13.3 illustrates this for any coefficient in the model. The key point is that a greater correlation between the regressors leads to larger standard errors for the estimated coefficients.

One consequence of larger standard errors is that the confidence intervals we make are wider; this is another way of saying that the estimators are less precise.

The consequence for hypothesis testing is more subtle. Consider the basic significance test with hypotheses

$$H_0: \beta_j = 0$$
$$H_1: \beta_j \neq 0$$
(13.14)

Whether the standard error is large or small does not affect the validity of the procedure or the decision rule that is set up in terms of critical t values. Also, the probability of making a Type I error is unaffected, because it is equal to the chosen level of significance.

However, a larger standard error leads to a greater probability of making a Type II error. That is, there will be a greater probability of not rejecting the null hypothesis when in fact it is false. Thus, considering a regressor that does have some effect on the dependent variable, a severe situation of multicollinearity makes it much less likely that we will correctly conclude that the associated coefficient is significant (i.e., significantly different from zero). In this sense, multicollinearity makes it hard to find significance.

Since there usually is some degree of linear dependence among the regressors, one might say that multicollinearity is usually present in regression models. It is standard, however, to reserve the term for situations that are especially

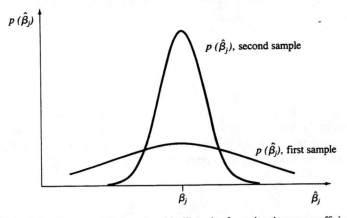

FIGURE 13.3 The consequences of multicollinearity for estimating any coefficient in the regression model (13.13) are shown by comparing the sampling distributions in two samples of data. In the first sample the correlation between the regressors is high, and in the second sample the correlation is low. A greater correlation between the regressors leads to a larger standard error for the estimator.

severe and in which the conclusions of statistical inference are somewhat disappointing.

What should be done if multicollinearity is present? Unfortunately, there is not much one can do about it easily. It is sometimes suggested that we should delete one of the correlated variables in order to reduce the multicollinearity, but this generally does not make sense because it leads to a specification error that biases the estimates of the remaining coefficients (see Section 13.4).

Since the degree of multicollinearity is a sample phenomenon, we might seek to reduce it by sample selection. It is helpful to make the sample as large as possible. However, in time-series work—where the problem is most acute— there are usually no more data to be had unless one is willing to wait for more history to happen. In cross-section work, there are occasions when control can be exercised in sample selection and the potential for severe multicollinearity can be reduced.

A difficulty of living in a multicollinear world is that some regression results are disappointing because the parameters of interest cannot be estimated with much precision. We must interpret our results with appropriate caution.

13.4 Misspecification

In Section 7.6 we considered the consequences of misspecifying the list of variables to be included in a linear multiple regression model. The previous discussion is extended here by incorporating the ideas of sampling theory. Two situations are distinguished: one occurs when a variable that belongs in the model is omitted from the specification of the estimated regression, and the other occurs when a variable that does not belong in the model is included. We present two related models for comparison, choosing one and then the other as the correct specification.

The first model supposes that a certain economic process is correctly described by

$$Y_i = \beta_0 + \beta_1 X_{1i} + \beta_2 X_{2i} + u_i \tag{13.15}$$

with u_i satisfying the assumptions of the normal regression model. The Gauss–Markov Theorem asserts that the OLS estimators (7.8)–(7.10) are the best linear unbiased estimators of the β_j. In this model the true impact of X_1 on Y is given by the coefficient β_1. Its proper OLS estimator is

$$\hat{\beta}_1 = \frac{(\sum x_1 y)(\sum x_2^2) - (\sum x_2 y)(\sum x_1 x_2)}{(\sum x_1^2)(\sum x_2^2) - (\sum x_1 x_2)} \tag{13.16}$$

using the deviation-from-mean notation of (7.7) for simplicity.

The second model supposes that the process is correctly specified by

$$Y_i = \gamma_0 + \gamma_1 X_{1i} + v_i \tag{13.17}$$

with the disturbance v_i satisfying the regular assumptions. In this model γ_1 gives the true impact of X_1 on Y, and its proper OLS estimator is

$$\hat{\gamma}_1 = \frac{\sum x_1 y}{\sum x_1^2} \tag{13.18}$$

which is equivalent to (5.59) rewritten in deviation form. Applying the Gauss–Markov Theorem again, this is the best linear unbiased estimator of γ_1.

The first type of misspecification that we consider occurs when a relevant variable is omitted from the estimated model. For this analysis we regard (13.15) as the correct specification of the process determining Y. Our attention is focused on the task of estimating the true impact of X_1 on Y, which is given by β_1. The OLS estimator of β_1 in the correctly specified model is (13.16).

Suppose, however, that we make the mistake of ignoring X_2 and carry out an estimation of a simple regression of Y on X_1, as though the correct model were (13.17). The OLS estimator for the slope coefficient on X_1 is given by $\hat{\gamma}_1$ in (13.18), but since we are interested in estimating the true (*ceteris paribus*) impact of X_1 on Y we can also denote this estimator by $\tilde{\beta}_1$. In other words, the OLS estimator (13.18) for the slope coefficient in a simple regression can be interpreted as an alternative estimator for the coefficient on X_1 in (13.15). Accordingly, $\tilde{\beta}_1$ is sometimes called an "omitted-variable estimator."

How do $\hat{\beta}_1$ and $\tilde{\beta}_1$ compare as estimators of β_1, the true impact of X_1 on Y? To answer this question we must examine and compare the two sampling distributions. With regard to their means, we know from sampling theory that

$$E[\hat{\beta}_1] = \beta_1 \tag{13.19}$$

so that $\hat{\beta}_1$ is unbiased. It turns out that

$$E[\tilde{\beta}_1] = \beta_1 + \beta_2 \frac{S(X_1, X_2)}{S^2(X_1)} \tag{13.20}$$

Thus $\tilde{\beta}_1$ is biased, unless the second term in (13.20) happens to be zero. Whether the bias, which is equal to the second term, is positive or negative depends on the sign of the true parameter β_2 and the sign of the covariance $S(X_1, X_2)$ in the data we have. Because of this bias, the procedures of hypothesis testing and interval estimation are no longer valid.

For example, in Section 7.6 we examined earnings functions involving *ED* and *EXP* as possible explanatory variables. Recasting these in terms of (13.15) and (13.17), X_1 plays the role of *ED* and X_2 plays the role of *EXP*. In the previous discussion, β_2 was presumed to be positive and the covariance was discovered to be negative in the data. Thus if the multiple regression specification were correct, the estimated impact of education on earnings in the simple regression would tend to be an underestimate of its true impact. That is, $\tilde{\beta}_1$ would be negatively biased.

Further understanding of the bias comes from noting that the ratio $S(X_1, X_2)/S^2(X_1)$ is equal to the slope of an OLS regression of X_2 on X_1. Thus (13.20) shows that the expected value of $\tilde{\beta}_1$ is equal to the true impact of X_1 on Y plus a combination of the true impact of X_2 on Y and the relation between X_2 and X_1 in the particular data we use.

A hypothetical comparison of the sampling distributions of the two estimators is given in Figure 13.4a for a case that corresponds to the earnings function example. The sampling distribution of the omitted-variable estimator, $p(\tilde{\beta}_1)$, is normal and its variance is less than that of the sampling distribution of $\hat{\beta}_1$. This opens the door to the possibility that the biased omitted-variable estimator may have a smaller mean squared error than the proper OLS estimator. Whether this

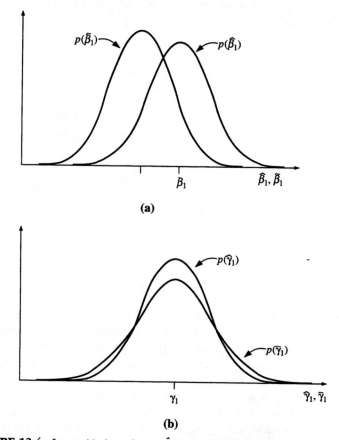

FIGURE 13.4 In part (a), the estimator $\hat{\beta}_1$ is the OLS estimator of β_1 in a correctly specified model, while $\tilde{\beta}_1$ is an omitted-variable estimator of the same coefficient. In the case illustrated, $\tilde{\beta}_1$ is negatively biased but has a smaller variance (and standard error) than $\hat{\beta}_1$. In part (b), the estimator $\hat{\gamma}_1$ is the OLS estimator of γ_1 in a correctly specified model, while $\tilde{\gamma}_1$ is an irrelevant-variable estimator of the same coefficient. Both estimators are unbiased, but the irrelevant-variable estimator has a larger standard error.

possibility represents a practical opportunity in any particular case is not easy to determine, and the sure bias of the omitted-variable estimator leads most researchers to avoid it in practice.

These results generalize easily. When a relevant variable is excluded from the specification of some economic process, OLS applied to the misspecified model yields biased estimators for all the coefficients. This invalidates the procedures of statistical inference in the estimated model.

The second type of misspecification that we consider occurs when an irrelevant variable is included in the estimated model. Turning around the comparisons just made, we regard the simple regression (13.17) as the correct model, but we suppose that (13.15) is chosen as the regression specification to be estimated. For example, it might be that the true process determining earnings depends only on education, but that experience is added to the regression specification by mistake or to test whether it has an effect.

The true impact of X_1 on Y is given by γ_1 in the correct simple regression, and its proper OLS estimator is given by (13.18). If instead the multiple regression specification (13.15) is estimated by OLS, the estimator of the coefficient on X_1 is given by the right-hand side of (13.16). This can be considered an alternative estimator of γ_1 and denoted by $\tilde{\gamma}_1$. Like the proper OLS estimator $\hat{\gamma}_1$, this "irrelevant-variable estimator" $\tilde{\gamma}_1$ has a sampling distribution that is normal and it is unbiased. However, the standard error for $\tilde{\gamma}_1$ is greater than that for $\hat{\gamma}_1$, and thus the irrelevant-variable estimator is inefficient. A hypothetical comparison of the two sampling distributions is given in Figure 13.4b. It should be noted that the two coefficient estimates calculated from the same data are different.

In this situation, when (13.17) is the correct model, (13.15) could be considered "correct" if the restriction that $\beta_2 = 0$ is added and somehow taken into account during estimation. The regular OLS estimator $\hat{\beta}_2$, which is given by (7.8) but does not take the restriction into account, has a normal sampling distribution with an expected value of zero. Of course, the actual estimate β_2^* will not be equal to zero, except by coincidence. In this misspecified model (13.15), a basic significance test for β_2 will usually conclude appropriately that the coefficient is not significant. However, a Type I error can occur (with probability α, equal to the level of significance), in which case we would mistakenly conclude that the irrelevant variable is significant.

The results of this special case generalize easily. When irrelevant variables are added to the correct regression specification of some economic process, OLS applied to the misspecified model yields estimators that are unbiased and have normal sampling distributions. These are inefficient estimators of the true coefficients in the correctly specified model, but the methods of hypothesis testing and interval estimation can be applied without alteration.

In comparing the two types of misspecification, we note first that including an irrelevant variable has relatively mild statistical effects. The standard errors of the coefficients are made greater than they should be, thereby decreasing the precision of our estimates. By contrast, excluding a relevant variable seems more serious; it leads to biased estimators and thereby undermines the validity of our statistical inference procedures. It should be remembered also that both types of misspecification can lead to substantial misinterpretation of reality.

Specification Strategy

Much research is guided by an exploratory strategy, in which various models are estimated and their results are tested for significance. Eventually the models must be compared, and perhaps one is chosen as the "best." In following this strategy, which is a reasonable one overall, the results of the hypothesis tests must be handled with special care. If a model is misspecified—and if several models are estimated most of them must be misspecified—the hypothesis testing procedure can yield misleading results.

In comparing various models or in proceeding along a search strategy, there is a tendency to act as though a variable that is found to be insignificant in a regression truly does not belong there. Often the next step taken is estimating a new version of the regression with the offending variable deleted. This is not always a wise procedure however. Even in a correctly specified model, pure sampling variability can lead a relevant variable to be judged insignificant. This is a Type II error in our testing procedure. One factor determining the chance of this is the level of significance: the lower is α, the greater is the chance of judging a relevant variable to be insignificant. A second, more general, factor is that the data may be such that the coefficients cannot be estimated with very much precision (i.e., the standard errors may be appropriately large). This leads to small t^* values and insignificance. The problem might be that there are too few observations, in which case a larger sample from the same economic process might show significance for the coefficient in question. Alternatively, it might be that the regression suffers from a severe case of multicollinearity, whose technical consequence is that the standard errors tend to be large.

In assessing a regression, if theory suggests that a variable belongs in the model and if the insignificance of the variable reasonably can be ascribed to a problem with the data or with the strictness of conventional levels of significance, good judgment calls for leaving it in. The ill consequences of mistaken exclusion are often worse than mistaken inclusion. Of course, if a variable does not belong in the specification of the model, there is no reason for having it there. The presence of an irrelevant variable imposes a statistical cost, and it may mislead the readers of the research report. With no strict rules to work by, the researcher needs to exercise care and judgment. This is the art of econometrics.

13.5 Sample Selection

In Chapter 2 we first noted the idea that a fundamental consideration for selecting data to be used in econometric regression analysis is that all the observations should have been generated by the same economic process. We maintain this idea. In addition, two further considerations regarding the selection of a sample of observations are suggested by sampling theory.

The first consideration is related to random sampling. Loosely speaking, a *random sample* taken from a random variable is one in which the observations are not selected on the basis of their values. For example, if we select the next ten values drawn from a random variable, the observations would constitute a random sample. All the samples dealt with in Chapter 9 are of this type. By contrast, if we select only the next ten *positive* values generated by a random variable, these observations would not constitute a random sample if there were some probability that negative values could occur.

The sampling theory presented in Chapter 11 presumes that the values of the disturbances in the Y_i are a random sample from the underlying disturbances. This means that care should be taken so that the values of the disturbances meet this criterion; otherwise the results of this sampling theory may not hold true. We usually cannot monitor this directly, because the disturbances are unobservable. However, selecting observations on the basis of the value of the dependent variable has the effect of selecting them on the basis of the value of the disturbances, and this should be avoided.

The situation and its consequences are illustrated in Figure 13.5, where the underlying true regression line is drawn first. Based on a given set of values for X, a set of observations resulting from this process is shown. If all these observations are used to make estimates of the coefficients, the sampling theory of Chapter 11 holds. Among other things, this implies that the OLS estimates are unbiased.

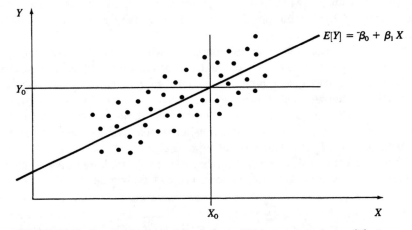

FIGURE 13.5 For the given set of X values, the Y values generated around the true regression line constitute a random sample. For these data, the OLS slope estimator is unbiased: $E[\hat{\beta}_1] = \beta_1$. If those observations for which $Y > Y_0$ are excluded, the slope estimator is biased: the estimated slope in the reduced sample will tend to be smaller than the estimated slope in the full random sample. However, if only those observations for which $X > X_0$ are excluded, the slope estimator remains unbiased.

Suppose, however, that a subset of these observations is selected by excluding from further consideration those with Y values greater than Y_0. For example, in a study of the earnings of low-skilled workers one might think of excluding workers who earn more than $20,000 per year. For the observations selected, each $Y_i \leq Y_0$, so

$$\beta_0 + \beta_1 X_i + u_i \leq Y_0 \tag{13.21}$$

or

$$u_i \leq Y_0 - (\beta_0 + \beta_1 X_i) \tag{13.22}$$

Thus, observations are selected only if their disturbances are smaller than a certain amount.

Further, and especially important, the upper limit for u_i among the selected observations decreases as X increases. Given this, the true mean of the disturbances decreases as X increases among the selected observations. The effect of this is that the estimated slope in the regression of Y on X in this selected sample will tend to be smaller than the true slope. In other words, the estimate of the slope will be biased. This problem of **selection bias** arises because observations were selected on the basis of the dependent variable. In some situations a correction can be applied, but it is better to avoid the problem in the first place.

It is interesting that these ideas do not carry over to possible selection of the sample on the basis of the explanatory variables, because these are taken to be fixed. For example, referring to Figure 13.5 again, if we were to exclude those observations having $X_i > X_0$, none of the previous difficulties would appear. The values of the disturbances for the observations remaining in the sample have not been influenced by the sample selection, and thus they constitute a random sample.

The second consideration we are concerned with here recognizes that it is appropriate to select observations on the basis of the values of the explanatory variables, as just discussed. Given this, is there any advantage to selecting one sample rather than another? Presuming that all the assumptions of the normal regression model hold, the only advantage that one sample can have compared with another is smaller standard errors. Smaller standard errors would mean that the coefficients are being estimated more precisely.

Consider first the task of estimating the slope in a simple regression model. As explained in Section 11.3, the standard error of $\hat{\beta}_1$ is given by

$$\sigma(\hat{\beta}_1) = \sigma_u \sqrt{\frac{1}{\Sigma(X_i - \bar{X})^2}} \tag{13.23}$$

That is, the standard error of $\hat{\beta}_1$ depends inversely on the total variation in X in the data. Thus, it would be better to have the total variation be large rather than small. Now, based on the definition (3.7) of the variance,

$$\sum (X_i - \bar{X})^2 = (n - 1)S_X^2 \qquad (13.24)$$

This provides some guidance for selecting a set of observations: it is better to have a large sample size (n) rather than a small one, and it is better to have a lot of dispersion among the values of X (as measured by S_X^2 or S_X) rather than a little. On both counts, the exclusion of observations with $X_i > X_0$ in Figure 13.5 would be a bad idea.

These principles apply in multiple regression also. In addition, as discussed in connection with multicollinearity in Section 13.2, standard errors tend to be smaller when correlations among the regressors are low. Hence, if one has control over the selection of observations, the sample could be selected with concern for the covariations among the explanatory variables as well as the variation in each one. Such selection is not easy.

Usually economists work with whatever appropriate data they can get, and they are not much involved with the actual selection of observations. The data are thought of as arising from natural experiments. In other fields, questions related to the selection of observations are treated as the problem of experimental design.

APPENDIX: Expectations _____

In Chapter 9, the expected value of a discrete random variable X was defined to be

$$E[X] = \sum X_k p(X_k) \qquad (13.25)$$

and this was simultaneously taken to be the definition of the mean of X in (9.10). The concept of "expected value" or "mathematical expectation" can be used in a more general way than this.

Consider a discrete random variable X whose probability distribution is given by $p(X)$. For notational simplicity, we eliminate the subscript k, which was used previously to index the possible values of the random variable. Now consider a function $g(X)$ of this random variable. We define the *expected value* of $g(X)$ to be

$$E[g(X)] = \sum g(X)p(X) \qquad (13.26)$$

where the summation is taken over the list of possible values for X. This definition says that for each possible value of X, the value of $g(X)$ is determined and then multiplied by $p(X)$. The sum of all these multiplications (products) yields the expected value of $g(X)$.

For example consider the discrete random variable X whose probability distribution is given in the second and third columns of Table 13.1. This is the same X as in Table 9.1, which describes the balls-in-hat example. Now consider the function defined as $g(X) = X^2$. Applying the definition given above,

TABLE 13.1 Probability Distribution of X and Expectations

k	X	p(X)	Xp(X)	X²	X²p(X)
1	5	.1	.5	25	2.5
2	6	.2	1.2	36	7.2
3	7	.3	2.1	49	14.7
4	8	.4	3.2	64	25.6
			7.0		50.0

$E[X] = \sum Xp(X) = 7.0$

$E[X^2] = \sum X^2 p(X) = 50.0$

$$E[X^2] = \sum X^2 p(X) = 50 \qquad (13.27)$$

as shown in Table 13.1.

In effect, the function $g(X)$ creates a new random variable, as discussed in Section 9.5 in regard to transformations. This new variable might be named Y. The expression $E[g(X)]$ gives the mean of Y, and it might otherwise be denoted by $E[Y]$ or μ_Y. In working with expected values of functions, this interpretation of $g(X)$ as creating a new variable Y is often not made explicit.

When $g(X)$ involves a linear combination of terms, the following rules simplify algebraic manipulations:

$$E[a + bX] = a + bE[X] \qquad (13.28)$$

$$E[bX] = bE[X] \qquad (13.29)$$

$$E[a] = a \qquad (13.30)$$

Note that (13.28) involves a linear transformation, and it is the same as (9.24). These results generalize to

$$E[aX + bY + cZ + \ldots] = aE[X] + bE[Y] + cE[Z] + \ldots \qquad (13.31)$$

That is, the expected value of a linear combination of random variables is equal to a linear combination of the expected values.

The new use of expected value notation allows us to rewrite the definition (9.11) of the variance of X as

$$\sigma^2(X) = \sum (X - E[X]^2)p(X) = E[(X - E[X])^2] \qquad (13.32)$$

and then show that

$$\sigma^2(X) = E[(X - E[X])^2]$$
$$= E[X^2 - 2XE[X] + (E[X])^2]$$
$$= E[X^2] - 2(E[X])^2 + (E[X])^2$$
$$= E[X^2] - (E[X])^2 \qquad (13.33)$$

Note that $E[X]$ gets treated like a constant in this derivation. Applying this to the random variable X in Table 13.1, we see that

$$\sigma^2(X) = E[X^2] - (E[X])^2 = 50 - 49 = 1 \qquad (13.34)$$

This provides a somewhat simpler computational procedure than the definitional method followed in Chapter 9.

For completeness we also note that the covariance defined in (9.27) can be reexpressed in expected value notation and shown equal to

$$\sigma_{YX} = E[(Y - E[Y])(X - E[X])] = E[YX] - E[Y]E[X] \qquad (13.35)$$

which is sometimes useful for computation or in theoretical derivations.

For a continuous random variable X whose probability density function is $p(X)$, the expected value of a function $g(X)$ is defined as in (13.26), except that an integral is used instead of a summation. The other rules and applications of expected values that are shown above hold in the continuous case also.

In Section 13.2, the bias of an estimator $\tilde{\beta}_j$ is defined as the expected value of its estimation error $\tilde{\beta}_j - \beta_j$. Equation (13.10) can be expanded slightly to show that

$$\text{bias of } \tilde{\beta}_j = E[\tilde{\beta}_j - \beta_j] = E[\tilde{\beta}_j] - E[\beta_j] = E[\tilde{\beta}_j] - \beta_j \qquad (13.36)$$

Note that the rule that $E[c] = c$ was applied in getting to the last expression.

Similarly, the mean squared error is defined as the expected value of the square of the estimation error that results when $\tilde{\beta}_j$ is used to estimate β_j. In (13.12) it is shown to be equal to

$$\begin{aligned}
MSE &= E[(\tilde{\beta}_j - \beta_j)^2] \\
&= E[\tilde{\beta}_j^2 - 2\tilde{\beta}_j\beta_j + \beta_j^2] \\
&= E[\tilde{\beta}_j^2] - E[2\tilde{\beta}_j\beta_j] + E[\beta_j^2] \\
&= E[\tilde{\beta}_j^2] - (E[\tilde{\beta}_j])^2 + (E[\tilde{\beta}_j])^2 - 2\beta_j E[\tilde{\beta}_j] + \beta_j^2 \\
&= (E[\tilde{\beta}_j^2] - (E[\tilde{\beta}_j])^2) + (E[\tilde{\beta}_j] - \beta_j)^2 \\
&= \sigma^2(\tilde{\beta}_j) + (E[\tilde{\beta}_j - \beta_j])^2 \qquad (13.37)
\end{aligned}$$

(In the fourth line a term is subtracted and then added.) That is, the MSE is equal to the sampling variance of $\tilde{\beta}_j$ plus the square of the bias.

Problems

Section 13.1

* **13.1** Based on the information in Section 13.1 construct a 95 percent confidence interval for predicting the value of aggregate consumption when disposable income reaches 2 trillion dollars.

  13.2 Based on the earnings function reported as regression (12.15), construct a 90 percent confidence interval for predicting the earnings of men with exactly 16 years of education. (Note that in the data the mean ED is 11.58 and its standard deviation is 3.44.)

* **13.3** Suppose that we know the true values of β_0, β_1, and σ_u in an economic process described by a simple regression model. How can we construct a 90 percent confidence interval for predicting the Y_p associated with a given X_p?

Section 13.2

  13.4 Suppose that we are seeking to estimate a coefficient β_j with two alternative estimators $\tilde{\beta}'_j$ and $\tilde{\beta}''_j$. In addition, suppose that it is very important to us that our estimate fall within the range $\beta_j \pm \delta$, where δ is some positive constant. Draw a figure showing the sampling distributions of the two estimates consistent with this: $\tilde{\beta}'_j$ is biased while $\tilde{\beta}''_j$ is unbiased, but $\tilde{\beta}'_j$ is definitely preferred over $\tilde{\beta}''_j$. Explain.

* **13.5** Consider a sample of size n taken from a random variable X whose variance is σ_X^2. The variance S_X^2 defined in (3.7) and applied to the sample values is an unbiased estimator of σ_X^2. Is the mean squared deviation (MSD_X) defined in (3.4) negatively biased, unbiased, or positively biased? How does the variance of the sampling distribution for MSD_X compare with the variance of the sampling distribution for S_X^2?

Section 13.3

  13.6 Examine the estimated regression (7.29) reported in Table 11.3 for the possible effects of multicollinearity.

* **13.7** Examine the estimated regression (7.46) reported in Table 11.1 for the possible effects of multicollinearity. (Note that the correlation between EXP and $EXPSQ$ is 0.98.)

Section 13.4

  13.8 Suppose that aggregate income and wealth both increase over time, as does aggregate consumption. Simple Keynesian theory assumes that consumption depends on income alone, whereas life cycle theory assumes that it depends positively on both income and wealth. What are the statistical implications of these theories for estimation of aggregate consumption functions?

★ **13.9** Suppose that we have control over the selection of our sample, so that we can have either a high correlation or no correlation between X_1 and X_2 in Equation (13.15). What impact would this choice have on the consequences of excluding X_2 and estimating a regression of Y on just X_1?

13.10 Compare the two Phillips curves reported in Table 11.5 with regard to what might be expected on the basis of possible misspecification.

Section 13.5

13.11 Consider a random variable X having a standard normal distribution. If all outcomes having a value greater than 1 are thrown away, would you anticipate that the mean of X in the remaining sample would equal zero? Explain.

13.12 Suppose that we considered estimating a simple earnings function using as observations only workers with annual earnings between 15 and 25 thousand dollars. What effect would this selection have on our estimation?

Appendix

13.13 Using expectations, show that if $Y = bX$, then $\sigma^2(Y) = b^2\sigma^2(X)$.

V

Topics in Econometrics

14

F Tests and Dummy Variable Outcomes

This chapter extends our basic knowledge of regression in two separate directions. In the first section we explain a procedure for testing hypotheses about more than one coefficient. In the second section we analyze models that have a dummy variable representing the outcome of the economic process.

14.1   *F* Tests in Multiple Regression _____

Standard *t* tests regarding single β_j coefficients are by far the most commonly examined hypothesis tests in regression analysis. Sometimes, however, we are concerned with more than one coefficient, and the *t* tests are inadequate for our needs.

For example, Table 14.1 reports the results of five variations of our earnings function with the dependent variable in its logarithmic form, *LNEARNS*. In this table the results of each regression are shown in separate columns and the presence or absence of values in particular rows indicates whether or not a particular regressor is included in the equation. Regression (1), which replicates (6.45), includes only *ED* as an explanatory variable; regression (2) adds *EXP* in order to examine the linear effect of experience, and regression (3) lets experience enter quadratically; regression (4) adds a dummy variable for race; and regression (5) adds three dummy variables for regional location.

TABLE 14.1   Earnings Functions (Dependent Variable: *LNEARNS, n* = 100)

	(1)	(2)	(3)	(4)	(5)
Constant	0.673	0.418	−0.0781	0.0746	0.119
	(0.158)	(0.289)	(0.390)	(0.3891)	(0.408)
ED	0.107	0.116	0.118	0.110	0.111
	(0.013)	(0.016)	(0.016)	(0.016)	(0.016)
EXP		0.00651	0.0542	0.0522	0.0500
		(0.00620)	(0.0263)	(0.0258)	(0.0260)
EXPSQ			−0.00103	−0.00101	−0.000942
			(0.00055)	(0.00054)	(0.000546)
DRACE				−0.381	−0.306
				(0.175)	(0.179)
DNCENT					0.0550
					(0.116)
DSOUTH					−0.135
					(0.119)
DWEST					−0.134
					(0.133)
R^2	.405	.412	.433	.460	.479
SER	0.446	0.446	0.440	0.432	0.431
SSR	19.5033	19.2844	18.6085	17.7241	17.0904

The significance of *ED* can be tested in each regression using a regular *t* test, as can the effect of *EXP* in regression (2). However, the effect of experience in regressions (3), (4), and (5) enters through two regressors: *EXP* and *EXPSQ*. The null hypothesis that experience has no effect on (the logarithm of) earnings, together with its contradictory alternative, is of the form

$$H_0\!: \beta_2 = 0 \quad \text{and} \quad \beta_3 = 0$$
$$H_1\!: \beta_2 \neq 0 \quad \text{and/or} \quad \beta_3 \neq 0 \tag{14.1}$$

which we have not seen before.

To preview the appropriate procedure for testing this null hypothesis, suppose that regression (3) in Table 14.1 is the basic specification that we believe characterizes the earnings function. The underlying regression model is

$$LNEARNS_i = \beta_0 + \beta_1 ED_i + \beta_2 EXP_i + \beta_3 EXPSQ_i + u_i \tag{14.2}$$

If the null hypothesis that $\beta_2 = \beta_3 = 0$ is true, the underlying regression model can be restated validly as

$$LNEARNS_i = \beta_0 + \beta_1 ED_i + u_i \tag{14.3}$$

In other words, the null hypothesis serves to restrict some of the coefficients in the underlying regression model. Equation (14.3) is referred to as the **restricted** form of the model, and (14.2) is the **unrestricted** form.

The essence of the test of the null hypothesis involves comparing the estimates of these two forms. In each regression, the sum of squared residuals (*SSR*) measures the overall error of fit. If the restricted form has a much poorer fit than the unrestricted form, this suggests that the restrictions (i.e., the implications of the null hypothesis) are quite different from the reality that generated the data. By contrast, if the error of fit of the restricted form is not much different from that of the unrestricted form, this suggests that the restrictions are fairly consistent with reality.

Theory

We start formally by considering a multiple regression model with regular assumptions:

$$Y_i = \beta_0 + \beta_1 X_{1i} + \beta_2 X_{2i} + \cdots + \beta_k X_{ki} + u_i \tag{14.4}$$

Consider a null hypothesis stating that several of the coefficients take on specific values or that there exists a certain relation among the coefficients (to be elaborated by example below). The alternative hypothesis is the denial of any one or more of the elements of the null.

Now we consider estimating two regressions and comparing the sums of squared residuals

$$SSR = \sum_{i=1}^{n} e_i^2 \tag{14.5}$$

from them. The first regression is of the full model (14.4) under consideration and the resulting sum of squared residuals is denoted by SSR_U, indicating that the estimation is unrestricted. The second regression results from somehow imposing a set of restrictions on the estimation in such a way that the null hypothesis is necessarily fulfilled. For example, in the earnings function (14.2) the null hypothesis that $\beta_2 = 0$ and $\beta_3 = 0$ is necessarily fulfilled by estimating (14.3). In general, other types of null hypotheses lead to other types of restriction. The restricted regression is estimated, yielding a certain sum of squared residuals denoted by SSR_R.

It turns out that SSR_R is always greater than SSR_U, unless they are equal by coincidence. Loosely speaking, this is because the unrestricted form allows the OLS technique to assign values freely to the $\hat{\beta}_j^*$ to make *SSR* as small as possible. By contrast the restricted form gives the technique less freedom to minimize the *SSR*, and thereby leads to a higher value for it. If the null hypothesis is true, SSR_R is likely to be only slightly greater than SSR_U because the estimated coefficients in the unrestricted form will differ from the values (perhaps implicit) in the restricted form only because of sampling variation. On the other hand, if the null hypothesis is false, SSR_R is likely to be much greater than SSR_U because the estimation of the restricted form must include (perhaps implicitly) some coefficients that are incorrect, leading to greater errors of fit.

Let n be the total number of observations, let k be the number of regressors in the unrestricted form, and let r be the number of restrictions. Generally, the number of restrictions r is equal to the number of fewer coefficients that are estimated in the restricted form as compared with the unrestricted form. We accept without derivation or proof the fact that if the null hypothesis is true, then the sampling statistic

$$F = \frac{(SSR_R - SSR_U)/r}{SSR_U/(n - k - 1)} \tag{14.6}$$

has an F distribution ($F_{r,n-k-1}$) with r degrees of freedom in the numerator and $n - k - 1$ degrees of freedom in the denominator. (The F distribution is discussed in the appendix to Chapter 10.)

The value of F reflects the increase in SSR resulting from estimating the restricted form of the model rather than the unrestricted form, as can be seen from (14.6). Following standard testing procedures, we choose a critical region consisting of values of F that seem unlikely to occur if H_0 is true but that would occur because of sampling variability with probability α, which is the level of significance. If the value of the statistic F^* is in the critical region, the null hypothesis is rejected. The logic is that if the restrictions inherent in the null hypothesis are wrong, F^* will tend to have a high value. Hence, large values of F^* cast doubt on the null hypothesis, and the critical region consists of values of F greater than a critical value F^c. This is illustrated in Figure 14.1. We recognize

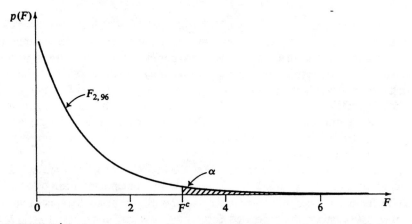

FIGURE 14.1 In carrying out an F test of linear restrictions on regression coefficients, the decision rule is to reject the null hypothesis if $F^* \geq F^c$. The critical value F^c is determined from Tables A.5 and A.6 for $\alpha = .05$ and $\alpha = .01$, respectively. The value of the test statistic is calculated according to Equation (14.9).

that there is a chance of mistakenly deciding to reject the null hypothesis when in fact it is true: this chance is equal to α. Appropriately enough, this whole procedure is known as an **F test.**

In brief, the decision rule is of the form

$$\text{Reject } H_0 \text{ if } F^* \geq F^c \tag{14.7}$$

where the critical value F^c is determined from

$$\Pr(F_{r,n-k-1} \geq F^c) = \alpha \tag{14.8}$$

and where the test statistic is

$$F^* = \frac{(SSR_R - SSR_U)/r}{SSR_U/(n-k-1)} \tag{14.9}$$

The specification of the hypotheses and formulation of the restricted and unrestricted regressions needed to calculate F^* vary from application to application. As in the case of t tests, it is a good idea to carry out the following five steps in conducting the test:

1. State the hypotheses clearly.
2. Choose the level of significance α.
3. Construct the decision rule.
4. Determine the value of the test statistic F^*.
5. State and interpret the conclusion of the test.

Most of the work comes in step 4.

Applications

The most common application of the F test involves the null hypothesis that in the regression model under consideration *all* the coefficients except the intercept are equal to zero:

$$H_0: \beta_1 = \beta_2 = \cdots = \beta_k = 0$$
$$H_1: \beta_j \neq 0 \quad \text{for at least one } j, \quad j = 1, \ldots, k \tag{14.10}$$

Essentially, H_0 says that all the regressors taken together have no effect on the dependent variable. This test is something of a straw man, in that we expect the null to be rejected in all but the most worthless of regression models.

The unrestricted form is the basic regression model under consideration and its sum of squared residuals is denoted by SSR_U. The restricted form, incorporating k restrictions, is simply

$$Y_i = \beta_0 + u_i \tag{14.11}$$

If this unusual regression were estimated, $\hat{\beta}_0^*$ would equal $\bar{Y}$ and SSR_R would equal the total variation in Y. Knowing this, we do not need to estimate the regression. Some algebraic manipulation shows that for this application

$$F = \frac{(SSR_R - SSR_U)/k}{SSR_U/(n - k - 1)} = \frac{R^2/k}{(1 - R^2)/(n - k - 1)} \qquad (14.12)$$

where R^2 is taken from the unrestricted form. Accordingly, this common F test is sometimes referred to as test of the significance of R^2.

Many computer programs for regression routinely calculate and report this F^* value, sometimes in conjunction with a display known as an analysis of variance table (see Chapter 19). It should be noted that it is possible for a regression to include at least one variable that is significant by its own t test and still not lead to rejection of the null hypothesis that the coefficients of all the regressors are equal to zero.

A second type of application involves a null hypothesis that *some* of the coefficients are equal to zero. For example, we return to the question of testing experience in the polynomial form of the earnings function. The relevant hypotheses are

$$H_0: \beta_2 = \beta_3 = 0$$
$$H_1: \beta_2 \neq 0 \quad \text{and/or} \quad \beta_3 \neq 0 \qquad (14.13)$$

Note that H_0 is specific and that it formalizes the statement that experience has no effect on earnings in this model. Also, H_1 is vague and it is the simplest denial of H_0. We choose the .05 level of significance. The unrestricted form of the model is (14.2) and the restricted form is (14.3). There are $r = 2$ restrictions imposed in the restricted form, there are $k = 3$ regressors in the unrestricted form, and there are the same $n = 100$ observations in both forms. The decision rule is to reject H_0 if $F^* \geq 3.1$ approximately, as determined from Table A.5. In Table 14.1 the restricted form is reported as regression (1) and the unrestricted form is regression (3). Thus the value of the test statistic is

$$F^* = \frac{(19.5033 - 18.6085)/2}{18.6085/96} = 2.308 \qquad (14.13)$$

Since F^* is not in the critical region we do not reject the null hypothesis, and we conclude that experience has an insigificant effect on the logarithm of earnings. However, the P-value is

$$P\text{-value} = \Pr(F_{2,96} \geq 2.308) = .105 \qquad (14.14)$$

(a computer is necessary to calculate this) which indicates that experience just misses being significant at the .10 level. This suggests that we should not simply discard experience as a relevant variable.

The results of an F test may seem to contradict those for t tests on the individual coefficients. Despite the fact that in regression (3) *EXP* is significant at the .05 level and *EXPSQ* is significant at the .10 level, the *F* test has shown that experience is not significant at the .10 (or .05) level. The *F* test is different from a simple combination of two *t* tests, and the results can be different. Note, however, that all the test statistics here are fairly close to the critical values and the differences between the statistical findings of the *F* and *t* tests are not really very great.

A similar procedure tests whether all the coefficients for a set of dummy variables are equal to zero. This is applied when a single qualitative characteristic leads to the construction of more than one dummy variable to represent the different categories. The test is related to a procedure known as the analysis of variance, which is discussed in Chapter 19.

For example, regression (5) in Table 14.1 reports an earnings function that includes three dummy variables to allow for shiftlike differences in earnings among the four regions of the U.S. (See Section 7.3.) The hypotheses used to test whether the region of residence affects earnings are

$$H_0: \beta_5 = \beta_6 = \beta_7 = 0$$

$$H_1: \beta_5 \neq 0 \quad \text{and/or} \quad \beta_6 \neq 0 \quad \text{and/or} \quad \beta_7 \neq 0 \tag{14.16}$$

The unrestricted regression is simply regression (5) in Table 14.1. The restricted form has the same specification except that the three dummy variables are excluded; this is regression (4). Carrying out the test is left as Problem 14.2.

Another application of this type involves just a single regression coefficient. The basic significance test described in Chapter 12 involves the hypotheses

$$H_0: \beta_j = 0$$

$$H_1: \beta_j \neq 0 \tag{14.17}$$

and is presented as a *t* test. The same hypotheses can be handled in the *F* test framework. In this situation, the *F* values are exactly equal to the squares of the corresponding *t* values, in terms of both test statistics and critical values. For the same level of significance, the conclusions of the two tests are identical. Since computer programs for regression routinely print out *t* statistics that are the appropriate t^* values for the basic significance test, this application of the *F* test is rarely needed.

A third type of application involves testing a hypothesis that specifies a relation among coefficients but not particular values for them. For example, suppose that we believe in a linear aggregate consumption function but want to examine whether or not the marginal propensity to consume labor income is the same as that for property income. We might have in mind a regression model of the form

$$CON_i = \beta_0 + \beta_1 LABINC_i + \beta_2 PROPINC_i + u_i \tag{14.18}$$

The null hypothesis and its alternative are formulated as

$$H_0: \beta_1 = \beta_2$$
$$H_1: \beta_1 \neq \beta_2$$

(14.19)

If the null hypothesis is true, then $\beta_1 = \beta_2$, and we can let β_1 stand for their common value. Imposing this restriction on the basic model, we see that

$$CON_i = \beta_0 + \beta_1 LABINC_i + \beta_1 PROPINC_i + u_i$$
$$= \beta_0 + \beta_1 [LABINC_i + PROPINC_i] + u_i$$

(14.20)

or

$$CON_i = \beta_0 + \beta_1 TOTINC_i + u_i$$

(14.21)

The restricted form of the model is simply the regression of CON on a newly constructed regressor $TOTINC$, which is equal to $LABINC$ plus $PROPINC$ for every observation. The number of restrictions r is equal to 1 because there is one fewer coefficient to estimate in (14.21) than in (14.18). We proceed with the F test as before, comparing SSR_R from (14.21) with SSR_U from (14.18).

All the F tests described in this section come under the general heading of *tests of linear restrictions* on the coefficients, and still other types of application are possible. For example, one might be interested in testing the proposition that $\beta_1 + \beta_2 = 1$ in some regression model. Given our current knowledge, all we need to do is formulate a restricted version of the model that incorporates this hypothesis.

The Chow Test

Another type of application of the F test is known as the *test for equality of coefficients* or the *Chow test* (after its originator, Gregory Chow). When the observations under study naturally fall into two or more groups, the question arises as to whether or not all the groups are subject to the same economic process. This, of course, is a fundamental consideration governing the selection of observations to be used in the estimation of a model. In time-series work, for example, it might be asked whether the whole consumption function permanently changed in a certain year. This establishes two groups, the "before" and the "after" observations. In cross-section work it might be asked whether the earnings function is substantially different for blacks and whites. This establishes two groups based on race.

We outline the test for a case in which the number of groups is two, but it may be extended to any larger number. If we estimate a multiple regression model (14.4) for a complete set of observations, we implicitly restrict the intercept and the effect of each of the regressors to be the same for all observations. But if we estimate the same model specification separately for each group, we allow the intercept and the effect of each of the regressors to differ between the groups.

The test for equality of coefficients considers the situation of possibly unequal coefficients for the groups to be the general, unrestricted model. The null hypothesis that every β_j has the same value for both groups is imposed on the general model by estimating the model just once, with the complete set of observations; this is the restricted form of the model.

In carrying out the test, SSR_U is obtained by adding the *SSR*s from the two separate regressions, and the corresponding number of degrees of freedom is equal to the number of observations minus the number of parameters estimated (counting both equations). The SSR_R is obtained directly from the combined regression, and the number of restrictions is equal to the number of fewer parameters in the restricted regression as compared with the total number of parameters in the unrestricted regressions. An underlying assumption of the test is that the standard deviation of the disturbance u_i is the same for all the observations, even if the β_j coefficients differ between the two groups.

For example, we may accept the general validity of the earnings function (14.2) but wonder whether the coefficients are the same for blacks and whites. The unrestricted form, allowing for differences, consists of two estimated regressions; for blacks,

$$\widehat{LNEARNS_i} = -1.408 + 0.129ED_i + 0.123EXP_i$$
$$\quad\quad\quad (2.282) \quad (0.083) \quad\quad (0.184)$$

$$\quad\quad\quad - 0.00220EXPSQ_i \quad\quad\quad\quad\quad\quad (14.22)$$
$$\quad\quad\quad (0.00377)$$

$$R^2 = .562 \quad SER = 0.473 \quad SSR = 0.6713$$

and for whites,

$$\widehat{LNEARNS_i} = 0.104 + 0.110ED_i + 0.0508EXP_i$$
$$\quad\quad\quad (0.401) \quad (0.016) \quad\quad (0.0264)$$

$$\quad\quad\quad - 0.000995EXPSQ_i \quad\quad\quad\quad\quad\quad (14.23)$$
$$\quad\quad\quad (0.000559)$$

$$R^2 = .391 \quad SER = 0.437 \quad SSR = 16.9793$$

Thus, $SSR_U = 0.6713 + 16.9793 = 17.6506$. The restricted form is regression (3) in Table 14.1. The coefficients seem to differ substantially, but this may be due just to sampling variability. The test statistic is

$$F^* = \frac{(18.6085 - 17.6506)/4}{17.6506/92} = 1.25 \quad\quad\quad (14.24)$$

The critical value at the .05 level of significance is $F^c \approx 2.47$, so the null hypothesis is not rejected. We judge that the earnings functions are not significantly different for the two races. It should be noted, however, that regression (4) in Table 14.1 shows a significant effect for the dummy variable *DRACE*.

In time-series work, the Chow test serves as a *test of structural stability*. The notion of stability here corresponds to our usual presumption that the true coefficients in the structural relation maintain the same values over all the time spanned by the data set. Such stability is of fundamental importance for our regression methods, for only if the relation is stable could all the data come from the same process. Of course, it is reasonable that economic processes might change over time (i.e., that they might be unstable), and whether a given set of data satisfies the criterion is always open to question and testing.

The most common form of the test divides the sample into two subperiods. The null hypothesis is that the coefficients of the basic structural relation are the same in both subperiods, and this leads to a restricted regression. The alternative hypothesis is that the corresponding coefficients are different in the two subperiods, and this leads to the unrestricted form. (Note that this is a very special characterization of the lack of stability: we are not considering a drift or a randomness for the coefficients.)

For example, consider the proposition that the coefficients of the simple logarithmic demand for money function

$$LNM_i = \beta_0 + \beta_1 LNGNP_i + u_i \tag{14.25}$$

were different in the 1971–1980 period from what they were in the 1956–1970 period. The null hypothesis is that there was structural stability:

$$
\begin{aligned}
H_0: \beta_0^{1956-1970} &= \beta_0^{1971-1980} &\text{and} &&\beta_1^{1956-1970} &= \beta_1^{1971-1980} \\
H_1: \beta_0^{1956-1970} &\neq \beta_0^{1971-1980} &\text{and/or} &&\beta_1^{1956-1970} &\neq \beta_1^{1971-1980}
\end{aligned} \tag{14.26}
$$

The restricted form of the model, which embodies the null hypothesis, was first reported as (6.38) and is given again as regression (1) in Table 14.2. The unrestricted form of the model consists of two separate regressions, one for the 1956–1970 period and the other for 1971–1980. These are reported as regressions (2) and (3) in Table 14.2, and SSR_U is the sum of their SSRs.

In this test the number of restrictions is $r = 2$ and there are a total of $25 - 4 = 21$ degrees of freedom in the unrestricted form. Choosing the level of significance to be $\alpha = .05$, the critical value for $F_{2,21}$ is 3.47. From Table 14.2 we see that $SSR_R = 0.021401$ and $SSR_U = 0.004727 + 0.006198 = 0.010925$. Hence the test statistic is

$$F^* = \frac{(SSR_R - SSR_U)/r}{SSR_U/(n - k - 1)} = \frac{(0.021401 - 0.010925)/2}{0.010925/21} = 10.07 \tag{14.27}$$

TABLE 14.2   Demand for Money—Chow Test (Dependent Variable: *LNM*)

	(1) $i = 1$ to 25	(2) $i = 1$ to 15	(3) $i = 16$ to 25	(4) $i = 1$ to 25
Constant	3.948	3.426	6.138	3.426
	(0.165)	(0.193)	(0.695)	(0.230)
LNGNP	0.215	0.292	−0.0910	0.292
	(0.024)	(0.029)	(0.0968)	(0.034)
D				2.712
				(0.614)
D · LNGNP				−0.383
				(0.086)
R^2	.780	.890	.100	.888
SER	0.0305	0.0191	0.0278	0.0228
SSR	0.021401	0.004727	0.006198	0.010925
n	25	15	10	25

Since $F^* > F^c$, the null hypothesis is rejected and we conclude that the relation was not stable over the whole period.

In assessing this result, we note that it could arise because of instability of the coefficients in (14.25), or it could arise because that equation does not give the true relation. Whatever the cause, the results of the Chow test indicate that the estimated regression (6.38) should be viewed with caution.

Although in this example and the previous one the unrestricted form of the model was estimated with two equations, it is possible to estimate this form in a single equation with the help of dummy variables. In the demand for money example, let $D_i = 1$ for the latter period and $D_i = 0$ for the earlier period. Consider the regression specification

$$LNM_i = \beta_0 + \beta_1 LNGNP_i + \beta_2 D_i + \beta_3 [D_i \cdot LNGNP_i] + u_i \quad (14.28)$$

where $[D_i \cdot LNGNP_i]$ is a single regressor that is constructed as the product of two other regression variables. When this specification is estimated for the whole sample period ($n = 25$), the fit is precisely the same as that of the two separate regressions of the unrestricted form. The results are reported as regression (4) in Table 14.2. We see that $\hat{\beta}_0^*$ and $\hat{\beta}_1^*$ in regression (4) are precisely the same as the estimated intercept and slope in the separate regression (2) for 1956–1970. Also, $(\hat{\beta}_0^* + \hat{\beta}_2^*)$ from regression (4) is the same as the estimated intercept in regression (3) for 1971–1980, and $(\hat{\beta}_1^* + \hat{\beta}_3^*)$ from regression (4) is the same as the corresponding estimated slope in regression (3). Further, *SSR* in regression (4) is equal to the sum of the *SSR*s from regressions (2) and (3), so it is precisely the SSR_U that is required for the Chow test.

This dummy variable estimation procedure can be used for any Chow test. In the demand for money example, the restricted form (14.25) is obtained from the unrestricted form (14.28) by imposing the null hypothesis "$H_0: \beta_2 = \beta_3 = 0$." Thus, the Chow test is another variant of the tests for linear restrictions. Note that the proper counting of the degrees of freedom for the F statistic should conform to the dummy variable procedure whether or not it is used in the Chow test; the use of n and k may be confusing when the unrestricted form is estimated as two separate regressions.

14.2   Models for Dummy Variable Outcomes ___

It sometimes is the case that the economic process under study leads to outcomes that are categorical, rather than measurable. For example, a person might take private or public transportation to work, a firm might go bankrupt or not, and a high school senior might go to college or not. In each case the outcome variable Y can be coded as a binary dummy variable: one outcome is assigned the value 0, and the other is assigned the value 1.

Suppose that the outcome Y depends on only one explanatory variable, X. Without further thought, one might estimate the model

$$Y_i = \beta_0 + \beta_1 X_i + u_i \tag{14.29}$$

by ordinary least squares. The results are illustrated generically in Figure 14.2.

We see immediately that something very special is at work. First, although the observed values of Y are all either 0 or 1, the fitted values take on a continuum of values from less than 0 to more than 1. Second, it is apparent that the disturbance terms in the regression model must be of a very special form.

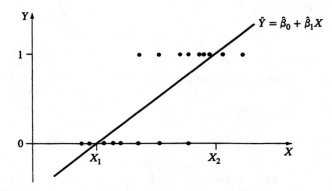

FIGURE 14.2   When the dependent variable is a dummy variable, which takes on values of 0 or 1 only, the scatterplot of the data takes on this special form. The regression is interpreted as a linear probability model, and $\hat{Y}$ values are interpreted as predicted probabilities. When $\hat{Y}$ is outside the 0 to 1 interval, these predictions are not reasonable.

In this setting, the simple regression specification (14.29) can be interpreted in a new way, as a type of probability model. For a given value X_i, let the probability that Y_i equals 1 be denoted by $\Pr(Y_i = 1)$ and also by the shorter form P_i. Since Y_i takes on only the values 0 and 1, it has a **Bernoulli distribution**—a binomial distribution with $n = 1$. Thus, by (9.15) and (9.16)

$$E[Y_i] = P_i \tag{14.30}$$

$$\sigma(Y_i) = \sqrt{P_i(1 - P_i)} \tag{14.31}$$

The goal of a probability model is to explain what determines P_i, the probability that the outcome of the process is of one kind ($Y = 1$) rather than another ($Y = 0$). Note how this contrasts with a regular regression model, in which the goal is to explain what determines the level of Y.

Linear Probability Model

The simplest approach is the *linear probability model* (LPM). We assume that

$$\Pr(Y_i = 1) = \beta_0 + \beta_1 X_i \tag{14.32}$$

Since P_i and $\Pr(Y_i = 1)$ are the same, this can be rewritten as

$$E[Y_i] = \beta_0 + \beta_1 X_i \tag{14.33}$$

using (14.30). This last equation then can be taken as the systematic component of a simple regression model, like (14.29).

The coefficients β_0 and β_1 can be estimated by OLS, and the results can be analyzed in a familiar way. For any given value X_i, the predicted probability $\hat{P}_i$ can easily be determined, as $\hat{Y}_i$. Similarly, we say that $\hat{\beta}_1^*$ gives the increase in $\hat{P}$ that results from a unit increase in X.

Several difficulties arise with this procedure. (1) As is apparent from Figure 14.2, the range of predicted probabilities can lie outside of the meaningful 0 to 1 range. (2) Since the disturbances clearly are not normal, we cannot apply our usual methods of statistical inference in small samples. (3) For a given observation, the disturbance is $u_i = Y_i - E[Y_i]$. Thus $\sigma(u_i) = \sigma(Y_i)$, and by (14.31) we see that $\sigma(u_i)$ will take on different values for different observations. This leads to the problem of heteroscedasticity, which is discussed in Chapter 15.

Despite these problems, the linear probability model is commonly used when the "dependent variable" in a regression is a dummy variable. Sometimes corrections are applied to yield better estimates than those from OLS.

For a somewhat contrived example, we take the data on *WEALTH* and *AGE* from the cross-section data set in Chapter 2. Suppose that the survey takers did not publicly release the actual wealth information about various families, but provided only the following code: *RICH* = 1 if a family's wealth is above the median, and *RICH* = 0 if it is below. We may expect that the greater is the age of the head of the family, the greater is the probability that the family would be "rich" (i.e., that it would have accumulated an above-average amount of wealth).

A linear probability model estimated by OLS yields

$$\widehat{RICH_i} = -0.491 + 0.0256 AGE_i$$
$$\phantom{\widehat{RICH_i} = }(0.251)\quad(0.0064) \tag{14.34}$$

At the minimum age of family heads in the data (26), the predicted probability of being rich is $-0.491 + (0.0256)(26) = .175$, or 17.5 percent. At the maximum age (54), the predicted probability is about 89.1 percent. Hence, in this example the problem of predicting probabilities outside the 0 to 1 interval does not arise. We interpret the coefficient on *AGE* by saying that being one year older increases the probability of being rich by .0256, or 2.56 percentage points.

The linear probability model can be extended to more than one explanatory variable in a natural way, appearing basically the same as a general linear multiple regression model. The "dependent variable" takes on only values 0 or 1. The coefficient β_j on variable X_j gives the increase in $\Pr(Y = 1)$ that would result from a unit increase in X_j, holding other variables constant. A predicted probability $\hat{P}_i$ can be calculated from the estimated coefficients in association with a set of specified values for all the explanatory variables, in the same way that $\hat{Y}_i$ is normally calculated.

Probit and Logit Models

Perhaps the major problem with the linear probability model is that it is linear. For a number of reasons, it might be thought that $\Pr(Y = 1)$ would be related to X by an "S-shaped" curve, as in Figure 14.3. Unfortunately, no simple transformation of Y is available that would allow us to estimate a nonlinear functional form in the fashion of Chapters 6 and 7.

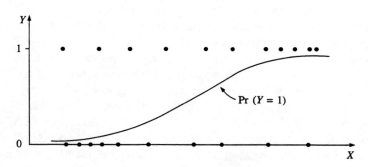

FIGURE 14.3   A reasonable probability model might specify that $\Pr(Y = 1)$ is an S-shaped function of X, as in this figure. All values for P_i are within the 0 to 1 interval. Probit and logit models both have these general features.

Instead, we move in a new and more complicated direction. The two models we look at here involve several departures from our previous work. Most important, the method of estimation is very different from what we have seen before. We cannot think of the method as fitting a line to data. Instead of developing these models fully, we aim to present some understanding of the essentials.

Both models involve using data on an outcome variable Y that takes on values 0 or 1. The models focus on determining how $\Pr(Y_i = 1)$ is related to the value of an explanatory variable X_i. In both cases, the ultimate relation is an S-shaped curve, as in Figure 14.3. From such a model we expect to be able to determine a predicted probability $\hat{P}_i$ for any given value X_i. Since the relation between P and X is nonlinear, the effect of changes in X_i on P_i will depend on the level of X_i.

We begin by presenting some new information about probability distributions. Let Z be a continuous random variable with a standard normal probability distribution, as defined in Chapter 10. Using $f(Z)$ instead of $p(Z)$ to denote the density function, (10.1) can be rewritten as

$$f(Z) = \frac{1}{\sqrt{2\pi}} \exp\left[-\frac{1}{2}Z^2\right], \quad -\infty < Z < \infty \tag{14.35}$$

Now, avoiding detail, let $F(Z)$ be a function that gives, for each possible value of Z, the probability that the random variable will be less than or equal to that possible value. For example, Table A.1 can be used to determine that $F(-0.5) = \Pr(Z \leq -0.5) = .309$ and that $F(1.5) = \Pr(Z \leq 1.5) = .933$. This function $F(Z)$ is called the cumulative normal density function, and it is graphed in Figure 14.4. As can be seen, it has the characteristics that we are seeking: it is an S-shaped curve, and it rises from a lowest possible value of 0 to a greatest possible value of 1.

This function provides the basis for specifying a **_probit model_**, in two parts:

$$\Pr(Y_i = 1) = F(Z_i) \tag{14.36}$$

where

$$Z_i = \beta_0 + \beta_1 X_i \tag{14.37}$$

Based on observed data on Y and X, the method of maximum likelihood can be used to estimate β_0 and β_1. Note, again, that the context is that for a given X_i the random variable Y_i has a Bernoulli distribution with possible values 0 and 1; we seek to estimate the parameters in the two-part relation that describes how $\Pr(Y_i = 1)$ is related to X_i. We delay the interpretation of this model for a short while.

A similar approach to the problem is based on using the logistic distribution, rather than the standard normal. A continuous random variable Z whose possibly

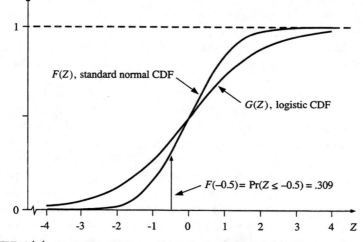

FIGURE 14.4 The height of the cumulative distribution function (CDF) above a particular value of Z gives the probability that the random variable Z will be less than or equal to that particular value. For example, for the standard normal distribution the height of the CDF at $Z = -0.5$ is $F(-0.5) = .309$. This can be determined from Table A.1. For the logistic distribution, the height $G(Z)$ can be calculated from Equation (14.39).

occurring values run all the way from $-\infty$ to ∞ is said to have a **logistic distribution** if its probability distribution (i.e., density function) is of the form

$$g(Z) = \frac{e^Z}{(1 + e^Z)^2}, \quad -\infty < Z < \infty \tag{14.38}$$

(For simplicity, we use Z for both the logistic and the standard normal.) The logistic distribution resembles a *t* distribution with a small number of degrees of freedom, and thus it is not too different from the standard normal. The cumulative logistic distribution function is given by

$$G(Z) = \frac{1}{(1 + e^{-Z})}, \quad -\infty < Z < \infty \tag{14.39}$$

and it is graphed in Figure 14.4. The height of the graph above a particular value of Z gives the probability that the random variable will be less than that particular value.

The function $G(Z)$ provides the basis for specifying the **logit model,** in two parts:

$$\Pr(Y_i = 1) = G(Z_i) \tag{14.40}$$

where

$$Z_i = \beta_0 + \beta_1 X_i \tag{14.41}$$

just as in the probit model. Based on observed data on Y and X, the method of maximum likelihood can be used to estimate β_0 and β_1.

To predict probabilities with these estimated models, we go through a two-step procedure. First, the estimated coefficients together with the chosen X_i determine a $\hat{Z}_i$ through

$$\hat{Z}_i = \hat{\beta}_0 + \hat{\beta}_1 X_i \qquad (14.42)$$

Then, the predicted probability $\hat{P}_i$ is determined from the appropriate cumulative density function as $F(\hat{Z}_i)$ or $G(\hat{Z}_i)$. A computer is helpful, although $F(Z)$ can be approximated by calculations from Table A.1, and $G(Z)$ can be calculated from (14.39).

In order to interpret the coefficients, we need to determine the slope $d\hat{P}/dX$ of the graph of the relation between $\hat{P}$ and X. Let $d\hat{P}_i/dX_i$ be the slope when $X = X_i$. It can be shown that in the probit model

$$d\hat{P}_i/dX_i = f(\hat{Z}_i) \cdot \hat{\beta}_1^{PROBIT} \qquad (14.43)$$

where $f(\hat{Z}_i)$ is simply the height of the standard normal density function evaluated at $Z = \hat{Z}_i$. For the logit model

$$d\hat{P}_i/dX_i = g(\hat{Z}_i) \cdot \hat{\beta}_1^{LOGIT} \qquad (14.44)$$

where $g(\hat{Z}_i)$ is the height of the logistic density function evaluated at $Z = \hat{Z}_i$. For completeness and comparison, we note that for the linear probability model

$$d\hat{P}_i/dX_i = \hat{\beta}_1^{LPM} \qquad (14.45)$$

which does not depend on X_i (i.e., the slope is constant).

Returning to our wealth–age example, recall that P gives the probability that $RICH = 1$, and let X stand for AGE. The estimated coefficients from the three models are reported in Table 14.3. As explained above, these coefficients can be used to determine the predicted probability of being "rich" at any age. Figure 14.5 shows the relation between $\hat{P}$ (the predicted probability) and AGE, based on the probit model. The relation based on the logit model is nearly identical to this, except at the low and high ends of the AGE range. The relation based on the linear probability model is given by a straight line that runs through the graphed probit relation. Hence, in an overall sense, the three models give very similar predictions in this example.

TABLE 14.3 Probability Model Estimates

	LPM	Probit	Logit
$\hat{\beta}_0$	−0.491	−2.773	−4.412
$\hat{\beta}_1$	0.0256	0.0703	0.114

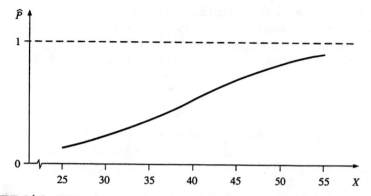

FIGURE 14.5 This graph shows the relation between the predicted probability of being "rich" ($\hat{P}$) and age (X), based on the estimated probit model. The graph of the relation based on the logit model is nearly identical to this. The slope of this graph, $d\hat{P}/dX$, gives the effect on $\hat{P}$ of being one year older. Table 14.4 gives the calculated slopes for various values of X.

TABLE 14.4 The Slope $d\hat{P}/dX$ at Various X Values

X	LPM	Probit	Logit
25	0.0256	0.0167	0.0163
30	0.0256	0.0225	0.0225
35	0.0256	0.0267	0.0273
40	0.0256	0.0280	0.0283
45	0.0256	0.0260	0.0251
50	0.0256	0.0213	0.0193
55	0.0256	0.0154	0.0133

In each model, the general way to interpret the estimated $\hat{\beta}_1$ is to calculate the slope $d\hat{P}/dX$, because this gives the effect on $\hat{P}$ of a unit increase in X. For the wealth–age models, Table 14.4 shows the slopes calculated at seven different ages that span the range of *AGE*. We see that for the Probit and Logit models, the effect ($d\hat{P}/dX$) of being one year older on the probability of being "rich" first increases and then decreases as *AGE* increases from 25 to 55. Also, we see that the calculated effects are very similar for the two models.

A briefer interpretation of the $\hat{\beta}_1$ coefficients in the probit and logit models can be provided by determining $d\hat{P}/dX$ at the point where $\hat{Z} = 0$. (This point occurs at different values of X in the two models.) At this point $\hat{P} = 0.5$, and $d\hat{P}/dX$ takes on its greatest value. For the probit model,

$$d\hat{P}/dX = f(0) \cdot \hat{\beta}_1^{PROBIT} = (0.399)(0.0703) = 0.0280 \qquad (14.46)$$

For the logit model,

$$d\hat{P}/dX = g(0) \cdot \hat{\beta}_1^{LOGIT} = (0.25)(0.114) = 0.0285 \qquad (14.47)$$

Based on these calculations we can then say, for example, that the estimated $\hat{\beta}_1$ in the probit model implies that a one-year increase in age increases the probability of being "rich" by no more than 2.80 percentage points. Note that not much can be said directly about the value $\hat{\beta}_1^{PROBIT} = 0.0703$ itself; one needs to determine some $d\hat{P}/dX$ in order to interpret the estimated coefficient.

Both probit and logit models can be extended to a multiple regression framework, by specifying

$$Z_i = \beta_0 + \beta_1 X_{1i} + \beta_2 X_{2i} + \cdots + \beta_k X_{ki} \qquad (14.48)$$

instead of (14.37) or (14.41). The method of estimation in both cases also provides estimates of the standard errors for the coefficients, and these can be used to assess the significance of the coefficients.

With more that one explanatory variable, the effect of a change in X_j on $\hat{P}$ is determined from the estimated $\hat{\beta}_j$ by equations similar to (14.43) and (14.44). Note that $\hat{Z}_i$ depends on the values of all the variables, through an equation like (14.48). Therefore, the effect of a change in X_j on $\hat{P}$ depends on the values of all the explanatory variables. However, without specifying the values of individual variables, one can determine the upper limit for each $d\hat{P}/dX_j$ by evaluating it at the point where $\hat{Z} = 0$.

Problems _____

Section 14.1

14.1 Use an F test to judge whether the explanatory variables in regression (2) of Table 14.1 help determine (the logarithm of) earnings.

★ **14.2** Based on regressions (5) and (4) in Table 14.1, test whether the region of residence significantly affects (the logarithm of) earnings.

14.3 Use an F test to judge whether EXP has a significant effect on (the logarithm of) earnings in regression (2) of Table 14.1.

14.4 Use a basic t test (two-tailed) to judge whether EXP has a significant effect on (the logarithm of) earnings in regression (2) of Table 14.1. Compare the squares of t^* and t^c with the corresponding F values in Problem 14.3.

★ **14.5** Suppose that we wish to test the hypothesis that the marginal propensity to consume out of property income is equal to 90 percent of the marginal propensity to consume out of labor income. Formulate the hypotheses and set up the procedure for carrying out this test.

14.6 Suppose that a dummy variable technique is used to combine the estimates of Equations (14.22) and (14.23). Explain how this regression is set up and determine each of its estimated coefficients.

★ **14.7** Explain intuitively why the standard errors in a dummy variable regression used for estimating the unrestricted form in a Chow test might be different from the corresponding standard errors in separate regressions. (Notice that they *are* different in Table 14.2.)

Section 14.2

14.8 Consider the disturbance u_i in a linear probability model. Graph its probability distribution. Using the basic methods for discrete probability distributions, show that if $P_i = \beta_0 + \beta_1 X_i$, then $E[u_i] = 0$.

★ **14.9** On one set of axes, graph the probability distributions of the disturbances corresponding to two different values of X_i in the linear probability model.

14.10 Using Equation (14.35), determine the value of the standard normal density function $f(Z)$ for $Z = 0, 0.5, 1.0, 1.5, 2.0$, and 2.5.

14.11 Using Table A.1, determine the value of the cumulative normal distribution function $F(Z)$ for $Z = 0, 0.5, 1.0, 1.5, 2.0$, and 2.5.

★ **14.12** Using Equation (14.38), determine the value of the logistic density function $g(Z)$ for $Z = 0, 0.5, 1.0, 1.5, 2.0$, and 2.5.

★ **14.13** Using Equation (14.39), determine the value of the cumulative logistic distribution function $G(Z)$ for $Z = 0, 0.5, 1.0, 1.5, 2.0$, and 2.5.

★ **14.14** Using each of the three models reported in Table 14.3, determine $\hat{P}$ for a family at $AGE = 65$.

14.15 Using each of the three models reported in Table 14.3, determine $d\hat{P}/dX$ for a family at $AGE = 65$.

15

Heteroscedasticity and Autocorrelation

The normal regression model presented in Chapter 11 is based on a set of assumptions about the disturbances. These assumptions provide the basis for deriving the sampling distributions for the coefficient estimators. In turn, these sampling distributions are used for making statistical inferences and for assessing the properties of the OLS estimators.

Two key assumptions of the normal regression model are (1) that the disturbances are independent random variables and (2) that all their standard deviations are equal. In this chapter we examine alternatives to these assumptions. If the disturbances do not have equal standard deviations, they are said to exhibit heteroscedasticity. If the disturbances are not independent, but related to each other in a special way, they are said to exhibit autocorrelation. These alternative assumptions are more plausible than the regular ones in certain situations, and we investigate their consequences for regression estimation. In both cases we extend the basic OLS estimation technique in order to get better estimates.

15.1 Heteroscedasticity

Heteroscedasticity is the situation in which the standard deviations of the disturbances are not the same for all observations. This most often arises in the analysis of cross-section data, although it may be present in time-series data also. Most of the discussion in this section addresses the situation in simple regression, but almost everything extends to multiple regression in an obvious way.

The Model and Its Consequences

Consider the simple regression model

$$Y_i = \beta_0 + \beta_1 X_i + u_i \qquad (15.1)$$

As presented in Chapter 11, the normal regression model includes the assumption that the standard deviations of all the disturbances are identical: $\sigma(u_i) = \sigma_u$ for all i.

We now consider the possibility that the standard deviation may take on a different value for each observation:

$$\sigma(u_i) = \sigma_i \qquad (15.2)$$

It could be that σ_i is purely idiosyncratic. However, only if there is a systematic relation between σ_i and some characteristics of the observation will it be possible to deal with the situation in practice. For our discussion, we suppose that σ_i is related to X_i, the value of the explanatory variable.

For example, consider a cross-section family consumption function, in which Y is consumption expenditure and X is family income. In order to clarify the presentation, suppose that only four different values of X are included in the data. The theoretical determination of Y is illustrated in Figure 15.1a. As X increases, the standard deviation (σ_i) of the relevant $p(Y)$ distribution increases also. This makes sense in this example, because families have much greater latitude in making expenditure decisions when incomes are high than when they are low. Now, among families with income level X_1, the observed values of Y are (theoretically) a set of outcomes generated from "$p(Y)$ for X_1," like those illustrated by the points having X_1 in Figure 15.1a. For greater values of X, the observations on Y will be less concentrated around their mean, and the process will generate a set of data resembling that in Figure 15.1b.

If we apply OLS directly to the estimation of (15.1) while ignoring (15.2), the OLS estimators are unbiased and consistent. However the estimators are no longer efficient: some other estimation method that produces unbiased estimators will have smaller sampling variances. If enough data were available so that the precision of estimation was already satisfactory, this would not be too troublesome.

Unfortunately, the calculations of the OLS standard errors based on the regular formulas are incorrect, because the formulas assume that there is no heteroscedasticity. Therefore, hypothesis tests based on these standard errors are invalid. An alternative method for determining the standard errors has been developed by Halbert White, and these yield consistent estimates of the sampling variances. Thus, at least in large samples, hypothesis tests can be carried out in

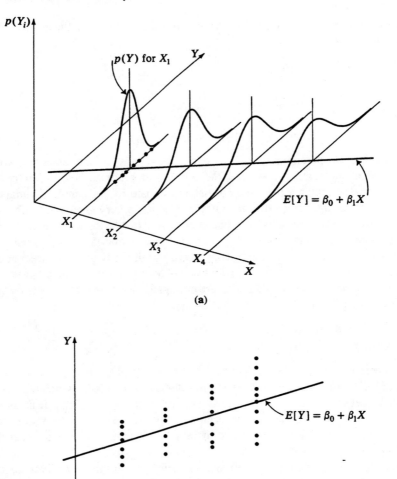

FIGURE 15.1 If the standard deviation of the disturbance increases with the value of X, we have a case of heteroscedasticity. The determination of Y in this case is illustrated in (a), which should be compared with Figure 11.2. The observed values of Y for several observations having X_1 in common are thought of as a set of outcomes from "$p(Y)$ for X_1." When only four distinguishable values of X are observed, this process leads to a set of data illustrated in (b).

the regular way. White's method is available as an option in many computer programs.

As an example, we consider the data on the *SAVING* and *INCOME* of families in the cross-section data set from Chapter 2. This can be used to estimate a saving function, which might display heteroscedasticity for the same reasons that a consumption function might. Assuming a simple linear form, the results are

$$\widehat{SAVING_i} = -1.062 + 0.295 INCOME_i$$
$$(0.851) \quad (0.075)$$
$$[1.233] \quad [0.152]$$
$$R^2 = .137 \quad SER = 4.154$$

(15.3)

The number in parentheses below each coefficient is the standard error calculated in the regular way, and the number in brackets below that is the standard error calculated from the consistent estimate of the sampling variance. The original standard error suggests that income has a very significant effect on saving ($t^* = 3.94$). The revised standard error is about twice as large, and the t statistic looks less impressive ($t^* = 1.94$). Since a one-tailed test would be appropriate, we would judge that income has a significantly positive effect at the 5 percent level. However, the coefficient would not be significant on a two-tailed test, and so the original standard errors might have led to a misleading assessment.

Detection

The essence of detecting heteroscedasticity involves estimating the original model (15.1) with OLS and then examining the residuals for evidence regarding a relation between $\sigma(u_i)$ and the characteristics of the observations. It need not be true that the relevant characteristics are variables that appear in the model, but this is usually the case. In any event, it may be difficult to ascertain what the relation is.

Sometimes it is possible to start with an informal, graphical analysis of the residuals. This is simplified somewhat by dealing with the absolute value of each residual, |e|. The pattern of the residuals in Figure 15.2a, for example, indicates

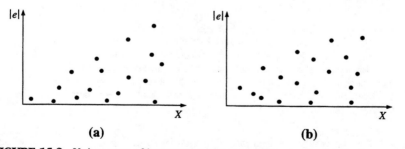

(a)   **(b)**

FIGURE 15.2 Various cases of heteroscedasticity show different patterns when the absolute value of the residual is graphed against X. In (a), |e| tends to increase with X and the pattern may be specified by Equation (15.9). In (b), |e| tends to increase with the square root of X, and the pattern may be specified in Equation (15.10).

that the standard deviation of the residuals associated with a given value of X is roughly proportional to X. This suggests that (15.2) should be specified as

$$\sigma(u_i) = \sigma X_i \qquad (15.4)$$

where σ now stands simply as a constant of proportionality.

Two general tests are commonly used, and these are sometimes computed automatically in regression programs. Both are applied after the main regression, like (15.1), is estimated by OLS. Each residual e_i is calculated and then squared. This produces a new variable whose values might be denoted by $RESIDSQ_i$ in computer applications or by e_i^2 in theoretical writing. This new variable is then used as the regressand in an auxiliary regression, which is estimated in order to produce a test statistic. The basic idea is that if $\sigma^2(u_i)$ is related to some characteristics of the observation, this would be reflected by e_i^2 being related to those characteristics in the auxiliary regression.

In the **White test,** the regressors in the auxiliary regression are all the explanatory variables in the main regression plus their squares and cross products (and also a constant). For instance, if the main regression included a constant and two regressors X_1 and X_2, the regressors in the auxiliary regression would be X_1, X_2, X_1^2, X_2^2, and $X_1 X_2$. Let P be the number of regressors in the auxiliary regression (not including the constant); in this case $P = 5$. White's test is based on the R^2 from this regression. If the null hypothesis that all $\sigma(u_i) = \sigma_u$ is true (i.e., if there is no heteroscedasticity), the test statistic nR^2 has a chi-square distribution with $P - 1$ degrees of freedom in large samples. Large values of R^2 imply that the regressors help explain the variation in the residuals, indicating heteroscedasticity. Hence H_0 is rejected when nR^2 is large.

With our family saving function, the auxiliary regression for the White test uses only $INCOME$ and $INCOMESQ$ as regressors:

$$\widehat{RESIDSQ_i} = -24.99 + 3.974INCOME_i + 0.0185INCOMESQ_i$$
$$\phantom{\widehat{RESIDSQ_i} = } (30.40) \quad (4.697) \qquad\qquad (0.1443)$$
$$R^2 = .0975 \quad SER = 78.11 \qquad (15.5)$$

Since $n = 100$, we see that $nR^2 = 9.75$. With $P - 1 = 1$, the critical value for the test statistic is $(\chi_1^2)^c = 3.84$ at the 5 percent level of significance (see Table A.4). Thus H_0 is rejected, and we take this as evidence in favor of heteroscedasticity.

In the **Breusch–Pagan test,** the k regressors in the auxiliary regression are whatever variables are thought to possibly affect $\sigma(u_i)$. A test statistic is constructed from the explained variation in the auxiliary regression and the sum of the squared residuals in the main regression:

$$\frac{\text{explained variation in } e_i^2}{2(\Sigma\, e_i^2/n)^2} \qquad (15.6)$$

The "explained variation" was defined in connection with R^2, and it is sometimes identified as the "explained sum of squares" or the "sum of squares due to the regression" on computer output. The term in parentheses is an estimate of the variance of the disturbance in the main regression (under the assumption of no heteroscedasticity). If the null hypothesis of no heteroscedasticity is true, this test statistic has a chi-squared distribution with k degrees of freedom in large samples. Values of the test statistic greater than a critical value indicate heteroscedasticity.

Some older, less general, tests are based on using a simple regression to explore the relation between the residuals (from the main regression) and a single explanatory variable X. These regressions themselves suffer from a variety of statistical problems, but they can be useful in providing some constructive information about the heteroscedasticity in the main regression.

The **Park test** is based on an auxiliary regression of the form

$$\ln e_i^2 = \beta_0 + \beta_1 \ln X_i + v_i \tag{15.7}$$

As discussed in Chapter 6, this log-linear specification permits a wide variety of relations between e^2 and X to be discovered. If $\hat{\beta}_1^*$ is statistically significant, we conclude that the disturbances are heteroscedastic. For example, a Park test on the residuals from the saving function (15.3) is carried out by estimating

$$\widehat{\ln RESIDSQ_i} = -3.885 + 1.796 \ln INCOME_i$$
$$(0.893) \quad (0.401)$$
$$R^2 = .170 \quad SER = 2.169 \tag{15.8}$$

In this regression we see that the (log of the) squared residual is significantly related to (the log of) income ($t^* = 4.48$). The estimated elasticity is not significantly different from 2, which is the value we would expect if the variance of the disturbance were proportional to the square of $INCOME$. This would mean that $\sigma(u_i)$ is proportional to $INCOME$, as in (15.4).

A similar approach leads to **Glejser tests,** in which the regressand in the auxiliary regression is taken to be $|e_i|$ rather than e_i^2. A variety of functional forms such as

$$|e_i| = \beta_1 X_i + v_i \tag{15.9}$$

and

$$|e_i| = \beta_1 \sqrt{X_i} + v_i \tag{15.10}$$

may be used. The specification (15.9) corresponds to a plot of $|e|$ against X that looks like Figure 15.2a, while (15.10) corresponds to a plot that looks like Figure 15.2b. If the estimated coefficient is statistically significant in these or other auxiliary regressions, we conclude that $\sigma(u_i)$ is not independent of X_i (i.e., we have evidence that the disturbances are heteroscedastic). Like the Park test, this procedure has the benefit of giving an indication of how $\sigma(u_i)$ is related to X_i.

Estimation

Suppose we have concluded that the disturbances in the main regression model (15.1) are heteroscedastic, as specified by (15.4). In this case the technique for estimating, or reestimating, the coefficients in (15.1) is straightforward to derive and apply. The object is to respecify the original model in such a way that the resulting disturbances are **homoscedastic** (i.e., free from heteroscedasticity).

The first step is to divide through the original model (15.1) by X_i, the measure to which $\sigma(u_i)$ is proportional in (15.4). Letting $\epsilon_i = u_i/X_i$, this yields

$$\left[\frac{Y_i}{X_i}\right] = \beta_0\left[\frac{1}{X_i}\right] + \beta_1 + \epsilon_i \tag{15.11}$$

which is a simple regression specification with regressand and regressor given in brackets (ϵ is lower case Greek "epsilon"). Note that the original intercept β_0 is the slope coefficient here, and the original slope β_1 now appears as the intercept.

Now, since X_i is fixed for each observation, the transformation $\epsilon_i = (1/X_i)u_i$ is a simple case of a linear transformation. Substituting from (15.4), we see that

$$\sigma(\epsilon_i) = \left|\frac{1}{X_i}\right|\sigma(u_i) = \frac{1}{X_i}\sigma X_i = \sigma \tag{15.12}$$

for $X_i > 0$. Thus (15.11) specifies a regression model that is free from heteroscedasticity. Since the ϵ_i satisfy all the regular disturbance assumptions, OLS can be used to make estimates of β_0 and β_1 that are unbiased, efficient, and consistent. The regressand and regressor in (15.11) are easy to construct, and therefore the technique is easy to apply.

For example, returning to our saving function, we saw that the Park test suggests that (15.4) may correctly characterize the heteroscedasticity in this situation. Proceeding on this basis, we estimate the regression

$$\left[\widehat{\frac{SAVING_i}{INCOME_i}}\right] = -0.228\left[\frac{1}{INCOME_i}\right] + 0.197 \tag{15.13}$$
$$(0.222)(0.044)$$

according to the approach in (15.11). It is common to present these results as

$$\widehat{SAVING_i} = -0.228 + 0.197INCOME_i \tag{15.14}$$
$$(0.222)(0.044)$$

and simply mention the method of estimation. This equation should be compared with (15.3). The standard errors here are substantially smaller than the correctly calculated ones reported earlier. This is in accord with the estimates here being efficient and the OLS estimates (reported earlier) being inefficient.

Other cases arise when the particular specification of heteroscedasticity is different from (15.4), and the resulting final models for estimation differ from (15.11). The general procedure is to divide through the original model by the measure to which $\sigma(u_i)$ is proportional. A common case starts from the specification

$$\sigma(u_i) = \sigma\sqrt{X_i} \tag{15.15}$$

Dividing through the original model by $\sqrt{X_i}$, one gets

$$\left[\frac{Y_i}{\sqrt{X_i}}\right] = \beta_0\left[\frac{1}{\sqrt{X_i}}\right] + \beta_1\left[\frac{X_i}{\sqrt{X_i}}\right] + \epsilon_i \tag{15.16}$$

It can be shown that $\sigma(\epsilon_i) = \sigma$, the constant of proportionality in this case. Notice that this is a multiple regression with no intercept (i.e., a regression through the origin).

These estimation procedures are special applications of the method of **generalized least squares** (GLS). Loosely speaking, GLS is a method that takes full account of the distribution of the disturbances. It does this by specifying a new equation involving transformed variables and then applying OLS to estimate the coefficients. The procedures used here are also known as **weighted least squares,** because the transformation is similar to attaching a separate weight to each observation.

Sometimes the best way to deal with heteroscedasticity is to think about it while formulating the original model. For example, if we are interested in family saving behavior, we might focus on the saving–income ratio, rather than the saving level, as the variable of interest. We would expect that the disturbances affecting this ratio would be relatively free of heteroscedasticity, especially in comparison with the disturbances affecting the saving level. Sometimes it is suggested that a relation be specified in log-linear rather than linear form, in order to reduce the apparent heteroscedasticity. However, the choice of functional form should be made predominantly on the basis of other considerations. It generally would not make sense to misspecify the systematic part of the model simply because OLS would be an inefficient estimator of coefficients in the correct model.

15.2   Autocorrelation _____

Autocorrelation (or, *serial correlation*) is the situation in which successive disturbances are related to each other rather than independent. Almost by definition this is a time-series problem, because the ordering of the observations plays a very special role. Accordingly, in this section we use t as a subscript (instead of i) to index the individual observations.

The circumstances surrounding time-series models make autocorrelation a plausible occurrence in many cases. Recall that one of the factors contributing to the disturbance term in a regression model is measurement error for the dependent variable. Measurement errors may be serially correlated because data-gathering techniques may be modified gradually over time. A second factor usually contributing to the disturbance term is the exclusion of some unimportant explanatory variables. Each of these is likely to vary systematically with time, and their combination may be serially correlated.

The Model

Consider the simple regression model

$$Y_t = \beta_0 + \beta_1 X_t + u_t \tag{15.17}$$

Under the assumptions of the normal regression model, the disturbances are independent. This means that the probability of different values occurring for one period's disturbance is not affected by the value that occurred for the previous period's disturbance. Therefore, the time plot of the values of the disturbances might look like Figure 15.3a. These disturbances, in association with the set of X values, are the basis for generating the data for Y through the regression model. The resulting set of observed data is shown in Figure 15.3b.

When autocorrelation is present, the time plot of the disturbances may resemble Figure 15.3c. In the figure, successive disturbances appear to be small deviations from the previous value, and the overall pattern is snakelike. If the values of X increase over time, which is common in time series, the Y values generated through the simple regression model will snake around the true regression line, as in Figure 15.3d.

In order to understand the consequences of this situation and to take corrective measures, we need to develop a formal model of autocorrelation. There are a variety of ways in which the disturbances may be related, and each requires a separate analysis. We examine only the most common one.

The model of *first-order autocorrelation* starts with the regression model (15.17). The disturbance u_t is assumed to be related to the previous period's disturbance according to

$$u_t = \rho u_{t-1} + \epsilon_t, \quad 0 < \rho < 1 \tag{15.18}$$

(ρ is lower case Greek "rho"). This specifies the case of *positive* autocorrelation, which is its most common form. The case of *negative* autocorrelation arises when $-1 < \rho < 0$. Because (15.18) suggests a regression of u_t on its own lagged value, the disturbances are sometimes said to follow a *first-order autoregressive process*, which is denoted by AR(1).

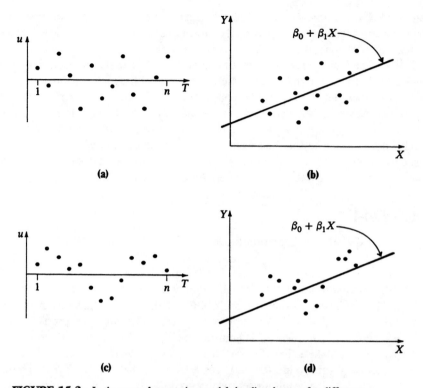

FIGURE 15.3   In the normal regression model the disturbances for different observations are independent. In (a), a typical time plot of disturbances shows a random pattern. In (b), these disturbances also show a random pattern around the true regression line. With positive first-order autocorrelation, successive disturbances are correlated, and a typical time plot of disturbances is given in (c). If the values of X increase over time, these disturbances show a snakelike pattern around the true regression line, as in (d).

In this model of autocorrelation, the value of each observation's disturbance is a random deviation from a portion of the previous disturbance. The ϵ_t are assumed to be random variables satisfying the same set of assumptions that were made for the u_t in the normal regression model: the ϵ_t are independent and have identical normal distributions with $E[\epsilon_t] = 0$ and $\sigma(\epsilon_t) = \sigma_\epsilon$. The ϵ_t are said to be *white noise*, or determined by a white-noise process; the terminology reflects its origin in scientific studies.

Given these assumptions regarding ϵ_t, the properties of the disturbances u_t, can be determined. It can be shown that all the u_t have unconditional normal probability distributions with $E[u_t] = 0$ and

$$\sigma(u_t) = \sigma_u = \frac{\sigma_\epsilon}{\sqrt{1 - \rho^2}} \qquad (15.19)$$

for all t. For any observation, the disturbance u_t has a greater standard deviation than the random term ϵ_t. We see that if ρ is large (close to 1 in absolute value), σ_u is much larger than σ_ϵ.

Notice that when we make the "regular" assumptions about ϵ in (15.18), all of them carry over to u_t except independence. That is, the u_t are normal with means of zero and identical standard deviations. But, it can be shown that the u_t have a joint probability distribution in which the correlation between successive observations is ρ. That is, ρ is the correlation between one period's disturbance and the next, or previous, one.

The impact of positive autocorrelation on the determination of Y is illustrated in Figure 15.4. Suppose that the value of the disturbance for the first observation is u_1^*. For the second observation, substituting (15.18) into (15.17), we see that Y_2 is determined from

$$Y_2 = \beta_0 + \beta_1 X_2 + \rho u_1^* + \epsilon_2 \tag{15.20}$$

The random term ϵ_2 causes there to be a (conditional) probability distribution for Y_2 that has a mean of $\beta_0 + \beta_1 X_2 + \rho u_1^*$ and a standard deviation of σ_ϵ. One

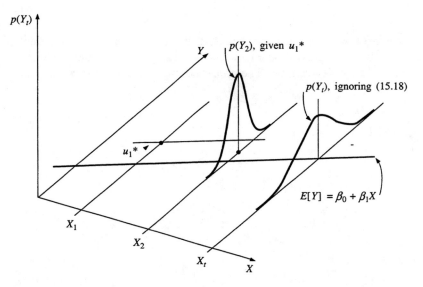

FIGURE 15.4 With first-order autocorrelation, each disturbance is thought of as a random variable whose mean depends on the value of the disturbance of the previous observation. Thus, for the second observation, Y_2 is thought of as an outcome from "$p(Y_2)$, given u_1^*." If we try to apply OLS directly, this is tantamount to assuming that each Y_t is determined from a probability distribution like "$p(Y_t)$, ignoring (15.18)," which has a larger standard deviation than the true distribution of Y_t. Thus OLS is no longer efficient. The determination of Y in the case of autocorrelation should be compared with that in the normal regression model, illustrated in Figure 11.2.

outcome from this distribution occurs, and the difference between this value (Y_2) and the unconditional mean $(\beta_0 + \beta_1 X_2)$ is the disturbance u_2^* (which is not shown). Similarly, for the third period (not shown) there is a conditional probability distribution for Y_3 that has a mean of $\beta_0 + \beta_1 X_3 + \rho u_2^*$ and a standard deviation of σ_ϵ. Its outcome includes a disturbance u_3^*, which helps determine the mean of the conditional distribution for Y_4. The process continues in this way, and for $0 < \rho < 1$ it leads to a set of Y values that may snake around the true regression line, as in Figure 15.3d.

The process of autocorrelation should be distinguished from one in which a misspecification of the model makes the disturbances appear to be serially correlated, when in fact they are not. For example, suppose that Y is a second-degree polynomial function of X,

$$Y_t = \beta_0 + \beta_1 X_t + \beta_2 X_t^2 + u_t \tag{15.21}$$

with regular disturbances. Figure 15.5 shows how the data generated from this process might look. If we mistakenly estimate a simple regression of Y on X,

$$\hat{Y}_t = \hat{\gamma}_0 + \hat{\gamma}_1 X_t \tag{15.22}$$

the residuals will seem to snake around the fitted line. We might think that autocorrelation is present when in fact the real problem is the exclusion of a relevant explanatory variable. The proper course of action when misspecification

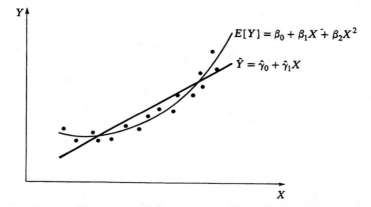

FIGURE 15.5 If an estimated model is misspecified, the pattern of residuals around the fitted regression line may resemble the pattern of autocorrelation. Here, the true regression model is quadratic, but a simple linear model is fit to the data. The proper procedure is to correct the misspecification, not to treat the situation as one of autocorrelation. Of course, it is not easy to know when the estimated model is misspecified, so some exploration may be appropriate.

is present is to correct the specification—it is not appropriate to assign the problem to the disturbance and treat the situation as one of autocorrelation.

Consequences of Autocorrelation for OLS

To assess the consequences of first-order autocorrelation for the problem of estimation, we reconsider the model determining the values of Y, as illustrated in Figure 15.4. As explained previously, the observed values of Y are generated from a series of probability distributions like "$p(Y_2)$, given u_1^*." The mean of each of these distributions depends (in part) on the value of the previous disturbance, and the standard deviation equals σ_ϵ. Now, if we ignore this information about the disturbances and simply apply OLS to (15.17), this is tantamount to assuming that the values of Y are generated from a series of probability distributions like "$p(Y_t)$, ignoring (15.18)." The standard deviation of this distribution is given by (15.19), and it is larger than σ_ϵ.

The consequence of this is that OLS applied directly to (15.17) is no longer efficient. Intuitively, a technique that does not take the disturbance structure (15.18) into account will yield larger sampling errors for its estimates than a technique that does. Further, and very important, when $\rho > 0$ and the values of X are increasing over time, the direct application of OLS to (15.17) tends to underestimate the appropriate standard errors, meaning that the t ratios based on these calculations are erroneously large. This tends to cause our hypothesis tests to reject a correct null hypothesis with a probability much greater than the chosen level of significance. In other words, our testing procedure is now invalid, and it errs in the direction of finding too much significance.

The presence of autocorrelation does not affect the unbiasedness and consistency of OLS under the other regular assumptions. However, if one of the regressors is a lagged value of the dependent variable, the OLS estimates are biased and inconsistent.

When first-order autocorrelation seems to be present, there are several methods of estimation that are preferable to OLS. If these methods are not used, OLS estimates are still worth examining. However, reports of the significance tests must be discounted.

Testing for Autocorrelation

In practice, one way to determine whether or not autocorrelation is present is to examine the time plot of the residuals. If they seem to cycle or snake around the time axis, positive autocorrelation should be suspected; if they are fairly random, the problem might be considered absent.

A rigorous approach to doing this is provided by the ***Durbin–Watson test.*** The null hypothesis is that there is no autocorrelation, specified as "H_0: $\rho = 0$." The alternative hypothesis can be specified in various ways, depending on the situation. Most commonly, the alternative hypothesis is "H_1: $0 < \rho < 1$," which is the case of positive autocorrelation.

The test statistic is

$$d = \frac{\sum\limits_{t=2}^{n} (e_t - e_{t-1})^2}{\sum\limits_{t=1}^{n} e_t^2} \qquad (15.23)$$

which ranges from 0 to 4. If the null hypothesis is true, then the sampling distribution of this statistic has a mean of about 2. If positive autocorrelation is present, differences like $e_t - e_{t-1}$ in the numerator tend to be smaller than the typical value e_t (neglecting sign) in the denominator, and d tends to be small. Hence, small values of d (close to 0) are evidence against the null hypothesis.

The decision rule for the test should be of the form "Reject H_0 if $d^* \leq d^c$," where d^c is the critical value of d that bounds exactly α probability in the lefthand tail of the sampling distribution of d when $\rho = 0$. Unfortunately, the critical value d^c cannot be determined exactly because the sampling distribution depends on the values of the regression variables. However, Durbin and Watson were able to derive upper and lower bounds for d^c, so that $d_l \leq d^c \leq d_u$ as illustrated in Figure 15.6. These upper and lower bounds depend on the number of regressors (k), the number of observations (n), and the level of significance for the test (α).

In practice, the decision rule for testing against the alternative of positive autocorrelation is

$$0 < d^* < d_l, \quad \text{reject } H_0$$
$$\text{If} \quad d_l \leq d^* \leq d_u, \quad \text{the result is indeterminate} \qquad (15.24)$$
$$d_u < d^*, \quad \text{do not reject } H_0$$

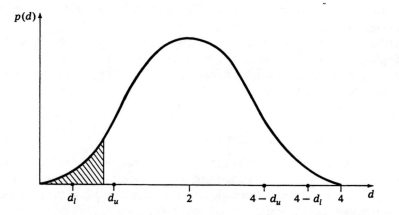

FIGURE 15.6 The exact sampling distribution of the Durbin–Watson statistic (d) depends on the values of the regression variables. Hence, the critical value d^c cannot be generally determined. However, lower and upper bounds have been derived, so we know that $d_l \leq d^c \leq d_u$. If the value of the test statistic, d^*, falls between these bounds, the conclusion of the hypothesis test is indeterminate.

For this one-tailed test, Table A.7 gives the d_l and d_u bounds at the .05 level of significance. Most econometric computer programs routinely calculate the value of the test statistic, d^*.

When we suspect negative autocorrelation, the alternative hypothesis is "H_1: $-1 < \rho < 0$." When negative autocorrelation is present, d tends to be large, and large values of d (close to 4) are evidence against the null hypothesis. The decision rule is

$$4 - d_l < d^* < 4, \qquad \text{reject } H_0$$

$$\text{If} \quad 4 - d_u \leq d^* \leq 4 - d_l, \quad \text{the result is indeterminate} \qquad (15.25)$$

$$d^* \leq 4 - d_u, \quad \text{do not reject } H_0$$

When there is no particular belief regarding the sign of ρ, a two-tailed test is appropriate. In this case, the critical and indeterminate regions are combinations of the corresponding regions for the one-tailed tests. Table A.8 presents the d_l and d_u bounds for two-tailed tests at the .05 level of significance.

For example, we consider again the simple aggregate consumption function (6.10) reported in Table 11.3:

$$\widehat{CON}_t = 0.568 + 0.907DPI_t$$
$$(6.973) \quad (0.010) \qquad\qquad (15.26)$$
$$R^2 = .977 \quad SER = 8.935$$

for which $d^* = 0.66$. With $n = 25$ and $k = 1$, we see from Table A.7 that $d_l = 1.29$ and $d_u = 1.45$. Since $d^* < d_l$, we reject the null hypothesis of no autocorrelation and suspect that positive autocorrelation is present.

It should be noted that calculation of the test statistic d^* demands that the observations be ordered from 1 to n corresponding to the passing of time. If the observations are shuffled, or ordered some other way, then the calculated d^* will be a different value. Shuffling the observations causes the d^* value to be close to 2, leading to a conclusion of no autocorrelation. It should be clear, however, that shuffling the data does not remove autocorrelation: it merely invalidates the test procedure.

Finally, the validity of the Durbin–Watson test depends on the regressors being truly fixed. If a lagged value of the dependent variable is specified as a regressor, this assumption is no longer tenable. In this case d is biased toward 2. We note that in this situation a useful test for autocorrelation is based on the **Durbin h statistic,** which can be calculated as

$$h = \left(1 - \frac{d}{2}\right) \sqrt{\frac{n}{1 - n \cdot V}} \qquad (15.27)$$

where d is the Durbin–Watson statistic and V is the square of the standard error of the coefficient on the lagged dependent variable. The test can be used only if $n \cdot V < 1$. In large samples, h has approximately a standard normal distribution if the null hypothesis of no autocorrelation is true, and Table A.1 can be used to determine the critical value of the test statistic.

Estimation Procedures

Suppose that the Durbin–Watson statistic indicates that autocorrelation is present. What should we do?

We first restate the first-order autocorrelation model for simple regression, given earlier as (15.17) and (15.18):

$$Y_t = \beta_0 + \beta_1 X_t + u_t \tag{15.28}$$

$$u_t = \rho u_{t-1} + \epsilon_t \tag{15.29}$$

in which ϵ_t satisfies the assumptions of the normal regression model. As noted earlier, the problem with OLS estimation in this case is twofold: (1) it is inefficient, and (2) the calculated standard errors tend to underestimate the true standard errors that OLS produces. A number of procedures have been developed to provide better estimators.

To understand these procedures, we begin with a hypothetical question: if we knew the true value of ρ, how would we estimate β_0 and β_1? Our answer to this is the method of generalized least squares (GLS), which takes into account all the characteristics of the disturbances. A new equation is specified in terms of transformed variables, and OLS applied to that equation produces unbiased and efficient estimates of the original coefficients β_0 and β_1.

The basic model (15.28) applies to every observation. The equation statement for period $t - 1$ can be multiplied through by ρ to yield

$$\rho Y_{t-1} = \rho \beta_0 + \rho \beta_1 X_{t-1} + \rho u_{t-1} \tag{15.30}$$

Subtracting (15.30) from (15.28) yields

$$[Y_t - \rho Y_{t-1}] = \beta_0[1 - \rho] + \beta_1[X_t - \rho X_{t-1}] + \epsilon_t \tag{15.31}$$

which holds validly for $t = 2, 3, \ldots, n$. The bracketed terms involving Y and X are known as **quasi differences** or **generalized differences**. Note that ϵ_t is present here because $u_t - \rho u_{t-1} = \epsilon_t$ by (15.29).

This equation provides the key to estimation. If ρ were known, the terms in square brackets could be constructed from the original data on Y and X. These new variables stand as the regressand and regressors in a multiple regression model with no intercept. The two coefficients β_0 and β_1 are the same as the coefficients in (15.28), and they can be estimated by applying OLS to (15.31). The benefit of doing these transformations is that the autocorrelation has been undone: the disturbance ϵ_t satisfies all the assumptions of the normal regression model.

The only problem with this procedure is that the first observation has been defined away. We can recover it by restating the basic model (15.28) for observation $t = 1$ and then multiplying through by $\sqrt{1 - \rho^2}$. This yields

$$[\sqrt{1 - \rho^2} Y_1] = \beta_0[\sqrt{1 - \rho^2}] + \beta_1[\sqrt{1 - \rho^2} X_1] + \epsilon_1 \tag{15.32}$$

As previously, the constructed values for the regressand and the regressors stand as a valid observation from a multiple regression process with coefficients β_0 and β_1 but with no intercept. It can be shown that the disturbance ϵ_1 is independent of all the other ϵ_t and that its probability distribution is identical to theirs. Thus the n different ϵ_t satisfy the assumptions of the normal regression model.

Put somewhat differently, the set of transformed and created variables can be thought of as n observations from the process

$$y_t = \beta_0 x_{0t} + \beta_1 x_{1t} + \epsilon_t \qquad (15.33)$$

which satisfies all the assumptions of the normal regression model. The coefficients β_0 and β_1 can be estimated by OLS, and in this model the OLS estimates are unbiased, efficient, and consistent. The ill consequences of autocorrelation have vanished.

Unfortunately, ρ is unknown and therefore this GLS estimation cannot be carried out exactly as described. However, the procedure can be approximated by making an estimate of ρ. A common way of doing this is by the following two-step procedure. In the first step, the main model (15.28) is estimated by OLS and the residuals e_t are calculated. In the second step, these residuals are used as data to estimate an auxiliary regression specified as

$$e_t = r\, e_{t-1} + v_t \qquad (15.34)$$

which is a simple regression with no intercept. This model mimics the autocorrelation specification (15.29). The value of $\hat{r}$ estimated from this regression stands as our estimate $\hat{\rho}*$ of ρ.

For example, continuing with the aggregate consumption function, the main model was already estimated and reported as (15.26). The 25 residuals e_t were calculated and used to estimate the regression

$$\widehat{RESID}_t = 0.679 RESID_{t-1} \qquad (15.35)$$

Note that the regressor here could be thought of as *RESIDLAG*, in the style of Section 6.3.

Using $\hat{\rho}* = 0.679$ in place of ρ, we construct the appropriate variables according to (15.31) and (15.32). Next, we estimate the equation corresponding to (15.33):

$$\hat{y}_t = -1.527x_{0t} + 0.911x_{1t}$$
$$\quad\;\; (13.406) \quad\;\; (0.018)$$

$$R^2 = .988 \quad SER = 6.723$$

$$(15.36)$$

Since our ultimate interest is in the main model, not the estimation procedure, these estimates are usually reported as

$$\widehat{CON}_t = -1.527 + 0.911 DPI_t$$
$$(13.406) \quad (0.018) \qquad\qquad (15.37)$$

$$R^2 = .997 \quad SER = 9.007 \quad \hat{\rho}* = 0.679$$

The R^2 and SER here have been recomputed from the actual and fitted values of CON, not y. Although this R^2 appears to be the same as that in (15.26), the value here is somewhat smaller (.99742 versus .99746). This reflects the fact that OLS provides the best fit to the data, even when it does not provide the best estimates of the coefficients.

The statistical properties of the applied GLS estimator are affected by our having to estimate ρ. In large samples the properties are approximately the same as those of GLS. In small samples, the exact properties depend on the particular application. The method is generally considered an improvement over OLS, especially when ρ is not small. In comparing the GLS and OLS estimates for the consumption function, we see that the standard errors are larger for the GLS estimates. This seems to reflect the fact that the standard errors calculated in conjunction with OLS are erroneous in the presence of autocorrelation.

Another popular approach to estimating models with an autocorrelated disturbance begins with (15.31) and rearranges it to yield

$$Y_t = \beta_0(1 - \rho) + \beta_1 X_t - \beta_1 \rho X_{t-1} + \rho Y_{t-1} + \epsilon_t \qquad (15.37)$$

This is quite different from other regression models we have dealt with, especially with regard to the presence of a term like $\beta_1 \rho X_{t-1}$. The parameters β_0, β_1, and ρ in this model can be estimated simultaneously by **nonlinear least squares**. In this procedure the estimates are arrived at by a numerical search rather than by the solution of formulas (as with OLS).

Some older methods focus on estimating an equation like (15.31). The **Cochrane–Orcutt procedure** is similar to the applied GLS procedure except that the first observation is ignored. The main equation like (15.28) is estimated, and the residuals are recovered. These are used to make an estimate of ρ through (15.34). The resulting $\hat{\rho}*$ is used to create the appropriate variables for estimating a regression like (15.31), which yields estimates of β_0 and β_1. This could be the end, but usually the procedure is iterated: the initial $\hat{\beta}_0$ and $\hat{\beta}_1$ estimates are used to calculate a set of fitted values $\hat{Y}$ from which a new set of residuals is calculated. Then a new estimate of ρ is made through (15.34) and so on. The procedure can be repeated over and over until successive values of $\hat{\rho}$ converge.

The **Hildreth–Lu** procedure begins with (15.31). Since ρ is not known, a set of trial values that span the relevant range for ρ are used, one at a time, to construct the regressand and the regressors and then estimate the equation. The trial value that leads to the equation with the smallest sum of squared residuals is designated to be $\hat{\rho}*$, and the equation estimated with this trial value is the final equation. A careful grid search of trial values can provide as much precision as is desired.

Durbin suggested that an estimate of ρ be made directly from the Durbin–Watson statistic calculated in the main regression: $\hat{\rho}* = 1 - d*/2$. This is then used to create the variables for estimating a regression like (15.31).

A special situation arises when it is assumed that $\rho = 1$, which is outside the range considered above. In this extreme form of autocorrelation, we see from (15.19) that $\sigma(u_t)$ is infinite or undefined. Also, the variables specified in (15.32) cannot be constructed. Despite these problems, the model can be partly estimated. The quasi differences defined in (15.31) are simply the first differences ΔY_t and ΔX_t, and they can be constructed easily. Thus, with $\rho = 1$ an equation of the form

$$\Delta Y_t = \beta_1 \, \Delta X_t + \epsilon_t \qquad (15.39)$$

can be estimated. (Note that β_0 drops out because $[1 - \rho] = 0$.) This is a simple regression through the origin. The ease of estimation makes this an attractive technique to use when one thinks that ρ is close to 1, even if it is not exactly equal to it.

Finally, when an estimated model is used to make forecasts, information about ρ should be taken into account. Suppose that we wish to forecast Y for period $t = n + 1$, the next period after the last in our data. We consider only the case in which X_{n+1} is known, which might arise if X is measured before Y or if X is a lagged variable. The last residual from the estimation is $e_n = Y_n - \hat{Y}_n$. Based on (15.29) we predict the value of the disturbance in period $n + 1$ to be $\hat{\rho}e_n$. (Note that ϵ_{n+1} is predicted to be zero.) Thus, our prediction for period $n + 1$ is

$$\hat{Y}_{n+1} = \hat{\beta}_0 + \hat{\beta}_1 X_{n+1} + \hat{\rho}e_n \qquad (15.40)$$

Similarly, if we were predicting for period $n + 2$, the adjustment for autocorrelation would be $(\hat{\rho})^2 e_n$. With $|\hat{\rho}| < 1$, this adjustment becomes smaller as the period of forecast moves farther beyond the end of the sample.

Problems _____

Section 15.1

★ **15.1** Suppose that measurement error in economic data has decreased over time. How might this affect the task of estimating a simple time-series regression model?

15.2 In the derivation leading to Equation (15.16), show that the disturbance ϵ is homoscedastic.

15.3 Draw a figure illustrating the following heteroscedastic specifications:
(a) $|e_i| = \beta_1 X_i^2 + v_i$ for $\beta_1 > 0$.
(b) $|e_i| = \beta_1(1/X_i) + v_i$ for $\beta_1 > 0$.
(c) $|e_i| = \beta_0 + \beta_1 X_i + v_i$ for $\beta_1 > 0$, $\beta_0 > 0$.
(d) $|e_i| = \beta_0 + \beta_1 X_i + v_i$ for $\beta_1 < 0$, $\beta_0 > 0$.

★ **15.4** In the functional forms suggested by Glejser (and those in Problem 15.3), is it correct to assume that the disturbance v_i has a normal distribution?

15.5 Draw figures showing the relation between e_i^2 and X_i indicated by the following results of the Park test:
(a) $\hat{\beta}_1 = -0.5$.
(b) $\hat{\beta}_1 = 0.5$.
(c) $\hat{\beta}_1 = 2.0$.

15.6 Suppose that we are formulating a model that explains the profitability of different firms. Is the specification more likely to be heteroscedastic if the dependent variable is the level of profits or the percentage rate of return on equity?

Section 15.2

15.7 Suppose that $\rho = .9$ in the first-order autocorrelation specification (15.18). If $u_1^* = 20$, what is the expected value of u_2 (i.e., $E[u_2]$)? Assuming that $\sigma(\epsilon_i) = 2$, name two values, u_2^* and u_3^*, that serve as good examples of results from this process.

★ **15.8** Repeat Problem 15.7 for $\rho = -.9$, a case of negative autocorrelation.

15.9 Draw a diagram in the spirit of Figure 15.3d that shows hypothetical data generated from a model with negative autocorrelation.

★ **15.10** Looking only at Table A.7, describe what happens to the sampling distribution of the Durbin–Watson statistic as the number of observations increases.

15.11 For $d^* = 1.50$, is positive autocorrelation indicated on a one-tailed test at the .05 level of significance if
(a) $k = 1, n = 20$?
(b) $k = 4, n = 20$?
(c) $k = 1, n = 60$?
(d) $k = 4, n = 60$?

★ **15.12** Taking $\hat{\rho}^* = 0.679$ and using the data on CON and DPI from Chapter 2, construct the regressand and regressors for the first three observations underlying the estimation of (15.36).

16

Regression
and Time Series

This chapter examines topics that apply to regression models of time-series processes. The first section, on distributed lags, deals with the specification of regression models in which the effects of the explanatory variable are spread over more than one period. The second section covers the use of regression for estimating trend and seasonality patterns in time series. The third section introduces the problem of nonstationary time series and spurious regressions.

Since all the discussion refers to time series, we use the subscript t (instead of i) to index the individual observations. Also, in order to simplify some of the notation, we depart from some usages that have been consistently maintained up to this point.

16.1 Distributed Lags

In economics it often is reasonable to think that a given time-series variable depends on previously occurring as well as contemporaneous values of its determinants. A process of decision making might well take into account the whole history of the determinant variables. For example, if persons are deciding how much to spend on consumption goods, they might take into account previous periods' incomes as well as the current period's amount. Sometimes economic processes have a gestation period that is longer than the time interval used to create the observations. For example, the production and sale of certain machine tools and other capital goods takes a long time; often the producing firms have backlogs of orders. Thus the firm's decision to purchase such equipment may occur a year or more before the actual purchase and delivery. This lag between decision and its measured fulfillment must be taken into account in modeling investment behavior.

The General Distributed Lag

Let Y be the dependent variable, and let X be its determinant. Suppose that the effects of X on Y do not all occur immediately, but that the total effect is distributed over several time periods. The general *distributed lag model* of the determination of Y is

$$Y_t = \alpha + \beta_0 X_t + \beta_1 X_{t-1} + \cdots + \beta_j X_{t-j} + \cdots + \beta_k X_{t-k} + u_t \quad (16.1)$$

In this notation, the current time period is t, the previous period is $t-1$, and so on. The model specifies that in period t, the value of Y is determined by the contemporaneous value of X and by the k previous values of X. In other words, the effect of X and Y is distributed over $k + 1$ periods.

Let us pursue a simple case in which the maximum length of the lag (k) is 2:

$$Y_t = \alpha + \beta_0 X_t + \beta_1 X_{t-1} + \beta_2 X_{t-2} + u_t \quad (16.2)$$

The effect of X on Y occurs partly with a lag, and it is distributed over three periods. For example, the idea that consumers' expenditures depend on their permanent incomes is sometimes formulated by hypothesizing that consumers have a three-period decision-making horizon: they view their "permanent incomes" as being a weighted average of three sequential years' incomes. In this example, Y is expenditures and X is income.

Some hypothetical data on Y and X are given in Table 16.1. As written, the model specified as (16.2) seems to involve just two variables, Y and X, but with multiple values of X. For example, the value $Y_3 = 415$ is determined by the contemporaneous value $X_3 = 475$, and by the previous values $X_2 = 425$ and $X_1 = 390$. This is not in regular regression form, which specifies a contemporaneous relation between a dependent variable and a set of regressors. The leap between the two specifications is made by constructing two new regressors, *XLAG1* and *XLAG2*, that contain the information of what the value of X was one and two periods previously, respectively. In Table 16.1 the values of *XLAG1* are constructed simply as the previous period's X value, and those of *XLAG2* are the values from two periods before. In (16.2), X_{t-1} corresponds to the value of *XLAG1* for period t in Table 16.1, and X_{t-2} corresponds to *XLAG2* for period t. Thus, for computational purposes we can think of rewriting (16.2) as

$$Y_t = \alpha + \beta_0 X_t + \beta_1 XLAG1_t + \beta_2 XLAG2_t + u_t \quad (16.3)$$

Notice that we start with n observations on Y and X, but that we have only $n - 2$ observations with which to estimate (16.3): the first two observations do not

TABLE 16.1   Hypothetical Data on Y and X

t	Y	X	$XLAG1$	$XLAG2$
1	350	390	—	—
2	380	425	390	—
3	415	475	425	390
4	445	505	475	425
.				
.				
$t-2$	Y_{t-2}	X_{t-2}	$XLAG1_{t-2}$	$XLAG2_{t-2}$
$t-1$	Y_{t-1}	X_{t-1}	$XLAG1_{t-1}$	$XLAG2_{t-1}$
t	Y_t	X_t	$XLAG1_t$	$XLAG2_t$
.				
.				
n	Y_n	X_n	$XLAG1_n$	$XLAG2_n$

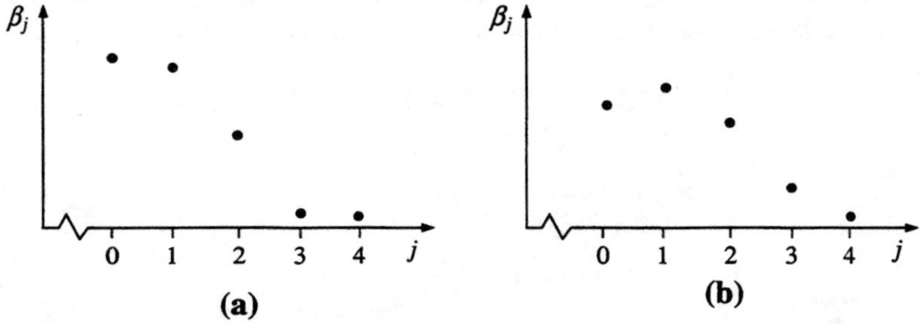

FIGURE 16.1   A graphical display of the values of the coefficients in a distributed lag model facilitates interpretation of the lag structure. The horizontal axis identifies the length of the lag. In (a), the one-period lagged value of X has almost as much impact on Y as the current-period X does, the second-period lag has half as much, and the third and fourth lags have much less. In (b), the one-period lag effect is greater than the current period's, but the importance of the effect smoothly decreases beyond there.

have values for $XLAG2$, and hence they cannot be used in the estimation. In this sense, constructing lagged variables leads to a loss of observations.

The actual reformulation of a distributed lag specification as (16.3) usually is understood implicitly in writing a model with notation like that of (16.2). With this understanding, equations like (16.2) should be viewed as properly specified regression models.

The relative importance of the current and lagged values of X in the determination of the current value of Y is given by the relative magnitudes of their regression coefficients. For example, consider a general distributed lag model like (16.1) with $k = 4$. A convenient way to compare the coefficients is in a graph like Figure 16.1. Here the values of the coefficients β_j are plotted vertically. They are spaced and identified along the horizontal axis by the length of the lag j. This is not a plot of data, but a convenient graphical depiction of the values of the coefficients. In Figure 16.1a, we have a case in which the current ($j = 0$) and one-period lag ($j = 1$) values of X have nearly equal effects on Y. The effect of the second-period lag is only about half as much as the current effect. The third and fourth lags have almost no effect compared with the current value of X. In Figure 16.1b, we have a different situation: the first lag effect is greater than the current effect, but after that the importance of the effect smoothly decreases with the length of the lag.

A distributed lag model like (16.1) or (16.2) can be estimated with the technique of ordinary least squares, yielding estimates of the coefficients that have the usual properties. Two difficulties arise, however. First, the regressors are likely to be highly correlated, since it is usually the case that X_t and X_{t-1} (for example) both increase over time. This results in a situation of multicollinearity that can be extremely severe. Second, if we specify that the effect of X on Y is distributed over a large number of periods, the consequent loss of usable observations compounds the difficulty of making precise estimates.

For example, adopting the permanent income theory's idea that current consumption depends on a three-year span of incomes, we estimate

$$\widehat{CON}_t = 0.735 + 0.886DPI_t + 0.0116DPILAG1_t$$
$$\quad\quad (8.768)\;\; (0.159) \quad\quad (0.2391)$$

$$\quad + 0.0100DPILAG2_t \tag{16.4}$$
$$\quad\quad (0.1762)$$

$$R^2 = .997 \quad SER = 9.825$$

for the 23 observations 1958–1980. We see that the lagged impacts of disposable income are of negligible importance in comparison with the current impact, casting some doubt on the permanent income theory. Further, the current effect is clearly significant, whereas the lagged effects are clearly insignificant. However, we note that the presence of multicollinearity makes it difficult to precisely estimate the coefficients.

These difficulties of estimation are ameliorated to some extent if a more structured specification for the distributed lag model is adopted, as discussed in the following sections. However, these specifications lead to other estimation difficulties. Also, if the adopted specification is not a reasonable characterization of the economic process, it will have created a misspecification problem.

The Koyck Model

A useful and important version of the distributed lag model involves the assumption that the β coefficients in (16.1) decline geometrically in value as the length of the lag increases. That is, it is assumed that

$$\beta_j = \beta_0 \lambda^j, \quad 0 < \lambda < 1, \quad j = 1, \ldots, k \tag{16.5}$$

(λ is lower case Greek "lambda"). For a given β_0, this means that $\beta_1 = \beta_0 \lambda^1 = \beta_0 \lambda$, $\beta_2 = \beta_0 \lambda^2$, and so on. The parameter λ reflects the relative importance of lag effects one period apart. Thus if λ is large, a change in X in a given period will have relatively large effects for many periods.

In the formulation known as the **Koyck model** or the **geometric lag model**, k is infinite. The factor λ^j gets very small as we push farther back in time (e.g., $0.5^{10} \approx 0.001$), so this assumption does not imply that the very distant past has an important effect on current Y.

Now, letting the length of the lag be infinite, (16.1) can be written [using (16.5)] as

$$Y_t = \alpha + \beta_0(X_t + \lambda X_{t-1} + \lambda^2 X_{t-2} + \cdots) + u_t \tag{16.6}$$

This relation holds for every period, and we can write it for period $t - 1$:

$$Y_{t-1} = \alpha + \beta_0(X_{t-1} + \lambda X_{t-2} + \lambda^2 X_{t-3} + \cdots) + u_{t-1} \tag{16.7}$$

Next, we multiply this equation through by λ to get

$$\lambda Y_{t-1} = \lambda \alpha + \beta_0(\lambda X_{t-1} + \lambda^2 X_{t-2} + \lambda^3 X_{t-3} + \cdots) + \lambda u_{t-1} \tag{16.8}$$

and then subtract (16.8) from (16.6) to get

$$Y_t - \lambda Y_{t-1} = \alpha - \lambda \alpha + \beta_0 X_t + u_t - \lambda u_{t-1} \tag{16.9}$$

Finally, moving λY_{t-1} to the right-hand side and letting $v_t = u_t - \lambda u_{t-1}$, we arrive at

$$Y_t = (1 - \lambda)\alpha + \beta_0 X_t + \lambda Y_{t-1} + v_t \tag{16.10}$$

This equation stands as the combination of the geometric lag assumption (16.5) with the infinite version of the general distributed lag model (16.1).

The regression model (16.10) can be estimated directly by OLS, with some difficulties to be discussed later. The specification of the geometric lag pattern enables us to replace an infinite stream of variables with just two regressors: the current value of X and the one-period lag of Y, the dependent variable. Only one observation is lost in the construction. This respecification has the beneficial effect of reducing the potential for severe multicollinearity that exists in the general distributed lag model. Notice that the coefficient on the lag of Y is λ, the geometric weight, which is to be estimated. The coefficient on the current value of X is β_0. Given (16.5), all the coefficients in the infinite distributed lag can be determined from these two values.

For example, consider the assumption that the importance of previous years' incomes in the determination of current consumption expenditures declines geometrically with the length of the lag. Our estimate of the Koyck model specification of the aggregate consumption function is

$$\widehat{CON}_t = 2.611 + 0.623DPI_t + 0.320CONLAG1_t$$
$$\quad\quad (7.476)\ \ (0.121)\quad\quad (0.136) \tag{16.11}$$
$$R^2 = .998 \quad SER = 8.483$$

for the 23 observations, 1958–1980. It should be noted that 24 observations are available here, but we have kept the same sample as that of (16.4) for comparison. The estimated coefficient on current income is $\hat{\beta}_0^* = 0.623$. The rate of geometric decline is estimated to be $\hat{\lambda} = 0.320$, implying an estimated impact of $(0.623)(0.320) = 0.199$ for the one-period lag of income, $(0.623)(0.320)^2 = 0.064$ for the two-period lag, and so on. The estimated structure of the distributed lag coefficients is illustrated in Figure 16.2.

The Koyck lag model (16.11) provides a dynamic specification of the process by which income affects consumption. In a given year, a 1 billion dollar increase in DPI leads to a 0.623 billion dollar increase in predicted CON; this is the *short-run* marginal propensity to consume. If the increase in DPI is maintained for a second year, predicted CON in that period will be higher than it otherwise would have been for two reasons: because DPI is higher and because CON_{t-1} is higher. From the viewpoint of the second year, CON_{t-1} is 0.623 billion dollars higher, leading CON_t to be $(0.320)(0.623) = 0.199$ higher through the lag effect. This, coupled with the current-period impact of the higher DPI, leads to a total *two-year* marginal propensity to consume of 0.822. The equilibrium, or long run, impact of a maintained increase in DPI can be determined from

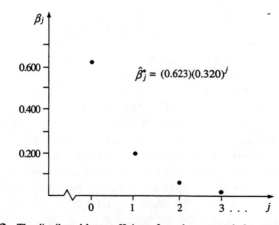

FIGURE 16.2 The distributed lag coefficients from the geometric lag specification of the consumption function, Equation (16.11), decline sharply with the length of the lag. The parameters β_0 and λ are estimated to be 0.623 and 0.320, respectively, and the implied value of each lag coefficient is determined from Equation (16.5).

$$\Delta \widehat{CON}_t = 0.623 \, \Delta \, DPI_t + 0.320 \, \Delta \, CONLAG1_t \qquad (16.12)$$

which is derived from (16.11). In equilibrium, the change in consumption above what it otherwise would have been is the same in each period: the effect has reached a plateau. Thus, $\Delta \, CON = \Delta \, CONLAG1$, and (16.12) can be solved to yield $\Delta \, CON = 0.916 \, \Delta \, DPI$. In this context, the *long-run* marginal propensity to consume is estimated as 0.916. In the general specification (16.10) of the Koyck model, the short-run impact of X on Y is given by β_0 and the long-run impact is given by $\beta_0/(1 - \lambda)$.

Partial Adjustment and Adaptive Expectations

We now briefly consider two other formulations that lead to estimating equations similar to (16.10). The first is the **partial adjustment** or **stock adjustment** model. The theory underlying this presumes that the behaviorally desired level of Y in period t is an unobservable variable Y^* and that this desired level is determined as

$$Y_t^* = \alpha + \beta_0 X_t + u_t \qquad (16.13)$$

Further, it is assumed that because of inertia, habit, costs, or other constraints, actual behavior each period is to close only part of the gap between last period's actual Y_{t-1} and this period's desired Y_t^* according to

$$Y_t - Y_{t-1} = \gamma(Y_t^* - Y_{t-1}), \quad 0 < \gamma < 1 \qquad (16.14)$$

A little substitution and algebra combines (16.13) and (16.14) to yield

$$Y_t = \gamma\alpha + \gamma\beta_0 X_t + (1 - \gamma)Y_{t-1} + v_t \qquad (16.15)$$

where $v_t = \gamma u_t$. We recognize that the coefficient on Y_{t-1} identifies the adjustment factor γ. Given this, the combined coefficient on X_t yields β_0, which is the impact of X on Y^*. The similarity of (16.15) and (16.10) should be noted: both specify a regression of Y_t on X_t and Y_{t-1}.

The second formulation is the **adaptive expectations** model, which characterizes a certain behavior by saying that the actual value of Y is determined by the expected (or desired) level of X according to

$$Y_t = \alpha + \beta_0 X_t^* + u_t \qquad (16.16)$$

The expected level of X is the unobservable variable X^* that is theorized to be a weighted average of last period's X^* and this period's actual X according to

$$X_t^* = \delta X_t + (1 - \delta)X_{t-1}^*, \quad 0 < \delta < 1 \qquad (16.17)$$

Substituting (16.17) into (16.16), we get

$$Y_t = \alpha + \beta_0(\delta X_t + (1 - \delta)X_{t-1}^*) + u_t \qquad (16.18)$$

Now, X^*_{t-1} depends on X_{t-1} and X^*_{t-2} in the same fashion as (16.17). Further substitutions lead to an equation that specifies Y_t to depend on an infinite distributed lag of X. We end up with

$$Y_t = \delta\alpha + \delta\beta_0 X_t + (1 - \delta)Y_{t-1} + v_t \qquad (16.19)$$

where $v_t = u_t - (1 - \delta)u_{t-1}$. Notice that δ plays a role that is similar to that of γ in the partial adjustment model. Also notice that both δ and γ correspond to $(1 - \lambda)$ in the Koyck lag model.

Since the partial adjustment and adaptive expectations models both lead to the same specification of regressand and regressors as the Koyck model, these models provide alternative frameworks for interpreting a regression with a lagged dependent variable. For example, consider the consumption function (16.11). Viewed through the partial adjustment model, the adjustment factor is estimated to be 0.680; this portion of the gap between desired consumption in a given year and actual consumption in the previous year is closed. We conclude that in the short run consumers adjust their actual consumption expenditures fairly completely to changes in desired expenditures. Also, using (16.15) we determine the marginal propensity to desire consumption [i.e., β_0 in (16.13)] to be $0.623/0.680 = 0.916$. It is no coincidence that this is the same as the long-run marginal propensity to consume [i.e., $\beta_0/(1 - \lambda)$ from (16.10)] in the Koyck interpretation. The formal correspondence between the estimating equations (16.10) and (16.15) leads to the correspondence between interpretations.

The results of (16.11) can be analyzed also through the framework of the adaptive expectations model. Expected income is fairly dependent on current actual income ($\delta = 0.680$), which is to say that through (16.17) expectations adjust rapidly to current reality. The marginal propensity to consume out of expected income is 0.916, although the mpc out of actual income is less: 0.623.

Estimation Problems

When the Koyck, partial adjustment, and adaptive expectations models are applied to the same economic process, they all lead to regression models having the same dependent variable and the same set of regressors. However, the error structures are not identical. To start with, we assume that the disturbance u_t in all the models satisfies the regular set of assumptions.

The situation is simplest for the partial adjustment model. The disturbance in the estimating regression (16.15) is $v_t = \gamma u_t$. Since v_t is proportional to u_t, it has the same properties. It can be shown that the OLS technique leads to consistent estimates of the parameters, although in small samples they will be biased because of the presence of the lagged dependent variable.

The Koyck model leads to a disturbance in the estimating regression (16.10) of the form $v_t = u_t - \lambda u_{t-1}$. Similarly, in the adaptive expectations model, the final (16.19) disturbance is $v_t = u_t - (1 - \delta)u_{t-1}$. This creates two difficulties.

First, v_t will be autocorrelated even if u_t is not. Unfortunately, the Durbin–Watson statistic cannot be used to test whether v_t is autocorrelated, because the presence of the lagged dependent variable biases d toward 2. Instead, we use Durbin's h statistic, defined by (15.27).

The second and more troublesome difficulty is that the inclusion of the lagged dependent variable Y_{t-1}, together with the autocorrelated disturbance, all but guarantees that these two terms will be correlated. This condition invalidates one of the assumptions used to show that OLS leads to unbiased estimates of the unknown coefficients, leaving us with the conclusion that OLS will be biased. Further, this bias will not disappear even in very large samples, so the estimates will be inconsistent. Some advanced estimation methods may be helpful here, but we do not cover them.

The Almon Lag Model and Other Lag Specifications

The geometric lag specification (16.5) is fairly flexible because various values of λ are consistent with various degrees of importance for the lagged variables. However, the specification restricts the values of β_j to decline geometrically with j, as in Figure 16.2. Although this pattern of decline is appropriate for many economic processes, it is not universally so.

A variety of forms for specifying the structure of the distributed lag have been developed, and each is appropriate in certain circumstances. Some of these structures are illustrated in Figure 16.3. In Figure 16.3a the relative importance of the coefficient decreases linearly with the length of the lag; in Figure 16.3b the importance first increases and then decreases.

The β_j coefficients in these lag structures can be determined by estimating the general distributed lag model (16.1) while imposing certain restrictions on the coefficients. For example, suppose we believe that the lag coefficients decrease linearly with the length of the lag (as in Figure 16.3a) and also that the maximum length of the lag is $k = 2$ periods. In this case, the general form of the estimating equation is the same as (16.2), but we need to impose some restrictions so that $\hat{\beta}_0$, $\hat{\beta}_1$, and $\hat{\beta}_2$ will lie along a straight line.

We do this by adopting the restrictions that $\beta_1 = \frac{2}{3}\beta_0$ and $\beta_2 = \frac{1}{3}\beta_0$. (Notice that extending this linear decline to β_{k+1} would result in $\beta_3 = \frac{0}{3}\beta_0 = 0$. By design, this linear lag structure satisfies an endpoint restriction that is consistent with the maximum length of the lag being 2 periods.) To impose these restrictions, we rewrite (16.2) as

$$Y_t = \alpha + \beta_0 X_t + (\tfrac{2}{3}\beta_0)X_{t-1} + (\tfrac{1}{3}\beta_0)X_{t-2} + u_t$$

$$= \alpha + \beta_0[X_t + \tfrac{2}{3}X_{t-1} + \tfrac{1}{3}X_{t-2}] + u_t \qquad (16.20)$$

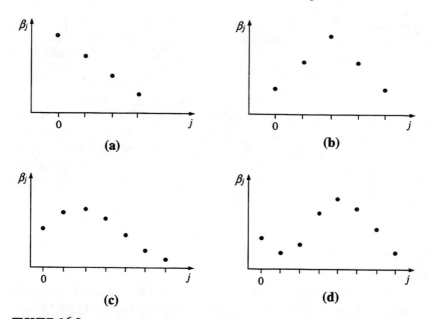

FIGURE 16.3 A variety of lag structures other than the geometric lag can be used. In (a), which is sometimes called the triangular lag, the relative importance of the coefficients decreases linearly with the length of the lag. In (b), the inverted-V lag specifies a special symmetric pattern for the coefficients. Parts (c) and (d) show two cases of the Almon lag structure, in which the lag coefficient values are specified to lie along a polynomial function of j, the length of the lag. These structures impose constraints on the relative values of regression coefficients and lead to the construction of a set of regressors that permit estimation by OLS.

The expression in brackets can be constructed as a regressor from the original data. Denoting this regressor by Z_0, (16.20) is equivalent to the simple regression

$$Y_t = \alpha + \beta_0 Z_{0t} + u_t \tag{16.21}$$

which can be estimated by OLS. This regression yields $\hat{\beta}_0^*$, and the other estimated lag coefficients are determined by multiplying this estimate by $\tfrac{2}{3}$ and $\tfrac{1}{3}$, respectively.

Figure 16.3c and d show cases of the **polynomial distributed lag,** which is also called the **Almon lag** (after its originator, Shirley Almon). In the Almon lag scheme, the β_j are specified to lie along a polynomial function of the length of the lag, j. A particular Almon lag structure is parameterized by the maximum length of the lag (k) and the degree of the polynomial $(2 = \text{quadratic}, 3 = \text{cubic},$ etc.). The cases in Figure 16.3c and d look like cubic relations between β_j and j. (The linear case in Figure 16.3a is a first-degree polynomial relation between β_j and j.)

To demonstrate the method in a fairly simple case, we show how the appropriate restrictions are imposed when a second-degree polynomial (i.e., a quadratic relation) with $k = 4$ is assumed to be the correct form of the lag structure. The general form of the model is

$$Y_t = \alpha + \beta_0 X_t + \beta_1 X_{t-1} + \beta_2 X_{t-2} + \beta_3 X_{t-3} + \beta_4 X_{t-4} + u_t \quad (16.22)$$

The assumptions about the lag structure can be formulated as

$$\beta_j = \gamma_0 + \gamma_1 j + \gamma_2 j^2, \quad j = 0, \ldots, 4 \quad (16.23)$$

Although this looks odd, it simply states that β_j is a quadratic function of j. Substituting this into (16.22) in five places and evaluating the quadratic expression for each j, we arrive at

$$
\begin{aligned}
Y_t = \alpha &+ (\gamma_0) X_t \\
&+ (\gamma_0 + \gamma_1 + \gamma_2) X_{t-1} \\
&+ (\gamma_0 + 2\gamma_1 + 4\gamma_2) X_{t-2} \\
&+ (\gamma_0 + 3\gamma_1 + 9\gamma_2) X_{t-3} \\
&+ (\gamma_0 + 4\gamma_1 + 16\gamma_2) X_{t-4} + u_t \quad (16.24)
\end{aligned}
$$

Now all this can be rearranged to isolate the estimatable parameters and thereby identify the regressors that need to be constructed:

$$
\begin{aligned}
Y_t = \alpha &+ \gamma_0 [X_t + X_{t-1} + X_{t-2} + X_{t-3} + X_{t-4}] \\
&+ \gamma_1 [X_{t-1} + 2X_{t-2} + 3X_{t-3} + 4X_{t-4}] \\
&+ \gamma_2 [X_{t-1} + 4X_{t-2} + 9X_{t-3} + 16X_{t-4}] + u_t \quad (16.25)
\end{aligned}
$$

Letting the three newly created regressors be denoted by Z_0, Z_1, and Z_2, we arrive at

$$Y_t = \alpha + \gamma_0 Z_{0t} + \gamma_1 Z_{1t} + \gamma_2 Z_{2t} + u_t \quad (16.26)$$

which is a regular multiple regression. After $\hat{\gamma}_0$, $\hat{\gamma}_1$, and $\hat{\gamma}_2$ are calculated, the five $\hat{\beta}_j$ coefficients are calculated from them following the quadratic relation specified in (16.23).

For example, we use Almon's original data to estimate the relation between business expenditures for new manufacturing capital and the appropriations (for such expenditures) made in the same and previous periods. The idea is that the capital expenditures often occur long after the actual budget appropriations, and the difference in timing varies from industry to industry and among different types of equipment. The data are aggregated for manufacturing industries in the U.S., and they are available quarterly for 1953–1961.

We specify a regression model with current expenditures as the dependent variable. The right-hand side is a distributed lag structure in which the maximum number of lag periods is $k = 8$ and the current and lagged coefficients for appropriations (i.e., the β_j) are specified to lie along a second-degree polynomial.

In addition, as explained in the next section, dummy variables are used to estimate seasonal patterns. This particular specification is different from Almon's, and it may not be the best one possible. Many econometric computer programs handle the creation of the regressors, and they report the calculated $\hat{\gamma}$ coefficients and the $\hat{\beta}_j$.

Rather than present the complete numerical results, we simply show the estimated lag structure as Figure 16.4. We notice that the expenditure of appropriated funds gradually builds up as time passes (after the appropriation was made), reaching a peak in about one year. Expenditures decrease after that, and the model shows no more expenditures occurring beyond two years from the original appropriation. (Of course, this latter statement results from the assumptions we made about the lag structure.) The sum of the $\hat{\beta}_j^*$ is 0.86, which indicates that only 86 percent of appropriated funds actually get spent. The shortfall from 100 percent may be due to cancellations and other business phenomena. It also may be due to misspecification of the model. A complete econometric analysis would deal with an assessment of the whole relation and would carry out various hypothesis tests.

A difficulty of working with any lag structure is that the resulting model may be misspecified. With the Almon lag, we need to specify both the length of the lag and the degree of the polynomial. (And, endpoint restrictions may be specified in more advanced variations.) Inevitably, this leads to a certain amount of searching among possible specifications, in order to find one that seems to be the best.

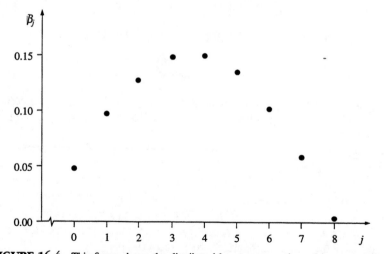

FIGURE 16.4 This figure shows the distributed lag structure estimated in a regression model that explains aggregate expenditures for new capital equipment on the basis of current and lagged values of the appropriations made for such expenditures. The lag structure is specified as a second-degree Almon lag in which the maximum length of the lag (k) is 8 quarters.

16.2   Trends and Seasonality _____

If we simply look at the plot of a time-series variable it is often possible to see a regularity that seems to permit forecasting into the near future. For example, Figure 16.5 plots the values of *GNP* from the time-series data set in Chapter 2 for the years 1956–1980. Intuition suggests that some method of extrapolation will be able to produce forecasts of *GNP* with relatively small error. If we are unable to specify and estimate a true structural model that determines *GNP* with predictive accuracy, then concentration on only the single time series may be the best thing to do. In this section we explore how regression techniques can be used for this purpose. This discussion scratches only the surface of a large and growing set of methods for time-series analysis.

Trends

For the example of *GNP* reported in annual data, the simplest procedure is to estimate the regression model

$$GNP_t = \beta_0 + \beta_1 T_t + u_t \tag{16.27}$$

where T is the time period number. The fitted regression line

$$\widehat{GNP_t} = \hat{\beta}_0 + \hat{\beta}_1 T_t \tag{16.28}$$

is interpreted as the **trend line** around which actual observations occur. Sometimes a nonlinear trend line is assumed, and a regression of *GNP* on T and T^2 is estimated. In either case, forecasts of *GNP* are made simply by determining

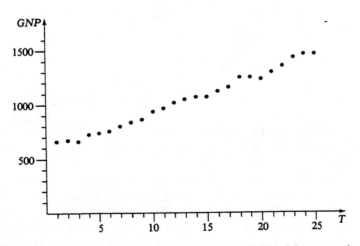

FIGURE 16.5   The time plot of *GNP*, based on the data of Table 2.3, suggests that extrapolation can be used to produce trend forecasts of *GNP*. A variety of regression specifications can be used to estimate this trend.

the value of predicted *GNP* that corresponds to the specified time period along the trend line. The choice of the proper functional form depends on theoretical considerations and on an analysis of the residuals that result from the regression.

Another type of trend model is based on the semilog specification. In Chapter 6 we estimated

$$\widehat{LNGNP}_t = 6.456 + 0.0354T_t$$
$$(0.012) \quad (0.00082) \tag{16.29}$$

$$R^2 = .988 \quad SER = 0.0297$$

which is based on the theoretical premise that *GNP* tends to grow at a constant proportional rate. This regression can be used to make predictions of *LNGNP* directly.

However, the best prediction of *GNP* is not simply the antilog of predicted *LNGNP*. Some adjustment is needed. To see why, we modify (6.47) to state the model underlying (16.29):

$$GNP_t = GNP_0(1 + r)^{T_t}e^{u_t} \tag{16.30}$$

where *e* is the base of natural logarithms. For a specific period *t*,

$$E[GNP_t] = GNP_0(1 + r)^{T_t}E[e^{u_t}] \tag{16.31}$$

Now, if u_t has a normal distribution with mean zero and variance σ_u^2, it turns out that e^{u_t} has a **lognormal distribution** with

$$E[e^{u_t}] = \exp(\sigma_u^2/2) \tag{16.32}$$

which is greater than 1. Thus

$$E[GNP_t] > GNP_0(1 + r)^{T_t} \tag{16.33}$$

In making predictions from (16.29), the antilog of predicted *LNGNP* corresponds to the right-hand side of (16.33). In order to make a better prediction of $E[GNP_t]$, we multiply this antilog by an estimate of $E[e^{u_t}]$, as suggested by (16.31). To obtain this estimate, we take $(SER)^2$ as an estimate of σ_u^2 in (16.32). In other words, our prediction of *GNP* is made by multiplying the antilog of predicted *LNGNP* from (16.29) by the antilog of $(SER)^2/2$.

For example, from (16.29) the prediction of *LNGNP* for 1981 ($T = 26$) is 7.376, yielding an antilog of 1597.2 billion dollars. This is then multiplied by the antilog of $(0.0297)^2/2$, which is about 1.0004, yielding a final *GNP* prediction of 1597.8 billion dollars. For cases in which *SER* is relatively large, the adjustment is more dramatic. (This adjustment procedure can be applied to making predictions from any regression model with a logarithmic dependent variable.)

Seasonality

All the time-series variables that we have dealt with before this chapter are measured on an annual basis. Shorter measurement periods are used for many actual time series. For example, the National Income Accounts data are available on a quarterly basis (January to March is the first quarter, April to June is the second, etc.), national unemployment rates are determined on a monthly basis, basic money supply data are determined on a weekly basis, and so on. Economists work with these data when short-period predictions are needed or when the dynamic behavior being studied displays itself naturally in these short periods.

Experience has shown that many variables are subject to regular patterns of variation during the course of a year, and this pattern is known as *seasonality*. For example, retail sales regularly go up in December because of holiday shopping, and the unemployment rate goes up in June because students leave school and enter the labor force searching for a job. Each time-series variable has its own seasonal pattern. Economic statisticians, who help prepare and analyze data, deal with seasonality in two ways. First, they may use a variety of seasonal adjustment procedures to adjust the data before any analysis: such data are said to be "seasonally adjusted." These procedures are complex and interesting, but we do not deal with them. Second, they may leave the data in their original form and take care of the seasonality as part of the analysis.

Table 16.2 displays quarterly data on expenditures for new plant and equipment, *NPE*, aggregated for all U.S. industries, 1966–1968. This short period exhibited relatively steady growth with a low rate of unemployment, and

TABLE 16.2   *NPE* and Seasonal Dummies

Obs.	T	NPE	Q1	Q2	Q3	Q4
1966-1	1	12.77	1	0	0	0
-2	2	15.29	0	1	0	0
-3	3	15.57	0	0	1	0
-4	4	17.00	0	0	0	1
1967-1	5	13.59	1	0	0	0
-2	6	15.61	0	1	0	0
-3	7	15.40	0	0	1	0
-4	8	17.05	0	0	0	1
1968-1	9	14.25	1	0	0	0
-2	10	15.86	0	1	0	0
-3	11	16.02	0	0	1	0
-4	12	17.95	0	0	0	1

Source: Business Statistics (a supplement to the *Survey of Current Business*), 17th edition (1969), p. 9.

therefore a simple trend model may be appropriate. However, as evident in the data and as shown in Figure 16.6, there is a strong seasonal pattern in addition to the simple trend. If we wish to construct a short-term quarterly forecasting model, we surely should take this pattern into account in addition to the steady trend of overall growth.

The most popular way to treat this kind of seasonality is to create a set of dummy variables that indicate in which quarter of the year each observation occurred. Following the treatment of regional location in Chapter 7, the dummy variables $Q1$, $Q2$, $Q3$, and $Q4$ are defined to be equal to 1 if the observation is in the corresponding quarter and 0 otherwise. These variables are displayed in Table 16.2.

In setting up a time-series regression model involving these seasonal dummies, it is essential that one of them be left out when the intercept β_0 is also present; it is not important which one of the dummy variables is excluded. Arbitrarily, we leave out the first quarter dummy and specify

$$NPE_t = \beta_0 + \beta_1 T_t + \beta_2 Q2_t + \beta_3 Q3_t + \beta_4 Q4_t + u_t \qquad (16.34)$$

All the observations, including those for first quarters, are used in the estimation. The results of the estimation are

$$\widehat{NPE}_t = 12.57 + 0.108T_t + 1.94Q2_t + 1.91Q3_t + 3.47Q4_t$$
$$\phantom{\widehat{NPE}_t = }(0.28)\ \ (0.025)\ \ \ \ (0.23)\ \ \ \ \ \ (0.23)\ \ \ \ \ \ \ (0.24) \qquad (16.35)$$
$$R^2 = .977 \quad SER = 0.281$$

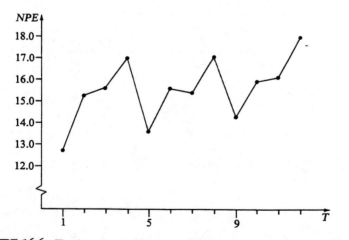

FIGURE 16.6 The time plot of *NPE*, which measures new plant and equipment expenditures on a quarterly basis, is based on the data in Table 16.2. The seasonal pattern around a positive trend stands out clearly. A regression model that includes a time trend and three seasonal dummy variables can be used to estimate the time pattern of *NPE*.

The coefficient on each dummy variable gives the difference in the predicted value of *NPE* that can be attributed to an observation's occurring in that quarter rather than in the first quarter. Each of the estimated coefficients is positive, indicating that the first quarter of each year tends to have the lowest *NPE*.

16.3   Random Walks and Spurious Regressions _____

As discussed in the previous section, a trend model of the form

$$Y_t = \gamma_0 + \gamma_1 T_t + u_t \tag{16.36}$$

can be used to describe a time series, and this description may be useful for forecasting values of Y in the near future. (Recall that $T_1 = 1, T_2 = 2, \ldots, T_t = t$, and so on.) Such a model can be applied, for example, with Y representing *GNP* or *LNGNP*. If the disturbance u_t arises from a first-order autoregressive process,

$$u_t = \rho u_{t-1} + \epsilon_t \tag{16.37}$$

better predictions might be obtained by taking this into account, as discussed in Section 15.2. Here and in what follows, ϵ_t is a white noise process. That is, the random variable ϵ_t has a zero mean and a constant variance (over time), and the ϵ_t are independent.

Now, if we restate (16.36) for period $t - 1$ and then subtract that from (16.36) itself, we get

$$\Delta Y_t = \gamma_1 + v_t, \quad \text{where} \quad v_t = u_t - u_{t-1} \tag{16.38}$$

(note that $\Delta T_t = 1$). That is, the change in Y_t from period to period is a constant amount (the trend) plus a random term. Further, if $\rho = 1$ (which is the extreme form of autocorrelation considered at the end of Section 15.2), this can be rewritten as

$$\Delta Y_t = \gamma_1 + \epsilon_t, \quad \text{when} \quad \rho = 1 \tag{16.39}$$

If ρ is close to 1, this holds as an approximation.

In the study of time series, a data-generating process of the form

$$\Delta Y_t = \delta + \epsilon_t \tag{16.40}$$

is called a ***random walk*** with drift (δ provides the drift). Comparing this with (16.38), we see that a random walk with drift specifies a process that is not too different from the trend model. (The processes are identical if $\rho = 1$.) It would not be too surprising, then, to find that both models provide fairly good descriptions of many economic time series. Indeed they do.

Now, suppose that Y and X are two time-series variables that are generated by independent random walk processes. In an economic sense, these variables are unrelated: there is no cause and effect relation between them. Suppose, however, that we estimate a regression of the form

$$Y_t = \beta_0 + \beta_1 X_t + u_t \tag{16.41}$$

in the belief that this model is the correct specification of the process determining Y. If ordinary least squares is applied in this situation, there is a tendency to find that (1) the R^2 is high, (2) the Durbin–Watson statistic is low (indicating ρ close to 1), and (3) standard t tests indicate a significant slope coefficient much of the time. Because we would often conclude that the model is appropriate when in fact it is not, this is called a *spurious regression.*

For example, consider the estimated regression of CON on PGNP,

$$\widehat{CON}_t = 167.02 + 4.914PGNP_t$$
$$(34.31)\quad(0.337) \tag{16.42}$$

$$R^2 = .902 \quad SER = 55.34 \quad d^* = 0.18$$

using data from the time-series data set of Chapter 2 (*PGNP* is the price deflator for GNP). On the basis of the large t statistic ($t^* = 14.59$) for the coefficient on *PGNP*, one would normally conclude that *PGNP* has a significant effect on *CON*. This might be explained by saying that consumers suffer from some form of "price illusion." However, the presence of the high R^2 coupled with the low Durbin–Watson statistic suggests that this might be a spurious regression.

Why does spuriousness occur in this situation? The random walk specified as (16.40) implies that

$$Y_t = Y_0 + \delta T_t + \sum_{j=1}^{t} \epsilon_j \tag{16.43}$$

The "disturbance" in this model is the sum of independent random terms. Although the mean of the disturbance is always zero, the variance of the disturbance increases over time. Thus the variance of Y increases over time also, and the mean of Y will increase if there is drift. Because of this, Y is said to be *nonstationary.* Since X is a random walk also, it too is nonstationary. In this situation the assumptions underlying the properties of least squares do not hold. Thus it is not surprising that the standard procedures for determining significance may be misleading.

Some progress can be made in the analysis of the relation (16.41) by recasting it in terms of first differences:

$$\Delta Y_t = \alpha + \beta_1 \Delta X_t + v_t \tag{16.44}$$

If Y and X are random walks, ΔY and ΔX both will be stationary series. A time series Z is *stationary* if the mean and variance are constant over time, and if the structure of covariances between Z_t and Z_{t-s} is fixed for all s. (When the series Z is the first difference of a random walk, such as $Z = \Delta Y$, the structure of covariances is simple: all the covariances are equal to zero for $s \neq 0$.) The least squares estimate of β_1 in this situation is a consistent estimate of β_1 in (16.41), and there is no special tendency to accept the coefficient as significant when in fact it is not.

This procedure can be applied to help assess the possible relation between CON and PGNP, which was considered above. A regression between the first differences yields

$$\widehat{\Delta CON_t} = 21.52 + 0.115\Delta PGNP_t$$
$$(4.16) \quad (0.669) \qquad\qquad\qquad (16.45)$$

$$R^2 = .001 \quad SER = 13.06 \quad d* = 1.30$$

The low t statistic ($t* = 0.17$) for the coefficient on $\Delta PGNP$ indicates that $\Delta PGNP$ does not have a significant effect on ΔCON, reinforcing the assessment that (16.42) shows a spurious relation.

The general advice is that one must be cautious in specifying regressions involving nonstationary time-series variables. There are a variety of tests for stationarity, but these are not covered here. Since taking first differences of a nonstationary series can produce one that is stationary, it may be prudent to carry out the analysis in first differences rather than levels. This would be especially true if a regression between levels, like (16.42), yields a high R^2 and a low Durbin–Watson statistic.

Problems

Section 16.1

16.1 Consider the distributed lag consumption function reported as Equation (16.4). Rewrite this model in difference form, as in Equation (16.12). Suppose that in period t, DPI is raised by 10 billion dollars above its actual historical value, but in succeeding years it remains at its actual historical values. What is the impact of this on CON in period t and in the four succeeding periods? Graph the results.

★ **16.2** Repeat Problem 16.1, except suppose that beginning in period t each value of DPI is raised by 10 billion dollars above its actual historical value.

★ **16.3** Suppose that Equation (16.3) correctly represents a certain economic process, but a simple regression of Y on current X is estimated. How will the estimate of the slope in the simple regression be related to β_0 in the correct model?

16.4 On one set of axes, display the structure of the distributed lag coefficients for a geometric lag model in which $\lambda = .9$, and for one in which $\lambda = .5$; for simplicity, let $k = 4$.

16.5 Suppose that beginning in year t, *DPI* in each year is raised one billion dollars above its actual historical values. Based on the estimated regression (16.11), compute and graph the impact of this on *CON* for the first five years of the change.

★ **16.6** Suppose that in period t, Y_t is less than Y_t^* in the partial adjustment model. If Y_t^* remains at a constant, flat amount for the next five years, what happens to Y_t during those years?

★ **16.7** Suppose that in period t, Y_t is less than Y_t^* in the partial adjustment model. If X grows at a constant absolute amount for the next five years, what happens to Y_t during those years?

16.8 Suppose that in period t, X_t is greater than X_t^* in the adaptive expectations model. If X_t remains fixed at a constant, flat amount for the next five years, what happens to Y_t during those years?

★ **16.9** Suppose that the Durbin–Watson statistic in Equation (16.11) is $d^* = 1.25$. Taking into account the presence of the lagged dependent variable, would you judge that positive autocorrelation is present?

16.10 Consider an Almon lag specification involving a third-degree polynomial with $k = 5$. Show how to construct the appropriate regressors for the estimating equation.

Section 16.2

16.11 Based on regression (16.29), make a simple (unadjusted) prediction of *GNP* for 1985.

16.12 If the standard error of the regression (*SER*) were 0.10, what would be the multiplicative adjustment factor for predicting *GNP* from Equation (16.29)?

★ **16.13** Based on Equation (16.35), determine the estimated coefficients in a seasonally adjusted trend model for *NPE* in which *Q4* is the excluded dummy variable.

16.14 How could we test whether seasonality plays a role in the determination of a time-series variable?

★ **16.15** Based on Equation (16.35), how much higher is predicted *NPE* in the third quarter as compared with the first quarter of the same year?

16.16 Suppose that $\rho^* = .7$ in regression (16.29). Make a simple prediction of *GNP* for 1981, taking autocorrelation into account. (*Hint:* You need Table 2.3.)

17

Simultaneous-Equation Models

Up to this point, we have viewed each regression equation as a complete model of an economic process. Such a model shows how a dependent variable is determined by a set of explanatory variables, which are taken as fixed by forces outside the process under study, and by a disturbance term. We now turn our attention to models in which more than one equation is necessary to adequately characterize the economic process. In these *simultaneous-equation models,* several "dependent" variables are jointly and simultaneously determined by a set of "explanatory" variables and disturbance terms. These models present us with new problems of specification and interpretation as well as new problems of estimation.

17.1 The Nature of the Models

We examine the nature of simultaneous-equation models by considering two examples. The first involves a cross-sectional analysis, and the second is based on time series.

The first model seeks to explain the hours worked and wages received by a relatively homogeneous group of workers. To simplify the economics, we assume that employers do not try to determine a worker's actual skill level or productivity. For concreteness, let us say that we are concerned with married women aged 25–34 who have college degrees with a major in economics. For a variety of reasons there is considerable variation in the wages received and (weekly) hours worked by these women, and our interest is in explaining how wages and hours are determined. From an employer's point of view, a worker who works more hours may be more valuable per hour because she provides continuity and can accept more responsibility. Hence, there is a demand-type relation between the hours an employer demands from a potential worker and the wage to be paid. From the individual woman's point of view, the hours she is willing to work depends on the wage, the other income her family receives, and the number of children in the family. In this context there are two economic behaviors exhibited: demand and supply.

These two patterns of behavior are combined to yield a ***structural model***, in which each equation describes a single type of economic behavior:

$$\text{(Demand)} \quad HOURS_i = \beta_0 + \beta_1 WAGE_i + u_i \tag{17.1}$$

$$\text{(Supply)} \quad HOURS_i = \gamma_0 + \gamma_1 WAGE_i + \gamma_2 OTHINC_i$$
$$+ \gamma_3 NKIDS_i + v_i \tag{17.2}$$

In this model, *HOURS* is the quantity demanded or supplied. These are observationally equivalent when our data are for women actually in jobs, but sometimes the conceptual distinction is made explicit by using $HOURS^d$ in (17.1) and $HOURS^s$ in (17.2) and then adding a third equation explicitly stating that $HOURS^d = HOURS^s$. For simplicity we have skipped this step. The disturbances *u* and *v* are regarded in the usual way. It should be noted that this model is different from standard market models, which deal with aggregate demand and supply: here we examine the behavior of individual employers and employees, and the observations are cross-section data on the characteristics of workers and their jobs.

To analyze this simultaneous-equation model, a new taxonomy of variables is necessary. The variables *HOURS* and *WAGE* are called ***endogenous*** because they are jointly determined inside the system (model). The variables *OTHINC* and *NKIDS* are called ***exogenous*** because they are determined outside the model. The variable *HOURS* appears on the left-hand side of both (17.1) and (17.2), while *WAGE* appears on the right-hand side along with the exogenous variables. This results from a fairly natural specification of the two patterns of behavior. Nonetheless, *HOURS* and *WAGE* have equal stature as endogenous variables. Despite appearances, *HOURS* is no more endogenous than is *WAGE*; both are jointly and simultaneously determined.

To illustrate how the endogenous variables *HOURS* and *WAGE* are determined, we first consider a set of observations that have the same values for *OTHINC* and *NKIDS*. This makes the terms $\gamma_2 OTHINC_i$ and $\gamma_3 NKIDS_i$ in (17.2) effectively constants. In Figure 17.1, the lines labeled "Demand" and "Supply" graph the systematic parts of (17.1) and (17.2), with the disturbances set to zero.

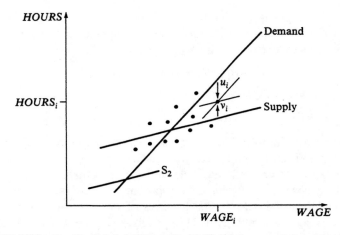

FIGURE 17.1 The lines labeled "Demand" and "Supply" represent the systematic components of Equations (17.1)–(17.2) for a set of observations having the same values for *OTHINC* and *NKIDS*. Suppose that for the *i*th observation, u_i is negative and v_i is positive. The effective demand and supply relations are represented by the light lines, and their intersection is the *WAGE–HOURS* combination that satisfies both equations. This point is the *i*th observation. The other observations are generated similarly. The line labeled "S_2" is the systematic part of the supply relation for a set of observations having in common a different pair of values for *OTHINC* and *NKIDS*.

Casual economic theory suggests that both slopes are positive, but we have no particular hypothesis with regard to their relative magnitudes.

Observations get produced from this process, and they differ from each other because of the randomness of the disturbances. Suppose that for the *i*th observation u_i is negative and v_i is positive. For this observation, the demand version of the *HOURS–WAGE* relation has a vertical intercept of $\beta_0 + u_i$ and a slope of β_1: it lies below the systematic demand relation by the negative amount u_i. Similarly, for this observation the supply version of the relation lies above its systematic form. Where the two lines intersect, both equations are satisfied; this is the *i*th observation illustrated in Figure 17.1. Similarly, other observations are produced in a scatter around the intersection of the systematic portions of the demand and supply relations. Given the values for its disturbances u_i and v_i, each observation then satisfies both equations of the model.

To illustrate the full workings of the model (17.1)–(17.2) requires a four-dimensional graph, which is beyond our capacity. However, we can see in Figure 17.1 that for another set of observations having common values of *OTHINC* and *NKIDS*, the supply curve could be graphed as another line (S_2) with the same slope but a different intercept. For example, women with more *OTHINC* and a greater number of *NKIDS* may be willing to work fewer hours at any available wage.

A second example is provided by a small macroeconomic model that is consistent with the simple *IS–LM* formulation of aggregate economic activity. The specification of its structure is

$$CON_i = \beta_0 + \beta_1 GNP_i + \beta_2 RTB_i + \beta_3 CON_{i-1} + u_i \tag{17.3}$$

$$GNP_i = CON_i + A_i \tag{17.4}$$

$$RTB_i = \gamma_0 + \gamma_1 GNP_i + \gamma_2 M_i + v_i \tag{17.5}$$

All but one of the variables have been used earlier in this book. *CON* is real consumption, *GNP* is real gross national product, *M* is the real money supply, and *RTB* is the treasury bill rate. The variable *A* denotes real autonomous expenditures, whose major conceptual components here are investment, government expenditures, and net exports. In terms of our data, *A* is a constructed variable that is defined implicitly by (17.4) as $A_i = GNP_i - CON_i$. We note that (17.3) and (17.5) appear to be single-equation models of specific economic behaviors. By contrast, (17.4) can be viewed as either an accounting identity or an equilibrium condition; in either case, it presents us with no task of econometric estimation. Nonetheless, it is a bona fide element of this simultaneous-equation model.

In economic terms, (17.3) and (17.4) make up the *IS* side of the model. They express a model of equilibrium in the real product market, albeit an unusual one in which investment is autonomous and consumption is interest sensitive. Equation (17.5) is the *LM* side of the economy, combining demand and supply elements in a single-equation model of equilibrium in financial markets.

The lagged value of consumption, CON_{i-1} gives the consumption function a dynamic character, as discussed in Chapter 16. We use *CONLAG* as the name of the regressor that is the one-period lag of *CON*. Whereas *CON* is an endogenous variable, *CONLAG* is not because its value is determined temporally prior to *CON*. In this way, *CONLAG* is similar to the exogenous variables, which are determined logically prior to *CON*. In the taxonomy of simultaneous-equation models, exogenous and lagged endogenous variables together make up a super-classification known as *predetermined variables.*

There are three endogenous variables in the system (*CON, GNP,* and *RTB*), which happen to be the left-hand side variables in the three equations. As we saw in the job market example, however, this is not an essential element in the specification of a simultaneous-equation model. The predetermined variables are *CONLAG, A,* and *M*. Taken as a whole, the model is a description of the process by which the economy simultaneously determines *CON, GNP,* and *RTB*.

The Reduced Form

A structural model is a set of equations, each of which describes a single type of economic behavior or is like an identity. Equation sets (17.1)–(17.2) and (17.3)–(17.5) are both structural models. We now consider certain algebraic properties and manipulations of these sets of equations in order to gain more insight into their nature.

We look first at the equations of the demand and supply model, (17.1)–(17.2). The spirit of the model is that the values of the exogenous variables are fixed outside the system, the coefficients are parameters (constants), and the values of the disturbances are established by a purely random process. The values of the endogenous variables are determined by all of these. In formal algebraic terms, the model consists of two linear simultaneous equations in two unknowns—the endogenous variables. Once the values of the disturbances are established for a particular observation, the economic process determines the values of the endogenous variables so as to satisfy both equations of the model simultaneously.

By standard algebraic methods, the original set of simultaneous equations can be solved for the unknowns, resulting in

$$WAGE_i = \left(\frac{\gamma_0 - \beta_0}{\beta_1 - \gamma_1}\right) + \left(\frac{\gamma_2}{\beta_1 - \gamma_1}\right) OTHINC_i$$
$$+ \left(\frac{\gamma_3}{\beta_1 - \gamma_1}\right) NKIDS_i + \left(\frac{v_i - u_i}{\beta_1 - \gamma_1}\right) \tag{17.6}$$

and

$$HOURS_i = \left(\frac{\beta_1\gamma_0 - \beta_0\gamma_1}{\beta_1 - \gamma_1}\right) + \left(\frac{\beta_1\gamma_2}{\beta_1 - \gamma_1}\right) OTHINC_i$$
$$+ \left(\frac{\beta_1\gamma_3}{\beta_1 - \gamma_1}\right) NKIDS_i + \left(\frac{\beta_1 v_i - \gamma_1 u_i}{\beta_1 - \gamma_1}\right) \tag{17.7}$$

[A simple solution method here is to solve (17.1) for *WAGE* in terms of *HOURS*, and then substitute (17.2) into that equation and rearrange terms, yielding (17.6). Next, the right side of (17.6) is substituted for *WAGE* in (17.1), which yields (17.7) after rearrangement.] For simplicity, (17.6) and (17.7) are conventionally rewritten as

$$WAGE_i = \pi_{10} + \pi_{11}OTHINC_i + \pi_{12}NKIDS_i + \epsilon_{1i} \tag{17.8}$$

$$HOURS_i = \pi_{20} + \pi_{21}OTHINC_i + \pi_{22}NKIDS_i + \epsilon_{2i} \tag{17.9}$$

where the π and ϵ terms are simply shorthand symbols for the corresponding terms in parentheses in the previous pair of equations. The π coefficients are complex combinations only of β's and γ's, and the ϵ's are combinations of u's, v's, β's, and γ's. Notationally, the first subscript on a π indicates whether it is in the first or second equation, and the second subscript indicates its left–right order in the equation.

In the analytics of simultaneous-equation econometric models, the solutions (17.6)–(17.7) or their simplified reexpressions (17.8)–(17.9) are called the **reduced form** of the original structural model (17.1)–(17.2). Each equation of the reduced form specifies how the value of a single endogenous variable is related to the values of the exogenous variables, the disturbances, and the structural coefficients. Loosely speaking, the interdependences among the endogenous variables are solved out. In (17.6)–(17.7), notice that each of the endogenous variables depends on both of the disturbances.

The reduced form of the small macroeconomic model (17.3)–(17.5) is obtained by solving those three linear simultaneous equations for the unknowns *CON, GNP,* and *RTB.* The simplified reexpression is

$$CON_i = \pi_{10} + \pi_{11}CONLAG_i + \pi_{12}A_i + \pi_{13}M_i + \epsilon_{1i} \qquad (17.10)$$

$$GNP_i = \pi_{20} + \pi_{21}CONLAG_i + \pi_{22}A_i + \pi_{23}M_i + \epsilon_{2i} \qquad (17.11)$$

$$RTB_i = \pi_{30} + \pi_{31}CONLAG_i + \pi_{32}A_i + \pi_{33}M_i + \epsilon_{3i} \qquad (17.12)$$

To generalize previous statements, each reduced-form equation has a single endogenous variable on the left-hand side and all the predetermined variables on the right-hand side. The laws of algebra lead the right-hand side of each reduced-form equation to be a linear expression involving the whole list of predetermined variables and disturbances. The π coefficients are complex combinations of β's and γ's, and the ϵ's are combinations of β's, γ's, u's, and v's.

If the equations in a structural model are all linear, then for the simultaneous system to be properly specified in an algebraic sense there must be exactly as many equations as there are endogenous variables. This ensures a unique solution for each endogenous variable. If the equations are not all linear, the nature of possible solutions is not so clear. Normally, however, econometric models are specified with the same number of equations and endogenous variables.

The structural and reduced-form versions of a simultaneous-equation model are equally valid formulations of the same economic process. However, the two versions present different problems of estimation and are suited for different applications. For example, if our only purpose is to make predictions of *WAGES* and *HOURS* conditional on specified values of *OTHINC* and *NKIDS,* then, after accepting the unestimated structural model (17.1)–(17.2) as theoretically valid, we can do all our practical work in terms of the reduced-form version of the model (17.8)–(17.9). Indeed, if we are interested only in making predictions of the *WAGE,* we can ignore (17.9) and just focus on (17.8). On the other hand, if we want to know how sensitive women's supply of *HOURS* is to changes in *WAGE* or if we want to calculate the impacts on *HOURS* and *WAGE* of the imposition of a payroll tax, we need to know the structural coefficients. The structural model also can be used to make the same kind of predictions that the reduced form produces. In general, it is more useful to estimate the structural model than the reduced form.

Estimation and Simulation

The econometric estimation of the parameters (π's) of the reduced form is relatively straightforward. Each equation stands as a single-equation model and can be estimated by the usual methods. As we have seen, if the disturbances do not meet the assumptions of the normal regression model, ordinary least squares may not be the chosen method.

The estimation of the equations in the structural model is more complicated. In some cases, discussed later, it is possible to estimate the coefficients of each equation by first estimating the reduced form and then solving algebraically to get estimates of the structural coefficients. This is not always fruitful, however, and we are interested in general methods for directly estimating them. Under appropriate circumstances, it is possible simply to use OLS on each of the equations. However, in Section 17.2, we see that even in these circumstances OLS turns out to be biased and inconsistent, and an estimation method having the property of consistency is presented.

An additional problem associated with the specification and estimation of a structural model is that for some reasonable-looking equations, it may be impossible for the coefficients to be estimated meaningfully. These are inappropriate circumstances for applying any estimation method, even OLS. One technical aspect of this, which is known as the problem of "identification," is that it is impossible to obtain consistent estimates of the coefficients. In source and solution this is a problem of specification, not estimation, and we put off its consideration until Section 17.3.

Reserving all these problems for later discussion, we consider here as an example the results of using OLS to estimate the econometric equations of the macroeconomic model (17.3)–(17.5) for the period 1957–1980 ($n = 24$):

$$\widehat{CON_i} = -29.36 + 0.335GNP_i - 4.23RTB_i$$
$$\quad\quad (6.62) \quad (0.050) \quad\quad\quad (1.08)$$

$$\quad\quad + 0.553CONLAG_i \quad\quad\quad\quad\quad (17.13)$$
$$\quad\quad\quad (0.083)$$

$$GNP_i = CON_i + A_i \quad\quad\quad\quad\quad\quad (17.14)$$

$$\widehat{RTB_i} = 5.10 + 0.0099GNP_i - 0.0455M_i \quad\quad (17.15)$$
$$\quad\quad (6.18) \quad (0.0019) \quad\quad\quad (0.0334)$$

This constitutes an estimated simultaneous-equation model.

One of the reasons for estimating the structural model rather than the reduced form is that it is now possible to look at each of the estimated equations and assess it as a single-equation model of economic behavior. The assessment would depend in part on an examination of the meaning and statistical significance of the coefficients and on a comparison of the results with other empirical work and with theoretical considerations. We do not do this for the example here, but for serious uses of models this kind of assessment is extremely important.

We proceed to consider the task of making predictions. Once a structural simultaneous-equation model has been estimated, the set of numerically specified equations is sometimes called a *simulation model* and the predictions it makes are called *simulations.* Algebraically, a prediction or simulation using the model involves solving (17.13)–(17.15) to obtain the values of the endogenous variables that result from a given set of values for the predetermined variables, with disturbances set to zero. When the equations are linear, as they are in this case, the algebraic solution can be based on the same methods that are used for determining the reduced form. In practice, however, most computer programs for simulation use an iterative solution algorithm that leads to the same results.

We also can use our estimated model to describe some rudimentary *policy analysis,* which usually involves two simulations over a period for which we have data on all the exogenous variables. For example, suppose that we wish to determine the effects of a 10 billion dollar increase in government expenditures beginning in period T. One simulation is made from period T forward, using the historical values of the exogenous variables. A second simulation is the same except that the value of A is set at 10 billion dollars above what it actually was in each period. The effects of the policy are studied by comparing the two simulated time paths for each of the endogenous variables.   -

A second type of policy analysis involves changes in the parameters. For example, suppose that economic theory and some extra calculations lead us to believe that a proposed decrease in federal tax rates is equivalent to raising the marginal propensity to consume out of GNP by 0.020 from whatever amount it now is. We can analyze the impact of this policy change on CON, GNP, and RTB by simulating the model twice, both times using the same historical data on the exogenous variables. First we carry out a simulation using the estimated model. In the second simulation we change the coefficient on GNP in (17.13) from 0.335 to 0.355 and carry out the simulation again. The differences in simulated values for the time paths of each of the endogenous variables is the basis for an analysis of the impact of the tax-rate change.

The first policy analysis described could be done using an estimated reduced-form model, because all that is involved is making predictions for alternative values of the exogenous variable A. By contrast, the second policy analysis requires an estimated structural model, because it involves a change in one of the structural coefficients—which cannot be isolated in the reduced form.

17.2 Estimation _____

In this section we focus on the task of estimating a single structural equation in a simultaneous-equation model. By doing this separately for each equation, the whole model can be estimated. We do not discuss some advanced procedures that involve estimating all the equations together. Also, in this section we presume that the equation of interest is appropriately "identified," so that meaningful estimation can be attempted.

Recall that in Chapter 11 it was shown that for the normal regression model, the technique of ordinary least squares yields unbiased estimates of the regression coefficients. In general, unbiasedness is a desirable property for an estimating technique to have. In the normal regression model we are willing to make the assumption that all the explanatory variables are fixed outside of the process under study, and hence that they are independent of the disturbance. Unfortunately, in simultaneous-equation models this assumption is no longer tenable, because the system implies that a right-hand endogenous variable is correlated with the disturbance in the equation. Hence, the unbiasedness of OLS no longer holds. Further, even as the sample size increases the biasedness remains, and consequently OLS is inconsistent. This situation is often referred to as *simultaneous-equation bias.*

To see the source of this bias, consider the task of estimating the demand relation (17.1). If this were an isolated single-equation model, we might accept the assumption that $WAGE_i$ is fixed (nonprobabilistic) and therefore uncorrelated with u_i. However, in (17.6), which is one of the reduced-form equations that is fully consistent with the structural model (17.1)–(17.2), we see that $WAGE_i$ depends in part on u_i. Therefore, $WAGE_i$ is correlated with u_i, except under extraordinary circumstances. This correlation of $WAGE_i$ and u_i cannot be assumed away if the structural model is accepted, and therefore the conditions for OLS to be unbiased are not present.

It may still be reasonable to use OLS despite the bias, and in large models this is often done. However, other techniques have been developed that yield consistent (but still biased) estimates of the parameters of each equation, although the appropriateness of some of these techniques is critically dependent on the correctness of the complete model's specification.

Two-Stage Least Squares

The most popular technique for obtaining consistent estimates for the parameters in equations of a simultaneous-equation model is known as *two-stage least squares* (TSLS). The essence of the technique is to replace each of the endogenous variables on the right-hand side of an equation with a constructed regressor that serves as a proxy for the original variable and that is essentially uncorrelated with the disturbance. Then OLS is applied to the equation. The resulting estimates of the (original) parameters of the equation may be biased, but this bias vanishes as the sample size increases.

The first stage of the technique is the construction of the proxy regressors. Let Y_j be one of the endogenous variables on the right-hand side of the equation, and let the list of predetermined variables in the entire system of equations be Z_1, $Z_2, \ldots, Z_m$ (there are m predetermined variables in the model). Using OLS, we regress Y_j on all of the Z's. Then, for each observation we calculate the fitted value $\hat{Y}_{ji}$ in the usual way, and this set of fitted values makes up our proxy $\hat{Y}_j$. It should be noticed that this procedure amounts to using OLS to estimate the jth reduced-form equation of the model, and calculating its fitted values. Formally, the proxy values are determined as

$$\hat{Y}_{ji} = \hat{\pi}_{j0} + \hat{\pi}_{j1}Z_{1i} + \hat{\pi}_{j2}Z_{2i} + \cdots + \hat{\pi}_{jm}Z_{mi} \tag{17.16}$$

In this notation i is the index for the observation number, with $i = 1, \ldots, n$ as usual. The index j identifies the endogenous variables: if there are three endogenous variables, then $j = 1$, 2, or 3, and there are three equations in the reduced form (as well as in the structural model). Equation (17.16) represents the estimated version of the jth reduced-form equation, and it is the fitted values of this equation that constitute the proxy for Y_j. This procedure is repeated separately for each of the endogenous variables on the right-hand side of the structural equation that we are seeking to estimate.

Regarding (17.16), we see that $\hat{Y}_j$, the proxy for Y_j, is a linear combination of all the predetermined variables in the system, Z_1 through Z_m. By definition, the predetermined variables are not related to any of the disturbances in the system of structural equations. However, the $\hat{\pi}$'s *are* related to the disturbances of the system, and therefore $\hat{Y}_j$ is correlated with the disturbances. In large samples, however, this correlation vanishes. Hence when $\hat{Y}_j$ is used as a proxy for Y_j in estimating a structural equation, the regressor $\hat{Y}_j$ is asymptotically uncorrelated with the disturbance of that equation.

The second stage of the TSLS technique is simply the OLS estimation of the modified structural equation, in which any endogenous variables that appear on the right-hand side are replaced by their proxy regressors. Whatever predetermined variables originally appeared in the regression remain there. The OLS estimates of the coefficients in this modified equation are consistent estimates of the parameters in the original equation. In finite-sized samples, which of course are the realm of practical applications, these estimates generally are still biased. The standard errors calculated in the regular way by OLS for this second stage are not correct, since they do not take into account all the information about the estimating procedure.

In practice, many econometric computer programs exist for making TSLS estimates in one fell swoop. From the researcher's point of view it is no more difficult to use TSLS than OLS. It should be noted that with TSLS, as well as with OLS in this context, hypothesis tests involving the estimated coefficients and their standard errors can be used only in an indicative way.

For example, the two-stage least squares estimates (1957–1980) of the small macro model (17.3)–(17.5) are

$$\widehat{CON}_i = -18.24 + 0.248GNP_i - 2.57RTB_i$$
$$\phantom{\widehat{CON}_i =} (11.74) \quad (0.064) \qquad (3.05)$$

$$\phantom{\widehat{CON}_i =} + 0.668CONLAG_i \qquad\qquad\qquad (17.17)$$
$$\phantom{\widehat{CON}_i =} (0.100)$$

$$GNP_i = CON_i + A_i \qquad\qquad\qquad\qquad (17.18)$$

$$\widehat{RTB}_i = 6.20 + 0.0104GNP_i - 0.0525M_i \qquad (17.19)$$
$$\phantom{\widehat{RTB}_i =} (6.14) \quad (0.0019) \qquad (0.0335)$$

The OLS and TSLS estimates of the interest-rate equation are quite similar, but the estimates of the consumption equation are more noticeably different.

There is no hard and fast rule for determining whether the OLS or TSLS estimates are better. When multicollinearity is strongly present, as in the consumption equation, the bias of both methods tends to be accentuated. It has been shown that under some conditions OLS can be superior to TSLS, especially if sampling variability as well as bias is taken into account. However, the weight of the evidence is that two-stage least squares is the preferable method, and it should be used when possible. Sometimes researchers report both OLS and TSLS estimates of the same simultaneous-equation model so that the reader can assess the differences.

17.3   Identification

As noted earlier, the task of **identification** is to determine whether the coefficients of a particular equation can be estimated meaningfully. This is a subtle and difficult problem, and we treat only the easy-to-handle aspects of it.

To begin with an example, we revise the simple job market model by excluding OTHINC and NKIDS from having an effect on HOURS supplied. Thus the structural model is

$$\text{(Demand)} \quad HOURS_i = \beta_0 + \beta_1 WAGE_i + u_i \qquad (17.20)$$

$$\text{(Supply)} \quad HOURS_i = \gamma_0 + \gamma_1 WAGE_i + v_i \qquad (17.21)$$

We note that there are two endogenous variables and no exogenous variables. The systematic part of each of these is graphed in Figure 17.2a, which is similar to Figure 17.1.

Figure 17.2b shows only the set of observations produced by this economic process. Our experience suggests that we can estimate a regression of HOURS on WAGE, but we have no basis for saying whether it is an estimate of the

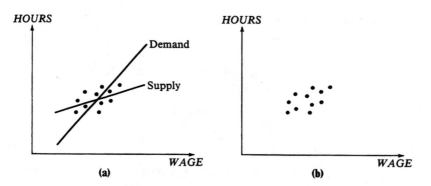

FIGURE 17.2 The model given by Equations (17.20)–(17.21) contains no exogenous variables. In (a), the lines represent the systematic components of the Demand and Supply equations. All the observations on WAGE and HOURS are produced by the process described for Figure 17.1. The lines are absent in (b), and there is no basis in the data for distinguishing separate demand and supply curves. This reflects the fact that both equations of the model are unidentified.

demand curve, the supply curve, or something else. In this sense, we have no way of *meaningfully* estimating the demand coefficients or the supply coefficients: they are **unidentified.**

Suppose instead that the correct model of supply includes the other income received by the family, but not the number of children. The full model is

$$\text{(Demand)} \quad HOURS_i = \beta_0 + \beta_1 WAGE_i + u_i \qquad (17.22)$$

$$\text{(Supply)} \quad HOURS_i = \gamma_0 + \gamma_1 WAGE_i$$
$$+ \gamma_2 OTHINC_i + v_i \qquad (17.23)$$

Figure 17.3 illustrates the systematic part of the demand and supply relations. As before, the systematic demand relation is the same for all observations. Now, however, the *HOURS–WAGE* supply relation differs among the observations because they have different values of *OTHINC*. The effective shifting of the supply curve serves to trace out the demand curve, although the disturbances make this imperfect. A set of data produced by this process provides the basis for estimating the demand version of the *HOURS–WAGE* relation, subject to the usual difficulties of estimation. The demand curve is now *identified,* although the supply curve remains unidentified.

What is special about the demand equation (17.22) that makes it identified, whereas the supply equation (17.23) is unidentified? Comparing the two, we see that the exogenous variable *OTHINC* is specifically excluded from the demand relation. The exclusion of exogenous variables is a key to identification.

The Order Condition

The conditions under which an equation within a simultaneous-equation model is identified or not are derived from a matrix algebra approach to

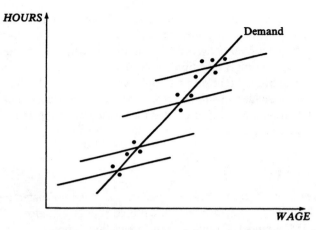

FIGURE 17.3 The model given by Equations (17.22)–(17.23) includes one exogenous variable for supply but none for demand. Observations are generated around various parts of the demand curve as the supply curve effectively shifts. The demand equation is now identified, and its coefficients can be meaningfully estimated.

simultaneous equations. We consider only one condition, which serves as a useful rule although it does not strictly guarantee the result.

As a preliminary, we recognize that in a complete structural model there are a certain number of endogenous variables and a certain number of predetermined (exogenous and lagged endogenous) ones. In a particular equation there must be present at least one endogenous variable—the one on the left-hand side of the equation. Usually, some endogenous variables are also present on the right-hand side, but not all the endogenous variables in the system need be in the equation; some may be excluded. Similarly, some of the predetermined variables in the system may be included in the equation, on the right-hand side, whereas some may be excluded.

The **order condition** for identification states simply that *if an equation is identified, then the number of predetermined variables excluded from the equation must be greater than or equal to the number of endogenous variables included on the right-hand side.*

If the order condition is satisfied with a "greater than" comparison, the equation is **overidentified,** whereas if "equal to" holds, the equation is *just identified.* Both cases satisfactorily meet the condition for identification of the equation. Technically, the order condition is necessary but not sufficient for identification. Although its satisfaction does not guarantee identification, it is widely used in practice.

We can apply this rule to the job market models. In all of these, there is one endogenous variable (*WAGE*) included on the right-hand side of each equation. In the simplest model (17.20)–(17.21), illustrated in Figure 17.2a, there are no exogenous variables in the system, so there are zero exogenous variables excluded from each equation. Since zero is not greater than or equal to 1, neither equation is identified. In the second model (17.22)–(17.23), illustrated in Figure

17.3, there is one exogenous variable ($OTHINC$) in the entire system. In the demand equation this one exogenous variable excluded; since this just equals the number of endogenous variables included on the right-hand side, the equation is just identified. In the supply equation zero exogenous variables are excluded; the equation is unidentified. In the original job market model (17.1)–(17.2), there are two exogenous variables in the system. Both of these are excluded from the demand equation, and since 2 is greater than 1, the equation is overidentified. The supply equation is unidentified.

Interpretation

What does it mean to say that an equation cannot be estimated meaningfully if it is not identified? Consider the unidentified supply equation (17.23) in the second job market model. Certainly, some estimation *is* possible; given the data, we can use OLS to run a multiple regression of $HOURS$ on $WAGE$ and $OTHINC$. The computer will accept the job and produce results. The crux of the identification analysis is that these estimated coefficients do not bear a determinate relation to γ_0, γ_1, and γ_2. Consistent estimation is impossible, with OLS or any other method. If we try to use TSLS on this unidentified equation, the technique breaks down. The reduced form proxy regressor for $WAGE$ is simply a linear combination of $OTHINC$, which is already in the equation. This situation of perfect multicollinearity violates a basic assumption of the technique and might cause the computer to stop or produce unpredictable results. Similarly, in any unidentified equation, OLS will "work" but produce meaningless results. The TSLS technique will break down because there will be too much overlap between the proxy regressors and the exogenous (predetermined) variables that are included in the equation.

Some additional insight into identification comes from looking at an estimating technique known as *indirect least squares*, ILS. Consider (17.8)–(17.9), which represent the simplified reexpression of the reduced form (17.6)–(17.7) of the job market model. The ratio π_{21}/π_{11} equals β_1, as may be seen by carefully inspecting the full form of the coefficients. Similarly, the ratio π_{22}/π_{12} exactly equals β_1 also. Thus, it seems that estimates of the β's can be obtained from estimates of the π's.

The π's of the reduced-form equations can be estimated by ordinary least squares, and the ratios $\hat{\pi}_{21}/\hat{\pi}_{11}$ and $\hat{\pi}_{22}/\hat{\pi}_{12}$ both are ILS estimators of β_1. Somewhat surprisingly, the two ILS estimators do not yield the same estimate of β_1. This situation of having more than one ILS estimator for a particular coefficient in a structural equation is characteristic of that equation's being overidentified. If an equation is just identified, there is just one ILS estimator for each of its coefficients. And if an equation is unidentified, it is impossible to form ILS estimators for all the coefficients. For example, there is no ratio or combination of the π's in (17.8)–(17.9) that yields γ_1, and the supply equation (17.2) is unidentified. In short, we can say that whether or not an equation is identified depends on whether or not the ILS estimators can be formed.

Indirect least squares estimators are biased but consistent. If an equation is just identified, ILS leads to exactly the same estimates as TSLS. If an equation is overidentified, ILS offers multiple estimates with no basis for choosing among them, whereas TSLS gives a single set of estimates. Hence, TSLS is usually preferred in practice.

Finally, we consider what can be done if an equation is unidentified. If the model is fully and correctly specified already, there is nothing to do. In most cases, however, the models we construct are considered to be only reasonable abstractions from the complexities of reality. Thus, respecifying the model can lead to another reasonable specification that may allow estimation of a previously unidentified equation. For example, if employers take a person's measured skill or productivity into account in setting their *HOURS–WAGE* relation, we would want to respecify the demand equation (17.1) to include this new exogenous variable. Presuming that skill or productivity does not affect the supply decision, the supply equation would now be identified, and it could be estimated.

Problems _____

Section 17.1

★ **17.1** Consider a structural model that is identical to equation set (17.1)–(17.2) except that *NKIDS* is not included. Solve for the reduced form.

17.2 Consider a structural model that is identical to equation set (17.1)–(17.2) except that *OTHINC* and *NKIDS* are not included. Solve for the reduced form.

★ **17.3** Consider the following structural model:
$$Y_i = \beta_0 + \beta_1 X_i + u_i$$
$$X_i = \gamma_0 + \gamma_1 Z_i + v_i$$

in which Y and X are considered endogenous. Analyze the logical structure of this *recursive model.*

17.4 Consider Equations (17.3) and (17.4) to be a two-equation model. Taking *CON* and *GNP* to be endogenous, solve for the reduced form.

★ **17.5** Suppose that the government decides to assure full employment by letting A adjust to whatever is necessary to fix *GNP* at a desired level. Taking Equations (17.3) and (17.4) to be a two-equation model, this makes *GNP* exogenous and A endogenous. Solve for the reduced form.

17.6 Suppose that Equation (17.13) is viewed as a single-equation model. Will the predicted value of *CON* for a given year (using the standard single-equation method) be the same as the simulated value of *CON* for the same year (using the systems method)?

Section 17.2

17.7 Consider a single-equation simple regression model. Draw a figure showing what the generated data look like if the disturbance is positively correlated with the explanatory variable. Sketch in the (hypothetical) fitted regression line.

17.8 Using the calculated standard errors to be indicators of estimation precision, would you judge the TSLS estimates of the macro model to be substantially different from the OLS estimates?

★ **17.9** Does OLS lead to simultaneous-equation bias for the equations in the recursive model discussed in Problem 17.3?

★ **17.10** Why are the $\hat{\pi}$'s in the first stage of TSLS related to the disturbances of the system? (*Hint:* The $\hat{\pi}$'s are OLS estimators.)

Section 17.3

★ **17.11** Assess the identification of Equations (17.3) and (17.5) in the macroeconomic model. [Equation (17.4) needs no estimation, and identification is not an issue.]

17.12 Consider the two-equation model of Problem 17.4. Is the consumption equation identified?

17.13 An alternative form of the order condition is "If an equation is identified, the number of excluded variables (counting endogenous and predetermined together) must be greater than or equal to the number of *other* equations in the model." Show that this is equivalent to the statement in the text.

★ **17.14** Consider the reduced-form model of Problem 17.1. How can ILS be used to estimate β_1 in the demand equation?

17.15 How does adding "productivity" as an exogenous variable to the demand equation (17.22) affect the identification of the demand and supply equations?

VI

Topics in Statistics

18

Inference for the Mean and Variance

In this chapter we develop and apply methods of statistical inference for the mean and variance of a random variable. The analysis parallels that in Chapters 11 and 12, which present a full discussion of inference in regression. The treatment here extends the earlier ideas and is much more brief.

To set the stage, suppose that there is a random variable having a known probability distribution $p(X)$ with a mean μ_X and variance σ_X^2. If we draw a sample of n observations from this random variable, we expect that the relative frequency distribution of the observed values will resemble the probability distribution $p(X)$ and that the calculated values of the sample data statistics $\overline{X}$ and S_X^2 will be similar to μ_X and σ_X^2. In large samples, we expect that the resemblance and similarities will tend to be great, whereas in small samples they will be less so.

The relations between the sample statistics and the corresponding parameters of the random variable are the subject of sampling theory. In turn, sampling theory is the basis for statistical inference.

18.1   The Sampling Distribution of $\overline{X}$

We focus first on characterizing the sampling variability that is associated with the mean, $\overline{X}$, in a sample taken from a given random variable. Let the random variable X have a known probability distribution $p(X)$ with mean μ_X and standard deviation σ_X. As in Chapter 11, we conduct a thought experiment to develop the theory; this is illustrated in Figure 18.1. Suppose that we draw N different samples each containing n observations, the same number in each case. In each sample, we calculate the value of the mean

$$\overline{X} = \frac{1}{n} \sum_{i=1}^{n} X_i \qquad (18.1)$$

and across the different samples these are denoted by $\overline{X}_1^*, \overline{X}_2^*, \ldots, \overline{X}_N^*$. (The asterisks indicate actually computed sample values.) Now, the N different $\overline{X}^*$ values can be collected and treated like data themselves: we can organize and determine the relative frequency distribution of the $\overline{X}^*$ values, $f(\overline{X}^*)$, and we can calculate the mean and the standard deviation of these values.

For example, suppose that the possibly occurring values of X range from 0 to 50, that $\mu_X = 20$, and that $\sigma_X = 10$. This specification corresponds to the top panel of Figure 18.1, which shows $p(X)$, the probability distribution of X, to be slightly skewed to the right. Suppose that the sample size (n) is 25, which statisticians consider large but not very large. And suppose that the number of samples (N), only three of which are represented in the figure, is quite large. The relative frequency distribution for each of the N samples bears a close resemblance to the probability distribution $p(X)$, and therefore they all resemble each other. However, the differences among them are noticeable. For each of the samples, the mean is calculated and the values shown are $\overline{X}_1^* = 18.2$, $\overline{X}_2^* = 21.4$, and $\overline{X}_N^* = 20.1$. Finally, the different $\overline{X}^*$ values are collected and their relative frequency histogram is given in the bottom of the figure.

The frequency distribution of the samples' $\overline{X}$ values, $f(\overline{X}^*)$, is constructed from samples that are drawn from the probability distribution of the random variable. Hence, we should expect that knowledge of $p(X)$ would give us information about the characteristics of $f(\overline{X}^*)$. Indeed, from $p(X)$ one can derive mathematically some knowledge regarding a new probability distribution, denoted by $p(X)$, which is a theoretical analog of the $f(\overline{X}^*)$ constructed from samples in our thought experiment. This probability distribution $p(\overline{X})$ is called the *sampling distribution* of $\overline{X}$. In theory, the sampling distribution $p(X)$ is the limiting form of the frequency distribution $f(\overline{X}^*)$ as the number of samples (N) increases to infinity. In other words, the sampling distribution of $\overline{X}$ is the probability distribution that governs the relative likelihood that different values will occur as the actual $\overline{X}$ in a sample that we draw.

Further mathematical analysis establishes the characteristics of the sampling distribution $p(\overline{X})$. First, if the form of $p(X)$, which is the distribution of the original random variable X, is normal, the form of $p(\overline{X})$ is also normal. Second, if the form of $p(X)$ is not normal, the form of $p(\overline{X})$ is approximately normal anyway if the sample size n is large. This result, which is rather marvelous, is known as the *Central Limit Theorem.* It holds true, as an approximation, when X is discrete as well as when it is continuous. The Central Limit Theorem is one

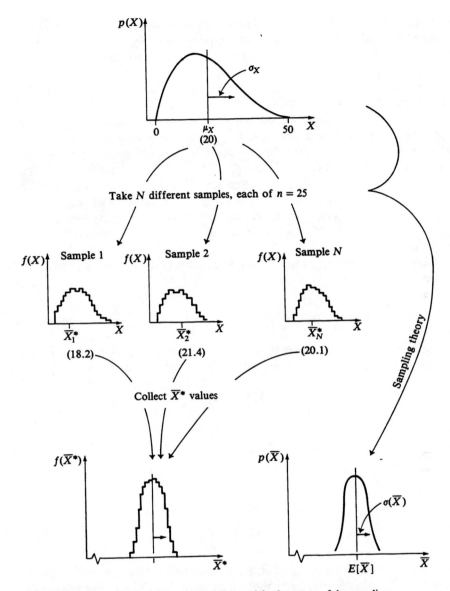

FIGURE 18.1 A thought experiment helps explain the nature of the sampling distribution of $\overline{X}$. We start with a continuous ramdom variable X whose probability distribution is shown at the top of the figure. Next, we take N different samples of size n, and in each sample we calculate the mean. These sample means are collected, and their frequency distribution is constructed. Theoretically, as the number of samples (N) increases to infinity, this frequency distribution reaches a limiting form. That limiting form is the sampling distribution of $\overline{X}$, which is the probability distribution that governs the likelihood of different values occurring for $\overline{X}$ in a sample of size n drawn from the original X.

of the reasons why the family of normal distributions is so important: other distributions lead to it in the context of sampling. How big does n have to be to make the approximation acceptable? Usually, 15 or 20 is big enough. Hence, for most practical applications we can treat the sampling distribution of $\overline{X}$ as though it were normal. As will be seen, this makes certain important probability calculations rather easy to handle.

The mean and variance of the sampling distribution can be derived by applying results from the appendix to Chapter 9. We now focus on one sample of n observations, rather than the N samples of the thought experiment. The values in the sample (i.e., $X_1, X_2, \ldots, X_n$), are usually thought of as being successive draws from the probability distribution $p(X)$ of the single random variable X. However, we also can think of them as being a set of single draws from n different independent random variables having probability distributions $p(X_1), p(X_2), \ldots, p(X_j), \ldots, p(X_n)$ that are all identical to $p(X)$, with $\mu_j = \mu_X$ and $\sigma_j^2 = \sigma_X^2$.

Now, consider defining a new variable named $\overline{X}$ in terms of the values of the n random variables $X_1, X_2, \ldots, X_n$:

$$\overline{X} = \left(\frac{1}{n}\right) X_1 + \left(\frac{1}{n}\right) X_2 + \cdots + \left(\frac{1}{n}\right) X_n = \sum_{j=1}^{n} \left(\frac{1}{n}\right) X_j \qquad (18.2)$$

Clearly, $\overline{X}$ is a linear combination of the n variables, and since they are independent (9.33) and (9.34) imply that

$$E[\overline{X}] = \mu_X \qquad (18.3)$$

and

$$\sigma^2(\overline{X}) = \frac{\sigma_X^2}{n} \qquad (18.4)$$

and thus

$$\sigma(\overline{X}) = \frac{\sigma_X}{\sqrt{n}} \qquad (18.5)$$

Why does it make sense to think of the n successive values of a single random variable X as being equivalent to the collection of single draws from each of n independent identically distributed random variables? The nature of a single random variable is that the value that occurs on one draw is not affected at all by what occurred on any previous draw, and this is the key to independence also.

Equation (18.3) shows that the mean of $\overline{X}$, which is denoted by $E[\overline{X}]$, is exactly equal to the mean of X. In other words, the expected value of the $\overline{X}$ calculated for a sample drawn from a random variable with a mean μ_X is exactly equal to that μ_X. This does not say, of course, that in taking one sample from X the $\overline{X}$ value will be equal to μ_X, but it says that on average it will be.

Since $\sigma(\overline{X})$ is greater than zero, we realize that in any sample there will be a difference between the value of $\overline{X}$ and the value μ_X. Since $\overline{X}$ is used to estimate the unknown μ_X, this difference is known as the *estimation error*, or *sampling error*:

$$\text{estimation error} = \overline{X} - \mu_X \tag{18.6}$$

The estimation error may be positive or negative, but on average it is zero [see (18.3)].

The typical (i.e., anticipated) magnitude of the estimation error (neglecting sign), is given by the *standard error* of $\overline{X}$; this is equal to its standard deviation $\sigma(\overline{X})$. As shown by (18.5), $\sigma(\overline{X})$ is exactly equal to $\sigma_X/\sqrt{n}$. As n gets larger, the standard deviation gets smaller. Because n enters the expression through $\sqrt{n}$, this relation is not proportional; in order to cut the standard error $\sigma(\overline{X})$ in half, the sample size (n) must be quadrupled. This is illustrated in Figure 18.2, which shows $p(\overline{X})$ for samples of sizes 10 and 40 from the same random variable X.

In summary, for most practical purposes, the sampling (probability) distribution of the mean

$$\overline{X} = \frac{1}{n}\sum_{i=1}^{n} X_i \tag{18.7}$$

in a sample of size n is normal, with

$$E[\overline{X}] = \mu_X \tag{18.8}$$

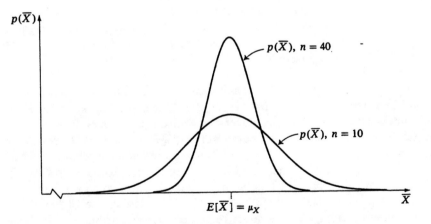

FIGURE 18.2 The sampling distribution of $\overline{X}$ is exactly normal if $p(X)$ is normal. When $p(X)$ is not normal, the sampling distribution of $\overline{X}$ is approximately normal if n is large, according to the Central Limit Theorem. The mean of $\overline{X}$ is equal to μ_X, and the standard error is equal to $\sigma_X/\sqrt{n}$. The sampling distributions of $\overline{X}$ shown here are for samples of sizes 10 and 40 drawn from the same random variable. When the sample size is quadrupled, the standard error is cut in half.

and

$$\sigma(\overline{X}) = \frac{\sigma_X}{\sqrt{n}} \tag{18.9}$$

For example, we considered earlier a random variable X that ranges from 0 to 50 and that has a probability distribution $p(X)$ with a mean $\mu_X = 20$ and a standard deviation $\sigma_X = 10$. Suppose that we consider taking one sample of size $n = 25$ and are interested in the $\overline{X}$ value that we will get. Even before all the theory, we might have guessed that it would be about 20, but this is rather imprecise. Sampling theory tells us that the probability distribution of $\overline{X}$ is approximately normal with a mean of $E[\overline{X}] = 20$ and a standard deviation equal to $\sigma(\overline{X}) = 10/\sqrt{25} = 2$.

Thus the theory confirms our intuitive guess, but it also allows us to make some probability calculations. Knowing that $\mu_X = 20$, we might wonder, for example, what the probability is that $\overline{X}$ will be within 1 of the true mean. Formally, we seek to determine $\Pr(19 \leq \overline{X} \leq 21)$. This notation highlights the fact that in thinking of the sampling distribution of $\overline{X}$, the $\overline{X}$ itself is the random variable being described. Now, since $\overline{X}$ is taken to be normal with $E[\overline{X}] = 20$ and $\sigma(\overline{X}) = 2$, we can solve this probability problem as we do with any one involving a normal distribution: we solve the equivalent probability problem in terms of Z, the standard normal distribution. The $\overline{X}$ value 19 corresponds to

$$Z_k = \frac{\overline{X}_k - E[\overline{X}]}{\sigma(\overline{X})} = \frac{19 - 20}{2} = -0.5 \tag{18.10}$$

and 21 corresponds to $Z_k = (21 - 20)/2 = 0.5$. Hence we want to determine $\Pr(-0.5 \leq Z \leq 0.5)$, because this probability amount is the same as $\Pr(19 \leq \overline{X} \leq 21)$. Table A.1 shows us that $\Pr(Z \geq 0.5) = .3085$. After drawing a diagram, recognizing symmetry, and doing a little arithmetic, we find $\Pr(-0.5 \leq Z \leq 0.5)$ to be .3830. Hence the probability that $\overline{X}$ will be within 1 of the true mean is 38.3 percent in this case.

Continuing the same example, what is the chance that the estimation error for μ_X will be as large as 3? (Note that "as large as 3" means "3 or larger" and that the context implies that we are concerned with negative as well as positive errors.) In other words, we seek to determine $\Pr(|\overline{X} - \mu_X| \geq 3)$. After drawing a diagram and noting that $\mu_X = E[\overline{X}] = 20$, we can restate the event $|\overline{X} - \mu_X| \geq 3$ as "$\overline{X} \leq 17$ or $\overline{X} \geq 23$." Thus we seek to determine $\Pr(\overline{X} \leq 17) + \Pr(\overline{X} \geq 23)$. Working with the normal distribution, we find the Z values to be -1.5 and 1.5, respectively, so the total probability is .1336. Thus the chance of having an estimation error as large as 3 is about 13.36 percent in this case.

18.2   Inference Regarding μ_X

When X has a normal distribution, the procedures for carrying out hypothesis tests and for making interval estimates for μ_X are basically the same as those presented in Chapters 11 and 12 for regression coefficients. These are reviewed here, and appropriate differences are noted. If the distribution of X is not normal, these procedures can be applied as good approximations when the sample size is large.

We start from the sampling theory summarized in (18.7)–(18.9). In practical applications we never know the standard error $\sigma(\overline{X})$ because it depends on σ_X, the standard deviation of X. Since S_X is used widely as an estimator of σ_X, we use it here to help estimate $\sigma(\overline{X})$. The resulting estimator of the standard error of $\overline{X}$ is given by

$$s(\overline{X}) = \frac{S_X}{\sqrt{n}} \tag{18.11}$$

Now, since the sampling distribution $p(\overline{X})$ is normal with a mean of μ_X and a standard deviation estimated by $s(\overline{X})$, the variable t defined by

$$t = \frac{\overline{X} - \mu_X}{s(\overline{X})} \tag{18.12}$$

can be expected to have a probability distribution that is similar to the standard normal. In fact, it turns out that this t has a t distribution with $n - 1$ degrees of freedom.

Since $\overline{X} - \mu_X$, which is the numerator in (18.12), is the estimation error involved in estimating μ_X, t can be interpreted as a measure of the estimation error in one sample relative to the typical estimation error. This sampling statistic t is the key to carrying out hypothesis tests and making interval estimates.

Hypothesis Tests

Hypothesis testing regarding μ_X can be carried out using the same five steps outlined in Chapter 12:

1. State the hypotheses clearly.
2. Choose the level of significance α.
3. Construct the decision rule.
4. Determine the value of the test statistic t^*.
5. State and interpret the conclusion of the test.

For example, suppose that we have a random variable X with a probability distribution that we believe is identical to the one used in Figure 18.1 and earlier examples in this chapter. We believe that $\mu_X = 20$. To test this belief we gather a sample of 36 observations on X.

The hypotheses are statements about an unknown parameter, here μ_X. The null hypothesis must be specific, stating that μ_X is equal to a particular value. The alternative hypothesis must be vague about the value of μ_X; its particular form determines whether the test is one-tailed or two-tailed. In our example we have no reason to believe that μ_X would be greater than 20 rather than less than 20, so the appropriate hypotheses are

$$H_0: \mu_X = 20$$
$$H_1: \mu_X \neq 20 \qquad\qquad (18.13)$$

The goal of the test procedure is to determine whether the data contradict the null hypothesis.

The level of significance α is chosen by the researcher, and it is usually taken to be a conventional amount such as 5 percent. The chosen α is used in the specification of the decision rule, and it is the probability that the null hypothesis will be mistakenly rejected (a Type I error).

The decision rule for a two-tailed test, which is called for by the hypotheses (18.13), is of the form

$$\text{Reject } H_0 \text{ if } |t^*| \geq t^c \qquad\qquad (18.14)$$

where

$$\Pr(|t| \geq t^c) = \alpha \qquad\qquad (18.15)$$

We recognize that t defined by (18.12) can take on any value from $-\infty$ to ∞. The logic of the decision rule is that the null hypothesis is to be rejected if the absolute estimation error is so large (relative to the standard error) as to be quite unlikely to have occurred if H_0 were true. Given α, the critical values $-t^c$ and t^c are determined from (18.15). The critical values are the boundaries of the critical region, which is indicated by the range of t values under the shaded areas in Figure 18.3. In our example, with $\alpha = .05$ and $n = 36$ (so df = 35), we see from Table A.3 that $t^c = 2.03$ approximately.

Only now, in the fourth step of the test, do we look at the findings of the sample. Suppose that $\overline{X}^* = 17.4$ and $S_X^* = 9$. The value of the test statistic is

$$t^* = \frac{\overline{X}^* - \mu_X}{s^*(\overline{X})} = \frac{17.4 - 20}{9/\sqrt{36}} = -1.73 \qquad\qquad (18.16)$$

That is, presuming that $\mu_X = 20$, the negative estimation error associated with finding $\overline{X}^* = 17.4$ amounts to 1.73 standard errors.

The conclusion of the test is to not reject H_0 because t^* is not in the critical region. Also, we say that the $\overline{X}^*$ value is not significantly different from 20. However, from Table A.2 we see that the chance of getting a negative sampling error as large as 1.75 standard errors is only about 4.5 percent. Therefore, finding $t^* = -1.73$ should make us somewhat suspicious of the validity of the null hypothesis even though it has not been rejected formally.

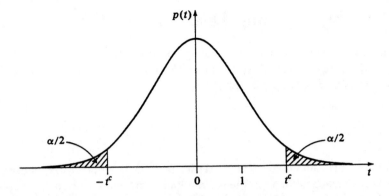

FIGURE 18.3 A hypothesis test regarding μ_X is based on the test statistic t, which is equal to $(\overline{X} - \mu_X)/s(\overline{X})$. This t has a t distribution with $n - 1$ degrees of freedom. In a two-tailed test, the decision rule is to reject the null hypothesis if $|t*| \geq t^c$. The critical values t^c and $-t^c$ each bound $\alpha/2$ probability in a tail, where α is the level of significance.

Interval Estimates

The procedure for constructing a confidence interval for estimating μ_X follows along the same lines as Chapter 11. The level of confidence $1 - \alpha$ is chosen by the researcher, with .95 being the most common amount.

It can be shown that the interval

$$\overline{X}* \pm h, \quad \text{where} \quad h = t^c s*(\overline{X}) \tag{18.17}$$

in which t^c is defined by

$$\Pr(|t| \geq t^c) = \alpha \tag{18.18}$$

can be used to construct an interval estimate of an unknown μ_X at the $1 - \alpha$ level of confidence.

For example, for the sample data used in the hypothesis test, we determine $t^c \approx 2.03$ from Table A.3 for a 95 percent confidence interval. The interval is

$$17.4 \pm (2.03)(9/\sqrt{36}) \quad \text{or} \quad 17.4 \pm 3.05 \tag{18.19}$$

which ranges from 14.35 to 20.45. We notice that the earlier null hypothesis value $\mu_X = 20$ lies within this interval. Indeed, it can be shown that there is a perfect correspondence between the findings of a $1 - \alpha$ confidence interval and a two-tailed test using an α level of significance: if the value of μ_X under the null hypothesis lies within the confidence interval, H_0 is not rejected, and if μ_X lies outside the interval, H_0 is rejected.

18.3   The Sampling Distribution of S_X^2

We turn now to characterizing the sampling variability that is associated with the variance S_X^2 to be calculated in a sample from a given random variable. The variance of data in a sample is defined as

$$S_X^2 = \frac{\sum\limits_{i=1}^{n}(X_i - \overline{X})^2}{n - 1} \qquad (18.20)$$

Following the same logic as in the earlier thought experiment, we realize that the variance calculated in a sample is a random variable S_X^2, with some sampling (probability) distribution denoted by $p(S_X^2)$. It can be shown that the mean is

$$E[S_X^2] = \sigma_X^2 \qquad (18.21)$$

which means that S_X^2 is an unbiased estimator of σ_X^2. This property would not hold true if the variance were defined with n rather than $n - 1$ in the denominator (i.e., if it were the mean squared deviation). Putting this in reverse, we see that the reason for defining S_X^2 with $n - 1$ in the denominator is to make this statistic an unbiased estimator of σ_X^2, the variance of the underlying random variable.

The other characteristics of the sampling distribution $p(S_X^2)$ depend crucially on the shape of $p(X)$. There is nothing like the Central Limit Theorem to point to a limiting form, except in special cases.

Consider the case of a random variable X having a normal distribution with mean μ_X and variance σ_X^2. It can be shown that the statistic

$$\chi^2 = \frac{(n-1)S_X^2}{\sigma_X^2} = \frac{\sum(X_i - \overline{X})^2}{\sigma_X^2} = \sum_{i=1}^{n}\left(\frac{X_i - \overline{X}}{\sigma_X}\right)^2. \qquad (18.22)$$

is a new random variable having a chi-square probability distribution with $n - 1$ degrees of freedom. To understand why, note that if $\overline{X}$ were replaced with μ_X in the rightmost expression, each term in parentheses would be a transformed variable having a standard normal distribution. Squaring and summing these would yield a χ^2 having a chi-square distribution with n degrees of freedom (see the appendix to Chapter 10). The true χ^2 defined by (18.22) has $n - 1$ degrees of freedom, the lost "1" being due to the algebra of isolating $\overline{X}$ and seemingly replacing it with μ_X.

18.4   Inference Regarding σ_X^2

When X has a normal distribution, hypothesis tests regarding the value of σ_X^2 can be carried out using χ^2 as the test statistic. If the null hypothesis "H_0: $\sigma_X^2 = \sigma_0^2$" is true, then

$$\chi^2 = \frac{(n-1)S_X^2}{\sigma_0^2} \tag{18.23}$$

has a chi-square distribution with $n-1$ degrees of freedom. Table A.4 permits us to find the critical values of χ^2 that bound selected areas in the left side and in the right-hand tail of the distribution, as appropriate.

For example, again using the sample explored earlier (with $n = 36$), suppose we believe that $\sigma_X^2 = 100$ (i.e., $\sigma_X = 10$). The hypotheses for testing this belief are

$$H_0: \sigma_X^2 = 100$$

$$H_1: \sigma_X^2 \neq 100 \tag{18.24}$$

Choosing the .05 level of significance, the left-side critical value is $(\chi^2)_l^c = 20.56$ and the right-hand critical value is $(\chi^2)_r^c = 53.22$. The decision rule is

$$\text{Reject } H_0 \quad \text{if} \quad (\chi^2)^* \leq (\chi^2)_l^c \quad \text{or} \quad (\chi^2)^* \geq (\chi^2)_r^c \tag{18.25}$$

The sampling distribution of χ^2 if the null hypothesis is true is illustrated in Figure 18.4, and the critical region is indicated. Based on the sample in which $S_X^2{}^* = 81$, the value of the test statistic is

$$(\chi^2)^* = \frac{(n-1)S_X^2}{\sigma_0^2} = \frac{(35)(81)}{100} = 28.35 \tag{18.26}$$

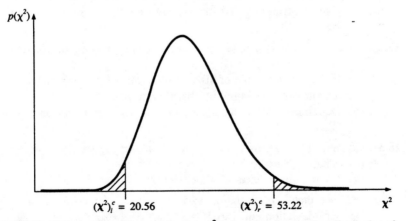

$(\chi^2)_l^c = 20.56$ $\qquad\qquad$ $(\chi^2)_r^c = 53.22$ $\qquad\qquad$ χ^2

FIGURE 18.4 A hypothesis test regarding σ_X^2 is based on the sampling distribution of the χ^2 test statistic, which is defined in Equation (18.23). This has a chi-square distribution with $n-1$ degrees of freedom. In a two-tailed test, the decision rule is to reject the null hypothesis if $(\chi^2)^* \leq (\chi^2)_l^c$ or $(\chi^2)^* \geq (\chi^2)_r^c$. As illustrated here, the critical value $(\chi^2)_l^c$ bounds $\alpha/2$ probability in the left side of the distribution, and $(\chi^2)_r^c$ bounds $\alpha/2$ in the right-hand tail; α is the level of significance.

Since $(\chi^2)*$ is not in the critical region, we do not reject the null hypothesis. Note, however, that this test is properly applied only if it is assumed that $p(X)$ is normal, which was not part of the original example.

Finally, confidence intervals can be constructed for estimating σ_X^2, based on the sample value S_X^2. Since the sampling distribution of S_X^2 is not symmetric, we are confronted with a new problem in constructing the interval. One approach leads to specifying the following

$$\text{confidence interval for } \sigma_X^2: \frac{(n-1)S_X^{2*}}{(\chi^2)_r^c} \quad \text{to} \quad \frac{(n-1)S_X^{2*}}{(\chi^2)_i^c} \qquad (18.27)$$

where $(\chi^2)_r^c$ bounds $\alpha/2$ probability in the right-hand tail and $(\chi^2)_i^c$ bounds $\alpha/2$ probability in the left side. For the sample data used above, this 95 percent confidence interval for estimating σ_X^2 ranges from 53.27 to 137.89.

Problems _____

Section 18.1

18.1 Suppose that X is a random variable having a normal distribution with a mean of 0 and a standard deviation of 4.
  (a) On one set of axes draw the probability distribution of X and also a hypothetical relative frequency distribution for a sample of $n = 16$ taken from it.
  (b) On another set of axes draw the probability distribution of X and also the sampling distribution $p(\overline{X})$ for the mean of a sample of size 16.

★ **18.2** Suppose that X is a random variable having a binomial distribution with $n = 100$ and $P = .5$.
  (a) If we take a sample of size 16, determine the mean and standard deviation of the sampling distribution $p(\overline{X})$.
  (b) Determine approximately the probability that $\overline{X}$ will be less than 48.

18.3 Consider the frequency distribution $f(\overline{X}*)$ in Figure 18.1.
  (a) What happens to it as N increases?
  (b) What happens to it as n increases?

18.4 Suppose that X is a random variable with an unknown mean and a standard deviation equal to 150.
  (a) How large a sample must be taken in order that the typical estimation error for μ_X will be 10 or less?
  (b) How large a sample must be taken in order that the typical estimation error for μ_X will be 5 or less?

★ **18.5** Suppose that X is a discrete random variable whose two possible values are -1 and 1, each occurring with probability 1/2. Determine the sampling distribution of $\overline{X}$ in a sample of size 2: what are its possible values and what are their probabilities?

Section 18.2

18.6 Suppose that X is a random variable. In a sample of size 81 we find $\overline{X}* = 103$ and $S_X = 15$. Test the hypothesis that $E[X] = 100$, using a 5 percent level of significance.

★ **18.7** Continuing Problem 18.6, suppose that the same values for the sample mean and standard deviation were found in a sample of size 400. How would the results of the test be affected?

★ **18.8** Determine the 95 percent confidence interval for estimating μ_X in the situation of Problem 18.6.

18.9 What happens to the width of the confidence interval for estimating μ_X if the sample size is quadrupled?

Section 18.3

18.10 Suppose that X has a normal distribution. If we consider taking a sample of size 10 from X, sketch (on separate graphs) the sampling distributions of $\overline{X}$ and of S_X^2.

★ **18.11** Suppose that X has a standard normal distribution. In a sample of size 10:
(a) What is the expected value of S_X^2?
(b) Determine (approximately) the probability that S_X^2 will be greater than 2.

Section 18.4

18.12 Suppose that X has a normal distribution. In a sample of size 16 we find $S_X^2* = 55$. Does this contradict the hypothesis that $\sigma_X^2 = 50$?

★ **18.13** Construct a confidence interval for estimating σ_X^2 in Problem 18.12.

19

Chi-Square Tests
and Analysis of Variance

This chapter surveys two statistical techniques that are used commonly in fields other than economics. The econometric approach usually involves a specification of the structure of the relationship among variables, and it permits the testing of behavioral hypotheses in that context. Chi-square tests lack this structure, and often are less powerful. By contrast, the analysis of variance specifies a structure, but it turns out that the resulting tests can be carried out easily using regression analysis.

19.1   Chi-Square Tests

In general, *chi-square tests* lend themselves to situations in which observations are categorized into a number of groups. This categorization may be on the basis of a single variable or more than one variable. Suppose that n observations are divided into a certain number of categories, with the absolute frequency in the kth category being denoted by n_k. Now suppose that a theory or belief leads to a prediction that out of the n observations a certain number should be in each category, with the number predicted to be in the kth category being denoted by p_k. The question arises as to whether the observed frequencies n_k are sufficiently different from the predicted frequencies p_k to cast doubt on the validity of the stated theory or belief. The question is answered by carrying out a hypothesis test.

We seek a test statistic that serves as an overall measure of how much difference there is between the n_k and the p_k. To be useful, the sampling distribution of the test statistic must be known under the condition that the underlying theory is correct. A statistic based simply on $\sum(n_k - p_k)$ will not serve, because this is always equal to zero. Squaring the differences gets rid of the canceling out of positive and negative values, and dividing these squares by p_k standardizes the measure in such a way that the sampling distribution can be determined. Formally, the test statistic is

$$\chi^2 = \sum \frac{(n_k - p_k)^2}{p_k} \tag{19.1}$$

where the summation is understood to include all the defined categories. It turns out that the sampling distribution of χ^2 is approximately chi-square. Generally, the approximation is good if all the p_k values are at least 5.

If the observed frequencies are exactly equal to the predicted frequencies (i.e., if $n_k = p_k$ for all k), then χ^2 equals zero. If the n_k are very different from the p_k, χ^2 is large. Hence large values of test statistic are used to reject the null hypothesis that the observed frequency distribution arises from a process that leads to the distribution of predicted frequencies. As with all hypothesis tests, we recognize that rejections using this decision rule will sometimes be mistaken. The probability of making this kind of mistake depends on the critical value for the test statistic, and the critical value is chosen so as to make this probability equal to a specified amount—the level of significance.

Test of Goodness of Fit

One major application of the chi-square test is in situations in which the predicted values p_k are derived from a theory that predicts a certain distribution for the values of a single variable. This *test of goodness of fit* examines whether the observed data fit the theoretical distribution, and vice versa. If the number of categories defined in the distribution is r, the χ^2 test statistic has $r - 1$ degrees of freedom. (Given the total number of observations, the number in the rth category is set by the numbers in the other $r - 1$ categories; hence there are $r - 1$ degrees of freedom here.)

For example, suppose we have a theory of organizations that predicts that for every manager in a certain type of firm, there will be 3 white-collar workers and 6 blue-collar workers. Thus, 10 percent of the total number of employees will be managers, 30 percent will be white-collar workers, and 60 percent will be blue-collar workers. Suppose also that we have complete personnel data for a firm of this type with 200 employees, and that the categorical breakdown shows 25 managers, 65 white-collar workers, and 110 blue-collar workers. Based on the organizational theory, the corresponding predicted frequencies (p_k) are 20, 60, and 120. These observed and predicted frequencies are displayed in Table

19.1. It looks as though this firm is a bit overloaded with managers and white-collar workers, possibly contradicting the theory in this case, but we need a hypothesis test to determine whether the differences could be due simply to chance variation.

The null hypothesis is that the distribution of predicted frequencies correctly characterizes the process underlying the generation of the observed data. We carry out the test at the .05 level of significance. With three occupational groups, the number of degrees of freedom is 2 (df $= r - 1$ here), and from Table A.4 we find that the critical value is $(\chi^2)^c = 5.99$. The sampling distribution of χ^2 and the critical region for the test are illustrated in Figure 19.1. Table 19.1 shows the calculations needed to determine the value of the test statistic, $(\chi^2)^* = 2.50$. Since $(\chi^2)^*$ is not greater than $(\chi^2)^c$, we do not reject the null hypothesis. The differences between actual and predicted frequencies are not so large as to be inconsistent with the organizational theory from which the predicted frequencies were determined.

TABLE 19.1   Observed and Predicted Occupation Frequencies

	Observed n_k	Predicted p_k	$n_k - p_k$	$\dfrac{(n_k - p_k)^2}{p_k}$
Manager	25	20	5	1.25
White-collar	65	60	5	0.42
Blue-collar	110	120	-10	0.83
				$\chi^2 = 2.50$

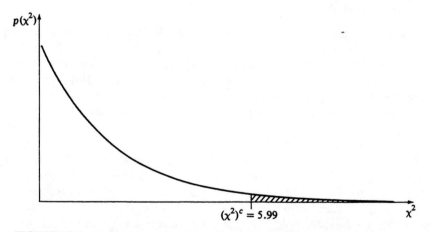

FIGURE 19.1   A chi-square test can be used to judge whether the observed and predicted frequencies in Table 19.1 are consistent. The test statistic χ^2 has a chi-square distribution with 2 degrees of freedom. The critical value that bounds 5 percent of the probability in the right-hand tail is 5.99, and the critical region consists of the values of χ^2 underlying the shaded area.

Test of Independence

A second application of the same basic approach leads to what is known as the *test of independence* in a contingency table.

Suppose that we wish to investigate whether an employee's gender plays a role in the process of occupational hiring or assignment. Continuing with the personnel data from the previous example, we use data on two variables: gender and occupation. One way to look at the data is given in Table 19.2, which shows the number of employees in each of the six gender-occupation categories. We see, for example, that among the 200 employees there were 21 managers who are men. The observed frequencies imply that 60 percent of the workers are men and 40 percent are women. Similarly, 12.5 percent of the workers are managers, 32.5 percent are white-collar workers, and 55 percent are blue-collar workers.

The numbers in parentheses show the frequencies that would be predicted if occupation were independent of gender in the data. These are determined by taking as given the overall proportions of workers of each gender. Based on the proportions, we would predict that if occupational hiring and assignment were independent of gender, then 60 percent of all managers would be men and 40 percent would be women. Given that there are 25 managerial jobs, this translates into predicted frequencies of 15 men managers and 10 women managers. The gender-specific predictions for the other occupations are made in the same way. It should be noted that the same predicted frequencies for the six categories are obtained when the total number of workers of each gender is multiplied by the overall proportion of workers in each occupation.

It appears from the data that women are found more frequently in white collar jobs than is predicted by independence (38 versus 26), and less frequently in managerial and blue-collar jobs. Put differently, managers and blue-collar workers are more frequently men than is predicted. Do these differences contradict the null hypothesis that gender and occupation are independent, or are they due just to chance fluctuation?

This question is answered by carrying out a hypothesis test using the test statistic χ^2 defined in (19.1). If the null hypothesis is correct, χ^2 has a chi-square distribution with $(r-1)(c-1)$ degrees of freedom, where r is the number of rows and c is the number of columns in the main body of the contingency table. (The counting of r and c excludes the marginal totals.) The proper number of

TABLE 19.2 Gender-Occupation Contingency Table

	Men		Women		Both
Manager	21	(15)	4	(10)	25
White-collar	27	(39)	38	(26)	65
Blue-collar	72	(66)	38	(44)	110
All occupations	120		80		

degrees of freedom can be interpreted as the number of unrestricted comparisons or differences that lead to the calculation of χ^2. In any column, the last entry can be determined from the $r - 1$ entries above it and the marginal frequency below it. Similarly, in any row the last entry can be determined from the $c - 1$ entries to the left of it and the marginal frequency to the right of it. Hence there are $(r - 1)(c - 1)$ unrestricted entries.

Returning to the example, with three rows and two columns there are two degrees of freedom for the relevant chi-square distribution. Large differences between observed and predicted frequencies in the categories lead to large values of χ^2. Hence large values of χ^2 constitute the critical region of values that lead us to reject the null hypothesis that gender and occupation are independent. At the .05 level of significance, Table A.4 gives $(\chi^2)^c = 5.99$. From Table 19.2 we calculate $(\chi^2)^* = 16.6$. Since $(\chi^2)^*$ is greater than $(\chi^2)^c$, we reject the null hypothesis and conclude that gender and occupation are not independent.

It should be noted that in going from the goodness-of-fit test to the test of independence for the same set of data, the nature of the analysis changes. In the first case we explicitly test a theory of occupational organization. In the second test, we take as given both the occupational structure and the relative numbers of men and women, and we test just for their independence.

19.2   Analysis of Variance and Regression

Analysis of variance, commonly referred to as ANOVA, is a statistical technique that seeks to determine whether differences in the values of a variable can be explained by categorization of the observations. This technique was developed for application to experimental data. Most of the results can be obtained through regression, and we approach ANOVA from this point of view.

ANOVA Table for Regression

The traditional framework for analysis of variance gives rise to a special format for organizing some of the results of regression estimation and hypothesis testing. This format, which is known as an ANOVA table, is shown generically for the results of a multiple regression in Table 19.3. Many computer programs print such a table for each estimated regression, replacing the formulas and symbols given here by their calculated values.

The core of the table is the column labeled "Sum of Squares." The three items here represent the identity derived earlier as (5.24), which states that the

TABLE 19.3 ANOVA Table for Regression

Source of Variation	Sum of Squares	Degrees of Freedom	Mean Square	F Ratio
Explained (by regression)	$\sum(\hat{Y}_i - \bar{Y})^2$	k	$\dfrac{\sum(\hat{Y}_i - \bar{Y})^2}{k}$	$\dfrac{\sum(\hat{Y}_i - \bar{Y})^2/k}{\sum(Y_i - \hat{Y}_i)^2/(n-k-1)}$
Unexplained (due to error)	$\sum(Y_i - \hat{Y}_i)^2$	$n - k - 1$	$\dfrac{\sum(Y_i - \hat{Y}_i)^2}{n-k-1}$	
Total	$\sum(Y_i - \bar{Y})^2$	$n - 1$		

total variation in Y can be decomposed into the explained variation and the unexplained variation:

$$\sum(Y_i - \bar{Y})^2 = \sum(\hat{Y}_i - \bar{Y})^2 + \sum(Y_i - \hat{Y}_i)^2 \tag{19.2}$$

The coefficient of determination R^2 can be computed as the ratio of the sum of squares in the first row to that in the third; equivalently, it is 1 minus the ratio of the second to the third:

$$R^2 = \frac{\sum(\hat{Y}_i - \bar{Y})^2}{\sum(Y_i - \bar{Y})^2} = 1 - \frac{\sum(Y_i - \hat{Y}_i)^2}{\sum(Y_i - \bar{Y})^2} \tag{19.3}$$

The assignment of values to the column labeled "Degrees of Freedom" is definitional, and it is made as an intermediate step to later results. The explained variation is assigned k degrees of freedom, and the unexplained variation is assigned $n - k - 1$. The sum of these, $n - 1$, is assigned to the total variation.

The "Mean Square" for each row is that row's sum of squares divided by its degrees of freedom. The mean square due to the regression is referred to as the explained variance, and the mean square due to the error is referred to as the unexplained variance. (Note that the unexplained variance is an unbiased estimator of the variance of the disturbance σ_u^2. The square root of this item is the standard error of the regression SER). Were we to calculate the mean square for the third row, it would be the variance of Y.

The only item in the "F Ratio" column is the ratio of the first mean square to the second, and it is sometimes called the variance ratio. This ratio is the same as the value of the F statistic (14.12) derived earlier to test the null hypothesis that all the regression coefficients (except the intercept) are equal to zero. To see that this is true, note that SSR_U in the earlier terminology is equal to the unexplained sum of squares in the present regression. SSR_R would be the sum of squared residuals in a "regression" of Y on an intercept, as specified in (14.11), but it also is equal to the total sum of squares in the present regression. Hence, $SSR_R - SSR_U$ is equal to the explained sum of squares (i.e., total − unexplained) in the ANOVA table. Thus, the F ratio here is the same as the F statistic.

One-Way ANOVA

We develop some of the ideas of analysis of variance with examples continuing from earlier in this chapter. Suppose that we have data on the salaries (or annual wage payments) made to the employees of a particular firm. This salary is denoted by Y, with the mean being $\bar{Y}$. Now suppose that the observations are categorized into three occupations: managers, white-collar workers, and blue-collar workers. The salary means within these three groups are $\bar{Y}_1$, $\bar{Y}_2$, and $\bar{Y}_3$, respectively. It seems natural to ask whether observed differences in these means reflect true interoccupational differences or just chance fluctuation.

Underlying the ANOVA technique is a set of assumptions about how salaries are generated. It is assumed that for the jth occupation, observed Y's are values of a normally distributed random variable with mean μ_j and variance σ^2. The means may differ among the occupations, but the variances are assumed to be the same. Our inquiry into the data is to test the null hypothesis

$$H_0: \mu_1 = \mu_2 = \mu_3 \qquad (19.4)$$

against the alternative that at least one of the means is different from the others.

Given data on salary (Y) and the categorization of observations into the three occupations, it is simple to determine the mean Y for all observations ($\bar{Y}$) and the mean Y within each occupation, denoted generically by $\bar{Y}_j$. These occupational means can be used to "predict" or help explain the observed Y values within each occupation. For an observation in the jth occupation, the predicted salary is simply $\bar{Y}_j$ and the error associated with this prediction is $Y_i - \bar{Y}_j$. For each observation,

$$(Y_i - \bar{Y}) = (\bar{Y}_j - \bar{Y}) + (Y_i - \bar{Y}_j) \qquad (19.5)$$

is a simple algebraic identity that can be interpreted as a decomposition of the total deviation of Y_i (from $\bar{Y}$) into two parts: the deviation of the group mean $\bar{Y}_j$ from the overall mean $\bar{Y}$, and the error associated with using this group mean to predict Y_i. This equation can be squared to yield another valid equation, and the n squared equations like that (one for each observation) can be added to yield, after extensive algebraic manipulation,

$$\sum (Y_i - \bar{Y})^2 = \sum (\bar{Y}_j - \bar{Y})^2 + \sum (Y_i - \bar{Y}_j)^2 \qquad (19.6)$$

This expression, whose evaluation requires careful attention to the correct j and i indices, can be reexpressed as

$$SS_T = SS_E + SS_U \qquad (19.7)$$

In this simplified expression, SS_T is the total variation of Y from its mean, and it is called the total sum of squares. SS_E is the portion of SS_T that is derived from terms like $\bar{Y}_j - \bar{Y}$, which help "explain" deviations of Y_i from $\bar{Y}$ on the basis of the occupational mean $\bar{Y}_j$. For this reason, SS_E is called the explained sum of squares. Finally, SS_U is the portion of SS_T that is derived from terms like

$Y_i - \overline{Y}_j$, which is "unexplained" even after occupational categorization. This SS_U is called the unexplained sum of squares.

These sums of squares can be arranged as in Table 19.4. Letting r be the number of groups (occupations), we assign $r - 1$ degrees of freedom to the explained variation and $n - r$ to the unexplained variation, adding up to $n - 1$ for the total. The mean square in each row is the sum of squares divided by the number of degrees of freedom. The F ratio is the ratio of the first two mean squares, and sometimes it is referred to as the variance ratio.

It can be shown that if the null hypothesis (19.4) is true, this variance ratio indeed has an F distribution, with $r - 1$ and $n - r$ degrees of freedom. Large values of the F ratio reflect considerable differences among the $\overline{Y}_j$, and therefore large values of F form the critical region for rejecting the null hypothesis.

We have avoided explaining the detail of this method and hypothesis test because exactly the same results can be obtained using regression analysis with dummy variables. To see this, let the dummy variable $D1$ take on the value 1 if the observation is a manager and 0 otherwise, and let the variable $D2$ take on the value 1 if the observation is a white-collar worker and 0 otherwise. The regression specification

$$Y_i = \beta_0 + \beta_1 D1_i + \beta_2 D2_i + u_i \tag{19.8}$$

can be estimated by OLS, and an ANOVA table like Table 19.3 could be produced.

A test of the proposition that $E[Y]$ is the same for each occupation is equivalent to testing the null hypothesis that occupation has no effect on Y (i.e., that $\beta_1 = \beta_2 = 0$). This test is carried out using the basic F test of regression, for which the value of the test statistic F^* is found in the regression ANOVA table. The validity of this test depends on the correctness of the assumptions underlying the regression model. In particular, the regular assumptions amount to saying that for each occupation the distribution of Y is assumed to be normal, with the same variance.

It turns out that $\hat{\beta}_0 = \overline{Y}_3$, $\hat{\beta}_1 = \overline{Y}_1 - \overline{Y}_3$, and $\hat{\beta}_2 = \overline{Y}_2 - \overline{Y}_3$. Hence the regression can be interpreted as "explaining" the observed values of Y on the basis of the mean value of the salary for the occupation to which each observation belongs. The unexplained variation $\sum (Y_i - \hat{Y}_i)^2$ measures the variation in Y that arises within each occupation. That is, within each occupation $\hat{Y} = \overline{Y}_j$ ($j = 1, 2, 3$),

TABLE 19.4   One-Way ANOVA Table

Source of Variation	Sum of Squares	Degrees of Freedom	Mean Square	F Ratio
Explained (by differences in $\overline{Y}_j$)	SS_E	$r - 1$	$\dfrac{SS_E}{r-1}$	$\dfrac{SS_E/(r-1)}{SS_U/(n-r)}$
Unexplained	SS_U	$n - r$	$\dfrac{SS_U}{n-r}$	
Total	SS_T	$n - 1$		

and for each worker therein $Y_i - \hat{Y}_i = Y_i - \overline{Y}_j$. Thus the unexplained variation within each occupation is the sum of squares like $(Y_i - \overline{Y}_j)^2$, and the unexplained variation in the whole regression is the sum of the three occupations' sums of squares. Thus regression and ANOVA lead to precisely the same decomposition of the total variation of Y, and the F statistics are identical.

Two-Way ANOVA

We extend our example further by recognizing explicitly that salaries may be explained by more factors than just occupation. Specifically, we suppose that the employee's gender is a variable that may help determine salary levels. It is natural to ask whether there are systematic differences in salary by occupation, given that salary is also related to the employee's gender. Symmetrically, one might ask whether there are systematic differences by gender, given occupation.

We approach this problem first through regression. Extending the previous specification (19.8), we let G be a dummy variable taking the value 1 for men and 0 for women. The resulting model is

$$Y_i = \beta_0 + \beta_1 D1_i + \beta_2 D2_i + \beta_3 G_i + u_i \tag{19.9}$$

In its theoretical specification, this model states that the expected salary within each group is as given in Table 19.5.

The null hypothesis that occupation has no effect on salary is H_0: $\beta_1 = \beta_2 = 0$, and this is tested by using a regression F test. The unconstrained model is simply (19.9), and the constrained model is

$$Y_i = \beta_0 + \beta_3 G_i + u_i \tag{19.10}$$

The null hypothesis that there is no difference by gender is H_0: $\beta_3 = 0$. This also can be tested with an F test in regression, but the same result is achieved simply by using the basic significance test (a t test) on β_3 in (19.9).

The analysis of variance treatment of the same questions is based on equivalent assumptions and leads to identical F tests. In the special case when the two factors are independent, as occurs in some experimental designs, there can be a decomposition of the total sum of squares into two explained sums of squares (one for each factor) and an unexplained sum of squares. The F tests are then based on the appropriate variance ratios. However, when the factors are not

TABLE 19.5 $E[Y]$ for a Regression Model

	Men	Women
Manager	$\beta_0 + \beta_1 + \beta_3$	$\beta_0 + \beta_1$
White-collar	$\beta_0 + \beta_2 + \beta_3$	$\beta_0 + \beta_2$
Blue-collar	$\beta_0 + \beta_3$	β_0

independent, this decomposition is not so simple and the tests are more easily handled through regression.

Problems _____

Section 19.1

★ **19.1** In the example leading to Table 19.1, suppose that there are 600 workers in the firm instead of 200 and that the actual proportionate breakdown by occupation is the same as in the example. Test to see whether the data contradict the organizational theory.

19.2 Using the 120 observations on men in Table 19.2, test to see whether the theory leading to the test in Table 19.1 is supported.

19.3 Suppose that 60 rolls of a die result in 15 occurrences of an ace (one spot) and 9 occurrences of each of the other possible outcomes. Test whether this is a fair die.

★ **19.4** Suppose that 100 observations occur as follows: 10 less than -1, 45 between -1 and 0, 30 between 0 and 1, and 15 greater than 1. Use a test of goodness of fit to determine whether these observations might have been taken from a standard normal random variable.

19.5 The following table shows the racial and poverty status breakdown among 900 people. Is being poor related to race?

	Blacks	Whites
Poor	22	113
Not poor	78	687

★ **19.6** The following table shows the educational attainment and earnings status of 600 people. Is income related to education?

	Grade School	High School	College
Less than $10,000	70	90	40
$10,000–$20,000	20	160	70
More than $20,000	10	50	90

Section 19.2

19.7 Given the specification of a regression, the values of R^2 and SSR from its estimation, and the value of n, explain how an ANOVA table can be created from this information.

For the next four problems, consider the following three regressions, which are hypothetical estimates of equations (19.8)–(19.10) with $n = 100$:

$$\hat{Y}_i = 12.0 + 18.0D1_i + 3.0D2_i$$

$$R^2 = .350 \quad SSR = 920.0$$

$$\hat{Y}_i = 13.0 + 16.0D1_i + 4.0D2_i - 3.0G_i$$

$$R^2 = .370 \quad SSR = 891.7$$

$$\hat{Y}_i = 19.0 - 7.0G_i$$

$$R^2 = .250 \quad SSR = 1061.5$$

19.8   In a one-way ANOVA for salaries, are there significant differences by gender?

★ 19.9   In a one-way ANOVA for salaries, are there significant differences by occupation?

★ 19.10   In a two-way ANOVA for salaries, are there significant differences by gender?

19.11   In a two-way ANOVA for salaries, are there significant differences by occupation?

Statistical Tables

Use of Table A.1: The Standard Normal Distribution

This table provides probability information about a random variable Z that has a standard normal distribution (see Section 10.1). In the following figure $Z*$ is a specific value of Z, and the shaded area equals $\Pr(Z \geq Z*)$. This probability amount can be denoted by α, so that $\Pr(Z \geq Z*) = \alpha$.

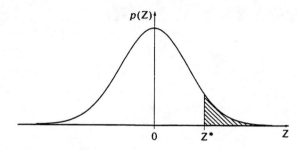

Each entry in the main body of the table gives $\Pr(Z \geq Z*)$ for the $Z*$ that is given by the sum of the values of the row and column labels for that entry. In other words, the entry is the α that corresponds to the $Z*$. The table is used to answer two types of probability problems.

The first type of problem has the form

$$\text{Find } \alpha \text{ such that } \Pr(Z \geq Z*) = \alpha$$

for a given $Z*$. The entry in the body of the table gives the probability α. For example, given $Z* = 1.53$, we look in the row labeled 1.50 and the column labeled .03; the table entry is .063. That is, $\Pr(Z \geq 1.53) = .063$.

The second type of problem has the form

$$\text{Find } Z^c \text{ such that } \Pr(Z \geq Z^c) = \alpha$$

for a given probability amount α. The table is used to determine the critical value of Z (denoted generally by Z^c, but corresponding to $Z*$ in the notation of this table) that bounds exactly α probability in the right-hand tail. For example, given that $\Pr(Z \geq Z^c) = .25$, we find two table entries .251 and .248 that bracket this probability ($\alpha = .250$). Looking at the row and column headings, we see that Z^c must lie between 0.67 and 0.68. For most purposes we can use the $Z*$ that corresponds to the closest table entry, so that we would say $Z^c = 0.67$. Interpolation can be used if greater precision is desired.

The lower section of the table gives a short reference list of several probabilities that are of special interest for statistical inference.

TABLE A.1   Standard Normal Distribution

	.00	.01	.02	.03	.04	.05	.06	.07	.08	.09
.00	.500	.496	.492	.488	.484	.480	.476	.472	.468	.464
.10	.460	.456	.452	.448	.444	.440	.436	.433	.429	.425
.20	.421	.417	.413	.409	.405	.401	.397	.394	.390	.386
.30	.382	.378	.374	.371	.367	.363	.359	.356	.352	.348
.40	.345	.341	.337	.334	.330	.326	.323	.319	.316	.312
.50	.309	.305	.302	.298	.295	.291	.288	.284	.281	.278
.60	.274	.271	.268	.264	.261	.258	.255	.251	.248	.245
.70	.242	.239	.236	.233	.230	.227	.224	.221	.218	.215
.80	.212	.209	.206	.203	.200	.198	.195	.192	.189	.187
.90	.184	.181	.179	.176	.174	.171	.169	.166	.164	.161
1.00	.159	.156	.154	.152	.149	.147	.145	.142	.140	.138
1.10	.136	.133	.131	.129	.127	.125	.123	.121	.119	.117
1.20	.115	.113	.111	.109	.107	.106	.104	.102	.100	.099
1.30	.097	.095	.093	.092	.090	.089	.087	.085	.084	.082
1.40	.081	.079	.078	.076	.075	.074	.072	.071	.069	.068
1.50	.067	.066	.064	.063	.062	.061	.059	.058	.057	.056
1.60	.055	.054	.053	.052	.051	.049	.048	.047	.046	.046
1.70	.045	.044	.043	.042	.041	.040	.039	.038	.038	.037
1.80	.036	.035	.034	.034	.033	.032	.031	.031	.030	.029
1.90	.029	.028	.027	.027	.026	.026	.025	.024	.024	.023
2.00	.023	.022	.022	.021	.021	.020	.020	.019	.019	.018
2.10	.018	.017	.017	.017	.016	.016	.015	.015	.015	.014
2.20	.014	.014	.013	.013	.013	.012	.012	.012	.011	.011
2.30	.011	.010	.010	.010	.010	.009	.009	.009	.009	.008
2.40	.008	.008	.008	.008	.007	.007	.007	.007	.007	.006
2.50	.006	.006	.006	.006	.006	.005	.005	.005	.005	.005
2.60	.005	.005	.004	.004	.004	.004	.004	.004	.004	.004
2.70	.003	.003	.003	.003	.003	.003	.003	.003	.003	.003
2.80	.003	.002	.002	.002	.002	.002	.002	.002	.002	.002
2.90	.002	.002	.002	.002	.002	.002	.002	.001	.001	.001
3.00	.001	.001	.001	.001	.001	.001	.001	.001	.001	.001

$\Pr(Z \geq 1.282) = .10$
$\Pr(Z \geq 1.645) = .05$
$\Pr(Z \geq 1.960) = .025$
$\Pr(Z \geq 2.326) = .01$
$\Pr(Z \geq 2.576) = .005$

Note: Table entry gives $\Pr(Z \geq Z^*)$, where Z^* is the sum of the values of the row and column labels.
Source: Computed using Fortran subroutines from the IMSL Library.

Use of Table A.2: The t Distribution

This table gives selected right-hand tail probabilities for a random variable that has a t distribution with df degrees of freedom (see Section 10.2). In the following figure, t^* is a specific value of the random variable t, and $Pr(t \geq t^*)$ is given by the shaded area. This probability amount can be denoted by α, so that $Pr(t \geq t^*) = \alpha$.

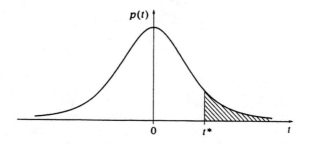

In the table, each row presents probability information for a particular member of the t family (with df indicated in the row label). Various t^* values are given in the column headings. Each entry in the table is the answer to a problem of the form

$$\text{Find } \alpha \text{ such that } Pr(t \geq t^*) = \alpha$$

for a given t^*. In hypothesis testing, this probability is known as the P-value.

For example, if df $= 15$, we find that $Pr(t \geq 1.50) = .077$ and that $Pr(t \geq 2.50) = .012$.

TABLE A.2 *P*-Values for the *t* Distribution

	$t^* = 0.50$	1.00	1.25	1.50	1.75	2.00	2.25	2.50	3.00
df = 1	.352	.250	.215	.187	.165	.148	.133	.121	.102
2	.333	.211	.169	.136	.111	.092	.077	.065	.048
3	.326	.196	.150	.115	.089	.070	.055	.044	.029
4	.322	.187	.140	.104	.078	.058	.044	.033	.020
5	.319	.182	.133	.097	.070	.051	.037	.027	.015
6	.317	.178	.129	.092	.065	.046	.033	.023	.012
7	.316	.175	.126	.089	.062	.043	.030	.020	.010
8	.315	.173	.123	.086	.059	.040	.027	.018	.009
9	.315	.172	.121	.084	.057	.038	.026	.017	.007
10	.314	.170	.120	.082	.055	.037	.024	.016	.007
11	.313	.169	.119	.081	.054	.035	.023	.015	.006
12	.313	.169	.118	.080	.053	.034	.022	.014	.006
13	.313	.168	.117	.079	.052	.033	.021	.013	.005
14	.312	.167	.116	.078	.051	.033	.021	.013	.005
15	.312	.167	.115	.077	.050	.032	.020	.012	.004
16	.312	.166	.115	.077	.050	.031	.019	.012	.004
17	.312	.166	.114	.076	.049	.031	.019	.011	.004
18	.312	.165	.114	.075	.049	.030	.019	.011	.004
19	.311	.165	.113	.075	.048	.030	.018	.011	.004
20	.311	.165	.113	.075	.048	.030	.018	.011	.004
21	.311	.164	.113	.074	.047	.029	.018	.010	.003
22	.311	.164	.112	.074	.047	.029	.017	.010	.003
23	.311	.164	.112	.074	.047	.029	.017	.010	.003
24	.311	.164	.112	.073	.046	.028	.017	.010	.003
25	.311	.163	.111	.073	.046	.028	.017	.010	.003
26	.311	.163	.111	.073	.046	.028	.017	.010	.003
27	.311	.163	.111	.073	.046	.028	.016	.009	.003
28	.310	.163	.111	.072	.046	.028	.016	.009	.003
29	.310	.163	.111	.072	.045	.027	.016	-.009	.003
30	.310	.163	.110	.072	.045	.027	.016	.009	.003
40	.310	.162	.109	.071	.044	.026	.015	.008	.002
50	.310	.161	.109	.070	.043	.025	.014	.008	.002
60	.309	.161	.108	.069	.043	.025	.014	.008	.002
70	.309	.160	.108	.069	.042	.025	.014	.007	.002
80	.309	.160	.107	.069	.042	.024	.014	.007	.002
90	.309	.160	.107	.069	.042	.024	.013	.007	.002
100	.309	.160	.107	.068	.042	.024	.013	.007	.002
125	.309	.160	.107	.068	.041	.024	.013	.007	.002
150	.309	.159	.107	.068	.041	.024	.013	.007	.002
200	.309	.159	.106	.068	.041	.023	.013	.007	.002
∞	.309	.159	.106	.067	.040	.023	.012	.006	.001

Note: Table entry gives $\Pr(t \geq t^*)$ for t^* in column heading.
Source: Computed using Fortran subroutines from the IMSL Library.

Use of Table A.3: The t Distribution

This table gives critical values for a random variable that has a t distribution with df degrees of freedom (see Section 10.2). The table is arranged to answer two types of problems. The first problem is of the form

$$\text{Find } t^c \text{ such that } \Pr(t \geq t^c) = \alpha$$

Various one-tailed α values are given in the column headings, and the corresponding critical values t^c are found in the row for the particular number of degrees of freedom. In the following figure, the shaded area corresponds to the given α, and t^c is the t value that bounds α probability in the right-hand tail of the distribution.

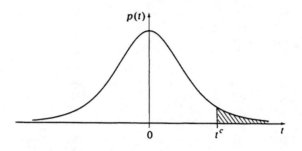

The second problem is of the form

$$\text{Find } t^c \text{ such that } \Pr\left(|t| \geq t^c\right) = \alpha$$

The probability amount α is split between the two tails of the distribution, each containing $\alpha/2$. Various two-tailed α values are given in the column headings, and the corresponding positive critical value t^c is given in the appropriate row (the other critical value is $-t^c$). In the following figure the two shaded areas together correspond to the given α, and t^c is the t value that bounds $\alpha/2$ probability in the right-hand tail.

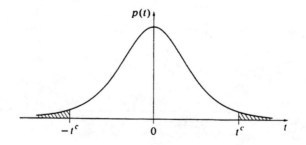

For example, if df = 15 and $\alpha = .05$, $t^c = 1.753$ for a one-tailed test, and $t^c = 2.131$ for a two-tailed test. Note that t^c for a one-tailed test with $\alpha = .05$ is the same as t^c for a two-tailed test with $\alpha = .10$.

TABLE A.3   Critical Values for the *t* Distribution

One-tailed α = .10	.05	.025	.01	.005
Two-tailed α = .20	.10	.05	.02	.01
df = 1 3.078	6.314	12.706	31.821	63.657
2 1.886	2.920	4.303	6.965	9.925
3 1.638	2.353	3.182	4.541	5.841
4 1.533	2.132	2.776	3.747	4.604
5 1.476	2.015	2.571	3.365	4.032
6 1.440	1.943	2.447	3.143	3.707
7 1.415	1.895	2.365	2.998	3.499
8 1.397	1.860	2.306	2.896	3.355
9 1.383	1.833	2.262	2.821	3.250
10 1.372	1.812	2.228	2.764	3.169
11 1.363	1.796	2.201	2.718	3.106
12 1.356	1.782	2.179	2.681	3.055
13 1.350	1.771	2.160	2.650	3.012
14 1.345	1.761	2.145	2.624	2.977
15 1.341	1.753	2.131	2.602	2.947
16 1.337	1.746	2.120	2.583	2.921
17 1.333	1.740	2.110	2.567	2.898
18 1.330	1.734	2.101	2.552	2.878
19 1.328	1.729	2.093	2.539	2.861
20 1.325	1.725	2.086	2.528	2.845
21 1.323	1.721	2.080	2.518	2.831
22 1.321	1.717	2.074	2.508	2.819
23 1.319	1.714	2.069	2.500	2.807
24 1.318	1.711	2.064	2.492	2.797
25 1.316	1.708	2.060	2.485	2.787
26 1.315	1.706	2.056	2.479	2.779
27 1.314	1.703	2.052	2.473	2.771
28 1.313	1.701	2.048	2.467	2.763
29 1.311	1.699	2.045	2.462	2.756
30 1.310	1.697	2.042	2.457	2.750
40 1.303	1.684	2.021	2.423	2.704
50 1.299	1.676	2.009	2.403	2.678
60 1.296	1.671	2.000	2.390	2.660
70 1.294	1.667	1.994	2.381	2.648
80 1.292	1.664	1.990	2.374	2.639
90 1.291	1.662	1.987	2.368	2.632
100 1.290	1.660	1.984	2.364	2.626
125 1.288	1.657	1.979	2.357	2.616
150 1.287	1.655	1.976	2.351	2.609
200 1.286	1.653	1.972	2.345	2.601
∞ 1.282	1.645	1.960	2.326	2.576

Note: Table entry gives t^c corresponding to $\Pr(t \geq t^c) = \alpha$ for one-tailed tests and $\Pr(|t| \geq t^c) = \alpha$ for two-tailed tests.

Source: Computed using Fortran subroutines from the IMSL Library.

Use of Table A.4: The Chi-Square Distribution

This table gives critical values for a random variable that has a chi-square distribution with df degrees of freedom (see the appendix to Chapter 10). Each entry in the table is the answer to a problem of the form

$$\text{Find } (\chi^2)^c \text{ such that } \Pr(\chi^2 \geq (\chi^2)^c) = \alpha$$

Various values of α are given in the column headings, and the corresponding $(\chi^2)^c$ is found in the row labeled by df. Critical values for areas in the left side of the distribution can be found by subtraction.

For example, if df $= 35$, $(\chi^2)^c = 53.22$ for $\alpha = .025$ and $(\chi^2)^c = 20.56$ for $\alpha = .975$. Thus $(\chi^2)^c = 53.22$ bounds .025 probability in the right-hand tail and $(\chi^2)^c = 20.56$ bounds .025 probability in the left side.

Use of Tables A.5 and A.6: The F Distribution

These tables give critical values for a random variable that has an F distribution with n degrees of freedom in the numerator and d degrees of freedom in the denominator (see the appendix to Chapter 10). Each entry in the tables is the answer to a problem of the form

$$\text{Find } F^c \text{ such that } \Pr(F_{n,d} \geq F^c) = \alpha$$

Table A.5 contains the F^c values for the .05 level of significance, and Table A.6 contains the F^c values for $\alpha = .01$. The entry for a particular distribution is in the column headed by n and the row labeled by d.

For example, if $n = 4$ and $d = 50$, $F^c = 2.56$ for $\alpha = .05$ and $F^c = 3.72$ for $\alpha = .01$.

Use of Tables A.7 and A.8: The Durbin-Watson Statistic

These tables give the critical values (significance points) of the lower and upper bounds, d_l and d_u, for the Durbin–Watson statistic (see Section 15.2). These bounds depend on the number of observations (n) and the number of regressors (k). Both tables are appropriate for use at the .05 level of significance: Table A.7 is for one-tailed tests, and Table A.8 is for two-tailed tests. (Table A.7 is also for two-tailed tests with $\alpha = .10$, and Table A.8 is also for one-tailed tests with $\alpha = .025$.)

For example, suppose that $n = 25$, $k = 3$, and $\alpha = .05$. For a one-tailed test, $d_l = 1.12$ and $d_u = 1.66$; if d^* falls between these values, the result of the test is indeterminate. For a two-tailed test, $d_l = 1.02$ and $d_u = 1.54$; on the right side of the distribution (see Figure 15.6) the range of indeterminacy extends from 2.46 to 2.98.

TABLE A.4 Critical Values for the Chi-Square Distribution

	α = .990	.975	.950	.900	.100	.050	.025	.010
df = 1	—	—	—	0.02	2.71	3.84	5.02	6.64
2	0.02	0.05	0.10	0.21	4.60	5.99	7.38	9.22
3	0.11	0.22	0.35	0.58	6.25	7.82	9.36	11.32
4	0.30	0.48	0.71	1.06	7.78	9.49	11.15	13.28
5	0.55	0.83	1.15	1.61	9.24	11.07	12.84	15.09
6	0.87	1.24	1.63	2.20	10.65	12.60	14.46	16.81
7	1.24	1.69	2.17	2.83	12.02	14.07	16.02	18.47
8	1.64	2.18	2.73	3.49	13.36	15.51	17.55	20.08
9	2.09	2.70	3.32	4.17	14.69	16.93	19.03	21.65
10	2.55	3.24	3.94	4.86	15.99	18.31	20.50	23.19
11	3.05	3.81	4.57	5.58	17.28	19.68	21.93	24.75
12	3.57	4.40	5.22	6.30	18.55	21.03	23.35	26.25
13	4.10	5.01	5.89	7.04	19.81	22.37	24.75	27.72
14	4.65	5.62	6.57	7.79	21.07	23.69	26.13	29.17
15	5.23	6.26	7.26	8.55	22.31	25.00	27.50	30.61
16	5.81	6.90	7.96	9.31	23.55	26.30	28.86	32.03
17	6.40	7.56	8.67	10.08	24.77	27.59	30.20	33.44
18	7.00	8.23	9.39	10.86	25.99	28.88	31.54	34.83
19	7.63	8.90	10.11	11.65	27.21	30.15	32.87	36.22
20	8.25	9.59	10.85	12.44	28.42	31.42	34.18	37.59
21	8.89	10.28	11.59	13.24	29.62	32.68	35.49	38.96
22	9.53	10.98	12.34	14.04	30.82	33.93	36.79	40.31
23	10.19	11.69	13.09	14.85	32.01	35.18	38.09	41.66
24	10.85	12.40	13.84	15.66	33.20	36.42	39.38	43.00
25	11.51	13.11	14.61	16.47	34.38	37.66	40.66	44.34
26	12.19	13.84	15.38	17.29	35.57	38.89	41.94	45.66
27	12.87	14.57	16.15	18.11	36.74	40.12	43.21	46.99
28	13.55	15.30	16.92	18.94	37.92	41.34	44.47	48.30
29	14.24	16.04	17.70	19.77	39.09	42.56	45.74	49.61
30	14.94	16.78	18.49	20.60	40.26	43.78	46.99	50.91
35	18.49	20.56	22.46	24.79	46.06	49.81	53.22	57.36
40	22.14	24.42	26.51	29.06	51.80	55.75	59.34	63.71
45	25.88	28.36	30.61	33.36	57.50	61.65	65.41	69.98
50	29.68	32.35	34.76	37.69	63.16	67.50	71.42	76.17
55	33.55	36.39	38.96	42.06	68.79	73.31	77.38	82.31
60	37.46	40.47	43.19	46.46	74.39	79.08	83.30	88.40
65	41.42	44.60	47.45	50.89	79.97	84.82	89.18	94.44
70	45.42	48.75	51.74	55.33	85.52	90.53	95.03	100.44
75	49.46	52.94	56.05	59.80	91.06	96.21	100.84	106.41
80	53.52	57.15	60.39	64.28	96.57	101.88	106.63	112.34
85	57.62	61.38	64.75	68.78	102.07	107.52	112.40	118.25
90	61.74	65.64	69.13	73.29	107.56	113.14	118.14	124.13
95	65.88	69.92	73.52	77.82	113.03	118.75	123.86	129.99
100	70.05	74.22	77.93	82.36	118.49	124.34	129.56	135.82

Note: Table entry gives $(\chi^2)^c$ corresponding to $\Pr(\chi^2 \geq (\chi^2)^c) = \alpha$.
Source: Computed using Fortran subroutines from the IMSL Library. Some values differ slightly from those in other published tables.

TABLE A.5 Critical Values for the F Distribution ($\alpha = .05$)

	$n = 1$	2	3	4	5	6	8	10	15
$d = 1$	161.4	199.5	215.7	224.6	230.2	234.0	238.9	241.9	245.9
2	18.51	19.00	19.16	19.25	19.30	19.33	19.37	19.40	19.43
3	10.13	9.55	9.28	9.12	9.01	8.94	8.85	8.79	8.70
4	7.71	6.94	6.59	6.39	6.26	6.16	6.04	5.96	5.86
5	6.61	5.79	5.41	5.19	5.05	4.95	4.82	4.74	4.62
6	5.99	5.14	4.76	4.53	4.39	4.28	4.15	4.06	3.94
7	5.59	4.74	4.35	4.12	3.97	3.87	3.73	3.64	3.51
8	5.32	4.46	4.07	3.84	3.69	3.58	3.44	3.35	3.22
9	5.12	4.26	3.86	3.63	3.48	3.37	3.23	3.14	3.01
10	4.96	4.10	3.71	3.48	3.33	3.22	3.07	2.98	2.85
11	4.84	3.98	3.59	3.36	3.20	3.09	2.95	2.85	2.72
12	4.75	3.89	3.49	3.26	3.11	3.00	2.85	2.75	2.62
13	4.67	3.81	3.41	3.18	3.03	2.92	2.77	2.67	2.53
14	4.60	3.74	3.34	3.11	2.96	2.85	2.70	2.60	2.46
15	4.54	3.68	3.29	3.06	2.90	2.79	2.64	2.54	2.40
16	4.49	3.63	3.24	3.01	2.85	2.74	2.59	2.49	2.35
17	4.45	3.59	3.20	2.96	2.81	2.70	2.55	2.45	2.31
18	4.41	3.55	3.16	2.93	2.77	2.66	2.51	2.41	2.27
19	4.38	3.52	3.13	2.90	2.74	2.63	2.48	2.38	2.23
20	4.35	3.49	3.10	2.87	2.71	2.60	2.45	2.35	2.20
21	4.32	3.47	3.07	2.84	2.68	2.57	2.42	2.32	2.18
22	4.30	3.44	3.05	2.82	2.66	2.55	2.40	2.30	2.15
23	4.28	3.42	3.03	2.80	2.64	2.53	2.37	2.27	2.13
24	4.26	3.40	3.01	2.78	2.62	2.51	2.36	2.25	2.11
25	4.24	3.39	2.99	2.76	2.60	2.49	2.34	2.24	2.09
26	4.23	3.37	2.98	2.74	2.59	2.47	2.32	2.22	2.07
27	4.21	3.35	2.96	2.73	2.57	2.46	2.31	2.20	2.06
28	4.20	3.34	2.95	2.71	2.56	2.45	2.29	2.19	2.04
29	4.18	3.33	2.93	2.70	2.55	2.43	2.28	2.18	2.03
30	4.17	3.32	2.92	2.69	2.53	2.42	2.27	2.16	2.01
40	4.08	3.23	2.84	2.61	2.45	2.34	2.18	2.08	1.92
50	4.03	3.18	2.79	2.56	2.40	2.29	2.13	2.03	1.87
60	4.00	3.15	2.76	2.53	2.37	2.25	2.10	1.99	1.84
70	3.98	3.13	2.74	2.50	2.35	2.23	2.07	1.97	1.81
80	3.96	3.11	2.72	2.49	2.33	2.21	2.06	1.95	1.79
90	3.95	3.10	2.71	2.47	2.32	2.20	2.04	1.94	1.78
100	3.94	3.09	2.70	2.46	2.31	2.19	2.03	1.93	1.77
125	3.92	3.07	2.68	2.44	2.29	2.17	2.01	1.91	1.75
150	3.90	3.06	2.66	2.43	2.27	2.16	2.00	1.89	1.73
200	3.89	3.04	2.65	2.42	2.26	2.14	1.98	1.88	1.72
∞	3.84	3.00	2.60	2.37	2.21	2.10	1.94	1.83	1.67

Note: Table entry gives F^c corresponding to $\Pr(F_{n,d} \geq F^c) = .05$.
Source: Computed using Fortran subroutines from the IMSL Library.

TABLE A.6   Critical Values for the F Distribution ($\alpha = .01$)

	$n = 1$	2	3	4	5	6	8	10	15
$d = 1$	4052.	4999.	5403.	5625.	5764.	5859.	5981.	6056.	6157.
2	98.50	99.00	99.17	99.25	99.30	99.33	99.37	99.40	99.43
3	34.12	30.82	29.46	28.71	28.24	27.91	27.49	27.23	26.87
4	21.20	18.00	16.69	15.98	15.52	15.21	14.80	14.55	14.20
5	16.26	13.27	12.06	11.39	10.97	10.67	10.29	10.05	9.72
6	13.75	10.92	9.78	9.15	8.75	8.47	8.10	7.87	7.56
7	12.25	9.55	8.45	7.85	7.46	7.19	6.84	6.62	6.31
8	11.26	8.65	7.59	7.01	6.63	6.37	6.03	5.81	5.52
9	10.56	8.02	6.99	6.42	6.06	5.80	5.47	5.26	4.96
10	10.04	7.56	6.55	5.99	5.64	5.39	5.06	4.85	4.56
11	9.65	7.21	6.22	5.67	5.32	5.07	4.74	4.54	4.25
12	9.33	6.93	5.95	5.41	5.06	4.82	4.50	4.30	4.01
13	9.07	6.70	5.74	5.21	4.86	4.62	4.30	4.10	3.82
14	8.86	6.51	5.56	5.04	4.69	4.46	4.14	3.94	3.66
15	8.68	6.36	5.42	4.89	4.56	4.32	4.00	3.80	3.52
16	8.53	6.23	5.29	4.77	4.44	4.20	3.89	3.69	3.41
17	8.40	6.11	5.19	4.67	4.34	4.10	3.79	3.59	3.31
18	8.29	6.01	5.09	4.58	4.25	4.01	3.71	3.51	3.23
19	8.18	5.93	5.01	4.50	4.17	3.94	3.63	3.43	3.15
20	8.10	5.85	4.94	4.43	4.10	3.87	3.56	3.37	3.09
21	8.02	5.78	4.87	4.37	4.04	3.81	3.51	3.31	3.03
22	7.95	5.72	4.82	4.31	3.99	3.76	3.45	3.26	2.98
23	7.88	5.66	4.76	4.26	3.94	3.71	3.41	3.21	2.93
24	7.82	5.61	4.72	4.22	3.90	3.67	3.36	3.17	2.89
25	7.77	5.57	4.68	4.18	3.85	3.63	3.32	3.13	2.85
26	7.72	5.53	4.64	4.14	3.82	3.59	3.29	3.09	2.81
27	7.68	5.49	4.60	4.11	3.78	3.56	3.26	3.06	2.78
28	7.64	5.45	4.57	4.07	3.75	3.53	3.23	3.03	2.75
29	7.60	5.42	4.54	4.04	3.73	3.50	3.20	3.00	2.73
30	7.56	5.39	4.51	4.02	3.70	3.47	3.17	2.98	2.70
40	7.31	5.18	4.31	3.83	3.51	3.29	2.99	2.80	2.52
50	7.17	5.06	4.20	3.72	3.41	3.19	2.89	2.70	2.42
60	7.08	4.98	4.13	3.65	3.34	3.12	2.82	2.63	2.35
70	7.01	4.92	4.07	3.60	3.29	3.07	2.78	2.59	2.31
80	6.96	4.88	4.04	3.56	3.26	3.04	2.74	2.55	2.27
90	6.93	4.85	4.01	3.53	3.23	3.01	2.72	2.52	2.24
100	6.90	4.82	3.98	3.51	3.21	2.99	2.69	2.50	2.22
125	6.84	4.78	3.94	3.47	3.17	2.95	2.66	2.47	2.19
150	6.81	4.75	3.91	3.45	3.14	2.92	2.63	2.44	2.16
200	6.76	4.71	3.88	3.41	3.11	2.89	2.60	2.41	2.13
∞	6.63	4.61	3.78	3.32	3.02	2.80	2.51	2.32	2.04

Note: Table entry gives F^c corresponding to $\Pr(F_{n,d} \geq F^c) = .01$.
Source: Computed using Fortran subroutines from the IMSL Library.

TABLE A.7 Durbin–Watson Statistic—Significance Points for d_l and d_u (For One-Tailed Tests, $\alpha = .05$)

	k = 1		k = 2		k = 3		k = 4		k = 5	
n	d_l	d_u	d_l	d_u	d_l	d_u	d_l	d_u	d_l	d_u
15	1.08	1.36	0.95	1.54	0.82	1.75	0.69	1.97	0.56	2.21
16	1.10	1.37	0.98	1.54	0.86	1.73	0.74	1.93	0.62	2.15
17	1.13	1.38	1.02	1.54	0.90	1.71	0.78	1.90	0.67	2.10
18	1.16	1.39	1.05	1.53	0.93	1.69	0.82	1.87	0.71	2.06
19	1.18	1.40	1.08	1.53	0.97	1.68	0.86	1.85	0.75	2.02
20	1.20	1.41	1.10	1.54	1.00	1.68	0.90	1.83	0.79	1.99
21	1.22	1.42	1.13	1.54	1.03	1.67	0.93	1.81	0.83	1.96
22	1.24	1.43	1.15	1.54	1.05	1.66	0.96	1.80	0.86	1.94
23	1.26	1.44	1.17	1.54	1.08	1.66	0.99	1.79	0.90	1.92
24	1.27	1.45	1.19	1.55	1.10	1.66	1.01	1.78	0.93	1.90
25	1.29	1.45	1.21	1.55	1.12	1.66	1.04	1.77	0.95	1.89
26	1.30	1.46	1.22	1.55	1.14	1.65	1.06	1.76	0.98	1.88
27	1.32	1.47	1.24	1.56	1.16	1.65	1.08	1.76	1.01	1.86
28	1.33	1.48	1.26	1.56	1.18	1.65	1.10	1.75	1.03	1.85
29	1.34	1.48	1.27	1.56	1.20	1.65	1.12	1.74	1.05	1.84
30	1.35	1.49	1.28	1.57	1.21	1.65	1.14	1.74	1.07	1.83
31	1.36	1.50	1.30	1.57	1.23	1.65	1.16	1.74	1.09	1.83
32	1.37	1.50	1.31	1.57	1.24	1.65	1.18	1.73	1.11	1.82
33	1.38	1.51	1.32	1.58	1.26	1.65	1.19	1.73	1.13	1.81
34	1.39	1.51	1.33	1.58	1.27	1.65	1.21	1.73	1.15	1.81
35	1.40	1.52	1.34	1.58	1.28	1.65	1.22	1.73	1.16	1.80
36	1.41	1.52	1.35	1.59	1.29	1.65	1.24	1.73	1.18	1.80
37	1.42	1.53	1.36	1.59	1.31	1.66	1.25	1.72	1.19	1.80
38	1.43	1.54	1.37	1.59	1.32	1.66	1.26	1.72	1.21	1.79
39	1.43	1.54	1.38	1.60	1.33	1.66	1.27	1.72	1.22	1.79
40	1.44	1.54	1.39	1.60	1.34	1.66	1.29	1.72	1.23	1.79
45	1.48	1.57	1.43	1.62	1.38	1.67	1.34	1.72	1.29	1.78
50	1.50	1.59	1.46	1.63	1.42	1.67	1.38	1.72	1.34	1.77
55	1.53	1.60	1.49	1.64	1.45	1.68	1.41	1.72	1.38	1.77
60	1.55	1.62	1.51	1.65	1.48	1.69	1.44	1.73	1.41	1.77
65	1.57	1.63	1.54	1.66	1.50	1.70	1.47	1.73	1.44	1.77
70	1.58	1.64	1.55	1.67	1.52	1.70	1.49	1.74	1.46	1.77
75	1.60	1.65	1.57	1.68	1.54	1.71	1.51	1.74	1.49	1.77
80	1.61	1.66	1.59	1.69	1.56	1.72	1.53	1.74	1.51	1.77
85	1.62	1.67	1.60	1.70	1.57	1.72	1.55	1.75	1.52	1.77
90	1.63	1.68	1.61	1.70	1.59	1.73	1.57	1.75	1.54	1.78
95	1.64	1.69	1.62	1.71	1.60	1.73	1.58	1.75	1.56	1.78
100	1.65	1.69	1.63	1.72	1.61	1.74	1.59	1.76	1.57	1.78

Note: n = number of observations, k = number of regressors.
Source: J. Durbin and G. S. Watson, "Testing for Serial Correlation in Least Squares Regression. II," *Biometrika* 38 (1951), p. 173. Reprinted with permission of the Biometrika Trustees.

TABLE A.8 Durbin–Watson Statistic—Significance Points for d_l and d_u (For Two-Tailed Tests, $\alpha = .05$)

n	k = 1 d_l	k = 1 d_u	k = 2 d_l	k = 2 d_u	k = 3 d_l	k = 3 d_u	k = 4 d_l	k = 4 d_u	k = 5 d_l	k = 5 d_u
15	0.95	1.23	0.83	1.40	0.71	1.61	0.59	1.84	0.48	2.09
16	0.98	1.24	0.86	1.40	0.75	1.59	0.64	1.80	0.53	2.03
17	1.01	1.25	0.90	1.40	0.79	1.58	0.68	1.77	0.57	1.98
18	1.03	1.26	0.93	1.40	0.82	1.56	0.72	1.74	0.62	1.93
19	1.06	1.28	0.96	1.41	0.86	1.55	0.76	1.72	0.66	1.90
20	1.08	1.28	0.99	1.41	0.89	1.55	0.79	1.70	0.70	1.87
21	1.10	1.30	1.01	1.41	0.92	1.54	0.83	1.69	0.73	1.84
22	1.12	1.31	1.04	1.42	0.95	1.54	0.86	1.68	0.77	1.82
23	1.14	1.32	1.06	1.42	0.97	1.54	0.89	1.67	0.80	1.80
24	1.16	1.33	1.08	1.43	1.00	1.54	0.91	1.66	0.83	1.79
25	1.18	1.34	1.10	1.43	1.02	1.54	0.94	1.65	0.86	1.77
26	1.19	1.35	1.12	1.44	1.04	1.54	0.96	1.65	0.88	1.76
27	1.21	1.36	1.13	1.44	1.06	1.54	0.99	1.64	0.91	1.75
28	1.22	1.37	1.15	1.45	1.08	1.54	1.01	1.64	0.93	1.74
29	1.24	1.38	1.17	1.45	1.10	1.54	1.03	1.63	0.96	1.73
30	1.25	1.38	1.18	1.46	1.12	1.54	1.05	1.63	0.98	1.73
31	1.26	1.39	1.20	1.47	1.13	1.55	1.07	1.63	1.00	1.72
32	1.27	1.40	1.21	1.47	1.15	1.55	1.08	1.63	1.02	1.71
33	1.28	1.41	1.22	1.48	1.16	1.55	1.10	1.63	1.04	1.71
34	1.29	1.41	1.24	1.48	1.17	1.55	1.12	1.63	1.06	1.70
35	1.30	1.42	1.25	1.48	1.19	1.55	1.13	1.63	1.07	1.70
36	1.31	1.43	1.26	1.49	1.20	1.56	1.15	1.63	1.09	1.70
37	1.32	1.43	1.27	1.49	1.21	1.56	1.16	1.62	1.10	1.70
38	1.33	1.44	1.28	1.50	1.23	1.56	1.17	1.62	1.12	1.70
39	1.34	1.44	1.29	1.50	1.24	1.56	1.19	1.63	1.13	1.69
40	1.35	1.45	1.30	1.51	1.25	1.57	1.20	1.63	-1.15	1.69
45	1.39	1.48	1.34	1.53	1.30	1.58	1.25	1.63	1.21	1.69
50	1.42	1.50	1.38	1.54	1.34	1.59	1.30	1.64	1.26	1.69
55	1.45	1.52	1.41	1.56	1.37	1.60	1.33	1.64	1.30	1.69
60	1.47	1.54	1.44	1.57	1.40	1.61	1.37	1.65	1.33	1.69
65	1.49	1.55	1.46	1.59	1.43	1.62	1.40	1.66	1.36	1.69
70	1.51	1.57	1.48	1.60	1.45	1.63	1.42	1.66	1.39	1.70
75	1.53	1.58	1.50	1.61	1.47	1.64	1.45	1.67	1.42	1.70
80	1.54	1.59	1.52	1.62	1.49	1.65	1.47	1.67	1.44	1.70
85	1.56	1.60	1.53	1.63	1.51	1.65	1.49	1.68	1.46	1.71
90	1.57	1.61	1.55	1.64	1.53	1.66	1.50	1.69	1.48	1.71
95	1.58	1.62	1.56	1.65	1.54	1.67	1.52	1.69	1.50	1.71
100	1.59	1.63	1.57	1.65	1.55	1.67	1.53	1.70	1.51	1.72

Note: n = number of observations, k = number of regressors.
Source: J. Durbin and G. S. Watson, "Testing for Serial Correlation in Least Squares Regression. II," *Biometrika* 38 (1951), p. 174. Reprinted with permission of the Biometrika Trustees.

Answers to Selected Problems

Chapter 1: Introduction

1.2 $\hat{C} = 0.568 + (0.907)(1000) = 907.568$.

1.5 $Q = \beta_0 + \beta_1 P + u$. This is formally similar to the demand model. In contrast to the demand model, however, we expect that $\beta_1 > 0$; the sign of β_0 is not clear.

1.7 No. The monthly survey and estimation of the unemployment rate are primarily based on general statistical techniques.

1.11 Moving from A to B, $\Delta y = 5.0 - 2.5 = 2.5$ and $\Delta x = 8 - 3 = 5$; thus the slope $= \Delta y / \Delta x = 0.5$.

1.12 Since the slope $= 0.5$, $\Delta y = 0.5 \, \Delta x$. If $\Delta x = 4$, $\Delta y = 2$; if $\Delta x = -1$, $\Delta y = -0.5$.

1.14 When $x = 2$, $y = 4$; at this point the slope equals $(2)(2) = 4$ and the elasticity equals $4/(4/2) = 2$. When $x = 4$, $y = 16$; the slope equals $(2)(4) = 8$ and the elasticity equals $8/(16/4) = 2$ again.

1.16 Using initial values of y and x as bases, the arc elasticity equals $(\Delta y/y)/(\Delta x/x) = (12/4)/(2/2) = 3$. Using average values as bases, the arc elasticity equals $(12/10)/(2/3) = 1.8$.

Chapter 2: Economic Data

2.2 The answer depends on the nature of the actual data. Most likely, the number of plants and the number of product lines are clearly discrete, and the number of employees and the amount of output can be considered practically continuous.

2.3 The objective in taking the sample is to make an estimate of the unemployment rate in the whole nation. If an unrepresentative sample is taken, such as from only a prosperous region or from only white-collar workers, the resulting estimate will be a distorted (or biased) estimate.

2.7 For this problem it is assumed that people correctly report their total wealth, but incorrectly report the savings account component. The failure to report any account leads to measured $S = 0$ for some individuals. The misreporting leads to measured S being greater than true S at low levels of W (hence low S), and oppositely for high W. The resulting pattern of data points has an apparent slope that is flatter than β_1, leading to an underestimate of it.

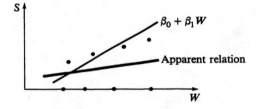

2.11 Predictions of future consumption are made along the line labeled "Continued process," which is an estimate of the behavior described in Equation (1.1). If the process changes, future values of consumption will lie around the line labeled "New process," and the model previously estimated gives distorted projections. Correct predictions would need to be based on knowledge of the new process.

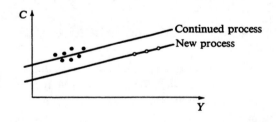

2.15 The calculations are based on a definition corresponding to Equation (2.4). For 1968, $CPI_{i-1} = 100$, and $RINF2_i$ is given in Table 2.3 as 4.200; hence $CPI_i = 104.20$. Similarly, for 1969, $CPI_i = 109.7997$, or about 109.80.

2.18 The four successive values of the absolute growth in X are $\Delta X = 5, 7, 9, 11$. The five values of $\ln X$ increase over time, but the successive differences are $\Delta \ln X = 0.41, 0.38, 0.34, 0.30$. Hence the absolute growth is increasing as time passes, but the rate of growth decreases as time passes.

2.20 When $r = -20$ percent, the graphs are

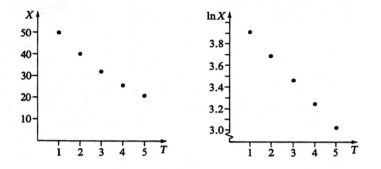

2.23 If a number is doubled, its logarithm is increased by adding $\ln 2$ ($= 0.693$). That is, if $y = 2x$, $\ln y = \ln 2 + \ln x$.

2.24 If $Q = AP^b$, $\ln Q = \ln A + b \ln P$.

2.28 If $\ln Y = a + Z \ln b$, $Y = e^a b^Z$.

2.29 Based on Equation (2.27), $\ln 42 = \ln 10 + 4 \ln(1 + r)$. Solving, this yields $\ln(1 + r) = 0.359$, so $r \approx 0.43$. [Note that $\ln(1 + r) \approx r$ is a poor approximation because r is so large.]

Chapter 3: Descriptive Statistics

3.1 The mean is 5.38; the median is 5.5.

3.4 No, the median cannot be determined this way.

3.8 With $\overline{X} = 5.38$ and $S_X = 0.914$, the one-standard-deviation interval runs from 4.466 to 6.294 and includes 60 percent of the observations. The two-standard-deviation interval runs from 3.552 to 7.208 and includes 100 percent of the observations.

3.11 Passing through the data once, we find $\sum X_i = 53.8$ and $\sum X_i^2 = 296.96$. Hence, $\sum d_i^2 = \sum X_i^2 - (1/n)(\sum X_i)^2 = 296.96 - (1/10)(53.8)^2 = 7.516$. These intermediate terms lead to a mean of 5.38, a variance of 0.835, and a standard deviation of 0.914. These are the same as in Problem 3.7, of course.

3.12 $\overline{Y} \approx 44$, $S_Y \approx 18$.

3.17 (a) $W_i = 24 + 12X_i$.
(b) $\overline{W} = 24 + 12\overline{X} = 240$; $S_W = 12S_X = 106.8$.

3.18 The standard deviation of income is increased by 20 percent, but the standard deviation of the logarithm of income is not affected.

3.21 Covariance $= -0.788$; correlation $= -.872$.

3.23 $S_{YZ} = bS_{YX}$.

Chapter 4: Frequency Distributions

4.3 The one-standard-deviation interval runs from 1.25 to 3.39 and contains 54 percent of the observations; the two-standard-deviation interval runs from 0.18 to 4.46 and contains 100 percent of the observations. (The uniform distribution assumption is not applied to discrete variables.)

4.6 Consider two low values of X with a given difference ΔX and two high values of X with the same ΔX between them. The transformation $Y_i = \ln X_i$ yields a set of four Y values such that the difference between the lower-valued pair is greater than that between the higher-valued pair (see Figure 2.4). If the original X has equal differences between all adjacent X values, the difference between adjacent Y values decreases as Y increases.

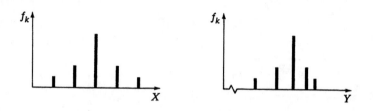

4.9 The frequency table is constructed like Table 4.2 with seven classes. The absolute frequencies are 3, 5, 30, 38, 14, 9, 1. The indicated class boundaries have a round number as the midpoint (3, 6, 9, etc.), and no observations can fall on a boundary.

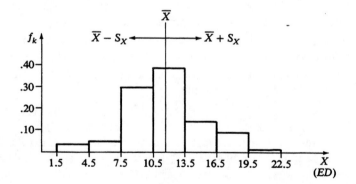

4.10 The mean is 11.58, and the standard deviation is 3.49. These statistics are not expected to be exactly equal to those calculated from the raw data on *ED* because in the computations we use the class marks instead of the actual values of *ED* for each observation. (In the raw data, the mean is 11.58 and the standard deviation is 3.44; hence, in this case the means computed from raw and grouped data are identical, but the standard deviations are slightly different.)

4.13 Inspection of the frequency table shows that the median lies in the fourth class. Its value is determined to be 11.45, based on the uniform distribution assumption. (Note that the lower boundary of the fourth class is 10.5.)

Chapter 5: Simple Regression: Theory

5.2 Yes. If all the disturbances are positive, all the actual Y_i values lie above the true regression line. This is an unlikely occurrence, however, except in very small samples.

5.6

5.11 The slope is flatter for observations 1–5 than for 26–30. Both slopes serve as estimates of the same β_1 value in the theoretical model. Since they are different, at least one of them must contain some error.

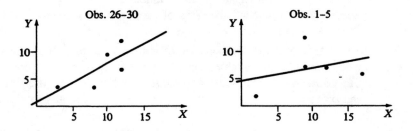

5.13 $R^2 = .507$, $SER = 2.992$.

5.18 $\hat{\gamma}_0^* = 763.9$ and $\hat{\gamma}_1^* = 701.8$. (Note that the new earnings variable is 1000 times greater than the original one.)

5.22 $\hat{Y}_i = 4.25 + 0.25X_i$ and $\hat{Y}_i = 1.343X_i$. In the second equation, $R^2 = -5.94$ when Equation (5.26) is applied.

5.25

$$\sum e_i^2 = \sum (Y_i - \hat{\beta}X_i)^2 \quad \text{see Equation (5.50)}$$

$$(d/d\hat{\beta})[\sum (Y_i - \hat{\beta}X_i)^2] = 0 \quad \text{see (5.52)}$$

$$-2 \sum (Y_i - \hat{\beta}X_i)X_i = 0 \quad \text{see (5.54)}$$

$$\sum Y_iX_i = \hat{\beta} \sum X_i^2 \quad \text{see (5.56)}$$

$$\hat{\beta} = \sum Y_iX_i / \sum X_i^2 \quad \text{see (5.59)}$$

Chapter 6: Simple Regression: Application

6.1   The disturbance equals -2.

6.5   The rest of the variation is accounted for by the residuals; we can say that this is due to the disturbances.

6.6   The 100 percent inflation means that all measured earnings in 1980 are twice as large as they would be in the 1963 data. Thus, an additional year of schooling increases predicted earnings by $(2)(0.797) = 1.594$ thousand dollars [see Equation (5.31)].

6.10 For 1974, $APC = CON/DPI = 763.6/858.4 = 0.890$. From Equation (6.14), for $T = 19$, predicted $APC = 0.907$. The error of fit is -0.017, which is somewhat larger (in absolute value) than SER.

6.12 Since $X = RM - RF$, we see that X remains the same. Thus, based on Equation (6.18), Y remains the same. Since $Y = RS - RF$, we see that RS increases by one percentage point.

6.14 DPI was 865.3 billion dollars in 1973 and 858.4 in 1974. Based on Equation (6.23), predicted CON for 1974 is $10.913 + (0.923)(865.3) = 809.6$ billion dollars. Based on Equation (6.10), predicted CON for 1974 is $0.568 + (0.907)(858.4) = 779.1$ billion dollars.

6.20 $Y = 8.60, 12.85, 15.29, 16.92$.

6.22 The increase in Y from 12.85 to 15.29 amounts to 18.99 percent. Since X increases by 100 percent, the ratio of proportionate changes is 0.1899. This is less than the point elasticity, 0.25.

6.24 If $Q = AP^b$, b is the elasticity of Q with respect to P (i.e., the price elasticity of demand). Such an elasticity is usually negative, corresponding to a downward-sloping demand curve as in Figure 6.3a. The elasticity b can be estimated by regressing $\ln Q$ on $\ln P$, as specified in Equation (6.35).

6.26 pc of $Y = \exp[(0.25)(0.693)] - 1 = \exp[0.1733] - 1 = 0.1892$, or 18.92 percent. This is identical to the change in Problem 6.22 (except for differences in computational rounding).

Chapter 7: Multiple Regression: Theory and Application

7.3   If income is fixed, the relation between predicted demand and price can be graphed as a straight line in a two-dimensional graph. For example, when $Y = Y_1$, predicted demand is a function only of price: this is a *ceteris paribus* relation. The vertical intercept depends on the regression constant, the amount of income, and its coefficient. When $Y = Y_2$ the intercept takes on a new value, and a new *ceteris paribus* relation between demand and price is established.

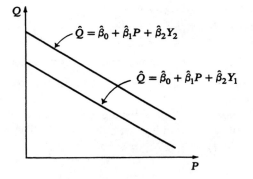

7.5 The first man has greater predicted earnings. Comparing the first with the second, $\Delta EARNS = 0.978\,\Delta ED + 0.124\,\Delta EXP = (0.978)(4) + (0.124)(-4) = 3.416$ thousand dollars.

7.12 For a black man with 16 years of schooling, predicted $EARNS$ is $-0.778 + 0.762(16) + 1.926(1) = 9.488$ thousand dollars. For a white man with 12 years of schooling, predicted $EARNS$ is $-0.778 + 0.762(12) = 8.366$ thousand dollars.

7.15 Let $M = 1$ if married, 0 if not; let $D = 1$ if divorced, 0 if not. The model is $EARNS_i = \beta_0 + \beta_1 ED_i + \beta_2 M_i + \beta_3 D_i + u_i$.

7.24 Let $Q =$ output, $L =$ labor input, and $K =$ capital input. The model is $\ln Q_i = \beta_0 + \beta_1 \ln L_i + \beta_2 \ln K_i + u_i$.

7.25 Extending the notation of Problem 7.24, let T be a time trend. The model is $\ln Q_i = \beta_0 + \beta_1 \ln L_i + \beta_2 \ln K_i + \beta_3 T_i + u_i$. As in a simple semilog specification, the coefficient on T equals $\ln(1 + g)$, where g is the rate of technical progress.

Chapter 8: Probability Theory

8.2 (a) Letting the first digit be the outcome on the first flip, and similarly for the second, the 16 outcomes are 11, 12, 13, 14, 21, 22, 23, 24, 31, 32, 33, 34, 41, 42, 43, 44.
(b) Since each is equally likely, $\Pr(e_i) = 1/16$.
(c) In a three-flip activity, there are $4^3 = 64$ outcomes.

8.6 (a) Since each is equally likely, $\Pr(e_i) = 1/10$.
(b) $\Pr(5) = 1/10$; $\Pr(6) = 2/10$; $\Pr(7) = 3/10$; $\Pr(8) = 4/10$.
(c) Letting A be "getting a number less than or equal to 7," $\Pr(A) = 6/10$.

8.7 (a) Yes.   (b) No.   (c) No.

8.8 (a) $E_1 = \{e_2, e_3, e_4, e_5, e_6, e_7\}$; $\Pr(E_1) = 6/8$.
(b) $E_2 = \{e_1, e_2, e_3, e_5, e_6, e_7\}$; $\Pr(E_2) = 6/8$.
(c) $E_3 = \{e_2, e_4, e_5, e_6, e_7, e_8\}$; $\Pr(E_3) = 6/8$.

8.10 (a) $\Pr(E_1) = 3/8 + 3/8 - 0 = 6/8$.
　　　(b) $\Pr(E_2) = 4/8 + 3/8 - 1/8 = 6/8$.
　　　(c) $\Pr(E_3) = 4/8 + 4/8 - 2/8 = 6/8$.

8.13 (a) 64 percent.　　(b) 32 percent.　　(c) 4 percent.

8.15 (a) The game ends with either 7 or 8. In this reduced sample space, $\Pr(8) = 5/11$.
　　　(b) The probability of establishing 8 as the point is 5/36, and then the probability of winning with 8 is 5/11. The total probability is $(5/36)(5/11) = 25/396$, or about 6.3 percent.

Chapter 9: Random Variables and Probability Distributions

9.3 No, because $\Sigma\, p(Y_k) = 21/20 \neq 1$.

9.5 $\mu_X = 7.0$, $\sigma_X = 1.0$.

9.6 $p(X) = 1/6$, $X = 1, 2, 3, 4, 5, 6$. $\mu_X = 3.5$, $\sigma_X = 1.71$.

9.11 No. If the sample size is not a multiple of 1000, then it is impossible for the relative frequency for $X = 2$ to be exactly .001. Also, even if n is a multiple of 1000, it is not necessary that $X = 2$ a specific number of times.

9.15 Since the number of offers has a binomial distribution, $E[X] = nP = 1$. Thus "getting fewer than the expected number" corresponds only to $X = 0$; $p(0) = 0.328$.

9.19 From Figure 9.6a it can be determined that $p(0.2) = .8$ and $p(0.8) = .2$. These density values give the relative likelihoods of these X values occurring. If we construct equal-width small intervals around each X value (such as 0.2 ± 0.001 and 0.8 ± 0.001), the probability of X occurring in the first interval (X about 0.2) will be four times the probability of X occurring in the second (X about 0.8) because the areas in the two thin rectangles will be in that ratio.

9.24 $\mu_Y = 2.5$, $\sigma_Y = 0.50$. The relations between these values and those from Problem 9.5 are in accord with Equations (9.24) and (9.26), of course.

9.26 In Problem 9.6 it was determined that $\mu_X = 3.5$ and $\sigma_X = 1.71$ for the toss of a single die. Let X_1 be the outcome of the first die and X_2 be the outcome of the second. Letting $W = X_1 + X_2$ and recognizing independence, we apply Equations (9.33) and (9.34) and find that $\mu_W = 7.0$ and $\sigma_W = 2.42$.

Chapter 10: The Normal and t Distributions

10.2 (a) $Z^c = 2.05$;　　(b) $Z^c = 1.28$;　　(c) $Z^c = 1.04$;
　　　(d) $Z^c = 2.326$;　　(e) $Z^c = 1.645$;　　(f) $Z^c = 1.44$.

10.5 (a) Since there is 20 percent probability in each tail, the corresponding $Z^c = 0.84$; thus the X values are 87.4 and 112.6.

  (b) For all normal distributions this probability is .382.

10.10 $\Pr(Z \geq 1.00) = .159$, as determined from Table A.1. In Table A.2, looking down the column for $t^* = 1.00$ we see that $\Pr(t \geq 1.00)$ decreases as df increases. Thus, as df increases the distribution becomes more compact about its mean (σ decreases). Also, we see that $\Pr(t \geq 1.00)$ approaches .159 as df increases, illustrating that the shape approaches the standard normal.

10.11 Using Table A.3,   (a) $t^c = 2.518$;   (b) $t^c = 1.721$;
  (c) $t^c = 1.323$;   (d) $t^c = 2.831$;   (e) $t^c = 2.080$;
  (f) $t^c = 1.721$.

10.16 For the chi-square family, the graph of the probability distribution (i.e., density function) shifts to the right as df increases.

10.17 Using Table A.5, we find that $F^c = 2.71$.

Chapter 11: Sampling Theory in Regression

11.2 $\Pr(u_3 > 0) = .5$. In the normal regression model, each disturbance is independent.

11.3 Let the disturbance be v. If $E[v_i] = \delta$, then $u_i = v_i - \delta$ conforms to Equation (11.2). The original model $Y_i = \beta_0 + \beta_1 X_i + v_i$ can be rewritten as $Y_i = (\beta_0 + \delta) + \beta_1 X_i + u_i$. The new intercept can be denoted by β_0', where $\beta_0' = \beta_0 + \delta$.

11.6 The mean slope estimate is 2.1, the standard deviation is 0.485.

11.10 From sampling theory we know that $p(\hat{\beta}_1)$ is normal with $E[\hat{\beta}_1] = 10$ and $\sigma(\hat{\beta}_1) = 8$. Hence $\Pr(\hat{\beta}_1 \leq 0) = \Pr(Z \leq -1.25) = .106$, or 10.6 percent.

11.12 In the first case $\Pr(\hat{\beta}_1 \leq 2) = .309$. In the second case $\Pr(\hat{\beta}_1 \leq 2) = .067$.

11.13 If the total variation in X is quadrupled, its square root is doubled. Hence, from Equation (11.10), the standard error is cut in half.

11.16 If $\beta_0 = 0$, the implied estimation error is $0.568 - 0 = 0.568$. This is much smaller than the standard error, so the results are not surprising.

11.18 Using the definition of t in Equation (11.24), its value is $(0.797 - 0.0)/0.128 = 6.2$. Looking at Table A.2 we realize that there is practically no chance that a random variable having a t distribution would turn out to be this large; it would not occur often.

11.19 From Equation (11.22), $\hat{\beta}_1^* = 0.797$ and $s^*(\hat{\beta}_1) = 0.128$. With $t^c = 1.98$, the 95 percent confidence interval for β_1 is 0.797 ± 0.253 or 0.544 to 1.050.

11.21 No. A 100 percent confidence interval for the marginal propensity to consume would be $-\infty$ to ∞. The interval definitely includes the true value of the parameter, but it is of no help in tax analysis.

11.22 **(a)** The confidence interval contains β_j in about 95 percent of the samples.

(b) No. We have 95 percent confidence that it contains β_j, but we cannot determine whether it does or not.

Chapter 12: Hypothesis Testing

12.1 (a), (b), and (d) can be only alternative hypotheses; (c) can be only a null.

12.4 Let β_2 denote the coefficient on *DRACE*. To judge whether a person's race affects his earnings, we set up H_0: $\beta_2 = 0$ and H_1: $\beta_2 \neq 0$. Since $t^* = -1.09$, we would conclude that race does not affect earnings (based on conventional levels of significance).

12.5 Let β_2 denote the coefficient on *EXP*. The appropriate hypotheses are H_0: $\beta_2 = 0$ and H_1: $\beta_2 \neq 0$. With df = 97, $t^c = 1.66$ for $\alpha = .10$ and $t^c = 1.98$ for $\alpha = .05$. Since $t^* = 2.07$, we would conclude that experience does affect earnings, at both levels of significance. (Note that experience is *not* significant at the 1 percent level.)

12.12 Let β_2 denote the coefficient on *LNRTB*. The appropriate hypotheses are H_0: $\beta_2 = 0$ and H_1: $\beta_2 < 0$. Since $t^* = -0.67$, we would conclude that the interest elasticity is not significantly negative (based on conventional levels of significance).

12.13 Using Table A.3, $t_1^c = 1.660$ and $t_2^c = 1.984$.

12.18 Let β_4 denote the coefficient on *LNMONTHS*. The appropriate hypotheses are H_0: $\beta_4 = 1$ and H_1: $\beta_4 \neq 1$. Since $t^* = -0.25$, the elasticity is not significantly different from 1 (based on conventional levels of significance).

Chapter 13: Estimation
and Regression Problems

13.1 Based on Equations (13.8) and (13.9), $\hat{Y}_p = 1814.57$ billion dollars, and $s_p = 15.36$. The 95 percent confidence interval is 1814.57 ± 31.78 or 1782.79 to 1846.35 billion dollars. (Note that the confidence interval is substantially wider than in the example in Section 13.1, where income was about one trillion dollars.)

13.3 If we know the true values of the parameters in the regression model, our predictions are not affected by estimation error. For the *p*th observation, as for every other one, the actual Y is viewed as a value of a normal random variable with mean $\beta_0 + \beta_1 X_p$ and standard deviation equal to σ_u. The 90 percent confidence interval is $(\beta_0 + \beta_1 X_p) \pm (1.645)(\sigma_u)$, where 1.645 is Z^c such that $\Pr(|Z| \geq Z^c) = .10$.

13.5 Based on their definitions, $MSD_X = [(n-1)/n]S_X^2$, so $E[MSD_X] < E[S_X^2] = \sigma_X^2$. That is, MSD_X is negatively biased. Also, by Equation (9.25), the variance of MSD_X is smaller than the variance of S_X^2.

13.7 *EXP* is significant in Equation (7.15), but in (7.46) *EXP* and *EXPSQ* are less significant ($t^* = 1.85$ and 1.40—not significant at $\alpha = .05$ on two-tailed tests).

13.9 If the correlation is zero, $\sum x_1 x_2 = 0$ in Equation (13.16), and $\hat{\beta}_1$ determined there is identical to $\hat{\gamma}_1$ in Equation (13.18). Thus in this case excluding X_2 has no effect on the value of the estimated coefficient. By contrast, in the case with a high correlation, excluding X_2 biases the estimate.

Chapter 14: *F* Tests and Dummy Variable Outcomes

14.2 The appropriate hypotheses are given by Equation (14.16). In the test, the number of restrictions is $r = 3$ and there are $k = 7$ regressors in the unrestricted form. Letting $\alpha = .05$, the critical value for $F_{3,92}$ is $F^c \approx 2.71$. In Table 14.1, $SSR_R = 17.7241$ and $SSR_U = 17.0904$. This leads to $F^* = 1.137$, which is not in the critical region. We conclude that the region of residence does not significantly affect earnings.

14.5 The unrestricted model is given by Equation (14.18):

$$Y_i = \beta_0 + \beta_1 LABINC_i + \beta_2 PROPINC_i + u_i$$

The appropriate hypotheses are H_0: $\beta_2 = 0.9\beta_1$ and H_1: $\beta_2 \neq 0.9\beta_1$. The restricted model incorporates the statement of the null hypothesis:

$$Y_i = \beta_0 + \beta_1 LABINC_i + 0.9\beta_1 PROPINC_i + u_i$$
$$= \beta_0 + \beta_1 [LABINC_i + 0.9 PROPINC_i] + u_i$$
$$= \beta_0 + \beta_1 ADJINC_i + u_i$$

where *ADJINC* is a new regressor representing adjusted income. In the *F* test, the number of restrictions is $r = 1$.

14.7 We see in Table 14.2 that, for example, the estimated coefficient on *LNGNP* (for $i = 1$ to 15) is 0.292 in regressions (2) and (4), but that the standard errors are different (0.029 versus 0.034). This difference arises because regression (4) estimates the standard errors on the presumption that σ_u is the same for all observations, whereas the separate estimation of regressions (2) and (3) allows for different variability in the disturbances for the two periods. Indeed, we find that $SER = 0.0191$ in the earlier period and $SER = 0.0278$ in the latter.

14.9 For each observation, the disturbance $u_i = Y_i - E[Y_i]$. For observation 1, suppose that $E[Y_i] = 0.25$; the outcome of u_1 is either -0.25 or 0.75. For observation 2, suppose that $E[Y_i] = 0.5$; the outcome of u_2 is either -0.5 or 0.5. The requirement that $E[u_i] = 0$ fixes the probability values.

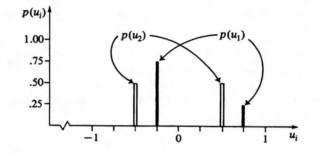

14.12 The values of $g(Z)$ are 0.250, 0.235, 0.197, 0.149, 0.105, and 0.070.

14.13 The values of $G(Z)$ are 0.500, 0.622, 0.731, 0.818, 0.881, and 0.924.

14.14 For LPM, $\hat{P} = 1.173$ is calculated directly. For Probit, $\hat{Z} = 1.7965$; then $\hat{P} = 0.964$ is determined from Table A.1 (using $Z^* = 1.80$). For Logit, $\hat{Z} = 2.998$; then $\hat{P} = 0.952$ is determined from Equation (14.39).

Chapter 15: Heteroscedasticity and Autocorrelation

15.1 Measurement error in the dependent variable is one of the factors incorporated into the disturbance. If this has decreased over time, the true disturbance is heteroscedastic.

15.4 The disturbance v_i cannot be normally distributed because the dependent variable is limited to being nonnegative in all these cases.

15.8 $E[u_2] = \rho u_1^* = (-.9)(20.0) = -18.0$. Taking $\epsilon_2 = 1.0$ as a possible outcome, $u_2^* = -17.0$. Then, taking $\epsilon_3 = -1.0$ as a possible outcome, $u_3^* = (-.9)(-17.0) - 1.0 = 14.3$.

15.10 We cannot expect to make a conclusive determination, because the table gives us information about the bounds for a critical value of d, not the critical value itself. In all cases in the table, the value of d_l increases with the number of observations, suggesting that the sampling distribution of d becomes more compact. However, when $k = 3$, 4, or 5, the value of d_u decreases as n increases up to a point, after which d_u starts to increase with n.

15.12 The first three values of y are 297.62, 138.53, and 137.03. The values of x_0 are 0.7341, 0.321, and 0.321. The values of x_1 are 327.57, 152.53, and 151.42.

Chapter 16: Regression and Time Series

16.2
$$\Delta CON_t = 0.886\Delta DPI_t + 0.0116\Delta DPILAG1_t$$
$$+ 0.0100\Delta DPILAG2_t$$

Period t: $\Delta CON = 0.886$
Period $t + 1$: $\Delta CON = 0.886 + 0.0116 = 0.8976$
Period $t + 2$: $\Delta CON = 0.886 + 0.0116 + 0.0100 = 0.9076$
Period $t + 3$: $\Delta CON = 0.886 + 0.0116 + 0.0100 = 0.9076$
Period $t + 4$: $\Delta CON = 0.886 + 0.0116 + 0.0100 = 0.9076$

16.3 If a simple regression of Y on X is estimated when Equation (16.3) is correct, the estimated regression suffers from an exclusion-of-variables type of misspecification. If X is increasing over time and if β_0, β_1, and β_2 are all positive, then the expected value of the slope coefficient in the simple regression will be greater than β_0. The slope in the simple regression captures the combined effects on Y of the current and past values of X.

16.6 With Y_t^* fixed, Y_t approaches Y_t^* over time.

16.7 If X grows at a constant absolute amount, so does Y_t^* [ignoring the disturbance in Equation (16.13)]. With Y_t^* growing at a constant amount, Y_t approaches Y_t^* over time.

16.9 In the presence of a lagged dependent variable, the appropriate test is based on Durbin's h statistic, calculated according to Equation (15.27). From (16.11) we have $n = 23$ and $V = (0.136)^2$. Given $d = 1.25$, we compute $h \approx 2.37$. In large samples Durbin's h has a standard normal distribution, so the one-tailed critical value is $Z^c = 1.645$. We conclude that positive autocorrelation is present. (Note that when $d < 2$, $h > 0$; thus the critical region for h is in the right-hand tail.) In this case, d is in the indeterminate region.

16.13 The dummy variable coefficients measure differences from the excluded category. If $Q4$ is excluded, the coefficient on $Q1$ would be -3.47, that on $Q2$ would be -1.53, and that on $Q3$ would be -1.56.

16.15 Compared with the first quarter, third quarter NPE is predicted to be 1.91 higher because of a seasonal effect and $(2)(0.108) = 0.216$ higher because of a trend effect. The total prediction is 2.126 higher.

Chapter 17: Simultaneous-Equation Models

17.1
$$WAGE_i = \left(\frac{\gamma_0 - \beta_0}{\beta_1 - \gamma_1}\right) + \left(\frac{\gamma_2}{\beta_1 - \gamma_1}\right) OTHINC_i + \left(\frac{v_i - u_i}{\beta_1 - \gamma_1}\right)$$

$$HOURS_i = \left(\frac{\beta_1\gamma_0 - \beta_0\gamma_1}{\beta_1 - \gamma_1}\right) + \left(\frac{\beta_1\gamma_2}{\beta_1 - \gamma_1}\right) OTHINC_i$$
$$+ \left(\frac{\beta_1 v_i - \gamma_1 u_i}{\beta_1 - \gamma_1}\right)$$

17.3 This is a special case of a simultaneous-equation model. Because X depends on Z but not on Y or u, the model can be thought of as a sequence of two single-equation models. Once X is determined, it serves as an "exogenous" variable in the first equation. The "reduced form" is

$$X_i = \gamma_0 + \gamma_1 Z_i + v_i$$
$$Y_i = \beta_0 + \beta_1\gamma_0 + \beta_1\gamma_1 Z_i + \beta_1 v_i + u_i$$

17.5 By making A endogenous and GNP exogenous, the model becomes recursive. The "reduced form" is

$$CON_i = \beta_0 + \beta_1 GNP_i + \beta_2 RTB_i + \beta_3 CON_{i-1} + u_i$$
$$A_i = -\beta_0 - (\beta_1 - 1)GNP_i - \beta_2 RTB_i - \beta_3 CON_{i-1} - u_i$$

17.9 No. The "endogenous" variable X on the right-hand side of the first equation is not related to the disturbance u, as can be seen in the "reduced form" given above. Thus there is no OLS bias in this case. The second structural equation, with no endogenous variables on the right-hand side, stands as a regular single-equation model.

17.10 Since the $\hat{\pi}$'s are OLS estimators of the reduced-form equations, they are linear combinations of the Y_j's. Each equation of the reduced form shows that each Y_j depends on the disturbances of the system. Hence the $\hat{\pi}$'s are linear combinations of the disturbances.

17.11 Equation (17.3) is just identified: two predetermined variables are excluded while two endogenous variables appear on the right-hand side. Equation (17.5) is over-identified: two predetermined variables are excluded while one endogenous variable appears on the right-hand side.

17.14 Considering the coefficients on $OTHINC$ in the reduced form, the ratio of that in the $HOURS$ equation to that in the $WAGE$ equation is simply β_1. Suppose that we estimate the reduced form equations. The ratio of the two estimated coefficients on $OTHINC$ is the ILS estimate of β_1.

Chapter 18: Inference for the Mean and Variance

18.2 X has a binomial distribution with $E[X] = 50$ and $\sigma(X) = 5$.
  (a) $E[\overline{X}] = 50$, $\sigma(\overline{X}) = 1.25$.
  (b) Treating $\overline{X}$ as approximately normally distributed, $\Pr(\overline{X} \leq 48) = \Pr(Z \leq -1.6) = .055$.

18.5 The possible values of $\overline{X}$ are $-1, 0, 1$, occurring with probabilities .25, .50, .25, respectively.

18.7 A two-tailed test is called for. With $n = 400$, $t^* = (103 - 100)/(15/20) = 4.0$ and $t^c \approx 1.97$. The conclusion of the test now would be to reject the null hypothesis that $E[X] = 100$.

18.8 With $n = 81$, $s(\overline{X}) = 15/9 = 1.67$ and $t^c = 1.99$. The 95 percent confidence interval is $103.0 \pm (1.99)(1.67)$, or 103.0 ± 3.32, which ranges from 99.68 to 106.32. (Since the confidence interval includes the value $\overline{X} = 100$, the null hypothesis H_0: $\mu_X = 100$ would not be rejected.)

18.11 **(a)** Since $\sigma_X^2 = 1$, $E[S_X^2] = 1$.
  (b) With $(n - 1) = 9$ and $\sigma_X^2 = 1$, $\chi^2 = 9S_X^2/1$ has a chi-square distribution with df $= 9$. $\Pr(S_X^2 > 2) = \Pr(\chi^2 > 18)$. In Table A.4 we see that with df $= 9$, $\Pr(\chi^2 \geq 16.93) = .05$ and $\Pr(\chi^2 \geq 19.03) = 0.25$. Hence $\Pr(\chi^2 \geq 18)$ is probably between 3 and 4 percent.

18.13 With df $= 15$, $(\chi^2)_l^c = 6.26$ and $(\chi^2)_r^c = 27.50$. Based on Equation (18.27), the 95 percent confidence interval extends from 30.0 to 131.8.

Chapter 19: Chi-Square Tests and Analysis of Variance

19.1 With 600 workers, $(\chi^2)^* = 7.50$. With $\alpha = .05$, $(\chi^2)^c = 5.99$, as before. Thus the null hypothesis is rejected, and we conclude that the data contradict the theory.

19.4 Based on the standard normal distribution, the predicted frequencies are 16 less than -1, 34 between -1 and 0, 34 between 0 and 1, and 16 greater than 1. Based on Equation (19.1), $(\chi^2)^* = 6.34$. There are four categories, so df $= 3$. With $\alpha = .05$, $(\chi^2)^c = 7.82$, and we do not reject the null hypothesis. We conclude that the observations might have been taken from a standard normal variable.

19.6 In the table, $(\chi^2)^* = 124.7$ and df $= 4$. With $\alpha = .05$, $(\chi^2)^c = 9.49$ and we reject the null hypothesis. We conclude that income is related to education.

19.9 The basic F test in the first regression corresponds to a one-way ANOVA by occupation. For $F_{2,97}$, $F^c \approx 3.09$ at $\alpha = .05$. Based on Equation (14.12), $F^* = 26.12$, and we conclude that there are significant differences by occupation.

19.10 In a two-way ANOVA, we test for differences by gender by comparing the second regression (unrestricted) with the first (restricted). For $F_{1,96}$, $F^c \approx 3.94$ at $\alpha = .05$. Based on Equation (14.9), $F^* = 3.05$, and we conclude that the differences by gender are not significant. (Note that $F^c \approx 2.8$ at the 10 percent level of significance, so the differences would be significant.)

Bibliography _____

The first three sections list standard texts in mathematical statistics and econometrics. The references for Chapter 2 provide the source information for the data sets presented in that chapter. The references for Chapters 14–17 are mostly citations to original contributions cited in the chapters.

Intermediate Mathematical Statistics

FREUND, JOHN E., and WALPOLE, RONALD E. *Mathematical Statistics.* 5th ed. Englewood Cliffs, N.J.: Prentice-Hall, 1992.

HOEL, PAUL G. *Introduction to Mathematical Statistics.* 5th ed. New York: Wiley, 1984.

HOGG, ROBERT V., and CRAIG, ALLEN T. *Introduction to Mathematical Statistics.* 4th ed. New York: Macmillan, 1978.

RAMANATHAN, RAMU. *Statistical Methods in Econometrics.* San Diego: Academic Press, 1993.

Intermediate Econometrics

GUJARATI, DAMODAR. *Basic Econometrics.* 2nd ed. New York: McGraw-Hill, 1988.

JUDGE, GEORGE G., ET AL. *Introduction to the Theory and Practice of Econometrics.* 2nd ed. New York: Wiley & Sons, 1988.

KENNEDY, PETER. *A Guide to Econometrics.* 3rd ed. Cambridge, Mass.: MIT Press, 1992. (A useful commentary; not a text.)

MADDALA, G. S. *Introduction to Econometrics.* 2nd Ed. New York: Macmillan, 1992.

PINDYCK, ROBERT S., and RUBINFELD, DANIEL L. *Econometric Models and Economic Forecasts.* 3rd ed. New York: McGraw-Hill, 1991.

438

Advanced Econometrics

GOLDBERGER, ARTHUR S. *A Course in Econometrics*. Cambridge, Mass.: Harvard University Press, 1991.

GREENE, WILLIAM H. *Econometric Analysis*. 2nd ed. New York: Macmillan, 1993.

JOHNSTON, J. *Econometric Methods*. 3rd ed. New York: McGraw-Hill, 1984.

Chapter 2: Economic Data

FERBER, ROBERT, ET AL. "Validation of a National Survey of Consumer Characteristics: Savings Accounts." *Review of Economics and Statistics* 51 (November 1969), 436–444.

PROJECTOR, DOROTHY S., and WEISS, GERTRUDE S. *Survey of Financial Characteristics of Consumers*. Washington: Board of Governors of the Federal Reserve System, 1966. (This describes and analyzes the survey from which the cross-section data set was taken.)

PROJECTOR, DOROTHY S. *Survey of Changes in Family Finances*. Washington: Board of Governors of the Federal Reserve System, 1968.

Economic Report of the President (Transmitted to the Congress February 1982). Washington: U.S. Government Printing Office, 1982. (This annual report includes a large appendix of statistical tables, from which the time-series data set was taken.)

Chapter 14: F Tests and Dummy Variable Outcomes

CHOW, GREGORY C. "Tests of Equality Between Sets of Coefficients in Two Linear Regressions." *Econometrica* 28 (July 1960), 591–605.

FISHER, FRANKLIN M. "Tests of Equality Between Sets of Coefficients in Two Linear Regressions: An Expository Note." *Econometrica* 38 (March 1970), 361–366.

MADDALA, G. S. *Limited-Dependent and Qualitative Variables in Econometrics*. Cambridge: Cambridge University Press, 1983.

Chapter 15: Heteroscedasticity and Autocorrelation

BREUSCH, T. S., and PAGAN, A. R. "A Simple Test for Heteroscedasticity and Random Coefficient Variation." *Econometrica* 47 (September 1979), 1287–1294.

COCHRANE, D., and ORCUTT, G. H. "Application of Least Squares Regression to Relationships Containing Autocorrelated Error Terms." *Journal of the American Statistical Association* 44 (March 1949), 32–61.

DURBIN, J., and WATSON, G. S. "Testing for Serial Correlation in Least Squares Regression. II." *Biometrika* 38 (June 1951), 159–178.

DURBIN, J. "Testing for Serial Correlation in Least-Squares Regression When Some of the Regressors Are Lagged Dependent Variables." *Econometrica* 38 (May 1970), 410–421.

GLEJSER, H. "A New Test for Heteroscedasticity." *Journal of the American Statistical Association* 64 (March 1969), 316–323.

HILDRETH, CLIFFORD, and LU, JOHN Y. "Demand Relations with Autocorrelated Disturbances." Michigan State University Agricultural Experiment Station, *Technical Bulletin* 276 (November 1960).

PARK, R. E. "Estimation with Heteroscedastic Error Terms." *Econometrica* 34 (October 1966), 888.

WHITE, HALBERT. "A Heteroscedasticity-Consistent Covariance Matrix Estimator and a Direct Test for Heteroscedasticity." *Econometrica* 48 (May 1980), 817–838.

Chapter 16: Regression and Time Series

GOLDBERGER, ARTHUR S. "The Interpretation and Estimation of Cobb–Douglas Functions." *Econometrica* 36 (July–October 1968), 464–472. (For making predictions with a logarithmic regressand.)

HARVEY, ANDREW. *The Econometric Analysis of Time Series.* 2nd ed. Cambridge, Mass.: MIT Press, 1990.

Chapter 17: Simultaneous-Equation Models

FISHER, FRANKLIN M. *The Identification Problem in Econometrics.* New York: McGraw-Hill, 1966.

Index

447

ISBN 0-02-381831-X

90000

9 780023 818318